*Oracle Press*™

Oracle Enterprise Manager 10g Grid Control Handbook

Werner De Gruyter

Matthew Hart

Daniel Nguyen

New York   Chicago   San Francisco
Lisbon   London   Madrid   Mexico City   Milan
New Delhi   San Juan   Seoul   Singapore   Sydney   Toronto

Cataloging-in-Publication Data is on file with the Library of Congress

McGraw-Hill books are available at special quantity discounts to use as premiums and sales promotions, or for use in corporate training programs. To contact a representative, please e-mail us at bulksales@mcgraw-hill.com.

Oracle Enterprise Manager 10*g* Grid Control Handbook

1 2 3 4 5 6 7 8 9 0   DOC DOC   1 0 9 8 7 6 5 4 3 2 1 0

ISBN   978-0-07-163422-9
MHID   0-07-163422-3

Sponsoring Editor	**Technical Editors**	**Production Supervisor**
Lisa McClain	Raj Aggarwal	Jean Bodeaux
Editorial Supervisor	Farouk Abushaban	**Composition**
Patty Mon	Sohail Zamurad	Glyph International
Project Manager	**Copy Editor**	**Illustration**
Harleen Chopra,	Margaret Berson	Glyph International
Glyph International	**Proofreader**	**Art Director, Cover**
Acquisitions Coordinator	Carol Shields	Jeff Weeks
Meghan Riley	**Indexer**	**Cover Designer**
	Karin Arrigoni	Pattie Lee

Written by and dedicated to the people who are in the heat of the debugging and diagnostics battles. May it help guide you in your quests for the truth…

—Werner De Gruyter

To the young and willing, the future authors of all things good.

—Daniel Nguyen

This book is dedicated to the, um, fascinating team that has sprung up around me, elevated my game, and become the enablers for my success: Eric (and Mr. Dobbs), Carl, Daniel, Ashok, Mike, Asim, and Oscar.

—Matthew Hart

About the Authors

Werner De Gruyter started his career with Oracle in Belgium, in the support organization back in 1996, right around the time Enterprise Manager 1.0 was released. After four years there, Werner moved to the United States in 2000, where he joined the System Management Products development organization, with the mission to help development eliminate the barriers to adoption for Enterprise Manager, based on the feedback provided by customers. In that time, he's seen the whole metamorphosis from Enterprise Manager (the JAVA/C++–based product) to Grid Control (the web-based product).

He has worked with every version of Enterprise Manager and Grid Control, and helped diagnose and troubleshoot issues raised by customers on all these releases.

Matthew Hart is the coauthor of five other Oracle books, including the upcoming *Oracle Database 11g RMAN Backup and Recovery* from Oracle Press. He has been working with High Availability technologies in Oracle since version 7.3, and database management technologies for most of that period. He currently works and lives in Kansas City, or at least at its airport anyway.

Daniel Nguyen holds an engineering degree from the University of Colorado and has over ten years of experience in the software industry. He has a deep-seated interest in technologies that change the space in which they compete. While employed at Oracle, Daniel took great strides to become principal across the technology stack where he addressed bugs, diagnostics, and escalations for Oracle Support Services. Daniel recently transitioned into the communications space where he has been gainfully employed by Avaya, a leading provider of communication technology, and serves as a transformation lead for various serviceability initiatives.

About the Contributor

Farouk Abushaban is a Senior Principal Support Engineer at the Oracle Rocky Mountain Support Center in Colorado. Farouk is a founding member of the Center of Excellence team, and is the Global Technical Lead for Enterprise Manager High Availability technology deployments. After spending over 20 years supporting customer information systems, and completing his Master's degree in Management of Information Technologies with emphasis on Project Management and Security, he was invited to contribute to the content of this book. The two chapters on RAC Cluster Management and Data Guard Management were written by Farouk. He was also a technical reviewer for several chapters of the book.

Farouk started his career as a hardware field engineer after completing his Bachelor's degree in Electrical Engineering at the University of Colorado in Colorado Springs. Farouk and his family reside in the Pike's Peak region of Colorado.

About the Technical Editors

Raj Aggarwal is a principal development lead at Oracle India and works in the framework team of Enterprise Manager. He has designed and developed some of the core framework services of Enterprise Manager. He works on performance, scalability, and high availability of Enterprise Manager Grid Control.

Sohail Zamurad is currently a Senior Technical Support Engineer for Oracle Enterprise Manager. He holds a Master's degree in computer science with a major in databases. Suhail holds Oracle certifications on the Oracle9*i* database, Oracle Database 10*g*, and Oracle Database 10*g* Real Application Clusters (RAC). Prior to joining Oracle, Suhail was an independent consultant. He has experience in day-to-day core DBA duties, RAC 9*i*/10*g*, Oracle ASM, Oracle Data Guard implementations, performance tuning at the database and application levels, and designing RMAN implementations and backup strategies.

Contents at a Glance

PART II
Grid Control Common Tasks and Functions

PART III
Enterprise Manager Power User's Guide

PART IV
Appendixes

Contents

PART I
Installing and Deploying Grid Control

ix

PART II
Grid Control Common Tasks and Functions

PART III
Enterprise Manager Power User's Guide

PART IV
Appendixes

Acknowledgments

wish we had science-fiction type technologies (already) to dump someone's brain on paper. Oh, and electronic paper would be fine, too...

This project started with that exact thought in mind: to bring the practical knowledge gained from helping customers all these years to paper, and present it in an easily consumable way for everyone to read and enjoy.

Dumping a brain and writing down all the tidbits, tips, and tricks turned out to yield quite a pile of information, considerably larger than I originally thought it would be. This led to some interesting debates on just how high the limit in the sky really was in terms of the size and scope of this book. The fact that the book is not bigger and thicker than it already is, is the direct result of my coauthors, and the publishers and editors at McGraw-Hill, constantly reminding me that there *were limits to adhere to,* and that we had to cap the book somewhere.

The result is right here: A comprehensive guide, designed to help you through the implementation and usage of Grid Control from the infrastructure standpoint. The brain dump is not complete, but this is the information essential for the start of the journey, that information you just need to start the quest. Time for a sequel, anyone?

—Werner De Gruyter

This book nearly broke me.

The fact that it did not do so must be attributed first and foremost to my coauthors, Daniel Nguyen and Werner De Gruyter, and the last-minute contributor Farouk Abushaban. I owe a deep debt of gratitude to each of these men for picking up where I left off, filling in holes, taking on coordination duties, and otherwise ensuring that this book actually made it out the door. The value of this book is primarily theirs, and its flaws so glaringly mine.

I must also thank the ever-patient (until it's time to not be patient) editor Lisa McClain and acquisitions coordinator Meghan Riley, who watched in horror as I went from being the predictable, on-time author to being *that* author. I am, truly, deeply sorry, as this is actually worse than being undependable from the get-go. Nevertheless, your dogged attitude and final ultimatums have lead to a hefty tome that we can all be proud of.

Almost literally minutes after we signed the contract for this book, my life was turned upside down by massive changes in my professional life and duties, and I found myself working harder than I ever thought possible, and testing the outer limits of my endurance. Through this, I had the irrepressible support of my ever-present mentor and friend, Martin Ingram. Without it, I would have crumbled. At the same time, I was introduced to a new mentor, who quickly inserted himself as a voice inside my head, becoming a filter for my day-to-day activities. A big thanks must go to Mr. Birtwell for that support, for believing in me, and for his relentless drive for excellence.

My team at Avaya, both the old one and the new one, must be thanked for muscling through a difficult year filled with frustration and loss, but also success and vindication. Many of them didn't know I was also trying to write a book at the same time as everything else, and to find this book on the shelves may serve as an "aha" moment for them, looking back at my short fuse on certain days when only an all-nighter would get me to done.

Finally, I must thank my wife and kids, for once again putting up with me, not only with the ridiculous travel schedule I kept, but the long hours for both my day job and this book, my night job. It was a long year, and without their support and love I would have succumbed to exhaustion months ago.

Finally, thank you, the reader, for wanting this book and reading it. I hope you find it as useful and relevant as we intended.

—Matthew Hart

I have been chasing time as long as I care to remember. As an athlete, it was all about streamlining techniques to shave milliseconds with each lap. College taught you that the mixture of midnight oil, caffeine, and music around 150 BPM were the necessary ingredients to cook up a diploma. As the reader of this book, you too, concur that time is an expensive commodity and the rewards of our profession stem from our ability to seek more with less. I thereby thank you; the reader, for wanting to arm yourself with this material and make use of it to cement a future success story.

I am sure I speak on behalf of all the authors when I say we are extremely grateful to Meghan Riley, Lisa McClain, and the rest of the McGraw-Hill staff. Not only do they source good talent, but they also have (just enough) patience to allow their authors the time, space, and emotional range of motion to look back while they looked forward. Without this kind of publishing expertise, you can bet there would be many more things that were not *write* as we sat down to *right*.

I'd be a fool to fuel the misconception that any achievement rests squarely on my smarts, ambition, or hustle. The outliers of any success are in large part due to a selected caliber of individuals at the most opportune moments of my life:

Maggie Wells: Thank you for taking that gamble and lifting the gates to the profession that I now call my own. Many executives attach batteries to those they mentor. I have a self-generating, hydrogen-powered flux supercapacitor.

Martin Ingram: For over a decade, I have remained grateful for your unwavering support, presence, and consideration. Through you, I have come to terms with the haphazard nature of life, which all too often produces progress in advance of understanding.

Matt Hart: It was just a matter of time before we worked closely with each other and needless to say… well, needless to say. If there were a science of superheroes, you could be an undercover one. Hmmm… Matt Hart *aka* Matt Hart: known for his extraordinary skills in transforming any planet of the apes to planet of the apps.

Lisa Tamura: Thanks for putting up with my personal and professional growing pains. I am building up all the good karma left in this world so my firstborn will only be half as difficult.

The trouble with doing things right the first time is that nobody appreciates how difficult it ever was. If this company ever needed an Avaya Select Services division, it would be the team of individuals I have worked with these past three years—they can be counted on to muscle through initiatives, just like that 800-pound gorilla.

Being a proud and complex individual, I face most of my struggles alone. But sometimes you need help pulling out from the lowest points of your life. This is to my circle: despite my missing many an occasion; I can always count on them to conjure up an army to cover my back (and balls). Such relationships are beyond rare and priceless in the truest sense of the word.

Finally, this is to my future wife and the cheerleader of my dreams. Before you, I was taught to never want anything that I couldn't stand to lose…

—Daniel Nguyen

Introduction

It's a Grid! It's a Cloud! It's a.... wild tangled mess!

Let's just look it right in the eye and call it out. We in the IT industries have been barraged with the buzzwords over and over again since we rolled into the new millennium: the transition to utility computing, or grid computing, or cloud computing (depending on the source/exact month/position of the stars in the sky). We've decided that we've hit fatigue in all of this, and there's nothing we can do about the language and jockeying for position that accompanies all of the PR.

But, underneath it all, a real transition has been taking place, based on real pressures in the global economy to leverage technology for business advantage, while suppressing costs and increasing reliability. This evolution can be characterized by the fulfillment of the promise of distributed computing (a whole room of commoditized computers, instead of one massive Cray); the move away from desktop applications to perform day-to-day tasks, and the move to the supremacy of the browser-as-everything-you-will-ever-need; and the rise of standards-based, open interfaces between computing elements. That's just for starters, but it's leading to innovations that help our companies get more from their data, more from their networks, and ultimately more productivity and innovation from their people.

So, people can look at it and brand it Grid, or Utility, and so on, but those of us who've been involved in it for the past decade understand the fundamental truth: the current technology landscape is one big wild mess.

And managing the hairy tangled mess of modern computing infrastructure elements is further complicated by pressures caused by the fact that we are spread all over the globe now, and are being asked to do more and more with less manual labor available. There's more to do, and less to do it with. These pressures have left most of us with a pile of tools that we use to monitor, manage, and administer all the distinct components that make up our borderless data centers.

But a few years ago, Oracle decided to take a step back, look at the big ecosystem mess, and stop tunneling in on specific technology components trying to solve these problems. Instead, Oracle started from scratch, and built a tool that tried to solve the overall ecosystem management problem, utilizing the patterns of management that exist across all components—host servers, operating systems, databases, application servers, the applications themselves, the network routing components, load balancers—everything (the kitchen sink is on the road map). At the same time, they wanted to leverage the elements of modern computing that they were also trying to manage: distributed computing, web-based applications, and standard, open interfaces. The result of this work is Oracle Enterprise Manager Grid Control.

Grid Control has been around for a few years now, and chances are, if you are reading this, you've had some exposure to it, and either really want to leverage and make good use of it, or you are already staring down a Grid Control implementation and you could use some help. If you are already working with Grid Control every day, helping users with the workflow, optimizing the performance and throughput or debugging issues, you will start seeing patterns and repeating issues popping up with every new deployment. These patterns and repeating issues often lead to real issues down the line, resulting in either downtime, or limitations in the rollout of Grid Control, preventing further growth of the ecosystem that EM is managing.

The Complete Grid Control Handbook

The idea driving this book is to give administrators of Grid Control the tips and tricks created for the common repeating issues and frequent mistakes people make. Most of these issues can be easily avoided if people are made aware of them up front, or by just pointing out the right set of checks and tests to perform. And this is where the information in this book comes into the picture.

In this book, we cover the entire life cycle of the Grid Control product, from the very beginning, with the preparation of the install of Grid Control, to the managing of the data center infrastructure, right down to the daily checks an administrator should be aware of to keep an eye on the product. This book is more than just an implementation guide; we packed it as full of real-world experience, ugly truths, head-scratchers, and gotchas as we reasonably could. We want you to take full advantage of Grid Control, and ensure that you can use it to manage the entire ecosystem. Getting it installed is just the beginning. Every step in the Grid Control life cycle is covered, giving you the background information required to succeed and flourish—with some real-life exercises and workshops to give any aspiring EM guru the chance to get his or her hands dirty.

Using This Book Effectively

Like all technical manuals worth their weight, this book is meant to be readable, cover to cover, as a way to familiarize yourself with Grid Control and its role in complete ecosystem management. The topics are approached in a format that allows each complex subject to build on previous chapters, slowly working forward from principles, to implementation, to configuration, to usage, and finally to diagnosing and troubleshooting.

The structure of this book is divided into three parts, mimicking the stages any Grid Control site will go through.

The first is the installation of the EM infrastructure itself. This crucial step is the one with which most problems and bottlenecks can be avoided, if the right choices are made for the rollout of the main EM application and the monitoring Agents.

The second stage involves the inner workings of Grid Control, to set up the right kind of monitoring and maintenance for both the EM and the IT infrastructure that is being monitored.

And last but not least is the managing of the IT infrastructure itself: Once Grid Control is rolled out and operational, the idea of the tool is to start monitoring the enterprise with all of its different applications and machines. We conclude Part III with detailed troubleshooting and diagnostics, as there are enough moving parts that knowing how to isolate faults and rectify them will consume much of your time.

We have also included a series of appendixes that provide fast reference points for Grid Control configuration files, parameters, the different log files, environment variables, and repository views that are available. There is also a command-line syntax guide and—no modern book is complete without it—an acronym guide should you find yourself scratching your head.

Grid Control Workshops

Not everyone reads a book cover to cover. We know this. Sometimes that's not the higher calling of a good technical book. A good book lives next to the computer, with pages dog-eared, sections highlighted, and little yellow post-its hanging off the side.

This book is meant to be a reference guide in addition to a conceptual explanation. We've packed this thing with useful techniques and timesaving practices that you can implement now, even if you're a little spotty on the architecture. Sometimes you just need to know *how to do it*, right? During a tough Grid Control implementation, or when you are hunting for a way to discover a database, there's nothing like a good cookbook approach to get you through an exercise and get you to where you are concentrating on your business again.

So, to help with the highlighting and dog-earing of pages, we utilized the Grid Control Workshop sections of the book. Whenever we provide useful code for performing a specific operation, or a series of steps to complete a certain project, we mark it in a larger font and box. When you see this box, you know the following pages will be filled with the actual steps you need to follow to get your job done fast. Think of Grid Control Workshops as recipes, providing the ingredients and the mixing instructions for a quick and easy meal.

To make your life even easier, we've compiled a separate Contents listing for every Grid Control Workshop in this book, with its descriptive title and the page number. You'll find this Grid Control Workshop reference as part of the Contents at a Glance at the beginning of the book. Using the Contents at a Glance, you can skip directly to the one you need and get right to work. That way, if you find our prose boring and concepts overblown, you can still get lots of specific use from this book.

Again, we encourage you to read the book chapter for chapter. Nothing can replace a conceptual understanding of a product, especially when that product is protecting your most valuable asset: the database.

So, good luck and happy hunting. We've done our best to give you the breadth and depth required to be on solid footing going into a new Grid Control implementation, or to take full advantage of an existing one. Get your highlighter out, start dog-earing the pages, and get ready to beat the big tangled mess of grid computing into submission.

PART
I

Installing and Deploying
Grid Control

CHAPTER
1

What Is Grid Control?
Enterprise Manager
Concepts

know it will sound like a cliché, but you are at the beginning of an important journey to help guide you through planning, deploying, and using a product that has an impact on your entire IT organization. And as with all other big undertakings, planning is a critical phase.

This chapter is important because it deals with and explains the very basics of the software called Enterprise Manager. I hope that, in reading this chapter, the one notion you will gather is that Enterprise Manager is more than just some application reporting data from a bunch of machines.

There are tips and tricks throughout this book to help you use this product more effectively. But the most important thing I hope people will learn from this book is that Enterprise Manager is indeed focused on the Enterprise, and can have a positive impact on the entire enterprise, in all of its aspects, and all of its diverse branches.

Enterprise Management Software

In 2003, Oracle took an unprecedented direction over the landscape of IT and proclaimed—with uncanny foresight—that its software, most notably Enterprise Manager, would be used to address key challenges that many companies would soon come to face. By that time, the dust over Internet technologies had settled, and IT professionals began to find themselves struggling for an end-to-end management solution, as the concept of *computing as a commodity* begun to catch on.

To address the challenges of companies whose business needs change faster than their IT departments can adapt, Oracle unveiled a suite of business software: Oracle Application Server 10*g*, Oracle Database 10*g*, and Oracle Enterprise Manager 10*g* Grid Control. The "g" in *10g* made an explicit call to address *grid computing*, a deployment topology that integrates all IT resources—storage, servers, databases, application servers, and network peripherals—to provide database services to applications on demand.

Oracle technology is typically arranged as a multitier architecture (commonly referred to as *n-tier*), in which the presentation, the application processing, and the data management are logically separate processes. It is worth noting that the concepts of *layer* and *tier* are often used interchangeably, when in fact there is one fairly common distinction between the two: a *layer* represents a logical structuring mechanism for the elements that make up a software solution, while a *tier* represents the physical structuring mechanism that make up a system infrastructure. With that in mind, a typical deployment using Oracle technology would be divided as follows:

- The *presentation layer*, represented as Tier-1, is the entry point for all application client connections seeking data. These requests originate from client machines or handheld devices, and communicate with the other layers by rendering the results from these requests.

- The *application-processing layer*, represented as Tier-2, consists of Java Enterprise Edition (J2EE) application servers and HTTP web servers, which Oracle provides in Oracle Application Server 10*g*. This tier is considered the "glue" to the other tiers and controls most of the application's functionality by performing detailed processing. If necessary, the communication to the database back end happens by means of various protocols and specifications such as Java Database Connectivity (JDBC) and Oracle Database Connectivity (ODBC).

■ The *data management layer*, represented as Tier-3, consists of databases and database storage subsystems. In the grid, databases are utilizing Oracle's Real Application Clusters (RAC) technology, which allows databases to run packages and custom applications unchanged across a set of clustered servers. The storage subsystem is usually a collection of low-cost disk devices that, when utilized against a solution such as Oracle's Automatic Storage Management (ASM), can easily partition and distribute data storage throughout the disk array.

Enterprise Manager 10*g* Grid Control weaves itself into the mix by effectively monitoring these tiers, and is even architected in the same manner; that is, components of Grid Control are built on Oracle technology that is even capable of monitoring itself. Because of this, no company needs to be fully immersed in grid technology to take advantage of what Grid Control offers. This is a cursory overview of the subject and is by no means complete, but it does place Enterprise Manager Grid Control in the correct context—this is the solution to gravitate toward if you seek to effectively monitor and leverage assets of a data center.

The monitoring of these data centers can be done from locations all around the world, making this suite of products a truly enterprise-class application. As Figure 1-1 illustrates, Grid Control can be used on local company networks, on subnets protected by firewalls, and even with targets on the Internet (outside the company network).

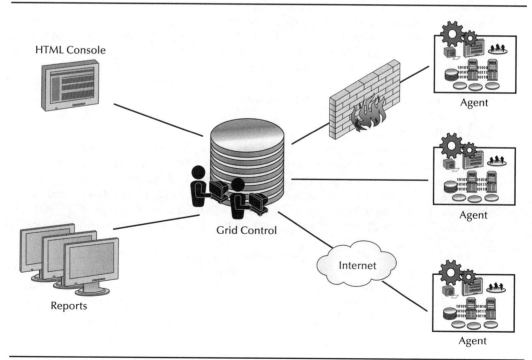

FIGURE 1-1. *The Grid Control architecture*

Administrators, who do not have to be in the same location as the management infrastructure, can use the information provided in Grid Control to manage and maintain their applications. With lights-out management capabilities, they can be alerted about outages and potential problems, giving Grid Control both proactive and reactive monitoring capabilities. Out-of-box, Grid Control supports monitoring of over 200 different types of targets and applications. On top of that, the infrastructure can be extended with additional monitoring plug-ins to support those types of business-critical targets that Grid Control is not aware of by default. This might sound like a lot, or even overkill. But the variety is required to even be considered a manageability solution in today's diverse IT environments. The days when a data center was nothing more than a few database machines put together in a single location are long gone.

Recall if you can, the days when you required specialized resources to maintain every implementation, and significant overhead was needed simply to make things work. The advent of Grid Control provides tremendous relief in this area, but requires a disciplined approach in changing the way we design and think about managing assets of a data center. Modern data centers have evolved into hubs of diverse IT infrastructure, ranging from simple staging machines to complex multimachine application setups and network devices needed to run today's enterprise-wide (and sometimes even world-wide) software.

The Various Management Tools

To respond to the rapid changes in a data center, a set of tools was introduced to manage the various components that make up a data center. Each of these tools manages and controls a set of Oracle products. They all follow the same multitier approach, with an Agent monitoring and gathering information, an application layer to collect and process the data, and a presentation layer to render the information to the administrator. While Grid Control is used to manage an enterprise and a variety of different things within that enterprise, there are other control tools managing some of the Oracle products. Two of those control tools, Database Control (DB Control) and Application Server Control (AS Control), are closely related to Grid Control, and often cause confusion in terms of setting them up and using them in conjunction with Grid Control.

DB Control

DB Control is a scaled-down and trimmed-down version of Grid Control, intended to manage a single database, or a single RAC installation. It contains a SYSMAN schema in the SYSAUX tablespace, and is monitored by an Agent designed specifically for that version of the database. Both the SYSMAN schema and the DB Control Agent have limited capabilities to monitor just that single installation. The software to run DB Control will be present in the *ORACLE_HOME* of the database. No additional software is needed to get the DB Control application—which includes the DB Control Agent—up and running.

If Grid Control is used to manage the enterprise, it replaces DB Control. The SYSMAN schema can then be removed from the target database and the DB Control Agent needs to be shut down, since it will no longer be used. The Grid Control Agent, installed on the same machine but outside of the database home, will then assume all monitoring and administration tasks, and report the data to the central Grid Control repository.

AS Control

AS Control is the main tool used to administer Oracle Application Servers. Like DB Control, AS Control consists of two parts: The main application, AS Control, and the AS Control Agent perform the basic monitoring and information gathering of each Oracle Application Server installation. No database schema is installed or used. This means that AS Control uses only real-time information, no historical information is kept, and no trending is done for any of the metric data. AS Control, like DB Control, is also installed together with the OAS software in the same *ORACLE_HOME*, requiring no further installation or configuration to get the tool up and running after the installation of the Application Server.

If Grid Control is used to monitor the Application Server, the Grid Control Agent will collect all the metrics directly from the Application Server components (bypassing the AS Control Agent), and upload that data to the central repository. The AS Control application is still needed to perform the main administration tasks like reconfiguring the Application Server, or deploying new applications.

Grid Control Concepts

Before we start diving deeper into the Grid Control application and what it can do, let's first review some basic concepts and explain some of the basic terminology used in the Enterprise Manager world.

Grid Control vs. Enterprise Manager

Take any piece of documentation, or any document or white paper written about Enterprise Manager, and you will see that the terms "Enterprise Manager" and "Grid Control" will be referenced multiple times. Besides the full term, there are also acronyms associated with each one: EM (Enterprise Manager) and GC (Grid Control). Historically speaking, the set of tools used to manage "things" (called "targets" in Grid Control–speak; see section "Metrics vs. Targets" later in this chapter) was called Enterprise Manager. Over the years the product has evolved and expanded into a suite of applications, with more than just the main management application. Hence the term Enterprise Manager nowadays points to the total infrastructure, with the entire suite of applications used to monitor and manage. Grid Control, on the other hand, is a relatively new term. It was first used as the management solution for the Grid Computing infrastructure. It refers to the main web-based management application, and the various components it needs to monitor and manage.

Going forward, the two will diverge even more: Enterprise Manager is the complete suite of applications used to manage and administer the enterprise, ranging from basic monitoring, top-down diagnostics, and performance monitoring of all the applications running in the enterprise, to rolling out and provisioning standardized environments defined as the corporate environment. It also includes tools like Oracle Application Diagnostics for Java (AD4J), Oracle Real User Experience Insight (RUEI), and Change Management Console, all add-ons installed on top of the base product. Grid Control, on the other hand, is still the same set of basic monitoring tools an Enterprise Administrator will get after installing the base software, designed to monitor and administer the enterprise.

NOTE
For the history buffs, a little side note: This web-based application was, in a previous incarnation, the Java application called Enterprise Manager. When the switch to Grid Computing and the web-based approach happened, the application was renamed to Grid Control, and the suite of tools and application kept the name Enterprise Manager.

In this book, we will focus primarily on the main application, and the IT infrastructure needed to use and maintain the product. As such, in the context of this book the terms Grid Control and Enterprise Manager mean and point to the same thing.

Acronym vs. Idiom

Every component in the Grid Control has its own acronyms and its own idioms:

- The OMA (Oracle Management Agent) is the Grid Control Agent. This is usually just referred to as the *Agent*.
- The OMS (Oracle Management Server) is the middle tier of infrastructure and is typically named the *Management Server*.
- The OMR (Oracle Management Repository) is the database used to store all the management data. Strictly speaking, the OMR only points to the schema used in the database that holds all the data (the SYSMAN schema), although the term "repository" is used several times to specify both the schema and the database the schema resides in.
- The last one in the list lacks a proper management acronym. The interface the users and administrators are using has several names: Console, UI, Browser. On the up side, each of these terms is descriptive enough to explain what it is pointing to.

For the sake of completeness, here are a few of the Application Server acronyms frequently used in documents and white papers:

- AS (Application Server) or iAS (Internet Application Server—the older term) points to an installation of the Oracle Application Server software.
- OC4J (Oracle Containers for Java) is a container that contains an entire application. It is deployed in an Application Server infrastructure. For Grid Control, there are two OC4J containers deployed: OC4J_EM (the main OMS application) and OC4J_EMPROV (Agent provisioning application). In the next release of Grid Control, Oracle has acquired BEA and plans to replace OC4J with JRockit as the new Java container.
- OHS is the Oracle HTTP Server, an OHS-based server used by OAS.

Metrics vs. Targets

Each enterprise asset is a *managed entity* in Grid Control (called a *target*) and provides the following information:

- State of this target (is it available for use?)
- Performance, resource, and usage indicators (how responsive is it?)
- Health statistics (is it working properly?)
- Configuration data (how is it configured?)

One should consider a target to be the management of just one thing—for instance, the DB Console is used to manage that one database, but it cannot also manage the environment in which that database exists. The ability to manage the combination of both is what is now commonly referred to as a *managed target*. When the monitoring capabilities expand to all technology elements required to keeping a business up and operational, then we consider that to be the management of a grid environment. The consumption of all such technology elements is what makes up a working ecosystem!

Each piece of information and each data point a target provides is modeled as a metric. A metric is computed through a command—or series of commands—that is executed on a regular basis to obtain data about the specified target. These commands can be specified as shell scripts, Perl scripts, SQL statements (or a PL/SQL block), SNMP requests, or even as Java commands. The metrics are combined into logical units called *collections* by the Agent. In most cases, a collection contains just one metric, but there are cases where several metrics are combined together to form one logical unit. An example of this is the storage information collected for a database: The storage collection consists of several metrics, gathering the tablespace and segment information for the database. All these collections are uploaded to a central location, where the information will be analyzed, to be used for trending and historical comparisons.

Metric data points can also have threshold conditions specified, to signal an abnormal condition of that metric on the target. These alerts, called *violations*, can then be used to notify the owner responsible for the target to take the appropriate action or artificially programmed to automatically address the issue.

The focus of Grid Control is to provide a centralized overview of all known targets and their metric information, to give the administrators managing those targets access to the current (and historical) state, and to interact with the targets for either regular maintenance, or to react to a problem condition found.

The two main parts in the management of targets are:

- ■ **Monitoring** Proactively gathering state information, raising alerts if needed, and uploading the state information to a central location. This data can then be used to do historical trending and compare information between targets at various points in time.

- ■ **Administration** Interaction with the targets via a centralized user interface to perform day-to-day operations. These tasks include regular maintenance and cleanup, as well as patching and upgrading targets.

When people log in to the Grid Control UI for the first time, the amount of data that is available usually overwhelms them. And it is true that there is a lot of information available. This is where this book can be a big help, to guide you through the initial installs, making available the things that you absolutely need, and giving suggestions on how to handle the continual stream of information.

Administrator vs. User

For any deployed application, an administrator maintains and monitors the application, while a user merely uses the product to do his or her daily work. And it's the same for Grid Control, although people tend to make the mistake of making users administrators. A Grid Control Administrator is someone who manages the (Enterprise Manager) infrastructure. These people typically do not manage the individual databases or application servers, or any other target discovered in Grid Control. A Grid Control User is a database administrator, a system operator, a network administrator, or an application DBA; in short, someone who uses Grid Control to manage the targets he or she is responsible for. Managing targets in Grid Control does not necessarily mean managing Enterprise Manager itself (meaning the infrastructure and the various components of the Grid Control application).

To make things easier to relate to, users in terms of Grid Control should be referenced as Enterprise Users or Enterprise Administrators:

- An Enterprise User is a mere user of Grid Control, with no special privileges or requirements to manage the Enterprise Manager infrastructure.

    These users only need access and privileges to manage and maintain the targets they are responsible for.

- An Enterprise Administrator is someone who manages and maintains Enterprise Manager, and will therefore need elevated privileges to be able to access the infrastructure components, and responds to alerts triggered by these targets.

- Every Grid Control administrator is by definition also a user of the application (but not every user is an administrator!). Some of these administrators will be super-users, with the necessary privileges to make changes to the infrastructure.

Grid Control Components

In order to provide a scalable architecture, which can grow and keep up with the growth of the IT environment in which it is installed, Grid Control has been split up into three different tiers, each with its own specific responsibilities, each performing a specific task. The high-level breakdown of these tiers is shown in Figure 1-2. The arrows in the figure describe the main communication flows between the various tiers in the architecture. The direction of the arrows is also important: The communication between the various components is strictly regulated, with only the central tier handling all the information requests, and dispatching the information as needed.

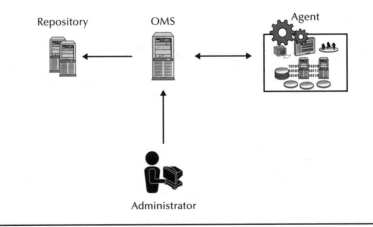

Repository   OMS   Agent

Administrator

FIGURE 1-2. *The three tiers of Grid Control*

Grid Control Console

Resting on the presentation layer, the Grid Control Console is the entry point to the Grid Control product and is commonly accessed from any web-based browser, making it a lightweight means of easily managing the entire environment from any location. With no additional setup, you can also extend subsets of Enterprise Manager to be managed by handheld devices using functionality provided by Enterprise Manager's EM2Go. The URL to access the Grid Control Console is `http(s)://<OMS-FQDN>:<PORT>/em`. By default, the communication between the browser and the Console is secured using SSL (HTTPS). The URL port differs depending on whether you are using Webcache or accessing the Oracle HTTP Server directly and on the operating system, Linux or Windows, that is hosting the Oracle Management Server. In addition to the web console, there are several optional client components that work with Grid Control:

- **EM Command Line Interface**   The EM CLI is for administrators who want to access the functionality of Grid Control, but use shell scripting or command-line interactivity in place of the Web Console.

- **Oracle Configuration Manager Client (OCM)**   Previously known as the Remote Diagnostic Agent, OCM is a tool to collect host configuration information to assist Oracle Support Services in performing diagnostics and root-cause analysis of your installations. This is a standalone utility that can be downloaded from My Oracle Support. It is also bundled with many Oracle products, and is installed and configured during the installation of the Oracle software.

The Grid Control Agent

It all starts with the Agent. This is the worker bee of the infrastructure. Without Agents, there is no data, and an administrator or user will have nothing to work with. Every managed server machine will have an Agent installed, which gathers and uploads information to the middle tier about the state and condition of all the targets it is responsible for running on this machine.

An Agent by itself will not do anything, or report anything. Only after it has been told to start monitoring a target, or when an OMS instructs it to execute a command on behalf of one of the targets, will the Agent start performing management tasks.

As soon as the install of the Grid Control Agent completes, there are at least two entities defined that the Agent will use as managed targets:

- The Agent itself, to report diagnostics information about itself

- The host the Agent was installed on

- A third entity (a target of the type "cluster") will be added if the Agent was installed on a cluster machine, and an Oracle CRS installation was found on the box.

These targets are the essential and mandatory minimum ones needed for the monitoring. Additional targets can be added to the Agent in three ways:

- **Auto-discovery**   After the install has added the Agent and Host targets, it will look for other common target types on the box. If any targets are found, they will be added to the list of managed targets.

The Agent will automatically look for these targets:

- Oracle Databases, RAC, and database listeners
- Oracle Application servers, and all Application Server components, such as HTTP Servers, Webcache servers, deployed OC4J applications, and so on.
- **A user requesting a rediscovery** When a user requests to add a target on an Agent in the Console (either via the Agent home page, or via the All Targets page), the Agent will rerun the discovery scripts of the standard types. If this rediscovery finds any new ones, these targets will be presented in the Console, so the user can decide to keep or ignore them.
- **Manual discovery of a target** If a standard target is not automatically discovered, or for those targets that do not have a discovery script, the user has the ability to manually add that target to the Agent via the Console.

When a target is discovered and visible in the Console, the Agent will monitor the target by providing useful data about it. At the same time, the Agent will accept requests from the Management Server and Grid Control users to execute administration tasks against the targets. For each target the Agent is monitoring, it has a set of collection data (the metrics and data points describing the state and condition of a target, as described earlier) that it will capture on a regular basis. These out-of-box collections are stored in the default collection files, one file for each type of target the Agent knows how to monitor.

By using these default collection files, the Agent will automatically start monitoring a specific set of metrics as soon as a target of that type is discovered. Each of the data points (called a *metric*) the Agent collects has the following characteristics:

- **A collection frequency** The agent will use this to schedule the metric on a repeating basis.
- **A metric category**
  - **Normal data metric** This is the most common type. The data is uploaded to the repository, where it gets rolled up, so the history of this metric can be shown in the Console. This rolled-up information can then be used for trending. Examples:
    - CPU utilization of a host
    - Tablespace usage of a database
  - **Configuration metric** These metrics are uploaded, but they are not rolled up, and they are not used for trending purposes. Differences between the current and previous values are kept, however, so changes to the configuration of the target can be tracked over time. Examples:
    - List of *ORACLE_HOME*s installed on a machine
    - List of network interfaces present on a host
    - List of OS patches installed on a host
  - **Real-time metric** These metrics are defined at the Agent, but without a formal schedule. They are run on demand, when a user specifically requests the data for this metric. They are also not uploaded to the repository, and no historical record is kept of the resulting values.

■ **An optional condition**   Only data metrics can have conditions. Configuration and real-time metrics do not have conditions. The condition is defined as a comparison between the data returned by the metric and the warning and critical thresholds defined in the condition. If the metric data point violates any of these threshold values, the Agent will generate an alert and send it to the OMS. This alert is sometimes also referred to as the *state* of the metric. Once this alert is uploaded to the repository, it can then be used to notify an user to take action.

Besides the metrics the Agent collects on a regular basis, the OMS can send information to run a specific command in the context of a target. This is the essence of a Grid Control Job: a command, or set of commands, sent to the Agent to be run at the appointed time in the context of a specific target.

The Management Server (OMS)

The Management Server (OMS) is the core of the infrastructure. It is the tier (and the only one) that communicates with all the other components. It rests in the application-processing layer and is installed as a standard Oracle Application Server, with two OC4J applications deployed (OC4J_EM, the main OMS server application, and OC4J_EMPROV to do Grid Control Agent provisioning). For deployments using version 10.2.0.5 or higher of Grid Control, a third OC4J application will be deployed: the OCMRepeater. This application is not part of the Management Server. It only serves to upload the OCM configuration data to Oracle.

The management server acts as an information broker in the infrastructure: It accepts all information the Agents are uploading, and stores it in the repository. When a user requests info about a specific target, the OMS will retrieve this information from the repository and report it back to the user. The OMS internally is broken up into a set of modules, each responsible for a specific aspect of the monitoring:

■ **The Console**   Responsible for retrieving and displaying all the information a user has requested in the browser.

■ **The Job subsystem**   Scheduling and dispatching of tasks and jobs defined either by the system itself, or by a user.

■ **The Loader subsystem**   All data uploaded by the Agents is parsed and inserted into the repository.

■ **The Notification subsystem**   Users and administrators need to be alerted of critical conditions happening in the environment. Once the data is loaded into the repository, and the triggered alert is detected by the notification system, all affected users and administrators will receive a notification of the violation.

■ **Self-monitoring**   This is often referred to as the MTM subsystem (Monitor The Monitor). This is a set of routines and automated tasks, which keep track of how the infrastructure itself is operating. If needed, alerts can be generated by the metrics the routines are collecting to alert an administrator of a potential problem.

The Grid Control Repository

The data management tier houses the data store in which all collected information from the managed targets resides. The size and resources used by this database will grow as the number of managed targets in your enterprise grows. To be able to handle growth, any Oracle Enterprise Edition Database can be used as the repository: The initial install can be done using a single-instance database, which later on is converted into a multinode RAC database, with a Data Guard instance in a remote location for disaster recovery. The database has to be an Enterprise Edition database, with the partitioning and object options enabled: These two options are needed for the repository schema.

The Enterprise Manager data is stored in a single schema (the SYSMAN user). This user controls and handles all management data. Besides acting as the central data store for all data, the repository will also perform some tasks that need to be done centrally, and not per Management Server. This includes housekeeping tasks, like data rollup, purging of the old data, and the old partitions. These tasks are performed via DBMS_JOBS, and can function and execute without the intervention of OMS servers.

The Flow of Information

We'll start with a basic overview of the main data flows of an Enterprise Manager infrastructure. More details for each of these flows will follow in the following chapters. But in order to make the right decisions when planning the rollout of Grid Control, understanding who talks to whom, and in what direction the data flows, is essential to make the right decisions on where to place and install which component.

Agent and OMS Communication

The communication between the Agent and OMS always uses HTTPS (SSL-encrypted HTTP traffic). Although it is technically possible to unsecure the Agent and have just normal HTTP communication (without the SSL encryption), the out-of-box default will always be secure.

The Agent will initiate contact with the OMS to upload metric data, update the target and metric configuration, or send over the result of a job or administration task the Agent has executed on behalf of the OMS. These communications are not on a fixed schedule: As soon as the Agent has information available to be sent over to the OMS, it will initiate a connection and send the information over. For secure communication from the Agent to the OMS, the default destination port 1159 will be used (Figure 1-3). This will be used by almost all the communications from the Agent to the OMS. For unsecure traffic initiated by the Agent, the default destination port 4889 is used. With the default rollout, the only unsecure connection the Agent will make is the first connection the Agent makes after install to obtain the secure wallet from the OMS. As soon as that secure wallet is obtained, all further communication done by the Agent will use the secure port 1159.

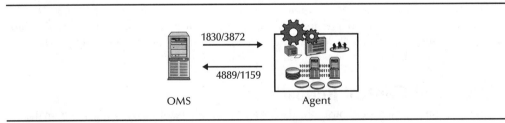

FIGURE 1-3. *Agent and OMS communication*

NOTE
To find out which ports are being used by the OMS for secure and unsecure communication, check the emoms.properties *file, located in the* $ORACLE_HOME/sysman/config *directory:*

oracle.sysman.emSDK.svlt.ConsoleServerPort=4889
oracle.sysman.emSDK.svlt.ConsoleServerHTTPSPort=1159

BEST PRACTICE
If there are multiple Management Servers running in the infrastructure, make sure all of them are configured to listen on the same ports. It is technically possible for each OMS to use different ports. But for obvious reasons, make the network administration a lot easier, and always use the same set of ports for each OMS. (Tips and tricks on how to force the install to use the same ports will be explained in detail in the next chapter, covering the install and setup of Grid Control.)

Similarly, the OMS can initiate a connection to the Agent to update the monitoring information of the Agent, or to send over job information with details on how to execute the various commands of the jobs. This type of communication is also not on a fixed schedule, and is initiated as needed.

Based on whether the Agent is running in secure or unsecure mode, the OMS will choose either HTTP or HTTPS to contact the Agent. The port it will use is the port the Agent has sent over with the initial configuration information of the Agent target that was discovered during the install. For 10gR1 installations, the port the Agent uses is 1830. For 10gR2 installations, port 3872 will be used by default.

NOTE
To find out which port the Agent is using to communicate with, check the emd.properties *file, located in the* <EMHOME>/sysman/config *directory:*

EMD_URL=https://myhost.acme.com:3872/emd/main/

The <EMHOME> *directory is the state directory the Agent uses. For regular Agents, this directory will be the same as the* $ORACLE_HOME *of the Agent software. But for some types of Agents, the state directory will be different from the* $ORACLE_HOME *(more about that in Chapter 4).*

To get the state directory the agent uses, run this command:

[oracle@agent ~]$ emctl getemhome

BEST PRACTICE
The same best practice applies to communication toward the Agents as well: Standardize on a single port to be used for the Agents. Having multiple ports in use for the Agent communication will make it a lot harder to configure firewalls. (The next chapter will shed some light on how to force the install to use the same port.)

An additional benefit of standardizing on a single port is the ability to spot the ugly duckling that got installed in a different way: Any Agent that is not using the standard port (3872 by default) can be easily identified.

The following query will list all Agents that have not used the default port 3872 during install. Run this as the owner of the Grid Control repository (SYSMAN user):

```
SELECT target_name
FROM   mgmt_targets
WHERE  target_type = 'oracle_emd'
  AND  SUBSTR(target_name,INSTR(target_name,':')+1) !=
3872;
```

All information the OMS and the Agent exchange is structured in XML format. There are various types of information:

- The OMS server sends changes to the configuration of a target (called the *monitoring configuration*) and the way the target is being monitored (metric settings and thresholds) to the Agent.

- The Agent will upload any monitoring information, including metric data and the generated alerts.

- For synchronous job tasks, the OMS server will send over the command, and wait for the Agent to reply using the same connection.

For long-running operations, the OMS server will send over the information, and close the connection. When the Agent has finished the task, it will initiate a new connection back to the OMS server to upload the results.

Because of the nature of the HTTP (or HTTPS) protocol, it is possible to have Agents scattered around the network. There are no restrictions on where to deploy Agents. As long as the OMS can communicate with the Agent, and the Agent can communicate and upload XML files to the middle tiers, Grid Control can monitor the server machine through the deployed OMS servers.

With the central function of the OMS server, however, the Management Servers will have to be strategically positioned in the network, to allow these machines to communicate with all the machines in the enterprise that require monitoring. Especially in enterprise-wide deployments, with (sometimes multiple) firewalls involved, this will be a factor that needs to be discussed and verified with the network administrators to successfully install Grid Control.

OMS-to-Repository Communication

The OMS is the only tier that makes a connection to the repository database (Figure 1-4). The Agents will communicate only with the OMS, and the logged-in users will also make all requests to the OMS. The Management Server will then take those requests, store and retrieve the necessary information to and from the repository, and send the resulting data back to the requestor.

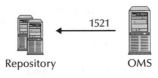

Repository   OMS

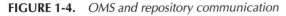

FIGURE 1-4. *OMS and repository communication*

The OMS server creates several thin JDBC connections to the repository database. These connections are split up in connection pools. Each pool is dedicated for a specific function. If a connection in a pool is not in use, it can be reused by another thread using the same connection pool in the OMS. If there are several OMS servers running, each middle-tier server will have its own connections for each pool.

NOTE
When you are checking the gv$session view in the database, you can find the connection pools by looking at OMS sessions, made from an OMS machine, which have the value of the Module column set to one of those pools.

Use the following SQL query to narrow this down:

```
SELECT inst_id, sid, serial#, machine, module, action
FROM    gv$session
WHERE   username = 'SYSMAN'
  AND   program = 'OMS'
  AND   module LIKE '%Pool';
```

There are four different connection pools the OMS uses, each with its own cryptic name. Each of the pools is part of a critical part (sometimes called a subsystem) of the OMS, performing either internal housekeeping tasks, or responding to requests made by the Administrators or the Agents:

- **OEM.BoundedPool**   Set of connections used to upload the Alert information from the Agents. This information also includes any updates to the condition of the targets the Agent is monitoring, and the setup and definition of the collections and metrics the Agent is monitoring (more about this in Chapter 7). This special connection pool is set-aside especially for this purpose, to guarantee no interruptions or delays when loading this type of data.

- **OEM.CacheModeWaitPool**   This pool is only used to process updates to the Grid Control jobs. More details about the Job system can be found in Chapter 10.

- **OEM.CacheModeWaitnPool**   All the processing notifications to inform an Administrator about a new Alert are done using connections from this pool. In-depth coverage about these notifications can be found in Chapter 9.

- **OEM.CacheModeWaitrPool**   Connections used by the Shared File System loader. This is a High-Availability (HA) feature. The details on how to use and set up this pool can be found in Chapter 3.

- **OEM.DefaultPool**   Every user logged in to the Grid Control application will use a connection from this pool. Since the connections are pooled and reused, multiple Administrators logged in to the Console can be using the same connection on the OMS to process the requests.

- **OEM.SystemPool**   This is used for all internal OMS operations and housekeeping tasks.

All data that needs to be persisted is saved in the repository. This can come from Agents in the form of metadata (target definitions, metric settings), state data (condition of the targets and metric run on that target), configuration data, and metric data.

Data can also come from Administrators who are logged in to the Console and updating configuration or providing new administration data.

NOTE
To find out which port the OMS server is using to create the database connections, check the emoms.properties *file:*

oracle.sysman.eml.mntr.emdRepPort=1521

In case of a RAC repository database, the port will be taken from the TNS descriptor used to connect to the database:

oracle.sysman.eml.mntr.emdRepConnectDescriptor=
(...TNS descriptor...(PORT\=1521)...rest of TNS
descriptor...)

An OMS server on startup will create several connections in the repository database. This includes the connections to perform the housekeeping tasks, handle the job requests, respond to the Administrators logged into the Console UI, and upload all the data send by the Agents.

With the out-of-box settings, each OMS server will create a minimum of 14 connections to the repository. More connections can be made depending on the number of Agents uploading data and administrators logging in to the system.

NOTE
More information about how to tune and change the OMS server settings to manage the database connections can be found in Chapter 12.

Based on this information, in combination with the overview of how the Agents communicate with the OMS server, we can now draw a second conclusion on how to deploy and where to put OMS servers in an Enterprise Manager deployment. With the OMS creating several connections to the repository database, and the fact that the information loaded into the repository through those connections will come in bursts, either from Agents uploading XML files or from users requesting information via the Console UI, the OMS server should be installed in the close vicinity of the repository database. The network latency should be kept to an absolute minimum between the OMS servers and the repository database to reduce the response time of the operations an OMS makes into the repository database: Any network hop that can be eliminated should be eliminated.

BEST PRACTICE
There are several tools available to monitor network activity, or to test network connectivity. For a quick-and-dirty approach to test the responsiveness of a remote machine, the standard command ping *can be used. Ideally, the response time returned by the* ping *command should be in the single digits, or the low double digits in milliseconds.*

There will be severe performance implications for the OMS server responsiveness to user requests (Console performance) and Agent upload request (XML file throughput) when the response time reported by ping *reaches 100 milliseconds and higher.*

User (Web-Client) to OMS Communication

A user connecting to the Grid Control Console will have to use a web browser to do so. Web browsers by definition only contact the HTTP server, and will never be the recipient of a connection from the server.

There are two sets of ports to access the OMS:

■ A direct access path to the OMS servers, using ports 1159 and 4889. These ports are used by the Agents to talk to the OMS.

BEST PRACTICE
For large enterprise-wide deployments, it is strongly advised to keep the traffic from the Agents separate from the communications between the users and administrators. The ports 1159 and 4889 should therefore only be used interactively (using a browser) to debug a problem, or when testing communication. All other UI-based activity done by users of Grid Control should use the Oracle HTTP Server (OHS) ports (or the Webcache ports if Webcache is used).

■ Access to the OMS servers using ports 7777/7778 and 4444/8250 (Figure 1-5). These ports are the main ones used by the users connecting via a console. Ports 7778 (unsecure, HTTP) and 8250 (secure, HTTPS) are defined by Webcache, and forwarded to OHS on ports 7777 and 4444 respectively.

NOTE
Webcache is not a strict requirement for the application rollout. Given the dynamic nature of Grid Control, with pages getting constructed on the fly based on the specifics specified by the logged-in user, the benefic of using Webcache to speed up the web pages is very limited. It is needed only if end-user monitoring is used to track the usage of specific URLs of the application.

Users logging in to Grid Control can use either of these two sets of ports. The reason for the second set of ports is to separate the traffic from the Agents from traffic from the people using Grid Control.

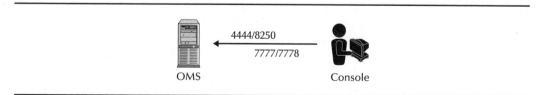

FIGURE 1-5. *Console-to-OMS communication*

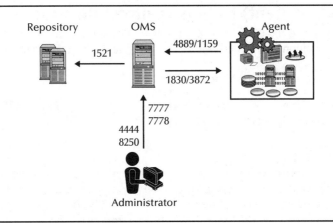

FIGURE 1-6. *TCP ports used by each tier*

TCP Ports Used by Enterprise Manager

Figure 1-6 shows all the TCP ports that Grid Control release 10.2.0.4 or higher uses. Table 1-1 describes the use of these ports.

Port	Used By	Communication To and From
1159	OMS Server	Used by the Agents to communicate to the OMS servers in a secure way.
1521	Repository	Used by the OMS servers to communicate to the repository database listener.
3872	Agents	Used by the OMS servers to communicate to the Agents. Can be either secure or unsecure.
4444	OMS Server	Used by the Administrator's browser UI to communicate to the OMS server (HTTP Server) in a secure way. The traffic will be redirected to port 8250.
4889	OMS Server	Used by the Agents to communicate to the OMS servers in an unsecure way (during securing requests).
7777	OMS Server	Used by the Administrator's browser UI to communicate to the OMS server (Webcache Server) in an unsecure way.
7778	OMS Server	Used by the Administrator's browser UI to communicate to the OMS server (HTTP Server) in an unsecure way. The traffic will get redirected to port 7777.
8250	OMS Server	Used by the Administrator's browser UI to communicate to the OMS server (Webcache Server) in a secure way,

TABLE 1-1. *TCP Port Details*

The Different Types of Targets

After this brief explanation of Grid Control and its basic functions, it's time for a list of the different types of targets that can be monitored. The idea is not to go into much detail at this point, but to give an idea of the capabilities and possibilities that Enterprise Manager can offer. Most people still are under the impression that Grid Control is just a database-monitoring tool. Over the years, the monitoring capabilities have been extended far beyond merely databases, making it possible to monitor a lot more targets that are typically present in today's data centers. Each different type of target added to the environment has its own requirements to keep track of. And with each new monitoring capability comes new preparation that needs to be done to make the monitoring and administration possible.

Besides drawing the attention of administrators beyond that of database monitoring, the intention of this list is also to make people aware of the additional steps and preparation that need to be completed to make the monitoring possible.

A lot of these targets are provided out of box with each install of Grid Control. Others are plug-ins (extensions) provided by either Oracle or partners to extend the default set of monitoring capabilities of Grid Control.

NOTE
For a complete list of all available monitoring extensions, check the Grid Control Extensions Exchange *web page on OTN (Oracle Technology Network):*

`http://www.oracle.com/technology/products/oem/`
`extensions/index.html`

Here is a brief overview of the type of targets to be monitored:

- **Host, Agent, and Cluster**   This is the cornerstone of all monitoring. Each monitored machine will have an Agent and a host target defined. If CRS is installed, a third target of the type "Cluster" will also be added to the default list of targets the Agent has after install.

- **Databases**   This goes beyond Oracle databases. Besides the single database instances, RAC databases, and Data Guard instances, other type of databases like Microsoft SQL Server, Times Ten In Memory Database, Sybase, or IBM DB2 databases can also be monitored.

- **Application Servers**   Besides Oracle Application Servers, Grid Control can monitor BEA Weblogic, JBoss Application Server, Microsoft Internet Information Server (IIS), Internet Security and Acceleration (ISA), Biztalk and Commerce Server, and IBM Websphere middle-tier installations.

- **Application Suites**   This includes Oracle Ebiz and Collaboration Suite, PeopleSoft and Siebel Application, Oracle Identity Management, and SAP installations.

- **Network devices**   Includes F5 Server Load Balancers, Juniper NetScreen, and Nortel Alteon Application Switch.

- **Storage devices**   Among the different storage devices are Netapp filers, Onara SANScreen, and EMC Celera, Clariion, and Symmetrix systems.

- **Grid Control–specific Container targets**   This includes Groups (logical groups of targets), Systems (set of physical targets that run a specific application), Services (logical definition of service, an application), and Beacons (network point to test connectivity with applications).

This list is not definitive. Additional plug-ins and monitoring extensions are uploaded regularly on OTN, and support for new target types is added to Grid Control with each new release of the product.

Summary

Now that we have been acquainted with the range of products that makes up Oracle's Enterprise Manager, two things should be clear by now. First, we can no longer profit from the luxury of placing live bodies to monitoring every new deployed database or middle-tier server. This solution doesn't scale in today's IT environment where environments exist in multi-national locations and accompanied by increased complexity from the applications that get deployed into them. Second, anytime an environment is scaled out, there is significant expense in ensuring the environment is effectively utilized and available. This is because prior to enterprise management technologies, the length of the feedback loop for discovering system imbalances then implementing corrective actions was lengthy and manually intensive. Throughout the rest of the book we will look at these various architectural challenges and now with Grid Control as part of the solution, we will discuss why the technology is a good fit.

CHAPTER
2

Preparing and Installing
the Environment

nstalling software is such a mundane task. It is something that we generally attend to in between other tasks or whenever we manage to find the time. However, if you use that approach with Enterprise Class software, you would be laying the groundwork for failure in the future. You must not rollout a technical solution for your entire IT organization without a proper plan that has been adequately discussed by all those involved.

Preparing for the Install

Like all traditional clichés, this chapter is likely the most important one you will read throughout the entire book. This is the point in time where the success or failure of a Grid Control deployment is determined: when someone knows enough about the product to be dangerous, but just not enough to really know what to do next. It is important to understand what Grid Control is and what it can do. And any administrator will need to acquire a basic understanding of the networking topology of the environment Grid Control will be installed in. But this is not enough to finish a project successfully. With the rollout of the managed targets comes a set of challenges. And the better prepared an administrator is to face these, the easier it will be to do the installations and get everything working.

The first question to ask when rolling out Enterprise Manager is this: What is the main business reason for using Grid Control? The typical reply for this question is always:

Monitoring of my *–insert your favorite target here–*

Rarely do people mention "data center management" (which actually means asset management), or "data center availability" or "application readiness" (which means keeping applications and software up to date and operational).

This might sound like a silly discussion, or nit-picking and debating semantics, but there are significant distinctions to be made with each of the responses. Each of them has a specific focus and will require special attention to certain aspects of the Grid Control management. The goal of the deployment has to be something that is known before the whole project starts. And this goal will probably be different depending on the people you talk to. Operators and the administrators working on the data center floor will have certain expectations about what they can do with the product, and how the product will help them in their day-to-day work. The work these people do is always hands-on, and will require specific setup to grant access to the necessary servers and applications through Grid Control. The remaining parts of this book cover the user and target setup of Grid Control, with all the tips and tricks on how to let the operators work effectively with the information available.

The Enterprise Administrators are a special breed of administrators, and have to be considered separately. They need to look at the infrastructure and all the managed targets on a different level: They don't need all the details, but they need to be able to see all the servers and the managed targets, to be able to intervene in case of a problem. Chapter 6 of this book is dedicated to the maintenance aspect of Grid Control, and how to make the changes that have been made in an enterprise visible in Grid Control.

And then there are the various levels of management, going all the way up to upper management (the C-levels). Depending on the business reason for the rollout, there will be a focus on a specific area, and specific information from that area. Features like reports and dashboards can roll up that information and make it accessible. Based on the requirements, though, these reports and dashboards will have to be customized. If the main purpose is to do asset management, reports about the various machines, the different types of hardware, software versions, and so on are needed.

On the other hand, if the main focus is on availability and data center readiness, outage reports, availability numbers, and detailed reports about maintenance windows will need to be made available.

It is usually an endeavor, requiring a series of steps, by multiple parties to take information and aggregate it into a dashboard view for quick reference. Examples of such reports will be outlined in more detail starting with Chapter 11.

As you can clearly deduce from all this, there will be a wildly varying set of features used in the deployment, beginning with the administrators who will get their hands dirty and work on the targets, all the way up to the rolled-up information and reports needed for the management chain. Each of the requirements will need to be mapped, planned, and put into a schedule.

Phased Rollout

This gets us to the deployment plan, another essential step in any Grid Control deployment. It's impossible to install everything at once, and bring all those custom reports, metrics, dashboards, and so forth online from the get-go. There are three essential phases, which every environment will need. They will be the same for each rollout, and need to be executed in this order: install the infrastructure, deploy the grid control agents, and manage required targets.

Install the Infrastructure

Without the OMS servers or the repository, there is no Grid Control. So it will make absolute sense to everyone to have this done first. But this phase goes beyond the simple rollout of the OMS server and the repository. The number of OMS servers will play a role here, too. So will the type of database used for the repository, and the network layout, with all the proxy servers, firewalls, and Server Load Balancers, which will need to be configured and adjusted to allow the Grid Control network traffic. Plus there is the whole availability question: How highly available does Grid Control need to be? Since this is such a big topic, with several things to point out and explain, the details about High Availability (HA) and Maximum Availability Architecture (MAA) for Grid Control are in their own separate chapter (the next one in fact). See Chapter 3.

Deploy the Grid Control Agents

Once the basic infrastructure is present, the Agents can be installed on the physical hosts that need to be monitored. This step is key to getting all the information that is required to manage your targets in the enterprise. Different mechanisms can be used to install Agents, depending on the requirements and restrictions imposed by the environment. For more information about how to appropriately roll out your Agents, see Chapter 4.

Manage All Required Targets

Finally, after the Agents are all happily brought online, talking to the OMS servers, and uploading all the standard monitoring information, comes the last step in the initial rollout plan of Grid Control: the management of all the required targets. Besides getting those targets configured and visible in the Grid Control UI, the configuration of these targets has to be completed: things like passwords, location of the software (*ORACLE_HOME*), communication ports used, and so on will need to be verified or updated. After the install of the Agents, some of the targets will already be discovered and present in Grid Control. Others will need to be added. The details on how to set up and configure targets are covered in Chapter 7. Logical groupings like Systems and Services, will need to be created by the administrators in the Console. An example of this is presented in Chapter 13.

Topology of the Management Framework

As we already discussed in the previous chapter, Grid Control requires communication on a set of TCP ports to the various parts of the infrastructure. The most typical of setups include multiple network domains with intranet or Internet access including one or many firewalls between each. Each addition will require a consistent management of ports to allow communication to and from the OMS servers.

BEST PRACTICE
Standardize the TCP ports used on both the Management Servers and the Agents. By using a consistent set of ports, you can minimize the changes on the firewalls and other network devices. And this will make the network administrators and security administrators very happy.

Another common network device that Enterprise Administrators will need to deal with is a proxy server. Grid Control uses HTTP and HTTPS to communicate with all the Agents in the environment. But it also requires external access to the My Oracle Support web site, to download information about the available releases, Critical Patch Updates (CPU), and other information about available patches. A proxy server, when specified, can affect both the Agent communication, and the external access to the Oracle web site.

TIP
Since Console UI and the Agent traffic can be separated, placing the entire EM infrastructure in its own demilitarized zone (DMZ) provides some interesting possibilities. With only two entry points into that management DMZ (one from Console and one from the Agents), both of which can be secured to use only SSL communication, the firewall can be configured with a few rules that tightly control access to the DMZ. If security is a concern, this option is one the Enterprise Administrator can consider to separate the traffic to and from the Enterprise Manager infrastructure.

Topology of the Managed Targets

Most people make the mistake of thinking that after the target has been discovered in Grid Control, all the work is done. It does not end with the discovery of the target. Making the target appear in the Console is only half of the work. The whole purpose of discovering targets in Grid Control is to manage them and report on unexpected behavior. And as Murphy's Law has demonstrated so many times, things *will* go wrong. And when they do, somebody will have to able to intervene and make the necessary corrections. To make sure people are capable of making changes to targets, make sure the following information is either known, or configured in Grid Control:

■ **Access to the Agent**   This might sound like a silly or an absurd point to make, but in a complex environment, with data centers all over the world, access to all the servers in the enterprise is not an obvious thing. Having access to an Agent is essential to do any kind of debugging, or perform any kind of intervention in case of a problem. This means not only having credentials to log in to the box, but also having the correct hostname and IP address to access this machine on the network. In a network with multiple domains, machines can have multiple network cards and multiple hostnames (access routes) to get to that machine.

■ **Access to the target**   This means having credentials (passwords) ready to go, or at least have a way to obtain the password in a timely fashion. Just as with the Agents, access also means being able to communicate with the target. In the case of an Application Server or a Database, an administrator has to be able to make a connection to that application.

■ **A contact person**   This can be either a specific person, or a group/division, as long as the information can lead, point, or allow a user or administrator to get in touch with a real live person to talk about the target. Once a contact person is specified for a given target, that person can update a property for the target he or she is responsible for in the Console. (These properties and how to specify them will be covered in more detail in Chapter 7.)

■ **Physical location details if applicable**   This is a "nice to have" item, but a *really* nice thing to have. Having a physical location to give people in order to do some work on a machine itself is a real bonus, and can speed things up quite considerably. The location information can also be stored as a property for each target. The value is a free-text field, and can be used to store a physical location like "Sydney, Australia"; an environment-specific value like "Building 20 - Floor 2"; or even a Data Center Grid comment like "Quadrant 2, Silo 4, Rack 7, Row 4."

Preparing for Future Growth

There's one certainty when data centers are managed: Things will change. The trick is to anticipate the change, and prepare the infrastructure to accommodate the coming changes. There are three types of changes that are relevant for Grid Control:

■ How many machines are getting decommissioned? This is the easiest one. The fewer machines, the less work for both the Agents and the Management Servers. Having to monitor fewer machines means more capacity and resources available in Grid Control.

■ How many new machines are being deployed? This is the big one. Installing new machines means new Agents. This means more managed targets, more work, and more information. And with this new information, the repository will grow, and the load of the OMS server will increase. At some point, an additional OMS server might be needed, or extra storage will need to be made available for the database.

■ How many applications and targets are getting moved? If a target or an application moves from one machine to another one, there is no increase in information, and therefore no change in the sizing of the repository and the OMS servers. But this will mean work to be carried out by the Enterprise Administrators, to relocate these targets to other machines, and have them properly discovered again with the correct settings on the new machines.

BEST PRACTICE
It's best to track the number of physical servers managed in Grid Control from a period of six to twelve months. By planning ahead, you can trend usage and predict when additional hardware will need to be brought online to accommodate new work. If dynamic conditions make predicting growth of the infrastructure impossible, there are still key indicators in Grid Control that make rudimentary sizing estimates a reality. Additional information on sizing estimates is in Chapter 5 and information about key metrics including how to interpret them, is covered in Chapter 6.

Naming Conventions for Physical Hosts

Enterprise-wide networks have evolved in recent years into a complex infrastructure requiring dedicated and specialized administrators to manage the various components of the network. Identification of machines via hostnames and IP addresses has become equally more complex and complicated. With technologies like network address translation (NAT), port address translation (PAT), Virtual Private Networking (VPN), virtual aliases, and so on, identifying a machine on the network is not always as straightforward as it seems. For the Agent and the OMS to be able to communicate with each other, they both need to need to be able to resolve the hostname of the other into a valid IP address. Tools like `ping` and `traceroute` can be used to verify the network connectivity. For example:

```
[oracle@oms ~]$ ping agent.acme.com
[oracle@oms ~]$ traceroute agent.acme.com
```

The names of the machines to be used in the Enterprise Manager infrastructure must conform to the RFC 952 and RFC 1034 standard networking definitions:

- Hostnames are case-insensitive.
- Only the special characters underscore (_) and hyphen (-) are allowed in hostnames.
- Hostnames cannot start with a numerical digit.

BEST PRACTICE
Even though hostnames are case-insensitive, the name of the target as it is discovered in Grid Control is case-sensitive. Always specify the hostnames in a consistent way (the common practice is to always use lowercase names), so anomalies can be tracked down easily.

In an enterprise deployment, where machines across multiple subnets will be monitored, always use fully qualified hostnames (FQDN notation). If just a hostname is used, based on the subnet where the Grid Control OMSes are located, the wrong machines can be used to communicate, resulting in communication errors. For example:

```
dns.au.acme.com
dns.es.acme.com
dns.us.acme.com
```

Trying to establish a connection to the machine's dns will be different based on where in the network the request was made. For generic network requests, like a hostname lookup, this will be okay (or even advisable), but for Grid Control, the communication to the machines needs to be fixed. The fully qualified name also gives a hint of the physical location (or at least the broad region) of the machine. And those domain names can be used to filter and classify targets in reports. Based on the previous example, here's a SQL statement to count all discovered machines in Australia:

```
SELECT COUNT(*)
FROM    mgmt_targets
WHERE   target_type = 'host'
AND   target_name LIKE '%.au.acme.com';
```

Related to the Fully Qualified Domain Name (FQDN) discussion, an additional thing to remember when discovering machines in Grid Control is to always make sure that each managed machine has a proper hostname. Here are the rules:

- Avoid having machines discovered with just their IP address. In theory, an IP address as the main means to locate and communicate a machine is fixed and will not change, making it possible for the Management Servers to communicate properly with that machine. However, the set of numbers can be a usability issue in the Console, with a very nondescriptive name visible for a machine. And more importantly, it removes some of the flexibility you have if the software on this machine ever needs to be migrated to another physical box. See also Chapter 6.

- Machines identifying themselves as localhost or 127.0.0.1 (the loopback addresses) will—for obvious reasons—not be able to communicate with any machine on the network using that name. Each machine discovered in Grid Control will need to have a unique hostname, and a unique IP address, that can be used to connect to the machine.

- It is possible to discover machines with a DHCP setup. If no special network setup is done, these machines will receive a hostname generated by the DHCP server. When the lease of the IP address ends, the DHCP name of the machine will change, as well as the IP address. This means that the discovered name in Grid Control will no longer match the name of the machine originally discovered in the Console, and this will create a problem with the upload of new data from the machine, as well as creating a problem for the OMS to update the Agent with any change made. If a machine with a DHCP setup needs to be discovered in Grid Control, make sure it has a fixed hostname, which will continue to be associated with that machine, even if the IP address lease has ended and a new IP address is assigned to the machine.

Using a Different Hostname for the Install

The Agent installer will always use the primary hostname of a machine as the main hostname for all the installation and configuration files. The primary hostname is the first name (not the aliases) associated with the IP address of the first network card in the machine.

Every operating system has its own specific configuration files, and specific network commands to define and determine the hostnames and IP addresses of a machine. In its simplest form, the name of the machine is the result of this command:

```
[oracle@oms ~]$ hostname
```

Note, the result is not complete as the domain name may not always be part of the output when using this specific command. There are additional approaches that can be used to get the complete hostname of a machine. But all these commands are OS-specific, and most of time they depend on certain network protocols or network services to be running. Some examples are:

```
[oracle@oms ~]$  nslookup hostname
[oracle@oms ~]$  ping -n 1 hostname
```

The way to get the "true" fully qualified hostname (meaning the FQDN, which is the name of the machine specified with the domain name) is by issuing the gethostbyname system call. This low-level call can be used in programming languages like C and Java, but also in scripting languages like Perl and Python. Here's a very simple (and perhaps cryptic to some) example to get the primary hostname of a machine using Perl:

```
[oracle@oms ~]$ perl -e 'use Sys::Hostname;($n,@l)=gethostbyname hostname;print $n;'
```

The way to specify an alternate hostname is to specify the new name as the value of the *ORACLE_HOSTNAME* environment variable. To use this with the Agent installer, specify it as both an environment variable (so the post configuration tools will pick it up after the base install completes), and also on the installer command line (so the base install uses the new name during the install):

```
[oracle@oms ~]$ ORACLE_HOSTNAME=virtual1.acme.com
[oracle@oms ~]$ export ORACLE_HOSTNAME
[oracle@oms ~]$ ./runInstaller ORACLE_HOSTNAME=virtual1.acme.com -debug
```

NOTE
Overruling of the hostname can only be done for those install methods that allow an option to overrule the default settings. Only the interactive install, the silent install, and the Agent download allow ways to overrule the hostname. Chapter 4 goes into more details about these methods, including the ways to overrule the defaults.

There are several reasons to want to overrule the primary hostname:

- On some machines, the main hostname is linked with an IP address that is not visible on the network (or at least on the parts of the network Grid Control is using). For those types of setup, an alternate hostname has to be used for the install, to make sure the communication with the other parts of the Grid Control infrastructure will succeed.

- In some deployments, a virtual hostname (an alias defined for the host) has to be used to abstract the physical box from the install. This is particularly interesting in high-availability installations (more about those in the next chapter).

Preinstallation Checks for the Installer and the Database

The OMS installer will run a set of prechecks when it starts. These prechecks can be run manually on the machine at any time using this command:

```
$ <staging area>/install/runInstaller
    -prereqchecker PREREQ_CONFIG_LOCATION=<staging area>/rdbms/Disk1/stage/prereq
    -entryPoint oracle.sysman.top.oms_Core -nowelcome
    -prereqLogLoc /tmp/gc_precheck.log -silent -waitForCompletion
```

GRID CONTROL WORKSHOP

Preparing the Repository

Workshop Notes

As a general best-practice rule, always deploy Grid Control in a dedicated database, installed for just this purpose. To take full advantage of all the features and capabilities of the database, always use the latest supported (and certified) database version for the repository.

Step 1. There are a few special requirements needed for a database to host the Grid Control repository:

- The repository database needs to be an Enterprise Edition database, with the Object and Partitioning options enabled. A Standard Edition database is not sufficient for Grid Control, as it does not have the partitioning option.

- No special tablespaces need to be created. The install will create all the necessary tablespaces in the database.

Step 2. Add the `dbms_pool` package for shared pool operations. From the database home, run this command in SQL*Plus:

```
SQL> CONNECT / AS SYSDBA;
SQL> @?/rdbms/admin/dbmspool.sql
```

Step 3. A set of `init.ora` parameters needs to be set in the database.

The following parameters need to be set with these values:

```
_b_tree_bitmap_plans=false
aq_tm_processes=1
db_block_size=8192
statistics_level=TYPICAL
timed_statistics=TRUE
undo_management=AUTO
```

NOTE
For 11g (or higher) databases, it is recommended to leave the parameter aq_tm_processes unset and let the database auto-tune the parameter.

The following parameters need to be specified with at least these minimal values:

```
job_queue_processes=10
log_buffer=1048576
open_cursors=300
processes=150
session_cached_cursors=200
undo_retention=10800
```

(continued)

These parameters can be set to higher values if the usage or specific installation of the database requires it. A full explanation of all the mandatory database parameters can be found in the *Grid Control Installation Guide.*

Step 4. Grid Control and DB Control cannot coexist in the same database. If DB Control is installed in the database, you will need to remove it using EMCA (the DB Control configuration assistant) before installing Grid Control.

Use the following command to remove the DB Control repository:

```
$ORACLE_HOME/bin/emca -deconfig dbcontrol db -repos drop
```

In the case of a RAC database, the `-cluster` option will need to be added to the command:

```
$ORACLE_HOME/bin/emca -deconfig dbcontrol db -repos drop -cluster
```

The best way to check for the existence of a DB Control or Grid Control repository is to simply search for a user named SYSMAN:

```
SELECT username
FROM   dba_users
WHERE  username = 'SYSMAN'
```

If the user exists, some type of repository is installed in the database. If there is ever some doubt about the type of repository installed in a database, this SQL query can be run as SYSMAN:

```
SELECT DECODE(component_mode
              ,'SYSAUX' ,'DB Control'
              ,'CENTRAL','Grid Control'
              ,component_mode)
FROM   mgmt_versions
WHERE  component_name = 'CORE'
```

This can help determine whether the system is ready for the install and all the system requirements to get the software deployed are met. If OS packages or patches are missing, they can be installed, and system/kernel parameters can be adjusted before running the actual install of Grid Control. The overview of all the prechecks run by the installer can also be found in the *Grid Control Installation Guide.*

NOTE
Make sure to run the `runInstaller` *command from the* `install` *subdirectory of the staging area, and not from the root of the staging area. If you do run the precheck command using the* `runInstaller` *from the root directory of the staging area, you will get this cryptic error message:*

```
The specified command line has invalid arguments:
    The command line arguments '-nowelcome' are not
valid options.
```

Modifying the Response Files

Typically, people will just start the Oracle installer in interactive mode, filling in the prompts and answering the questions the install routine is asking. For automation, an interactive install experience is not going to work: You need to be able to script the install, and start specifying the values of all these prompts and questions somehow. And this is where the command-line install (aka silent install) comes into the picture.

The installer will use response files in case of a silent install (when the `-silent` command-line option is used). These files are located in the response directory of the install staging area, and contain the values and settings the user would typically enter during an interactive install (see Table 2-1).

These response files will have to be modified by the database administrator before doing the install. Parameters like the operating system users and groups, location of software, and environment-specific settings like proxy servers and so on will need to be specified.

NOTE
Response files are only used for silent installs (the `-silent` command-line switch is used). Any kind of interactive install will ignore the response files, even if one is specified on the command line.

Hardware Requirements

Determining which hardware is absolutely necessary for Grid Control is not an easy task. There are so many variables and environmental factors to be considered, making it impossible to come up with a definitive set of hardware requirements. There are a couple of guidelines, though, that should be followed.

Dedicated Hardware

Unless you have a small site, with a fixed number of machines to monitor, the biggest challenge in keeping Enterprise Manager running is anticipating the growth of the environment and the monitoring of that environment. To allow the infrastructure to grow, the machines used for the infrastructure boxes and the way the various components have been installed are key to have the possibility to grow Grid Control.

Response File	Description
`em_with_new_db.rsp`	The first install option: Install a new Grid Control site, and put a new repository database on the same machine
`em_using_existing_db.rsp`	The second install option: Install a new Grid Control site, but use an already existing database as the repository
`additional_mgmt_service.rsp`	Add a new management server to the existing Grid Control environment
`additional_agent.rsp`	Add an Agent to the Grid Control environment.

TABLE 2-1.   *Response Files*

Use a dedicated RAC database for the repository with a couple of commodity server-class machines for the OMS. The rule of thumb machine-wise is a set of two 4 × 4 machines (four CPUs, 4GB of memory) for the repository to have a two-node RAC database, and two 2 × 2 (two CPUs, 2GB of memory) for the Management Servers. The RAC database gives the flexibility to add another instance to the RAC database if additional capacity is needed. And with two OMSes to start with, the minimal HA requirements are met (see Chapter 3), with the possibility to add more if the need arises.

Focus on IO Throughput, CPU, and Memory for the Repository Machine(s)

A constant flow of data is getting updated and inserted into the repository, while administrators and some of the housekeeping jobs (like the data rollup) query the old data again. The nature of this kind of activity is typical for an OLTP type of database, requiring decent IO throughput to be able to read and write all this data in a timely fashion. To keep the SQL responses snappy for users working with Grid Control, and to keep the housekeeping tasks running smoothly, the database should have sufficient CPU power and a properly sized System Global Area (SGA) to work with (a 2GB SGA is not an exception for a large enterprise deployment). If you are presented with a choice of machines to use for Grid Control, always choose the machine with the most CPU power for the repository.

Focus on Network Throughput and Network Latency for the OMS Machine(s)

The OMS is the hub of activity for Grid Control: All information passes through the OMS. This makes the network connectivity the most important aspect of the OMS machines (it's also typically the first bottleneck people hit when a deployment grows). Network throughput is key to the performance of the OMS. All traffic from the middle-tier machines to the database is time-critical: Keep the network latency (and thus automatically also the number of hops) between the OMS and repository database as small as possible. Network response times are expressed in milliseconds. Despite the fact that this is a very short period of time, it still should be either in the single-digit or the very low double-digit range.

An OMS machine will need some CPU capacity, but there are no "burst" activities or any other kind of intense operations happening on the Management Server side. The minimum of 2GB of memory that the Application Server requires is also quite sufficient for an OMS.

Installing Grid Control

Here is the moment of truth: If the Enterprise Administrators have done all the necessary homework, and prepared everything properly, the actual install of the Grid Control software should be a piece of cake: just a matter of clicking the button, and waiting for the install to finish copying all the software on the disc. When you are starting the installation of the Grid Control software, four different options are available for the install, as shown in Figure 2-1.

Enterprise Manager 10*g* Grid Control Using a New Database

This type of install is sometimes referred to as the "collapsed install," since it installs everything (repository, OMS, and Agent) on a single box. It is only suitable for small deployments, test environments, or prototypes. For any kind of production environment, which might grow beyond what it is initially monitoring, this option should *not* be used. This option can only be used for a new environment, and cannot be used to add a Management Server to an existing environment.

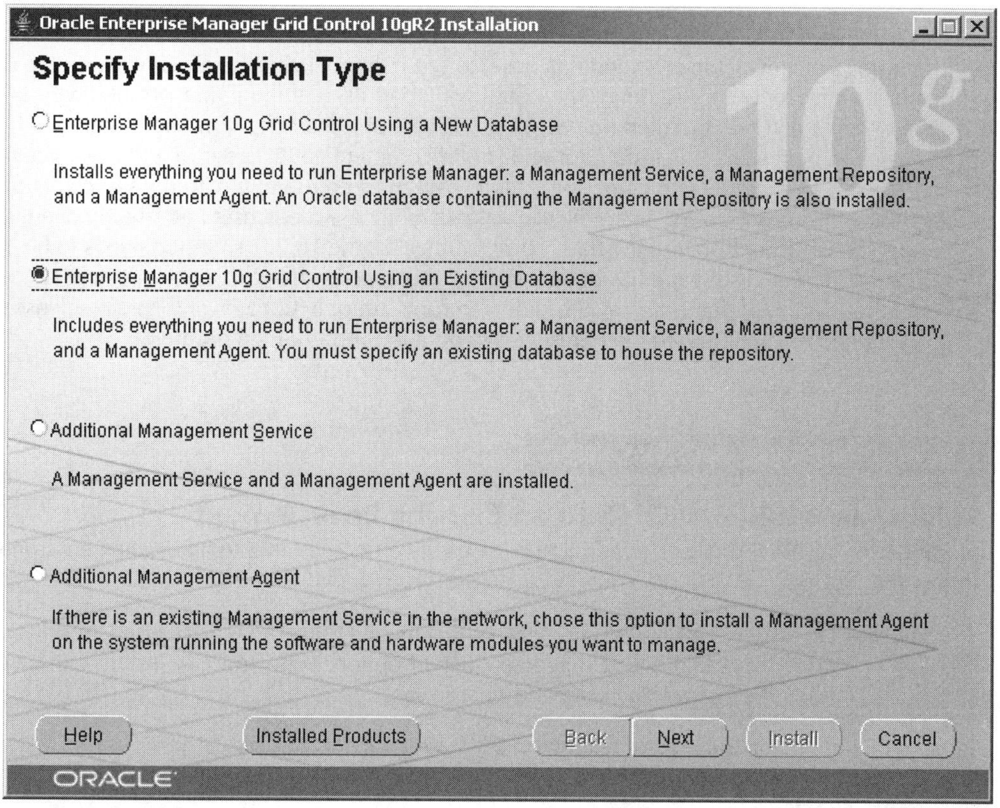

FIGURE 2-1.   *Oracle Universal Installer – Grid Control installation*

BEST PRACTICE
*The seed database deployed in this type of install is a 10.1.0.4
database. For production environments, it is advised to upgrade the
repository database to the latest 10gR2 (or higher) compatible version.*

Enterprise Manager 10*g* Grid Control Using an Existing Database

The option of using an existing database is the recommended way of installing Grid Control. For
any enterprise rollout that has to scale, the repository database should be kept separate from the
Management Servers on its own dedicated hardware. The install of the first OMS of the infrastructure
will then create the Grid Control schema in that remote database. This is also a way to install a
new Grid Control infrastructure, but must not be used to add an additional Management Server
to an existing environment.

Additional Management Server

This is the option to use to add an additional Management Server to a deployed environment. The install will check the specified database, to see if the repository is already present in that database. If no repository is found, the install will abort itself. If the Grid Control environment has already had a patchset installed (in case of a 10.2.0.2 or higher deployment), adding an OMS to that environment using this install option is not recommended. In order to add a Management Server to an existing infrastructure, the added OMS must be running with the same version as the rest of the infrastructure. To get to the same version (in case a patchset has already been installed to upgrade Grid Control from the base 10.2.0.1 release), the 10.2.0.1 version needs to be installed first. After the initial software has been installed, the appropriate Grid Control patchset needs to be applied on top of that base OMS install: Patchsets are only updates of the base release of a product, and cannot be used by themselves to do a full install of the product.

GRID CONTROL WORKSHOP

Adding an Additional OMS to an Existing Environment

Starting from 10*g*R4 (10.2.0.4), to add a non-base version of the OMS to an existing environment, follow these steps:

Step 1. Do a software-only install of the base version (10.2.0.1, 10.2.0.2 on Windows), using the Additional Management Server option. Software-only installs can be done using the -noconfig command-line option:

```
$ ./runInstaller -noconfig -force -waitForCompletion
```

NOTE
An overview of the command-line switches is available in Chapter 17.

Step 2. After that base install completes, the software of both the OMS and the Agent needs to be upgraded to the latest version.

Step 3. Two software-only upgrades will have to be done: one to upgrade the OMS, and one for the Agent. Use the same -noconfig option, combined with the b_softwareonly=true option to perform the upgrade:

```
$ cd <latest version stage directory>

$ export ORACLE_HOME=<ORACLE_HOME of the OMS>
$ ./runInstaller -noconfig -force -waitForCompletion b_
softwareonly=true

$ export ORACLE_HOME=<ORACLE_HOME of the Agent>
$ ./runInstaller -noconfig -force -waitForCompletion b_
softwareonly=true
```

Step 4. When those two install sessions finish, the software installed on the machine will be an upgraded OMS install. No configuration will be done yet, and none of the OC4J applications will be deployed yet. To run the configuration manually, run the postconfiguration tool:

```
$ export PERL5LIB=${ORACLE_HOME}/perl/lib/5.6.1
$ ${ORACLE_HOME}/perl/bin/perl
        ${ORACLE_HOME}/sysman/install/ConfigureGC.pl ${ORACLE_BASE}
```

Step 5. With 10.2.0.5, a new way to export and import configuration settings has been added. This can be used to import the runtime settings of an existing OMS into the newly installed Management Server, to make sure that all the Management Servers are running with the same configuration:

```
$ emctl importconfig oms -file <backup file>
```

Step-by-step instructions for the software-only install are available in the *Grid Control Installation Guide*, Section 3: *Installing Enterprise Manager.*

Additional Management Agent

An Agent can be installed using the install CD on a new server. However, there are a couple of other ways to deploy and install Agents in the enterprise, which might be better suited for a mass rollout (compared to an interactive install on each of the machines to be monitored). Chapter 4 covers the various ways to deploy Agents.

Postconfiguration on the Repository Server

The most important thing for the repository is to have an Agent installed on all the database servers running the database. The install will add an Agent automatically on each of the OMS server installs. But if the repository database is running on a different set of servers, no Agents will be added on the database machines by default. After the install completes on the Management Servers, add an Agent on all the repository database machines (also including the Data Guard if one is used for the repository). Without an Agent monitoring the repository database, important information about the health and throughput of Grid Control will not be available. The repository database is the heart and soul of Grid Control: If it is not available, Enterprise Manager will not be available either. This means that extra care should be given to this database, to make sure it is running smoothly and nothing bad is happening.

Of course, there are more aspects to setting up and configuring a database: Having the right properties set for the database is one of them. Having the right backup and recovery strategy is another. An overview of the settings needed to strengthen the database is covered in the next chapter, on High Availability.

Postconfiguration on the OMS Server

After the install of the OMS software, a couple of additional tweaks are needed to get the application ready for an enterprise-wide deployment. These tweaks are specific to the environment, and the actual values of the parameters specified in this section can change depending on the size and the scale of the Grid Control deployment.

Loader Setup and Shared File System Loader

All metric data files uploaded by the Agents are first stored in temporary file storage at the OMS server, before they are loaded into the database. This will allow the Agents to send over the data faster in bursts, while the loader can continuously take the top file from the queue and upload it in the repository. If the environment consists of a single OMS server, this file storage area is a simple directory that can reside anywhere on the local server. The location of that directory to put the XML files in is specified in the `emoms.properties` file:

```
ReceiveDir=<directory>
```

The default value for this parameter is always `$ORACLE_HOME/sysman/recv`. If space is limited on the disk with the OMS software installed, the value of this parameter can be changed, to point to another directory on another disk, to store the files.

When there are multiple servers, the OMS can be configured to use a common shared area to upload the files to, and process them from that central location.

NOTE
If the Grid Control infrastructure is going to include a Server Load Balancer to virtualize the access to the Management Servers, the loaders will have to be configured for Shared File System.

BEST PRACTICE
Even in the case of a single OMS server, it is still advisable to have Shared File System enabled on the box itself to store the XML files from the Agents. The shared loader system will give much faster access to the files, streamlining the upload process and increasing the throughput.

All OMS servers, however, must use the same mechanism for storing the XML files, and use the same name for the mount-point in case of shared loading. As soon as the OMS receives a new XML file from an Agent, it will store the file in the shared location, and put the filename of the XML file in an AQ (Advanced Queue) in the database. This allows any of the operational OMS servers to pick up the XML file to be loaded.

To configure the shared loading, use this command:

```
[oracle@oms ~]$ emctl config oms loader -shared <yes|no> -dir <loader dir>
```

Example:

```
[oracle@oms ~]$ emctl config oms loader -shared yes -dir /u09/oms10g/recv
```

BEST PRACTICE
*Never use the mount-point itself as the receive directory. Always
create a subdirectory on the mount-point and specify that as the
shared loader area. This will give you more control over the location
in case it needs to be re-created, renamed, or cleaned up. Example:*

- *The shared storage area is mounted on /u09/oms10g.*

- *Create a subdirectory called /u09/oms10g/recv, and specify that as the shared directory.*

There are different types of shared file systems that can be used: You have Network File
System (NFS)-based solutions, NAS, Storage Area Network (SAN), and cluster file system add-ons
like Oracle's Cluster File system Version 2 (OCFS2). Due to the usage of this file system by the
OMS, any NFS-based file systems are not really a good option for this.

- Network latency has to be kept to an absolute minimum. Activity on the loader directory
  will always be in bursts, where the XML receivers upload a set of files from the Agents,
  and the multiple loaders start reading and processing the files.

- There are always multiple threads working in the loader directory, which makes fast and
  optimized file locking and file handling very important.

- And lastly, the file system has to be capable of handling lots of files. In an environment
  with several thousands of Agents uploading files, it's not uncommon to have 100,000 files
  present in the receive directory waiting to get processed during an abnormal spike in usage.

NOTE
*Every Management Server needs to have the same loader parameters
specified in the emoms.properties file. This way one OMS can
continue to process files in case an OMS is taken offline, or is shut
down. This applies to the number of loader threads, as well as the
type of loading method defined. Example:*

`em.loader.threadPoolSize=5`
`em.loader.coordinationMethod=sharedFilesystem`

*To check the loader parameters defined per OMS, use this SQL
statement:*

```
SELECT DISTINCT host_url, name, value
FROM   mgmt_oms_parameters
WHERE  LOWER(name) LIKE 'loader%'
ORDER BY host_url, name
```

*If any differences are found between the OMS servers, update the
emoms.properties file of the involved servers, and restart them so
the changes will get picked up and saved in the repository.*

Out-Of-Band Notifications

Administrators can be alerted when the OMS server goes down, or gets restarted, either
intentionally through emctl or opmnctl commands issued by an administrator, or after a reboot
or a crash of the machine, or a forced restart by the OPMN watchdog. Although administrators

can get notified on the default OMS server down condition, it is advisable to have the OOB (Out-Of-Band) messages enabled as well, to keep track of what's happening with the OMS server and what OPMN is doing with the OC4J_EM application.

NOTE
This feature will only work on UNIX platforms. Support to run the event scripts from the OPMN layer is not present on Windows platforms.

The main difference between the standard OMS server down notification (which is generated, handled, and dispatched by Grid Control itself), and the OOB way of alerting people is the time when the notification is sent. In the case of an OOB message, as soon as the OMS is shut down, the message is sent to the specified administrator, regardless of how many Management Servers are still operational. For the standard Grid Control notification, you need an operational OMS server to dispatch and send the notification. If all the OMS servers are down, the standard Grid Control notification will not be sent until one server is brought back online again to dispatch the notifications. This means that in case of a real disaster with all the Management Servers being unavailable, the Enterprise Administrators will not be notified of the OMS server down condition. The OOB parameters can be changed in the emoms.properties file as described in Table 2-2.

In addition to the changes in emoms.properties, the opmn.xml file in the directory $ORACLE_HOME/opmn/conf will also need to be updated, to call the event scripts in case of a restart. Insert the event-scripts block in the definition of the OC4J_EM script right before the timeout definitions:

```
</module-data>
<event-scripts>
  <pre-start path="<PERLHOME>/bin/perl <ORACLE_HOME>/bin/omsstart.pl"/>
  <pre-stop  path="<PERLHOME>/bin/perl <ORACLE_HOME>/bin/omsstop.pl"/>
</event-scripts>
<start timeout="900" retry="2"/>
```

Property Name	Description
em_email_address	E-mail address to use to send OOB messages to. Any valid e-mail address can be specified.
em_from_email_address	E-mail address to use as source e-mail address in OOB messages.
em_email_gateway	E-mail server to be used to send the OOB messages.
em-oob_crash	Boolean flag. Send OOB messages on crash.
em-oob_shutdown	Boolean flag. Send OOB messages on shutdown. Default is FALSE.
em_oob_startup	Boolean flag. Send OOB messages on startup.

TABLE 2-2. *OOB Parameters in the emoms.properties File*

The preceding code assumes the following:

- `<PERLHOME>` refers to the location of Perl installed on the system.
- `<ORACLE_HOME>` refers to the location of the OMS software.
- (Specify the full pathname for both these directories in the `opmn.xml` file.)

Log and Trace Files and Rotation

Out-of-box, AS components, such as HTTP Server and Webcache, generally do not rotate or reset their logs. This means that over time, these log files will grow and consume enough space to cause performance problems.

Oracle HTTP Server (OHS/Apache) Log Files

All of the OHS log files should never reach a size of 2GB. If they do reach this size, a resource limit will be reached, causing logging and tracing to stop. There are four main files used by the HTTP server that require special attention. Each of those files should use the OHS `rotatelogs` option, to age out a file after a certain amount of time specified in seconds.

access_log   Configured in the `$ORACLE_HOME/Apache/Apache/conf/httpd.conf` file. After the install, the `access_log` configuration will look something like this:

```
CustomLog "|<ORACLE_HOME>/Apache/Apache/bin/rotatelogs
              <ORACLE_HOME>/Apache/Apache/logs/access_log 86400" common
```

(Specify this directive on a single line.)

error_log   Configured in the `$ORACLE_HOME/Apache/Apache/conf/httpd.conf` file. After the install, the `error_log` configuration will look something like this:

```
ErrorLog "|<ORACLE_HOME>/Apache/Apache/bin/rotatelogs
              <ORACLE_HOME>/Apache/Apache/logs/error_log 86400"
```

(Specify this directive on a single line.)

ssl_engine_log   Configured in the `$ORACLE_HOME/Apache/Apache/conf/ssl.conf` file. This file should be rotated on a regular basis, to prevent overflow of this file.

```
SSLLog "|<ORACLE_HOME>/Apache/Apache/bin/rotatelogs
              <ORACLE_HOME>/Apache/Apache/logs/ssl_engine_log 86400"
```

 (Specify this directive on a single line.)

ssl_request_log   Configured in the `$ORACLE_HOME/Apache/Apache/conf/ssl.conf` file. This file should be rotated on a regular basis, to prevent overflow of this file.

```
CustomLog "|<ORACLE_HOME>/Apache/Apache/bin/rotatelogs
              <ORACLE_HOME>/Apache/Apache/logs/ssl_request_log 86400"
              "%t %h %{SSL_PROTOCOL}x %{SSL_CIPHER}x \"%r\" %b"
```

(Specify this directive on a single line.)

The amount of time specified for the log rotation depends on the activity taking place on the site. For most small and medium deployments, the value of 86400 (a full day) will be quite sufficient. On other sites that are used quite heavily, this value might have to be decreased to 43200 (half a day), or even less.

OC4J Applications Log Files

This includes the home, the OC4J_EM, the OC4J_EMPROV, and the `OCMRepeater` (starting from 10.2.0.5) applications. For the OC4J applications, there are two possibilities to get more control over the log files written:

- Split the log files after a certain amount of time using the `split` tag with the logging parameters. The following time periods can be used to split the log files:

  - None

  - Hour

  - Day

  - Week

  - Month

- Enable ODL (Oracle Diagnostic Logging). This will write the log files in XML format, but it allows more control over the size of the log files and the rotation of those files.

There are various files used by the OC4J framework. All the logging changes will have to be made in the OC4J configuration files. The location of the file depends on the application, as shown in Table 2-3.

In the following XML examples, ODL is enabled wherever possible and the standard logging is enhanced with the `split` attribute.

Changes in the `application.xml` file:

```
<log>
  <!--
  <file path="../log/global-application.log" split="day"/>
    -->
  <odl path="../log/global-application/" max-file-size="1000"
       max-directory-size="10000"/>
</log>
```

OC4J Application	Location of Configuration Files
home	$ORACLE_HOME/j2ee/home/config
OC4J_EM	$ORACLE_HOME/j2ee/OC4J_EM/config
OC4J_EMPROV	$ORACLE_HOME/j2ee/OC4J_EMPROV/config
OCMRepeater	$ORACLE_HOME/j2ee/OCMRepeater/config

TABLE 2-3. *Location of Configuration Files for OC4J Applications*

Changes in the `default-web-site.xml` file:

```
<access-log path="../log/default-web-access.log" split="day" />
```

This file does not allow the ODL tags to be used. So only standard log file rotation based on time can be done for this file.

Changes in the `jms.xml` file:

```
<log>
    <!-- <file path="../log/jms.log" split="day" /> -->
    <odl path="../log/jms/" max-file-size="1000"
        max-directory-size="10000"/>
</log>
```

Changes in the `rmi.xml` file:

```
<log>
    <!-- <file path="../log/rmi.log" split="day" /> -->
    <odl path="../log/rmi/" max-file-size="1000"
        max-directory-size="10000"/>
</log>
```

Changes in the `server.xml` file:

```
<log>
    <!-- <file path="../log/server.log" split="day" /> -->
    <odl path="../log/server/" max-file-size="1000"
        max-directory-size="10000"/>
</log>
```

For the OC4J_EM application, there is one extra file that needs special attention: the em-application.log file. This log file is defined in the `orion-application.xml` configuration file in the directory $ORACLE_HOME/j2ee/OC4J_EM/application-deployments/em:

```
<log>
  <file path="../../log/em-application.log" split="day" />
</log>
```

OPMN Log Files

For OPMN, there are a couple of standard files, created and managed by OPMN. And then there are the application log files that are created when OPMN starts an application. For the OPMN-controlled files (`ipm.log` and `ons.log`), the parameters are specified in the OPMN.XML file. By default, these files are rotated after reaching a size of 1,500,000 KB (~1.5GB). If the rotation size has to be changed, edit the `opmn.xml` file. Example:

```
<log-file path="$ORACLE_HOME/opmn/logs/ons.log"
          level="4" rotation-size="1000000"/>

<log-file path="$ORACLE_HOME/opmn/logs/ipm.log"
          level="4" rotation-size="1000000"/>
```

After the change, update the configuration, and restart the services:

```
$ dcmctl updateConfig -ct opmn
$ opmnctl stopall
$ opmnctl startall
```

Each process started by OPMN writes its own STDOUT and STDERR to an application specific log file in the $ORACLE_HOME/opmn/logs directory. The OPMN daemon does not have any control over these files except to define the directory path of these files. The log file rotation size for these log files is the same as the one defined for ipm.log and ons.log. The rotation settings, however, will only be checked by OPMN on component startup, before starting the managed process. While the AS components are running, no more validation is done on the log file sizes.

On UNIX systems, these log files can be rotated by using the following commands:

```
$ cp /dev/null HTTP_Server~1
$ cp /dev/null OC4J~OC4J_EMPROV~default_island~1
$ cp /dev/null OC4J~OC4J_EM~default_island~1
$ cp /dev/null OC4J~home~default_island~1
$ cp /dev/null WebCache~WebCacheAdmin~1
$ cp /dev/null WebCache~WebCache~1
$ cp /dev/null dcm-daemon~dcm-daemon~dcm~1
```

However, this cannot be done on Windows: A restart of AS services is required to force a rotate of the log files.

Webcache Log Files

There are only two files that require attention for Webcache: the access_log file, containing all the incoming requests, and the event_log file with all the events and Webcache encountered.

access_log   Configured in the $ORACLE_HOME/webcache/webcache.xml file. After the install, the access_log configuration will look something like this:

```
<ACCESSLOG XLFFORMATNAME="WCLF" TIMESTYLE="LOCAL"
           ROLLOVERNAME="daily" FILENAME="access_log"/>
```

(This XML line is specified on a single line.)

event_log   Configured in the $ORACLE_HOME/webcache/webcache.xml file. By default, this file is not rotated, allowing it to just grow over time. The install defaults will need to be changed to:

```
<EVENTLOG FILENAME="event_log" TIMESTYLE="LOCAL">
   <ROLLOVER FREQUENCY="DAILY"/>
</EVENTLOG>
```

NOTE
If chronos is configured, the Webcache files will be archived in the directory $ORACLE_HOME/webcache/logs/archive. However, these archived files will not be cleaned up. A cleanup script will need to be run on the OMS server on a regular basis to clean up the oldest archived files.

Oracle HTTP Server Configuration

The Oracle HTTP server uses a file to use as interprocess locking and synchronization method for the various operational threads. The location of this semaphore file is defined in the configuration file $ORACLE_HOME/Apache/Apache/conf/ssl.conf:

```
#    Semaphore:
#    Configure the path to the mutual expulsion semaphore the
#    SSL engine uses internally for inter-process synchronization.
SSLMutex file:/u01/app/oracle/oms10g/Apache/Apache/logs/ssl_mutex
```

To allow fast interaction of OHS, and prevent any kind of delays and waits on the processing of HTTP requests, this semaphore file should be stored on a fast, local file system. Even in the case where the Oracle software is installed on a shared drive, not local to the machine, this file pointer should be updated to point to a file on the local machine.

SMTP Server

One of the notification mechanisms used by Grid Control is e-mail. In order to use e-mail as a notification method, however, the e-mail server and some basic SMTP parameters will need to be provided, to allow the OMS server to send these notifications. To set these parameters:

1. Log in to the Console.

2. Go to the Setup page, and choose the Notification Methods page.

3. On the main page, the Mail properties can be specified.

4. The outgoing SMTP server field can contain a comma-separated list of machine names. If no port is specified for the e-mail server, the default port 25 is assumed. Starting with 10gR5, secure SMTP is supported, which means that SSL or TLS (Transport Layer Security) can now be used also when defining the SMTP server and port.

5. If the Mail server is configured to use a username to log in and send an e-mail, the username and password of a valid Mail server user have to be specified. That account will be used to send all the e-mails from Grid Control.

6. The Identify Sender As value is the friendly name of the e-mail account used to send the mail. This can be any value, but in order to know the source of the e-mail, it is advised to put in something like Grid Control or Enterprise Manager, so that the source of the e-mail can be identified immediately.

7. The Sender's E-mail Address value needs to be a valid e-mail address. This is for convenience, to allow administrators to reply to the e-mails they have received from Grid Control.

Best practice here is to have a mailing list set up with the Enterprise Administrators responsible for the Grid Control architecture, and use that mailing list here as the address to use.

Securing the Environment

Having the application available is a first step in a rollout. But in a modern-day enterprise rollout, with monitoring of machines happening in multiple data centers for all kinds of applications and company services, security is an aspect that is gaining more and more importance. Enterprise-class deployments require special attention in terms of restricting the access and securing the information they provide.

Setting Up Advanced Networking Option (ANO)

The usual database communication between the OMS and the repository database is one of those layers of security that can be enabled.

GRID CONTROL WORKSHOP

Enabling the Advanced Networking Option

To enable the Advanced Networking Option (ANO), make the following changes:

- On the repository database (or each instance in case of RAC), make the following changes in the `sqlnet.ora` file:

```
SQLNET.ENCRYPTION_SERVER=required
SQLNET.ENCRYPTION_TYPES_SERVER=(<encryption type to use>)
SQLNET.ENCRYPTION_CLIENT=requested
SQLNET.ENCRYPTION_TYPES_CLIENT=(<encryption type to use>)
```

 BEST PRACTICE
For obvious reasons, if ANO is mandated for the Grid Control rollout, the encryption of the SQL*Net traffic should be set to required, *forcing all access to the repository database to use the same ANO setup.*

After making these changes, restart the database listener:

```
[oracle@db ~]$ lsnrctl stop  listener
[oracle@db ~]$ lsnrctl start listener
```

- On each of the Management Servers, edit the `emoms.properties` file, and add the following parameters:

```
oracle.sysman.emRep.dbConn.enableEncryption=TRUE
oracle.net.encryption_types_client=(<encryption type to use>)
oracle.net.encryption_client=REQUIRED
```

After making these changes, restart the OMS:

```
[oracle@oms ~]$ emctl stop  oms
[oracle@oms ~]$ emctl start oms
```

All servers should be configured in the same way, to guarantee access to the repository database in the same way.

Configuring HTTP Server to Use SSL for Console UI

When the Grid Control middle tiers are installed, a default SSL certificate is installed as well. This certificate uses strong encryption, and its primary use is for the Agent-to-OMS communication.

GRID CONTROL WORKSHOP

Adding a Third-Party SSL Certificate for Console Access

To add a third-party SSL certificate for Console access, follow these steps:

Step 1. Create a new wallet, to be used for the SSL communication.

Use the Oracle Wallet Manager (OWM) to create a wallet based on the certificate that will have to be used by Grid Control.

Step 2. Copy the new wallet files to the wallet directory of the OHS server. The location of this directory is specified by the SSLWallet property in the file $ORACLE_HOME/Apache/Apache/conf/ssl.conf:

```
SSLWallet file:/scratch/10gr4/oms10g/Apache/Apache/conf/ssl
.wlt/default
```

Step 3. If the wallet is not an auto-login wallet, then get the obfuscated wallet password by running the following command. On Windows:

```
C:\ > %ORACLE_HOME%\Apache\Apache\bin\osslpassword.exe -p
<wallet pwd>
```

On UNIX:

```
$ $ORACLE_HOME/Apache/Apache/bin/iasobf -p <wallet pwd>
```

After obtaining the obfuscated password, add the SSLWalletPassword directive also in the $ORACLE_HOME/Apache/Apache/conf/ssl.conf file:

```
SSLWalletPassword=<obfuscated password>
```

Step 4. Restart the AS server:

```
$ opmnctl stopall
$ opmnctl startall
```

If the OMS is running 10gR5, all the preceding steps can be condensed to the following two tasks:

a. Create the wallet for the Console access.

b. Issue this command on the OMS:

```
$ emctl secure console -wallet <location of wallet>
```

One thing to point out, though, regardless of the version of Enterprise Manager, is that any SSL wallet added to the environment has to be added on all the OMS servers if there is any kind of failover or redundancy built into the infrastructure: If a Server Load Balancer (SLB) has to reroute user traffic to another OMS, or a failover happens, and another OMS is now serving the UI pages, those other OMS machines will need the same SSL wallet to serve those connections.

Although it is technically possible to use the same certificate for the web-based application access Administrators are using, the recommendation is to use either the company-enforced certificates for web applications, or a certificate generated by a well-known certificate authority for the web-based access to Grid Control.

EMKEY Operations

The EMKEY is the encryption key the OMS servers will be using to encrypt and decrypt information in the repository. After the install, an EMKEY file called `emkey.ora` will be created in the directory `$ORACLE_HOME/sysman/config`, but the encryption key will still be present in the repository, too. To prevent access to the key by anyone logging in to the repository (which can be potentially from various machines), the security best practice is to remove this key from the repository after the install, and keep it only on the OMS file system:

```
$ emctl config emkey -remove_from_repos
```

When the EMKEY file is created on the file system, the location of the file is specified in the `emoms.properties` file:

```
oracle.sysman.emkeyfile=<ORACLE_HOME>/sysman/config/emkey.ora
```

If the default location of the file is not the desired one, or in cases where the file needs to be moved to another location, the following command can be used to repoint the EMKEY file to a different location:

```
$ emctl config emkey -emkeyfile <path> -force [-sysman_pwd <pwd>]
```

The `-force` option will need to be specified, if the EMKEY is already stored on disk somewhere, to overrule the current location.

NOTE
Before any upgrade of Grid Control, the EMKEY needs to be restored back in the repository, to allow the PL/SQL routines access to the secure key while running data upgrade scripts.

If the EMKEY is removed from the repository, the file on the file system of the OMS server will be the only location where this file still exists. If this file is lost or damaged, all encryption and decryption of data will fail. The only way to recover in this scenario is to reset the key, re-create the SSL wallets on all the OMS servers, re-secure all Agents in the infrastructure, and re-enter all previously stored target credentials in repository.

To prevent this very painful work, make sure a good backup—preferably more than one—is made of this file.

Locking and Unlocking the OMS Server

An OMS server can be configured to respond to incoming Agent requests in two ways: unlocked and locked.

Unlocked

Unlocked is the out-of-box default for the OMS server for all installations prior to 10.2.0.5, to allow both secure and unsecure communication from the Agents.

This is an easier mode, to allow Enterprise Administrators to set up an infrastructure to roll out secure Agents. However, it also means that any Agent can point to the OMS and start uploading data, since there is no verification on the OMS to recognize a rogue Agent that should not be discovered in that Grid Control environment. This is the command to use:

```
$ emctl secure unlock
```

If an OMS is already in an unlocked mode, this command is ignored, and nothing is changed.
Starting with 10.2.0.5, the `lock` and `unlock` commands have two extra switches to do selective operations:

- To unlock the upload traffic:

    ```
    [oracle@oms ~]$ emctl secure unlock -upload
    ```

- To unlock the console traffic:

    ```
    [oracle@oms ~]$ emctl secure unlock -console
    ```

Both options can be specified on the same command line. If no option is specified, both are assumed.

Locked

When an OMS is marked as locked, it will no longer accept communication of the Agent using HTTP (no SSL). This forces all Agent communication to be secured, and therefore forces Agents to register themselves first with the OMS before they can upload any data. This is the command to use:

```
[oracle@oms ~]$ emctl secure lock -upload
```

If an OMS is already in a locked mode, this command is ignored, and nothing is changed.

BEST PRACTICE
It is possible to have OMS servers working in both unlocked and locked mode. However, it is advisable to lock down the all the OMS servers once all the network components have been configured to use SSL communication.

To find out which OMS is in locked mode, and which OMS is in unlocked mode, run this SQL statement as SYSMAN in the repository:

```
SELECT DISTINCT p.host_url, p.timestamp,
       DECODE(p.value,0,'Unsecure',1,'Secure',2,'Locked'
                      ,'error:'||p.value) lock_status
FROM   mgmt_oms_parameters p,
       (
        SELECT host_url, name, MAX(timestamp) last_time
        FROM   mgmt_oms_parameters
        WHERE  name = 'oms_secure_status'
        GROUP BY host_url, name
       ) l
```

```
WHERE   p.host_url  = l.host_url
  AND   p.TIMESTAMP = l.last_time
  AND   p.name      = l.name
ORDER BY p.host_url
```

The locked or unlocked status of an OMS is transparent to an SLB. Since the load balancer is just routing traffic, it is not aware of the lock status of the Management Servers, and is not functionally impacted if the lock state changes.

Securing the Database and the Application Server

On top of securing the communication, there are a few more database-specific and application-server–specific configuration changes that can be made to make the infrastructure more secure. These are the most common things to do for a Grid Control rollout:

- **Apply the latest CPU**   The repository database and the application server Grid Control is using are just like any other Oracle application in the enterprise. Each released CPU bundle with all the critical (and security) updates should be applied on those components, too.

- **Shut down unneeded services**   Since the repository database should be a dedicated database, all nonessential services like the Oracle XML Database (XDB) should be shut down in the database. And all nonessential OS services, like portmap, FTP, and so on are not essential for the operations of Grid Control, and should not be left running on both the OMS and the repository database servers.

- **Revoke access to some PL/SQL packages in the repository database**   Revoke EXECUTE privileges from the PUBLIC user on the PL/SQL packages UTL_FILE and UTL_TCP.

  ```
  SQL> REVOKE EXECUTE ON utl_file FROM public;
  SQL> REVOKE EXECUTE ON utl_tcp  FROM public;
  ```

- **Enforce password policies on all database accounts**   Every user and administrator defined in Grid Control will have an account in the repository database. Enforce password policies on all these accounts, except SYSMAN and MGMT_VIEW. The two special Grid Control accounts require specific actions to be taken to update the passwords. See also Chapter 7 for more information on how to modify and change the passwords of these two accounts.

- **Restrict access to the repository database**   Put restrictions on the listener to only accept connections from the OMS servers, and the machines of the Enterprise Administrators managing the repository database. Restrict remote logging from machines on the network. Only allow the repository database administrators to log in to the repository database box. Parameters are available for this in the protocol.ora file, located in the directory $ORACLE_HOME/network/admin, to restrict network access to the listener:

  ```
  tcp.validnode_checking = YES
  tcp.excluded_nodes = <list of IP addresses>
  tcp.invited_nodes  = <list of IP addresses>
  ```

■ **Prevent SYSMAN from logging in to the Console (UI)**   To prevent SYSMAN from logging in, execute this SQL statement in the repository:

```
DELETE
FROM   mgmt_created_users
WHERE  user_name = 'SYSMAN'
;
```

To allow SYSMAN to log in again, execute this SQL statement in the repository:

```
INSERT INTO mgmt_created_users
  (user_name, system_user )
VALUES
  ('SYSMAN',1)
;
```

For a complete overview of the all the security configuration settings, see the *Oracle Database Security Guide.* That book covers a lot more topics, and has a lot more detail on all the specific security settings for an Oracle database. There is also Enterprise Manager–specific security documentation: See the Enterprise Manager Security chapter of the *Oracle Enterprise Manager Advanced Configuration Guide.*

Using Firewalls

Firewalls are a commonplace thing these days, especially in a company environment with multiple locations, data centers, subnets, and so on. And with the installation of Grid Control comes the need to have certain routes of traffic enabled to allow the various pieces of the infrastructure to communicate with each other. The key to setting up Grid Control with firewalls is to simplify the access methods to the application. This will reduce the amount of work that needs to be done on the firewall side, and limit the number of ports and exceptions that network administrators will have to create to allow all access to Grid Control. With Figure 2-2 illustrating the TCP ports used, this means:

■ Only allow secure access to the application using HTTPS on either 4444 (direct OHS communication) or 8250 (access to the Console via Webcache). Eliminate the use of the HTTP ports 7777 and 7778.

■ If an SLB is configured, allow only access to Grid Control via the SLB, for both the Agents and the users and administrators working with Grid Control. Direct OMS communication should only be allowed when performing maintenance to the application software, like installing patches, or upgrading Grid Control.

Using these rules to simplify the flow of communication between the various parts of the Grid Control infrastructure, the following rules will be needed on a firewall:

■ Between the Management Servers and the repository:

```
OMS -> Database - Port 1521 (Oracle Net)
```

Allow Oracle Net traffic from the Management Servers to the repository database on the port used by the repository database listener (default is 1521).

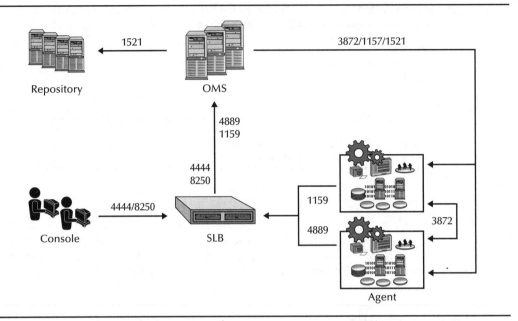

FIGURE 2-2. *Grid Control TCP ports used*

- Between the SLB and the Management Server:

```
SLB -> OMS - Port 1159 (HTTPS - Agent - Normal traffic)
SLB -> OMS - Port 4889 (HTTP  - Agent - Secure requests only)
SLB -> OMS - Port 4444 (HTTPS - Console - Apache)
SLB -> OMS - Port 8250 (HTTPS - Console - Webcache)
```

If an SLB is used, the traffic the SLB receives from the Agents and the web browsers of the Administrators must be forwarded to the appropriate OMS servers. Allow secure HTTP traffic from the SLB to the Management Servers:

- On the port used by the Management Server for Agent traffic (default is 1159)
- On the port used by the Oracle HTTP Server for Console traffic (default is 4443)
- On the port used by the Webcache Server for Console traffic (default is 8250)

- Allow HTTP traffic from the SLB to the Management Servers:

- On the port used by the Management Server for Agent traffic (default is 4889). This port is only used for requests of the Agent to secure. All normal operations from the Agents to Grid Control will use the secure port 1159.

- Between the Grid Control Console and the SLB:

```
UI Console -> SLB - Port 4444 (HTTPS)
UI Console -> SLB - Port 8250 (HTTPS)
```

Allow secure HTTPS traffic from the Console machines to the SLB on the ports used by the OHS (default is 4443) and Webcache (default is 8250).

- Between the Agents and the SLB:

```
Agent -> SLB - Port 1159 (HTTPS)
Agent -> SLB - Port 4889 (HTTP)
```

Allow secure HTTP traffic from the Agents to the SLB on the port used by the Oracle OHS (default is 1159). This port is used for all the data the Agent has to send to the OMS. Allow unsecure HTTP traffic from the Agents to the SLB on the port used by the OHS (default is 4889). This port is only used to obtain the wallet to configure the secure communication between the Agent and the OMS.

- Between the Management Servers and the Agents:

```
OMS -> Agent - Port 3872 (HTTPS)
```

The OMS servers will need to be able to talk to the Agents for the following operations:

- **Updating monitoring settings for managed targets**   This includes adding new targets, updating the monitoring properties like passwords and *ORACLE_HOME* settings, as well as the metric settings, and so on.
- **Requesting real-time information from the managed targets**   If an administrator requests real-time metrics, or requests the data point for a specific metric in the Console, the OMS will forward that request to the Agent.
- **Submitting jobs and tasks to run on the managed targets**   When an Enterprise Manager job needs to run on a particular target, the OMS will forward the job details to the Agent.

In order to get the requests sent over, the OMS will use the EMD_URL property of the Agent (which includes the protocol and the port number) to contact the Agent.

- Between the Management Server and the managed targets

In the case of a database:

```
OMS -> Database target - Port 1521 (SQL*Net)
```

To manage a database target via the Console, an administrator will make a connection from the Management Server to the managed database to perform these actions.

In the case of an Application Server:

```
OMS -> Application Server target - Port 1157 (HTTPS)
```

The same applies for a managed AS target: If an administrator is performing administration tasks in the Console for an AS target, the Management Server will contact the AS Agent on the box to perform certain tasks.

- Between the Agent and another Agent:

```
Agent -> Agent - Port 3872 (HTTPS)
```

When cloning targets from one Agent to another, the source Agent will make a connection to the destination Agent, to get the cloned data across. This approach is done to prevent the data from getting sent over the network twice (from source to OMS, and from OMS to destination).

Postconfiguration for Patching and Provisioning

In order to apply patches or implement scripted changes to targets, the patching and provisioning framework needs to be configured in Grid Control. Things like the setup of the My Oracle Support (MOS) account, and identifying a directory on the Management server for the staging of patches and deployment procedures (DP's) are some of the necessities for using Grid Control's patching and provisioning features.

Software Library

Another postconfiguration task that needs to be done, to get the patching and provisioning going, is the setup of the Software Library. This is a location on a shared disk, available on all OMS servers, where the patches and provisioning archives will be stored. Take the following steps:

- Log in to the Grid Control UI.
- Go to the Deployments menu tab, click the Provisioning submenu tab, and go to the Administration tab (see Figure 2-3).
- The Software Library Configuration option is the last one on the page. Use the Add button to specify the shared location for the library.

BEST PRACTICE
Since the software library needs to be available on all OMS servers, and mapped as the same directory on each server, the physical location of this directory should be similar to the shared storage of the XML receive directory used by all the OMS servers.

ORACLE Enterprise Manager 10*g*
Grid Control

Setup   Preferences   Help   Logout

Home | Targets | **Deployments** | Alerts | Compliance | Jobs | Reports

General | Provisioning

Administration >
Add Software Library Location

Cancel   OK

Add new Software Library by specifying directory location. In case of multiple Oracle Management Service (OMS) setup, specify normal preferred credentials for each host running OMS.

∗ Software Library directory location. [   ]

Provisioning Archives(par) located at $OMS_ORACLE_HOME/sysman/prov/paf will be uploaded

Cancel   OK

Home | Targets | **Deployments** | Alerts | Compliance | Jobs | Reports | Setup | Preferences | Help | Logout

Copyright © 1996, 2007, Oracle. All rights reserved.
Oracle, JD Edwards, PeopleSoft, and Retek are registered trademarks of Oracle Corporation and/or its affiliates. Other names may be trademarks of their respective owners.
About Oracle Enterprise Manager

FIGURE 2-3. *Setting up the software library*

Proxy Server Settings

All the communication the OMS servers do is based on the HTTP protocol. In order to communicate with external machines, outside the local network, a proxy server can be defined to allow communication with machines on the Internet. The setup of the proxy servers is different based on the versions of Grid Control:

- For all versions prior to 10.2.0.5, there was only one set of proxy settings available. These settings apply for Internet access (like the My Oracle Support links), but also for the normal monitoring access to all the Agents.

- With the release of 10.2.0.5, two sets of proxy settings are possible: one for the external (Internet) access, and one for the internal (monitoring) access to the Agents and Grid Control infrastructure.

- To define the proxy settings for Grid Control version prior to 10.2.0.5:

  - From the Setup link, choose the Patching Setup menu item.

  - Select the Proxy & Connection Settings subtab to get to the page shown in Figure 2-4.

  - Select the Manual Proxy Configuration radio button. If no proxy server is needed, the default Direct Connection to the Internet option should be used.

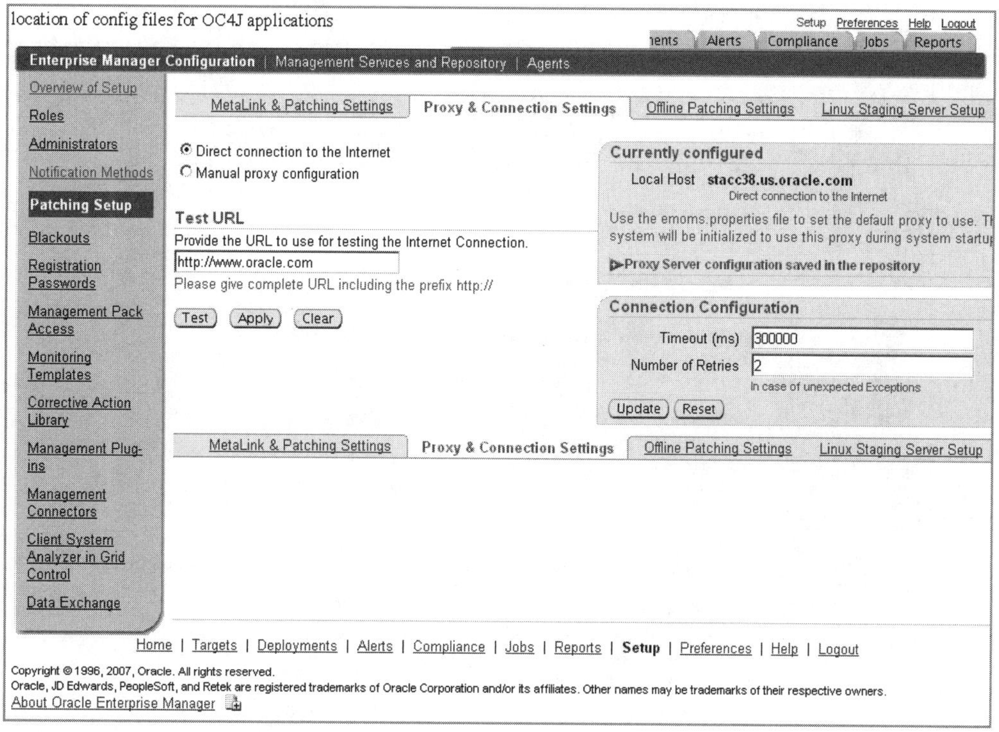

FIGURE 2-4. *Setting up proxy servers*

To define the proxy settings for Grid Control versions 10.2.0.5 or higher:

- From the Setup link, choose the Patching Setup menu item.
- Select the My Oracle Support and Proxy Connection subtab to get to the new page, as shown in Figure 2-5.
- Specify the proxy setup for both My Oracle Support and for the Agent Connection Setting.

BEST PRACTICE
Always specify the proxy settings in the Console UI. Do not put them in the emoms.properties *file of any of the Management Servers.*

My Oracle Support Setup

In order to get the latest CPU information, and to be able to get patch information, a connection to the My Oracle Support web site is needed. The configuration for this is on the same pages as the proxy setup. Besides specifying the proxy servers, to allow access to the internet, also specify

---

ORACLE Enterprise Manager 10*g*
Grid Control

Setup Preferences Help Logout

Home | Targets | Deployments | Alerts | Compliance | Jobs | Reports

Enterprise Manager Configuration | Management Services and Repository | Agents

Overview of Setup
Roles
Administrators
Notification Methods
E-mail Customization
Patching Setup
Blackouts
Registration Passwords
Management Pack Access
Monitoring Templates
Corrective Action Library
Management Plug-ins
Management Connectors
Client System Analyzer in Grid Control
Data Exchange
Manage Privilege Delegation Settings

Patching Setup

(Apply)

My Oracle Support and Proxy Connection | Online and Offline Settings | Linux Patching Setup

This page is used to set the network proxy details for My Oracle Support and Agent connection separately. Apart from communication with 'My Oracle Support', all other communication is considered as agent communication. "Direct connection to internet" means proxy will not be used for communication. "Manual proxy configuration" option allows setting proxy for OMS communication. 'My Oracle Support' connection details set from this page applies to all OMSes in a multi-OMS environment. To ensure that the agent proxy in the repository is used by all OMSes in a multi-OMS environment, all OMSes need to be bounced, preferably in a rolling mannner.

My Oracle Support

Username john.doe@acme.com
Password
Patch Search URL https://updates.oracle.com   (Test)

My Oracle Support Connection Setting
◉ Direct connection to the Internet ○ Manual proxy configuration

Connection Configuration

(Reset)

Timeout (ms) 300000
Number of Retries 2
☑ **TIP** Reset button is used to set the proxy connection parameters to default values.

Agent Connection Setting
◉ Use My Oracle Support connection settings ○ Direct connection to the Internet ○ Manual proxy configuration

Test URL
Test with an agent URL to ensure that the Agent is reachable.

URL https://mydesktop.acme.com:1830/emd/main/   (Test)
Provide complete URL including the protocol https:// or http://

My Oracle Support and Proxy Connection | Online and Offline Settings | Linux Patching Setup

---

FIGURE 2-5. *Setting up proxy servers in 10.2.0.5*

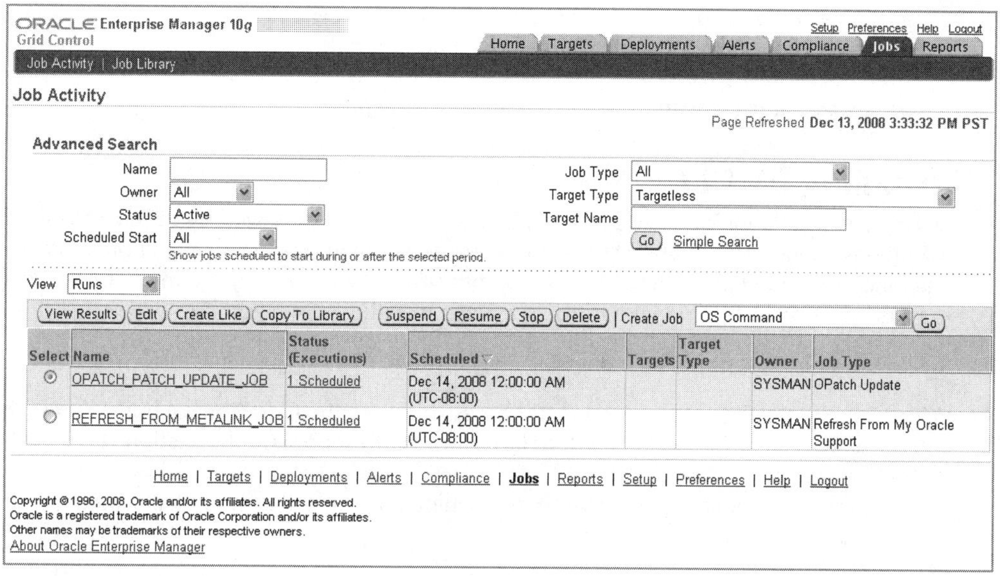

FIGURE 2-6. *Searching for OPatch and Critical Patch Advisory jobs*

a valid My Oracle Support account, and test the setup with the Test button. On success, Grid Control will automatically download the latest information from the My Oracle Support web site on a daily basis via two jobs:

- **OPatch update job**   Download and stage the latest version of `OPatch` in the software library.
- **Refresh From My Oracle Support**   Download the latest information about CPUs and product updates.

Both of these jobs can be found in the Job Activity page. In the Advanced Search option, look for all jobs that have the target type `Targetless`. An example of such a search is shown in Figure 2-6.

EMCLI

Doing work in the Console is the standard and most common way of performing tasks in Grid Control, for both the monitoring and administration part. However, Console work is not very practical for scripting purposes, or to automate things. In order to allow users and administrators to automate things, there is EMCLI, a command-line version of Grid Control, to perform a couple of repetitive actions directly from a shell window.

BEST PRACTICE
EMCLI is deployed by default on each of the installed OMS servers.
It can also be rolled out on additional machines the Enterprise
Administrators are using. It should not be deployed in the enterprise
as regular client software on a large number of machines.

Installing EMCLI

During the installation of each OMS, EMCLI is installed and deployed by default: No special
operations are needed on any Management Server machine. To install EMCLI on another
machine that is not part of the Grid Control infrastructure, a special page in the Console (shown
in Figure 2-7) can be used to download the kit to install:

```
https://<host>:<port>/em/console/emcli/download
```

With 10.2.0.5, the EMCLI page is directly accessible from the Grid Control home page: The link
Enterprise Manager Command Line Interface from the Resource Center section gets you directly
to the EMCLI page.
　　Follow the instructions on this page to download and install EMCLI on a separate machine.

NOTE
The jar file to be used to install EMCLI (`emclikit.jar`) can be found
in the `$ORACLE_HOME/sysman/jlib` directory of any OMS install.

ORACLE' Enterprise Manager 10*g*　　　　　　　　　　　　　　Setup　Preferences　Help　Logout
Grid Control　　　　　　　　　Home｜Targets｜Deployments｜Alerts｜Compliance｜Jobs｜Reports

Enterprise Manager Command Line Interface Download

The EM CLI Client can be installed on any machine within your managed network and provides a subset of the functionality available in the Enterprise Manager Grid Control console. It is designed to allow scripting access to some of the EM Grid Control functionality.

Requirements
Before installing EM CLI, you will need the following:

- Java version 1.4.1 or greater
- Workstation running Solaris, Linux, HPUX, Tru64, AIX, or Windows with NTFS (client installation)

Installing the EM CLI Client
- Download the EM CLI <u>kit</u> to your workstation
- Set your JAVA_HOME environment variable and ensure that it is part of your PATH. You must be running Java 1.4.1 or greater. For example

  　　setenv JAVA_HOME /usr/local/packages/j2sdk1.4.1_02
  　　setenv PATH $JAVA_HOME/bin:$PATH

- Install the EM CLI Client. You can install the client portion of EM CLI in any directory either on the same machine as the OMS or on any machine on your network (download the emclikit.jar to that machine).

  　　java -jar emclikit.jar client -install_dir=<emcli client dir>

- Execute "emcli help setup" from the EM CLI Client for instructions on how to use the "setup" verb to configure the client for a particular OMS.

FIGURE 2-7. *EMCLI download page*

Setting Up EMCLI

Before you can use EMCLI, it has to be initialized, using a valid Grid Control account and the pointer to the Grid Control URL. Beginning with 10.2.0.5, EMCLI behaves like any other browser an administrator is using to log in to Enterprise Manager. This means that the URL used to set up EMCLI must be the same one as that used for the regular administrator's logins. Especially when an SLB is configured that has specific persistence rules set up for the regular UI interaction, choosing the right URL with the correct persistence model is important when setting up EMCLI.

GRID CONTROL WORKSHOP

Install and Configure EMCLI

- For all versions of EMCLI prior to 10.2.0.5, when running EMCLI from the OMS home, you still need to set the *JAVA_HOME* environment variable first before issuing any commands. To get around that limitation, add this at the beginning of the `emcli` shell script:

```
if [ -z "$JAVA_HOME" ]; then
    if [ ! -z "$ORACLE_HOME" ]; then
        if [ -d $ORACLE_HOME/jdk ]; then
            JAVA_HOME=$ORACLE_HOME/jdk
            export JAVA_HOME
        fi
    fi
fi
```

- If EMCLI is installed as a standalone tool on a machine that does not have an OMS installed on it, make sure the *JAVA_HOME* environment variable is set to a valid location of Java installed on the box.
- Commands to set up EMCLI:

```
$ emcli setup -url="https://myslb.acme.com/em" -username="JOHN.DOE"
$ emcli sync
```

The value for the URL command line option is the main Console URL of the Grid Control application, which can be a Server Load Balancer if one is used in the infrastructure (more about that in Chapter 3).

It is possible to specify any of the working Grid Control URLs for the setup of EMCLI. However, since EMCLI is a client tool, the best practice is to specify a UI-based URL for EMCLI, to clearly separate the Agent traffic from the Console traffic the users and administrators are using.

The username specified on the command line must be a valid user defined in Grid Control that can log in to the application.

 BEST PRACTICE
It's tempting to specify SYSMAN as the user, to be able to do just about anything with EMCLI. For security purposes, and to be able to track who is doing what, EMCLI should be set up using a specific account, depending on the type of work that EMCLI will be doing.

(continued)

There is no requirement to use a super-user account for the setup. Any Grid Control account can be used for EMCLI.

- If the command-line kit has been installed on a machine of an Enterprise Administrator, the username of that administrator should be used.

- If EMCLI is going to be used by some scripting framework, or as a back end for an application, use a specific dedicated account that has access and privileges only to the objects it need to perform the actions.

An optional parameter -dir can be specified on the command line. This will point EMCLI to an alternate location to store the runtime information of EMCLI. If this parameter is not specified, a hidden directory named .emcli will be created in the OS home directory of the user invoking the setup command. That directory will contain the information about the setup being done.

> **NOTE**
> *You cannot be logged in to the machine using PBRUN, SU, or SUDO (or any command that allows the user to execute commands with the privileges of another user) when running the setup command for EMCLI.*

- If there are common options that must be specified with the EMCLI command invocation, the environment variable *EMCLI_OPTS* can be used for that.

A simple example:

```
$ export EMCLI_OPTS=-Djava.awt.headless=true
$ emcli <rest of the EMCLI command-line options>
```

Files Used by EMCLI

EMCLI is just a small client-side application with only a handful of files that are required for EMCLI to work. The following chart gives an overview of the files:

EMCLI Component	Description
emcli / emcli.bat	The shell script (or BAT file on Windows) used to execute an EMCLI command.
emCLI.jar	Main application JAR file.
.emcli	All runtime information is stored in a special hidden directory called .emcli, created in the home directory of the user that is using EMCLI.
	With 10.2.0.5, the install will automatically configure and set up EMCLI with the installation of a Management Server. All log and trace files generated during the install for the setup of EMCLI will be stored in the OMS-based directory $ORACLE_HOME/sysman/emcli/setup/.emcli.

Filename	Description
.cookies	File with the session cookie the EMCLI session is using. This allows EMCLI to behave as a browser application, and use the same login mechanisms as a standard user.
.emcli	Binary encoded setup file, which contains the specifics on how EMCLI will contact the Management Server. This file gets updated when the EMCLI setup is run.
.emcli.log	Log file of all the EMCLI operations.
.omsinv	Text file with the location of the JAR files EMCLI needs to establish the connection with the Management Server.

TABLE 2-4. *EMCLI Directory Contents*

On UNIX, the location of the .emcli directory will be under the $HOME directory. On Windows, the location will be under the C:\Documents and Settings\<user> directory. This directory will contain the following files as listed in Table 2-4.

Synchronizing EMCLI Software

If a patch is applied on the management server that contains fixes or updates for the EMCLI software, those updates need to be propagated to the client installation, to make sure that the client-side EMCLI software is using the same version with the same capabilities as the server.

This synchronization can be done using the sync command on the client:

```
$ emcli sync
```

Command Overview

There are many commands available in EMCLI; so many, in fact, that a separate book is available in the standard set of Grid Control documentation with all the details on the commands you can run: *Oracle Enterprise Manager: Command Line Interface*. Just to give a brief overview of the capabilities of EMCLI, here's a short high-level overview of the types of operations that are possible using EMCLI:

- **Infrastructure commands** Among the available commands are the adding, deleting, and relocation of targets, auditing operations, and performing backup and recovery of the infrastructure.

- **Configuration and maintenance of targets** Common tasks, like updating target settings (passwords, *ORACLE_HOME*, and so on), creating and managing groups, and working with systems and services, are all possible via the command line.

- **User and Administrator management** All operations to create users and roles and assigning privileges can be done via the command line.

- **Patching, provisioning and cloning** Common patching and provisioning operations, like cloning a target, launching a deployment procedure, or applying a patch on the target.

Setting Up a Test Environment

The main production site is always the primary focus of every rollout of Grid Control. But for large deployments, with complex environments, having a test and/or a staging site available is equally important. In an ideal environment, the test site should be a replica of the main production site. It can be a scaled-down one (especially in the case of an enterprise deployment with thousands of Agents), with only a limited number of targets discovered. But it should have all the major functionality of the main site, including all the plug-ins, extensions, and customizations made. There are several benefits of having this staging site:

- Any new functionality that needs to be rolled out can first be installed and tested on this site, without impacting anything on the production site.

- Patches and upgrades can first be done on the staging site, to have a playbook ready for the change on the production environment.

- Any change made on the network infrastructure in the enterprise can first be tested and validated on the test staging site. This means that any changes made to the firewall, the network routes, proxy servers, and so on, should always be done first and verified on the test site, before making these kinds of (major) changes to the production environment.

Installation and Deployment Best Practices

Before we get to best practices, we should cover the most common mistakes that we should endeavor to avoid.

Common Mistakes

There are four mistakes people commonly make when rolling out Grid Control:

- **Installing a collapsed environment (aka the one-button install)**   For a production environment, a collapsed environment—where all three main infrastructure tiers are installed on the same server machine—is probably the worst kind of install you can do. Besides limiting yourself severely in terms of flexibility to handle future growth of the environment, it also makes it pretty difficult to separate resource utilization of each tier. A collapsed environment is fine for a sandbox or staging environment, but for a rollout in a production environment, this is not the type of install you want to do.

- **No room for additional growth in the infrastructure**   The repository and OMS should be installed and configured in such a way that you can grow the environment, and handle more targets and more administrators. If you know the number of managed servers is going to double or even triple (and then some) in a year, starting out with a single-instance database is not a wise move. Although it is possible to migrate a single-instance database to a RAC, starting out with a single-instance RAC and adding a RAC node to that database is a lot easier. On a similar note, not starting with a SLB solution, knowing you'll have multiple OMS servers in a short while is only going to create a major headache when you have to reconfigure and resecure all the managed Agents to point to the SLB once it's there.

- **No test and staging environment**   Although a Grid Control rollout might start out as a noncritical and nonessential application in your enterprise, you'll find out that pretty soon a lot of people will depend and rely on the information provided by the Application. As a result, adding or installing new features, rolling out infrastructure patches, or even trying out that new monitoring script directly on the production environment is not a good idea. All testing and playing with new features should be done on a staging or development system, to prevent visits from Murphy (and those angry phone calls from your boss).

- **No deployment plan**   If everything is rolled out using non-disciplined approaches, such as inadequate documentation, scheduling, and outstanding action-items, the problems (which can be operational, configuration related, or just plain human error) will start to consume the entire manageability initiative. This can lead to such a huge number of problems (often creating even bigger ones) that the whole infrastructure from an operational and financial standpoint can end up in jeopardy. Sadly, this is generally the time when panic sets in and people typically ask for assistance to help get the deployment back on track. The only way to fix this is to scale back, and start putting a schedule and disciplined practice in place.

Best Practices

The next few sections give you a recap of all the best practices and all the sound advice given in this chapter.

Understand the Network Topology the Infrastructure Will Be Deployed In

With data centers spread out geographically, chances are that firewalls, proxy servers, and several network domains will be part of the network topology. To simplify things for the network administrators, and to keep your own sanity when watching the management infrastructure grow:

- *Make sure that all machines have a valid hostname.* Discovering a machine using an IP address is not a good way of keeping that machine available over time when changes are made in the network.

- *Use the same ports for the Agent on every machine.* This will reduce the number of changes that will need to be made on firewalls and other network (security) devices.

- *Make sure all the hostnames of the server machines to be managed are fully qualified (using a valid domain name!), and are accessible from the all the OMS servers.* Especially in High Availability (HA)/Disaster Recovery (DR) environments, where there are multiple OMS servers, the name resolution of the server machines must be kept constant, even after a failover to a recovery site.

Design with HA in Mind

Not everyone needs a full-blown MAA Grid Control environment to anticipate all kinds of natural and not-so-natural disasters. However, in every Grid Control environment, monitoring a set of critical server machines will require increased uptime. Make sure the repository database and OMS servers can survive minor incidents (like HW failures, OS problems, one-off patches, and so on) to allow administrators to continue to monitor and work on their targets.

Have Spare Capacity

Accidents happen. Problems will occur. That's the one certainty there is. In a perfect world, there would be no problems (but then again, you would not need management software monitoring in the perfect world either). But the simple truth is that a data center consists of hardware (which will fail), software (which has bugs), and is operated by people (who make mistakes). And no matter how well you protect the environment against these problems and failures, things will fall through the cracks. And in case of failure, you'll need extra capacity in order to maintain the level of monitoring, and to keep on top of the extra alert and notification information generated.

Here's a rule of thumb: If you have two OMS servers, make sure you have 50 percent spare capacity on both servers. That way, in case of an OMS failure, the other OMS will be able to handle the complete load without a service interruption. This extra capacity is also your safeguard against failures in the enterprise and the spikes in resource consumption due to the increased volume of alerts and notification this will incur. For an enterprise rollout of Grid Control, this means:

- If you have three OMSes, have 33 percent spare capacity.
- If you have four OMSes, have 25 percent spare capacity.
- If you have five OMSes, have 20 percent spare capacity.
- and so on.

Know and Identify the Managed Targets Ahead of Time

Allowing server machines to be discovered in Grid Control means that these servers will start uploading data into the repository. In case of alerts and error floods being generated for these new targets, an Enterprise Administrator has to be able to intervene and contact the Agent on that machine. It is, therefore, imperative that either the owners of these machines are known and can be contacted immediately in case of an emergency, and/or the right authentication methods are known and set up to access all discovered machines. Here's an example:

1. A machine was renamed without alerting the Enterprise Administrators, or making the necessary changes in Grid Control to correctly identify this machine.

2. This meant that the Agent was trying to upload the data for that machine using the new name the OMS and repository didn't know and recognize.

3. The OMS naturally rejected the information, causing the Agent to get into a loop, continuously trying to upload the gathered information.

4. However, when the Enterprise Administrator detected this problem, he was not authorized to log in to this box and correct the problem, causing this problem to go on for a long time before the right system administrator for that machine was found to fix this problem.

Grid Control Is as Critical as the Most Critical System You Monitor

Identify the service level agreements for each system and application you monitor. In order for Enterprise Manager to meet this service level, Grid Control itself must be configured to at least the same service level. Examples:

- If a manufacturing application cannot be down for more than two hours, the maximum downtime Grid Control can have is also two hours.

■ If the management infrastructure is down for a longer period of time, you run the risk of not being able to detect a problem with the manufacturing application, and, therefore, violating the service level agreements for that application.

Implement a Backup Strategy on All the Tiers

And the backup strategy goes beyond just making the backup itself. It requires a scheduled backup operation (preferably automated), which has been verified and restored. And the test and staging system can again play a role here: to test the backup and restore procedure, and to make sure that, when disaster strikes, the restore can be done quickly and effortlessly.

GRID CONTROL WORKSHOP

Implementing a Grid Control Proof of Concept

Workshop Notes

This exercise describes how to install Enterprise Manager 10*g* Grid Control Release 5 using an existing Oracle 11*g* Database Enterprise Edition.

Overview   As you are now well aware, Enterprise Manager offers many installation scenarios in an effort to accommodate the vast number of environments currently deployed by Oracle's customer base. This workshop will walk you through installing the latest release of Oracle Enterprise Manager Grid Control (10.2.0.5.0) using the latest Oracle Database Enterprise Edition (11.1.0.7.0) as the repository. This will be the perfect opportunity to use the latest software releases and implement a working proof-of-concept that could possibly be scaled to address your entire enterprise at some later point.

Architectural Design Decisions   There will be three servers of x86 architecture running Oracle Enterprise Linux Release 5.

■ Server A, labeled *stage.acme.com*, will host the software used throughout this exercise.

■ Server B, labeled *repodb.acme.com*, will host the installation of the Oracle Managed Repository Release 5 (10.2.0.5.0), which is based on an existing installation of the Oracle Database 11*g* Enterprise Edition Release (11.1.0.7.0).

■ Server C, labeled *oms.acme.com*, will host the installation of the Oracle Management Server Release 5 (10.2.0.5.0) and the Oracle Management Agent Release 5 (10.2.0.5.0).

Minimum network requirements: All servers will be within the same subnet and communication between Grid Control components will have a maximum `ping` latency of no more than:

■ Grid Control Console to Oracle Management Server: 300ms

■ Oracle Management Agent to Oracle Management Server: 300ms

■ Oracle Management Server to Oracle Management Repository: 20ms

■ Oracle Management Repository to Oracle Management Repository Storage: 10ms

(continued)

The communication to the Management Servers from the outside world should be optimized (since we all want to see snappy updates in the web browser): The 300ms number is a general best practice, and an objective to stride for. A higher latency number for an Agent on a remote part of the network will not cause the Agent to be nonfunctional. What it does mean, however, is that special precautions need to be taken for these remote Agents, to make sure the Management Servers can communicate with these machines in a productive way. The amount of data will have to be verified and tweaked to make sure that all the data can be transferred to the OMS (see Chapter 7), and the OMS will have to be made aware of these slower Agents to scale back the heart-beating the Agents will be doing (see Chapter 6).

The network latency between the Management Servers and the repository database and the Storage devices, however, is critical for the entire infrastructure: The bigger and more complex the infrastructure, the better this network link between these components needs to be tuned. In order for the Management Servers to process and handle all the data coming into the system, the database and storage devices need to be very responsive. For large deployments of several thousands of Agents, these numbers of 10ms and 20ms can even be on the high side.

Prerequisites   In order for this exercise to work successfully, you will need to verify that all of the requirements listed in *Installing Enterprise Manager Grid Control Using An Existing Database* are met as described in the *Oracle Enterprise Manager Grid Control Installation Guide, 10g Release 5 (10.2.0.5.0)*.

NOTE
A default installation of an Enterprise Edition database is not sufficient to support a Grid Control repository.

Synchronized OS Timestamps and Time Zones are particularly important for all hosts running Grid Control OMS, Repository, and/or Agent software. This is particularly helpful when encountering the following scenarios:

- Performing detailed log reviews rendered by the Grid Control Console or directly on the operating system.

- Investigating interconnectivity issues between Grid Control Repositories in a RAC environment.

- When installing the Oracle software in a cluster, the Oracle installer will initially install the software on the local node and then remotely copy the software to the remote node. If the date and time of the nodes are not synchronized, you will likely receive errors:

```
/bin/tar:./Apache/Apache/conf/dms.conf: time stamp  2009-04-26
10:30:02 is 25 s in the future
```

The recommended approach is to synchronize timestamps by running a Network Time Protocol (NTP) service on all the hosts. To check that the NTP daemon is running, execute the following command:

```
[root@stage ~]$ /sbin/service ntpd status
```

or check for the presence of the `ntpd` process, whose output is similar to the following:

```
[root@stage ~]$ ps -ef | grep ntpd | grep -v grep
ntp    17081    1    0 Mar29 ?     00:08:02 ntpd -u ntp:ntp -p /var/run/ntpd.pid
```

If you plan on scaling your Grid Control implementation across multiple OS time zones, the suggestion is to consider using the UTC time zone for all Grid Control hosts, including managed target hosts. By doing so, you will save your administration team the burden of converting time zones when performing detailed log reviews.

Section A: Staging the Grid Control Software

We advise that you begin downloading and staging the Grid Control Software so it can easily be accessible by all servers in your network. The easiest and most preferred method would be to utilize the Oracle Technology Network (OTN). You can download the latest full Grid Control software releases from the OTN web site: `http://www.oracle.com/technology/index.html`.

> **NOTE**
> *Please note the distinction between Full Installers and Patch Installers. Full Installers contain the OMR, OMS, OMA, and Management Packs, whereas Patch Installers only contain updates to the OMS, OMA, and Management Packs. Since Oracle does not provide Full Installers for any of the latest releases of Grid Control technology, you will need to download and stage the Full Installer archive of an earlier release (10.2.0.1.0), followed by the Patch Installer of Release 5 (10.2.0.5.0).*

Once you obtain the software releases and unzip them into their respective staging directories, you need to allow access to the software via several methods, depending on whether the target system is local or remote. If the target machine is local, access the Grid Control software directly on that system. If the target system is remote, access the staging directory using common remote access methods; in the case of Linux, the preferred method is via a Networked File System (NFS) server. NFS servers are relatively easy to configure. All that is required is to export a file system, either generally or to a specific host, and then mount that file system from a remote client.

In the case of this example, we have two servers: *stage.acme.com* and *oms.acme.com*; where *stage.acme.com* hosts the Grid Control software and NFS server to be mounted by the remote client, *oms.acme.com*.

On the NFS server, *stage.acme.com*:

Step 1. Stage the base product of the Grid Control software in the following directory:

```
/u02/stage/apps/ORCL/EMGC_10G/FI/emgc/
```

Step 2. As root, export the file-system by simply adding the following line to the /etc/ exports file:

```
/u02/stage/apps/ORCL/EMGC_10G/     *(rw, no_root_squash)
```

(continued)

Step 3. As root, issue the following command to activate the new directory:

```
[root@stage ~]$ exportfs -r
```

Step 4. Verify that the exported file directory is activated:

```
[root@stage ~]$ showmount -e
Export list for stage.acme.com:
/u02/stage/apps/ORCL/EMGC_10G/
```

From the client server, *oms.acme.com*:

Step 1. As root, mount the partition to a pre-existing /mnt/grid10g directory using the following command:

```
[root@oms ~]$ mount -t nfs stage.acme.com:/u02/stage/apps/ORCL/
EMGC_10G/ /mnt/grid10g
```

You should now be able to access all the staged Oracle Grid Control software. For instance, launching the 10.2.0.1.0 Grid Control installer requires the execution of the following command:

```
[oracle@target Disk1]$ ./mnt/grid10g/FI/emgc/Disk1/runInstaller
```

Subsequently, with the NFS server active, you now have the ability to centrally mount software from many other clients seeking to stage and install the Grid Control software.

Section B: Mapping Out the Directory Structures and Naming Conventions for This Exercise

Common problems that manifest with proof-of-concepts typically stem from neglecting to recall key decisions regarding the implementation of the Grid Control solution and providing incorrect input from what seems to be an overwhelming range of choices. Table 2-5 is a mapping exercise that will help in deterring such problems by outlining the sequence of events, and Table 2-6 lists the correct parameters that must be used to successfully complete the exercise.

Section C: Installing Operating Systems Used to Host Enterprise Manager Grid Control

This section does not cover the details behind the installation of the Linux operating systems; rather, we will focus on what options you should choose to ensure that all the necessary packages are available to complete the Oracle installs.

Step 1. For this example, Oracle Enterprise Linux 5 was installed from OTN with these options selected during the installation:

Applications	*Networking and Publishing*
	Engineering and Scientific
Development	*Development Libraries*
	Development Tools
Base System	*System Tools*

Sequence	Action	Component Installed/ Configured	Comments
1	Repository Database	Prepare an existing Database for a Grid Control Repository	Perform tasks as outlined in the prerequisites and throughout this chapter.
2	Oracle Management Server	Install the 10.2.0.1.0 Oracle Management Server	Install on host, *oms.acme.com*
3	Upgrade of 10.2.0.1.0 OMS and Agent.	Install the 10.2.0.5.0 patch set to the 10.2.0.1.0 OMS and Agent.	The OMS install includes the Management Agent.
4	Configure Grid Control	Configure Grid Control for 10.2.0.5.0.	Configures 10.2.0.5.0 release of Grid Control for the OMS and Repository (*oms.acme.com* and *repodb.acme.com*)
5	Verifying Grid Control	Verifying that Grid Control 10.2.0.5.0 is installed.	Ensures the integrity of the install.

TABLE 2-5. *Sequence of Events*

Step 2. Oracle Enterprise Linux 5 and Red Hat Enterprise Linux 5 require a link titled libdb.so.2 to be created by the root user:

```
[root@oms ~]$ ln -s /usr/lib/libgdbm.so.2.0.0 /usr/lib/libdb.so.2
```

Step 3. To ensure that all software package requirements are met, the following simple command can be issued by the root user or placed in a script on the local server to be run and compared against the software prerequisites of the installation guide:

```
rpm -qa --qf '%{name}-%{version}-%{release}.%{arch}\n'| egrep 'comp
at|glibc|gcc|binutils|make|elfutils|libaio|libstdc|sysstat'| sort
```

Section D: Verifying That the 11.1.0.7.0 Oracle Database Is Prepared for a Grid Control Repository

Step 1. Verify that your existing 11.1.0.7.0 database fits the characteristics needed for a Grid Control Repository. The documentation is available on OTN: *Oracle Enterprise Manager Grid Control Installation Guide 10g Release 5 (10.2.0.5.0)*.

Referencing Part II, "Installing Enterprise Manager Grid Control," Chapter 7, "Installing Enterprise Manager Grid Control," and the link labeled "Installing Enterprise Manager Grid Control Using an Existing Database," you will find that there is a table of prerequisites listing the steps needed to prepare an existing database for repository use. Note that a default installation of an Enterprise Edition database is not sufficient to support a Grid Control Repository.

(continued)

Installation Parameters	Suggested Value	Comments
10.2.0.1.0 Full Installer FULL_INSTALLER_ STAGE	/mnt/grid10g/ FI/10.2.0.1.0/	Software staging directory.
10.2.0.5.0 Patch Installer PATCH_INSTALLER_ STAGE	/mnt/grid10g/ PI/10.2.0.5.0/	Software staging directory.
ORACLE_SOFTWARE	/u01/apps/oracle/ product/	The directory where all Oracle software resides.
Grid Control Base Directory ORACLE_BASE $ORACLE_SOFTWARE/ emgc	/u01/apps/oracle/ product/emgc/	The base directory for Grid Control product installation. The installation process will specifically request the location of this directory.
Oracle OMS Home Directory OMS_HOME $ORACLE_HOME/oms10g	/u01/apps/oracle/ product/emgc/oms10g	Automatically generated under Grid Control Base Directory.
Oracle Agent Home Directory AGENT_HOME $ORACLE_HOME/ agent10g	/u01/apps/oracle/ product/emgc/agent10g	Automatically generated under Grid Control Base Directory.
Location of the oradata $ORACLE_SOFTWARE/ oradata	/u01/apps/oracle/ product/oradata	Location for the database repository files.
Location of the oraInventory $ORACLE_SOFTWARE/ oraInventory	/u01/apps/oracle/ product/oraInventory	Oracle Universal Installer (OUI) uses this directory as a repository of the Oracle products that are installed on the machine.
Access passwords	welcome1	All OS, EM, and DB access passwords; for the sake of simplicity.
Repository Database SID	repodb	The global identifier of the Grid Control Repository database.

TABLE 2-6.   *Required Parameter Values*

Section E: Installing Oracle Management Server

Step 1. Taking the previously staged directory for the Grid Control software, `/mnt/grid10g/FI/10.2.0.1.0/`, into account, we will be modifying the install response file, `em_with_existing_db.rsp`, for the *Grid Control Using An Existing Database* install-type, located in the `/mnt/grid10g/FI/10.2.0.1.0/response/` directory.

Step 2. Make a copy of the `em_oms_repodb.rsp` response file for our specific customizations using the following command:

```
[oracle@stage ~]$ cp
/mnt/grid10g/FI/emgc/response/em_with_existing_db.rsp
/mnt/grid10g/FI/emgc/response/em_oms_repodb.rsp
```

Step 3. Edit the `em_oms_repodb.rsp` file and alter the following parameters:

```
UNIX_GROUP_NAME="dba"
FROM_LOCATION="/mnt/grid10g/FI/emgc/stage/products.xml"
BASEDIR="/u01/apps/oracle/product/emgc/"
INSTALLATION_NAME="oms10gr5"
s_reposHost="repodb.acme.com"
s_reposPort="1521"
s_reposSID="repodb"
s_reposDBAPwd="welcome1"
s_mgmtTbsName="/u01/apps/oracle/product/emgc/oradata/mgmt_01.dbf"
s_ecmTbsName="/u01/apps/oracle/product/emgc/oradata/mgmt_ecm_
depot_01.dbf"
s_securePassword="welcome1"
s_securePasswordConfirm="welcome1"
b_lockedSelected=false
s_reposPwd="welcome1"
s_reposPwdConfirm="welcome1"
```

Be aware of the following when working with response files:

■ For the parameter UNIX_GROUP_NAME, the value dba must be a valid OS user group.

■ For the parameter INSTALLATION_NAME, a value must be provided.

■ For the parameters s_mgmtTbsName and s_ecmTbsName, the directories specified as values must pre-exist. The installer will not create these on your behalf, and if they do not exist, you will receive errors, which can be difficult to diagnose without detailed log review and starting the entire process over.

■ Use the examples in the response file templates to include double quotes ("") or curly braces ({}) where indicated. Omission of these character string conditioners will lead to errors that can be difficult to diagnose without detailed log review and starting the entire process over.

(continued)

Step 4. Install the base Oracle Management Server for Linux using the following command:

```
[oracle@oms ~]$ ./mnt/grid10g/FI/emgc/runInstaller -noconfig
b_skipDBValidation=true -ignoreSysPrereqs -silent -responseFile
/mnt/grid10g/FI/emgc/response/em_oms_repodb.rsp use_prereq_
checker=false
```

The generic parameter is of the following form:

```
FULL_INSTALLER_STAGE/runInstaller -noconfig b_skipDBValidation=true
-ignoreSysPrereqs -silent -responseFile FULL_INSTALLER_STAGE/
response/ em_oms_repodb.rsp use_prereq_checker=false
```

Be aware of the following:

■ The installation must take place in an existing, empty directory.

■ Product installations will always be logged and the naming conventions are
  pre-appended with installActions followed by a timestamp (for example,
  installActions2009-03-25_11-34-29AM.log). These log files are located in:

  ■ ORACLE_BASE/oraInventory/logs/

  ■ ORACLE_HOME/oms10g/cfgtoollogs/oui/

  ■ ORACLE_HOME/agent10g/cfgtoollogs/oui/

Step 5. Launch a new terminal session as the user root and run the following scripts on the
host, when prompted by the installer:

Run the orainstRoot.sh script from the Oracle central inventory directory:

```
[oracle@oms ~]$ ./u01/apps/oracle/product/oraInventory/orainstRoot.sh
```

Run the allroot.sh script from the Oracle home directory of the OMS:

```
[oracle@oms ~]$ ./u01/apps/oracle/product/emgc/oms10g/allroot.sh
```

Step 6. Certain OPMN processes will be running merely as a result of installation, in spite
of the fact that no configuration of the OMS Oracle Home has been performed. In
order to continue with the 10.2.0.5.0 patch installation, these OPMN processes
must be stopped by issuing the following command from the Oracle Home directory
of the OMS:

```
[oracle@oms ~]$ ./u01/apps/oracle/product/emgc/oms10g/opmn/bin/op-
mnctl stopall
```

Section F: Applying the 10.2.0.5.0 Patch Set Release
to the Oracle Management Server and Agent Install

Step 1. Taking the previously staged directory for the Grid Control software, /
mnt/grid10g/PI/10.2.0.5.0/, into account, we will be modifying
the install response file, patchset.rsp, located in the /mnt/grid10g/
PI/10.2.0.5.0/3731593/Disk1/response/ directory.

Step 2.   Since the Grid Control base install includes both the OMS and Agent, we will need to make a copy of the `patchset.rsp` response file in order to individually upgrade both:

```
[oracle@oms ~]$ cp /mnt/grid10g/PI/10.2.0.5.0/3731593/Disk1/
response/patchset.rsp /mnt/grid10g/PI/10.2.0.5.0/3731593/Disk1/
response/oms_patchset.rsp

[oracle@oms ~]$ cp /mnt/grid10g/PI/10.2.0.5.0/3731593/Disk1/
response/patchset.rsp /mnt/grid10g/PI/10.2.0.5.0/3731593/Disk1/
response/agent_patchset.rsp
```

The generic parameter is of the following form:

```
PATCH_INSTALL_STAGE/3731593/Disk1/response/patchset.rsp
```

Step 3.   Alter the following parameters from default as follows in the `oms_patchset.rsp` file:

```
ORACLE_HOME="/u01/apps/oracle/product/emgc/oms10g"
b_softwareonly=true
s_sysPassword="welcome1"
sl_pwdInfo={ "welcome1" }
oracle.iappserver.st_midtier:szl_InstanceInformation={ "oms10gr5" }
```

> **NOTE**
> *The password login credentials for the ias_admin user, (the* `oracle.iappserver.st_midtier` *parameter) are set after the initial setup and install of Grid Control to the same value as the SYSMAN user. However, the Application Server administrator can change the password independently from the SYSMAN password at a point in time.*

Step 4.   Alter the following parameters from default as follows in the `agent_patchset.rsp` file:

```
ORACLE_HOME="/u01/apps/oracle/product/emgc/agent10g"
b_softwareonly=true
s_sysPassword="welcome1"
sl_pwdInfo={ "welcome1" }
```

Step 5.   Apply the 10.2.0.5.0 patchset to the OMS Oracle Home by issuing the following command:

```
[oracle@oms ~]$
./mnt/grid10g/PI/10.2.0.5.0/3731593/Disk1/runInstaller -noconfig
-silent -responseFile
/mnt/grid10g/PI/10.2.0.5.0/3731593/Disk1/response/oms_patchset.rsp
```

(continued)

The generic parameter is of the following form:

```
PATCH_INSTALLER_STAGE/3731593/Disk1/runInstaller -noconfig -si-
lent-responseFile PATCH_INSTALLER_STAGE/3731593/Disk1/response/
oms_patchset.rsp
```

Be aware of the following:

■ While the Grid Control base product installation requires the use of the
  -ignoreSysPrereqs option, the patchset does have the ability to check for OEL5,
  RHEL5, and SLES10 prerequisites, so the ignore option should not be used for
  patchset installation.

■ Product installations will always be logged and the naming conventions are
  pre-appended with installActions followed by a timestamp (for example,
  installActions2009-03-25_11-34-29AM.log). These log files are located in:

   ■ *ORACLE_BASE*/oraInventory/logs/

   ■ ORACLE_HOME/oms10g/cfgtoollogs/oui/

■ Expect the logs for the OMS patchset to be stamped with a later date than the
  three original files created during installation. This pattern will continue with
  subsequent attempts in the event any retries are taken.

Step 6. Execute the root.sh script as the root user:

```
[root@oms ~]$ ./u01/apps/oracle/product/emgc/oms10g/root.sh
```

No feedback will be given on successful execution in this case.

Step 7. Apply 10.2.0.5.0 patchset to the Management Agent of the Oracle Home:

```
[oracle@oms ~]$ ./mnt/grid10g/PI/10.2.0.5.0/3731593/Disk1/
runInstaller -noconfig -silent -responseFile /mnt/grid10g/
PI/10.2.0.5.0/3731593/Disk1/response/agent_patchset.rsp
```

The generic parameter is of the following form:

```
PATCH_INSTALL_STAGE/3731593/Disk1/runInstaller -noconfig -silent
-responseFile PATCH_INSTALL_STAGE /3731593/Disk1/response/agent_
patchset.rsp
```

Be aware of the following:

■ Product installations will always be logged and the naming conventions are
  pre-appended with installActions followed by a timestamp (for example,
  installActions2009-04-26_10-30-00AM.log). These log files are located in:

   ■ *ORACLE_BASE*/oraInventory/logs/

   ■ ORACLE_HOME/agent10g/cfgtoollogs/oui/

■ Expect the logs for the OMS patchset to be stamped with a later date than the
  three original files created during installation. This pattern will continue with
  subsequent attempts in the event any retries are taken.

Step 8. Run the `root.sh` command as root:

```
[root@oms ~]$ ./u01/apps/oracle/product/emgc/oms10g/root.sh
```

Section G: Configuring the Grid Control Installation with the ConfigureGC.pl Script

Step 1. Ensure that the `runConfig.sh` file has `execute` permission.

```
[root@oms bin]$ chmod 777
/u01/apps/oracle/product/emgc/oms10g/oui/bin/runConfig.sh
```

Step 2. Use the following procedure to preserve and set the *PERL5LIB* environment variable:

Make a backup of the *PERL5LIB* variable value:

```
[root@oms ~]$ export PERL5LIB_BACKUP $PERL5LIB
```

Set the *PERL5LIB* variable to the correct path:

```
[root@oms ~]$ export
PERL5LIB=/u01/apps/oracle/product/emgc/oms10g/perl/lib/5.6.1
```

Step 3. Configure Enterprise Manager Grid Control by running the ConfigureGC.pl script:

```
[root@oms ~]$ ./u01/apps/oracle/product/emgc/oms10g/perl/bin/perl
u01/apps/oracle/product/emgc/oms10g/sysman/install/ConfigureGC.pl
u01/apps/oracle/product/emgc/
```

The generic parameter is of the following form:

```
ORACLE_HOME/oms10g/perl/bin/perl
ORACLE_HOME/oms10g/sysman/install/ConfigureGC.pl ORACLE_BASE
```

Be aware of the following:

■ Product configurations will always be logged and the naming conventions are pre-appended with `configActions` followed by a timestamp (for example, configActions2009-04-26_10-30-00AM.log). These log files are located in:

   ■ `ORACLE_HOME/agent10g/cfgtoollogs/oui/`

■ As the configuration assistants are run through the progress of the script, your `ORACLE_HOME/cfgtoollogs/cfgfw/` files will begin to populate with the results of these configuration actions for each Oracle Home in its respective directory (for example, *ORACLE_BASE*/oms10g/ or *ORACLE_BASE*/ agent10g/). As operational actions are taken in the configuration steps, logs will be populated in the following locations:

   ■ `ORACLE_HOME/sysman/log/`

   ■ *ORACLE_BASE*/oms10g/opmn/logs/

   ■ *ORACLE_BASE*/oms10g/j2ee/OC4J_EM/log/

   ■ *ORACLE_BASE*/oms10g/Apache/Apache/logs

(continued)

Step 4. The configuration may take around an hour with little command-session update at times. It may be instructive to follow the progress of the configuration in these files:

- For the progress of the OMS Configuration Assistants: *ORACLE_BASE*/oms10g/ `cfgtoollogs/cfgfw/CfmLoggertimestamp.log`

- For the upgrade progress of the Grid Control Repository: *ORACLE_BASE*/ `oms10g/sysman/log/emrepmgr.log.*`

Section H: Completing Postinstallation Tasks after Setting Up Grid Control Proof-of-Concept

For this exercise, the following postinstallation tasks are recommended:

- Verifying the Grid Control Install of 10.2.0.5.0
- Backing up critical OMS Files
- Setting up the Oracle SHELL environment on all nodes

Verifying the Grid Control Install of 10.2.0.5.0   It is a useful task to verify the integrity of Grid Control and the success of the upgrade to Release 5. There are several methods of doing this:

- **Method 1**   From the main page of the Grid Control Console, select the link labeled About Enterprise Manager on the bottom left of the page. The output should reflect:

  ```
  Oracle Enterprise Manager 10g Release 5 Grid Control 10.2.0.5.0
  ```

- **Method 2**   Issue the following command from the ORACLE_BASE/oms10g directory:

  ```
  [oracle@oms oms10g]$ ./OPatch/opatch lsinventory
  ```

  The output should result in the following:

  ```
  [Installed Top-level Products (2):
  Enterprise Manager Patchset                    10.2.0.5.0
  Oracle Enterprise Manager Grid Console         10.2.0.1.0
  ```

- **Method 3**   Launch the Oracle Universal Installer and select the Installed Products view.

  From the drop-down list of the respective Oracle Home of both the OMS and Agent there should be this listing:

  ```
  [Enterprise Manager Patchset 10.2.0.5.0
  ```

- **Method 4**   From the *ORACLE_HOME* of the OMS, issue the emctl status oms command and verify the following output:

  ```
  [oracle@oracle oms10g]$ emctl status oms
  Oracle Enterprise Manager 10g Release 5 Grid Control
  Copyright (c) 1996, 2009 Oracle Corporation.  All rights reserved.
  Oracle Management Server is Up.
  ```

■ **Method 5** From the *ORACLE_HOME* of the Agent, issue the `emctl status agent` command and verify the following output:

```
[oracle@oracle agent10g]$ emctl status agent
Oracle Enterprise Manager 10g Release 5 Grid Control 10.2.0.5.0.
Copyright (c) 1996, 2009 Oracle Corporation.  All rights reserved.
----------------------------------------------------------------
Agent Version    : 10.2.0.5.0
OMS Version      : 10.2.0.5.0
Protocol Version : 10.2.0.5.0
```

■ **Method 6** If you maintain a Metalink Support account, you have the ability to download the EMDIAG utility. The main intent of this utility is to help identify and verify the repository and the repository data for any problems that can impact the normal functions of Grid Control. The content can be sent to Oracle Support for further diagnosis and analysis should there be any cause for concern. Reference Metalink Note:421953.1 and issue the following command for the most descriptive output:

```
[oracle@oracle agent10g]$ repvfy -tns alias -pwd pwd -level 9 -details
```

Backing Up Critical OMS Files It is always a good idea to outline business continuity plans, especially around backup and recovery. Although a complete cold backup is the ideal approach, it doesn't hurt to back up the following OMS files:

■ **$ORACLE_BASE/oms10g/sysman/emd/targets.xml** This file contains managed target information for the Application Server Control Agent and comes populated with agent discovery during the installation of Enterprise Manager.

■ **$ORACLE_BASE/agent10g/sysman/emd/targets.xml** This file contains managed target information for the Grid Control Agent and comes populated with agent discovery during the installation of Enterprise Manager. Common failures when using the Agent Configuration Assistant (agentca) are generally due to file corruption, and restoring these files will aid in the rediscovery or removal of managed targets. It is also recommended to back up this file for all target hosts not containing an OMS.

■ **$ORACLE_HOME/webcache/internal.xml** Abrupt reboots often cause corruption to this file, resulting in Webcache's inability to start. Backing up this file regularly will ensure that you have a working file to restore should you encounter this problem.

■ **$ORACLE_HOME/sysman/config/emoms.properties** This file contains the obfuscated SYSMAN password. In the event of disk failure and file corruption, this file must be restored in order to gain access to the Grid Control Console. The line containing the obfuscated password is of the following form:

```
oracle.sysman.eml.mntr.emdRepPwdSeed=1508149684005275721
```

■ **$ORACLE_HOME/sysman/config/emkey.ora** This file contains the hash key needed to encrypt and decrypt the SSL wallets from the Agents and the credential information stored in the repository. If this file is lost and cannot be recovered, a new key needs

(continued)

to be generated, every Agent will have to be resecured, and all credentials stored in the repository will have to be re-entered. Although the default location of this file is $ORACLE_HOME/sysman/config, its properties can be changed by updating the emkeyfile parameter in the emoms.properties file:

```
oracle.sysman.emkeyfile=<directory>/emkey.ora
```

Setting Up the Oracle SHELL Environment on All Nodes   Aside from setting the necessary file permissions for Oracle products and performing other root-related configuration activities, executing the orainstRoot.sh and root.sh scripts provides you with the ability to set up a working SHELL environment should you ever find yourself at the terminal. By default, the oraenv, coraenv, and dbhome scripts are created in the /usr/local/bin directory and the oratab script is in the /etc directory. We will leverage these by building a simple wrapper script that will allow you to customize the Oracle environment based on your personal preferences and needs.

Step 1.   Create a script directory in the home of the Oracle user:

```
[oracle@oms ~]$ mkdir /home/oracle/bin
```

Step 2.   Using your favorite text editor, create a wrapper script named gcenv with the following content:

```
#!/bin/bash
clear
echo "\o/\o/\o/\o/\o/\o/\o/\o/\o/\o/\o/\o/\o/\o/\o/\o/\o/\o/\o/\o/\o/"
echo "||          Self-identifying banner - insert text here          ||"
echo "\o/\o/\o/\o/\o/\o/\o/\o/\o/\o/\o/\o/\o/\o/\o/\o/\o/\o/\o/\o/\o/"
echo ""
echo "Type one of the following ORACLE_SID's to setup the SHELL for an
ORACLE ENVIRONMENT:"
echo " oms to set up paths to the 10.2.0.5.0 Oracle Enterprise Manager
OMS."
echo " agent to set up paths to the 10.2.0.5.0 Oracle GRID Control Agent."
echo " repodb to set up paths to the 11.1.0.7.0 Database EE Repository. "
. oraenv

# Initialize generic parameters.
alias cdo='cd $ORACLE_HOME'
cd $ORACLE_HOME
LD_LIBRARY_PATH=$ORACLE_HOME/lib:$ORACLE_HOME/network/lib:/usr/lib; export
LD_LIBRARY_PATH
PATH=/home/oracle/bin:/bin:/usr/bin:/usr/local/bin:/usr/local/bin/X11:/
usr/X11R6/bin:/usr/kerberos/bin:$PATH; export PATH
clear
DISPLAY=oms.acme.com:0.0; export DISPLAY
echo ""

TEMP_PATH=/home/oracle/bin:/bin:/usr/bin:/usr/local/bin:/usr/local/bin/
X11:/usr/X11R6/bin:/usr/kerberos/bin; export TEMP_PATH
if [ $ORACLE_SID == "oms" ] ; then
# Oracle Management Server  - Adding opmnctl, opatch and dcmctl paths to
$PATH
```

```
PATH="$TEMP_PATH"; export PATH PATH="$ORACLE_HOME/bin:$ORACLE_HOME/opmn/
bin:$ORACLE_HOME/OPatch:$ORACLE_HOME/dcm/bin:$PATH"; export PATH
fi
fi
if [ $ORACLE_SID == "agent" ] ; then
# Management Agent - Adding agentca and emctl paths to $PATH
PATH="$TEMP_PATH"; export PATH
PATH="$ORACLE_HOME/bin:$ORACLE_HOME/OPatch:$PATH"; export PATH
fi
if [ $ORACLE_SID == "repodb" ] ; then
# Repository Database - Adding lsnrctl, opatch, sqlplus, and isqlplus
paths to
# $PATH

PATH="$TEMP_PATH"; export PATH
PATH="$ORACLE_HOME/bin:$PATH"; export PATH
fi
echo "Congratulations. You are now set to the following Oracle home: " pwd
echo "You can use [cdo] to change to ORACLE_HOME anytime."
cdo
```

Step 3. Administration of Grid Control is easier when you can specify a Grid Control component's home directory path with environment variables. This helps administrators when referencing variables in other scripts or running common executables without having to specify the full path. In the case of this exercise, the command for stopping and starting `opmnctl` components without setting the Oracle user's environment would be:

```
[oracle@oms ~] $ ./u01/apps/oracle/product/emgc/oms10g/opmnctl
startall
```

versus

```
[oracle@oms ~] $ opmnctl startall
```

You can further customize the Oracle user's environment for each Oracle Home by adding parameters in each `if/fi` statement block.

Step 4. As root, edit the `/etc/oratab` script and ensure that there are correct entries reflecting the *ORACLE_SID*s referenced in the wrapper script. The entries must be in the form of `$ORACLE_SID:$ORACLE_HOME:<N|Y>` and in the case of our exercise:

```
oms:/u01/apps/oracle/product/emgc/oms10g:N
agent:/u01/apps/oracle/product/emgc/agent10g:N
```

Step 5. Ensure that the `/home/oracle/bin` path is correctly accessible in the Oracle shell. For our example, the `.bash_profile` file was modified to include the following entry:

```
# User specific environment and startup programs
PATH=$PATH:$HOME/bin
```

(continued)

Step 6.   Finally, you can set the appropriate environment by calling on the `gcenv` wrapper script and passing the correct *ORACLE_SID* as input:

```
[oracle@oms bin]$ . gcenv
```

NOTE
If you issue the command `. /home/oracle/bin/gcenv` *the script will execute, but your environment will not be correctly set. This is an idiosyncrasy of Linux, and since we require the Oracle environment variables to persist throughout the session, you must simply use "." because including "/" spawns another shell to execute the script, and upon successful completion, it will exit leaving you with the original session and no environment!*

Summary

As time passes, your solution will find itself deeply rooted into the enterprise so, it is important to understand that no amount of careful planning or precisely followed procedures will make up for a poorly designed architecture. The root of most Grid Control problems is that poorly designed architectures are prone to failures under stress, and lack the capacity for real-time diagnosis and course correction. The successful management of large ecosystems stem from sound engineering. A successful Grid Control architect must be able to see above and beyond a set of business requirements and their corresponding "quick-and-dirty" engineering plans. Careful analysis of this chapter and constant surveillance for opportunities in which your Grid Control solution can prove that it is the right technological fit, before using it as the building block in a much larger architecture, will result in relatively pleasing outcomes.

CHAPTER
3

Grid Control and
Maximum Availability

n business-critical environments, stakeholders choose what they believe to be vital aspects to the continuity of their business. When discussing business-critical environments, the first thing that comes to mind should be the concept of high availability. Without it, a simple system failure could cause a service outage, and service outages to a business are much like a missing groom in a wedding ceremony.

From a technical perspective, high availability is simply taking a single "service" and ensuring that a failure of one of its components will not result in an outage. So very often, high availability is thought to be at the physical server level—one host server is failed over for another. However, this is not the business intent of the CEO and CIO alike—where the goal is to ensure that the services provided by business applications are functional and accessible a majority of the time. To get to this level is much like creating a masterpiece: It can only be accomplished with hard work, careful deliberation, and the right resources.

The rule of thumb throughout this chapter is simple: You need (at least) a count of two. Note that the count of two applies to the aspects of business continuity, not just components. This isn't solely about equipment and software; it is also about policies and procedures. The count of one is bad because it leads to a single point of failure, with nothing to lean on in the event of a failure, or backup policies to reallocate responsibilities and work. Even in the event of an unexpected failure, the services provided should always remain (perhaps not at the level of efficiency before the failure). Regardless, to effectively manage and maintain a sizable Grid Control environment, both aspects and components of business continuity must be mastered.

Why High Availability?

As the Enterprise Manager Environment grows, so will the importance of the infrastructure. More and more people will start to rely on the available information and will need this for their day-to-day operations. And with increased visibility of the product comes the increased need to keep the infrastructure alive. And this is where High Availability (HA) comes into the picture.

HA is actually only one part of the equation. This focuses on keeping the application alive in case of a small failure (like tripping over a power cable, a disk failing in a machine, or a patching that needs to be done on the OS or the application software). It typically means adding redundancy to the various components on a local level, so that when a failure occurs, the redundant components will still continue to function and keep the application alive. All of these solutions require some kind of cluster software to be present, to link several machines together into one working entity. You can achieve HA in two big ways:

- *Running redundant components concurrently.* All nodes in the cluster will run all the components. And if one node becomes unavailable, the other surviving nodes simply continue, taking on the load of the failed node. A good example of this approach is the RAC solution for Oracle databases. One can even distinguish two different types of concurrent redundant component setups: The most common case is when the redundant components are just running side by side, as with a RAC database: Both nodes run at the same time, handling the work. For some setups, people set up a primary component and a backup component, not necessarily next to each other, but potentially even in a different data center, or in a different location. And even though these targets are separated distance-wise, they both are active and running. When both the primary and the secondary component are running at the same time, that type of configuration is known as an Active/Active setup.

■ *Running in an Active/Passive mode.* A component runs on only one node in the cluster (or several machines in case of a multinode cluster), and will fail over to an idle node in case of failure. In this scenario, there is always at least one operational (active) node, and one idle (passive) node, waiting to run the component in case of a failure.

HA is only one part of the equation. There is also Disaster Recovery (DR). This focuses more on the not-so-small failures—like a failure of a complete tier of the multitier application, a complete data center power blackout, or a major network failure—by adding failover capabilities to the application. This usually means an offsite duplication of the environment. In the event of a catastrophe in one data center, another data center can take over and continue to run the application from the different (unaffected) location. These two combined (HA+DR), form the Maximum Availability Architecture (MAA).

To make Grid Control maximally available, we'll have to first strengthen the architecture to be highly available, and then add infrastructure components into the picture to make it resilient to disasters. Let's start with the basic simple rollout of Grid Control shown in Figure 3-1: We have a three-tier application, so we'll need to focus on each of those three tiers to get the problem points eliminated.

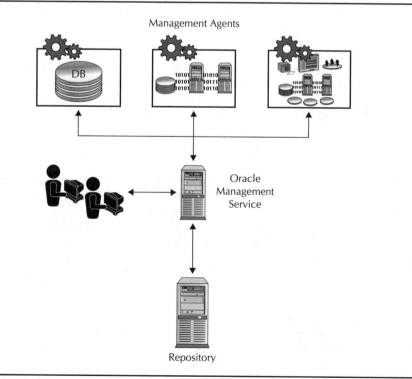

FIGURE 3-1. *The basic Grid Control architecture*

HA: Eliminating the Single Point of Failure

Making an application High Available is nothing more than the art of eliminating the single points of failure in the infrastructure. It's a simplification (and the MAA guys might not really agree with my oversimplification 100 percent), but it makes the goal of the exercise pretty visible: In order to be highly available, redundant components will need to be present, so that no single point in the entire chain of machines and software running the application will render the Grid Control application inaccessible. And this will require administrators to deploy each of the tiers of Enterprise Manager with HA in mind:

- Multiple instances on the database side (meaning RAC)

- Multiple OMS servers, with an additional piece of hardware called a Server Load Balancer (SLB) fronting the traffic and balancing the application traffic from the Agents as well as the Administrators

Repository Database

Since the Grid Control repository can be *any* Enterprise Edition Oracle database, a RAC database is the solution for this tier. By switching from a standalone, single-instance database to a multinode RAC database, this single point of failure has effectively been eliminated: If one instance fails, Grid Control will continue to work without any downtime on the remaining database nodes. The OMS(s) must be configured to connect to all the RAC instances as described in the next section. The MAA guide lists a set of recommendations and best practices, to further strengthen the database. To save some trees and not make this chapter too big, we'll put the spotlight on a few of the very obvious ones:

- **Setup of the database** *ASM:* The preferred option for high-availability installs is to use Oracle Automatic Storage Management to manage database storage. If ASM storage is used, there is no need to enable any space management storage settings for tablespaces and/or data files: The ASM layer takes care of all the file handling. *CRS with RAC:* By converting a standalone database into a RAC database, you get both high availability (with the surviving RAC instances continuing to be available if one goes down), and scalability (by simply adding a RAC instance if the database requires more processing capacity).

- **DB configuration** *Init.ora changes:* All the necessary changes are covered in the prerequisite checks of Grid Control. Any good Enterprise Administrator who has read the documentation (and don't we all read the documentation religiously cover to cover?) should already be ready for this. *Enable archivelog mode:* This is a mandatory feature for any decent backup and recovery strategy. Hot backups, online RMAN recoveries, and any kind of Data Guard setup all require archivelogging to be enabled on the database. To make it extra secure, multiple archivelog destinations can be used, to eliminate the failure of a single archivelog file corruption, or a disk failure of the main archive directory. *Block checksums:* To safeguard the repository against logical IO corruptions, enable block checksums. Enabling the block checksums has a performance impact (slowing down the IO processing a few percentage points). But if high availability and data protection are high on the list of requirements, this is something that has to be calculated into the capacity planning of the infrastructure.

■ **Backup and Recovery policy** We'll run slightly ahead here for this point: Failures can occur at several levels, starting with the hardware, all the way up to the human error of someone issuing a wrong command, or clicking the OK button when it should have been the Cancel button. For some of these failures, the redundant hard- or software pieces are the solution. But for most common types of human error, the answer typically is a backup or a piece of a backup that needs to be restored to get the data back into its original state. To prepare for these kinds of failures, implement a backup policy on the repository database. Equally important is the routine to test the recovery of the backup. Making backups religiously is only a good thing if you know you can restore them. This is another use the test and staging site can have: to test the backup and restore policies, to make sure a backup *can* be restored in case of a failure.

More information about these database deployment best practices can be found in the MAA (Maximum Availability Architecture) guide:

`http://www.oracle.com/technology/deploy/availability/htdocs/maa.htm`

OMS—Application Server

The most obvious thing to do at the middle tier is to have multiple OMS servers running. Not only does this guarantee High Availability (in case one of the servers goes down), but it also provides scalability, as work will be evenly distributed between all operational management servers. In case of a failure, the surviving servers can continue the work: Any pending work will be automatically rebalanced between the operational Management Servers, and any partial work the failed OMS was doing will get rescheduled.

■ In terms of configuring the different Management Servers, there is only one golden rule: Every OMS needs to be configured in the same way, using the same shared storage, the same software, and having the same patches applied. It is *not* possible to run OMS servers with different versions in the same infrastructure. All OMS servers need to run with the same version of Grid Control, pointing to a repository using the same version of the SYSMAN schema in the database.

NOTE
This might be overkill, and stating the obvious, but the best practice is always to run the latest version of Grid Control. Always upgrade the infrastructure to the latest available version: That means both the Management Servers (which includes the SYSMAN repository schema upgrade), and the Grid Control Agents. The most recent version of Grid Control has all the monitoring capabilities to support the newer hardware and software (including newer versions of the operating systems).

■ Although in theory it is possible to run Management Servers in a mixed operating system environment, this should be avoided at all costs in an operational environment. The main issue with running OMS servers on different operating systems is keeping them exactly in sync in terms of software and patches: All machines must be running with the exact same set of patches, fixes, and updates. And this goes beyond just Grid Control software: It also includes the Application Server stack, the Java versions used, and so on.

NOTE
There is one exception case where we can break this rule, and allow the mixed environment for a short period of time: In cases where there is a migration of hardware from one platform to another similar platform, you can plan the migration to have Management Servers running on different operating systems for the duration of the migration, as long as the exact same set of updates is applied on all the Management Servers. This way, a migration from 32-bit to 64-bit Linux, or from HP PA-RISC to HP Itanium, is possible without any downtime of the Grid Control application.

But there is more to keep in mind than just the versions and the operating systems and hardware of the Management Servers. There are also the changes made to the OMS servers: All the changes and tweaks explained in this book to optimize the performance and streamline the operations of an OMS need to be made on *all* the Management Servers.

During the install, the connection to the repository database will be set up as a host-port-SID descriptor to connect to a specific database instance. If the repository database is a RAC database, this will need to get changed to use a TNS descriptor to connect to any instance of the RAC database for the monitoring. The change will need to be done in three places:

- Update the connect descriptors in the `$ORACLE_HOME/sysman/config/emoms`
  `.properties` file. The connect descriptor should have the following information as a bare minimum:

```
(DESCRIPTION=
    (ADDRESS_LIST=
        (FAILOVER=ON)
        (ADDRESS=(PROTOCOL=TCP)(HOST=<db1-vip>)(PORT=<num>))
        (ADDRESS=(PROTOCOL=TCP)(HOST=<db2-vip>)(PORT=<num>))
    )
    (CONNECT_DATA=(SERVICE_NAME=<name>))
)
```

- Update the `emdRepConnectDescriptor` parameter in the `emoms.properties` file with the updated database connect string:

```
oracle.sysman.eml.mntr.emdRepConnectDescriptor=(DESCRIPTION\=...)
```

NOTE
*Change the TNS descriptor to escape all the "=" characters with "\="
for the update of the connect descriptor in the `emoms.properties` file.*

- The monitoring configuration of the OMS And Repository target. On the Monitoring Configuration page (see Figure 3-2), remove the host, port, and SID value, and use the Connect Descriptor field to put in the full TNS connect descriptor.

One *gotcha* should be pointed out, though: Even with multiple OMS servers running, there is only one OMS server that will monitor the OMS And Repository target. After an initial rollout of the infrastructure, the first installed OMS server will always have this target defined and configured.

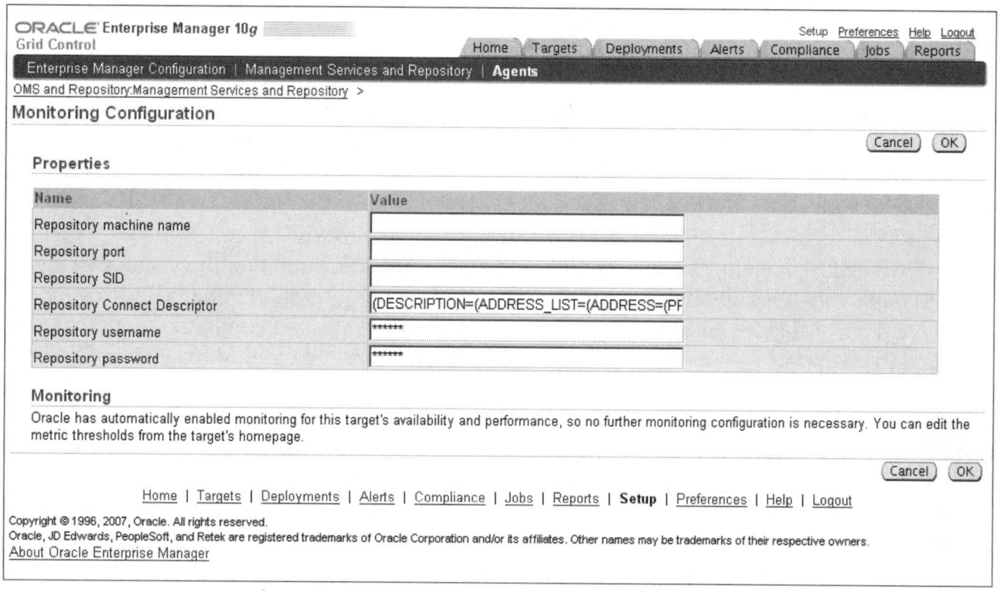

FIGURE 3-2. *OMS and Repository setup*

NOTE
If the first OMS server is decommissioned or replaced by another machine, the OMS And Repository target will need to be rediscovered on another OMS machine. More information on how to handle the decommissioning and moving of OMS servers can be found in Chapter 6.

Another one of these configuration changes is the definition of the storage areas the Management Servers will use for temporarily storing the data the Agent is uploading. As soon as multiple OMS servers are operational, the receive directory to store the XML files will need to be moved to a common shared file location. All XML files uploaded by the Agent have data with timestamps, which need to be loaded in sequence. If the directory stays locally on an OMS server, as soon as that OMS is unavailable, all XML files present on that machine that were not uploaded yet in the repository will not be accessible any more. This will create a gap in the monitoring data shown in the Console. And as soon as the failed OMS server is brought back up again, those pending files waiting for that OMS will be obsolete, since the internal marker timestamps in the repository will already be beyond the time of the data in the XML files.

To prevent gaps in the monitoring data, and this potential data loss, the XML receive directory should be put on a common shared disk location (preferably with mirroring enabled, to be able to recover a disk crash). To switch to a shared file location for the XML files, use this emctl command:

```
$ emctl config oms loader -shared yes -dir <loader dir>
```

NOTE
As a general best practice, the location specified for the receive directory should be the same on each OMS server. Although it is technically possible to have different directories specified for the receive directory per OMS, the directories should be kept the same on each OMS, to simplify operations like backup and recovery (including the import and export configuration; see the section "Backup and Recovery" later in this chapter).

When a Management Server is added to an existing infrastructure, the install will always install and deploy the OMS with the out-of-box defaults (meaning no shared load directory, and no Server Load Balancer [SLB] setup). After the install completes, the configuration of that OMS will need to be updated to point to the same shared location as the other Management Servers.

BEST PRACTICE
All OMS servers need to use the same type of mechanism for the receive directory: Either all machines use local storage (not recommended), or all servers use the shared location. If both loading mechanisms are used by the OMS servers, files could get loaded out of sequence, creating logical problems with the rollup and handling of the metric data in the repository.

Server Load Balancer (SLB)

The main reason to think about a Server Load Balancer (SLB) is to "abstract" the physical OMS location from the Agents and the Administrators, and make them talk to a fixed address, hiding the true identities of the deployed OMSes.

The Agents need a fixed point of contact to talk to, and upload their information to. And with the secure communication taking place, the SSL wallet requires the two endpoints used in the communication to be fixed. In an environment where there is no SLB, and the OMS servers have not been virtualized, any failover of an OMS to another server will require the following changes:

- All Agents talking to the old OMS will need to be updated, to make them point to the new OMS server.

- After making this change, the Agents will need to be resecured, so that the SSL wallet will once again contain two valid endpoints to be used in the communication. If Grid Control only has 10 Agents discovered, performing these two tasks is just going to be an annoyance. It will take some time, but it's not an impossible task, and in half an hour, those 10 Agents will be online again, and talking to the new online OMS server. If we scale up the environment now to 1000 Agents or more, this whole idea of changing and resecuring the Agent becomes a pretty impossible task to complete in a timely fashion.

For any rolled-out Grid Control environment, which is going to have a fair number of Agents (triple digits and up), you'll need a way to prevent this problem of resecuring the Agents in case of OMS server failures. And there is only one mechanism to do this: Virtualize the addresses of the OMS servers, so that these addresses can be reused on other boxes in case of a failure. This can be achieved in two ways:

■ **A hardware Server Load Balancer (active/active solution)** For the bigger deployments, this is the preferred solution. The hardware solution has a couple of benefits: Besides being a physical device, which is dedicated and optimized to perform this function of load-balancing network connections, this solution also has options and extensions available to do failover of that device, so the SLB device itself does not become the single point of failure.

■ **Virtual IP addresses to be used on the OMS server (active/passive solution)** This is a poor man's failover solution. The idea here is to give each OMS a virtual IP address (VIP) and a virtual hostname. And in case of a failure, this virtual name and address is reassigned to another OMS. As far as the Agents are concerned, it's valid, since the two endpoints are still there, and they are still valid, even though it's not the same physical machine any more. The major drawbacks here are scalability and flexibility. Although it's technically possible to make the failover of the hostname and IP address transparent, it will either require some fancy scripting, or cluster software to perform the failover. And in terms of resources, there will need to be enough spare capacity available, to continue to process the load of the application without interruption.

NOTE
The virtual IP address and virtual hostname solution has one big drawback, though. For the SSL communication, the wallet generated to allow the secure communication has a well-known single endpoint. That hostname is fixed and cannot be changed: A running OMS cannot be working and responding to two virtual hostnames at the same time using the same secure wallet. Therefore, any failover of a virtual IP and virtual hostname has to be to a new additional server.

Any SLB solution used for Grid Control should be used in combination with the Shared File System loader mechanism. The whole purpose of the Server Load Balancer is to have the Agents upload to a virtual address that can be any OMS behind the scenes. To prevent the data files sent by the Agents from being loaded out of sequence, the OMS servers should upload the XML files to the shared XML receive location, so all servers can see and upload the data in the repository in the right order.

To set up an SLB solution in the Grid Control infrastructure, the following steps will need to be taken:

■ Obtain an IP address and a hostname for the SLB. This is the point of contact the Agents will use to talk to the Management Servers.

■ Resecure the OMS servers again, using that SLB server name, so that the SSL wallets on the OMS servers will contain the same endpoint the Agent will be using.

```
$ emctl secure oms -host <slb hostname>
```

■ Update the Oracle HTTP Server configuration, so that the OMS will identify itself as the SLB to the Agent. Edit the ssl.conf file in the $ORACLE_HOME/Apache/Apache/conf directory, and change the ServerName parameter. The value should be set to the hostname the SLB is using:

```
ServerName <slb hostname>
```

NOTE
Starting from 10.2.0.5, this step is no longer needed. The resecure operation will automatically update the Oracle HTTP Server configuration too, to make the OMSes point to the SLB.

- Configure two traffic routing rules on the SLB.

  - One for the secure traffic (port 1159 by default). This is the main pool the Agents will be using to upload data and send updates to the Management Servers.

  - The second one is for the Administrators logging into Grid Control, which can either be secure (port 4444 by default) or unsecure (port 7777 by default). Based on company policy and company rules, one of them (or even both these access methods) can be defined to allow Administrators to work with Grid Control: The recommended access is always the secure way, of course. Although in theory the same 1159 pool can be used for UI access as well, the recommendation is to split up the administration traffic (meaning Administrators working via a browser) from the Agent traffic (meaning all the uploads and updates the Agent sends over).

NOTE
For Grid Control versions prior to 10.2.0.4, a third route was needed. This third route, referred to in the documentation as the "genWallet pool," was needed to do the actual securing requests from the Agents to the OMS. This route needed to have a fixed endpoint for the whole secure operation: Every secure request had to be routed to the same Management Server during the exchange of information to get the secure wallet. The way to fix the endpoint is to either route the traffic to one particular OMS (single point of failure, so no HA, and therefore not the recommended way!), or set a persistence rule for the traffic on this port that guarantees the client will continue talking to the same OMS.

Each of these routes follows the same setup:

- Start point (called the Service Name in F5 terminology) is always the SLB with the port number of the specific traffic to be routed. Example:

  ```
  slb.acme.com:1159
  ```

- The endpoint (called the Virtual Pool in F5 terminology) is the set of Management Servers that will accept the traffic. Example:

  ```
  oms1.acme.com:1159
  oms2.acme.com:1159
  ```

- No special persistence needs to be specified for the Agent routes. Any option the Load Balancer provides to evenly distribute the traffic to the various servers can be used. For the UI traffic, the session the Administrator initiated on the client browser should persist to the same OMS, in order to continue to serve the UI pages in the context of the work the administrator is doing. Therefore a form of persistence should be specified for that traffic:

  - For SSL-based communication, the SSL session ID, or Client IP (simple persistence) can be used to track the OMS working for the client connection. Since SSL traffic is encrypted, any persistence model that requires inspecting the HTTP headers or looking at the traffic cannot be used.

■ For straightforward HTTP communication (if used), any kind of persistence, even a simple IP-based routing mechanism, is fine.

Each of the persistence mechanisms typically requires some kind of timeout value to be set. This timeout value should be set to match the UI timeout values defined in the infrastructure (or set to a slightly higher value to be safe). See also Chapter 6 for more info on how to set up and define the timeouts on the various pieces of the Grid Control stack.

NOTE
Some older versions of Internet Explorer renegotiate the SSL session ID every couple of minutes. If SSL communication is used together with older versions of IE for Console access, the persistence cannot be based on the SSL session ID, and needs to fallback to another persistence method defined by the Load Balancer.

Each of the virtual pools will need to be monitored, so the SLB will know when to redirect the traffic to another (surviving) OMS machine in case of a failure. The monitor is a health check the SLB will make to make sure the referenced application on the Management Server is still alive and operational. The way the monitor is usually set up is to have a dummy transaction going from the SLB to the defined server, to see if the server responds. For Grid Control, the typical operation used for a health-check for UI access is this:

```
GET /em HTTP/1.0\n
```

This translates to a simple HTTP request to get to the logon page of the Grid Control application.
To mimic Agents uploading files, the monitor for the Agent upload ports should be defined as:

```
GET /em/upload HTTP/1.0\n
```

Once the URL to use to monitor is defined, the SLB needs to be instructed what to expect as the answer to the specified URL (the *receive rule*). The answer can be defined as an HTTP return code (200 [the all-clear] and 302 [redirect] being the most common return codes to define success), or as a word or phrase found in the web page returned by the application. To help in defining a proper success string for the F5 to use, the /em/upload URL will always return the phrase "Http Receiver Servlet active!" on success: That exact phrase can be used as the receive rule for the monitor.
Having a Server Load Balancer present in the infrastructure has a couple of important benefits to the infrastructure:

■ By virtualizing the Management Server URLs, an administrator can add and remove an OMS without having to reconfigure the Agents.

■ The names of the infrastructure machines can change, since no Agent has any knowledge of the actual machines working for the Grid Control environment.

■ There is automatic load balancing of the work between the OMS machines. Since an Agent talks to a virtual machine, which then hands off the work to the actual Management Server, any OMS can participate and help with the work that needs to get done.

Setting Up Management Servers in a Dynamic Environment

In a dynamic environment, where changes to the Management Servers in terms of hostnames and available machines will occur, the OMS hostnames should be virtualized by default:

- Set up an alias for the virtual hostname of the OMS machine. This alias should be known on the SLB and Management Server machine.

- The software should be installed using the virtual hostname, using the ORACLE_ HOSTNAME environment variable:

```
$ ORACLE_HOSTNAME=virtual1.acme.com
$ export ORACLE_HOSTNAME
$ ./runInstaller ORACLE_HOSTNAME=virtual1.acme.com -debug
```

- Set up the virtual pools on the SLB using the virtual hostname. With the hostname of the Management Server virtualized, the physical box can be changed at any point in time, as long as the alias to the virtual hostname is associated with the new physical machine.

The benefit you get for setting it up this way is that automatic operations like failover (in active/passive configurations) or recovery/relocation of service to an other machine (cloud setups) can happen without having to make a change to any of the EM infrastructure.

There is one important prerequisite, though, for using an SLB: As soon as an SLB is used, all the Management Servers need to be configured with a shared XML receive directory. The whole point of the SLB is to have any OMS pick up any request from the Agents. This also means that data uploaded from the Agents can now be handled by any of the running Management Servers. In order to preserve the order of the received files, the common XML receive directory needs to be configured.

GRID CONTROL WORKSHOP

Setting Up an SLB for Grid Control

So let's put all this together now in a workflow, to set up the Grid Control environment with an SLB solution.

Assume the following environment:

- A 10.2.0.5 Grid Control infrastructure installation.

- A hardware SLB solution (F5 load balancer).

- Two OMS server machines, each using 1159 as the secure port and 4889 as the unsecure port. The names of the machines are *oms1.acme.com* and *oms2.acme.com*.

- The name of the virtual OMS server URL will be *gridcontrol.acme.com*.

- Administrators will access the Console via the secure port 4443.

The steps to take are as follows:

Step 1.   Secure the OMS with the SLB name. During the install, the OMS server will be secured using the primary hostname of the OMS server machine. Since we're using an SLB now, the Agents need to communicate using that hostname. The following is the command to use on the two OMS machines:

```
$ emctl secure oms -reg_pwd ready4em -sysman_pwd myempwd
      -host gridcontrol.acme.com
```

(Command to be run on a single line.)

Prior to 10.2.0.5, an additional manual step was needed to update the port in the `ssl.conf` file from the `$ORACLE_HOME/Apache/Apache/conf` directory to specify the port the SLB is using to forward the web traffic.

A new set of switches is added in 10.2.0.5, to specify the UI port to use on the SLB side and to automatically lock the OMS after securing it:

```
$ emctl secure oms -reg_pwd ready4em -sysman_pwd myempwd
      -slb_console_port 4443 -host gridcontrol.acme.com -lock
```

(Command to be run on a single line.)

Step 2.   Next we'll need to define the two access points into Grid Control:

■   One used by the Agents using 1159 for secure communication:

Virtual Pool: `agent_upload_https`
Persistence: Client IP (simple persistence)
Members of the pool: *oms1.acme.com:1159, oms2.acme.com:1159*

■   One used by the Administrators using 4443 for Console access:

Virtual Pool: `ui_access_https`
Persistence: Client IP (simple persistence)
Members of the pool: *oms1.acme.com:4443, oms2.acme.com:4443*

Step 3.   Each of these virtual pools that was defined needs to be monitored by the SLB. Define a monitor for the various pools:

```
GET /em/upload HTTP/1.0\n
```

If the virtual pool monitors an application using SSL, define the monitor as follows:

```
GET /em/upload HTTPS/1.0\n
```

The receive rule for the upload pool should look for this response in the returning HTML page:

```
Http Receiver Servlet active!
```

Step 4.   Change the agent download script. All the response files to do remote Agent installations can be found in the version-specific subdirectories under `$ORACLE_HOME/sysman/agent_download`. Each version will have an `agent_download.rsp` file,

(continued)

which controls the settings needed to do the Agent install. In that file, change the following parameters:

```
s_OMSHost="gridcontrol.acme.com"
s_OMSPort="4889"
```

Step 5. Finally, once all the SLB work is done, we need to resecure the Agents on the OMS machines so that they will use the SLB too, and will not be dependent any more on the availability of the OMS server on that box.

Prior to the 10.2.0.5 release, this means changing the wallet URL first in the Agent configuration and then resecuring the Agent:

■ Find the location of the runtime files used by the Agent:

```
$ emctl getemhome
```

■ In the `<EMHOME>/sysman/config/emd.properties` file, change the `emdWalletSrcUrl` property:

```
emdWalletSrcUrl=http://gridcontrol.acme.com:4889/em/wallets/emd
```

■ And finally, resecure the Agent:

```
$ emctl secure agent ready4em
```

Starting with 10.2.0.5, this has process has been simplified. On the two Management Server machines, go to the Agent `ORACLE_HOME` and issue this command using the new command-line option for the secure operation:

```
$ emctl secure agent ready4em
        -emdWalletSrcUrl https://gridcontrol.acme.com:1159/em
```

(Command to be run on a single line.)

Step 6. After the all the Management Servers have been brought up, the command-line interface for the Grid Control will need to be reconfigured again to use the new URL:

```
$ emcli setup -username=SYSMAN -password=myempwd
        -url="https://gridcontrol.acme.com:1159/em" -trustall
```

(Command to be run on a single line.)

Step 7. The 10.2.0.5 release also gives administrators the ability to define the URL that will be used when e-mail notifications are sent out, and URLs in reports are mailed to administrators. Without this feature, the e-mails sent regarding the notifications of alerts or the generation of reports will contain the URL of the OMS that has processed the request. Since the whole purpose of the SLB setup is to route all the traffic through the SLB, the OMS can be instructed to use the URL of the SLB in the e-mails it sends out. To specify the address, go to the Management Server and Repository page in the Console, and click the Add button (or Edit if one already exists) next to the Console URL label on the top-left part of the screen.

Agent

On the Agent tier, there is not much to be done to make it HA. All of the things to do revolve around the reliability and resilience of the Agent:

- **The OMS_URL**   The Agents should be configured to use the SLB hostname for all communication with the Management Servers. This way, even if one OMS server is down, the Agents will remain available (meaning operational and able to upload data), since the SLB will route the traffic to the surviving Management Servers. The information for this OMS pointer gets updated automatically when resecuring the Agent using the SLB hostname:

  ```
  $ emctl secure agent
  ```

- **Out-of band notifications**   The Agent can send out notifications to an administrator to alert them of a potential problem. This proactive measure can prevent an outage of the Agent, and increase the availability of the monitoring of the targets. More information about these additional configuration steps can be found in Chapter 4.

- **The Agent watchdog**   Part of the Agent software is the watchdog, which keeps an eye on the main Agent process, and if needed restarts the program (this by itself is already a High Availability feature). The next section of this chapter will go into much more detail on how to tune and tweak the settings for the Agent, and how to configure the watchdog for large systems. See Chapter 4.

Wrapping Up the HA Part

Now that we have eliminated the single points of failure, we have achieved High Availability. We are one step closer to the MAA Grid Control architecture (Figure 3-3)!

Making Grid Control Disaster Recovery–Ready

The art of making an application Disaster Recovery–ready is to be prepared for the impossible. The saying "TRUSTNO1" is not some meaningless gibberish for the Enterprise Administrator implementing a DR solution: It's a way of life, and the only way to really have everything covered.

Repository Database

The usual way to make an Oracle Database Disaster Recovery–ready is to use Data Guard. There are two distinct types of Data Guard setups typically used:

- **Physical standby**   An exact copy of the database is kept in recovery mode. All transactions from the primary database are shipped across the network to the standby database and applied on the copy. Because the standby database is in constant recovery mode, no queries can be run on the standby. With the release of the 11*g* database, there is a new feature called Active Data Guard (ADG), which allows a Data Guard instance to be opened in read-only mode. With this option, the standby database can be used for queries and reporting (for tools like Portal and Oracle Reports) or to do data mining or business intelligence reporting. More information about the Active Data Guard feature can be found in the Maximum Availability Architecture section of the Oracle web site.

- **Logical standby**   In this mode, the standby database can be opened. It is typically used to have some form of query or reporting copy of the database available, to run reports and business intelligence logic on. However, the mechanism used to apply the updates

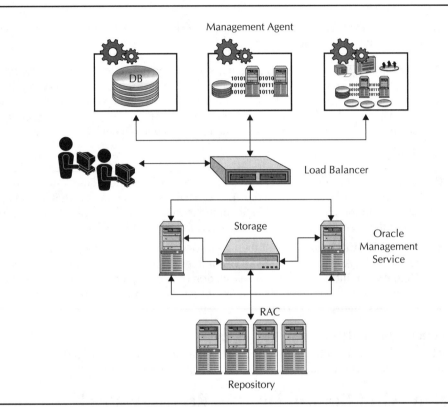

FIGURE 3-3. *The Grid Control HA architecture*

from the primary database does not support all the datatypes defined in the database: Special features, like Nested Tables and Advanced Queues are not supported for Logical Standby. Since Grid Control is using these database features, a Logical Standby database cannot be used as the standby mechanism for the Grid Control environment.

When you are setting up Data Guard between the primary repository database, and the standby database, the Data Guard Observer needs to be configured as well. This is a kind of watchdog that will keep an eye on the databases, and will determine if a failover from the primary to the standby site is needed. Although in theory this observer runs on a separate machine somewhere between the primary and the standby site, as a best practice, the observer can be installed and configured in the same home as the standby database software: If the standby site is not available (and thus the observer is not there to detect a disaster), failing over to it in case of a disaster is not going to be possible anyway.

Server Load Balancer
Having a Load Balancer in play is already a step to abstract the direct OMS access, and therefore have some kind of virtualization to allow the Agents to communicate with *some* Management Server, even if some of the Management Servers are not available. But in essence, just putting the

SLB in the infrastructure is fixing the single point of failure with just another one: If that SLB fails, we now have a *complete* failure of all communication between the Agents and the OMS.

This is why hardware SLB solutions are typically rolled out in pairs, with two devices operational, each aware of the other, and routing traffic from the Agents to the Management Servers. With some automatic TCP safeguards in place at the hardware level, a failure of one of the SLB devices will cause the other one to just assume the identity and responsibilities of the failed one, making the failure completely transparent to the rest of the network. If the SLB does not have some kind of automatic failover, a 3DNS solution or a manual update of the DNS/YP servers can help route traffic from a failed device to a surviving device or machine, without having to reconfigure any servers on the network.

The main message for the SLB is to have some kind of automatic failover at the TCP level, to route traffic—at the network level—from the Agents to any of the surviving SLB devices/machines.

OMS—Application Server

Making the Management Server DR–ready is pretty much the same as making it High Available: All it takes is a set of Management Servers that can take over on a standby location if the primary site fails. There are two ways of deploying this:

- The set of Management Servers on the standby servers is shut down (passive). In case the primary site fails, the repository is failed over to the DR site, and the Management Servers on the standby site are started. If a new machine has to be installed or configured, a copy or a clone of an active OMS can be taken, and brought online if needed. (More information will be provided about this in the "Backup and Recovery" section of this chapter.)

- The set of Management Servers on the standby servers are online (active). Since the OMS servers are operational, they will be helping out loading XML files, dispatching jobs, sending notifications, and so on. This also means the Management Servers on the standby site need access to the shared directory for the XML file loading, the software library for patching and provisioning, and most important of all, they need a fast and low-latency link to the repository database.

If Management Servers are active in both the primary and standby location, the network latency between the OMS machines and the repository database, as well as the latency between the OMS machines and the shared XML loader directory, has to be kept to a minimum: With the standby servers also participating in the day-to-day operations, they have to be able to make the updates in the repository, and process the loader files in a timely fashion just like the primary servers.

If Management Servers on both the Primary and Standby site have to connect to the repository database on either site, the TNS descriptor used to make the connections to the database will need to be resilient to handle failovers.

An Oracle Net service name can be used for that purpose. Create a new TNS descriptor using all primary and standby machine names. The service is started on the primary site, preventing connections to be made on the standby database. When the primary site fails, and the standby site takes over, a database trigger starts the service on the standby site, allowing the connections now to get established on the standby database. Example:

- Database `emgc`, with service name `emgc_failover`
- A two-node primary RAC database on *active1* and *active2*

■   A two-node standby RAC database on *passive1* and *passive2*

```
EMGC =
  (DESCRIPTION =
    (LOAD_BALANCE=yes)
    (ADDRESS_LIST=
      (ADDRESS=(PROTOCOL=TCP)(HOST=active1.acme.com)(PORT=1521))
      (ADDRESS=(PROTOCOL=TCP)(HOST=active2.acme.com)(PORT=1521))
      (ADDRESS=(PROTOCOL=TCP)(HOST=passive1.acme.com)(PORT=1521))
      (ADDRESS=(PROTOCOL=TCP)(HOST=passive2.acme.com)(PORT=1521))
    )
    (CONNECT_DATA =
      (SERVER=DEDICATED)
      (SERVICE_NAME=emgc_failover.acme.com)
    )
  )
```

More information on how to set up the services on the primary and the standby database, with the information on how to handle the failover, can be found on the MAA site:

http://www.oracle.com/technology/deploy/availability/htdocs/maa.htm

Look for the document named: *Client Fail-over in Data Guard Configurations for Highly Available Oracle Databases.*

To make the whole failover transparent to the Agents in the infrastructure if an SLB is used, the setup of the virtual pools needs to include all the OMS servers, of both the primary and standby site. In case of a site failure, the servers from the primary site won't be accessible any more, and the SLB servers will automatically reroute the traffic to the standby machines without any of the Agent machines in the enterprise noticing the switch.

NOTE
If some kind of IP failover is used for the Agents in the environments, and a hostname can be tied to a different IP address, the Java startup parameters of an OMS will need to be updated to make sure the OMS can detect the change in the IP address of the Agent. The default behavior in Java is to cache the resolved hostnames indefinitely. However, if the link between a hostname and an IP address changes, this default behavior of the networkaddress.cache.ttl *parameter will need to be changed. More information about this can be found in Chapter 6.*

OMS—Shared File Areas

Using the Shared File System loader mechanism eliminates the single point of failure for the Agent data upload. But unless the file system itself is mirrored, or synchronized with some secondary server, there is a chance of a failure if the file system crashes or becomes unavailable. Special hardware (of file system-level) precautions need to be taken to allow the file system to recover in case of a catastrophe. The same applies for the other file system areas the Management Servers use, like the Software Library and the RPM repository used by the Provisioning pack.

Agent

The changes made to make the Grid Control infrastructure HA compliant are all that are needed at the Agent side: As long as the Agent is working against a *virtual OMS hostname* (the SLB name), no further changes are needed to make the Agent aware of the changes made for the Disaster Recovery setup.

Wrapping Up the DR Part

After adding the DR setup to the architecture, we now have a more complete picture of an MAA architecture rolled out for Grid Control (Figure 3-4).

Backup and Recovery

Strictly speaking, backup and recovery is not really an HA feature. But in order to be High Available, you will need to come up with some kind of a backup and recovery strategy. So in a sense, being able to back up and recover the application is a requirement for making it High Available. To further re-enforce the HA mantra: The most important part of High Availability is the "availability" part of it.

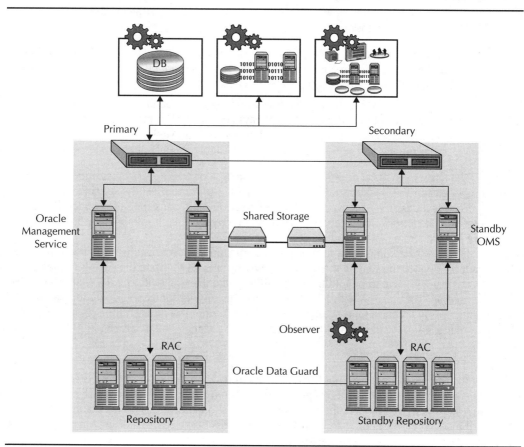

FIGURE 3-4. *The Grid Control HA+DR architecture*

Part of keeping an application available (with minimal downtime) is to make sure the Application can be brought back online again after a crash or a corruption at any level of the Application stack (starting with the hardware, all the way down the configuration files and the setup-specific data in the repository).

A big part of the work here is to have a good backup, and if necessary, regular refreshes of that backup. But it does not end there. Even a rigorous backup strategy that takes a full backup of everything every day can be flawed if nobody has ever tried, documented, and verified a restore of that backup.

Backup and Recovery of the Repository

There is no one single recommended backup strategy, or one type of backup that is superior to another one. It all depends on the environment (and the size) of the database in question.

With a small Grid Control deployment, where a few minutes of downtime are not an issue, taking the Management Servers and the repository down to make a full cold backup of the database might be a perfectly valid backup strategy. For an enterprise-wide rollout, however, the option to take a full cold backup will usually not be available. For those cases, a database in archivelog mode with an RMAN script to back up and restore the database is a more likely candidate.

For the implementation of any kind of backup and recovery strategy, the same two questions need to be asked (and answered):

- *How much downtime can I afford?* This usually translates into: How many minutes do I have before somebody higher in the management chain calls me to ask about the availability of the application?

- *What kind of disasters do I have to prepare for?* Although this will sound like a silly question (isn't the answer to this always "everything"?), it's a matter of budget and time that drives this question: The more (and bigger) disasters you have to prepare for, the more money and resources need to be available to make the disaster recovery possible.

The answers to these questions will drive the type of backup strategies and the various components in this backup strategy you will need in order to meet the specified goals.

The ideal case for a recovery is to restore the complete backup, and get back to the state right before disaster struck (for database backup and recovery, this should be the normal scenario if the right backup strategy was used).

However, if a complete restore is not possible, and a point-in-time recovery is the only available option, the state in the repository will not match the state the Agents in the enterprise have: They will have to be told to resend all the state they have. If 10.2.0.5 Management Servers are used, in combination with 10.2.0.5 Agents, this resynchronization operation can be done from a central location (one of the OMS machines). After the point-in-time restore of the database completes, issue this command *before* restarting the Management Servers on just one of them:

```
$ emctl resync repos -full -name "My resync"
```

All this command does is to put the repository in resynchronization mode. As soon as the Management Servers are started after running this command, they will sent a signal to all the Agents requesting them to resend all the state and configuration information to update the repository again.

Once the Grid Control site is online, the progress of the resynchronization operation can be viewed in the Console. From the Management Services and Repository tab, select the Repository Synchronization link from the bottom of the page. On this page all the known recovery operations are listed, as shown in Figure 3-5.

ORACLE Enterprise Manager 10g   Setup   Preferences   Help   Logout
Grid Control

Home | Targets | Deployments | Alerts | Compliance | Jobs | Reports

Enterprise Manager Configuration | **Management Services and Repository** | Agents

Repository Synchronization

Page Refreshed **Feb 10, 2009 12:07:35 PM**

Repository Synchronization is used to synchronize state between agents and the repository. Use this page to monitor the most recent resynchronization operation.

✔ TIP Repository synchronization only works for agents of version 10.2.0.5.0 or newer. Older agents need to be synchronized manually.

Agent Name [stajo%]

Show Status [All ▼] (Go)

(Stop) (Resubmit)

Select All | Select None

Select	Resync Name ▲	Agent Name	Started	Ended	Status	Message
☐	My DR operation	stajo14.us.oracle.com:1830	Feb 10, 2009 11:57:30 AM	Feb 10, 2009 11:58:25 AM	Finished	
☐	My DR operation	stajo09.us.oracle.com:3872	Feb 10, 2009 11:57:30 AM	Feb 10, 2009 11:58:35 AM	Finished	
☐	My DR operation	stajo15.us.oracle.com:1830	Feb 10, 2009 11:57:30 AM	Feb 10, 2009 11:58:25 AM	Finished	
☐	My DR operation	stajo10.us.oracle.com:3872	Feb 10, 2009 11:57:30 AM	Feb 10, 2009 11:58:35 AM	Finished	

Related Links

Past Repository Synchronization Summary

FIGURE 3-5. *Repository resynchronization operations*

For all machines running with an Agent version prior to 10.2.0.5, the resynchronization operation will need to be done on the Agent side. Run these commands on each of the Agents:

```
$ emctl stop agent
$ emctl start agent
$ emctl clearstate agent
```

The restart of the Agent, in combination with the clearstate command, will make the Agent resend all the target metadata and the current state of all the targets.

NOTE
Never issue a `clearstate` *command when the Agent is down. The Agent needs to be able to detect the* `clearstate` *signal, and reset the state of all the targets. If it is not up and running when the command is issued, the state of the targets will not be reset.*

Backup and Recovery of the OMS

Installing software does not (usually) take too much time. The sticky point is always all the changes and tweaks that administrators made after the install is complete. Those are always much harder to track, and much harder to keep synchronized. Restoring an OMS can be broken up into two parts: the binaries (the software), and the configuration of the Management Server.

For the binaries, a restore of the entire ORACLE_HOME from a backup is always the quickest way to recover an OMS. If there is no file-level backup (or it is not available), the other way to restore an OMS, is to simply reinstall the software again on the box.

For the Grid Control application, there are a couple of configuration files, that require some attention. This includes the settings for the OMS, the Oracle HTTP Server definitions specific for Grid Control, and the way Grid Control interacts with Oracle HTTP Server.

- **$ORACLE_HOME/sysman/config/agent_download.conf**   Contains the definition of the agent_download area on the Oracle HTTP Server to allow remote Agent download installs, or Agent push installs via the Console.

- **$ORACLE_HOME/sysman/config/emoms.properties**   Contains all the parameters needed for the OMS. All the settings in this file are captured and restored with the `exportconfig` and `importconfig` commands.

- **$ORACLE_HOME/sysman/config/emomslogging.properties**   Contains all logging and tracing parameters for the OMS. All the settings in this file are captured and restored with the `exportconfig` and `importconfig` commands.

- **$ORACLE_HOME/sysman/config/httpd_em.conf**   Contains the specific setup for the OC4J_EM application used by Oracle HTTP Server.

- **$ORACLE_HOME/sysman/config/emkey.ora**   Contains the part of the secure key used by the OMS to encrypt and decrypt passwords in the repository.

For these files, starting with 10.2.0.5, a set of commands has been added to the EMCLI command, to allow a backup and a restore of these configuration settings.

```
$ emctl exportconfig oms [-dir <dir>] [-keep_host] [-sysman_pwd <pwd>]
```

This command takes all the configuration data, including the OMS wallet and the EMKEY, and exports all the data in an encrypted file.

Commandline Option	Description
`-dir`	Directory to store the export file. If this parameter is not specified on the command line, the default location `$ORACLE_HOME/sysman/backup` will be used.
`-keep_host`	This option can be used to save the hostname of the OMS when exporting the configuration. In case of the recovery of a crashed machine, keeping the hostname of the original OMS the same in the configuration files prevents the need to make additional changes on the Server Load Balancer: As long as the hostname is resolved to the new machine, the OMS configuration can assume the identity of the old OMS machine.
`-sysman_pwd`	The password of the SYSMAN user to grab the relevant configuration from the repository. If this parameter is omitted, `emctl` will prompt the user to specify the password.

Similarly to the `export` command, a new command is also introduced in 10.2.0.5 that can import the configuration:

```
$ emctl importconfig oms -file <bka file> [-key_only] [-no_resecure]
        [-sysman_pwd <pwd>] [-reg_pwd <pwd>]
```

Commandline Option	Description
-file	Name of the exported configuration file to use for the import. This has to be a valid `bka` file that was generated by an `exportconfig` command.
-key_only	This option allows you to just import the `EMKEY` again. The `EMKEY` is part of the encryption key used to encrypt and decrypt passwords stored in the repository. If this EMKEY is out of sync, and cannot be restored from a file backup, the key can be imported again via this option.
-no_resecure	The `importconfig` command can also be used to restore something trivial like the emkey file. In those cases, where the overall configuration has not changed, there is no need to do a resecure, and this command-line option can be used to skip this step.
-sysman_pwd	The password of the SYSMAN user to grab the relevant configuration from the repository. If this parameter is omitted, `emctl` will prompt the user to specify the password.
-reg_pwd	Used to validate the import of the configuration. This registration password has to match the password already defined in the infrastructure.

Both the `exportconfig` and `importconfig` commands are ways to quickly and efficiently back up and restore the identity of an OMS.

These commands should be used for disaster recovery alone: If an `ORACLE_HOME` is restored from a backup (or in the worst case, reinstalled), the `importconfig` command can be used to restore the settings saved in a bka file to the installation.

BEST PRACTICE
To avoid any confusion about the setup of the Management Servers and the hostnames the OMS is using and in the way the Agents communicate (with or without an SLB involved), the procedure to import the OMS configuration should always be:

```
$ emctl importconfig oms -file <bka file> -no_resecure
        -sysman_pwd <pwd> -reg_pwd <pwd>
$ emctl secure oms -host <slb hostname>
```

For all versions prior to 10.2.0.4, a manual restore of these configuration files will be needed: Either reapply all the changes made to these configuration files, or restore the entire files from a valid backup. The two commands do not safeguard the Application Server configuration, or the other components of the AS stack (like the Oracle HTTP Server or Webcache): All configuration settings and files of these components will still need to be backed up.

Besides the Grid Control files, there are a few Application Server–specific files that will need to be recovered as well:

- **OPMN configuration**

  `$ORACLE_HOME/opmn/conf/opmn.conf`

  Contains the Application server setup, including the startup and shutdown commands for all components of the Management Server stack.

■ **Oracle HTTP Server configuration**

`$ORACLE_HOME/Apache/Apache/conf/httpd.conf`

Contains the main Oracle HTTP Server configuration, and defines the access points to the Management Server for both the Agents and the Administrators.

`$ORACLE_HOME/Apache/Apache/conf/ssl.conf`

Contains the secure HTTP access definitions for Oracle HTTP Server.

■ **Webcache configuration**

`$ORACLE_HOME/webcache/internal.xml`

Contains the internal settings of the Webcache, including the WebCacheAdmin configuration.

`$ORACLE_HOME/webcache/webcache.xml`

Contains the main information on how to cache and route the traffic.

■ **AS Control**

`$ORACLE_HOME/sysman/config/emagentlogging.properties`

Contains all the logging and tracing settings for the AS Control Agent.

`$ORACLE_HOME/sysman/config/emd.properties`

Contains all the settings for the AS Control Agent.

`$ORACLE_HOME/sysman/emd/targets.xml`

Contains the list of all the Application Server components the AS Control Agent is managing.

If the software is reinstalled on a box, any custom changes made to the Application Server prior to the recovery will have to be remade in these files.

Backup and Recovery of the Agent

The first thing that comes to mind when talking about recovery is the ability to restore the Agent software. Luckily, several deployments are available, each with their own strengths and limitations, that can help with this problem. If a file system backup is available, that is the obvious way to restore the Agent binaries. Short of that, redeploying the Agent software is just a matter of choosing the right type of installing the Agent. The second part of this problem is the state the Agent keeps locally on the machine. And just as with the OMS, there are a few files the Agent keeps around. All these files are kept in the state directory structure of the Agent. The location of this state directory can be requested from the Agent by issuing this command:

```
$ emctl getemhome
```

Target and Monitoring State   There are three pieces in this area:

■ The list of targets the Agent is monitoring is stored in the targets.xml file. This is a crucial piece of information, as it determines what the Agent is monitoring, and what targets are visible in Grid Control.

File: `<EMHOME>/sysman/emd/targets.xml`

- Each of the monitored targets can have specific metric monitoring requirements specified for it (when templates are applied, metrics changed, or User Defined Metrics [UDMs] added). The Agent keeps this metric state locally, so it can restart and continue the required monitoring without any intervention of the OMS.

  Files: All files in the `<EMHOME>/sysman/emd/collection` directory

- The current monitoring state of the targets is kept in the blackout.xml file. This file controls which targets are in blackout and should not be monitored.

  File: `<EMHOME>/sysman/emd/blackouts.xml`

Starting from 10.2.0.5, there is a way to recover this state in case of a disaster: A resynchronization routine is available, both in the UI, and via EMCLI to send the information from the Grid Control repository back to the Agent. If the OMS has detected a problem with the Agent state, a button will appear in the Console on the Agent home page to force a sync-up of the Agent state. A new EMCLI verb is also available, to do the resynchronization operation on the command-line:

```
$ emcli resyncAgent -agent="Agent Name"
```

NOTE
These resync operations require both a 10.2.0.5 OMS and a 10.2.0.5 Agent. Both tiers have to be using 10.2.0.5 software in order to be able to resynchronize the information. For all versions prior to 10.2.0.5, the only way to recover these state files is by ensuring that a copy of these files is available, to be able to restore them in case of a disaster.

Configuration Changes   Depending on the type of targets the Agent is monitoring, a couple of specific files might contain configuration changes and additional settings to enable the monitoring. All these files contain manual changes made by administrators to enable specific monitoring. In case of a recovery, either these changes will have to be redone, or a backup copy of the file has to be restored during the recovery as well:

- The most commonly updated file is the Agent configuration file itself. This file contains all the tuning and optimizations made to the Agent.

  File: `<EMHOME>/sysman/config/emd.properties`

- If there are multiple Oracle software inventories installed on the machine, the Agent has to be made aware of these different inventories. This information is kept in the OUIinventories.add file, which has to be manually updated.

  File: `$ORACLE_HOME/sysman/config/OUIinventories.add`

- One of the metrics the Agent is collecting for the host target is the storage information. For certain specific storage solutions, additional configuration is needed to correctly monitor the specific storage devices. The settings stored in this file are also manually updated.

  File: `<EMHOME>/sysman/emd/emagent_storage.config`

- For SAP and Siebel monitoring, two properties files contain the specific settings needed to monitor these targets. These files are also manually updated.

  File: `<EMHOME>/sysman/config/nimsoft.properties`

  File: `<EMHOME>/sysman/config/siebelremotelogging.properties`

■ If a beacon is installed on the Agent, monitoring third-party web applications via HTTPS, the SSL wallet information needs to be changed to add the certificate information of these web sites.

File: `<EMHOME>/sysman/config/monwallet/cwallet.sso`

File: `<EMHOME>/sysman/config/monwallet/ewallet.p12`

Plug-ins and Additional Monitoring Software   Besides the default out-of-box monitoring capabilities of the Agent, additional modules can be added to the Agent to monitor additional resources in the enterprise. These plug-ins are staged on the Management Server, deployed to the Agent. In case of a software reinstall, or an incomplete file-level recovery, not all plug-ins might be present on the Agent any more.

For 10.2.0.5, part of the recovery process is to redeploy any plug-in that was present in the Agent software tree prior to the recovery. For all versions prior to 10.2.0.5 however, plug-ins will have to be redeployed manually in the Console to the recovered Agent.

The list of all deployed plug-ins is kept in the repository. Prior to the recovery, get a list of all plug-ins installed on an Agent. After the recovery, use the list as a sanity check to make sure all software was reinstalled, and is present on the Agent. To get the list of all deployed plug-ins for a particular Agent, use this SQL statement:

```
SELECT target_type, mp_version, deploy_date,
       TO_CHAR(deploy_date,'DD-MON-YYYY HH24:MI:SS') deploy_date
FROM   mgmt_management_plugins p, mgmt_mp_deployments d
WHERE  p.mp_guid = d.mp_guid
  AND  agent      = '<name of the Agent>'
  AND  status     = 1
ORDER BY target_type, mp_version
```

Strengthening the Extended Infrastructure

Besides the base infrastructure of Grid Control, a lot more machines, devices, and targets are involved to ensure that the entire enterprise can be monitored properly. These additional targets require monitoring and follow-up too.

Firewalls and Proxy Servers

Grid Control will need both local access to the machines it is monitoring, as well as access to the external server updates.oracle.com to get the product and Critical Patch Update information. For the Management Servers to have access to both intranet and internet, it is not uncommon to have firewalls and proxy servers involved to manage the network traffic. These will also have to be included in the HA picture when designing the Grid Control infrastructure. Backup servers and fallback scenarios will need to be in place to allow Grid Control to continue getting the CPU information from the Oracle web site.

Hostname Resolution

Grid Control does not work with IP addresses (if the discovery has not been forced to use them). But this leaves Grid Control to rely on the hostname resolution to work properly when trying to contact a monitored target. And that hostname resolution is dependent on TCP services like DNS and YP to provide the resolution capabilities. If these services are not available to Grid Control, all communication with monitored Agents and targets will become impossible.

Email Servers

And this should get expanded to any service or network device that is used to deliver notifications. Machines seldom go down in a heartbeat (barring a disaster, but then we're talking about DR strategies). Usually there are subtle signs that there is a problem dawning at the horizon: Performance problems, or hiccups in the functionality, are typically the first signs of a bigger impeding problem.

Grid Control monitors these conditions, and can, therefore, send proactive notifications out to the administrators to act on these problems before they start impacting the availability of the application. But this means that the notifications have to be delivered to the right people, which means the HA strategy will have to be expanded to the SMTP servers, and any other type of servers or applications used to deliver the Grid Control notifications.

Summary—EM HA in the Real World

The complete HA+DR architecture as described in this chapter is the *ideal* situation. Not every site will have to implement this complete solution in order to guarantee uptime. It all depends on the requirements of the environment, and the amount of resources available to build the environment.

For some environments having a complete DR site that is an exact mirror of the active site is not necessary (or possible, budget- and/or resource-wise). In other environments, it might be acceptable to have downtime of EM in case of disaster, which gives administrators the time to manually fail over applications and/or the shared disk storage to other servers.

Forming a strategy to guarantee uptime of an application is always a balancing act between the amount of time, money, and hardware resources you can dedicate to the architecture. Based on the recommendations and the possibilities laid out in this chapter, the Enterprise Administrators can pick and choose those things they need for their environment, to build the MAA Grid Control architecture according to the requirements and needs of the enterprise.

CHAPTER
4

Deploying Agents
into the Enterprise

n order to give something, you first have to get something, and the same goes for Enterprise Manager. To get to the level of enterprise management, you must first have an enterprise full of machines to monitor and manage.

In some cases you will find machines to be added, sometimes in the weirdest and most unusual places. In other cases, you will find a new machine suddenly appearing in the Console, discovered by another administrator.

But it all starts with the rollout of the Agents, the piece of software that will do the monitoring and the maintenance of the targets in the enterprise.

Preparing the Server Machine

There aren't a lot of requirements to install an Agent. And most of the requirements are just plain common sense. For other things, it is more a question of configuring the machine in a certain way, to allow the Agent to manage and monitor it better.

Hostnames and Hostname Resolution

The Agent requires a unique hostname, which will be used to uniquely identify the machine this Agent is monitoring in the enterprise.

In today's TCP environment, though, where firewalls, NAT, PAT, and all other kinds of name translations are occurring, the hostname of a machine might not be as fixed or deterministic as one wants it to be.

The Agent and the OMS, however, will require a fixed hostname to be used, which resolves to the same IP address on both ends, to communicate with each other.

During the install of the Agent, the installer will request the primary hostname of the machine (by issuing a `gethostbyname` system command). That hostname will be used in all the configuration files to identify this Agent.

That hostname will be sent to the OMS, stored in the repository, and subsequently used by the OMS to communicate back to the Agent.

To get the hostname the Agent is using, use this command:

```
$ emctl config agent getlocalhost
```

If the primary hostname is not the hostname the Agent should use to communicate with the OMS, specify the `ORACLE_HOSTNAME` environment variable prior to installing and using the Agent. Example:

```
$ ORACLE_HOSTNAME=newname.acme.com
$ export ORACLE_HOSTNAME
```

If the `ORACLE_HOSTNAME` is used to overrule the default hostname of a machine, make sure the value is set each time prior to launching and using the Agent. The easiest way to accomplish this is to put it in the profile of the user starting the Agent, or as part of a shell script used to start the Agent.

User Accounts

No matter which user is used to install the Agent software, that user must be able to monitor and administer the targets on that machine (meaning: running OS commands if needed).

For Oracle databases and Oracle Application servers, this means that the user who owns the Agent software has to be in the same OS group as the databases and application servers it is monitoring.

If the Agent is installed with a different user as the database, access will have to be granted to the Agent user on a few of the database files. The Agent needs to be able to access and read the `alertlog` file, and access the files in the background destination directories (`adump`, `bdump`, `cdump`, and `udump`). For the health-check metric, the Agent also needs read access to the `hc_<sid>.dat` file in the `$ORACLE_HOME/dbs` directory.

For AS monitoring, the Agent will need access to the following files:

- The `$ORACLE_HOME/opmn/bin/opmnctl` commands and the `opmn.xml` file from the `$ORACLE_HOME/opmn/conf` directory

- The `$ORACLE_HOME/dcm/bin/dcmctl` command and the `dcm.conf` file from the `$ORACLE_HOME/dcm/conf` directory

- The `$ORACLE_HOME/Apache/Apache/bin/apachectl` command and the `httpd.conf` file in the `$ORACLE_HOME/Apache/Apache/conf` directory, including all the files the `httpd.conf` includes and needs

- The `ias.properties` file from the `$ORACLE_HOME/conf` directory

In the case of a cluster, the Agent software owner has to be able to launch commands on the other nodes of the cluster using `rsh` and `ssh`.

Time Zone and OS Clock

Another common issue frequently encountered is the setup of the OS clock and the time zone of the server.

If all machines are pretty much concentrated in the same geographical location, time zones and time differences are not much of a problem.

In today's enterprise environment, though, data centers are scattered around the globe, and administrators are accessing data from all corners of the globe, making time zones and time conversions a big thing.

- When the machine initially gets rolled out, the OS clock is set to the current data and time. However, OS clocks have this nasty habit of drifting, causing the correct date and time to be (increasingly) different from the time and date the machine is using. Over time, this drift (even the typical small microsecond discrepancy per hour) will start to add up, and cause the timestamps between the various machines not to line up any more.

- By itself, a machine reporting an incorrect time is not a functional problem for Grid Control. However, the problems become pretty obvious when you start to compare or correlate reported occurrences between various machines over time. Especially on clusters, where services are running on several machines concurrently, having an accurate date and time to properly compare with is essential for day-to-day operations.

- Keeping the OS clocks in sync between the machines is a best practice, and should be done from the very beginning when rolling out machines. A time daemon like NTPD on UNIX can help automate this, and keep all servers in (time) sync.

- During the install of the Agent software, the time zone of the server is retrieved from the OS and used in the Agent configuration. This *TZ* variable is then sent over to the OMS and stored in the repository.

  Forcing a wrong time zone on the Agent (like using the *TZ* environment variable and setting it to a wrong value) will result in incorrect timestamps being stored in the repository. As long as information about this Agent only is requested from the repository, there will be no functional impact due to *TZ* mismatch. But as soon as comparisons between machines are performed, the result will have a skew in the comparison, which can lead to people drawing the wrong conclusions.

  To get the current *TZ* configured at the Agent, use this command:

  ```
  $ emctl config agent getTZ
  ```

  The value the Agent is currently using can also be found in the `emd.properties` file. Example:

  ```
  agentTZRegion=US/Pacific
  ```

If the time zone is changed on the machine, the converted times in the repository will no longer match the real ones on the server, creating a discrepancy when trying to correlate data from this machine with either other targets on other machines, or even with historical data from this Agent sent over before the change.

NOTE
For more information about how to handle a time zone and the OS time changes of a machine, see Chapter 6.

Available Disk Space

To calculate the available space needed for an Agent, there are a couple of variables that need to be taken into account. It's more than just the size of the binaries.

The Agent consists of two main areas:

- **The Agent software itself (the binaries)**   This will be a fixed size, but dependent on the OS and version of the Agent.
- **The Agent state (the runtime state)**   This consists of the log and trace files, the state file for the monitored targets, and the data pending upload. Each of these components of the runtime state is controlled by settings and parameters specified in the `emd.properties` file.

The maximum size of the XML files the Agent will keep locally on disk before sending it to the OMS is set as follows:

```
# The maximum number of megabytes(MB) the upload manager will support in
# the upload directory before temporarily disabling collections, logging
# and tracing
UploadMaxBytesXML=50
```

The size of the log and trace files is set as follows:

```
# Default log file maximum size before rolling in Kilobytes
LogFileMaxSize=4096
# Maximum number of log file roll files to maintain before deletion
LogFileMaxRolls=4
# Default trace file maximum size before rolling in Kilobytes
TrcFileMaxSize=4096
# Maximum number of trace file roll files to maintain before deletion
TrcFileMaxRolls=4
# EMAGENT_PERL_TRACE_FILESIZE default to 5M
EMAGENT_PERL_TRACE_FILESIZE=5
```

Adding to that files for all the target and metric definitions and the collection files, we end up with a little over 100MB of possible runtime information stored by the Agent.

NOTE
Although it is tempting to reduce the footprint of the Agent, and change the settings for the maximum number of XML files allowed by the Agent, and to reduce the size of the allowed log and trace files, it is strongly advised to keep these minimal default settings. For Agents monitoring large systems, or if the Agent is monitoring a large number of targets, these parameters should even be increased.

Different Types of Install

There are quite a few ways of installing Agents. This multitude of mechanisms is not a clever and devious way to confuse and confound people, but a mere fact of the historical requirements that came out of rolling out Grid Control to an ever-increasing number of machines.

Standard OUI Interactive Install

The "mother of all install types," this install is the basic interactive install using the Oracle installer. All other install mechanisms still use this mechanism in one form or another behind the scenes.
Why should you use this type of install?

- This is the last line of defense when doing and debugging installs. If any of the install mechanisms cannot be used, for whatever reason, this is the best way to still get the Agent rolled out on the server machine.

Why should you not use this type of install?

- Since it's an interactive install, it requires administrator intervention, and is, therefore, not a mechanism to use when automating or scripting is involved. It also requires the Agent install area to be accessible on the server machine.

Silent OUI Install

The silent install is nothing more than an interactive install, where the user input is encapsulated in a response file (typically named agent.rsp). This response file is then played back during the install, to mimic the administrator typing in all the required info and finishing the install.

Why should you use this type of install?

- It is a simple way to script an install.
- The response file allows enough flexibility to script the install in a generic way.

Why should you not use this type of install?

- A silent install still requires access to all the individual machines.
- A silent install requires access to the install area to install from, which means either mounting the install media with the software from a central location, or going to the individual machine and inserting the install media.

Agent Download

The Agent Download mechanism is perhaps the install type that is the most misunderstood. It's nothing more than a script to do a silent OUI install, which downloads the necessary install information from the OMS server. This install type eliminates the problem of the silent OUI install of having the install media available and accessible on each server: When the script to do the install runs, the installer and the install staging area are downloaded from the OMS server. These downloaded staging bits are then used to install the Agent.

Limitations of this install type:

- The Agent Download script installed by default is using wget as the transfer mechanism to get the necessary bits from the OMS server. If wget is not available, or cannot be used, the download script can be customized to use another transfer mechanism.

Why should you use this type of install?

- It can easily be scripted.
- All information is by default available on the OMS server to do this type of install out of the box.

Why should you not use this type of install?

- It still requires access to all the individual machines to start the Agent Download script.

Agent Push (aka UI-Based Push)

An install mechanism added in 10gR2, Agent Push is nothing more than a wrapper around an Agent Download type of install, which can be pushed from the Grid Control Console.

Limitations of this type of install:

- This mechanism uses the OC4J_EMPROV OC4J application deployed on the iAS middle tier.
- It requires SSH access to be configured on the box prior to launching the push install.

Why should you use this type of install?

- Installs are done from the UI, centrally, without having to be logged on to the destination box.
- It can push out installs to multiple machines at the same time.

Why should you not use this type of install?

- The SSH requirement still means that initial preparation needs to be done on the box. If not all machines have this SSH setup, it might take longer to do the SSH setup on the box first and push out the install from the UI than it would to do the Agent Download type of install directly on the box.

Shared Agent (aka State-Deployed Agent/NFS Agent)

Shared Agent is a hybrid type of install. An install of the Agent is done in a shared location, used by several agents running on several boxes, each using their own state directory with runtime information, while sharing the same binaries from the shared location.

Here are the limitations of this type of install:

- The agent must be installed on a shared location using any of the previously mentioned install mechanisms.
- The master Agent (the one whose binaries will be shared by the multiple operational Agents) and the deployed Agent must be running on identical OS platforms. This means: same OS, and same OS release. This is to avoid problems with versions of shared libraries.
- A shared storage area needs to be present on the network with all the Agents sharing the binaries. This means that the network between the shared storage and the various agents needs to be in pristine condition, to avoid network timeouts and network outages.

Why should you use this type of install?

- It will reduce space used by the various Agent installs. Instead of rolling out the Agent on each machine, the install is only done once, and the runtime state (which is considerably smaller than a full install) is the only overhead per machine.

Why should you not use this type of install?

- It requires a shared location, which is mounted/shared on several machines. This shared location then becomes a single point of failure: If that central location vanishes, several machines will not be monitored any more.
- Maintenance of a shared Agent (like patching, upgrading, and so on) also becomes a factor, since multiple machines are affected by every intervention done on the shared Agent install.

An overview of these install types, with some basic tips and tricks to use, can be found in the Agent deployment best practice guide, located on OTN:

http://www.oracle.com/technology/products/oem/pdf/10gr2_agent_deploy_bp.pdf

Using the Agent Download Install

So, let's take a look under the hood of the main install mechanism: The Agent Download. This type of install is always present as soon as an OMS is installed and deployed in the environment, making it a quick and easy way to deploy an Agent of the same version on a machine running the same operating system. For some operations (like installing on other operating systems, or deploying a different version of the Agent), additional setup and configuration is required.

The Default Installed Software

With the installation of the OMS, the necessary bits to do an Agent download install for Agents of the same operating systems are staged in the ORACLE_HOME.

The following directory structure is used for this:

```
$ORACLE_HOME/sysman/agent_download
$ORACLE_HOME/sysman/agent_download/10.2.0.1.0
$ORACLE_HOME/sysman/agent_download/10.2.0.1.0/agentdeployroot.sh
$ORACLE_HOME/sysman/agent_download/10.2.0.1.0/agent_download.rsp
$ORACLE_HOME/sysman/agent_download/10.2.0.1.0/<os>
$ORACLE_HOME/sysman/agent_download/10.2.0.1.0/<os>/agentDownload.<os>
$ORACLE_HOME/sysman/agent_download/10.2.0.1.0/<os>/agent
$ORACLE_HOME/sysman/agent_download/10.2.0.1.0/<os>/oui
$ORACLE_HOME/sysman/agent_download/10.2.0.1.0/<os>/..other directories..
```

- The $ORACLE_HOME/sysman/agent_download directory is the starting point of the whole structure. This directory is also exposed to the Oracle HTTP Server, to allow requests to be made to download the Agent download files.

- Under the main directory, a subdirectory will be present for each applicable version of the Agent. After the install of an OMS, only the version 10.2.0.1.0 will be present, and contain all the software needed to install a 10.2.0.1 Agent of the same OS as the OMS. For newer versions of the Agent, and for support for different operating systems, visit the OTN web site to download the additional versions and platforms.

- For each version, there is a response file (agent_download.rsp). This response file is OS independent, but is specific for that release of the Agent. Minor differences are possible in this file for each version of the Agent. During the install, all the necessary parameters like the OMS server name and the location of the staging area, and so on, will all have been instantiated in this file.

- Each operating system has its own OS directory under the version directory, which contains the two main parts:

  - The script to do the actual Agent install (agentDownload.<os>)

  - And the directories with the Install software (/oui) and the staging area with the Agent software (/agent).

GRID CONTROL WORKSHOP

Adding Support for Other Operating Systems

Workshop Notes

After the install of an OMS server, the software for the 10.2.0.1 Agent for the platform on which the OMS server was installed will be present. For every other version and platform that is needed in the enterprise, the software for that Agent will need to be downloaded from OTN, and staged on the OMS server.

A new feature for this was added in 10.2.0.5. In the Deployments tab of the UI, there is a new page, which allows you to select the required version and platform and stage it on all the OMS servers. To get to the new page:

■ On the Grid Control home page, click the Deployments tab.

■ On the Deployments page, select the Download Agent Software link from the Agent Installations section:

```
https://<host>:<port>/em/console/ecm/prov/agentpush?event=DOWNLOAD_
AGENT_KIT
```

■ Once on this page, select the required version and operating system of the Agent software.

For versions prior to 10.2.0.5, or in case you want to manually download and stage the software on the Management Servers, follow these steps:

Step 1. Download the Agent download software for the required OS from the Oracle Support web site or OTN:

```
http://www.oracle.com/technology/software/products/oem/htdocs/
agentsoft.html
```

Step 2. Some of the archives downloaded from OTN will be CPIO archives. For most platforms, the Agent download archive is a CPIO file, which needs to be extracted using this command:

```
$ cpio -Hhpodc -idmv < filename.cpio
```

In case of a normal ZIP archive, the usual commands like unzip or gunzip can be used to extract it:

```
$ unzip filename.zip
```

Step 3. The archive will contain the following files (example for AIX):

```
agentDownload.aix
agentdeployroot.sh
agent_download.rsp
aix/
```

Step 4. Create the necessary directories for the download. For a new version of the Agent, a version directory will need to be created first in the agent_download directory:

```
$ mkdir $ORACLE_HOME/sysman/agent_download/<version>
```

(continued)

The version used in the directory will always be the full five-digit version number of the Agent software. Example:

```
$ mkdir $ORACLE_HOME/sysman/agent_download/10.2.0.4.0
```

The next step is the creation of the subdirectory for the OS needed for that version:

```
$ mkdir $ORACLE_HOME/sysman/agent_download/<version>/<os>
```

Step 5. Customize the `agent_download.rsp` file. If the file `agent_download.rsp` is not present in the `agent_download` destination directory, a copy of the response file will need to be customized and put in the version directory.

The following variables in the response file will need to be tweaked:

- **s_OMSHost**   The name of the OMS (or the name of the SLB) the Agent has to talk to in order to communicate with Grid Control.

- **s_OMSPort**   Port used by the OMS. This is always the unsecure port. The install will use this port to obtain the wallet with the SSL key during the secure operation. Example:

```
s_OMSHost=oms.acme.com
s_OMSPort=4889
```

Step 6. Copy the files. The files `agentdeployroot.sh` and `agent_download.rsp` are version specific, but OS independent. If they are already present in the version directory, they will not need to be copied over again. If they don't exist, copy the files to the download staging area:

```
$ cp agentDownload.<OS>
$ORACLE_HOME/sysman/agent_download/<version>/<OS>
$ cp agentdeployroot.sh
$ORACLE_HOME/sysman/agent_download/<version>/<OS>
```

This leaves us with just one thing to do, the copying of the Agent install staging area:

```
$ cp -r <OS> $ORACLE_HOME/sysman/agent_download/<Version>
```

After installing some additional versions, and adding some operating system to the download area, the `agent_download` structure will look something similar to this:

```
$ORACLE_HOME/sysman/agent_download
$ORACLE_HOME/sysman/agent_download/10.2.0.1.0
$ORACLE_HOME/sysman/agent_download/10.2.0.1.0/agentdeployroot.sh
$ORACLE_HOME/sysman/agent_download/10.2.0.1.0/agent_download.rsp
$ORACLE_HOME/sysman/agent_download/10.2.0.1.0/linux
$ORACLE_HOME/sysman/agent_download/10.2.0.1.0/linux/agentDownload
.linux
$ORACLE_HOME/sysman/agent_download/10.2.0.1.0/linux/agent
$ORACLE_HOME/sysman/agent_download/10.2.0.1.0/linux/oui
$ORACLE_HOME/sysman/agent_download/10.2.0.4.0
$ORACLE_HOME/sysman/agent_download/10.2.0.4.0/agentdeployroot.sh
$ORACLE_HOME/sysman/agent_download/10.2.0.4.0/agent_download.rsp
$ORACLE_HOME/sysman/agent_download/10.2.0.4.0/hpi
$ORACLE_HOME/sysman/agent_download/10.2.0.4.0/hpi/agentDownload.hpi
$ORACLE_HOME/sysman/agent_download/10.2.0.4.0/hpi/agent
```

```
$ORACLE_HOME/sysman/agent_download/10.2.0.4.0/hpi/oui
$ORACLE_HOME/sysman/agent_download/10.2.0.4.0/linux
$ORACLE_HOME/sysman/agent_download/10.2.0.4.0/linux/agentDownload
.linux
$ORACLE_HOME/sysman/agent_download/10.2.0.4.0/linux/agent
$ORACLE_HOME/sysman/agent_download/10.2.0.4.0/linux/oui
$ORACLE_HOME/sysman/agent_download/10.2.0.4.0/solaris
$ORACLE_HOME/sysman/agent_download/10.2.0.4.0/solaris/agentDownload
.solaris
$ORACLE_HOME/sysman/agent_download/10.2.0.4.0/solaris/agent
$ORACLE_HOME/sysman/agent_download/10.2.0.4.0/solaris/oui
```

The name of the operating system–specific directory used as the subdirectory for the version is fixed. Here's the list of the possible OS-specific names used for the download scripts:

Abbreviation Used	Operating System (OS) Details
aix	IBM AIX (64-bit)
decunix	HP Tru64 (64-bit)
hpi	HP-UX Itanium (64-bit)
hpunix	HP-UX PA-RISC (64-bit)
linux	Linux (32-bit)
linux_ia64	Linux Itanium (64-bit)
linux_ppc64	IBM Linux PowerPC (64-bit)
linux_x64	Linux (64-bit)
linux_zseries64	IBM z/OS Linux (64-bit)
solaris	Sun Solaris SPARC (64-bit)
solaris_x64	Sun Solaris Intel (64-bit)
solaris_x86	Sun Solaris Intel (32-bit)
win32	Windows XP (32-bit)
windows_ia64	Windows Itanium (64-bit)
windows_x64	Windows XP (64-bit)

Customizing the Agent Download Script

Out of the box, the Agent download script is using wget as the tool to transfer the installer and the install staging area for the Agent from the OMS to the machine where the Agent needs to be installed.

Even though wget is not guaranteed to be available on every machine in the enterprise, the reason it was chosen as the default tool for this install method is twofold:

1. The protocol used by the OMS and the Agent is HTTP. It is, therefore, guaranteed to be available, and removes any additional requirement needed to access files from the middle tier.

2. Unlike `ftp`, `scp`, or `rcp`, wget does not require any form of authentication to access files from the middle tier. And since the OMS is already configured to serve the files, no additional handling is required to get the files from the HTTP server on the OMS. If wget is not available, or cannot be used to transfer the files, the download script can be customized to use an alternate way of obtaining the files.

Starting with 10.2.0.5, the `agent_download` has a clear abstraction of the file transfer routines. This makes it easy to change the script to use an alternate transfer mechanism to transport the files from the OMS to the Agent machine.

For Agent versions prior to 10.2.0.5, customizing the script is not a matter of changing a single line in the script. A few changes will be needed to tweak this script. The changes required are:

1. Need to define a routine for the protocol that will be used to transfer the file:

```
# ---------------------------------------------------------------------
# BEGIN User-defined variables -- edit for your environment
# ---------------------------------------------------------------------

# check if /usr/local/bin/wget exists use that
WGET="wget"
if [ -x /usr/local/bin/wget ]
then
    WGET="/usr/local/bin/wget"
else
    if [ -x /usr/bin/wget ]
    then
        WGET="/usr/bin/wget"
    fi
fi

# WGET proxy settings if needed
# export http_proxy=http://your.proxy.server:port

# WGET way of downloading a file
wget_get_file () {
  ${WGET} --dot-style=mega --verbose --tries=5 ${AgentDownloadURL}/$1
  return $?
}

# We need the location of the OMS ORACLE_HOME, to be able to access
# the files on that server in case of file copy or ftp-like downloads
OMS_ORACLE_HOME=/u01/app/oracle/product/oms10g

# FTP example way of downloading a file
ftp_get_file () {
  omsFILE=${OMS_ORACLE_HOME}/${AgentDownloadDIR}/$1
  omsDIR=`dirname ${omsFILE}`
  ftp -i -g -v -n ${OMShost} <<@EOF@
user anonymous anonymous
bin
cd ${omsDIR}
```

```
get $1
close
bye
@EOF@
  return $?
}
```

```
# Command that will be used by the installer
InstallerDownloadCmd=wget_get_file
```

```
# Generic routine to download/get a single file, with error trapping
download_file () {
  ErrMsg="Command failed: $InstallerDownloadCmd $1"
  $InstallerDownloadCmd $1 #2>&1 | tee -a $LogFile
  stat=$?
  echo "Finished Downloading $1 with Status=$stat"
  if [[ ${stat} -ne 0 || ! -f $1 ]]
  then
    false
    ErrHandler
    exit 1
  fi
  return ${stat}
}
```

```
# Log patch check warnings, but do not prompt; set to null to make
patch check interactive
silentPatchCheck=TRUE
# Script default is to initiate automatic target discovery and start
the agent
doDiscovery=TRUE
startAgent=FALSE
```

```
# ------------------------------------------------------------------------
# END User-defined variables
# ------------------------------------------------------------------------
```

In this example, a routine is used to get the files via `ftp`:

- Change the anonymous anonymous to the real username and password.

- And put the correct ORACLE_HOME in there for `ftp` to pick up the files from the OMS ORACLE_HOME.

- Change the InstallerDownloadCmd from wget_get_file to ftp_get_file to use the `ftp` method.

2. Change the download command for the three main files:

```
DownloadResponseFile () {
  download_file agent_download.rsp
  stat=$?
}
```

```
DownloadInstaller () {
  download_file ${os}/oui/oui_${os}.jar
  stat=$?
}

DownloadUnzipUtility () {
  download_file ${os}/agent/install/unzip
  stat=$?

  echo  "Adding execute permissions to unzip ..."
  mkdir -p $InstallerLocalStage/Disk1/UnzipUtl
  ErrMsg="Command failed: mv unzip $InstallerLocalStage/Disk1/UnzipUtl"
  mv unzip $InstallerLocalStage/Disk1/UnzipUtl
  chmod 0754 $InstallerLocalStage/Disk1/UnzipUtl/unzip
}
```

3. Add a variable to give the absolute location of the file:

```
# -- Begin change
AgentDownloadURL="http://${OMShost}:${httpPort}/agent_
download/${EmVersion}"
AgentDownloadDIR="sysman/agent_download/${EmVersion}"
# -- End change
```

Using a staticports.ini File

In order to keep the ports used by the installer fixed across all installs, a special file can be used during the install, to fix the ports. Using the default ports used with a 10gR2 install, this file should have the following values:

```
Enterprise Manager Central Agent Port=3872
Enterprise Manager Central Console Port=4889
Enterprise Manager Central Console Secure Port=1159
```

BEST PRACTICE
When rolling out Agents in an enterprise, keep this file around in the agent_download *structure. When copying over the* agent_
download.<os> *script to the target box, also copy over the* staticports.ini *file, and use the* -p *command-line switch to specify the file. This way, all Agents will be installed in the same way, using the same ports.*

Command-Line Options for the Agent Download Script

The agent_download script has quite a few command-line options to use. To get the complete overview, use the -h command-line option to get the full list of available options:

```
$ ./agentDownload.linux -h
Usage: agentDownload.linux [-bcdhimnoprstuxN]
   b - baseDirectory of the Agent OracleHome
   d - Do NOT initiate automatic target discovery
   h - Usage (this message)
   i - Inventory pointer location file
```

```
m - To specify the oms hostname for downloading the agent install
n - To specify the cluster name
o - OLD_ORACLE_HOME during Upgrade
p - Static port list file
r - Port for connecting to oms hostname
t - Do NOT start the Agent
u - Upgrade
x - Debug output
c - CLUSTER_NODES
N - Don't prompt for Agent Registration Password
R - To use virtual hostname(ORACLE_HOSTNAME) for this installation.
```

Commandline Options	Description
-b	Parent directory of the Agent, to be used to do the install. This value for this option should be the same as the ORACLE_BASE environment variable.
-d	After the install completes, do not perform an auto-discovery of targets on the box. If this option is used, only the Agent and the host target—and a cluster target if CRS software is present on the box—will be discovered.
-h	Help screen, with the overview of all command-line options.
-i	Pointer to the inventory location. This is the location of the oraInventory directory, as specified in the oraInst.loc file.
-m	Hostname to be used to contact the OMS.
-n	Name of the cluster. Only use this in combination with the -c option if CRS software is present on the machine. The CRS_HOME environment variable must also contain the correct location to the CRS software.
-o	Only use this parameter when upgrading the Agent. This is the old ORACLE_HOME of the Agent.
-p	Location of the staticports.ini file, with the fixed TCP ports to be used by the Agent.
-r	Port to use when connecting to the OMS. This will typically be 4889.
-t	Do not start the Agent after completing the install. By default the Agent will be started as soon as the install finishes.
-u	Upgrade the Agent. An out-of-home upgrade of the Agent will be done, moving the runtime information from the old Agent to the new Agent ORACLE_HOME.
x	Enable additional debugging.
-c	List of all the nodes participating in the cluster. Only use this in combination with the -n option if CRS software is present on the machine.
-N	Do not prompt for the secure password. The default action is to secure the Agent, which will prompt for a password. If the install is scripted, this option has to be used to not block the script.
-R	New option added in 10.2.0.5. This parameter gives the option to specify an alternate hostname to be used for the install (the ORACLE_HOSTNAME setting).

BEST PRACTICE
When using the `agent_download`, *use this command line:*

```
$ agent_download.linux -b <base directory for
software> -t -x
        -p <location of staticports.ini>
```

After the install completes, check the install log, to make sure the install completed successfully, verify the list of discovered targets, and then secure the Agent. After this has completed, start the Agent.

Using the Agent Push Install

This type of Agent deployment uses the Console as the central starting point to push out the installation request. This method can be used either to install a standalone Agent on a single box, or to roll out the Agent on all the nodes of the specified cluster (cluster install).

The Prerequisites for Push Installs

In order to be able to use this method for installing Agents, the following requirements need to be met:

- The OC4J_EMPROV application needs to be up and running. If it is not running, start it on all the OMS servers:

  ```
  $ $ORACLE_HOME/opmn/bin/opmnctl startproc type=oc4j
  instancename="OC4J_EMPROV"
  ```

- The proper Agent Download software (for the operating system of the machine and the selected version) must be available on all the OMS servers. More importantly, the software needs to be accessible from *all* the OMS servers, so that the job that pushes out the software to the machine can use any of the Management Servers to do so.

- There must be SSH connectivity between the OMS servers and the machines to install the Agents on. The OMS will make a connection using SSH to the target machine to log in and install the software in the specified directory.

Installation Steps

Whenever a push install is initiated, behind the scenes, the following steps will be executed when this install method is used:

- Ask the Administrator for the details to install with, like the machine name, the username, and password to use.

- Run the prechecks and some verification and validation to make sure the install can actually start on that machine.

There are two phases for the prechecks.

- **Local precheck** Validates the information specified by the administrator, to see if the install is possible. The log files for this phase will be written in the directory

  `$ORACLE_HOME/sysman/prov/agentpush/<timestamp>/prereqs/local`.

■ **Remote prechecks** Checks the state of the machine to install the Agent on. The log files for this phase will be written in the directory:

`$ORACLE_HOME/sysman/prov/agentpush/<timestamp>/prereqs/<hostname>.`

Once everything has been verified, the actual work will begin: Create an SSH connection to the selected machine (or set of machines if multiple machines are specified), drop the Agent download shell script, and start a silent install of the Agent using the Agent download method. The log and trace information for these operations will be written to the directory `$ORACLE_ HOME/sysman/prov/agentpush/<timestamp>/logs/<hostname>`.

Using the Shared Agent Install

The Shared Agent install is the odd one out in this whole line-up: In order to get to a Shared Agent install, you must first install the shared software, and make sure that it is *not* used as a regular agent. In a second phase, the actual Agents are deployed, referencing the shared software. This two-phase approach makes this install a little trickier to set up, but it can save some time and resources in the long run.

The Prerequisites for Shared Agent Installs

There are a couple of restrictions an administrator needs to be aware of in order to use the Shared Agent mechanism as a method for installing Agents on machines:

■ The Shared Agent install will only work on UNIX platforms.

■ The Agent software needs to be available on a mount-point that is visible on all machines in the same location: The ORACLE_HOME used to install the shared Agent software has to match the name of the mount-point on each machine mounting the shared software.

Installation Steps

As soon as the mount-points have been set up on all the required machines, perform the following steps:

■ *Install the master Agent on the shared location.* This will install the actual binaries of the Agent in the central location, mounted by all the machines. This master should never be started or used as an actual agent: It's just to stage the files, and make the software available on the share. If an Agent is needed on the box, instantiate an Agent on the box, using the regular deploy operations for the Shared Agent install. To prevent the Agent from the shared software location from getting started after a reboot of the machine, rename the agent startup file:

```
$ cd $ORACLE_HOME/install/unix/scripts
$ mv agentstup agentstup.do_not_use
```

If the install discovered the Agent in the Console, it will have to be removed from the repository using this SQL statement:

```
SQL> exec mgmt_admin.cleanup_agent('<agent name>');
```

- *Prepare the new machine.* Any machine that will use the shared location has to mount the shared location from the master Agent. If the new machine does not have any Oracle software installed, the inventory will need to be initialized. A special script is available for that purpose in the Oracle inventory of any box that already has Oracle software installed: `<oraInst dir>/orainstRoot.sh`.
  Make this script available on the new machine, either by copying it to the shared location, or copying it to the new box, and then execute it. Example:

```
# cat /etc/oraInst.loc
inventory_loc=/u01/app/oracle/oraInventory
inst_group=dba
# cd /u01/app/oracle/oraInventory
# scp orainstRoot.sh root@new_machine.acme.com:/tmp
# ssh root@new_machine.acme.com /bin/sh -c /tmp/orainstRoot.sh
```

- *Deploy the Agent software.* Once the software is mounted, and the inventory is OK and ready to go, the actual install of the Agent software can be done. Installing the Agent on the new machine is nothing more than instantiating a state directory for this machine, where the Agent will be able to write the runtime state and the collection information. The state directory is instantiated with the `nfsagentinstall` command. The command takes the following two arguments:

  - **-s <local state directory>**   The state directory is the location where the Agent on the new box will write the files for the monitoring. This location has to be a directory local on the new box that is only available on that box.

  - **-p <port number>**   The port number to use for this Agent. As with any other Agent installation, the recommendation here is to specify the same port for all the Agents. This will simplify the administration and the reporting of all the Agents in the enterprise. Example:

    ```
    $ cd $ORACLE_HOME/sysman/install
    $ ./nfsagentinstall -s /home/mystate/emagent -p 3872
    ```

- *Use the Agent on the new box.* When the Agent is instantiated on the new box, the state directory will also contain a `bin` directory with the `emctl` command to stop and start the Agent. That command has to be used to perform all the operations for that Agent, and not the one from the shared home location. Using the same example:

```
$ cd /home/mystate/emagent/bin
$ ./emctl start agent
```

Although the `emctl` command from the shared location will still be used behind the scenes to access the binaries, the local state-specific `emctl` command has the pointers specified to write to the correct state directory, using the local Agent configuration.

Postinstallation and Configuration Steps

After the install of the Agent has completed, the software can be tailored to the specific needs of the system. Although most settings will be quite adequate for most systems, and require no change, some of these settings might need to be altered to meet the specific requirements of the machine.

Enabling OOB Messages

OOB messages are Out-Of-Band notifications the system can send. These messages do not follow the standard route through the Enterprise Manager framework, but use a direct shortcut to send messages (notifications) directly. This mechanism can be used to alert administrators in cases where the standard framework is not available, or when Grid Control cannot be used to trigger the notification. There are two types of notifications the Agent can send out in case of an emergency on the Agent side:

■ If the Agent watchdog cannot restart the Agent, or cannot keep the Agent operational, it will execute the OS script specified in the `emd.properties` file. This script can then execute any OS commands to alert or trigger a notification. To enable this feature, specify the following property in the `emd.properties` file:

```
emdFailureScript=<any valid OS script>
```

A default template script is provided in the `$ORACLE_HOME/bin` directory called `emdfail.command`, which can be used to specify the commands to inform an administrator in case of a failure. It contains a simple example on how to report info about the failure to the administrator:

```
#
# Mail to specified user
#
if [ "$1" = "upload" ]; then
    echo "Upload failure at `date`" >/tmp/upload$$
    echo "Last 100 lines of log file:" >>/tmp/upload$$
    tail -100 $EMDROOT/sysman/log/emd.trc >>/tmp/upload$$
    mailx -s "Cannot upload files" john.doe@acme.com </tmp/upload$$
    rm -f /tmp/upload$$
else
    echo "emdfail.command: unknown failure code: $1"
fi
```

The script can be further customized to perform specific tasks, or notify multiple people in multiple ways if needed. To use this default script, specify it as the failure command for the property:

```
emdFailureScript=<ORACLE_HOME>/bin/emdfail.command
```

NOTE
If the Agent does not find a script defined for the failure condition, it will log a message in the `emagent.trc` file about this:

WARN upload: Upload manager has no Failure script: disabled

■ The agent can send an e-mail if the repository is no longer accessible (this is a result of the fact that the OMS and Repository target is not monitored because a connection cannot be established to the database). If the repository is not available, the middle-tier servers cannot use it to send notifications. Therefore the Agent has to be able to send an e-mail on its own. In order to enable this feature, specify the following three properties in the emd.properties file:

```
emd_email_address=<destination email address>
emd_email_gateway=<email gateway machine to use>
emd_from_email_address=<source email address>
```

Configuring the Monitoring Space

There are several controls available to prevent the Agent from using up too much disk space. All of these mechanisms are controlled by parameters in the emd.properties file:

Property Name	Property Description
UploadMaxBytesXML	Total size the upload directory can be. If the size grows beyond that, metric collections will be suspended until the size of the upload directory goes down. Default is 50MB.
UploadMaxDiscUsedPct	The percentage to which the disk containing the runtime files for the Agent can be filled. If the disc fills up to more than this percentage, metric collections will be suspended until the percentage again drops below the specified floor value. Default is 98 percent.
UploadMaxDiscUsedPctFloor	The percentage of free space needed on the disk to resume metric collections again, after the disc has filled up above the maximum allowed value. Default is 95 percent.
UploadMaxNumberXML	The total number of files allowed in the upload directory. If the number of XML files exceeds this value, metric collections will be suspended until the number of XML files drops below this value. Default is 5000 files.

On a typical deployment, these default settings will be more than adequate. However, if the Agent is monitoring a large number of targets, or if there are special disk space requirements, some of these values might need to be adjusted.

Logging and Tracing

Log and trace files will be created and updated by the Agent and the watchdog as soon as the Agent gets started. To keep these files small, and limited in size, some tweak might be needed after the install, to make sure the Agent will be able to store all the information on the available disk space. The main Agent log and trace files (emagent.log and emagent.trc) can be controlled by parameters in the emd.properties file:

LogFileMaxRolls	Number of rotated log files the Agent will keep. Default is 5.
LogFileMaxSize	Size of one log file. Default is 256KB.
TrcFileMaxRolls	Number of rotated trace files the Agent will keep. Default is 5.
TrcFileMaxSize	Size of one trace file. Default is 256KB.

These values control how many times the log and trace files roll over before information is aged out, and how big each log and trace file will be.

BEST PRACTICE
A minimum of at least two files, each of 256KB, should be kept to allow some basic debugging and diagnostics to be done on the Agent in case of a problem. If the Agent is monitoring a larger number of targets (more than 20), the number of rotated log and trace files should be kept to five at the very least.

To minimize the impact of the Agent on the system, and to minimize the logging and tracing the Agent is doing, all the trace levels for the modules specified in the `emd.properties` file should be set to WARN. Do not increase these values except for debugging purposes, or if asked to do so by Oracle Support or Oracle development.

Besides the main Agent log and trace files, Perl scripts executed by the Agent can also write in the Perl-specific log and trace files:

EMAGENT_PERL_TRACE_DIR	Directory to store the metric Perl trace file. Default location is $ORACLE_HOME/sysman/log.
EMAGENT_PERL_TRACE_FILESIZE	Maximum size in megabytes for the metric Perl trace file. Default value is 5 (MB).

NOTE
For the Perl trace files, only two copies are ever kept: the main active ones, one rotated log and one rotated trace. There is no option to increase the number of archived log and trace files for the Perl tracing.

On UNIX systems, if there is a problem on the system, the Agent can create a core file in the `<EMHOME>/sysman/emd` directory. By default, the Agent will keep only the last three core files (and associated traceback file with the stack trace of that core file). To change that default number, use the `EMAGENT_MAX_CORES` environment variable:

```
EMAGENT_MAX_CORES=2
Export EMAGENT_MAX_CORES
```

The internal SQL fetchlet, gathering data from Oracle databases, will use standard SQL*Net to make the connections to the database. Since it's using the standard Oracle Net features, all failures will be logged to the `sqlnet.log` file. This file, if no directory is specified for the Oracle Net log file, is created in the starting directory of the Application. For the Agent, that starting location is `<EMHOME>/sysman/emd`. To avoid having a `sqlnet.log` file in the middle of the runtime state information of the Agent, create a `sqlnet.ora` file in the directory `$ORACLE_HOME/network/admin` (or `$TNS_ADMIN` directory if defined on the machine) with the following content:

```
TRACE_LEVEL_CLIENT = OFF
TRACE_FILE_CLIENT = sqlnet.trc
TRACE_DIRECTORY_CLIENT = <<ORACLE_HOME>>/network/trace
LOG_FILE_CLIENT = sqlnet.log
LOG_DIRECTORY_CLIENT = <<ORACLE_HOME>>/network/log
```

The Oracle Net log and trace directory can be any directory the Agent can write to. The default (and most commonly used) location for these directories is always the log and trace directories in $ORACLE_HOME/network.

TIP
If you want to keep all the Agent log and trace files together in one location, make the LOG_DIRECTORY_CLIENT and TRACE_DIRECTORY_CLIENT point to the <EMHOME>/sysman/log directory. This way, the sqlnet.log file will also be written to the same directory as the Agent log and trace files.

Timeout Configuration

The Agent has a built-in thread called the Health Monitor, which checks any pending operation, and verifies to see if that operation is not timing out, or taking too much time to complete. If the Health Monitor detects a thread taking too much time, it will abort the task, and restart the Agent.

■ **Metric engine and target properties** The following emd.properties settings can be used to change the default behavior of the metric collector thread (these settings are case-sensitive):

dynamicPropsComputeTimeout	Time in seconds the collector can take to evaluate a target property. These properties are retrieved from the monitored target each time the Agent starts, and each time the target is marked Up (available) again after downtime. Default is 30 seconds.
NMUPM_TIMEOUT	Number of seconds a request to the OS-specific utility nmupm can take. This utility is only used for the Host target to retrieve some OS-specific metric data. Default is 15 seconds.
CannotScheduleThreadTimeout	Amount of time the Agent will retry if no OS resources are available to perform the basic monitoring. If the timeout has been reached, the agent will restart. Default is 20 minutes.

■ **Agent heartbeat** The Agent heartbeat thread sends regular heartbeats to the Management Server to let it know the Agent is still up and running. Every heartbeat is just an HTTPS (or HTTP if the Agent is not secured) request to the OMS with a timestamp, and the identification of the Agent. The OMS will parse that information and mark the Agent as responsive. If the OMS detects an Agent that stopped sending heartbeats, it will mark the Agent as unresponsive, and will verify to see if the Agent is really down. If the Agent cannot be reached, the Agent and the host will be marked as Down.

It is the OMS that defines the frequency of the heartbeats: It responds to an Agent heartbeat with the time for the next heartbeat.

To catch TCP/IP anomalies and communication hangs and timeouts, the following emd.properties settings can be used to change the default behavior of the Agent heartbeat thread:

PingHangMaxAttempts   Number of heartbeat timeouts the Health Monitor will allow before it shuts down the Agent. Default value of 3.

PingMaxTime   Maximum amount of time (in minutes) before the Health Monitor times out a pending heartbeat request and shuts down the Agent. Default value of 15 minutes.

■ **HTTP transfer and XML file upload**   Every XML file the Agent sends is also sent via the HTTPS protocol. A specific set of emd.properties settings is also available to catch the communication irregularities for the file transfers:

httpTimeoutBody   Time in seconds the Agents will use to transmit the body of a message to the OMS. If the OMS does not respond within the specified time, the Agent will time out the request, and retry the operation again at a later time. Default is 60 seconds.

httpTimeoutPrimaryHeader   A similar type of timeout, but in this case for the HTML headers of a message update the Agent sends to the OMS. Default is 30 seconds.

HttpTimeoutSecondaryHeaders   This parameter controls the timeout for the secondary headers (with the additional HTTP protocol properties). Default is 30 seconds.

uploadTimeout   Maximum amount of time, in seconds, the upload thread will wait for a response from the Management Server to complete the upload of a file before timing out. Default is 1800 seconds (30 minutes).

The SNMP Subagent

The Agent has the capability of responding to SNMP requests made for Oracle databases and listeners from third-party applications. To be able to accept these incoming requests, the subagent has to be started and running on the Agent. For the SNMP solution to work, the SNMP peer daemon needs to be the SNMP master process, with the regular SNMP daemon from the OS as a slave to that peer daemon. The subagent of the Agent will listen for requests coming in from the SNMP peer process, retrieve the necessary values, and respond to the SNMP request without any intervention of the OS daemon.

To set up the SNMP peer daemon, the native SNMP process on the OS has to be changed to switch the ports it is listening on to alternate ports. Typically, the ports used by the SNMP process by default are 161 (for getting SNMP requests) and 162 (for sending SNMP traps). These ports have to be changed to a different set, usually defined as 1161 for requests and 1162 for traps. On UNIX, this can be done in the file /etc/snmpd.conf for most operating systems. After this change, stop the OS SNMP daemon, and use the start script from the Agent ORACLE_HOME to start the SNMP peer daemon, which will in turn restart the native OS daemon.

NOTE
The specifics on how to set up SNMP and configure the SNMP daemon are different for each operating system. The steps outlined here are just to give a high-level overview of what is needed to make the SNMP solution work. For the exact steps for each operating system, read the OS-specific instructions on how to configure the SNMP daemon, and check the Oracle Install Guide for that platform for the specific integration of the OS daemon with the peer daemon.

To start the SNMP subagent, follow these steps:

- Log in as root, and start the SNMP peer Agent:

```
$ su root
# cd $ORACLE_HOME/network/snmp/peer
# start_peer -a
# exit
```

- Verify that the main SNMP processes are running:

```
$ ps -ef | grep peer
$ ps -ef | grep snmpd
```

- If all the system SNMP processes, including the peer process, are running, start the SNMP subagent:

```
$ emctl start subagent
```

Securing the Agent

Security at the Agent is always a concern too. There is no direct user interaction with the Agent software (making that part easier to manage): The only communication the Agent does with the outside world is via the Management Server. But because the Agent is monitoring services and applications on the box, that monitoring needs to be done in a secure way.

Registration Passwords

Securing the Agent is more than just switching it to use SSL when communicating with the OMS. When an Agent is secured against an OMS, the Agent becomes a trusted part of the infrastructure of that Grid Control deployment. To prevent rogue Agents from securing themselves against an OMS, and getting inserted as a member of the infrastructure, a password must be specified during the secure process. Without the correct password, the secure operation will abort, and the Agent will not be able to obtain the wallet with the SSL key from the OMS.

The initial secure password (IPW) is defined during the install. That password is used to secure the Agent installed with the OMS, and is kept in the repository to allow additional agents to secure themselves against that deployment. These registration passwords can be managed from the Console, giving Enterprise Administrators the possibility to rotate the password, create multiple specific ones, or even remove the initial one.

In the Console, from the Setup page, use the Registration Passwords link:

```
https://<host>:<port>/em/console/admin/rpw/rpwAdmin
```

NOTE
Since this is an operation that impacts the infrastructure of Grid Control, only users with the SUPER USER *privilege will be able to get to this page.*

When creating a new registration password, the Enterprise Administrator has a couple of options:

- A password can be defined as a *one-time* or a *persistent* password. Persistent passwords can be used multiple times, and should typically be used in conjunction with an expiration date. A one-time password can only be used once. As soon as an Agent uses the password, the password will be flagged as expired. For situations where an Agent has to be reinstalled (or recovered from a disaster), or when an additional ad-hoc Agent is added to the infrastructure, a one-time password is a good way of getting just that Agent into the infrastructure.

- Every password can have an expiration date. Regardless of the type of password created, an end date should be specified for the password (see Figure 4-1). This will limit the exposure of the password, and also force people to finish the deployments of the Agents before the deadline. When the password expires, the definition will still be in the repository, but Agents won't be able to use that password any more for the secure operation.

Especially when different groups are involved with the rollout of the Agents, each deploying their own Agents against the infrastructure, having a set of registration passwords (with one for each group) can be a useful thing to prevent rogue Agents from getting into Grid Control.

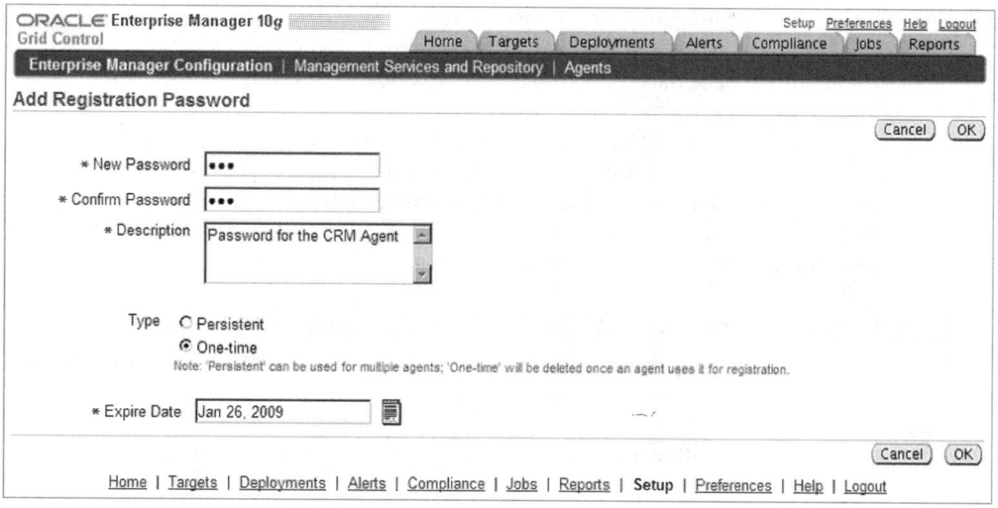

![Screenshot of Oracle Enterprise Manager 10g Grid Control "Add Registration Password" page. It shows fields for New Password, Confirm Password, Description ("Password for the CRM Agent"), Type (Persistent / One-time, with One-time selected), and Expire Date (Jan 26, 2009). Note: 'Persistent' can be used for multiple agents; 'One-time' will be deleted once an agent uses it for registration. Cancel and OK buttons appear.]

FIGURE 4-1. *Adding Agent registration passwords*

Securing and Unsecuring the Agent

When any install of a 10*g*R2 or higher Agent is done, it will be secured after the install, using SSL and HTTPS to communicate with the OMS. The Agent can be unsecured to debug an issue, or to fix a problem in the network configuration (like changing a firewall setup). However, the best practice is to keep all Agents secured, so that all communication between the OMS and the Agent is done via a SSL-encrypted channel: The Agent should never be left running in an unsecure mode. To temporarily unsecure the Agent, use this command:

```
$ emctl unsecure agent
```

To resecure the Agent again, or to update the SSL wallet of the Agent, just use the `secure` command again:

```
$ emctl secure agent
```

NOTE
An Agent should only be resecured for three reasons:

- *The Agent was running in an unsecure mode, and secure communication is now needed.*
- *The OMS server setup changed, and the hostname the Agent knew as the OMS server to communicate with is no longer there.*
- *The Agent was removed from Grid Control and needs to be rediscovered.*

Advanced Networking Option and Database Monitoring

The Agent uses the Oracle Net libraries for all connection requests. If the Advanced Networking Option (ANO) is installed and used on the machine for the databases that the Agent is monitoring, the `sqlnet.ora` and `protocol.ora` files in the Agent ORACLE_HOME will need to be updated with the necessary ANO parameters to allow the communication with the target databases. As soon as the parameters are added to the Oracle Net files, and the Agents are restarted (so the Oracle Net libraries will reread the configuration files, and reinitialize the libraries to use the secure options), the secure communication will be in effect.

More information about the Advanced Networking Option, including the overview of all the parameters to specify in the Oracle Net files, can be found in the Oracle documentation: *Oracle Database Advanced Security Administrator's Guide.*

Configuring the Agent for PAM Authentication

Every operating system has its own little tweaks for Pluggable Authentication Modules (PAM) and Lightweight Directory Access Protocol (LDAP) configuration. But the overall steps to set it up and make it work are (more or less) the same.

For UNIX systems, follow these steps to set up the Agent to work with PAM:

1. *Make sure PAM is configured on the system.* The `libpam.so` file is typically located in the `/usr/lib` directory. There are variations on some operating systems, so consult the OS-specific documentations for the details of configuring PAM on the system.

2. *Configure PAM to recognize the Agent.* In order for PAM to recognize the Agent, the Agent executable must be added to the system configuration. Create a new file called `/etc/pam.d/emagent`, with the following content:

```
#%PAM-1.0
auth required /lib/security/pam_ldap.so
account required /lib/security/pam_ldap.so
password required /lib/security/pam_ldap.so
session required /lib/security/pam_ldap.so
```

On RHEL4, the PAM configuration file looks a little different:

```
#%PAM-1.0
auth required pam_ldap.so
account required pam_ldap.so
password required pam_ldap.so
session required pam_ldap.so
```

On AIX, there is just one main PAM file, which contains the configuration for all programs. Add the following lines in the `/etc/pam.conf` file:

```
emagent auth       required   /usr/lib/security/pam_aix
emagent account    required   /usr/lib/security/pam_aix
emagent password   required   /usr/lib/security/pam_aix
emagent session    required   /usr/lib/security/pam_aix
```

3. Adjust the Agent configuration. Edit the `$ORACLE_HOME/bin/commonenv` file of the Agent and add the directory of the `libpam.so` file.

```
if [ "$LD_LIBRARY_PATH" = "" ] ; then
   LD_LIBRARY_PATH=<path to libpam.so>
else
   LD_LIBRARY_PATH=<path to libpam.so>:$LD_LIBRARY_PATH
fi
```

After the Agent has been restarted, authentication of user accounts will now pass through the PAM modules configured on the system.

Configuring the Agent for Large Systems

When the Agent is initially rolled out, the parameters and settings in the `emd.properties` files are set for an average amount of work the Agent has to do. However, if the machine the Agent is running has an abnormally high number of targets to monitor, these default settings will need to be adjusted.

Incoming Connections

The Agent limits the number of incoming connections it can accept concurrently from the OMS to 25. Once these connections are all used up, the Agent will refuse any additional request the OMS makes, forcing the OMS to retry the request again a little while later. The number of connections an Agent can accept simultaneously can be specified in the `emd.properties` file:

```
MaxInComingConnections=25
```

If the Agent has more than 25 targets of the same type discovered, chances are that a bulk request from the OMS to change monitoring settings or update parameters will cause the Agent to reach that limit of 25. On those machines, where there are more than 25 targets of the same type discovered that are actively used for management, increase this parameter to the number of targets of the same type discovered. From the `emagent.trc` file:

```
WARN resman.socket: Incoming Socket max=25 reached !!
```

NOTE
Every incoming connection is a TCP socket that will be used by the Agent. Once you have more than 50 targets of the same type of a box, blindly updating this value to a value beyond 50 might cause the Agent to reach an OS limit, and fail when trying to make the extra connections. Consult the OS-specific documentation of the machine, and more importantly, observe the behavior of the machine itself to make sure the extra connections are possible, before making changes like this. Also, the more connections an Agent will accept simultaneously, the more work will be done at the Agent at the same time. Blindly adding more connections will lead to contention at the Agent while processing all this at the same time, which can cause severe performance degradations.

Threads and Processes

Every target the Agent is monitoring will have metrics that need to be executed against it. All these metrics are either threads (in the case of direct Agent access to the target) or processes (in the case of external scripts like shell or Perl scripts). When the number of targets the Agent is monitoring exceeds any of these values, metrics cannot be executed, causing potentially vital data not to be collected in a timely manner. Two parameters in the `emd.properties` file can help control the number of threads and processes the Agent can create:

```
MaxSpawnedProcesses=64
MaxThreads=100
```

- **Processes** Each time an external metric, like an OS script or a Perl script, needs to be executed, the Agent will spawn a process. Also, jobs submitted via the Grid Control will require the Agent to spawn a new process. Every process the Agent starts will also have a thread associated with it, so the Agent can keep track of all the commands that are getting executed.
- **Threads** Besides a set of internal housekeeping threads, the Agent will need one thread for each metric it's executing, and one thread for each external process that is running.

Once the Agent has reached the maximum number of threads (and therefore also processes), the following error message will be written to the agent trace (`emagent.trc`):

```
ERROR ThreadPool: Could not create thread, ERROR=12:Not enough space
```

For a large system, with more than 50 targets to be monitored, the number of threads and processes can easily be doubled, even tripled.

NOTE
Given the fact that each process the Agent creates requires a thread too, the value of the MaxThreads *parameter should always be higher than the* MaxSpawnedProcesses *one. As a best practice, make the thread count at least 30 higher than the process count.*

Watchdog Monitoring

As soon as the Agent is started on a machine, there are two processes that are getting started: the main Agent process (emagent), and the Agent watchdog (emwd.pl). The purpose of the watchdog is to make the sure the Agent is operational and running properly on the machine. It performs the following checks:

- *See if the Agent process is running.* If the emagent process is not running, the watchdog will restart the Agent. To prevent the watchdog from trashing and constantly restarting the Agent in case of a fatal problem on the machine, the watchdog will only try to restart the Agent three times in a row. If, after these attempts, the Agent is still not running, the OOB messaging settings are called to inform the Administrator of the failure, and the watchdog will abort too. The number of retries can be changed with the following environment variable:

```
$ EM_MAX_RETRIES=3
$ export EM_MAX_RETRIES
```

- *Make sure the Agent is healthy and responding.* Every minute, the watchdog will see if the Agent is responding to a heartbeat signal. If the Agent does not respond, the watchdog will assume the Agent is hung, and restart the emagent process. When the watchdog detects a hung agent, an error stack similar to this will be written to the emagent.nohup file:

```
--- Tue Jan 15 10:00:59 2009::Abnormality reported for EMAgent : 6320 ---
--- Tue Jan 15 10:00:59 2009::Debugging component EMAgent ---
--- Tue Jan 15 10:00:59 2009::generate first core file for diagnosis ---
--- Tue Jan 15 10:01:01 2009::core file
    /emgc/agent10g/sysman/emd/core.hung.6320_1213516881 generated ---
```

The generated core file (and the associated traceback file containing the stack trace of the core file) can be used by Oracle Support and Oracle Development to determine the cause of the hang.

- *Check the Agent resource consumption.* A final set of checks the watchdog performs is a verification of the amount of memory the main Agent process is consuming. If it crosses the thresholds, the watchdog will force the Agent to restart. The default of 600MB total memory and 20MB increase in between checks can be adjusted with the following environment variables:

```
$ EMAGENT_RECYCLE_MAXMEMORY=600
$ export EMAGENT_RECYCLE_MAXMEMORY
$ EMAGENT_MAXMEM_INCREASE=20
$ export EMAGENT_MAXMEM_INCREASE
```

Oracle Database Connections

Every Oracle database (RAC, RAC instance, Single Instance, Data Guard) the Agent is monitoring will have at least two connections (for 8*i* and 9*i* databases) or three connections (in the case of 10*g* or higher) established. More connections can be made per database, to allow several metrics to be collected at the same time.

For versions prior to 10.2.0.5, the Agent had a maximum total number of connections it could establish across all targets. Once that limit was reached, any request for another connection was put in a queue. The request then had to wait until another connection disconnected from any of the monitored databases, before it could continue its work. With work queued up like this, metrics could be waiting to get executed on the database, causing critical data not to be collected on time.

There are two parameters available that can influence this pre-10.2.0.5 behavior:

■ The total number of connections an Agent can make, regardless of how many databases it is monitoring. (Default is 100.)

`MaxOCIConnection=100`

■ The total number of concurrent connections the Agent can make against a single database. (Default is 7.)

`MaxOCIConnectionPerTarget=7`

With a little math, we can deduce that once we have more than 14 monitored databases (100/7), there is a potential problem, and with more than 33 databases monitored (100/3), there will be metric queuing going on by the Agent. There are two ways of changing this:

■ *Increase the total number of OCI connections.* The number of OCI (Oracle Call Interface) connections can be increased to accommodate the extra connections the Agent will make per database. Example: If there are 100 databases on a single machine, the value for this parameter can be set to 400 (to allow two metrics to be running simultaneously for each database).

But since multiple connections can be made for a single database, depending on the amount of work (metrics) the Agent has to do, continuing to increase this number might not be the complete solution.

■ *Limit the number of concurrent connections to a single target.* In cases where there are more than 150 databases on a single server, simply increasing the `MaxOCIConnection` value is not going to be the solution. At some point, the number of connections per databases has to be limited, to prevent starvation of the total number of connections per Agent. In cases like this, limit the total number of connections per target, in combination with setting an increased limit on the total number of OCI connections per Agent.

NOTE
Keep in mind that the Agent needs a minimum of three connections per database for a 10g database (one for the server-generated alerts, one for the Response Up/Down, and a minimum of one extra connection to run metrics).

Allowing four connections per database on a large system with lots of databases is a reasonable compromise, to allow some concurrency when collecting metrics, while at the same time limiting the total number of OCI connections made by the Agent.

Starting with 10.2.0.5, the behavior is a little different. There is still a limit per target, handled by the same parameter, `MaxOCIConnectionPerTarget`, but the overall pool limit is gone (no more `MaxOCIConnection`). In terms of tuning and tweaking the Agent parameters, this means that the only thing to look for now is the total number of file descriptors that are available to the Agent, compared to the number of database targets the Agent is monitoring.

Property Timeouts

Every target can have a set of properties and additional variables, which can only be calculated during runtime. For a database, for instance, the main one is the database version. Depending on the database version, different metrics will be executed, and SQL queries will slightly change. These variables, used to properly monitor the target, need to be calculated each time the Agent is started, and each time a target is reported back as operational after downtime. The Agent has a default timeout of 30 seconds to calculate all the properties for a target. This value will be used for all the target types, unless a specific value is specified to change the timeout for that particular target type. If it takes longer than that to finish the calculation, a timeout will be raised, and the target will remain in a Down or an Unknown state. If such a timeout is encountered, the Agent will write the following message in the `emagent.trc` file:

```
ERROR TargetManager: TIMEOUT when compute dynamic properties
       for target database.acme.com
```

There are two possible ways of changing this timeout in the `emd.properties` file:

- There is the generic value, which will be used for all targets of all types:

  ```
  dynamicPropsComputeTimeout=60
  ```

- There is also a target-type–specific value that can be used. There can be a value for each of the various target types the Agent is monitoring. Example:

  ```
  dynamicPropsComputeTimeout_oracle_database=120
  ```

BEST PRACTICE
The timeouts can be increased from the default of 30 to 60, 120, or even 180 on a heavily loaded system. Increasing it beyond 180 seconds is not recommended.

Certain metric collections require OS-specific code to be executed to get the data. All this code is combined in a single executable, the `nmupm` executable, to get that data. On some systems, especially if there is resource starvation of any kind going on, getting that OS-specific data might take longer than usual. For any nmupm timeout, the following message will be written to the emagent.trc file:

```
ERROR fetchlets.oslinetok: Process stdout =
        em_error=nmupm child process timed out. Terminated
```

There is a special parameter in the emd.properties file that can be used to change the default behavior of the nmupm executable. The default value for this parameter is 15 (seconds). Example:

```
NMUPM_TIMEOUT=30
```

BEST PRACTICE
As with all timeouts, they can be increased. But they should not be increased to some extreme or absurd value. Setting the nmupm timeout to 30 or even 60 seconds might be necessary on a heavily loaded server machine. Setting that value to extreme values like 600 or 900 might give the illusion of fixing the problem, but it will only hide problems on the box, and delay the reporting of those issues to the administrators.

OMS Server Request Timeouts

Every time the OMS server sends a request over to perform an administration task, like updating the monitoring configuration of a target, or setting/unsetting a blackout, and so on, the Agent will create a thread to work on this operation and report back the result. This thread has a default timeout of 300 seconds to complete the task, which is typically plenty of time to complete the specified in task on a normal machine. On a machine with lots of targets, or a machine running with a heavy load, this timeout might not be enough for the more complex tasks, like doing a full Agent reload and restarting the collections for all the targets.

Here's an example of a hang from the emagent.trc file:

```
ERROR Dispatcher: The remote api of type 10624 has timed out.
        We will bounce the agent
```

A unique number in the trace files identifies each of these remote API calls. The following table contains the most common potentially lengthy operations the OMS server can send to the Agent:

10624	Update target configuration
10634	Remove target from Agent
10635	Update target configuration
10648	Get blackout details (single blackout)
10649	Get blackout details (multiple blackouts)
10650	Remove blackout from Agent
10651	Create new blackout
10658	Reset target state on Agent
10661	Recompute the target properties on Agent
10662	Set new master Agent for cluster target

The parameter to control this is also in the `emd.properties` file. The default value of 300 seconds (5 minutes) can be increased up to 600 seconds (10 minutes) on a heavily loaded machine. Example:

```
RemoteAPITimeout=450
```

Summary

Now that we have a management infrastructure (installed according to the MAA specifications off course), and we have successfully deployed Agents on all the machines that need monitoring and administration, we have concluded the roll-out of the Enterprise Manager software. But this is not the end of the story. Getting the software installed is only the beginning! Now comes the fun part of actually using the software to make life easier...

CHAPTER
5

Grid Control: Sizing the Environment and Other Best Practices

izing an enterprise-class application is one of the hardest things to do. This usually means the "storage size" or "disc footprint" of the data the application stores.

In the Grid Control context, or shall I say, in the context of this chapter, the size of the OMS servers and the repository is actually not the most important thing to keep in mind: It's the processing of data.

Getting all the data processed and made available to everyone requesting it is the main thing to keep in mind. This will require resources on both the OMS and the repository database.

To calculate the necessary resources, this chapter contains a couple of tips and tricks to give Enterprise Administrators a general idea of the magnitude of the infrastructure.

However, predicting size and resources is not an exact science. Keep in mind that we're only talking about "estimates", or even better, "guesstimates", with the only intention of giving an idea of the magnitude to help with the planning of the Grid Control rollout.

Just How Many OMS Servers Do I Need?

This is the most typical question that people ask when they are either rolling out or thinking about rolling out Grid Control. And it's also the most difficult one to answer. The answer is always: *It depends.* And despite the fact that people always think that this is a clever ploy to avoid answering the question, or to keep some absurd requirement hidden, it *really* does depend, on several factors. There is no simple answer to this question. A lot of environmental factors need to be considered, and real operational data will need to be analyzed to make a (good) educated guess about the number of OMS servers needed for Grid Control.

Besides the obvious one (the number of targets the infrastructure is monitoring), there are several other factors that play a role, including:

- The number of jobs running in the system

- The number of administrators that will log on and work simultaneously in the Console

- Available resources in the database to perform the housekeeping tasks

- Network bandwidth, and how fast data can get transferred to and from the OMS servers

- The number of violations that get triggered in the system, and how many of those need notifications to the administrators

- The speed and stability of the IO system that the database uses

- The speed and stability of the IO system the OMS servers use

Each of these factors can become a serious bottleneck, throttling the throughput of information. And it's easy enough to throw resources at this problem, from either a depth perspective (just get a bigger box) or a breadth perspective (install an extra box in the environment) to push the bottleneck away. But at some point, some limit will be reached. After installing that 128th CPU in a machine, either you'll be hitting the physical limit of the server, or you'll notice no change in the resource usage, since some other bottleneck will now be the one throttling the throughput.

Similarly, just adding boxes will have its limit too. Besides running out of floor space in the data center, having dozens of OMS servers will create such a strain on the other components like the network interfaces and the repository database that adding that one extra box to that environment will gain you nothing in terms of performance and scalability.

All the planning and preparing to roll out and expand the environment has to be properly analyzed. In some conditions, a faster and bigger server might be a good solution. For other bottlenecks, adding another OMS box to the environment will be a big benefit. But with each expansion of the infrastructure, and each change made to the hardware, you will have to look at the amount of work that is getting done in Grid Control, and ask questions like:

- Do we really need to collect all the metrics for this target?
- Do we need to generate alerts and violations for all these metric conditions?
- Do the administrators really need to be notified of all these violations?
- Do we really need to keep all this data around for this long?

The answers to these questions can help reduce the amount of work coming into Grid Control, and getting pushed out. And with less work, fewer resources will be needed, giving the configured hardware some reprieve.

There are some big chunks of work being done, which can give an idea of just how stressed the environment is, and how much capacity is still left:

- The amount of metric info coming in
- The number of notifications being sent out
- The number of jobs being dispatched to the Agents
- Housekeeping the repository has to do to analyze all the metric data

Each of these factors can give a good indication of how Grid Control is behaving, and whether there is still sufficient capacity available to process all the data.

NOTE
Grid Control has indicators available for these major areas that can help identify the bottlenecks. More information about how to find and use those indicators and what to do to keep Grid Control alive and kicking is provided in Chapter 6 of this book, which covers all the aspects needed to maintain the Grid Control infrastructure and keep it operational.

Adding an Additional OMS Server

When you have determined that you are at the point where an additional OMS is required for your environment, the steps required to add it match those used to prep the environment for an initial install, as discussed in Chapter 2. In order to add a Management Server to an existing infrastructure, the added OMS must be running with the same version as the rest of the infrastructure. To get to the same version (if a patchset has already been installed to upgrade Grid Control from the base 10.2.0.1 release), the 10.2.0.1 version needs to be installed first. After the initial software has been installed, the appropriate Grid Control patchset needs to be applied on top of that base OMS install: Patchsets are only updates of the base release of a product, and cannot be used by themselves to do a full install of the product.

GRID CONTROL WORKSHOP

Adding an Additional OMS to an Existing Environment

Starting from 10*g*R4 (10.2.0.4), to add a nonbase version of the OMS to an existing environment, follow these steps:

Step 1. Do a software-only install of the base version (10.2.0.1), using the Additional Management Server option. Software-only installs can be done using the -noconfig command-line option:

```
$ ./runInstaller -noconfig –force -waitForCompletion
```

NOTE
An overview of the command-line switches is available in Chapter 18.

Step 2. After that base install completes, the software of both the OMS and the Agent needs to be upgraded to the latest version.

Step 3. Two software-only upgrades will have to be done: one to upgrade the OMS, and one for the Agent. Use the same -noconfig option, combined with the b_softwareonly=true option, to perform the upgrade:

```
$ cd <latest version stage directory>

$ export ORACLE_HOME=<ORACLE_HOME of the OMS>
$ ./runInstaller -noconfig –force -waitForCompletion b_
softwareonly=true

$ export ORACLE_HOME=<ORACLE_HOME of the Agent>
$ ./runInstaller -noconfig –force -waitForCompletion b_
softwareonly=true
```

Step 4. When those two install sessions finish, the software installed on the machine will be an upgraded OMS install. No configuration will be done yet, and none of the OC4J applications will be deployed yet. To run the configuration manually, run the postconfiguration tool:

```
$ export PERL5LIB=${ORACLE_HOME}/perl/lib/5.6.1
$ ${ORACLE_HOME}/perl/bin/perl
        ${ORACLE_HOME}/sysman/install/ConfigureGC.pl ${ORACLE_BASE}
```

Step 5. With 10.2.0.5 a new way to export and import configuration settings has been added. This can be used to import the runtime settings of an existing OMS into the newly installed Management Server, to make sure all the Management Servers are running with the same configuration:

```
$ emctl importconfig oms –file <backup file>
```

Step-by-step instructions for the software-only install are available in the *Grid Control Installation Guide*, Section 3: *Installing Enterprise Manager*.

XML Loaders

Each OMS has a set of loader threads loading all the information the Agent has accumulated into the repository. Since the Agent is structuring all the data in XML format, these loaders are commonly referred to as the XML loaders.

There are three types of data that need to be uploaded into the repository:

- **Metadata** The Agent uploads all monitoring configuration, and metric settings are uploaded as *metadata*. Metadata files are always loaded first, since Grid Control needs to know about the targets and the metrics that are being collected and evaluated by the Agents before any monitoring state and any metric data can be uploaded. These files are loaded synchronously: All other XML loading for this Agent stops until the metadata is uploaded and processed. The internal notation for this is the A channel: "A" files generated by the Agent contain all the metadata information.

- **State information** The state of all monitored targets and the state of each metric with thresholds defined are uploaded as state information. State information can only be uploaded after the metadata is present. But it will be loaded before the actual data points are loaded, to speed up the delivery of notifications. These files are also loaded synchronously: All other XML loading for this Agent stops until this state file is uploaded and processed. This is the B channel: Any "B" file generated by the Agent contains either a state change (change in availability of a target), or a metric condition (like a threshold violation or an error evaluating the metric).

- **Metric data** This is all the normal metric data the Agent gathers for the targets. All other channels (C and D) are used for the metric loading. The Agent will generate these C and D XML files depending on the importance and type of data generated. The files are uploaded asynchronously. The Agent batches all uploads to the OMS server. And the OMS will store these metric files temporarily in the XML loader directory specified: C and D files will be treated and handled the same on the OMS.

The throughput these loader threads can handle is determined by two main factors:

- The time it takes for an OMS server to read and parse an XML file, to turn it into SQL statements.

- The time it takes for those generated SQL statements to get executed and committed in the database.

All these factors rely heavily on the hardware the OMS server and the database is running on, and very little can be done to actually tune or optimize the throughput of these loader threads from a Grid Control perspective.

Tuning the XML Loaders

The following parameters are available in the `emoms.properties` file of the OMS, to tune and tweak the XML loaders. Each of these parameters can be specified on each OMS. Although the values can technically be specified differently on each OMS, the recommendation is to keep the values of all these parameters the same on each OMS:

- **em.loader.maxMetadataThreads** The number of simultaneous loads for metadata loading is controlled by this parameter. The default value of 10 is sufficient for most cases.

In the unlikely event that this parameter does need to be increased, for every connection added for the metadata threads, also add a connection to the `maxConnForDataLoad` parameter in the `emoms.properties` file:

```
oracle.sysman.emRep.dbConn.maxConnForDataLoad=26
```

If that parameter is not specified in the properties file, the default of 25 connections is used.

- **em.loader.threadPoolSize**   The number of threads the Management Server will use to load metric data into the repository. For each loader thread present, a connection into the repository database is created. The default is 1. The maximum value that can be specified for this parameter is 10. To reduce the overhead on both the OMS (number of threads) and the repository database (active connections), specify only the number of threads needed to load all the data: Do not max out the loader threads just because you can.

- **ReceiveDir**   Directory where all the metric data files uploaded from the Agents are stored temporarily before they are uploaded into the repository by the XML Loaders threads. Only metric data is stored in the receive directory. Target configuration data and any metric threshold violation data are loaded directly in the repository.

TIP
A typical installation will load an average of about 500 rows per second into the repository. On a well-tuned site, this number can go up to 1,000, or even higher. To get the exact number for this throughput, check the Loader Throughput (rows per second) metric for the OMS and Repository target. If the number falls below 500 rows/ second, it means there is a bottleneck preventing optimal throughput of rows. This can be either:

- *IO throughput, with the database not being able to write all the data in a timely fashion*

- *Network throughput, with the OMS not being able to transmit all the SQL statements in a timely fashion*

- *CPU contention, causing the transactions in the database not to be completed in time*

- *Unusual database waits, due to improper redo and undo configuration*

As a general rule of thumb, to guarantee optimal throughput for each of the types of data, the XML loaders should be used 75 percent of the time to load metric data, leaving 25 percent of the time for the loading of metadata and state information.

The 25 percent parameter is in reality too high: Unless the thresholds for metrics are very poorly defined and are generating violations constantly, the loading of metadata and severity information will rarely go above 10 percent. However, the extra spare capacity is critical: The whole purpose of Grid Control is to detect problems. And as Murphy has already shown time after time, problems rarely come spread out nicely, where you can look at them one at a time. When disaster strikes, or even when there is a limited outage of network segment, several violations will be generated in a short period of time, causing a spike in the amount of violation data coming in. The Management Servers need the spare capacity to be able to process and notify the users and administrators for the unusual peak in state information, without overwhelming the infrastructure and taking up all the resources to process the information created during the spike.

Load per Target Type

To give some rough guidance on what to expect in terms of load on a per-day basis for the metrics each target type is uploading, we offer you Table 5-1. The numbers in this table are just rough estimates of how many rows an average target of that type uploads per day: They are based on the number of metric data records that all the targets of that given type uploaded into the repository. These numbers were then mined from various repositories and averaged out to come up with the sizing estimates per type of target

The size per day is split up per rollup mechanism:

- ■ **RAW** indicates the raw data points as they are loaded by the Agent.
- ■ **HOUR** indicates the hourly rollups of the raw data.
- ■ **DAY** indicates the daily rollups of the raw data.

The actual number of rows for a target of this type may vary, depending on the size and usage of the target. The company 10-petabyte data warehouse will upload a lot more data points per day than a small test database with only the scott/tiger schema installed.

	Size / Day			
Target Type	**RAW**	**HOUR**	**DAY**	**Records/Day**
Agent	60KB	20KB	1KB	900
Oracle HTTP Server	600KB	450KB	20KB	9,000
ASM Instance	2MB	1MB	50KB	30,000
BC4J	12KB	3KB	0.1KB	200
Cluster	50KB	5KB	0.2KB	800
CSA Collector	15KB	1.5KB	0.1KB	250
Database Instance	4MB	500KB	25KB	60,000
Host	1.2MB	300KB	15KB	20,000
Application Server	120KB	100KB	5KB	1,800
Listener	40KB	6KB	0.2KB	600
Netapp Filer	1MB	1MB	50KB	15,000
OC4J	1MB	300KB	15KB	15,000
OC4J JVM	300KB	200KB	10KB	5,000
RAC Database	120KB	80KB	4KB	2,000
Webcache	60KB	40KB	2KB	900

TABLE 5-1. *XML Load Based on Target Type, per Day*

There are also some obvious target types missing from Table 5-1:

■ **Groups, Systems, and Services** These aggregate targets will only generate data points if aggregate metrics are defined for these targets. Since an administrator has a choice to define these or not, the number of records for targets of this type cannot be predicted. The number of records, though, can be calculated quite easily knowing the exact definition of these targets.

■ **Beacons and Web sites** A beacon does not generate any data unless transactions are defined for web applications. And the frequency of these transactions is also configurable. This means that putting *any* kind of generic numbers up there in that list will be completely wrong. The math can be easily done, though: Each transaction, checked every 10 minutes, will generate 144 raw records, 12 hourly ones, and 1 daily rollup point. This might not seem like a lot of data, but since beacons are typically distributed in various part of the network, each running multiple transactions, the numbers will start to add up.

GRID CONTROL WORKSHOP

Calculating the Number of Servers for an Environment

Workshop Notes
Assume the following environment:

■ The loader threads upload 500 rows per second in the database.

■ The system includes 2000 server machines to monitor:

   ■ Five hundred two-node RAC databases

   ■ Five hundred two-node Oracle Application servers, each with the default home and an additional OC4J applications deployed

The question is: How many OMS servers do I need to be able to upload all the monitoring data for this environment?

Step 1. To calculate this properly, let's break this down into its individual pieces. With the numbers provided, we can deduce the number of rows as shown in Table 5-2.

Step 2. Next we need to calculate the number of rows per second as shown in Table 5-3.

Step 3. And finally, knowing the rows per second, we can now calculate the number of loader threads we'll need to handle this load, as seen in Table 5-4.

With a maximum of 10 loader threads per OMS, and given the fact that we need some extra capacity in case an OMS goes down, we need one OMS server to be able to load all this data. But given the HA recommendations, we'll use two Management Servers in this deployment, which gives us plenty of spare capacity for future growth.

Keep in mind that this is only a rough estimate, only intended to draw a *very* big picture, and give an idea of the amount of capacity you will have to consider for the rollout. The actual throughput of rows will need to be monitored on a regular basis using the statistics Grid Control gathers, to track the capacity that is currently being used. Based on this, we can extrapolate the additional capacity needed in the infrastructure to handle more targets.

This exercise can easily be extended to calculate the number of records for any Grid Control deployment: Just put in the number of targets for each type, and do the math to get an estimate on the number of rows this will produce.

2,000 Agents	× 900 rows per day	= 1,800,000 total
2,000 Hosts	× 20,000 rows per day	= 40,000,000 total
1,000 Clusters	× 800 rows per day	= 800,000 total
500 RAC databases	× 2,000 rows per day	= 1,000,000 total
1,000 database instances	× 60,000 rows per day	= 60,000,000 total
1,000 database listeners	× 600 rows per day	= 600,000 total
1,000 Application Servers	× 1,800 rows per day	= 1,800,000 total
2,000 OC4J Applications	× 15,000 rows per day	= 30,000,000 total
1,000 Oracle HTTP Servers	× 9,000 rows per day	= 9,000,000 total
1,000 Webcache servers	× 900 rows per day	= 900,000 total
	Grand total:	= **145,900,000** total

TABLE 5-2. *Number of Rows Produced Based on the Environment*

145,900,000	Rows per day
/ 86,400	Seconds per day
* 75%	Maximum activity a loader thread should be using for metric data
= **1,267**	Rows per second

TABLE 5-3. *Number of Rows per Second*

1,267	Rows per second
/ 500	Rows per second defined as our upload speed
= **3**	Loader threads needed

TABLE 5-4. *Number of Loader Threads Needed*

GRID CONTROL WORKSHOP

Calculating the Number of Targets an Environment Can Handle

Workshop Notes

Assume the following environment:

- Four OMSes, each configured with 10 loaders.
- Each loader threads uploads 500 rows per second in the database.

The question is: How many two-node RAC databases can this environment load?

Step 1. Let's begin by calculating the number of rows one complete two-node RAC database will upload, as shown in Table 5-5.

Step 2. Next, we calculate the rows per second as shown in Table 5-6.

Step 3. We have four OMS servers. Given the fact that we must have spare capacity, we can only put three of those to work, to allow the fourth one to be unavailable without jeopardizing the entire infrastructure.

This means:

Three OMS servers × 10 loader threads × 500 rows/seconds = 15,000 rows/second maximum

Step 4. Finally, to calculate the total number of two-node RAC installs, do the calculations shown in Table 5-7.

Two Agents	× 900 rows per day	= 1,800 total
Two Hosts	× 20,000 rows per day	= 40,000 total
One Cluster	× 800 rows per day	= 800 total
One RAC database	× 2,000 rows per day	= 2,000 total
Two database instances	× 60,000 rows per day	= 120,000 total
Two database listeners	× 600 rows per day	= 1,200 total
	Grand total	= **165,800** total

TABLE 5-5. *Rows from a Two-Node RAC Database*

165,800	Rows per day
/ 86.400	Seconds per day
* 75%	Maximum activity a loader thread should be using for metric data
= **1.5**	Rows per second

TABLE 5-6. *Rows per Second from Two-Node RAC Database*

15,000	Rows per second maximum capacity
/ 1.5	Rows per second for each RAC setup
= 10,000	Two-node RAC installs can be installed with the 4 OMS install

TABLE 5-7. *Total Number of RAC Databases to Be Monitored*

Metric Data Rollup

Data rollup is another critical function that the repository itself provides (there is no interaction with the Agents or the Management Servers for this). All metric data uploaded by the Agents is rolled up to an hourly and a daily level for trending and analysis by a DBMS_JOB running regularly in the repository database. The math for measuring the throughput and the capacity for this function is pretty simple:

- The number of rows this module is rolling up per second must be higher than the number of rows the loaders are loading per second.

- As soon as the number for the rollup job drops below the loader throughput, we'll start building a backlog for the rollup function.

The current speed (meaning throughput, or rows/second for the loader job) can be retrieved from the self-monitoring that Grid Control is doing (more about this in Chapter 6). The SQL statement to get the current rows/second for the Rollup job would look like the following snippet:

```
SELECT TO_CHAR(collection_timestamp,'DD-MON-YYYY HH24:MI:SS') collected,
       value
FROM   mgmt$metric_current
WHERE  target_type   = 'oracle_emrep'
  AND  metric_name   = 'DBMS_Job_Status'
  AND  metric_column = 'jobthroughput'
  AND  key_value     = 'Rollup'
```

In case of a low throughput, or a throughput that is getting dangerously close to the loader upload throughput, the database will need to be checked for the potential performance bottleneck.

- **Database bottleneck** Automatic Workload Repository (AWR) and Automatic Database Diagnostic Monitor (ADDM) are your friends here. These diagnostic features are the first thing to do and will check to see where a potential bottleneck might exist.

- **IO bottleneck** The very nature of this operation will be highly IO intensive: Large amounts of data from the raw metrics table are read, rolled up, and then written to the rollup tables. This means large amounts of data will be read and written by the database.

In cases where the bottleneck is simply database power, a few options are available:

- **More CPUs and more memory** As a wise man once said: Any performance problem can be solved by just adding more CPU and memory. Besides the fact that this wise man surely must have had a stake in a chip manufacturing company, there are limitations to this approach. A machine can only be extended up to a certain point before it becomes physically impossible to add more resources. And blindly adding resources to a box is never a good solution. Increasing the System Global Area (SGA) of the database is not going to make it run any faster if the machine is CPU-bound. Similarly, adding additional CPUs to the machine in cases where the database is constantly waiting for IO operations is not going to do much good: It's just going to wait faster! Any change made to the repository machines must be the result of a careful analysis of the specific bottleneck encountered.

■ **Add a RAC instance** This is where the power of a RAC database becomes evident: If the Grid Control repository is deployed in a RAC database, adding computational power to the database can be as simple as adding a new instance to the RAC database.

Agent Heartbeating

Every Agent sends a heartbeat signal on a regular basis to the Management Servers. The OMS will use this signal to keep track of which Agents are still working properly, and which ones have fallen off the radar. In case an Agent stops heartbeating, the OMS will try to determine if the Agent or the machine is down, and update the status of the affected targets appropriately. The interval used for these signals is stored in the repository, and is set to 120 (seconds) by default.

This means that the throughput for these Agent signals can be defined as follows:

$$\frac{\text{\# Total Agents}}{120 \text{ seconds} \times \text{\# OMS Servers}} = \text{Minimal throughput per second required}$$

There is no specific metric to calculate the throughput per second for Agent heartbeats. But you can get the total number of Agents that are heartbeating per minute, and perform some basic statistical analysis with those numbers:

```
SELECT MIN(cnt) min_agent, MAX(cnt) max_agents,
       ROUND(AVG(cnt),2) avg_agents
FROM   (
       SELECT TRUNC(last_heartbeat_ts,'MI') heartbeat, COUNT(*) cnt
       FROM   mgmt_emd_ping
       WHERE  status = 1
       GROUP BY TRUNC(last_heartbeat_ts,'MI')
       )
```

In order to make sure that all Agents will be able to send their heartbeat signal to the OMS, only two things can be done:

■ **Increase the default ping interval** The default of 120 seconds can be increased in the repository on a per-Agent basis.

■ **Add another OMS server** In cases where the ping interval cannot be increased, the only other viable option is to add another Management Server to the infrastructure.

More information on how to tune the Agent heartbeating can be found in Chapter 6.

Job Handling

There will never be a problem with job dispatching during the initial rollout of Grid Control: EM Jobs are the result of administrators using and administering the discovered targets in EM. This means that during the ramp-up phase, with Grid Control getting rolled out across the enterprise, the minimal HA rollout of two Management Servers will be more than sufficient to get started.

It is only when everything is operational, and activities like the application of templates, patching and provisioning, and RMAN backups against databases, and so on, are getting scheduled that job processing will be a factor to look at in terms of processing power. For Grid Control job handling, there are two main process groups involved:

- **The Job Dispatcher**   There is only one Job Dispatcher per OMS. The function of the dispatcher is to check on a regular basis to see if there are steps (units of work for a job) that need to be dispatched to an Agent. If there is outstanding work, the Dispatcher will pick up the details, and give it to a Job Worker to have them send the information to the appropriate Agent.

- **The Job Workers**   These are threads running as part of the OMS that are waiting for work given to them by the Job Dispatcher. There are three types of job workers running on the Management Server:

  - **Short-running pool**   This pool is used for short-running commands. These are commands run synchronously: The Worker thread sends over the information, and it will wait until the Agent has completed the command and get the result immediately.

  - **Long-running pool**   All long-running commands that can potentially take a long time to complete are put in the long-running pool. These commands run asynchronously: The Job Worker will just send the info over and disconnect, and then let the Agent · come back as soon as the command completes.

  - **System pool**   The system pool is reserved for internal commands run by the infrastructure itself. This includes operations like removing or updating targets on the Agent side, blackout operations, metric and metric thresholds updates, and so on.

More details about the Grid Control job system can be found in Chapter 10.

To correctly size the job system and the number of Management Servers needed, a few things will have to be taken into consideration. The key performance metrics of the Job System are available from the Management Server And Repository target:

- **Size of the job backlog**
  Metric: Repository Job Dispatcher
  Column: Job Dispatcher Job Step Average Backlog
  SQL statement to get the current value of this metric:

```
SELECT value,
       TO_CHAR(collection_timestamp,'DD-MON-YYYY HH24:MI:SS') collected
FROM   mgmt$metric_current
WHERE  target_type   = 'oracle_emrep'
  AND  metric_name   = 'Repository_Job_Dispatcher'
  AND  metric_column = 'repository_job_backlog'
```

The backlog is defined as the number of steps (units of work) that are waiting to be delivered to the appropriate Agent. This is the first thing that will have to be verified: If there is no (continued) backlog, no action is needed. A temporary spike in backlog can be an indication that an administrator has just submitted a job (or a set of jobs) against a large number of targets. However, if the backlog continues, more investigation is needed to see what the bottleneck is.

- ■ **Job Dispatcher performance**
  Metric: Job Dispatcher Performance
  Column: Job Dispatcher Processing Time (% of Last Hour)
  SQL statement to get the current value for this metric:

```
SELECT  key_value, ROUND(value,2) value,
        TO_CHAR(collection_timestamp,'DD-MON-YYYY HH24:MI:SS') collected
FROM    mgmt$metric_current
WHERE   target_type   = 'oracle_emrep'
  AND   metric_name   = 'Job_Dispatcher_Performance'
  AND   metric_column = 'processing'
ORDER BY key_value
```

- ■ **Metric:** Job Dispatcher Performance
  Column: Steps Per Second
  SQL statement to get the current value for this metric:

```
SELECT  key_value, ROUND(value,2) value,
        TO_CHAR(collection_timestamp,'DD-MON-YYYY HH24:MI:SS') collected
FROM    mgmt$metric_current
WHERE   target_type   = 'oracle_emrep'
  AND   metric_name   = 'Job_Dispatcher_Performance'
  AND   metric_column = 'throughput'
ORDER BY key_value
```

The throughput of the dispatcher (steps per second), and the total time spent working (processing time) are the main indicators of the performance of the Job Dispatchers.

There is a clear indication of not enough available processing power if the job dispatcher is always busy more than 75 percent of the time (and getting close to that 100 percent mark). This is usually the sign that another OMS will be needed to get all the jobs dispatched in a timely fashion.

A low steps-per-second number is not necessarily a bad thing (it could be just the fact that there is very little job work to be done). But if the number is low, in combination with a continuous job backlog, the job dispatcher is not working at full capacity.

There are a few potential causes for this:

- ■ **Not enough job worker threads** The OMS is configured by default to use a set of default worker threads per type of job activity. However, if a particular job type has more jobs being submitted than the number of available threads on a regular basis, the number of worker threads might not be sufficient (more details on how to tune this in Chapter 6).

- ■ **Communication latency with the repository database** There is no single metric or data point that can be queried to get this value. But a high latency between the OMS and the repository database always leads to low performance and very slow operations, and not even limited to the job system. The AWR and ADDM reports of the repository database can highlight problems in this area, with high numbers for network waits.

■ **Network saturated** If the network is saturated, the information the OMS has to send to the Agents will take considerably more time. And during that communication exchange, the job worker threads will be marked as busy, and the Job Dispatcher will have to wait for the next available job worker thread. Use the networking statistics of the OMS host machine to see if there is a network bottleneck: Use the Network Interfaces metric and the collected data for this metric to verify the trends for the read, write, and total IO sizes.

More details on how to track and use the Grid Control job statistics can be found in Chapter 6.

Notification Handling

This section is just added for the sake of completeness. Any problem encountered for notifications is always a matter of tuning the notification delivery mechanisms, or changing the monitoring setup in case of a notification dispatching issue.

Notification handling can be broken down into two pieces:

■ **Notification dispatching** There should *never* be a bottleneck with notification dispatching. If there is one, the whole Grid Control environment is not configured correctly: Too many alerts are being generated and loaded into the system. Besides the impact this has on the XML loaders and the repository, it will drive the administrators and users crazy getting constantly woken up in the middle of the night to respond to alerts. The biggest impact to make when faced with a flood of alerts is to roll out a unified set of thresholds for the affected metrics, to reduce the number of incoming alerts. This set of thresholds can be grouped together into something called a *template* (see Chapter 9 for more details).

■ **Notification delivery** This is a little trickier. If a notification is getting delivered via e-mail, and the operation to send an e-mail takes 20 seconds, you can start to pile up notifications in case of a sudden spike in generated alerts. The times of the delivery will vary based on the type of notification (for example, e-mail versus the execution of an OS command). But the Management Server dispatching the notification can also be a factor: One OMS could potentially—for whatever reason—deliver e-mail notifications at a much slower pace than the other OMS servers.

To get an idea of how many milliseconds it takes to dispatch a single notification for a specific type of notification, use this SQL statement:

```
SELECT name, host_url,
       ROUND(AVG(duration/DECODE(value,0,1,value)),2) msec_per_notif
FROM   mgmt_system_performance_log
WHERE  job_name = 'EMD_NOTIFICATION.NotificationDelivery Subsystem'
  AND  is_total = 'Y'
  AND  name != 'RCA_TASKS'
GROUP BY name, host_url
ORDER BY name, host_url
```

More details on how to get the necessary performance data and the appropriate course of action can be found in Chapter 9.

How Big Does the Database Need to Be?

After having successfully deflected the OMS server question, this is always the follow-up question. And the answer to this one might cause eyebrows to be raised again: *It depends!* There is no magic formula to give, or any tricks to get a number representing the size of the repository. There are just too many variables, and too many environment-specific factors in play to come up with a simple way of calculating the database size. However, there are a couple of indicators that can be used to estimate the size of certain parts of the repository, and to give an idea of the magnitude of the database. For any kind of space calculation for the repository, the biggest factor will always be the metric data. This will be by far the biggest contributor to the size and growth of the repository. All the information the Agent is uploading needs to be stored. So naturally, the number of monitored targets will play a big role in determining the size of the repository database. But other aspects, like the number of jobs, number of administrators, amount of configuration history, and the number of alerts and violations in the system will also significantly influence the size of the repository.

Alerts and Errors

Errors and alerts are always a sore point, especially when presenting numbers in this area to upper management. But the reality is that errors and alerts (both policy and metric threshold violations) *will* happen. A big part of the reason for the existence of Grid Control is precisely to alert administrators about these violations, so they can be acted on before they become an operational problem.

Even with an error rate of 2 percent (which is reasonable), the total numbers will start to add up across the enterprise. With over a hundred metrics being collected for a single database, even an error rate of 2 percent for 1,000 monitored databases will result in 2,000 alerts and errors in the Grid Control system.

The only way to combat this problem is by watching the influx of alerts and errors, and responding to any notification send out by Grid Control:

- *Make sure the metric and policy thresholds are set appropriately.* Use templates to roll out the settings to all targets across the enterprise.

- *Resolve metric errors.* Any error reported means a failure to collect the data and also means that no validation will be done to see if there is a violation for this metric.

To give some idea of the size of an alert/violation: An alert, triggered by the Agent, that has gone through all the motions of getting reported, triggering a notification, and having the administrator write an annotation for this alert will take about 1.5KB in the repository. Using this rough number, an estimate of the total size of all alerts in Grid Control can be calculated as follows:

```
SELECT  ROUND((num_rows*1.5)/(1024*1024),2) size_gb
FROM    user_tables
WHERE   table_name='MGMT_VIOLATIONS'
```

Configuration History

All targets monitored by the Agent will upload configuration data (some more than others). That configuration data is stored in the repository in "snapshots" (configuration data for a given point in time), and the differences between the current and the previous snapshot are flagged.

Calculating or predicting the size of configuration data is very difficult, since there are big differences between the different types of targets regarding the amount of data getting uploaded.

A second problem is the number of recorded changes and updates: The more the configuration changes for a target, the more data will be recorded in the repository.

For production data-center targets, the configuration might not change that much, but for test and development systems, there will most likely be lots of updates and changes, resulting in a lot of snapshots, and a lot of flagged differences and updates.

In order to give some idea of the size of the configuration data, this *guesstimate* can be used: 500 KB per snapshot. This number was calculated using data from several repositories, and averaging out the size of all the snapshots in the repositories across all the monitored targets. It's a rough number, which might vary depending on the type of monitoring being done. But it will give a starting number and a rough estimate of how big the configuration piece can be. Using this number, the total size of the configuration history in Grid Control can be calculated as follows:

```
SELECT  ROUND((COUNT(*)*500)/(1024*1024),2) size_gb
FROM    mgmt_ecm_gen_snapshot
WHERE   is_current='Y'
```

Jobs

For jobs, calculating the size is just as difficult as with the configuration data. A simple job that executes merely an `ls` on a single target will be a *lot* smaller in size than a job submitted against a group of 2,000 databases, executing a series of steps to do something like an RMAN backup. Another aspect of the size of a job is the output a job sends back: Even a complicated job, run against thousands of targets, that returns a single line of output, can take up less space than a job that dumps every file on the file systems. Using the same guesstimate technique as with the configuration data, the following number can be used as a starting point to get the job size: 1 MB per job. Keep in mind, though, that this is just a *very rough number*, which will vary from site to site. The total size of all jobs in Grid Control can be estimated as follows:

```
SELECT  ROUND(num_rows/1024,2) size_gb
FROM    user_tables
WHERE   table_name='MGMT_JOBS'
```

Users

The user definition itself is negligible in size compared to any of the other pieces. But it's the work this administrator does in the Console that will cause the increase in size: Any groups, blackouts, templates, notification rules, and annotations this user makes will be stored in the repository. And all of these objects will use space and add to the size of the repository. Coming up with an estimated size for a user is not possible: There are too many links to the various subsystems of Grid Control to come up even with a guesstimate for this.

Size per Target Type

There is one aspect of the repository size that can be predicted (more or less): the metric data, meaning the data points collected for the all the monitored targets. Based on the table with the average record statistics loader per target type per day, we can build a new table, assuming the default retention periods for the rollup tables:

- RAW data points are kept for 7 days.
- HOUR data points are kept for 31 days.
- DAY data points are kept for 365 days.

| Target Type | Size / Day | | | Total Size (MB) |
	RAW	HOUR	DAY	
Agent	60KB	20KB	1KB	1.37MB
Oracle HTTP Server	600KB	450KB	20KB	24.85MB
ASM Instance	2MB	1MB	50KB	62.82MB
BC4J	12KB	3KB	0.1KB	0.21MB
Cluster	50KB	5KB	0.2KB	0.56MB
CSA Collector	15KB	1.5KB	0.1KB	0.18MB
Database Instance	4MB	500KB	25KB	52.05MB
Host	1.2MB	300KB	15KB	14.44MB
Application Server	120KB	100KB	5KB	5.63MB
Listener	40KB	6KB	0.2KB	0.53MB
Netapp Filer	1MB	1MB	50KB	55.82MB
OC4J	1MB	300KB	15KB	21.43MB
OC4J JVM	300KB	200KB	10KB	11.67MB
RAC Database	120KB	80KB	4KB	4.67MB
Webcache	60KB	40KB	2KB	2.33MB

TABLE 5-8.   *Calculating Target Data Increases in Database Size*

Once the repository is in a steady state (meaning more than one year old), the influx of data coming in will be nullified by the amount of data being purged. The amount of data for a target can then be calculated, based on an exercise demonstrated in Table 5-8.

GRID CONTROL WORKSHOP

Estimating Repository Size for Metrics

Workshop Notes

Let's reuse the setup from our previous workshop, "Calculating the Number of Servers for an Environment," with 2,000 server machines to monitor:

- Five hundred two-node RAC databases
- Five hundred two-node Oracle Application servers, each with the default home and an additional OC4J applications deployed

The question is: How much metric data will be present in the repository for these targets?

Using the table with the sizes per target type, we can break this down into the individual pieces:

2,000 Agents	× 1.37 MB	= 2.67 GB
2,000 Hosts	× 14.44 MB	= 28.20 GB
1,000 Cluster	× 0.56 MB	= 0.54 GB
500 RAC databases	× 4.67 MB	= 2.28 GB
1,000 Database instance	× 52.05 MB	= 50.83 GB
1,000 Database listeners	× 0.53 MB	= 0.51 GB
1,000 Application Servers	× 5.63 MB	= 5.49 GB
2,000 OC4J Applications	× 21.43 MB	= 41.85 GB
1,000 Oracle HTTP Servers	× 24.85 MB	= 24.26 GB
1,000 Webcache Servers	× 2.33 MB	= 2.27 GB
	Grand total	**= 158.90** GB

Installing and Deploying Grid Control: Common Mistakes

Now that we have installed our Grid Control infrastructure, hardened it for availability, made it foolproof, and sized it appropriately, we are almost ready to learn about maintaining it and then (of course!) using it to get a grip on our ecosystem management tasks. But first, let's spend a few minutes recapping our journey. To do that, we need to discuss again the most common mistakes and pitfalls that are encountered when rolling out EM Grid Control. An ounce of prevention is worth a pound of cure.

For a small environment these problems will typically not exist, since there will only be a handful of people working with Grid Control. Finding the culprit to chase a problem is not going to be difficult if only a handful of people have access to the application. For larger rollouts, however, especially those with data centers located around the globe, having a structure defining who can do what is an absolute must! The typical problems for the larger deployments are discussed next.

■ **No deployment plan for adding targets** If the Grid Control site is just going to have an open invitation for everyone to add his or her favorite machine to the infrastructure, not only will there be an explosion of new targets appearing in the Console, but it will also lead to trouble with the monitoring and the number of alerts coming in. And with no real tracking or auditing of who's adding which target in the Console, tracking down the right person to fix metric settings or resolve some problems on the box generating errors can be a very painful exercise.

■ **No user and privilege model** Usually, this anarchy of users and roles typically leads to a lot of users being granted the SUPER_USER privilege, just because it's easier to do than it is to specify every individual's privileges. Every security office and auditor is not going to like this approach.

■ **No standardized monitoring**   Making one-off changes to metric settings on all targets individually is a recipe for trouble. Since all targets will have different settings, with no standardization whatsoever, any kind of comparison between similar targets, or troubleshooting an outstanding issue will be a very difficult thing.

Summary: Best Practices

It's not all bad news. The Enterprise Administrator has tools available to help control the infrastructure, and keep track of who's adding what to Grid Control (and more importantly, *when*). So, if you are avoiding the common mistakes, it's also time to internalize the best practices for success.

■ **Have the full self-monitoring rolled out**   It starts with having all the Management Servers discovered, and installing Agents on all the machines running the repository database. But it goes further than that: The system and service created specifically for EM can be a huge benefit for an Enterprise Administrator to get a high-level overview of what's going on with the application. All these components can be grouped together into a System target, representing the EM infrastructure. Keep this system and service up to date, and make any changes to it as soon as the infrastructure changes (like a new OMS, or an additional RAC instance for the repository database). More details about Groups, Systems, and Services can be found in Chapter 13.

■ **Restrict access to Grid Control**   The number of users logging in to the Console is only one aspect of this. Avoid group accounts, since the passwords of those group accounts (I refer to them sometimes as anonymous users) have a tendency to become public knowledge. And with more random people accessing the site, the more potential harm can be done. The second part of this is equally important: Use a registration password, preferably with an expiration date, to restrict the adding of Agents to Grid Control: Prevent random agents from getting discovered in the infrastructure. As soon as an Agent is discovered, it becomes part of the monitoring and administration infrastructure. But that also means it can upload alerts, errors, metric data, and so on. And more data means more load on the application.

■ **Have accountability**   Define users and roles for everyone who has to access the Console. Group the privileges in groups aligned with the business units or business groups accessing Grid Control. Enable auditing whenever possible to get a history of all the actions performed in Grid Control.

■ **Define groups, systems, and services**   "Monitor many as one" is a mantra the Helpdesk and system operators will like very much. Define systems and services for all major applications and services in the enterprise. If the enterprise is complex enough, roles can be created specifically for these applications to have even more fine-grained access control defined.

■ **Use templates for monitoring**   Once the targets are all discovered, and the groups, systems, and services have been defined, create templates with standardized monitoring settings that can be used to roll out to all targets in the enterprise. Consistency is the key here: Standardize the metric settings, with only those thresholds defined on metrics that people need to be alerted on.

That's it, that's the stuff you need. We will be discussing these topics in some depth later in the book, so keep reading! You are well on your way to a successful implementation!

CHAPTER

6

Maintaining and Managing the EMGC Infrastructure

hings change. They always change. That's the one constant you can count on. And a data center is no exception to this rule. Whether it's because of resource restrictions, increased capacity, or a new company direction, new machines will come in, old machines will be removed, and existing machines will be upgraded.

All these changes mean work for the system administrators. Some of it can be done in Grid Control itself. Other things will be done directly on the machines involved, and the changes will be recorded in Grid Control. There is always something changing somewhere out there...

Monitor the Monitor

The most useful feature an Enterprise Administrator has to keep an eye on Enterprise Manager is the self-monitoring: The Monitor The Monitor (MTM) functionality. It is composed out of a series of UI pages, and a set of data-points designed to help administrators determine the health and performance of Enterprise Manager.

The OMS and Repository Target

Every Grid Control installation has one target (and only one) defined, called "Management Services and Repository." This target represents the complete Grid Control infrastructure, and forms an essential part of the self-monitoring framework. The target is installed and configured by default on the first OMS installed. The monitoring user defined for it is always the SYSMAN user (and this cannot be changed to another account). All the self-monitoring metrics and data points gathered are dependent on this target being defined properly, and working properly. This makes the target a vital part of the Grid Control architecture, and a target that should be closely watched by all administrators at all times.

Initial Target Definition

The repository target is created during the install and setup of the first OMS in the infrastructure. The Agent installed with the first OMS will have a target of the type `oracle_emrep` defined, using the information specified during the install as the monitoring information. To see which agent is monitoring the target, and how it is configured, go to the Management Services and Repository page from the Setup pages. There, the Agent responsible for the target will be shown in the Overview page, and the related links at the bottom include a link to see and change the monitoring setup of this target.

The information can also be queried from the views in the repository:

```
SELECT target_name, host_name, timezone_region
FROM   mgmt$target
WHERE  target_type = 'oracle_emrep'
```

And to get the monitoring properties of this target, use this SQL statement:

```
SELECT property_name, property_value
FROM   mgmt$target_properties
WHERE  target_type = 'oracle_emrep'
```

The monitoring of this target happens in two places: The Agent collects just two metrics for this target. All the rest of the metrics are collected and evaluated directly in the database. For the Agent-side monitoring, the most important one is the availability of the repository (which should be interpreted as "Can the repository be reached by the Application?"). The other is the status of the notification system. The reason both these metrics are evaluated at the Agent side is to give the Agent the ability to send an Out-Of-Band notification: If the Management Server is down, or the notification system is not working, Grid Control cannot send the notification to alert the administrators of this condition, and therefore an external mechanism must be used to send the alert. Since the Agent can use a Response Action without any intervention from the OMS, these two metrics can use that mechanism for alerts for those metrics. All the other metrics for this target are collected and evaluated directly in the repository, without any involvement of an Agent or an OMS, and stored directly in the necessary metric data table.

Checking the Repository Target

The validation of this target should always start with the Agent:

- The Agent monitors the availability state of the target. This means not only that the Agent has to be up and running, but it also must be able to connect to the repository database, to get the necessary data from the tables to determine the state of Grid Control.

- Once the Agent has established a connection to the repository, it will execute a query to see if any the Management Servers are running. This is done by checking the heartbeats the OMS machines insert into the repository: If no recent heartbeat is detected, the Agent will mark the Grid Control application as down.

TIP
If the Management Services and Repository pages show the Grid Control application to be down (which is a contradiction, since a user is logged in to the application and looking at the Grid Control data), it is always an indication that there is a problem on the Agent with the monitoring of this target. This could be the fact that the Agent is down, the monitoring properties are not correct (like an invalid password), or a problem occurred while executing the SQL to get the current state of the Management Servers (which will be logged in the emagent.trc *file).*

Besides the Agent-side metrics, the repository is also calculating and evaluating a set of metrics on behalf of this target. This DBMS_JOB Repository Metrics is responsible for evaluating these metrics. If that job is not running, or has a backlog (more about that later in this chapter), the other metrics for the oracle_emrep will be affected as well.

Management Server Metrics

Most of the Management Server metrics are metrics calculated in the repository itself and by the Repository Metrics job. The list of all available metrics can be found by using the All Metrics link in the related links section on every Management Server and Repository page:

- **Active Agents**   Upload status of the Agent. If the Agent is not uploading any data, there is a communication problem between the Agent and OMS that needs to be investigated.

- **Active Loader Status**   Vital XML loader statistics, gathered for each loader per OMS server7.

- ■ **Active Management Servlets**   More loader statistics, but rolled up to the infrastructure level.

- ■ **Agent Status**   Number of restarts per Agent. If the Agent is getting restarted too frequently, either an administrator is doing some very naughty things, or the Agent process is having a problem.

- ■ **Configuration**   Basic Grid Control numbers, concerning the number of users, number of targets, and so on.

- ■ **DBMS Job Status**   Status of the internal housekeeping jobs running in the repository.

- ■ **Duplicate Targets**   Number of targets with the same name, discovered on Agents. Only the first one will be allowed into the system. All the other ones will be marked as duplicates.

- ■ **Job Dispatcher Performance**   Performance of the Grid Control job system.

- ■ **Notification Method Performance**   Throughput of the outgoing notification. This measures the throughput (in absolute numbers) and time it takes to deliver an email, run OS commands, and so on.

- ■ **Notification Performance**   Overall notification system performance.

- ■ **Notification Status**   Status of the notification system. This is an external metric, evaluated on the Agent monitoring the OMS and Repository target.

- ■ **Repository Collections Performance**   Statistics about the internal repository metrics the system is executing.

- ■ **Repository Job Dispatcher**   Job system backlog indicator.

- ■ **Repository Sessions**   Number of SYSMAN connections made to the repository by the OMS servers.

- ■ **Response**   Overall status of the OMS(s) and repository. External metric, calculated by the Agent monitoring the OMS and Repository metric.

What Is MTM?

MTM (short for Monitor The Monitor) is a framework built into Grid Control that monitors Grid Control itself. It collects statistics from the various subsystems and keeps track of backlogs accumulated in the various parts of the infrastructure. For an Enterprise Administrator, this is the first stop in the Console for any kind of debugging effort done on the infrastructure. There are four main UI pages defined for this. To get to these pages, go to the Setup pages and click the Management Services and Repository subtab. Each of these pages deserves a little bit more of an explanation.

Overview

The overview page has the basic data points from the Monitor The Monitor system available. This includes the main statistics of the infrastructure, like the number of Management Servers, number of Agents, deleted targets, administrators, and so on. The page has been divided into several sections, to group the data together:

- ■ **General section**   This contains the general information about the availability of the Grid Control, and the Agent monitoring the repository target. *New in 10.2.0.5:* Part of the general overview is the ability to specify a Console URL. This URL will be used in email notifications to point to the web link administrators can use to access the Grid Control site.

This way, any SLB configuration (including a port override) can be specified in the emails instead of the URL to the Management Server that is delivering the email notification.

- **Overview section**   This has the links to all the main pages for the infrastructure: the list of Agents, all the targets in a Pending Delete state, the list of administrators, and so on.

- **Repository Details section**   This contains some details about the repository. A very important thing to point out here is the fact that there *should* be a link to the repository database target in this section. If no link is present, it means no Agent was installed on the repository database box (or the Agent does not have the repository discovered as a target to monitor), and nothing inside Grid Control is monitoring the repository database. Without the database present as a monitored entity, there is no way to drill down into the database for the reported issues from the either the Application Server or from the self-monitoring framework.

- **Job Activity section**   The section displays the basic statistics from the job system, including the backlog and the throughput (performance) of the job system.

- **Alerts section**   All outstanding alerts for the Management Servers, the repository target itself, and the alerts on the OMS machines and the machines the repository is running on will be displayed in this section.

- **Audit section**   This section was added in 10.2.0.5, to show the status of the Auditing framework, and give a link to the audit log page, to search for specific audited events.

- **Backlog bar charts**   The right side of the page shows the backlog of the loader and the notification system in a bar chart. Any continuously rising trend visible in the line charts is a cause for alarm.

Repository Operations

All the internal housekeeping Grid Control does directly in the repository is controlled via DBMS_JOBS in the database. These do not require any interaction with the OMS servers, and can function on their own, without any intervention with the rest of the framework. For each of these internal housekeeping jobs, the following information is available:

- **Status**   The most obvious thing to point out is to make sure the jobs are running, and processing the data successfully.

- **Last Error**   If an error was encountered during the processing of the job, the timestamp of the last error will be listed here. The timestamp of the last error links to the Error page, to allow searches on the errors encountered in the system.

- **Throughput**   Measured in number of records per second. Throughput is a valuable piece of information, but unfortunately it can be quite deceiving. With throughput, people typically associate high numbers, the higher the better. In the case of this metric, though, a value of 0.00 does not necessarily mean a problem. The throughput numbers for the jobs are calculated every 10 minutes by default. But some of these jobs run only once per day (like the Purge and Maintenance jobs), and will, therefore, not generate any throughput numbers most of the time. Hence the 0.00 throughput number, which is *not* a problem in this case. For some of the other jobs, like Compute Metric Baseline Statistics or Set Adaptive Metric Thresholds, low numbers can simply mean that there is not a lot of baselining going on, and the jobs have therefore very little work to do, generating low throughput numbers. This leaves us with just a few jobs left that need to be looked at more closely:

Agent Ping	The job that keeps track of the health of the host machines in Grid Control. Any Agent that is failing to heartbeat will be put on the suspect list, to be investigated by the OMS. A nonzero number for this job means that there are machines that are suspected to be down. Although the goal of this number will be to keep this at zero all the time, realistically speaking in a production environment, there will also be a small number of machines that are taken offline, undergoing maintenance, or are having a problem. As long as the number is low compared to the total number of machines in the discovered enterprise, there is no immediate threat to the health of the system.
Notification Check	Number of violations coming into the system that require filtering for notification delivery. The higher this number is, the more violations are coming in. The goal is to keep this number as low as possible.
Repository Metrics	It's tricky to predict a good number here for throughput, since the work the repository metrics are doing depends heavily on the number of discovered targets, and the number of aggregate metrics defined on the systems and services. The key here is to keep this number in the same range: Spikes in the numbers (going all of a sudden from 10 to 50 or higher for instance) usually mean there is an unusual occurrence happening in the system, generating more work (like lots of outages on servers, or lots of violations for web application transactions, and so on).
Rollup	This will have a number that will increase every time new targets are added to the system. The more targets in the system, the more data the Agents will be uploading, and the more rows the rollup job will have to roll up on a regular basis. There should be no spikes in the number reported for this job, as the number of rows per hour should always be roughly the same. If there are spikes reported for this number, there are Agents that have piled up data and are uploading the metric data in bursts. If the spikes continue, this could be an indication of communication problems between the Agents and the OMS.

■ **Processing time**   Time per hour (in percentages) this job is working. This is a very useful parameter to keep track of. For obvious reasons, this value should never get to 100 percent. It should not even get close to 100 percent. The number can give you the first indication of a resource problem in the database. If a job is consistently running for more than 75 percent, the infrastructure is at risk: Since there is very little headroom left, the slightest spike in work can cause the system to get into a state where it cannot keep up with the amount of work coming in, creating a permanent backlog problem that will only grow over time.

BEST PRACTICE
As a rule of thumb, use these guidelines for this number:

- *If the number is consistently more than 50 percent, you should worry, and start looking at the database performance to see what can be tweaked or changed to improve the throughput in the database.*

- *If the number is consistently more than 75 percent, the word "panic" will be more appropriate. Then it's time to start scheduling an increase of capacity for the database, by adding a RAC node, increasing the SGA, or making any other modification to the database as advised by the database performance reports (ADDM, ASH, or AWR).*

- **Scheduling information** These two timestamps can, together with the status of the job, give some clue as to when and how these jobs are scheduled. If there is no next or last scheduled time listed, the job is not submitted in the database, and it will need to be resubmitted. If the next scheduled time is set for the year 4000 (the way the database says: *I've stopped scheduling this job*), you will know there is a problem with this job.

Let's look at the list of DBMS_JOBS used by Grid Control. Each of these should be present (and getting scheduled and run) all the time in the repository:

- **Agent Ping** Heartbeat verification, to make sure all Agents are communicating properly with the OMS. Job frequency: Every 30 seconds

- **Beacon Availability Computation** Calculation of web application availability based on all the beacon data. Job frequency: Every minute

- **Clear Expired Suppressions** New job introduced in 10.2.0.5. This job is responsible for removing and re-evaluating any stale suppressed policy violations specified by users. Job frequency: Every day, one minute after midnight

- **Composite Target Availability Computation** Calculation of the availability for all composite targets. Job frequency: 1 minute

- **Compute Metric Baseline Statistics** Calculates the statistical numbers for the base metrics, to be used to set the statistical metric baselines for the metric. Job frequency: Every day, a half hour before midnight

- **EM Audit Externalization Service** New job introduced in 10.2.0.5. This job will write the audit data if enabled for the external files specified in the audit setup. If no external files have been defined for the audit data, this job will perform no action. Job frequency: Every day

- **Job Purge** Remove all finished job runs (both succeeded and failed) older than the specified retention times. More information about the job purge retention times can be found later in this chapter in the sections "Data Purging" and "Data Rollup." Job frequency: Every day

- **Maintenance (Analysis)** Daily maintenance of the repository. This includes gathering statistics on tables with stale Cost-Based Optimizer (CBO) statistics and rebuilding indexes for some of the highly fragmented indexes. Job frequency: Every day, at 3:10 A.M.

- **Notification Check** Check all new severities, and filter out the ones that need to be pushed to the notification system. Job frequency: Every 30 seconds

■ **Purge Policies**   Purge old data in the repository based on the retention times. This includes metric data, alert and violation data, configuration data, and error information. More information about the purge policies is also available later in this chapter in the sections "Data Purging" and "Data Rollup." Job frequency: Every day at midnight

■ **Repository Metrics**   Collection and evaluation of repository-side metrics. This includes the MTM metrics and the aggregate metrics specified for the systems and services. There are two types of metrics in this category:

   ■ **Short-running metrics**   Metrics that can be obtained by running a straightforward query.

   ■ **Long-running metrics**   This category of metrics takes a longer time to evaluate and collect. This can be evaluating a larger set of data, or querying various data points before returning the rollup or aggregate data point.

   Starting from 10.2.0.5, this job is broken up into two separate jobs: *Repository Metrics 1* (short-running jobs) and *Repository Metrics 2* (long-running jobs). Job frequency: Every minute

■ **Rollup**   Hourly and daily rollup of the metric data collected by the Agent and by the Repository Metrics job. Job frequency: Every hour

■ **Root Cause Analysis Purge**   New job introduced in 10.2.0.5. This job removes all stale RCA data in the repository. Job frequency: Every day

■ **Set Adaptive Metric Thresholds**   Updates the thresholds for the metric using baselines, based on the generated statistics. Job frequency: Every hour, on the hour

■ **Web Application End-User Data Rollup**   Rollup of the Webcache page performance data (Chronos). Job frequency: Every hour

■ **Web Application OC4J Data Rollup**   Rollup of the end-to-end performance numbers for OC4J applications. Job frequency: Every hour

There are two PL/SQL API calls available to stop and restart the DBMS_JOBS in the repository. For those who have already patched an OMS server, these commands will look very familiar. The only downside is that these routines have an all-or-nothing approach: There is no way to specify stopping or restarting a single job.

■ Stopping the Grid Control–specific DBMS_JOBS:

```
exec emd_maintenance.remove_em_dbms_jobs;
COMMIT;
```

■ Starting the Grid Control–specific DBMS_JOBS:

```
exec emd_maintenance.submit_em_dbms_jobs;
COMMIT;
```

Management Services

This page has the list of all known management servers of the infrastructure. For each active OMS server, the availability and the basic loader stats are displayed.

NOTE
The name used on this page is the value from the emoms
.properties *file of the parameter* oracle.sysman.emSDK.svlt
.ConsoleServerName *of each of the OMS servers. Even if an SLB
is used to virtualize the Management Servers, the name of the OMS
should be kept as it was initially configured, to have it show up on
this page using the real name of the OMS.*

If an OMS server is not available, the administrator has the option to remove this server from the list on this UI page. Use this feature if an OMS server has been decommissioned.

Errors

If one of the subsystems of a Management Server or a repository job encounters an error during the processing of data, an error will be logged in the system error log. The errors are cataloged by module and error level. If there was an Agent involved with the operation, the Agent will be referenced as well. Basic searching capabilities allow an administrator to filter out specific messages by module, by Agent, or by error text. As with the other log and trace files, the most important things to look for are repeating error messages: These are the operations that need to be verified, to fix the underlying issue to resolve the problem.

NOTE
*The system errors are not being archived or purged by Grid Control.
The administrators are responsible for cleaning up the errors and
removing any errors that are either resolved or no longer relevant.*

Errors can be generated for one of the following components (modules):

- **Agent Heartbeat Recorder** Module responsible for updating the heartbeat timestamps the Agent is sending to the OMS servers.
- **Agent Ping** The module verifying the state of an Agent if it is not heartbeating any more.
- **Beacon Availability Computation** Repository-side calculation of the web application availability, based on the values of all the beacons.
- **Beacon Transactions** Manipulation of the beacon test data, including the setup and maintenance of the beacon tests, and evaluation of the data the beacons have provided.
- **Blackouts** Blackout subsystem. All repository-side administration tasks performed on blackouts.
- **Compute Metric Baseline Statistics** Calculation of the statistical data needed for metric baselines.
- **End-To-End Trace Rollup** The rollup of the Application Server end-to-end metric data.
- **End User Performance Rollup** Rollup of the end-user data Webcache data (Chronos).
- **General Maintenance** Daily maintenance module. This job performs vital housekeeping operations in the repository, like gathering stale statistics, checking the fragmentation of the indexes, and performing maintenance tasks on the partitioned metric tables.
- **Jobs** All operations performed by the Job Dispatcher and the Job Scheduler.

- ■ **Loader** All operations related to the loading of the metadata, state information, and metric data provided by the Agents.
- ■ **Maintenance (Analysis)** Repository maintenance module. A subset of the General Maintenance tasks, specifically for the part of gathering the stale statistics and checking the health of the indexes.
- ■ **Management System Metrics** The evaluation of the Management Server metrics. This is a specific subset of the Repository Metrics module.
- ■ **Notification Check** Notification verification module. This module validates each incoming alert, and determines if this alert needs to be dispatched to an administrator.
- ■ **Notification Delivery** Notification delivery subsystem.
- ■ **Purge** Metric data purge module.
- ■ **Purge Policies** Data purge subsystem.
- ■ **Repository Metrics** Repository-based metric calculation module.
- ■ **Severity Evaluation Sub System** The verification of the repository-side metric data, to see which data point violated the defined thresholds.
- ■ **Severity Sub System** Processing of the incoming alerts uploaded by the Agents and the repository evaluation subsystem.
- ■ **Target** Target manipulation (discovery and monitoring configuration).

Administration Pages

Besides the main MTM pages, there are a couple of other pages available in the Console that can be quite useful to the Enterprise Administrator.

Discovered Agents The source of all information is the Agents that are registered in Grid Control. The list of all available Agents is available as a special page in the Console. It shows the availability and the basic statistics of each Agent. The page is available as a subtab from the main Setup page:

```
https://<hostname>:<port>/em/console/admin/rep/emdList
```

A second page is added in 10.2.0.5 for the Agent monitoring, available in the Console as another tab from the Agent page.

```
https://<hostname>:<port>/em/console/admin/rep/emdBadAgents
```

Any Agent that is trying to upload to the infrastructure that does not have a valid SSL wallet, or is not able to communicate correctly on the Agent side, will be marked as misconfigured.

Some misconfigurations (like SSL errors) are fatal, and will make the OMS mark the Agent as blocked immediately.

Other minor errors will simply be logged, and displayed on the same Agent monitoring page. An Enterprise Administrator can look at these warnings, and decide to manually block an Agent if needed.

When an Agent is added on the blocked list, no further communication from this Agent is accepted by the OMS, and an Enterprise Administrator will have to make a manual intervention to resolve the communication problem, and then unblock the Agent from this page.

Unconfigured Targets   Every target that does not have a complete set of monitoring properties, or has errors while trying to get the runtime properties for the target, will be listed on this page. The message column will actually clarify the exact issue with the target listed. In an ideal situation, no targets should be in an unconfigured state: Every configuration problem needs to be fixed in order to have proper monitoring for this target.

This page is available from the Agent overview page, as well as the All Targets page, only if there are unconfigured targets in the repository.

```
https://<hostname>:<port>/em/console/admin/rep/emdConfig/targetUnconfig
```

A target can be marked as unconfigured for any of the following reasons:

- **Incomplete monitoring configuration**   If the monitoring properties are either incomplete (missing a vital piece of information like the ORACLE_HOME), or wrong (incorrect password), the target will be marked with the message "Missing Properties." To resolve these kinds of issues, use the Monitoring Configuration link on the home page of the target to update and correct the properties.

- **Timeouts encountered by the Agent**   If the Agent cannot evaluate and verify the properties of the target in time, the target will be marked with the message "Compute dynamic property takes too long." The timeouts can be controlled on the Agent side by editing the emd.properties file. (This is covered in Chapter 4.)

- **Property computation errors**   If the Agent encounters an error during the computation or validation of a target property, the target will be marked with the message "Get dynamic property error" or "Dynamic Category property error" based on the type of property that threw the error. All property errors should be treated as metric failures on the Agent side, and have to be investigated as such. Details on how to debug these kinds of issues, and the steps on what to do are outlined in Chapter 18.

- **Target removed from the Agent**   A target can only be discovered in the Console from an Agent if there is an entry in the targets.xml file of the Agent that got uploaded to the repository. However, if the target entry is removed from that file after the target has been uploaded, the repository will know of the existence of a target the Agent is no longer monitoring. All targets in this condition will be marked with the message "Target deleted from agent." This can happen in case of a crash (incomplete) recovery, or when an administrator made an error and either copied a bad file or manually edited the file in a bad way. There are only two possible ways to resolve this:

  - Remove the target from the repository if it is no longer valid. This can be done in the Console.

  - Restore the correct copy of the targets.xml file, or add the deleted target back into the targets.xml file.

To list all broken targets, with the reason why they are marked as broken, this query can be run in the repository:

```
SELECT host_name, target_name, target_type, broken_str
FROM   mgmt_targets
WHERE  broken_reason > 0
```

Duplicate Targets   Duplicate target names are not allowed in Grid Control. A target will be flagged as a duplicate as soon as a second Agent tries to upload target metadata for a target that already exists with that same name in the repository.

When a duplicate is detected, the Administrator has two choices:

- Either remove the target from the second Agent.

- Or remove the target from the first Agent, and move the monitoring of this target to the second Agent.

These options are available from the Duplicate Targets page, which is available from the Overview MTM page. The link to this page will only be visible if there are duplicate targets present in the repository.

```
https://<hostname>:<port>/em/console/health/healthDupTarget
```

BEST PRACTICE
Keep a consistent naming strategy for all targets in Grid Control, both in naming convention, as well as the case used to identify the target. Having a strict naming convention makes it easier to detect anomalies and misconfigured targets. It also makes it easier to automate certain tasks through EMCLI.

NOTE
Target names are case-sensitive in Grid Control. Although two targets like ORCL.WORLD and orcl.world might both be considered the same for a DBA, in Grid Control, these are two distinct targets.

Pending Delete Targets   Just as targets can be added to Grid Control, decommissioned or obsolete targets will have to be removed from Grid Control. Targets can only be removed from either the Agent home page, or from the pages from the Target tab. When a target is removed, it first goes into a Pending Delete state (logical removal). For every target delete operation, an internal EM job is launched, which performs two distinct steps:

- The first step is to contact the Agent to remove the target from its list of monitored targets.

- When that operation is finished, the job will remove all traces of this target from the repository tables.

As long as the internal job is still running and finishing the two steps, the target will be listed on the UI page with an empty "Time delete completed" time. If a target needs to be deleted right away, the Force Delete option can be used on a selected target, to run a cleanup of that target then and there (this might still take a minute or two to complete).

This page is available from the main MTM page, only if there are targets still in a pending delete state.

 `https://<hostname>:<port>/em/console/health/healthDeletedTargets`

Broken Corrective Actions   A corrective action (CA) in a broken state will not be used if a violation comes that has this CA defined for it. This can result in alerts being left in an unattended state. This list of all broken CAs is available from the All Targets page, only if there are broken ones in the repository.

```
https://<hostname>:<port>/em/console/jobs/fixCA
```

The Reason column on the page will give details about the exact issue with the CA.
A Corrective Action can be broken for three reasons:

- **Reassign of the CA after a user was removed**   When an administrator is removed from Grid Control, part of the remove operation is to reassign the jobs and corrective actions this user owns to another user. Any corrective action reassigned to the new user will be marked as broken, to let the new administrator verify and if necessary adjust the CA.

- **Credential problem**   If the credentials specified for the CA (or the preferred credentials if nothing was specified during the creation of the CA) are wrong and cannot be used, it will be marked as broken.

- **Privilege problem after a reassign**   The new user who got the CA assigned to him or her has to have at least operator privileges on the target for the CA to work properly. If the new user lacks the necessary privileges, the CA will be marked as broken.

Machines with Missing Configuration Data   Configuration data is more than just some parameter values for a target. It contains vital information about the setup and configuration of any of the monitored targets, providing information like software version, parameter settings, configuration files used, and so on. It is needed to do any kind of asset management. It's also the source for all Oracle software inventories, and is vital for patching and provisioning Oracle software.
The Collection Problems link can be used from either the Grid Control home page or from the main Deployments page:

```
https://<hostname>:<port>/em/console/ecm/track/missingConfig
```

After you have navigated to the Configuration Collection Problem page, there are two subtabs available to list the two types of problems:

- **Missing Configuration Information**   Each host discovered in Grid Control will run a configuration metric called Inventory once a day. This metric collects the hardware statistics, the OS software information (including installed patches), and the Oracle Software Inventory details. This information is uploaded to the repository in the repository, to make all this configuration information available to all the Grid Control features. If specific pieces of the collection are incomplete, or the Inventory metric encounters an error while collecting the information, the collection problem will be recorded on this page.

- **Software targets without Inventory**   This page will contain a specific subset of targets with missing configuration information. It will only contain Oracle Software targets that do not have any inventory information registered in the repository. For each of these targets, the patching and provisioning framework will not be able available. Every unique host associated with all of the targets listed on this page will have an entry on the Missing Configuration Information page with the details about the inventory failure.

Resolving errors and problems with the configuration collection needs to be handled like any other metric error: Check the agent trace files for the exact error condition. The specifics on how to debug metric issues are explained in Chapter 18.

Health-Checks

Like any other application, Grid Control will need a spot-check or a health-check on a regular basis, to make sure everything is still running smoothly. Many people simply assume that because Grid Control is making administration of applications and machines easier, the infrastructure itself therefore does not require any administration or checkup. Nothing is further from the truth. As far as maintenance and follow-up are concerned, Grid Control is just another application, running on several server machines, and requires the same kind of attention you give any other application.

Backlog Indicators

The main thing to keep an eye on is the throughput of the data in Grid Control, and to make sure nothing is getting piled up. These pile-ups can occur in two different places:

- **Things getting in**   The main backlog can occur here for the XML files the Agents are sending over. If the metric data is not getting loaded in a timely fashion, the data in the Console will be stale, and can pose problems debugging issues in real time. A second more hidden backlog indicator is for the repository-side metrics being calculated. This includes all rollup metrics for Groups, Systems and Services, as well the metrics for the management infrastructure itself (MTM).

- **Things going out**   Several things are going out of Grid Control:

    - **Notifications for alerts and violations**   Administrators have to be alerted about the threshold violations on the managed targets.

    - **Jobs defined by administrators**   Scheduled work needs to run on the managed targets in a timely fashion. A backup job scheduled to run at midnight should not be delayed till 8 A.M., when people are getting back into the office.

These backlog indicators are all available in the Console, but they are not brought together in one single location. A workshop later in this chapter will fix that, with a practical example of how to query the repository to get the actual backlog values. The four main backlog indicators are

- **Loader backlog**   Available on the overview page of the MTM page (chart top right) The metric column Files Pending Load for the metric Active Management Servlets is defined for the loader backlog. It reports the number of files in backlog per OMS.

- **Job backlog**   Available as a link on the Overview MTM page. The link drills down to the metric details of the metric Repository Job Dispatcher for the column Job Dispatcher Job Step Average Backlog.

- **Notification backlog**   Available on the overview page of the MTM page (chart bottom right). The backlog is defined per notification subsystem. The metric Notification Method Performance with the column Notifications Waiting will show the backlog for each notification method type.

The listed notification types will be:

EMAIL   All e-mail notifications

JAVA   All Java-based notifications (used by the connector framework)

OSCMD   All OS command notifications

PLSQL   All PL/SQL-based notifications

SNMP   All SNMP traps to be sent

TICKET   All notifications for the helpdesk connectors (Remedy, PeopleSoft CRM, and so on)

■ **Repository Metric backlog**   Only available from the All Metrics page from the related links section of any of the Management Services and Repository pages. Look for the Collections Waiting To Run column of the Repository Collections Performance metric.

BEST PRACTICE
All of these metrics are critical to the health of Grid Control. Each Enterprise Administrator should be notified of any threshold violation for any of the backlog metrics.

Repository Operations: DBMS_JOBS

As already mentioned previously in this chapter, the DBMS_JOBS running in the database are a vital part of the infrastructure. They perform key internal housekeeping tasks that need to be run on a regular basis in order to keep the system healthy. These jobs need to be monitored, and their status and throughput are critical metrics an Enterprise Administrator needs to be alerted on.

The metric DBMS Job Status is evaluated if the OMS and Repository target is operational in Grid Control. It has the following columns:

■ **DBMS Job Invalid Schedule**   A validation of the scheduled time and interval the database uses for the job. If the schedule is invalid (like the year 4000, meaning "stopped scheduling" in Oracle RDBMS-speak), the value for this metric column will show INVALID. Here's a SQL example to check for invalid schedules:

```
SELECT key_value job_name
FROM   mgmt$metric_current
WHERE  target_type  = 'oracle_emrep'
  AND  metric_label = 'DBMS Job Status'
  AND  column_label = 'DBMS Job Invalid Schedule'
  AND  value        != 'OK'
```

■ **DBMS Job Processing Time (% of Last Hour)**   Time spent per hour running the DBMS_JOB. If the value gets above 50 percent, administrators will need to investigate the performance and throughput of the database and this routine. If the value gets above 75 percent, there is very little headroom left for spikes and sudden changes in the environment. If this value continues to be above 75 percent, more database capacity will be needed to run the job. All Enterprise Administrators should be alerted on the warning and critical levels of this metric. The following SQL example checks for +75 percent usage jobs in the last day:

```
SELECT  key_value job_name,
        TO_CHAR(rollup_timestamp,'DD-MON-YYYY HH24:MI:SS') collected,
        ROUND(average,2) average
FROM    mgmt$metric_hourly
WHERE   target_type  = 'oracle_emrep'
  AND   metric_label = 'DBMS Job Status'
  AND   column_label = 'DBMS Job Processing Time (% of Last Hour)'
  AND   average         > 75
  AND   rollup_timestamp > SYSDATE-1
ORDER BY key_value, rollup_timestamp DESC
```

■ **DBMS Job UpDown**   This will flag the job if it's broken, or has failed, or is not running on schedule. If the execution of the job takes longer than the schedule interval, work might not be processed in a timely fashion. This is another metric all the Enterprise Administrators should be notified on. Here's a SQL example to look for all down jobs:

```
SELECT  key_value
FROM    mgmt$metric_current
WHERE   target_type  = 'oracle_emrep'
  AND   metric_label = 'DBMS Job Status'
  AND   column_label = 'DBMS Job UpDown'
  AND   value        != 'UP'
```

■ **Throughput Per Second**   Number of records processed per second. By itself, this is not too useful. This number should always be looked at in the context of the function it is providing. Also, the trending of this number over time can give some evidence of how much more work is coming in, and how much the infrastructure has grown. Use this SQL example to look for the current throughput of the Rollup job:

```
SELECT  ROUND(value,2) current_value
FROM    mgmt$metric_current
WHERE   target_type  = 'oracle_emrep'
  AND   metric_label = 'DBMS Job Status'
  AND   column_label = 'Throughput Per Second'
  AND   key_value    = 'Rollup'
```

The EMOMS Log and Trace Files

The Management Server writes all its messages to two files: the emoms.log and emoms.trc file:

■ Regardless of the type of debugging parameters specified for the OMS (more about those in Chapter 18), the emoms.log file will always contain the English version of only the error and warning messages logged by the OMS.

■ The emoms.trc file, however, will contain all the messages as defined by the logging properties (again, Chapter 18 will go into more detail on the whats, hows, and wheres of this).

The main thing to look for in the log and trace files is repeating error messages: If an error just keeps on repeating, there is a consistent problem, which will not go away unless its cause is fixed.

GRID CONTROL WORKSHOP

Report for All the Backlog Indicators

Knowing which pieces to keep an eye on is already the first step toward better monitoring of any application. But in order to really track these backlog numbers, they should all be put together in one place so we can get an overview of what's happening inside Grid Control. And although there is no single Console UI page that shows all these types of information, we can, however, create our own report, and put all this data on one single page.

This will already demonstrate a little bit about the power and flexibility of the Reporting framework in Grid Control. More information about what features are available in the reports to a user can be found in Chapter 11.

These are the steps to create the backlog indicator report:

Step 1.   Create the report (see Figure 6-1). First provide the title and a descriptor of the report:

Title: Repository backlog indicators

Description: Overview of all the backlog indicators in the repository

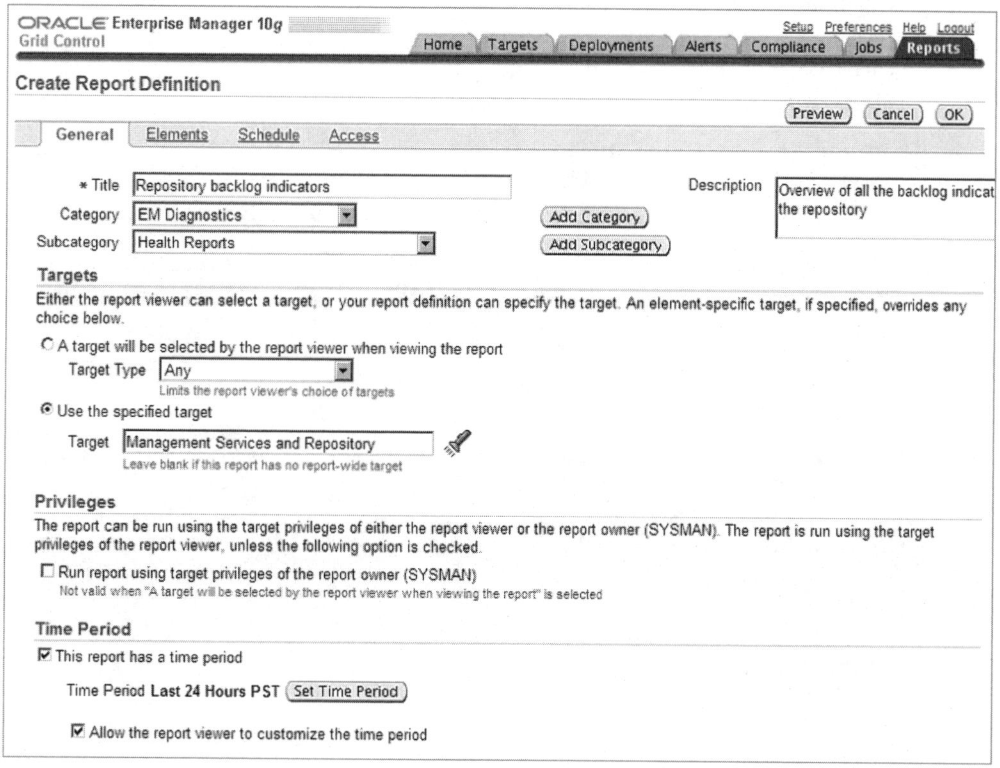

FIGURE 6-1.   *Report creation for Repository backlog indicators*

(continued)

Since this is a diagnostics report, doing some basic health checks, we'll reuse the same category and subcategory we used before:

Category: Grid Control Diagnostics

Subcategory: Health Reports

For this report, we do want to specify a target: the OMS and Repository target, since the queries will use the metric data of that target.

Check the This Report Has a Time Period option in the Time Period section. This means the user generating the report will be able to specify a custom time period.

Step 2. Create all chart elements (see Figure 6-2). Go to the Elements tab, to create eight elements: four charts and four table elements. This report will have an overview of the four major backlog indicators discussed in this chapter. For each indicator, a line chart will graph the evolution of the backlog, while a simple table will show the current (last known) values.

XML loader backlog:

■ For the first element (graph), select Chart From SQL as the element type, and specify this information:

Header: XML Loader Backlog - Historical
Chart Type: Time Series Line Chart
Statement:

```
SELECT key_value, rollup_timestamp, average
FROM    sysman.mgmt$metric_hourly
```

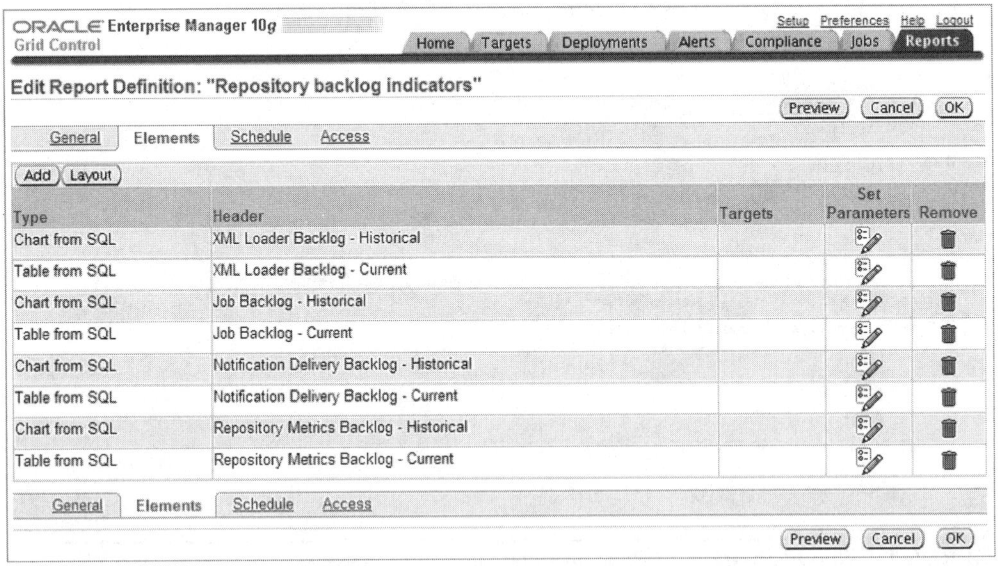

FIGURE 6-2. *Elements for Repository Backlog Indicators report*

```
WHERE  target_guid = ??EMIP_BIND_TARGET_GUID??
  AND  metric_guid = HEXTORAW('B72713257822A65853FDF0C77554F660')
  AND  rollup_timestamp
       BETWEEN ??EMIP_BIND_START_DATE?? AND ??EMIP_BIND_END_DATE??
ORDER BY rollup_timestamp, key_value
```

■ The second element (the current values) is a Table From SQL element, with this information:

Header: XML Loader Backlog - Current
Statement:

```
SELECT key_value, value
FROM   sysman.mgmt$metric_current
WHERE  target_guid = ??EMIP_BIND_TARGET_GUID??
  AND  metric_guid = HEXTORAW('B72713257822A65853FDF0C77554F660')
ORDER BY key_value
```

Job backlog - Historical:

■ The third element is again a graph (Chart From SQL) with these specifics:

Header: Job Backlog - Historical
Chart Type: Time Series Line Chart
Statement:

```
SELECT 'System', rollup_timestamp, average
FROM   sysman.mgmt$metric_hourly
WHERE  target_guid = ??EMIP_BIND_TARGET_GUID??
  AND  metric_guid = HEXTORAW('CA4FF4BB045B18ADD7CA465C47A696F5')
  AND  rollup_timestamp
       BETWEEN ??EMIP_BIND_START_DATE?? AND ??EMIP_BIND_END_DATE??
ORDER BY rollup_timestamp
```

■ The accompanying element with the current values (Table From SQL) is defined as:

Header: Job Backlog - Current
Statement:

```
SELECT 'System', value
FROM   sysman.mgmt$metric_current
WHERE  target_guid = ??EMIP_BIND_TARGET_GUID??
  AND  metric_guid = HEXTORAW('CA4FF4BB045B18ADD7CA465C47A696F5')
```

Notification Delivery backlog:

■ For this Chart From SQL element, specify:

Header: Notification Delivery Backlog - Historical
Chart Type: Time Series Line Chart
Statement:

```
SELECT key_value, rollup_timestamp, average
FROM   sysman.mgmt$metric_hourly
```

(continued)

```
      WHERE  target_guid = ??EMIP_BIND_TARGET_GUID??
        AND  metric_guid = HEXTORAW('F4450F5AD8E95174CBFA21A261D5993C')
        AND  rollup_timestamp
             BETWEEN ??EMIP_BIND_START_DATE?? AND ??EMIP_BIND_END_DATE??
        AND  key_value != 'RCA'
      ORDER BY rollup_timestamp, key_value
```

- The current values for this backlog indicators are defined as follows:

  Header: Notification Delivery Backlog - Current
  Statement:

```
      SELECT key_value, value
      FROM   sysman.mgmt$metric_current
      WHERE  target_guid = ??EMIP_BIND_TARGET_GUID??
        AND  metric_guid = HEXTORAW('F4450F5AD8E95174CBFA21A261D5993C')
        AND  key_value != 'RCA'
      ORDER BY key_value
```

Repository Metrics backlog:

- The final Chart From SQL is created like this:

  Header: Repository Metrics Backlog - Historical
  Chart Type: Time Series Line Chart
  Statement:

```
      SELECT key_value, rollup_timestamp, average
      FROM   sysman.mgmt$metric_hourly
      WHERE  target_guid = ??EMIP_BIND_TARGET_GUID??
        AND  metric_guid = HEXTORAW('5175E215E86BCCD6A55CF3D883B6AF2D')
        AND  rollup_timestamp
             BETWEEN ??EMIP_BIND_START_DATE?? AND ??EMIP_BIND_END_DATE??
      ORDER BY rollup_timestamp, key_value
```

- And finally, the last Table From SQL element:

  Header: Repository Metrics Backlog - Current
  Statement:

```
      SELECT key_value, value
      FROM   sysman.mgmt$metric_current
      WHERE  target_guid = ??EMIP_BIND_TARGET_GUID??
        AND  metric_guid = HEXTORAW('5175E215E86BCCD6A55CF3D883B6AF2D')
      ORDER BY key_value
```

Step 3. Specify the layout of the elements (see Figure 6-3). To get the graph and the current values to be shown side by side, we can use the Layout button, and move the graph (Historical) and the current values (Current) at the same row.

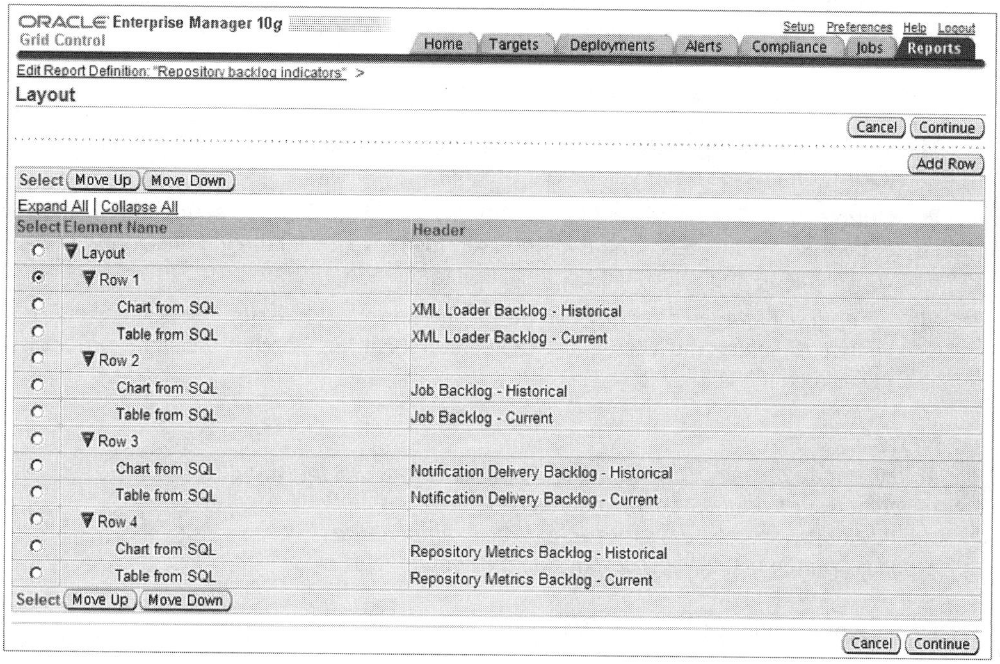

FIGURE 6-3.   *Layout for Repository Backlog Indicators report*

Step 4.   Schedule and Access. These settings can be kept to their defaults. For a normal report, which does not require any special scheduling, these settings will be fine. Since the target we have selected for this report is the OMS and Repository target, only super-users and users that have the MONITOR ENTERPRISE MANAGER or VIEW ANY TARGET privilege will be able to access this report.

Step 5.   All done. After you click the OK button, one more report will now be present in the list, ready for use.

Cleaning Up Files

During the normal operations of Grid Control, all log and trace information will be written and stored in various files in the ORACLE_HOME of the Management Server. Some of these files and directories will need to be cleaned up on a regular basis.

Using the Grid Control Job System to Rotate Log Files

There is a special job available in Grid Control called the Log Rotation job. It is a special type of job, only available for the Application Server types OC4J, Oracle HTTP Server, and Web cache. In cases where no special setup is done for the log files for these types of targets, this job can be used to schedule a rotation of the log files. However, if the Enterprise Administrator has done due diligence and modified the log file settings for the Application Server components as explained in Chapter 2 (like enabling ODL logging), the files will automatically rotate and archive, and this job will not have to be run on the Management Servers.

These are the guidelines for setting up the job:

■ The job can run against one or multiple targets, but all targets must be of the same type (OC4J, Oracle HTTP Server, or Web cache).

■ During the definition of the job, the job "knows," based on the configuration and setup of the specified targets, where all the used log files are. All the log files found in the configuration and setup will be presented to the administrator.

■ An optional archive directory can be specified in the job. If nothing is specified for the archive directory, the job will use the default location, which is the same directory where the rotated file is located.

NOTE
To prevent an outage of the Grid Control application, this job should never be run on all the Management Servers at the same time. Always run this job on specific days for each OMS. Example: Run it on Mondays on the first OMS, Tuesdays on the second, and so on.

Here's how the job works:

■ When the job executes, it will shut down the specified components of the Application Server, to archive the file to the specified archive directory (or the current one if nothing is used).

■ After the file has been archived, the components are restarted.

Archiving Log and Trace Directories

In the previous chapters of this book, the log and trace directories used by the Application Server software were already covered. Log files can grow pretty big (watch out for the 2GB file sizes!). The setup of the Application Server and Grid Control can be changed to archive or rotate the log files. To prevent overflow of these archive files, check the following directories, and either back up and/or remove the old log files in the following directories:

```
$ORACLE_HOME/Apache/Apache/logs
$ORACLE_HOME/j2ee/home/log/OC4J_EM_default_island_1
$ORACLE_HOME/j2ee/OC4J_EM/log/OC4J_EM_default_island_1
$ORACLE_HOME/j2ee/OC4J_EMPROV/log/OC4J_EM_default_island_1
$ORACLE_HOME/webcache/logs
$ORACLE_HOME/webcache/logs/archive
```

The archival process will be most likely driven by the amount of disk space available on the Management Servers. With the rotation intervals commonly set to a daily schedule, a cleanup script should typically be run once a week (if available disk space is low on the OMS server), or once a month (just to keep a little bit more history if needed).

Image Cache

One additional directory is the image cache directory used by the OMS server. Any cached image used in the Console will be removed and cleaned up as soon as the session is disconnected.

```
$ORACLE_HOME/j2ee/OC4J_EM/applications/em/em/images/chartCache
```

In case of a crash, or an abrupt termination of the OMS server, files might be left behind in this directory. Every file older than one day can be safely removed from this directory.

Defining Timeouts

Every login made by an administrator takes up resources. And for normal operations, that is OK. But if a logged-in administrator takes the rest of the day off, those resources used for that idle connection should be freed, so they can be reused by other administrators. Controlling these idle connections and setting up timeouts to reclaim the used resources can be specified at various levels in the infrastructure.

Management Server (OMS)

The OMS itself also keeps track of connections. Every connection idle for more than 45 minutes is closed by the OMS by default.

For people who are logged on to Enterprise Manager the entire day, this default does not give much time to go for a coffee, or answer a telephone call. For those people, the default can be changed with the `maxInactiveTime` parameter in the `emoms.properties` file from the `$ORACLE_HOME/sysman/config` directory:

```
oracle.sysman.eml.maxInactiveTime=15
```

Oracle HTTP Server

The main timeout parameter for Oracle HTTP Server is the `Timeout` parameter specified in the `httpd.conf` file, located in the `$ORACLE_HOME/Apache/Apache/conf` directory. The default for this parameter is set to 300 seconds (5 minutes).

This parameter controls the time the Oracle HTTP Server will wait for the completion of a response or an update from the client. If the client does not respond within that time period, it will close the HTTP or HTTPS connection, forcing the client to reinitiate the communication. This timeout is for the TCP requests handled by Oracle HTTP Server, and does not include any interaction with the Enterprise Manager application itself (meaning: the handling of the HTTP request by the application).

This timeout parameter, however, also applies for the Agents, trying to upload data to the OMS. The Agent can send over large files if it's monitoring a large set of targets (20MB files are quite possible). If part of the monitored infrastructure is on a slow network, with limited bandwidth, and with particularly large machines on that part of the network, a transfer can take more than 5 minutes to upload. The Oracle HTTP Server will time out, causing the upload to fail, and forcing the Agent to resend the file again (which will most likely time out again). In cases like this the timeout value of Oracle HTTP Server should be increased to allow the transfers to finish.

The installation of Enterprise Manager overrides this default setting from the `httpd.conf` file with its own value. The file `httpd_em.conf`, located in the `$ORACLE_HOME/sysman/config` directory, specifies a value of 900 seconds for the virtual servers EM needs. Example:

```
# Timeout: The number of seconds before receives and sends time out.
Timeout 900
```

Server Load Balancer (SLB)

Because of the nature of the work it is doing, the load balancer also has timeouts built in. On top of the regular network traffic timeout, the SLB will also have some kind of persistence defined, a kind of definition for preferential forwarding of the information, to route traffic from a given client to the same server if it is within a certain time limit of the previous conversation these two endpoints had.

If the persistence timeout defined on the SLB is higher than that of the OMS Server, the SLB might route traffic to a server that is not expecting anything any more. Although this is not a problem for the OMS (as it would treat this as a new fresh connection), it does mean that the load balancing on the SLB side is not managing the connections the way the OMS servers perceive them.

If the timeout is lower than that of the OMS Server, the SLB might already consider a conversation as finished, and start a new one if additional information from that client comes in, while the OMS Server is still waiting for updates and keeping the old connection open. The connection on the OMS server will eventually time out and get cleaned up. But the SLB will potentially route any additional traffic to a different OMS that is not expecting the information: That OMS will treat this as a new connection, and force a new login. The result is that an administrator using a web browser will all of a sudden be forced to log in again, even though he or she was already authenticated and working in the Console.

> **BEST PRACTICE**
> *The rule of thumb for any persistence timeout defined on the SLB is to have this value defined slightly higher (single-digit seconds) than the timeouts on the OMS and Oracle HTTP Server timeouts, just to account for the routing, the network latency between the SLB, and the OMS servers and traffic processing overhead.*

OPMN Ping Interval

The ping interval does not directly impact the Console or the application, but it does impact the overall Application Server. OPMN (the main Application Server watchdog) will by default ping all OC4J applications every 20 seconds, with a timeout of 5 minutes to respond. On a heavily loaded OMS system, where the Enterprise Administrators have established that the Application Server is running just fine, these intervals can be changed, to reduce the amount of local traffic the OPMN process is doing (reducing load and CPU consumption of all the AS components). To change the `ping` interval, with the response timeout, edit the `opmn.xml` file in the `$ORACLE_HOME/opmn/conf` directory:

- Change the following:

```
<process-type id="OC4J_EM" module-id="OC4J">
  ...
  <start timeout="900" retry="2"/>
  <stop timeout="120"/>
  <restart timeout="720" retry="2"/>
  ...
</process-type>
```

- into:

```
<process-type id="OC4J_EM" module-id="OC4J">
  ...
  <start timeout="900" retry="2"/>
  <stop timeout="120"/>
  <restart timeout="720" retry="2"/>
  <ping timeout="300" interval="60" />
  ...
</process-type>
```

In this example: The timeout is kept to 5 minutes (`timeout="300"`), but the interval is set to once per minute (`interval="60"`). This change can be made for each of the deployed OC4J applications:

- **home**   The standard application, used for the monitoring and administration of the Application Server
- **OC4J_EM**   The Grid Control Management Server
- **OC4J_EMPROV**   The Grid Control Agent provisioning application

Managing the Core Infrastructure

The Grid Control infrastructure has a couple of key components: The obvious ones people will point out are the Management Server and the repository itself. Every one of them has a couple of vital tasks to perform that are key to the operational health of the entire application. And they all have some indicators and statistics administrators can look at to assess the status.

XML Loaders

The loading of the data is one of the cornerstones of Grid Control. Without information from the Agents getting uploaded, nothing will be visible in the Console, and nothing will be available for the users and administrators.

What is commonly referred to as the *loaders* is in fact a set of two distinct threads and processes:

- **The XML receivers, accepting the files from the Agent**   For A (metadata) and B (state) files, the data will be uploaded directly into the repository by the loaders, to have this info available ASAP. For all other files (metric data files), the receivers will simply write the file to the directory defined in the `emoms.properties` file to be uploaded on a first-come, first-serve basis.

- **The XML loaders, uploading the metric data into the repository**   Since the receiver already uploaded the metadata and state information to the repository, the only thing left to do is the upload of the metric data. The "only" part is relative, as the XML loaders will be the most active threads of the loaders as a whole. These threads will load all the metric data into the repository, to get the data for the metric details (the graphs and the home page data) in the Console up to date.

The reason for this split is twofold:

- To optimize the loading of metadata and state information. It is critical to have the definitions of target and metrics, and the current state of those targets and the metrics, available as soon as possible, to be able to alert administrators in a timely fashion about any violation that might have occurred.

- To avoid lengthy processing times. To upload all the metric data in the repository, the receivers can quickly accept the info the Agent is sending out, preventing a pile-up of files on the Agent side.

Based on this architecture, the two potential hot spots are obvious:

- The receivers can have a backlog when they cannot accept the files fast enough from the Agents.

- The loaders can have a backlog when they cannot process the metric data in time.

Backlog Indicators for the Receivers

For the receivers, there is no metric available to measure the throughput or calculate the backlog, since this depends on the Agents. And if the Agents are having a backlog, having a metric data point in that backlog describing just how many files there are in backlog is pretty pointless (the classic "chicken and egg" problem). On a typical system, even a heavily loaded one, there is seldom an issue with the receivers. Since the receivers can only handle the incoming requests as fast the network card allows, the bottleneck for the receivers is always the throughput of the network on the machine.

> **TIP**
> *To see just how busy the network is on the OMS boxes, check the Network Interfaces metric. The Network Interface Combined Utilization (%) metric will give an idea just how busy the network cards really are.*

In the rare case that there is a bottleneck with the receivers, the best way to scale the receivers is by increasing the number of database sessions responsible for processing of the incoming HTTP requests When all the database connections are used, any new request coming in will be rejected. And the OMS will log a Server Busy error message in the MGMT_SYSTEM_ERROR_LOG table. These error messages can be found with the following SQL statement:

```sql
SELECT  SUBSTR(host_url,1,INSTR(host_url,':')-1) oms,
        TO_CHAR(TRUNC(time,'HH'),'DD-MON-YYYY HH24:MI') slot,
        SUM(value) "Server busy count"
FROM    mgmt_system_performance_log
WHERE   job_name = 'LOADER'
  AND   module   = 'ReceiverPool'
  AND   name     = 'ServerBusyRejects'
  AND   TIME     > SYSDATE-1
GROUP BY host_url, TRUNC(time,'HH')
ORDER BY host_url, TRUNC(time,'HH');
```

The default for the Oracle HTTP Server is 150, and can be increased if the machine can handle the extra HTTP sessions.

Change the following parameter in the `httpd.conf` file from the directory `$ORACLE_HOME/Apache/Apache/conf`:

```
# Limit on total number of servers running, i.e., limit on the number
# of clients who can simultaneously connect
MaxClients 150
```

BEST PRACTICE
Before increasing the number of HTTP clients of the Oracle HTTP Server, always check the network throughput and the network bandwidth of the machine first. Having more clients connecting to the machine at the same time will only mean more network traffic coming in. And the machine has to be able to cope with the extra incoming networking traffic. If there are too many HTTP clients specified, and the network data will not come in, the connections will start to time out, creating problems on both the OMS and the Agent with work that has to be redone.

Backlog Indicators for the XML Loaders

For the XML loaders, on the other hand, there are quite a few metrics available that can help in debugging performance issues. The values for these metrics can be found from the All Metrics page on any of the Management Services and Repository pages.

Active Loader Status   This metric has the following columns:

- **Loader Throughput** (rows per hour)   This metric will usually report some huge number that is only interesting to get a feel of how much work is done on an hourly basis. This data is collected per OMS, per loader thread.
  SQL statement to get the current value:

```
SELECT TO_CHAR(collection_timestamp,'DD-MON-YYYY HH24:MI:SS') collected,
       key_value oms_loader, ROUND(value,2) value
FROM   mgmt$metric_current
WHERE  target_type   = 'oracle_emrep'
  AND  metric_name   = 'Management_Loader_Status'
  AND  metric_column = 'loader_processing_hour'
```

- **Loader Throughput** (rows per second)   This metric is a lot more interesting to look at, since it will be a good measure of the throughput of the loader system. These values are also gathered per OMS loader thread. On a well-tuned system, this number should report at least 1000 per thread (preferably higher). If this number goes below 200, it's time to start using the word "panic," as the throughput of the loaders is really below par.
  SQL statement to get the current value:

```
SELECT TO_CHAR(collection_timestamp,'DD-MON-YYYY HH24:MI:SS') collected,
       key_value oms_loader, ROUND(value,2) value
FROM   mgmt$metric_current
```

```
WHERE  target_type   = 'oracle_emrep'
  AND  metric_name   = 'Management_Loader_Status'
  AND  metric_column = 'load_processing'
```

Since this data is collected per loader per OMS, the values can be analyzed to see if all the Management Servers are performing at roughly the same rate. If one OMS is loading at a much slower rate, it usually means a specific bottleneck is preventing that OMS from reaching its *optimal* throughput.

■ **Total Loader Runtime in the Last Hour** (seconds)   Since an hour only has 3600 seconds, it is pretty easy to determine just how busy the loaders are. If the number of seconds goes above 2700 (75 percent), it's time to start thinking about making changes to the loader system. SQL statement to get the current value:

```
SELECT TO_CHAR(collection_timestamp,'DD-MON-YYYY HH24:MI:SS') collected,
       key_value oms_loader, ROUND(value,2) value
FROM   mgmt$metric_current
WHERE  target_type   = 'oracle_emrep'
  AND  metric_name   = 'Management_Loader_Status'
  AND  metric_column = 'load_run'
```

Active Management Servlets   This metric has the following columns:

■ **Files Pending Load**   This is the actual backlog indicator: the number of files that are waiting to be uploaded into the repository per OMS. On a well-tuned and well-performing system, the number of files pending upload should be roughly the same per OMS. If one OMS has a much higher number of files in backlog, there is a bottleneck specific to that Management Server. The pain threshold can only be determined by looking at this number over time, and see how it fluctuates. Any number above 100,000, though, is a bad one. If there are more than 100,000 files waiting to be uploaded, a lot of information will not be available in the Console for administrators to look at. SQL statement to get the current value:

```
SELECT TO_CHAR(collection_timestamp,'DD-MON-YYYY HH24:MI:SS') collected,
       key_value OMS, ROUND(value,2) value
FROM   mgmt$metric_current
WHERE  target_type   = 'oracle_emrep'
  AND  metric_name   = 'Management_Servlet_Status'
  AND  metric_column = 'load_backlog'
```

■ **Oldest Loader File**   This value represents the difference in time, specified in minutes, between the current time and the time of the oldest file, waiting for upload per OMS. This can be useful when debugging issues with data in the Console. SQL statement to get the current value:

```
SELECT TO_CHAR(collection_timestamp,'DD-MON-YYYY HH24:MI:SS') collected,
       key_value OMS, ROUND(value,2) value
FROM   mgmt$metric_current
WHERE  target_type   = 'oracle_emrep'
  AND  metric_name   = 'Management_Loader_Status'
  AND  metric_column = 'load_run'
```

Detecting Loader Backlog Issues

With this loader metric data, a couple of simple checks can be made to see what kind of a backlog is present on the system:

■ **Loader throughput per second is low** (below 500)   The loader throughput is largely defined by the following environmental factors:

■ **Performance of the database**   The database has to be able to handle large bulk inserts and updates of data. If there are serious waits happening in the database while these bulk operations from the loaders are executing, the performance of the loaders will suffer. Sessions in the database for the loaders can be identified by the module and action set at the session level. To find the loader session in the repository database, run this SQL statement:

```
SELECT inst_id, sid, serial#, machine, action
FROM   gv$session
WHERE  username = 'SYSMAN'
  AND  program  = 'OMS'
  AND  module   = 'OEM.SystemPool'
  AND  action LIKE 'XMLLoader%'
ORDER BY machine, action
```

■ **Performance of the disk containing the XML files**   There is heavy IO activity happening on the receive directory: The XML receivers will first write the files, while the loaders will read the files, parse them, and then upload the data in the repository. In order to allow fast read and write access of a large number of files (which can be both small and large), you will need a well-performing storage system.

TIP
NFS file systems are notorious for having performance bottlenecks with a heavily used receive directory. Always use a true clustering file system as the shared loading area for the OMS servers.

■ **Performance of the network between the OMS and the Repository database**   The network latency between the OMS servers and the database also plays a factor when determining the throughput. If the network is slow, with a slow response, the SQL statements executing against the database will also be impacted by this.

BEST PRACTICE
Keep the OMS servers as close as possible to the repository database. Keep the number of network hops as small as possible.

■ **Total runtime per hour is more than 75 percent** (2700 seconds)   If the loader is too busy, it's time to add a loader thread. As long as the network between the OMS server and the database can handle the additional load, and the database has enough spare capacity for another connection coming in, the number of loaders can be increased. The default number of loaders per OMS server is always set to 1 during the install.

This parameter can be increased in the `emoms.properties` file, up to 10 loader threads per OMS server. Example:

```
em.loader.threadPoolSize=5
```

BEST PRACTICE
Although it's always tempting to go directly for the max, and put the number of loaders directly to 10, always increase the number of loaders with just the number you need to run comfortably. So if you can run the system with two loader threads, you can set the number to 3, just to have a spare in case of a spike and a burst of data, but don't waste resources on the OMS server and the database by setting it to 10.

■ **Loader backlog keeps increasing** (+10,000 files and climbing) If the number of files in backlog keeps increasing, there is most likely a combined problem: On the one hand too many files coming in, while on the other hand the throughput of the loaders is not sufficient enough to upload everything in time. The solution to fixing this problem is rarely a single change, tweak, or modification made to any of the infrastructure components. It will always be a combination of improving the database throughput, changing the OMS server configuration, and reducing or streamlining the files send by the Agents. On the Agent side, there is the following parameter from the `emd.properties` file to control the size of the XML files to be uploaded to the repository:

UploadFileSize   Maximum size (in KB) for the metric XML file to be uploaded to the OMS. This value acts only as a guide for the Agent to close the file and start a new one as soon as the size has been reached. The actual size of the XML file can be a little bigger than the specified value. Default is 2048 (2MB).

Adding an OMS server can be a beneficial thing, if there are several indicators that an additional machine will improve the throughput and performance of Grid Control overall. But if the decision to add an OMS server is solely based on loader statistics, there is another question any administrator has to ask him/herself before going the route of additional hardware: Do we really need to upload all this data? Not all targets might need all the data points. Not all metrics have to be collected at the same interval on all targets. For some development machines, less detail might be quite okay. All of these things will reduce the amount of data uploaded to the OMS servers, and will lessen the strain on the loaders.

Cleaning Up Old Loader Files

Besides files in the receive directory, there are two other subdirectories that will contain files:

■ **clob directory** All the files in this directory are data uploads from the Agent with large objects. The files the Agent sends over are stored temporarily in this directory, and the OMS will load these in the order they got received. Once the files are loaded, the saved files are removed from this location. In case of an abnormal termination of the OMS, or in case the machine was rebooted unexpectedly, some files could be left behind in this directory. Any files older than one day can be safely removed in this directory.

■ **errors directory**   Every file with metric data the Agent uploads to the OMS that cannot be loaded completely in the repository by the loader system will be moved to the `errors` directory, and a message will be logged in the system error log (available on the Errors tab of the Management Servers And Repository pages in the Console). Under normal circumstances, no files will be present in that directory. If there is a load failure, the error message in combination with the error file will provide enough information to diagnose the problem. There are a few parameters available on the OMS side to control the automatic cleanup of the error files. Depending on the infrastructure, and the amount of work (and errors) generated by all the Agents, these parameters can be changed:

`em.loader.errorDirPurgePeriod`	The period in time, specified in seconds, the OMS waits to run the purge cycle to cleanup the old files. The default for this is set to 1 day (86,400 seconds).
`em.loader.maxAgeErrorFiles`	The maximum time in seconds a file can reside in the errors directory. If a file is found during the purging cycle that is older than the set value, it will be purged. The default for this is 30 days (2,592,000 seconds).
`em.loader.maxNumErrorFiles`	Maximum number of files that can be present in the error directory. If more files are present at the time the purging routine runs, the oldest files will be removed until the number of allowed files is reached. The default is set to 10,000 files.

Grid Control Jobs

The Grid Control job system is not to be confused with the DBMS_SCHEDULER or DBMS_JOB capabilities of the database: It is an entire job-scheduling and execution framework inside Grid Control. Jobs are defined and created in the Console by Administrators. They can either be a simple command or a series of commands, submitted against a single target or multiple targets across various machines in the infrastructure. Several scheduling options can be given for a job, ranging from running immediately, to running on a repeated schedule every *x* minutes/hours/ days, all the way to running at a particular point in time. Besides the jobs created by people using Grid Control, the system will use the job system behind the scenes, to perform maintenance tasks like updating monitoring properties on machines, synchronizing settings between nodes on a cluster, pushing out monitoring settings via templates, and performing blackout operations.

All scheduling of the job and the units of work to be executed is done on the OMS server. A special thread in the OMS server—the Job Dispatcher—is responsible for picking up the job tasks and dispatching them to their appropriate destination. The Agent will just receive the request to execute a task, and send the output of that task back to the OMS server. Any of the OMS servers can pick up a job task, and send it to the Agent for execution. This means that all OMS servers must be capable of communicating to all of the Agents, since there is no fixed relationship between the OMS server and the Agent.

Backlog Indicators

Job backlog can be measured as the number of job tasks that have reached their scheduled time and are waiting to be picked up by the Job Dispatcher threads of the running OMS servers. If job tasks are piling up, either the dispatcher cannot keep up with the number of tasks waiting to be delivered, or it cannot hand off the work to the job worker threads to do the actual execution of the job task.

Each OMS server will have a job dispatcher thread running, which will check every second to see if there are tasks waiting to be dispatched. The dispatcher works with batches of 30 at a time; it will pick up those tasks and give them to the worker threads to be executed. If there are more than 30 job tasks coming in per second on a regular basis, one OMS server will not be sufficient to do all the work, and a second middle tier might be needed.

Once the job dispatcher is happily working, and has retrieved a batch of up to 30 job tasks waiting to be executed, it will check the type of each task, and based on the type, send it to the appropriate job pool. These job pools are local to each OMS server. Each pool has its own characteristics and is controlled by a parameter in the emoms.properties file. Every middle tier will have its own set of worker threads, all waiting to receive instructions from the Job dispatcher to execute tasks:

`em.jobs.shortPoolSize`	Short-term thread pool for agent operations that are short-lived and do not require long to complete. Examples: Typical user job commands like OS commands or SQL scripts to execute. Default is 25.
`em.jobs.longPoolSize`	Long-term thread pool for operations that are known to take up some time, like transferring files, or executing patch/upgrade operations. Examples: User job commands like patching or file transfers. Default is 12.
`em.jobs .systemPoolSize`	Internal thread pool for internal operations (System jobs). This includes operations like removing or updating targets on the Agent side, blackout operations, metric and metric thresholds updates, and so on. Default is 25.

If no job worker of the pool needed for the tasks is available, the job dispatcher has to wait until a thread of that type becomes available. The longer the dispatcher has to wait, the more chance there is that tasks waiting to be scheduled will not be picked up.

RULE OF THUMB
The default settings for the job pools are quite sufficient for most systems, even under heavy (job-related) load. Only increase the size of job pool if there is evidence of a continued backlog for that specific type of job, with the Job Dispatcher spending more than 75 percent of its time processing job steps.

There is a fourth emoms.properties parameter that needs to be looked at for jobs. All the job workers threads need repository database connections, to pick up the details of the job steps to execute. The number of database connections available for job workers is limited by default to 25 per OMS. This can be controlled by a parameter in the emoms.properties file:

```
oracle.sysman.emRep.dbConn.maxConnForJobWorkers=10
```

If all the job worker connections are in use, any worker thread that receives a job from the Job Dispatcher will have to wait until a connection becomes available in the pool.

BEST PRACTICE
On a busy system, the number of job worker connections in the pool should at least match the total number of threads from the short-term pool. If there are many jobs running, of various job types, including regular user jobs, patching and provisioning, and template operations, and so on, the number of job worker connections should even be made high enough to accommodate both the short-term and long-term pool.

Grid Control itself is keeping track of some of the key job-processing statistics. These metrics are accessible from the All Metrics page of the Management Services and Repository target. A set of metrics is available for the job processing. All of these metrics can be inspected on the All Metrics page linked on any of the Management Server and Repository UI pages.

Job Dispatcher Performance   This metric has the following columns:

- **Job Dispatcher Processing Time** (% of Last Hour)   Amount of time per hour the Job Dispatcher is busy picking up steps, and giving them to the job worker threads. If this number remains above 75 percent for long periods of time, this could indicate that an additional OMS server might be needed to process the Job load of the infrastructure. SQL statement to get the current value:

```
SELECT TO_CHAR(collection_timestamp,'DD-MON-YYYY HH24:MI:SS') collected,
       ROUND(value,2) value
FROM   mgmt$metric_current
WHERE  target_type   = 'oracle_emrep'
  AND  metric_name   = 'Job_Dispatcher_Performance'
  AND  metric_column = 'processing'
```

- **Steps Per Second**   Number of job tasks (steps) processed by the dispatcher per second. This will be roughly the number of tasks the dispatcher picks up from the queue each time it checks the system.
SQL statement to get the current value:

```
SELECT TO_CHAR(collection_timestamp,'DD-MON-YYYY HH24:MI:SS') collected,
       ROUND(value,2) value
FROM   mgmt$metric_current
WHERE  target_type   = 'oracle_emrep'
  AND  metric_name   = 'Job_Dispatcher_Performance'
  AND  metric_column = 'throughput'
```

Repository Job Dispatcher   This metric has the following column:

- **Job Dispatcher Job Step Average Backlog**   This is the main backlog indicator. This number represents the number of job tasks waiting to be picked up by the Job Dispatcher. These tasks can be from either user-defined jobs, or internal system jobs

created by Grid Control itself.
SQL statement to get the current value:

```
SELECT TO_CHAR(collection_timestamp,'DD-MON-YYYY HH24:MI:SS') collected,
       ROUND(value,2) value
FROM   mgmt$metric_current
WHERE  target_type   = 'oracle_emrep'
  AND  metric_name   = 'Repository_Job_Dispatcher'
  AND  metric_column = 'repository_job_backlog'
```

Detecting Job Backlog Issues

The backlog number for jobs in Grid Control is unfortunately a single number, which does not make any distinction between the various job pools. But, with a little SQL magic, we can break down the job backlog number, and get a per-pool backlog number:

```
SELECT DECODE(command_type,0,'Short',1,'Long',2,'System') JobPool,
       COUNT(*) cnt
FROM   mgmt_job_execution
WHERE  step_type IN (1,8,9,12,13)
  AND  step_status = 1
  AND  start_time  < MGMT_GLOBAL.SYSDATE_UTC
GROUP BY DECODE(command_type,0,'Short',1,'Long',2,'System')
ORDER BY JobPool
```

All of the work done by the OMS to dispatch the jobs is done in PL/SQL inside the database. Any noticeable backlog of the job system always needs to be verified first in the database, via ADDM, AWR, and ASH, to check for abnormal wait conditions and heavy SQL activity. Once the database has been verified, in case of consistent backlog for a particular type of job, the job system itself can be tweaked and adjusted to increase the various job pools if needed using the `emoms.properties` parameters `em.jobs.shortPoolSize`, `em.jobs.longPoolSize`, and `em.jobs.systemPoolSize`.

NOTE
The short and system job pools can be adjusted based on the needs of the infrastructure, as long as the Application Server has enough resources available (memory- and CPU-wise) to run the additional threads. Increasing the number of long pool threads can have a negative effect on the network performance, though: Since that pool typically performs the lengthy operations, like transferring patches to Agents, or retrieving files from the Agents, the operations these threads are doing will be very network intensive. Having a lot more of them will reduce the bandwidth the Agents have available to send information to the OMS servers.

BEST PRACTICE
Although nothing is preventing the rollout of different values for the job pool sizes per OMS, it is strongly advised to keep these values the same on each of the active Management Servers.

Retention Time for Job Information

Job information is purged by its own purge policy rules, and its own routine. There are three types of retention periods used to clean up jobs in Grid Control:

- System jobs (jobs initiated by Grid Control itself, without the intervention of an administrator) are cleaned up as soon as the job finishes. The purge policy for system jobs cannot be changed. All system jobs will be purged as soon as they finish.

- User jobs (jobs initiated by an administrator) have a default retention period of 30 days. The daily purge routine will purge any job older than that (for both completed and failed ones). The default retention time for user jobs is stored in the MGMT_JOB_PURGE_POLICIES table:

```
SELECT time_frame num_days
FROM   mgmt_job_purge_policies
WHERE  policy_name = 'SYSPURGE_POLICY'
```

Depending on the requirements of the site, the retention time of the user jobs can either be increased or decreased.

BEST PRACTICE
It's possible to increase the retention time, and store a lot more job history in the repository. Increasing the purge time too much will have a negative effect on the performance, though, since all job searches in the Console do use the history table to report on. Reducing it too much can also be a problem, since you lose track of what jobs have run. The recommendation is to keep at least seven days of data, to be able to get some data and history on weekly running jobs.

- All other internal jobs regarding the Critical Patch Advisories, the OPatch updates, and the cleanup and purge of the Software Libraries are on a separate purge schedule for each of these types of jobs. The default retention time is set to seven days for each of these in the MGMT_JOB_PURGE_POLICIES table:

```
SELECT policy_name, time_frame num_days
FROM   mgmt_job_purge_policies
WHERE  policy_name != 'SYSPURGE_POLICY'
```

BEST PRACTICE
The retention time for these jobs can be changed and made smaller. However, some history should be kept for these jobs, to get a history of what happened with the communication with the My Oracle Support server. A minimum of three days should be kept in the repository to backtrack any updates and issues with the jobs.

Notification Dispatching

The notification system is a subscriber model: All incoming alerts and notifications are checked to see if an administrator has specified an interest for that type of alert. If so, the notification handlers will send out the notification based on the delivery specifics defined by the administrator. The first step in the notification handling is the setup of the *notification rules*. These are the subscription rules that define which types of alert and notification the administrators are interested in. When a notification rule has matched an incoming alert, and determined that an administrator needs to be alerted of this, the handler will use the *notification method* to dispatch the alert in the specified way. All notification handling is based on alerts loaded in the repository. These alerts can come from a couple of different places:

- **Threshold violations uploaded by the Agent**   All metrics the Agent is evaluating and checking will upload any threshold violation. This violation will then be stored as-is in the repository, and dispatched to the notification system.

- **Job alerts and notifications**   Any state change of a job will also be reported as an alert, and dispatched to the notification system.

- **Repository-side threshold violations**   These are just like Agent-side thresholds. The only difference is that the repository has detected the condition, and inserted the violation directly in the repository, bypassing the loader system.

Every OMS will participate in the notification handling, and any OMS can potentially pick up any notification. Therefore, any configuration done to handle notifications, like giving access to SMTP servers for email dispatching, or setting up an SNMP trap manager to accept traps from Grid Control, should be done on all the OMS servers, and any third-party machine involved in the receiving of the notifications should expect incoming data from any of the Management Servers. There are several mechanisms available to deliver notifications:

- **E-mail**   The alert details are e-mailed to the address specified by the Administrator. This requires an SMTP server to be defined, and a valid e-mail address specified by the Administrator account.

- **OS command**   The alert details are passed to a script or an executable defined in the notification method.

- **SNMP**   An SNMP trap is sent to the specified server, port, and community of the notification method.

- **PL/SQL**   A notification PL/SQL object is passed to the specified PL/SQL procedure. Although the OMS makes the PL/SQL call to get the notification handled, for this type of notification delivery, the repository database will actually do the work.

- **Java**   This is an internal notification method, used by the connectors and plug-ins to communicate with third-party notification tools like Remedy and PeopleSoft.

Backlog Indicators

There are quite a few metrics available for monitoring notification performance. And although there is an explicit backlog indicator (Notifications Waiting), that number by itself is not enough to diagnose any kind of performance bottlenecks with the notification system.

Notification Performance   This metric has the following columns:

- **Notification Delivery Time**   Average time in seconds to deliver a notification. This is a rollup number for all notifications delivered for all notification methods.
  SQL statement to get the current value:

```
SELECT  TO_CHAR(collection_timestamp,'DD-MON-YYYY HH24:MI:SS') collected,
        ROUND(value,2) value
FROM    mgmt$metric_current
WHERE   target_type   = 'oracle_emrep'
  AND   metric_name   = 'Notification_Performance'
  AND   metric_column = 'delivery_avg'
```

  Since there is a wide range of notification methods (with fast and slow delivery mechanisms), this number by itself is not sufficient to determine a bottleneck. If the average is consistently above three seconds, though, more investigation will be needed to see where the time is spent, and what notification type is taking up the most time.

- **Notification Processing Time** (% Last Hour)   As with the other processing time metrics, the important thing for this metric is to make sure there is no consistent high usage.
  SQL statement to get the current value:

```
SELECT  TO_CHAR(collection_timestamp,'DD-MON-YYYY HH24:MI:SS') collected,
        ROUND(value,2) value
FROM    mgmt$metric_current
WHERE   target_type   = 'oracle_emrep'
  AND   metric_name   = 'Notification_Performance'
  AND   metric_column = 'notificationprocessing'
```

  If the notification handling is taking up too much time per hour, there is a notification delivery bottleneck and/or a spike in alerts getting generated by the system. Both these avenues will need to be investigated to see where the time is spent.

- **Notifications Waiting**   This is the main backlog indicator. This number represents the total number of notifications waiting to be delivered.
  SQL statement to get the current value:

```
SELECT  TO_CHAR(collection_timestamp,'DD-MON-YYYY HH24:MI:SS') collected,
        ROUND(value,2) value
FROM    mgmt$metric_current
WHERE   target_type   = 'oracle_emrep'
  AND   metric_name   = 'Notification_Performance'
  AND   metric_column = 'waiting'
```

  This is a rollup number, though, for all notification delivery mechanisms, across all the Management Servers. If there is a consistent backlog, more details are needed here to find out which notification delivery mechanisms are affected, and how many notifications are waiting per OMS per notification delivery mechanism.

- **Throughput Per Second** Number of notifications delivered per second. This number signifies the number of notifications that completed delivery per OMS per second. SQL statement to get the current value:

```
SELECT TO_CHAR(collection_timestamp,'DD-MON-YYYY HH24:MI:SS') collected,
       ROUND(value,2) value
FROM   mgmt$metric_current
WHERE  target_type   = 'oracle_emrep'
  AND  metric_name   = 'Notification_Performance'
  AND  metric_column = 'notificationthroughput'
```

A low number here does not necessarily mean a problem with the notification system. In the case of a consistent backlog and a low throughput number, more investigation is needed to determine what type of notifications indicate a throughput problem, and which ones do not have one.

Detecting Notification Backlog Issues

Based on these metrics, we can come up with a few simple rules of thumb:

- A consistent notification backlog, but with a low processing percentage, is an indication of a delivery problem, where one type (or more) of notification has a problem in delivering the notifications in a timely manner. The first step to do in these cases is to get a breakdown of how many notifications are waiting per OMS per notification delivery method, using this SQL statement:

```
SELECT f.host_url, b.consumer_name, b.cnt
FROM   mgmt_notify_queues q, mgmt_failover_table f,
       (SELECT consumer_name, COUNT(*) cnt
        FROM   aq$mgmt_notify_qtable
        WHERE  msg_state = 'READY'
          AND  consumer_name NOT LIKE 'ADM%'
          AND  consumer_name NOT LIKE 'RCA%'
        GROUP BY consumer_name) b
WHERE  q.qname  = b.consumer_name
  AND  q.oms_id = f.failover_id
ORDER BY b.consumer_name
```

Based on the breakdown of the backlog, a couple of things can be looked at:

- If one OMS is significantly slower in processing notifications of a particular type than the other OMS servers, the setup of the machine will need to be verified to find that bottleneck.

- If all notifications of a certain type are slow across the board, the delivery of the notification itself might be the problem.

- For delivering emails, this could mean a slow SMTP server.

  Besides the breakdown of the backlog, an additional piece of data can be obtained by running a query against the performance log table, to find out what the delivery time of the notification and total delivery time (including the Grid Control housekeeping overhead) are for a certain notification delivery mechanism:

```
SELECT name, ROUND(AVG(duration/1000),2) avg_duration
FROM   mgmt_system_performance_log
WHERE  job_name = 'EMD_NOTIFICATION.NotificationDelivery Subsystem'
  AND  is_total = 'N'
  AND  name IN ('EMAIL_DELIVERY_TIME','EMAIL_TOTAL_DELIVERY_TIME')
GROUP BY name
```

For the notification delivery mechanisms, the names used in the performance log are:

EMAIL	*EMAIL_DELIVERY_TIME* and *EMAIL_TOTAL_DELIVERY_TIME*
PLSQL	*PLSQL_DELIVERY_TIME* and *PLSQL_TOTAL_DELIVERY_TIME*
SNMP	*SNMP_DELIVERY_TIME* and *SNMP_TOTAL_DELIVERY_TIME*
JAVA	*JAVA_DELIVERY_TIME* and *JAVA_TOTAL_DELIVERY_TIME*
OS Command	*OSCMD_DELIVERY_TIME* and *OSCMD_TOTAL_DELIVERY_TIME*

■ When the Notification Processing Time percentage is high all the time, in combination with a high Throughput Per Second value, it means too many notifications are coming into the system, which is usually an indication that the metric and policy settings are not specified correctly. Having too many notifications coming in can cause serious performance problems throughout the infrastructure: The settings for the metrics and policies will need to be updated to reduce the rate of incoming alerts.

■ A consistent backlog for a particular type of notification, in combination with a reasonable throughput and a low delivery time, is an indication of just not enough horsepower available to deliver all the notifications in time. The first thing to do in these cases is verify that all the generated alerts and notifications are indeed needed: The best way to get rid of a backlog is always to make sure we don't have anything to put in the backlog in the first place. If the alerts are valid, and there are no perceived bottlenecks in the delivery mechanism, two things can be done to increase the throughput:

   ■ *Increase the number of notification delivery threads per OMS.* The maximum number of threads can be changed in the emoms.properties file by setting the following property:

   ```
   em.notification.max_delivery_threads=24
   ```

   Starting with 10.2.0.5, the Set_Number_Queues procedure inside the MGMT_NOTIFICATION package can be used to increase the number of queues per notification method if needed.

   ■ **Add an OMS** This is the last resort, since adding an OMS has implications to all the other subsystems and activities Grid Control is doing. But in some cases, it just might be necessary to add an OMS to the infrastructure to make sure everything gets delivered in time.

Agent Heartbeating

The Grid Control infrastructure needs to be able to keep track of which Agents are still operational and working, and which ones are offline. The mechanism that is used for this is a simple heartbeat the Agent sends over on regular intervals to the OMS.

Setting the ping Interval for Agents

The interval for this heartbeat is specified in the `MGMT_EMD_PING` table in the repository. The column `MAX_INACTIVE_TIME` defines the time in seconds the OMS will wait to check for the next heartbeat of the Agent. Each time an Agent sends a heartbeat over, the response of the OMS always includes the interval to inform the Agent when to send the next heartbeat The default value for every Agent discovered in the infrastructure is always 120 seconds. An administrator can change the `MAX_INACTIVE_TIME` value for an Agent. Increasing the value too high can have negative consequences, though, to the up/down reporting of an Agent and a host:

- The OMS expects an Agent to respond within the interval specified (which is the default 120 seconds).

- If an Agent fails to send a new heartbeat, the OMS will flag this Agent as potentially down. It will then wait for another interval period (another 120 seconds) before it will make a state change, just to give the Agent the chance to still respond.

- If after this second interval the Agent still has not sent a heartbeat, the OMS will try to contact the Agent, and see if it can get a response:

  - If the Agent is still responding, the OMS will not take any action.

  - If the Agent is not responding, the status of the Agent and host will be marked as Agent Unreachable.

  The message recorded with the state change will distinguish between a mere Agent Down situation or a Machine Unavailable.

This means that with the default of 120 seconds, it will take a little over 4 minutes (twice the interval, plus the time it takes the OMS to try to contact the Agent) before a machine will be marked as unavailable and an alert is raised. If the `ping` interval is increased to 180 seconds, the time it takes to mark a machine as unavailable is then raised to beyond 6 minutes.

Setting the Startup Grace Time

When an OMS starts, it waits for a few seconds before it will start checking for potentially down Agents. This is done to give all the Agents the opportunity to send their latest state, and prevent the unnecessary work of verifying Agents that have not sent a heartbeat signal in time.

The default value for this grace period is 10 seconds. This is sufficient for a small number of Agents, but as soon as the managed infrastructure contains hundreds of Agents, this default grace time is not big enough. After an outage of the Management Servers, especially if the outage was for more than just a few minutes, the Agents will have gathered some information to upload to the OMS. Under these conditions, recording 20 heartbeats per second is a reasonable figure to use for calculating throughput of heartbeats. To calculate the grace period time needed to have all Agents report in, use the following formula:

```
            # Total Agents
    --------------------------------  =  Minimal number of seconds required
    20 per second x # OMS Servers
```

Example:

■ With 6000 Agents and four Management Servers, the formula becomes:

```
6000
------- =  75 seconds
20 x 4
```

To set the startup grace time, insert the `PING_START_GRACE_TIME` property. Example, assuming the 75-second grace period:

```
INSERT INTO mgmt_parameters
  (parameter_name, parameter_value, parameter_comment, internal_flag)
VALUES
  ('PING_START_GRACE_TIME',75,'Initial wait time after an OMS bounce to
resume checking the Agent heartbeats',0);
COMMIT;
```

Repository Metric Calculations

The agent collects almost all the metric data for the specified targets. But some metrics cannot be obtained from the target directly, and can only be calculated once dependent data is available, or other targets have reported in. The affected metrics can be put in the following categories:

■ **Metrics defined on logical targets** Any aggregate metric defined on a group, a system, or a service can only be calculated once all the dependent data is available.

■ **Rollup metrics for clustered targets** For targets that have members running on several machines, some metrics are calculated as a function of the results of the member targets. A good example of this is the availability of a RAC database target: The RAC database is only considered as up as long as one of the database instances of that RAC is up and running. This means that the availability of the RAC target can only be calculated once the availability of at least one instance is known.

■ **Self-Monitoring (the MTM metrics)** All metrics Grid Control is collecting about itself are a function of the operational data and overall throughput of Grid Control.

These metrics are calculated in the repository, by the repository database, based on the scheduled frequency defined for these metrics. The OMS will put the scheduled metric request in an AQ. A set of DBMS_JOBs is defined on the repository that will pick up these requests from the AQ, run these metric collections, and store the data directly in the appropriate metric tables together with the other metric data. There are two distinct types of DBMS_JOBS scheduled in the database for the whole repository collection framework:

■ **The worker threads** There will be worker threads submitted by default: at least one for short-running jobs, and one for long-running tasks. Each of these worker threads will pick up the tasks from the queue based on its type. Use the following SQL statement to get the details for these jobs:

```
SELECT job, last_date, last_sec, broken, failed
FROM   user_jobs
WHERE  what LIKE 'EM_TASK.WORKER%'
```

Information about these jobs is available in the Console, on the Repository Operations page of the Management Services and Repository page.

Starting from 10.2.0.5, these workers threads show up as Repository Metrics 1 (short-running) and Repository Metrics 2 (long-running). For all versions prior to 10.2.0.5, these jobs were grouped together under the heading Repository Metrics.

■ **The watchdog** This job just keeps an eye on the worker threads, and if needed reschedules any failed worker thread. The schedule is set to run every minute, which is quite sufficient for any kind of Grid Control implementation. The following SQL statement can be used to get the details for this job:

```
SELECT job, last_date, last_sec, broken, failed
FROM   user_jobs
WHERE  what='EM_TASK.RESUBMIT_FAILED_TASK();'
```

This job runs silently in the background, and will not show up in the MTM pages on the Repository Operations page.

Backlog Indicators

For all repository-side operations, the metric Repository Collection Performance can be used to get some useful statistics on what is happening. This metric is evaluated every 10 minutes, and will report the statistics for those last 10 minutes of activity in the repository.

Repository Collection Performance This metric has the following columns:

■ **Collection Duration** (seconds) Total number of seconds the execution of the collections took.
SQL statement to get the current value:

```
SELECT TO_CHAR(collection_timestamp,'DD-MON-YYYY HH24:MI:SS') collected,
       key_value ROUND(value,2) value
FROM   mgmt$metric_current
WHERE  target_type  = 'oracle_emrep'
  AND  metric_label = 'Repository Collection Performance'
  AND  column_label = 'Collection Duration (seconds)'
```

■ **Collections Processed** Total number of collections processed.
SQL statement to get the current value:

```
SELECT TO_CHAR(collection_timestamp,'DD-MON-YYYY HH24:MI:SS') collected,
       key_value ROUND(value,2) value
FROM   mgmt$metric_current
WHERE  target_type  = 'oracle_emrep'
  AND  metric_label = 'Repository Collection Performance'
  AND  column_label = 'Collections Processed'
```

■ **Collections Waiting To Run** Number of collections in the queue waiting to be picked up, per type (long- or short-running). This is an exact backlog number that can be used to

track the progress of the repository worker threads.
SQL statement to get the current value:

```
SELECT  TO_CHAR(collection_timestamp,'DD-MON-YYYY HH24:MI:SS') collected,
        key_value ROUND(value,2) value
FROM    mgmt$metric_current
WHERE   target_type    = 'oracle_emrep'
  AND   metric_label   = 'Repository Collection Performance'
  AND   column_label   = 'Collections Waiting To Run'
```

■ **Total Throughput across Workers**   Number of collections each type of worker processed.
SQL statement to get the current value:

```
SELECT  TO_CHAR(collection_timestamp,'DD-MON-YYYY HH24:MI:SS') collected,
        key_value ROUND(value,2) value
FROM    mgmt$metric_current
WHERE   target_type    = 'oracle_emrep'
  AND   metric_label   = 'Repository Collection Performance'
  AND   column_label   = 'Total throughput across workers'
```

Detecting Repository Metric Backlog Issues

The Collections Waiting To Run metric is the clear way of detecting a backlog of repository-side tasks. If this number continues to rise, or stays high for a prolonged period of time, actions have to be taken to resolve the problem:

■ All repository-side operations are SQL and PL/SQL commands executed in the database. Any performance bottleneck the database is facing will also impact these repository tasks. The database diagnostics framework (ADDM, AWR, and ASH) can be used to verify the database performance.

■ Any errors the repository worker threads report will also impact the execution of the tasks. The Errors page of the Management Services and Repository page will have all the errors from the workers listed with the Repository Metrics module.

■ If the backlog is still high with a high throughput, even with a well-performing database and no errors from the worker threads, the number of worker threads might be too low. The number of workers can be increased, for both the short and long running tasks, with the set_worker_count PL/SQL call. To set the number of short-term workers to 3, use this command:

```
SQL> exec mgmt_collection.set_worker_count(0,3);
```

To set the number of long-term workers to 2, use this command:

```
SQL> exec mgmt_collection.set_worker_count(1,2);
```

BEST PRACTICE
Never increase the number of worker threads too much. For each worker thread, a new DBMS_JOB is created in the database.

After each modification to the number of worker threads, the workers themselves will need to be restarted:

```
SQL> exec mgmt_collection.start_workers();
```

Data Rollup

Grid Control collects a lot of information from all the discovered targets. This information gets rolled up into manageable chunks, but at the same time the old data will need to be purged from the system to prevent the repository from getting too big.

For the rollup of the metric data, there are two tables containing the aggregate values of the raw metric data:

- **1-HOUR rollups (MGMT_METRICS_1HOUR)**   Contains the aggregate values (min, max, avg) over one-hour periods of time. Each hour, the raw data is rolled up in a partition of the MGMT_METRICS_1HOUR table. This data is used in the default last week views in the Console.

- **1-DAY rollups (MGMT_METRICS_1DAY)**   Contains the aggregate values (min, max, avg) over one-day periods of time. Each day, the raw data is rolled up in a partition of the MGMT_METRICS_1DAY table. This data is used in the default last month views in the Console.

Backlog Indicators

The rollup job runs once per hour, to roll up all the raw metric data into the hourly partitions for the MGMT_METRICS_1HOUR table. And once per day it also rolls up the data into the daily table for the MGMT_METRICS_1DAY table. If more data is coming in than the rollup job can aggregate in one hour, a backlog will start to pile up. Although there is no exact backlog number for the rollup job, the best indicator for the rollup job is the metric that keeps track of how long a certain job is running in the system:

```
SELECT TO_CHAR(collection_timestamp,'DD-MON-YYYY HH24:MI:SS') collected,
       value
FROM   mgmt$metric_current
WHERE  target_type  = 'oracle_emrep'
  AND  metric_label = 'DBMS Job Status'
  AND  column_label = 'DBMS Job Processing Time (% of Last Hour)'
  AND  key_value    = 'Rollup'
```

The DBMS Job Processing time will show how much time the job takes up per hour. If the rollup job is running 100 percent of the time (or getting dangerously close to that magical number 100), the rollup job is at risk of hitting a backlog.

Detecting Rollup Backlog Issues

All of the work the rollup job is doing is inside the repository, and is purely SQL and PL/SQL work. As already mentioned for similar cases, the first stop to look for any kind of performance trouble is the database itself. Backlog for the rollup jobs will not create any kind of functional problem in Grid Control: Only the Console is affected, with missing values or delays in showing the latest details for the Last Week and Last Month display options for the metric details pages. The nature of the rollup job means that it will read all the raw data, calculate the aggregate values for all the found data points, and the write the rolled-up values back to the database. To tune the repository database for this operation, one must, therefore, optimize the IO throughput of the database, as well as allow some processing power to be available to make to calculate the aggregations:

- To find IO bottleneck, look for excessive read or write wait events. Both AWR and ADDM will list these types of events as the wait class `User I/O`.

- For database CPU usage, look for the `CPU Time` wait class in the AWR reports or ADDM recommendations. If the repository database is a target visible in the Console (and this should always be the case), the performance page, accessible from the database homepage, can also help break down the CPU usage of the database and spot problems with the CPU consumption of the database.

Data Purging

Grid Control collects a lot of information from all the discovered targets. This information gets rolled up into manageable chunks, but at the same time the old data will need to be purged from the system to prevent the repository from getting too big.

The purge framework will remove all old data once a day, based on the settings specified in the purge policy framework:

- **Metric data**   Old partitions will be truncated first, and if the repository database version is 10.2.0.1 or higher, the partitions are also dropped.

- **Alert and violation data**   All cleared violations older than the specified retention time are purged.

- **Configuration history data**   Old configuration snapshots and configuration changes older than the retention time are purged.

- **Job data**   The job data is being purged by a special job, and not by the generic purge policy routine.

Backlog Indicators

A backlog situation for the purge routine is very unlikely, since the purging of the data consists mainly of truncating and deleting the old (stale) partitions of the metric data, and cleaning up the old and marked obsolete data for the alerts, configuration history, notifications, and jobs. As with the rollup job, there is no backlog number that can be queried directly. The only thing available and gathered by the MTM system, as with the rollup job, is the amount of time the DBMS_JOB is running:

```
SELECT  key_value,
        TO_CHAR(collection_timestamp,'DD-MON-YYYY HH24:MI:SS') collected,
        value
FROM    mgmt$metric_current
WHERE   target_type  = 'oracle_emrep'
  AND   metric_label = 'DBMS Job Status'
  AND   column_label = 'DBMS Job Processing Time (% of Last Hour)'
  AND   key_value IN ('Job Purge','Purge Policies')
```

And the same rules apply here too: The number should never be more than 75 percent for a prolonged period of time. Anything getting close to, or reaching the 100 percent, is an indication of a potential backlog problem of the purge routines.

Detecting Purge Backlog Issues

The job processing time is the best indicator for a performance problem in this area. The only remedy for a too-high percentage of time spent for the purging of data is to give the database more horsepower to be able to finish the work in less time. Truncating partitions will be a relatively quick and painless operation in the database, with very little overhead. For the purging of the old and obsolete data, a lot of IO activity will be happening during the purge. As a result, a typical performance problem in this area will lead to an investigation of the IO activity, and making sure the underlying storage used for the repository database is working fast enough to process all the work. The two key things to focus on for this are

- **DB processing**   If there is a problem with the database performance at the time the purge routine is running, try to reschedule some of the tasks (like reports, or EM jobs working against the repository) to another time slot to avoid contention with the purge job.

- **IO waits**   Due to the intense IO operations for finding and deleting the old and obsolete alert, configuration, job, and notification history, the database will have to be tuned to optimize the IO throughput, and keep the IO waits to a minimum.

Retention Time for Metric Data

The metric data collection by the Agent and the repository metrics is retained by default using the following default criteria:

Type	Repository Table	Default Retention
RAW data	MGMT_METRICS_RAW	7 days (1 week)
1HOUR rollup	MGMT_METRICS_1HOUR	31 days (1 month)
1DAY rollup	MGMT_METRICS_1DAY	365 days (1 year)

The three metric tables are created as partitioned tables in the repository:

- For each hour of RAW data, a new partition will be created. With 5 days of future partitions always created ahead of time, and the default 7 days of history, this means that the RAW table will always use around 288 partitions in the database (give or take one or two, depending on how many hours apart the purge routine and partition maintenance routine run).

- For each day of 1HOUR and 1DAY data, a new partition will be created. For 1HOUR data, with 31 days of history, and 5 extra days already available, the total in use will always be 36. For 1DAY data, the total will be 370 (1 year, plus the extra 5 days).

The number of partitions that are currently allocated for each of the metric tables can be queried from the repository:

```
SELECT table_name, COUNT(*) cnt
FROM   user_tab_partitions
WHERE  table_name IN
          ('MGMT_METRICS_RAW','MGMT_METRICS_1HOUR','MGMT_METRICS_1DAY')
GROUP BY table_name
ORDER BY table_name
```

NOTE
If a 10gR2 database is used for the repository, the purge and delete of the old partitions of the metric tables is done automatically. If an older version is used for the repository, a special partition cleanup routine has to be called manually to remove the old partitions:

`SQL> exec emd_maintenance.partition_maintenance;`

This routine has to be run with all the Management Servers down and not running.

These default retention times for these three metric tables are stored in the repository, and can be retrieved from the MGMT_PARAMETERS table. If a parameter is not specified in the parameters table, the default value for it is assumed:

```
SELECT parameter_name, parameter_value
FROM   mgmt_parameters
WHERE  parameter_name IN ('mgmt_raw_keep_window'
          ,'mgmt_hour_keep_window','mgmt_day_keep_window');
```

To change the retention times of the metric data, insert or change the value in the repository table. Example to set the raw retention in the table for the raw data to 14 days (two weeks):

```
INSERT INTO MGMT_PARAMETERS
   (PARAMETER_NAME, PARAMETER_VALUE)
 VALUES
   ('mgmt_raw_keep_window','14');
```

NOTE
Increasing the retention times for the partitioned metric tables will not have any functional impact on Grid Control, but it will affect the size of the repository, and the performance of the repository. Before increasing the retention windows, check the current size of the partitioned tables, and make sure no wait events are reported in the database for the metric tables.

Retention Time for Alert and Violation Data

All threshold violations and policy violations including the availability data are purged by the ALERTS policy group. With the out-of-box settings, all data older than 4320 hours (180 days, approximately six months) will be purged.

The purge routine for the Alert data will remove the following items:

- **Availability** All state information older than six months from all the targets in Grid Control.
- **Alerts** All alerts and violations older than six months that have cleared and are no longer outstanding will be removed.
- **Notifications** All information about notification sent for the purged alerts will be purged.
- **Annotations** All messages administrators logged for the purged alerts will be removed as well.

The default retention time for this type of data is specified in hours, is stored in the MGMT_PURGE_POLICY_GROUP table:

```
SELECT group_retention_hours
FROM   mgmt_purge_policy_group
WHERE  group_name = 'ALERTS'
```

BEST PRACTICE
When reducing the retention time of the ALERTS group, keep in mind that the availability data for all targets will also be purged. Making the time too short (less than one month) will cause data to be incomplete on various pages in the Console.

NOTE
Since this category contains both availability and alert information, the retention time should always be kept long enough for the Console to show relevant data for all the metrics and metric detail pages. Always keep at least two months (1440 hours) of data in the repository.

Retention Time for Configuration and Change History Data

The configuration data collection for each target, including the configuration changes detected during the upload of the new configuration snapshots, can be purged on a separate schedule from the metric data.

All configuration data is kept for 8784 hours (366 days, approximately one year) by default. The retention time for this type of data is also stored in the MGMT_PURGE_POLICY_GROUP table using the group name CONFIGURATION:

```
SELECT group_retention_hours
FROM   mgmt_purge_policy_group
WHERE  group_name = 'CONFIGURATION'
```

The amount of data to keep for this category can also be changed and altered. There should always be enough history in the repository, however, (and preferably more) to show in combination with severities and availability information. Practically speaking, this means that the value of the CONFIGURATION group should be set to a higher value than the ALERT group in the MGMT_PURGE_POLICY_GROUP table:

```
SELECT DECODE(SIGN(c.num_days-a.num_days),
           -1,'Not correct!',
            0,'Cutting it close...',
              'OK') validation
FROM   (SELECT group_retention_hours/24 num_days
        FROM   mgmt_purge_policy_group
        WHERE  group_name = 'ALERTS') a,
       (SELECT group_retention_hours/24 num_days
        FROM   mgmt_purge_policy_group
        WHERE  group_name = 'CONFIGURATION') c
```

Metric Cleanup for Target Deletion

Whenever a target is being removed from the system, a PL/SQL routine in the database will clean up all references and links to this target in the repository. Part of that cleanup includes the partitioned metric tables, which contain the metric data history for the targets. If these partitioned tables contain large amounts of data, deleting the data will consume quite some time. And since they are being purged on a regular basis anyway, the delete action can be deferred until the partitions are being purged. To stop the target deletion from cleaning up the metric data in the partitioned tables, run the following SQL statements in the repository, as the EM repository owner:

```
SQL> connect SYSMAN;
SQL> exec mgmt_admin.disable_metric_deletion;
```

Keeping Up with Changes in the Data Center

It was already hi-lighted in the beginning of the chapter: A modern data center is not a static thing. There is always something that changes. It can be either an upgrade of an application, some new application getting rolled out, or a refresh of hardware. There is always something changing in a global data center!

And for an Enterprise Administrator, the most important changes are those that directly impact Enterprise Manager.

Infrastructure Changes

These are the most critical changes, since they will directly impact the interaction with the Agent and the administrators using Grid Control. All new machines, and decommissioned old machines, have to be properly defined and removed from the Grid Control infrastructure.

Moving the Repository

Any standard database feature, like RMAN, Data Pump, or a physical file copy can be used to copy the repository database to another machine. Once the database copy has been verified and validated, and it has been brought online again, some pointers in the Grid Control infrastructure will need to be updated to reflect this change:

- All the OMS servers will need the new connect string to the database. Update the `emdRepConnectDescriptor` parameter in the `emoms.properties` file with the updated database connect string:

  ```
  oracle.sysman.eml.mntr.emdRepConnectDescriptor=(DESCRIPTION\=...)
  ```

NOTE
To distinguish the separator of the parameter and value of the `emoms` `.properties` file, and the different settings of the TNS descriptor to connect to the database, all the "=" signs in the TNS descriptors must be escaped with the "\" character. So the following code

```
(DESCRIPTION= ... (CONNECT_DATA=(SERVICE_NAME=db
.acme.com) ... )
```

becomes:

```
(DESCRIPTION\= ... (CONNECT_DATA\=(SERVICE_NAME\=db
.acme.com) ... )
```

- The OMS and Repository target needs to be adjusted too, to point to the correct database location.

  - In the Grid Control Console, go to Setup.

  - Click the Management Services and Repository subtab.

  - On the bottom of the Overview page, click the Monitoring Configuration link.

  - Update the connect information, and click the OK button.

- If there is no Grid Control Agent installed on the new repository database machine (or machines in case of RAC), install one. Make sure the repository database is properly discovered, to have all the information available from the MTM pages.

- Update the Grid Control System and web application to reflect the changes. The targets we added in the first section of this book, to represent the Grid Control infrastructure, have to be updated too.

Changing the RAC Database Repository

When the repository is created in a RAC database, nodes can be added or removed from this RAC database at any point in time. If there is a change in the number of nodes of the RAC database, make the following changes to the infrastructure:

- *Update the emoms.properties for each OMS server.* The connect descriptor the OMS server is using needs to be updated to reflect the new number of machines in the RAC database. This change needs to be made on all the OMS servers, to have each server connect to the repository database in the right way. Update the emdRepConnectDescriptor parameter in the emoms.properties file with the updated connect string:

  ```
  oracle.sysman.eml.mntr.emdRepConnectDescriptor=(DESCRIPTION\=...)
  ```

- *Update the monitoring configuration for the OMS and Repository target.* The OMS and Repository target should be configured with the connect string, to connect to the service defined on the RAC nodes. If a node gets added or removed, the address list of the connect string will change. And this change needs to be made also in the monitoring configuration of the target. The easiest way to get to the monitoring configuration is:

  - From the Setup page, click the Management Server subtab.

  - Use the Monitoring Configuration link at the bottom of the page.

  - Edit the configuration, and save the changes.

- *Make sure there is a Grid Control Agent running on each of the RAC nodes, with the repository database instance properly discovered.*

- *Update the Grid Control System and web application to reflect the changes.* Any change made in the infrastructure has to be made in the definition of these targets, to reflect the current deployment of the infrastructure.

Decommissioning an OMS Server

Sometimes a machine needs to be replaced, and the old machine will either be removed from the environment, or reused for another application. If the OMS server will no longer be part of the management infrastructure, a couple of cleanup steps will need to be taken:

- *Repoint the Agents if no SLB is used.* In cases where the Agents are talking directly to the OMS servers, the Agents will have to be updated to point to a surviving OMS before it gets removed. To get the list of which Agents talk to which OMS, run this query in the repository:

```
SELECT p.heartbeat_recorder_url, t.target_name
FROM   mgmt_emd_ping p, mgmt_targets t
WHERE  p.target_guid = t.target_guid
ORDER BY p.heartbeat_recorder_url, t.target_name
```

NOTE
This heartbeat URL is the OMS that has accepted the heartbeat from the Agent. If there is no SLB in use, this URL will define the OMS this Agent is talking to. If there is an SLB involved, the URL will point to the OMS that the SLB routed the traffic through. The Agent, though, is configured to talk to the SLB even though this is not reflected in the data in the SYSMAN schema.

- *Remove OMS targets from Grid Control.* Remove first all targets on that Agent, and finally remove the host and the Agent target itself from Grid Control. If the OMS was the first installed OMS, the additional OMS and Repository target on the Agent is discovered. This target will have to be moved, or removed and rediscovered on a new OMS server if the first OMS gets decommissioned. Starting with 10.2.0.5, the OMS and Repository target can be moved to a new Agent with a new EMCTL command. This command has to be run from the ORACLE_HOME of any of the OMS machines:

```
$ emctl config emrep -agent <new agent>
```

- *Remove the OMS server from the MTM pages.* On the server management page, remove the server to be deleted from the list of available OMS servers.
    - From the Setup menu, click the Management Services and Repository subtab.
    - Go to the Management Services page.
    - Select the decommissioned OMS server, and remove it.
- *Re-create the OMS and Repository target if needed.* If the OMS server to be removed was the first installed OMS, and the target has not been moved via EMCTL or relocated using EMCLI, the OMS and Repository target will need to be re-created on another OMS server.
    - From the Setup menu, click the Agent subtab.
    - Search for the Agent of one of the OMS servers.

- From the Add list box, select the OMS and Repository option and click Go.
- Enter the name **Management Services and Repository** (just to keep it consistent with the out-of-box defaults) and put in the connect information to connect to the repository.

NOTE
Before you re-create the OMS and Repository target, make sure the old one is no longer present in the repository. Check the deleted target page to see if the target is deleted.

Adding an OMS Server

When the infrastructure grows and needs more capacity and resources, a new OMS server might be needed in the environment. When a new server is added, the following additional steps are needed to get it operational:

- *Install the OMS server software.* Apply all the patches applied on the other OMS server. All OMS servers must have the same set of patches applied, to run the same code in the same way.

- *Any changes made to the emoms.properties on the other OMS servers have to be made on the new server too.* With the release of 10.2.0.5, a new command has been added to make things a little easier here: Instead of having to make all the changes manually to the configuration files, the configuration of an existing OMS can be imported into the new OMS. First export the configuration from an existing OMS in the infrastructure.

```
$ emctl exportconfig oms -sysman_pwd <pwd>
```

Copy the `bka` file with the saved configuration to the new OMS machine, and import the configuration:

```
$ emctl importconfig oms -file <bka file>
        -sysman_pwd <pwd> -reg_pwd <pwd>
```

- If `importconfig` was not used to update the configuration of the new OMS (if this is a pre-10.2.0.5 release), the loader settings need to be manually updated if needed. If a shared file system for the loading of XML files is used, this new OMS server will also have to be switched to the shared file system loader too. It is not supported to have both the shared and non-shared file system used by the various OMS servers. All servers must use the same method for loading XML files.

```
$ emctl config oms loader -shared <yes|no> -dir <loader dir>
```

- When a Server Load Balancer is used, the newly installed OMS will need to be made aware of the SLB. After the install completes, the OMS server will need to be resecured, using the hostname and the port the SLB is using to communicate with the Agents:

```
$ emctl secure oms -reg_pwd <pwd> -host <slb> -slb_port <port>
```

After the new OMS server has been secured, the SLB configuration itself will need to be updated, to allow the routing of traffic to the new OMS server.

- Update the Grid Control System and web application to reflect the changes. Keep those container targets up to date in the Console!

Moving an OMS Server

During the lifecycle of a machine, the machine might need to physically move. If the distance the machine has to be moved is small enough, typically there are no network changes, which makes it easier to handle the change: nothing to do in this case. However, if the machine is moved to another building, or even another data center, the network changes might be a little bit more involved. These changes typically mean a change of the IP subnet used, or in some cases even a change of the network domain the machine is in.

- If there is only an IP address change, there is no work needed to reconfigure the Management Server in Grid Control. All Agent communication, and all the configuration files contain the hostname, and will never use the IP address. As long as the Agent is discovered using a hostname, and not an IP address, and all managed targets have identified themselves using a hostname, no changes need to be made in Grid Control.

- If the hostname changes (for example, a new network domain), a few changes are needed to the OMS infrastructure:

  1. Remove the Agent from the Grid Control environment. Since the hostname changes, the name of the Agent and the host will change. This means that for Grid Control, a set of new targets will be appearing after the hostname change. To avoid confusion with the previous targets, the old Agent and all of its targets should be removed from Grid Control:

     ```
     SQL> exec mgmt_admin.cleanup_agent('<old agent name>');
     ```

  2. Make the hostname change on the box. These steps are the normal networking steps to configure the machine, and all networking configuration files, to point to the new hostname.

NOTE
If firewalls are used, make sure the rules on the firewalls are updated to reflect the hostname change of the OMS. The same applies for any Server Load Balancer used in the environment: A new machine will need to be added to the load-balancing rules and configuration.

  3. Change the hostname of the AS infrastructure. A special script is present in the ORACLE_HOME of the Application Server software to make the hostname change:

     ```
     $ cd $ORACLE_HOME/chgip/scripts
     $ ./chgiphost.sh -mid
     ```

  4. Force a rediscovery of the targets of the Agent. With the new hostname, and the new AS targets, the Agent will need to rebuild the list of monitored targets, and configure those targets.

     ```
     $ cd $ORACLE_HOME/bin
     $ ./agentca -f -d
     ```

NOTE
After the discovery is done, the Agent has been resecured, and the metadata has been uploaded to the repository, check the monitoring configuration of all the rediscovered targets. Properties like passwords will be reset to the default (usually blank), and will need to be updated again.

5. Resecure the Agent and restart the Agent. Since the name of the Agent changed, the certificate the Agent has is no longer valid. A new one will need to be generated. After the new wallet has been downloaded to the Agent, the Agent can be restarted, to start uploading all the updated metadata back into the repository:

```
$ emctl secure agent
$ emctl start  agent
```

NOTE
All changes made to metric collection frequencies or threshold updates will have to be resubmitted again to the targets on the Agent. This can either be done via the Console directly per target, or via a template operation. Notification rules also need to be updated to include these new targets.

6. Remove the old Management Server from the Management Server page. The repository will still have pointers and configuration data of the old OMS server (which used the old hostname). Remove the old OMS server from the configuration on the Management Services page:

```
http://<console URL>/em/console/health/healthServices
```

■ Time zone changes can also be a part of the physical relocate: If the relocating is to a new geographical area, the time zone of the machine might also change. This will typically go hand-in-hand with a hostname change (a new domain the server is in, is also a hostname change). Since the Agent is getting reconfigured as part of the hostname change, no additional time zone-specific actions are needed. However, if the hostname stays the same, and only the time zone is changed as part of the move, some additional steps will need to be done to update the configuration of the targets in the repository to point to this new time zone. More details are provided in this chapter in the section "Change the Time Zone of a Server Machine."

Repointing the OMS to a New Repository

The Management Server does not keep any state about the infrastructure locally. Seven things will need to be changed to move an OMS to a new environment:

■ *Extract or copy the EMKEY.* If the repository the OMS server needs to point to is just the old repository, but in a new location, the EMKEY (which handles the encryption) is the same and does not to change. But more likely, the repository is a new one, and the OMS server needs to obtain the EMKEY relevant for this repository. The location of the EMKEY file is specified in the `emoms.properties` file:

```
oracle.sysman.emkeyfile=<location of emkey.ora>
```

This key file can be copied or extracted in two ways:

- If the environment has multiple Management Servers, copy the EMKEY file from another OMS server.
- If the key has not been exported out of the repository database, the EMKEY file can be grabbed from the repository.

```
$ emctl config emkey -emkeyfile <location of EMKEY file>
```

- *Update the repository pointer.* Update the `emdRepConnectDescriptor` parameter in the `emoms.properties` file with the updated repository connect string:

```
oracle.sysman.eml.mntr.emdRepConnectDescriptor=(DESCRIPTION\=...)
```

- *Resecure the OMS to obtain a valid wallet to use for the new environment.*

```
$ emctl secure oms -reg_pwd <pwd> -host <slb> -slb_port <port>
```

- *Update the loader configuration.* The OMS needs to be able to use the shared loader directory to store the XML files, and load them in the repository. The way this directory is visible on the OMS must be same as on all the other Management Servers of the infrastructure.

```
$ emctl config oms loader -shared <yes|no> -dir <loader dir>
```

- *Verify the provisioning configuration.* On the Administration tab of the Provisioning section, check all the settings specified, to make sure the OMS can use those settings.
- *Check the My Oracle Support setup.* This really boils down to checking the configuration of the proxy servers and the setup of the SMTP servers.
- *Update the SLB configuration.* Any SLB used in the environment must be updated to allow the traffic from the Agents now also to be routed to the new management server.

Server Machine Operations

A data center is always changing. Machines come and go. Hardware failures might happen, causing machines to be rebuilt, or changed to a new server. All these changes have to be reflected in Grid Control, to make sure the view of the enterprise is up to date.

Removing a Machine from the System

Every time an administrator removes a target from Grid Control, an EM Job is submitted to the monitoring Agent to remove that target from its list of monitored targets. As soon as the Agent replies that the target is removed, the second part of the job will then remove all traces of that target from the repository. On completion of that second part of the job, the delete operation will be marked as completed, at which time the target can be rediscovered again to the environment. Sometimes, a machine is already decommissioned (and no longer available on the network) even though it is present in the Grid Control Console. The standard removal of the targets in the UI will not work, since the OMS servers will not be able to contact the Agent any more, to remove the targets. In cases like this, there are two options:

■ *Delete the targets in the Console.* Once they are marked as pending delete, go to the Deleted Targets page in the Console, and use the Force Delete button to remove the targets from the repository.

```
https://<oms hostname>:<port>/em/console/health/healthDeletedTargets
```

NOTE
You can only remove the host and Agent target after all the other targets have been removed. After those have been removed with the Force Delete button, the Agent and the host can then be removed.

■ *Use the PL/SQL API to remove the Agent and all the targets.* This is a one-shot deal: This API call will remove all targets, including the host and the Agent, in the right order, without contacting the Agent.

```
SQL> mgmt_admin.cleanup_agent('<agent name>');
```

BEST PRACTICE
Only use this call if you know for sure that the Agent is no longer available on the network. If the Agent is still running and gathering information, it will not be notified of the changes in the list of monitored targets. And this will cause upload problems if this Agent then tries to upload information for a nonexisting target.

Relocation of Monitored Targets

In some environments (like any type of on-demand monitoring), the targets are pretty dynamic. And even though the managed target itself does not change, the machine monitoring targets might change frequently: A target might get relocated to a new server with more (or sometimes even less) resources.

Starting from 10.2.0.4 there is a new option to move a target from one Agent to another Agent:

```
$ emcli relocate_target
    -src_agent=currentOwner -dest-agent=<new agent>
    -target_name=<name> -target_type=<type>
```

As part of the procedure to physically move the target from one machine to another, this EMCLI command can be used to update the configuration in the repository, and make this target point to the new Agent. It prevents the need to remove the target from the Console from the old agent (which removes all customizations in terms of monitoring and notifying), and rediscover a new target on the new Agent. By keeping the original target intact, all customizations are preserved, and the monitoring of the targets and notifications sent to the administrators will stay the way it was.

Change of Hostname or IP Address

In the case of an IP address change, no special operations need to be done on the Agent side: The Agent does not store the IP address of the machine.

NOTE
Even though no actions are needed on the Agent or the Agent configuration, the networking configuration will need to be updated to make sure the hostname of the machine is getting properly resolved to the correct IP address. This means making changes to DNS servers, YP servers, or even the local hosts file, depending on the network configuration.

On the OMS side, however, a change is needed. By default, any Java program using the Java Net libraries will cache the IP address of any connection made to a remote machine indefinitely. If there is a chance of an IP address changing for a machine, or if there are scheduled network changes coming up, the caching Java algorithm can be changed. It is controlled by the parameter `networkaddress.cache.ttl` in the `java.security` file or by using the `sun.net.inetaddr.ttl` parameter on the command line. The default for this parameter is `-1` (meaning indefinite), but it can be changed to any positive number, which indicates the number of seconds Java will keep the IP address cached. To set the DNS caching of IP addresses to 15 minutes, add the cache switch to the `opmn.xml` file:

■ Edit the file `OPMN.XML` from the `$ORACLE_HOME/opmn/conf` directory.

■ For the startup parameters for the OC4J_EM application, add the switch:

```
<category id="start-parameters">
  <data id="java-options" value=".. other parameters..
      -Dajp.keepalive=true -.Dsun.net.inetaddr.ttl=900"/>
  <data id="oc4j-options" value="-properties"/>
</category>
```

The `sun.net.inetaddr.ttl` property is only valid for the current Java Runtime Environment (JRE) and Java Developer's Kit (JDK) releases and will not necessarily be supported in future releases of Java. The preferred way of doing this, though, is by specifying the `networkaddress.cache.ttl` parameter in the `java.security` file. This file is located in the `$ORACLE_HOME/jdk/jre/lib/security` directory:

```
networkaddress.cache.ttl=900
```

■ Update the OPMN configuration, so that with the next restart of the OMS, this new parameter will be used:

```
$ dcmctl updateConfig -d -v
```

NOTE
Disabling the DNS caching of IP addresses (by specifying the value 0) is not a recommended approach, as this means that the OMS will have to do the hostname lookup every time it has to initiate communication with an Agent.

When the name of the machine changes, the necessary modifications needed to continue the monitoring are a little bit more extensive: The name of the Agent and the host target changes.

And a new name means a new target that will need to be discovered in Grid Control. To successfully transition the old Agent and its targets to the new Agents, follow these steps:

- Stop the old Agent. The old Agent needs to be shut down so that no more interactions can occur from the Management Servers to this Agent.

  ```
  $ emctl stop agent
  ```

- Unsecure the old Agent. The new name requires a new SSL wallet, so we have to unsecure the old Agentbefore we can properly resecure the Agent with the new name again.

  ```
  $ emctl unsecure agent
  ```

- Make the hostname change on the machine, via the OS- and network-specific commands.

- Update the emd.properties and targets.xml files:

  ```
  $ emctl getemhome
  $ cd <that EMHOME>
  $ cd sysman/config
  $ vi emd.properties
  $ cd ../emd
  $ vi targets.xml
  ```

  In both these files, replace the old hostname with the new hostname throughout the entire file, and save the changes. Make sure to keep a backup of these files around, just to be on the safe side!

- Remove the old state files. Any state or temporary file that the old Agent generated is no longer valid and will have to be removed:

  ```
  $ emctl getemhome
  $ cd <that EMHOME>/sysman
  $ rm -fr log/*
  $ rm -fr emd/state/*
  $ rm -fr emd/upload/*
  $ rm emd/agntstmp.txt
  $ rm emd/blackouts.xml
  $ rm emd/lastupld.xml
  $ rm emd/protocol.ini
  ```

- Resecure the Agent. Since we have a new Agent with a new name, a new SSL wallet will need to be generated to allow secure communication with the Management Servers.

  ```
  $ emctl secure agent
  ```

- Start the Agent. On startup, the Agent will send over the updated target information, effectively discovering the new Agent in Grid Control:

  ```
  $ emctl start agent
  ```

- Repoint the targets to the new Agent. Go to the duplicate targets page, and change the monitoring Agent for all the involved targets.

  ```
  https://<console url>/em/console/health/healthDupTarget
  ```

On that page, use the Change Monitoring Agent button to switch all the monitored targets from the obsolete Agent to the new Agent.

■ Remove the old agent in the repository:

```
SQL> exec mgmt_admin.cleanup_agent('<old hostname>:<port>');
```

BEST PRACTICE
To avoid having trouble with renaming targets if the name of machine changes, do not use the hostname as part of the monitored target that has the potential to move or be changed. If necessary, manually discover targets via the Console, or use EMCLI commands to add targets to the enterprise using a specific custom name.

Change the Time Zone of a Server Machine

A server in a data center might physically move, while keeping the same identity (meaning IP and hostname). Or a new configuration policy might require machines to be put in a new time zone. For cases like this, the information in the repository will need to be adjusted, to reflect this change of time zone. This includes updating the timestamps for the last known metric states, as well as the latest availability state of the target. Here are the steps to follow to change the time zone of a machine:

■ Stop the Agent on the machine:

```
$ emctl stop agent
```

■ Make the change on the OS for the new time zone.

■ Run the resetTZ command to update the Agent information:

```
$ emctl resetTZ agent
```

■ Update the repository with the new time zone for this Agent:

```
SQL> EXEC mgmt_target.set_agent_tzrgn
          ('<agent name>',''<new TZ>');
SQL> COMMIT;
```

The new specified time zone region must be a valid time zone region recognized by the database. To get a list of all known time zones, recognized by the database, run this SQL statement:

```
SELECT TZname, TzAbbrev
FROM   V$TIMEZONE_NAMES
ORDER BY TzAbbrev;
```

Use the value of the TZname column to update the Agent.

■ Start the Agent on the machine:

```
$ emctl start agent
```

DST Changes

In recent years, we have seen a surge in DST issues, as rules were changed and updated almost every year. Just because of these many changes, always check My Oracle Support for any alerts or DST updates for the software used.

For Oracle software, there are two things that will need to be checked and verified:

■ **The version of the Core Required Support Files** These support files contain the libraries and the rules for the DST and are an integral part of any Oracle product installed on a machine. Based on the version of these support files, the appropriate DST fix will need to be installed. To find the current version of the Core Required Support Files, use this command:

```
$ cd $ORACLE_HOME/OPatch
$ opatch lsinventory -details | grep "Oracle Core Required Support
Files"
Oracle Core Required Support Files         10.1.0.2.0
Oracle Core Required Support Files         10.1.0.5.0
```

In this example:

The main release installed was 10.1.0.2.0. Additionally, the 10.1.0.5.0 patchset was installed.

For Grid Control, this means that these files will have to be checked on the repository, all the middle tiers, and all the Agents.

■ **The version of the time zone files** The time zone data files are part of the Core Required Support Files. In some cases, though, these files might have been patched and updated directly. So to avoid any confusion about the current version of the time zone files, always check these files too. To find out the current version of the time zone files of an installation, check the `readme.txt` file in the `$ORACLE_HOME/oracore/zoneinfo` directory. The first two lines of this file contain the versions of the time zone files. Example:

```
$ head -2 $ORACLE_HOME/oracore/zoneinfo/readme.txt
Current Structure version: 2
Current Content Version  : 4
```

The following chart shows the version matrix of the default core time zone files per Grid Control version:

Grid Control	Management Server	Agent
10.2.0.1	Version 2	Version 2
10.2.0.2	Version 2	Version 2
10.2.0.3	Version 2	Version 3
10.2.0.4	Version 4	Version 4
10.2.0.5	Version 7	Version 7

The installed Java software in both the Agent and the OMS ORACLE_HOME need to be updated too to keep up to date with the DST changes. For updating the Java software, there are two possibilities:

■ Upgrade to a newer 1.4.2 release JRE and JDK release that contains the required DST updates.

■ Run TZUPDATER. This tool is an add-on for Java, which can be downloaded and installed in the JDK home. It will update the DST rule engine of the currently installed Java software, without having to upgrade the Java software to a higher version. To test if there are changes needed in the Java software that can be updated by the tool, run this command:

```
$ cd oms10g/jdk/bin
$ ./java -jar tzupdater.jar -t
```

To update and then retest the software, run this command:

```
$ cd oms10g/jdk/bin
$ ./java -jar tzupdater.jar -u
$ ./java -jar tzupdater.jar -t
```

Pointing the Agent to a New Infrastructure

In some cases, an existing Agent will need to be repointed to a new infrastructure. This can happen if a machine gets promoted from test to production, or in cases where the infrastructure is getting moved and partitioned differently.

NOTE
The <EMHOME> directory referred to in the following workflow is the directory that contains the runtime configuration files of the Agent. To get the value of that directory, issue the following command:
$ emctl getemhome

1. Stop the Agent:

    ```
    $ emctl stop agent
    ```

2. Remove the Agent from the previous Grid Control infrastructure. If the infrastructure the Agent was pointing to is still operational, the Agent will need to be removed from that repository. Run the following command in the repository of the old infrastructure:

    ```
    SQL> exec mgmt_admin.cleanup_agent('<agent name>');
    ```

3. Unsecure the Agent. The SSL wallet the Agent has of the old infrastructure will not be valid for this new Grid Control install. Therefore, switch the Agent back to normal HTTP traffic, so it can be resecured again against the new infrastructure later on:

    ```
    $ emctl usecure agent
    ```

4. Update the `emd.properties`, and change the following properties: Since the Agent now needs to report to a new OMS, the hostname of the OMS (or SLB in case of load balancing) needs to be specified in the `emd.properties` file.

    ```
    $ cd <EMHOME>
    $ cd sysman/config
    $ vi emd.properties
    ```

    Make the following change:

    ```
    REPOSITORY_URL=http://<oms>:<port>/em/upload/
    emdWalletSrcUrl=http://<oms>:<port>/em/wallets/emd
    ```

    ```
    machine  = Name of the new OMS (or SLB) machine
    port    = Unsecure port (Port using HTTP)
    ```

5. Clean up the current state files. Since we have to start with a clean slate on the new OMS, the existing state of the Agent needs to be flushed.

    ```
    $ cd <EMHOME>
    $ cd sysman/log
    $ rm -f em*
    $ cd ../emd
    $ rm -f agntstmp.txt blackouts.xml lastupld.xml protocol.ini
    $ rm -f state/*
    $ rm -f upload/*
    ```

6. Resecure the Agent, to get the updated wallet from the new OMS:

    ```
    $ emctl secure agent
    ```

7. Start the Agent:

    ```
    $ emctl start agent
    ```

Patching and Upgrading the Infrastructure

Just like any of the other targets in the IT infrastructure, the EM infrastructure components will also require patching and updating: All three tiers of the infrastructure will require maintenance. Each of these tiers have their own preparation and configuration that can be done to make the patching and updating easier.

Patching and Upgrading the Agents

The Agent is the easiest tier to talk about regarding patches. It's a relatively small and confined problem compared to the other tiers. But it's the sheer volume of Agents that make this something to really think about, before rolling out a procedure to patch or upgrade. Even a gain of five minutes in execution time for a patch or upgrade, can start adding up to quite some time if you have to upgrade a thousand Agents in the enterprise.

Preparing for an Upgrade or Patch As far as the Agent is concerned, there is not much in terms of physical preparation that needs to be done on the machine. The most important thing to do before any kind of maintenance on the Agent side is to make sure that there is enough free disk space available to roll out the patch or upgrade.

There is something at the Enterprise Level, though, that people typically forget when performing maintenance on a machine: Any patch or upgrade operation will require a restart of the Agent. If availability and SLAs are important, any maintenance done at the Agent will have to be coordinated with the administrators of the machine, and a planned outage (meaning a "blackout" in Grid Control terminology) will have to be defined for the operation. The last thing the operators and administrators of a machine want to have happen is to be awakened in the middle of the night with an alert generated from Grid Control saying the Agent of their application machines is down, only to find out it's due to a scheduled outage for a patch.

Patching the Agent   There are several ways to apply a patch on the Agent:

- **Directly using OPatch**   This is the easiest way, and the most direct one. The downside of this approach, though, is that you need to be physically logged on to the box with the Agent software, and an administrator will have to type the commands for the actual patch installation. Once the patch has been manually staged on the box, and unzipped in an empty directory, the patch can be applied using `opatch`:

```
$ ${ORACLE_HOME}/bin/emctl start blackout my_patch -nodeLevel
$ ${ORACLE_HOME}/bin/emctl stop agent
$ cd <location of unzipped patch>
$ ${ORACLE_HOME}/OPatch/opatch apply
$ ${ORACLE_HOME}/bin/emctl start agent
$ ${ORACLE_HOME}/bin/emctl stop blackout my_patch
```

> **NOTE**
> *It is possible to script patching with* `opatch` *for any Oracle product, and apply patches in a silent mode without any user interaction using the* `-silent` *command-line option. If this switch is used, starting from* `OPatch` *version 10.2.0.4.5, you will need a configuration file for OCM. To generate this OCM response file, use the tool provided with* `OPatch`*:*
>
> `$ cd $ORACLE_HOME/OPatch/ocm/bin`
> `$ ./emocmrsp -output <location of OCM response file>`
>
> *This response file must then be specified when applying the patch in silent mode:*
>
> `$ opatch apply -silent -ocmrf <location of OCM`
> `response file>`

- **Using the Patch Wizard**   The advantage of the Patch Wizard, shown in Figure 6-4, is that it can push and apply patches to one or more Agents in the infrastructure from the browser, without the need to log on to the machines. The patch job will take care of the downloading of the patch from My Oracle Support, the staging of the patch on the machine, the creation of a blackout to consider the outage of the Agent a planned one, and finally the application of the patch itself.

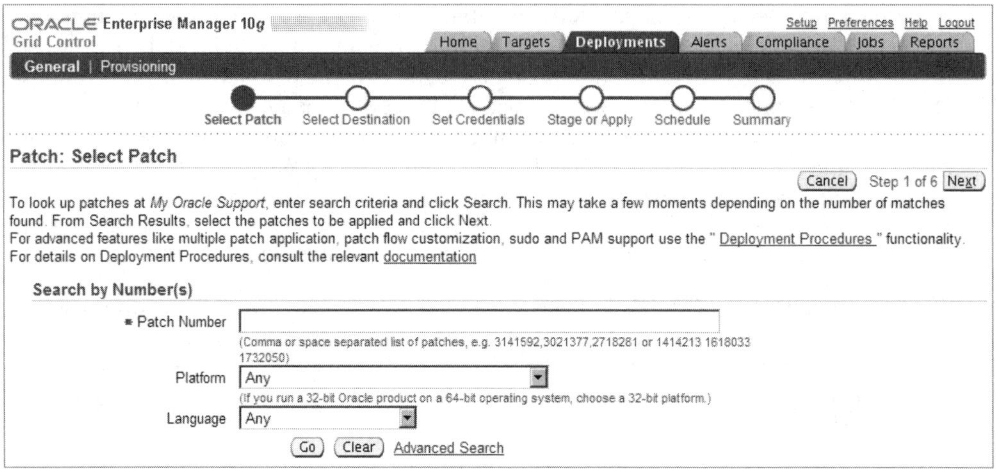

FIGURE 6-4. *Patch Wizard*

Several new features were added to the Patch Wizard with 10.2.0.5, to help streamline the patch application for Agents:

■ **Apply multiple patches in one patch operation** In previous releases, only one patch could only be applied to one or more Agents. Starting with 10.2.0.5, multiple patches can be selected, and applied in a single patch session.

■ **Support for NAPPLY patches** All one-off patches containing multiple patches (patch bundles) require special commands to be applied. Support for these patch bundles got added for Agent patches as well.

Upgrading the Agent

There are two possible scenarios for upgrading the Agent:

■ **A minor upgrade (patchset)** Patchsets can be applied directly on the ORACLE_HOME, and do not require any special preparation. Any of the available installer mechanisms can be used to run the upgrade:

   ■ The easiest way is to run the Oracle Universal Installer, and run the upgrade directly on the box. It's also the most labor-intensive one, requiring the administrator to log on to the box, manually stop and black out the Agent to perform the upgrade.

   ■ The upgrade can also be done using the agentDownload mechanism, giving administrators the capability to automate the upgrade. The -u switch can be used to specify the upgrade:

   ```
   $ agent_download.linux -b <base directory for software> -u -x
   ```

NOTE
Since an upgrade means more than one version of the Agent is already known in the agentDownload *directory of the OMS, make sure the script from the patchset is downloaded and used to run the upgrade!*

- For every Grid Control patchset, there is also a special patch released to upgrade the Agent. This patch can then be used by the Agent Patch Wizard to apply the upgrade.

- **A major upgrade (new major release)**   Any new major release will have to be applied out of home. This means that any new major version of the Agent will have to be installed next to the existing one. The final stage of the upgrade will migrate the state of the old Agent to the new one. A major upgrade is not a patch upgrade. The regular install mechanisms can be used to do a major upgrade, but some special consideration is needed to do the upgrade:

    - The install will create a second ORACLE_HOME on the machine. So there has to be enough free disk space available to install a new Agent in a new ORACLE_HOME.

    - The agentDownload mechanism can also be used to do this type of upgrade, but an additional parameter is required to specify the location of the old ORACLE_HOME:

    ```
    $ agent_download.linux -b <base directory for software> -u -x
                     -o <OLD ORACLE_HOME>
    ```

NOTE
Same note for the agentDownload *mechanism applies here: Make sure the correct version of the script is used to run the upgrade.*

Upgrading Java in the Agent Home   A Java Developer's Kit (JDK) is installed in the Agent ORACLE_HOME in the directory $ORACLE_HOME/jdk. It is possible to replace this Java version with a newer version of Java released for that platform in case of a critical fix in the Java software, as long as the new version is a maintenance release. To get the version of the JDK, use this command:

```
$ $ORACLE_HOME/jdk/bin/java -version
```

For all versions up to 10.2.0.4, you can only put a newer 1.4.2 version of the Java software in the Agent home. The versions 1.5 and 1.6 are not supported with all Agent versions 10.2.0.1 up to 10.2.0.4. The 10.2.0.5 Agent will have Java version 1.5.0 installed. Any higher Java 1.5 version can be used in the Agent ORACLE_HOME. The Java versions 1.4.2 and 1.6 are not supported, though.

NOTE
An important thing to point out here is that with each upgrade, the Java installed in the Agent home will be replaced with whatever the install has provided. If a newer Java maintenance release was installed in the Agent home, always check to see if the version after the upgrade is the same or higher as the replaced one that was there before the upgrade.

BEST PRACTICE
Always keep the original version of the JDK around (rename the current one to jdk.old, for instance). The Agent software has been thoroughly tested using the version dropped during the install. And although a newer version of Java should be compatible with an older version, it's better to have a fallback in case there is a problem with the newer software.

Patching and Upgrading Management Servers

Patching the OMS machines is already a little trickier. Any discussion about upgrading the OMS needs to broken up into two parts:

- **Maintenance of the Grid Control application**   Although this technically means just the OC4J application deployed on the Application Server (OC4J_EM and OC4J_EMPROV), the Grid Control application has a third component in there (the repository, with the schema and the data Grid Control uses), which needs to be patched and updated at the same time the application changes.

- **Maintenance on the Application Server**   This is the middle-tier infrastructure Grid Control uses. The Application Server itself also has patches and CPUs that need to be applied.

Patching the Grid Control Application   There is only one way to apply a patch to Grid Control itself: Since any kind of patching framework involves having an operational Management Server, the patching framework (meaning the Patching Wizard and the Deployment Procedures) cannot be used to patch. The only mechanism available to apply a Grid Control patch is through `opatch`.

Depending on the type of patch, either it will require a shutdown of all the Management Servers, or it can be applied in a rolling fashion. Instructions on what is possible and how the patch can be applied will be in the README file of the patch itself. If the patch requires a shutdown of the entire Grid Control application on all the Management Servers, a few tricks can be done to minimize the downtime:

- Stage the patch first on all Management Servers. This will allow the patch to be applied in parallel on several machines at once.

- As a first step, shut down all redundant Management Servers, and apply the patch, without making any repository changes. We'll call these servers the First Wave set of machines. At the end of this step, we now have patched OMS machines, without the patch itself being visible in the application yet.

- As soon as the First Wave machines are patched, bring down all the remaining Management Servers.

- When all Management Servers are shut down, a few things can be done in parallel:

  - Pick one machine from the First Wave set of machines and follow the instructions in the README file to execute all the commands needed for the patch application. (We'll call this OMS the Master Server for reference purposes.)

  - While those commands are running, apply the patch with `opatch` on all the other unpatched OMS machines.

- As soon as all the instructions have been executed on the Master Server, all the First Wave machines can be started. The remaining OMS servers can then be started as soon as the `opatch` command finishes applying the patch.

Upgrading Grid Control Application   The complexity of a Grid Control upgrade is just the same as that of a patch with repository changes. The only difference between the patch and the upgrade will be the time it takes to complete: An upgrade typically takes a bit more time to complete.

A similar trick can be used to minimize the downtime for an upgrade. The only gotcha for the upgrade case is the fact that the install is smart in the way it detects the condition of the repository: If an OMS is getting upgraded, and the repository has not been upgraded yet, the upgrade operation itself will also upgrade the schema and the data in the repository. When the second OMS gets upgraded, the schema is already upgraded, and the upgrade will finish after updating the OC4J applications.

Since we cannot preupgrade the spare Management Servers while they are pointing to the production repository, we need to involve the test and staging site in this case. If you want to minimize the downtime of an upgrade, both the test site and the redundant (spare) Management Servers might come in handy.

■   The test site can be upgraded independently from the production site. This can even be done days or even weeks before the scheduled upgrade of the production site. The benefit of doing this is to be able to walk through an entire upgrade process, and have time to verify Grid Control after the upgrade, before touching the production environment.

■   As soon as the schedule is made for the upgrade of the production environment, the next step is to upgrade the redundant Management Servers. For each OMS server:

   ■   Stop the OMS and all the Application Server components:

   ```
   $ $ORACLE_HOME/opmn/bin/opmnctl stopall
   ```

   ■   If an SLB is used, make sure the SLB is updated to no longer route traffic to the stopped Management server.

   ■   Point the OMS server to the test site. The only place that needs to be updated to make an OMS point to a specific repository is in the emoms.properties file. The connect descriptor and the SYSMAN password have to change to make the OMS point to the test environment:

   ```
   oracle.sysman.eml.mntr.emdRepPwd=<sysman pwd>
   oracle.sysman.eml.mntr.emdRepPwdEncrypted=FALSE
   oracle.sysman.eml.mntr.emdRepConnectDescriptor=(DESCRIPTION\=...)
   ```

   ■   Upgrade the OMS. Since the test site is already upgraded, the upgrade of the OMS will only install the new files, update the OC4J applications, and not run any of the schema changes.

   ■   When the upgrade of the OMS is done, and it has been functionally verified, point it again to the production site, but leave it down. The quickest way here is to restore the backup of the emoms.properties file before the upgrade changes were made: This file has the original settings of the OMS, and can, therefore, be copied over as-is to get back to the original settings.

■   After the set of spare Management Servers have all been upgraded, shut down the remaining OMS servers, and upgrade the first OMS. This upgrade will also upgrade the repository schema and perform all the database tasks in the production environment.

- As soon as the upgrade operation finishes, and the OMS is back online, start the redundant OMS servers (the ones that were preupgraded against the test environment) to give the infrastructure enough CPU power to catch up on all the work.

- The final step is then to upgrade any of the remaining Management Servers one by one in the normal way.

Patching and Upgrading the Application Server   Grid Control is just an OC4J application running on top of an Application Server. All patches and CPUs the AS server needs can and should be applied on the Application Servers the Management Servers are using as well. The main difference between applying an Application Server patch and a Grid Control patch is that an AS patch does not touch or change the Grid Control application. With each OMS install having its own separate Application stack, any patch to apply can be applied in a rolling fashion on each OMS individually, preventing a total downtime of Grid Control.

NOTE
Applying an AS patch to an OMS install via the Patch Wizard or via a DP (Deployment Procedure) creates a chicken-and-egg problem: In order for the patch to be applied via the Console, you need an OMS. And in order to apply the patch on the Application Server, the entire AS stack will have to be shut down (including the OMS). Luckily, if the HA best practices were followed, there is a way out: If multiple Management Servers are used, one Application Stack can be shut down completely. As soon as the Console has detected the down condition of all the AS targets, the patch can be applied via an operational OMS. As long as the operational OMS can talk to the Agent of the machine with the to-be-patched AS stack (which should be the case anyway) and the agent points to the SLB and not the local OMS, the patch can be pushed out and applied on the machine. This trick can be used in a rolling fashion, to patch the Application Servers one at a time.

Any installation of Grid Control 10gR2 prior to 10.2.0.5 will install the Application Server 10.1.2.0.2. All compatible CPU bundles and one-patches can be applied on top of that 10.1.2.0.2 Application Server stack, but any upgrade of the Application Server to a version higher than 10.1.2.0.2 is not supported and not certified.

Starting from 10.2.0.5, the 10.1.2.3 Application Server stack is used. The same rule for compatible CPU bundles applies: All those CPU patches for 10.1.2.3 can be applied on the 10.2.0.5 Application Server stack.

Upgrading Java in the OMS Home   As with the Agent software, it's possible to install a newer maintenance release of the Java software in the OMS home. The same restrictions apply here as well: You can only replace the existing Java software with a newer 1.4.2 maintenance release. Versions 1.5 and 1.6 are not supported with 10gR2. To get the version of the JDK and JRE software, use this command:

```
$ $ORACLE_HOME/jdk/bin/java -version
$ $ORACLE_HOME/jre/1.4.2/bin/java -version
```

For the OMS server, both a JDK and a JRE are installed:

- **JDK** `$ORACLE_HOME/jdk`
- **JRE** `$ORACLE_HOME/jre/1.4.2`

NOTE
The same important note applies as with the Agent: An upgrade will replace the JDK and JRE in the OMS home. Always check the version of JDK and JRE after an upgrade, to make sure the same or higher version is used.

BEST PRACTICE
The same good advice as that for the Agent applies here as well: Always keep the old version of the Java software around. It's better to keep a backup handy, just in case.

Keeping Track of Changes

The biggest danger for any data center is the threat of the undocumented, unknown little change that crept onto a machine. It seems that no matter how strict the change control procedures are, some change, sometimes a very trivial one, just happens to be made. And, as Murphy has demonstrated so many times, these trivial changes are usually the ones creating the biggest trouble. To stay ahead of all these problems, it's absolutely necessary to keep track of all the changes and all the modifications made on a system.

The configuration management features in Grid Control can help here. Besides regular metric data points, the Agent also collects a group of configuration data. As far as the Agent is concerned, this data is just another set of metrics that have to be collected and uploaded to the OMS. The difference with the configuration data is how the repository handles that data. Configuration data is not rolled up like regular metrics: There is very little value in calculating the average number of CPUs for the last seven days. During the loading of the data in the repository, the old configuration (called the old snapshot) is compared against the current set of data (the current snapshot). Any difference in the data is marked as a change, and a special record with the details of the found change is inserted together with the new data. This gives administrators the ability to find the setup and configuration of a target at any point in time, and also highlight all the changes that got made leading up to that setup.

Accessing the Configuration Information

Several targets have configuration data in the repository that is accessible in the Configuration section of the Deployments tab. Only the host target has an additional link to get to the configuration data: The Configuration tab on the host home page is the point of entry into the configuration data (see Figure 6-5). This page is the starting point to view the current configuration, the history of all changes made on the target, and the ability to compare this information with other targets of the same type.

The current configuration snapshot is always displayed by default, showing the current configuration settings for the target.

- The Save button allows the current configuration snapshot to be saved. This can either be in the repository itself (to have a point-in-time snapshot to compare against at a later point in time), or it can be saved to an XML file.

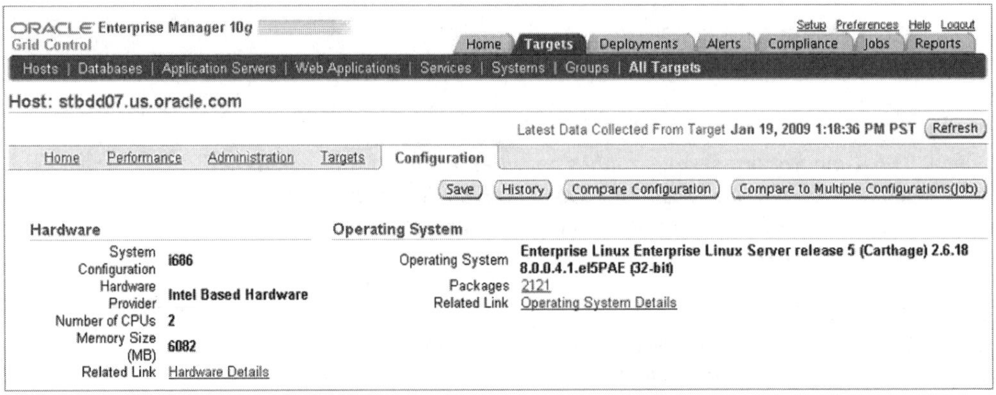

FIGURE 6-5. *Host configuration example*

■ The History button gives the ability to view all the past changes, or even filter on just the changes a user is interested in.

■ The Compare Configuration and Compare to Multiple Configurations buttons are options to use the current target as a baseline, and find all the differences between either one (for the first button), or a set of other similar targets (for the second button).

Browsing the Configuration History

There are two ways to get to the configuration history page:

■ Either by using the History button for a specific target (the Target Name will be filled in, to filter out just those changes for the target in question).

■ Or by going to the Deployments tab, and selecting the Configuration History link (see Figure 6-6). In this case, no filtering will be done by default, allowing the user to choose all the filtering options to pick and choose the changes he or she is interested in.

Once the filtering is complete, and just the required changes are visible, that set of changes can be saved to a CSV file using the Save To File button on the page.

Comparing Configurations

Here's a typical data-center mystery: An application is running smoothly on one machine, while on another machine, which is identical to the first one (or at least: it *should* be identical), it's misbehaving. These day-to-day treasure hunts to find the differences on machines can be very time-consuming.

Comparing configurations is the solution here, to find the differences between two targets that *should* be configured identically. A comparison can be done directly in the Console between two targets. If two or more targets need to be compared, a Grid Control job is submitted that will compare all the configuration data, and report all the differences between the selected targets. To make it even more interesting, a Saved Configuration can also be selected as the starting point to compare with: This will help debug any issues, where the configuration has drifted away from a gold standard or a standard setup.

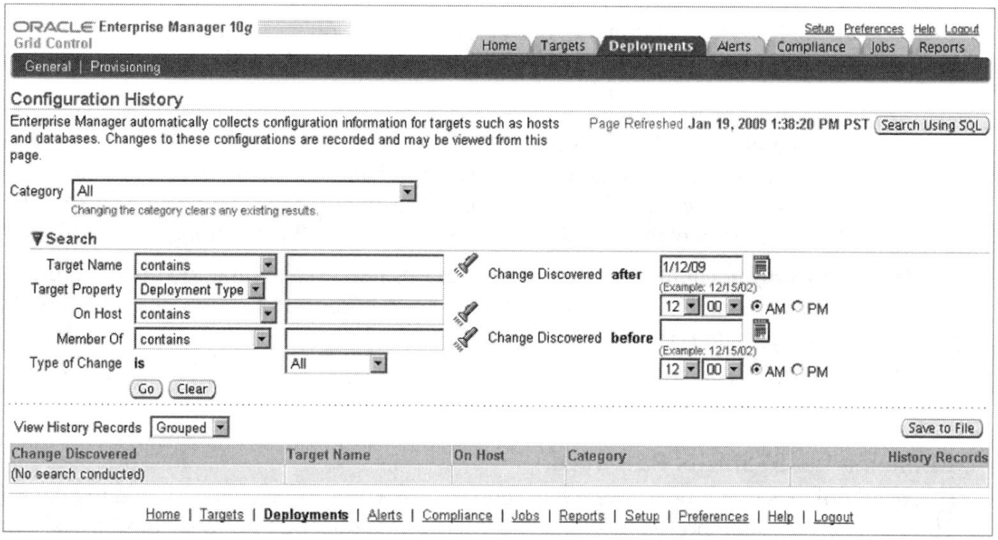

FIGURE 6-6.   *Searching the configuration history*

Figure 6-7 is an example of a database instance compare, between two instances of a RAC database. Although the instances should be configured identically, the compare *did* find a couple of interesting differences.

And yes, this was a staged example to highlight the benefit of a compare. But these kinds of subtle differences between targets that are supposed to be the same are quite common in a data center rollout. Cases like this are more common than one might think!

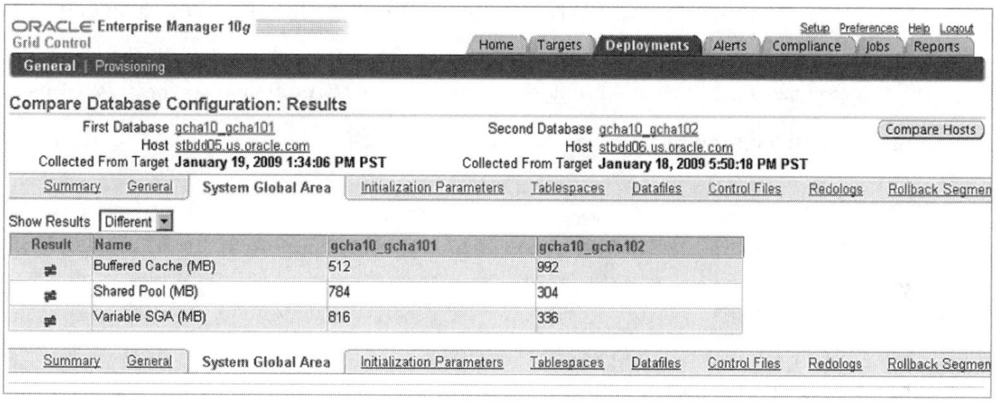

FIGURE 6-7.   *Configuration history comparison*

Administrator Management

Every enterprise has some kind of password management and password lifecycle procedure to update passwords for application account. In Grid Control there are three types of users known in the system:

- **Application users**   For Grid Control, all user and administrators defined in the application can be changed and updated via standard mechanisms. There are two special Grid Control accounts, however, which require special attention in terms of updating passwords: the SYSMAN (owner of the repository) and the MGMT_VIEW (reporting framework) user.

- **Monitoring accounts**   Targets like databases require a login to do the monitoring. These users are defined in Grid Control as monitoring users, and are specified as part of the monitoring setup of the target.

- **Preferred Credentials**   These are accounts specified for Grid Control users to perform administrator tasks.

Changing the SYSMAN Password

Password policies might be in effect that require passwords to be changed on a regular basis. The SYSMAN account, however, is one of those database accounts that is not so trivial to change: Since every OMS is using this database user to create connections to store and retrieve information from the repository, any change made to this user will immediately affect all the Management Servers.

Starting from 10.2.0.5, there is a new EMCTL command to help streamline this operation to change the password:

- Stop all the OMS servers:

  ```
  $ emctl stop oms
  ```

- On the first OMS, run this command to update the local settings, change the password in the repository database, and update the monitoring settings:

  ```
  $ emctl config oms -change_repos_pwd -change_in_db
          -old_pwd <pwd> -new_pwd <pwd> -use_sys_pwd -sys_pwd <pwd>
  ```

  On all other Management Servers, only the local settings will need to be updated to use the correct new password:

  ```
  $ emctl config oms -change_repos_pwd -old_pwd <pwd> -new_pwd <pwd>
  ```

- Start all the OMS servers:

  ```
  $ emctl start oms
  ```

  Prior to 10.2.0.5, a few more things had to be done to change the SYSMAN password:

- Stop all the OMS servers:

  ```
  $ emctl stop oms
  ```

- Change the password in the database:

  ```
  SQL> ALTER USER sysman IDENTIFIED BY <new password>;
  ```

■ Modify the emoms.properties file on each OMS server:

```
oracle.sysman.eml.mntr.emdRepPwd=<new password>
oracle.sysman.eml.mntr.emdRepPwdEncrypted=FALSE
```

After the OMS gets restarted, the clear-text password will be encrypted, and the emdRepPwdEncrypted parameter will be changed back to TRUE.

■ Restart all the OMS servers:

```
$ emctl start oms
```

■ Log in to the Console, and update the monitoring password for the OMS and Repository target. Go to the Management Services and Repository page in the Console.

```
https://<oms name>:<oms port>/em/console/health/healthHome
```

On the bottom of the page, in the Related Links section, click the Monitoring Configuration link, and update the Repository password parameter with the new password of the SYSMAN user.

Regardless of how the SYSMAN password got changed on the Management Servers, any EMCLI client installation that is using the SYSMAN account will also have to be updated to use the new password:

```
$ emcli setup -url <Grid Control URL> -username SYSMAN
$ emcli sync
```

Changing MGMT_VIEW Password

The reporting framework is the only system in Grid Control using the MGMT_VIEW account. Nobody needs to know the password of this account, and no configuration file contains a reference to this account. The repository owner (SYSMAN) manages this account. If the account has to be changed due to a security policy, follow these steps:

1. Change the password of the MGMT_VIEW account, using the PL/SQL API.

```
SQL> exec mgmt_view_priv.change_view_user_password('<new PWD >');
```

Do not use any ALTER USER command to change the password. When the password change is being done directly in the database, SYSMAN will not know of the change, and the reporting framework will not be able to log in any more. After the password has been changed, all the OMS servers have to be restarted, to have the application pick up the new password for the MGMT_VIEW account.

2. Starting from 10.2.0.5, there is an EMCTL command to change the MGMT_VIEW password:

```
$ emctl config oms -change_view_user_pwd [-sysman_pwd <sysman_pwd>]
         [-user_pwd <user_pwd>] [-auto_generate]
```

The recommendation is to use the -auto_generate flag to generate a completely random password that nobody knows. After running this EMCTL command, the OMS will still have to be bounced, to make the OMS pick up the new password, and reinitiate the MGMT_VIEW connections to render the reports.

Regardless of how many Management Servers are operational, the command to update the MGMT_VIEW password only needs to be changed once. Each OMS will have to be restarted, though, to pick up the new password.

Changing Password of Grid Control User

Like any other application using an Oracle database, the passwords of the Grid Control users can be managed directly in the database. There is also a UI page available for making, creating, and updating Grid Control users. The Administrators page, which is part of the Setup menu, allows any Grid Control user to modify his or her password (only super-users can modify other accounts).

NOTE
Starting from 10.2.0.5, Grid Control users can be associated with a password profile, to make the administration and the rules for setting and modifying passwords consistent across accounts.

The password can also be updated via EMCLI:

```
$ emcli modify_user -name="<username>" -password="<new password>"
```

Changing Monitoring Password

DBSNMP is the default user, used for monitoring databases. The account information to do the monitoring of databases is kept both in the repository, and on the Agent side (`targets.xml` file).
Prior to 10.2.0.5, changing of accounts in the target databases has to be done in two steps:

1. Change the account in the database. This step is not automated in EM. So a DBA still has to go into the database, and alter the monitoring user to give it a new password.

2. Update the monitoring configuration in Grid Control. Without this update, the Agent will not be able to log in to the database any more. To change the password of the monitoring user in Grid Control, follow these steps:

   - In the Grid Control Console, go to the target's home page.
   - Click the Monitoring Configuration link at the bottom.
   - Update the password of the monitoring account (typically DBSNMP).
   - Save the changes, to update the settings at the Agent.

   You can also use EMCLI to update the monitoring password for the target:

   ```
   $ emcli update_password -target_type=oracle_database
           -target_name=<db name> -credential_type=DBCreds
           -key_column=DBUserName:dbsnmp
           -non_key_column=DBPassword:<old pwd>:<new pwd>
   ```

   (The complete command should be on a single line.)
   For security reasons, the old password needs to be specified while updating the password, to prevent rogue administrators from getting access to an account. The difference between updating the monitoring credentials in the UI and running the EMCLI is that the Console update will only update one password on the specific page the administrator is using. With the EMCLI command, all references of the specified account will be changed, across all users and all administrators defined in Grid Control.

It streamlines the updates with a single command, but it will update the password for all users defined in the enterprise.

With the release of 10.2.0.5, some new EMCLI verbs were added to make the updating of passwords a little bit more streamlined. For databases, the new commands do the two tasks needed to update the password in one command: This both changes the account on the target database itself and updates all the references of that user used for monitoring and preferred credentials:

```
$ emcli update_db_password -target_name=<db name>
        -user_name=<user name> -change_at_target=yes
```

If nothing else is specified on the command line, ECMLI will ask the user to input the old password, the new password, and a confirmation of the new password. To prevent EMCLI from asking the questions and having to enter the values interactively, additional command-line options are available to specify the values for these password questions. The way this works for EMCLI is to have a file available containing the value of the option you want to specify. The three options for the password questions are:

- **old_password**   The current password of the user that is being modified. For security reasons, the password change will not succeed if this value is not specified, or if a wrong password is specified.
- **new_password**   The new password for this user.
- **retype_new_password**   A confirmation of this new password.

Using these three options, the full command line becomes:

```
$ emcli update_db_password -target_name=<db name>
        -user_name=<user name> -change_at_target=yes
        -inputfile="old_password=/tmp/file1;
                new_password=/tmp/file2;
                retype_new_password=/tmp/file2"
```

Changing Preferred Credentials

Preferred credentials are just references to users and passwords to be used to do administration on targets. These credentials are stored as part of a Grid Control user. And like the monitoring credentials, an update of the password for these accounts requires two things to happen:

- The password needs to change on the target.
- The preferred credentials need to be updated to specify the new password.

The same commands and steps used for the monitoring credentials can be used to update the preferred credentials as well.

- From 10.2.0.5 onward, use the EMCLI command to perform both operations in sequence. The same commands used to change the monitoring credentials can also be used for changing the preferred credentials: The second part of the command will replace all references of the old password with the new password for the specified user.
- Prior to 10.2.0.5, the two steps just mentioned must be executed, to first change the password on the target, and then either change the preferred credentials in the Console, or use the EMCLI command to update all the references of the account.

Removing Users

Just as new administrators can be created, old ones may need to be removed from the system. When an account is removed from the system, Grid Control will verify the following:

- If this account owns any objects defined in Grid Control, like blackouts, jobs, groups, and templates, another valid Grid Control user will need to be specified to reassign the objects to that administrator account: If no valid administrator account is specified during the delete operation, it will fail.

- Except in case of an external user (for example, LDAP), the removal of the account will also mean the removal of the database account created in the repository for this administrator.

NOTE
Only super-administrators can remove users from the system, and no user is capable of deleting him- or herself. The SYSMAN account is also protected, and can never be removed from the system, since this would mean the removal of the repository from the database.

There are a few ways to remove a user from Grid Control:

- **Via the Console**   Go to the Administrators page of the Setup option to manage administrator accounts. Once an administrator is selected for removal, the UI will ask you for a new account to use to reassign any object owned by the administrator to be removed.

- **Via EMCLI**   The command-line interface has a simplified way of removing a user: There is no option to specify the account to use for the reassignment. The command to use is:

```
$ emcli delete_user -name="<user_name>"
```

For the EMCLI use, all jobs and blackouts the user owns must be stopped and be no longer active. If there are active jobs and blackouts found, the delete operation will fail. All other objects owned by the administrator (like templates and groups) will be reassigned to the user SYSMAN.

Summary

Like any other enterprise-wide application, Grid Control will require some attention and some maintenance. And this is usually what Enterprise Administrators are *not* doing.

The Common Mistakes

- **Follow-up on the MTM metrics**   Grid Control has a lot of metrics and data points available by default to inform the Enterprise Administrators about the status of the application. All of this is accessible from the MTM pages (the Management Services and Repository pages) in the Console. Strangely enough, these pages are typically underutilized, causing critical and warning alerts about the infrastructure to be missed.

- **Using a test or staging site**   A test or staging site is critical to test out new procedures. Without a test site around to play with, all modifications have to be done in the production environment directly. This means that any mistake of any nature will automatically cause some downtime of the production application. This also includes testing patches, and running the patch and/or upgrade procedure on the test site to document the steps and actions to take when doing the same on the production site.

- **Redundancy for the OMS and repository**   For any enterprise-wide production Grid Control deployment, there needs to be redundancy at the OMS and the repository level. Without this redundancy, any kind of operation that requires a reboot or a downtime of the machine will result in downtime of the application.

- **Alert floods**   The flow of incoming alerts needs to be checked and validated on a regular basis. Any metrics generating frequent alerts, warnings, and clears need to be verified, and the thresholds should be adjusted if needed. Any unwanted alerts should either be disabled or have the thresholds removed to stop the metric from sending more alerts. If the flood of alerts is not kept under control, in case of a real problem happening on a set of servers (like a network outage, or a problem with multiple servers), the extra alerts will cause even more strain on the infrastructure.

Best Practices

There are plenty of data points and pages available in the Console to give administrators the necessary data to check on Grid Control. The following list gives a rollup of the major areas to look at:

- **Regular health-checks**   This is perhaps the single most important thing to point out:

> **Check the infrastructure on a regular basis!**

   Grid Control is not a zero-administration tool. It's a tool that will help and assist administrators to manage targets and applications. But Grid Control is an application too, running on server machines, and therefore will need the same kind of attention you give to other critical applications. Check the backlog indicators. Check for repeating errors in both the Console, as well as the log and trace files of the OMS.

- **Failure and problem reports**   Errors rarely happen only once or twice. As soon as an error is reported, the underlying cause must be investigated, and if possible resolved or worked around to prevent further escalation of the problem and prevent multiple errors from getting logged in Grid Control.

- **Spare capacity**   Any of the Management Servers should never be busy all the time, for any of the Grid Control routines, or even for the CPU utilization on the box. There should also be enough spare resources available to handle any failure of a single OMS in a multi-OMS environment. The amount of spare capacity is dependent on the number of Management Servers:

  - At least 50 percent spare capacity in case of two servers
  - At least 33 percent spare capacity in case of three servers
  - At least 25 percent spare capacity in case of four servers

PART
II

Grid Control Common Tasks and Functions

CHAPTER
7

Principles of Target Monitoring

arget monitoring is all about getting the information from the Agents and interpreting it which already means that you have to be sure that you are getting all the information you need. But it also means that you need to get just the information you need, and not get overloaded by all kinds of noise.

The default set of information collected from the monitored targets is good enough for most of the targets. But for some extreme cases with either mission-critical machines, or development and test machines of lower importance, the monitoring settings and the information collected for these targets will have to be tweaked.

In the end, it boils down to this simple principle: The information you will get from Grid Control, is only as good as the existing monitoring setup for all the targets on the Agents.

Monitoring and Managing a Target

Life would be pretty dull without targets in Grid Control. The console would have nothing to show, and an Administrator would have nothing to do or click on. A target is one of the key things Grid Control needs to have. By default, Grid Control will have a base number of targets, because it has registered itself—the Grid Control components (repository, middle-tier, and application) are all there to peruse. A target needs to be added in the environment through a discovery procedure: a method, either run by the Agent to detect and find possible targets on the machine where the Agent is running, or through a manual procedure initiated by an Administrator in the Console. Once a target is available to the Agent, the definition is uploaded to the OMS and added to the repository. Then three types of operations are possible:

- **Monitoring** Every target managed by a Agent will be monitored by that Agent. A set of metrics will be executed on a regular basis, determining the current condition of that target. The metric data collected by the Agent also forms the basis for determining the state of that target.

- **Administration** For all Oracle products discovered in Grid Control, there are specific areas in the Console to allow an Administrator to manage and maintain those targets. For all non-Oracle products and plug-ins added to Grid Control, the most effective method of administration is always to use the tools provided by the vendor for those targets. The administration of these products is therefore not added in Grid Control.

- **Running tasks** All targets discovered by an Agent can be used to run tasks—Grid Control jobs—on the server where the target resides. These tasks are either run directly against the target itself (for instance, a SQL statement run against a target database), or as a set of OS commands run in the correct context of the target (that is, starting and then stopping a database listener). Chapter 10 goes into more detail on the setup and configuration of the tasks.

In addition to individual targets discovered by the Agents, Administrators can also bundle targets together in special container targets called *Groups*. The main purpose of groups is to give Administrators the ability to logically combine targets, and perform all the usual monitoring and maintenance on all the members of the group via a single operation. This principle of combining targets is commonly referred to as the "manage many as one" principle. It allows the administrators to standardize the monitoring, and perform identical tasks on all the members of the group. Groups can be used in all major areas of Grid Control, starting with the monitoring, and including the running of jobs, and the creation of reports and dashboards. For each of these, a group can be selected. And the action taken on the group will result in the action being replicated on each member of the same type in the group.

Grid Control itself utilizes Groups to create specialized containers that are utilized internally for different purposes. These groups are displayed along the topmost tab of Grid Control so that they can be quickly linked to—Systems and Services are the most obvious examples. Systems and Services serve specific business purposes, and are described in detail in Chapter 13.

Setting Up a Target for Administration and Monitoring

Every target that is discovered and uploaded into the repository will have a set of properties associated with it, to identify the target, and allow the Management Server and the Agent to monitor and administer this target. The properties can be split up into a couple of broad categories:

- **Credential information**   Username and passwords to access a target are commonly referred to as *credential information*. This login information is needed to be able to perform tasks in Grid Control.

- **Monitoring properties**   These are all the settings the Agent needs to monitor the target. These properties will exist on both the Agent side (in the `targets.xml` file), and in the repository for the users to see and validate.

- **Target properties**   These are custom properties that an Administrator can specify to further identify the target. These are kept only in the repository. The Agent will not know these properties.

Credential Information

For every administration or maintenance operation a user does in Grid Control, a login will have to be specified for the user to be able to access the target and perform the operation. Even simple and straightforward operations, like looking at the performance of a database or checking the logging and tracing levels of an Application Server, will require the Administrator to authenticate him- or herself. Once a valid username and password information are entered, the user then has a choice to save this credential information as the default account to use for that target. This information is securely stored, and only the Administrator will be able to modify the credential information. And just to put any security concerns at rest: There is no way to *see* credential information anywhere in Grid Control: not via the Console, not via some (undocumented) PL/SQL routine, not via an Agent command. Once credentials are stored, only the user who owns the credentials can change them.

There are several types of credential information in Grid Control:

- **Monitoring credentials**   These are needed for any target that requires a login in order to obtain information from it. Not all targets require monitoring credentials, but some types of targets do to be able to get the data and statistics of the target. A typical example here is an Oracle database: Without a username and a password, you will not be able to get any information from this database. Monitoring credentials are part of the monitoring properties, and are kept both on the Agent side, and in the repository. For all those targets that require monitoring credentials, a link called Monitoring Configuration will be on the bottom of the target homepage: On that page, an Administrator can configure the account to use for monitoring a target. Figure 7-1 shows this monitoring configuration screen for a database target.

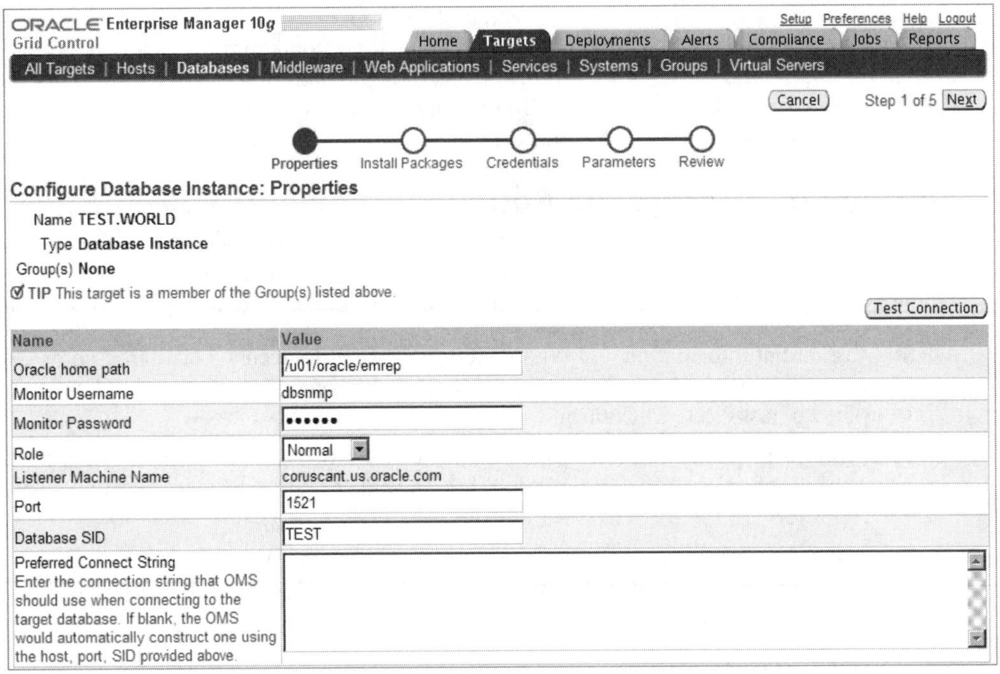

ORACLE Enterprise Manager 10g
Grid Control
Setup Preferences Help Logout
Home Targets Deployments Alerts Compliance Jobs Reports
All Targets | Hosts | Databases | Middleware | Web Applications | Services | Systems | Groups | Virtual Servers
Cancel
Step 1 of 5 Next
Properties Install Packages Credentials Parameters Review
Configure Database Instance: Properties
Name TEST.WORLD
Type Database Instance
Group(s) None
TIP This target is a member of the Group(s) listed above.
Test Connection
Name
Value
Oracle home path
/u01/oracle/emrep
Monitor Username
dbsnmp
Monitor Password
••••••
Role
Normal
Listener Machine Name
coruscant.us.oracle.com
Port
1521
Database SID
TEST
Preferred Connect String
Enter the connection string that OMS should use when connecting to the target database. If blank, the OMS would automatically construct one using the host, port, SID provided above.

FIGURE 7-1. *Monitoring Configuration page for an Oracle Database*

NOTE

Although people will typically associate credentials and login information with a username and password, it does not always have to be exactly that. Any target that is monitored via SNMP (network devices, firewalls, and so on) requires an SNMP domain and an SNMP port to be able to access the target. And even though this is not strictly speaking a login, the Agent (and therefore also the OMS and repository) treats these monitoring properties as credentials.

- **Preferred credentials** This will be the most commonly known and most widely used type of login information. Every user in Grid Control can specify a default username and password to use for every target he or she has access to. Once specified, this login information will then always be presented first in the Console when performing operations that require a login: The user then has the option to either use these default ones, or specify another username and password, to be used for that operation only. Figure 7-2 gives an example of the database login page: Although the username was already saved as the default credential, the administrator can still overrule this, and specify another account if needed.

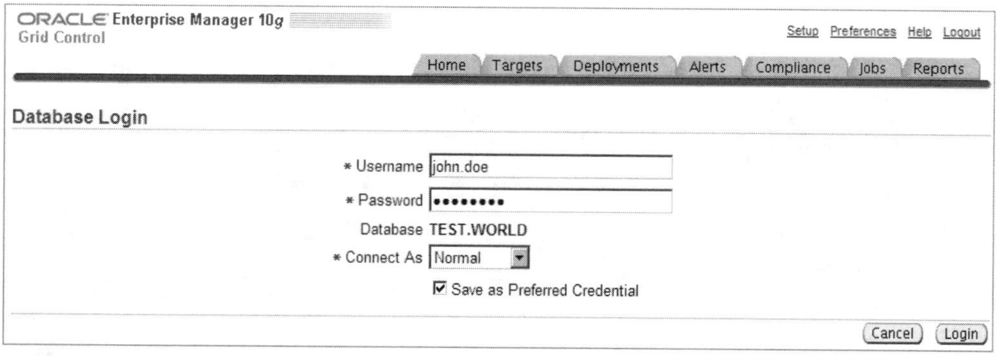

ORACLE Enterprise Manager 10*g*
Grid Control

Setup Preferences Help Logout

Home | Targets | Deployments | Alerts | Compliance | Jobs | Reports

Database Login

* Username [john.doe]

* Password [••••••••]

Database TEST.WORLD

* Connect As [Normal ▼]

☑ Save as Preferred Credential

(Cancel) (Login)

FIGURE 7-2. *Database Login page*

TIP
In some cases, an Enterprise Administrator might want to give access to a specific target to a specific user, without actually handing out the password. For super-users (and all Enterprise Administrators should be super-users), it is possible to set preferred credentials for another user via EMCLI commands. This gives the super-users the ability to set a password in Grid Control that a regular user working in Grid Control does not know, but can still use in the Console when working with that target.

Every user has to manage his or her own preferred credentials. Use the Preferred Credentials link from the Preferences menu to get to the page in the Console (as shown in Figure 7-3).

When an administrator enters his or her credentials for a given target, or for a set of targets, two sets of username and password can be specified:

- The normal one to be used for the regular operations. The typical examples of this are the login account of the administrator on a machine, or the regular named account of that administrator in a database.

- A privileged account that an administrator can specify. (Think root on a machine, or the SYSDBA account on a database). This account is to be used for specialized operations, like rebooting a machine, or shutting down (or starting up) a database or an Application Server.

Any administrator who has snooped around a little bit in the Console and played with some of the targets will notice two strange things on this page:

- There are target types listed on the Preferred Credentials page, which do not require a login. Examples of this are the Agent and the Oracle Application Server.

- A second set called the Default Credentials Set is also listed on this page per target type.

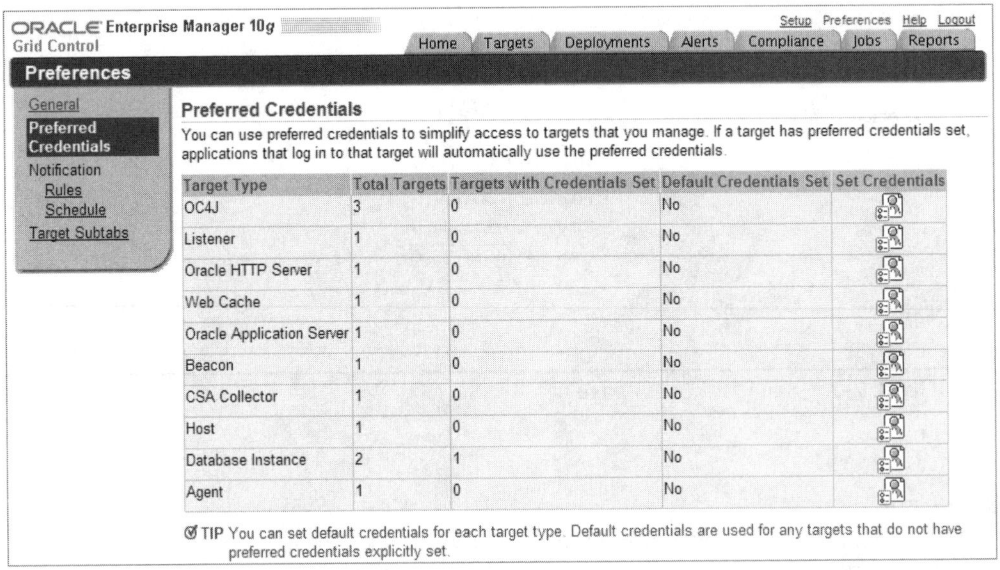

FIGURE 7-3. *Setting up preferred credentials*

To understand the first strange thing, consider this: In order to perform any kind of administration task, like stopping or starting the target, or patching/upgrading the software of a target, you will need to run the commands on the same machine on which the target is running. The owner of the Agent software (and thus the user that is running the Agent process) is not always the same as the owner of the target software. This means that any attempt to run commands or update files will most likely not work when the Agent user is used. Hence the need for an OS login to the machine, to be able to perform these administration tasks. This login (an OS login in this case, and not a target-specific login) will be required for each target discovered in the Console. And therefore it must be defined in the Console. This is why we have Preferred Credentials for each target in the enterprise.

The second weird thing showing up on this page is actually a feature to help reduce the time it takes to set up all the login information. For every distinct target type discovered in Grid Control, there are two ways to specify preferred credentials:

- *A Default Credentials Set can be defined.* Any login information specified as the *default set* will be used for every target of that type. In deployments where the passwords have been synchronized across targets and machines, this feature can help in setting up access to the targets: Instead of specifying a username and password on a per-target basis, it is only specified once at the *type* level.

- *Credentials can be defined on a per-target basis.* Any login information specified on the target level will overrule the default set defined for the target type. This can be used to specify the exceptions from the generic type set.

Starting from 10gR3 (10.2.0.3), support was added for PDP (Privilege Delegation Provider) authentication for OS logins. With the increased security restrictions, common accounts like the Agent or database software user have been locked down: No end user can log on to a machine using these common (or group-based) accounts. They first have to log in as themselves, and then use commands like `sudo` or `pbrun` to become the common user. This way, there is a trace of when a user logged on, which is important for the accountability of operations done on the machine. To allow this kind of login behavior, for each login into a physical box, SUDO and Powerbroker information can be specified when defining the preferred credentials. If `sudo` or `pbrun` is configured on the machine, this feature allows the Agent to become a specific OS user while executing tasks, without actually logging in to the machine with that account.

- **Job credentials**   This includes both the Grid Control job system, as well as the provisioning framework (which is using the job system behind the scenes). For any command the job system executes on a machine, OS login information will need to be provided. The preferred credentials will always be presented first, but the user always has the choice to either confirm the preferred credentials, or specify an alternate login for each job definition.

- **ORACLE_HOME credentials**   This is a type of credential that is slightly different from the other previously mentioned ones. All the prior ones are target related and provide credentials to access a particular target. An ORACLE_HOME, on the other hand, can contain multiple targets all working from that one home. ORACLE_HOME credentials are specified for only one reason: to patch or upgrade the software installed in that home. This is again to prevent problems when the user running the Agent does not have the necessary permissions to write and update the software in the ORACLE_HOME installed by another user. When the specific owner of the ORACLE_HOME software is specified as the credentials, any patch and upgrade operation will run without a permission problem. These home credentials can also be set via the command-line tool:

```
$ emcli set_credential
        -target_type=host -target_name=mydb.acme.com
        -credential_set=OHCreds
        -user=em_ui_user
        -column="OHUsername:osusr;OHPassword:ospwd"
        -oracle_homes="mydb_home"
```

Monitoring Properties

Targets discovered by the Agent need to be monitored. For the Agent to be able to monitor these targets, it will require some information (called *properties*) to do the monitoring. Some of the properties can be determined from the target itself (these are the dynamic properties the Agent collects when it starts). Other properties require specific knowledge about the setup and configuration of the target. This last type of information forms the *monitoring properties*: properties the Agent must know in order to locate and communicate with the target. They have to be specified by an Administrator when the target is added in the Console, or gathered from the machine by a discovery script.

All known monitoring properties are stored in the `targets.xml` file on the Agent side. They are uploaded to the repository as part of the target metadata, to make them visible in the Console to all users administrating the targets. Any user with operator privileges on the target can look up those properties, and modify them if needed. Any changes made in the Console will be saved in the repository and sent over to the Agent as well, to make the Agent aware of the changes in the monitoring.

Target Properties

Besides the credential information and the monitoring properties, there are a couple of additional properties an administrator can define for each target in Grid Control. These properties are a set of free-text fields a user can update to specify some environment-specific information like a comment, the type of target (Production, Test, Acceptance, and so on), the line of business (to specify the group in the enterprise responsible for this target), a contact person (very useful if you have to track down somebody to fix a problem on this target), and a location (which can be practical if you need to give operations some information on what and where to do some work). These standard properties are created and available as soon as the target is discovered in the Console. There is no specific checking done on the values of these fields. They are just plain free-text fields. In the Related Links section on the home page of each target supporting these additional properties, there will be a link called Target Properties. Use that link to display and modify the target properties of that target.

Prior to the 10.2.0.5 release of Grid Control, this list of properties was fixed, and could not be changed. In some cases, though, there might be a need to add an additional property or an additional piece of information for a particular type of target (like an asset number, a helpdesk ID, and so on).

With the release of 10.2.0.5, a couple of new verbs are available in EMCLI (the command-line tool), to give administrators the ability to add a particular property to a given target type:

- **Adding and removing new properties to a given target type** To add the property to a target type, use this EMCLI command:

  ```
  $ emcli add_target_property -target_type="<type>" -property="<name>"
  ```

  Any new property added to a given target type will be available to every target of that type. The value for this property can be set on each target individually, but the property itself is defined at the target type level. No property can be defined on just one target: It is always tied to a target type, and available to all targets of that type.

  Example: If an Asset Number property is added to the type Database (oracle_database), every database discovered in Grid Control will have the additional property Asset Number displayed on the target property page.

  ```
  $ emcli add_target_property
          -target_type="oracle_database" -property="Asset Number"
  ```

  Similar to the adding of the property, a new EMCLI command is also available to remove the property again:

  ```
  $ emcli remove_target_property -target_type="oracle_database"
  -property="Asset Number"
  ```

- **Show a list of all available properties for a given target type** As soon as a couple of properties are added to some specific target types, the need to know what properties are there becomes pretty obvious. That list of available properties can be displayed using EMCLI also:

  ```
  $ emcli get_target_properties -target_type="<type>"
  ```

■ **Setting the value of a specific property**   And the final command is the one to set the actual values for properties.

```
$ emcli set_target_property -property_records="<target:property:value>"
```

Example:

```
$ emcli set_target_property
    -property_records="oms1.acme.com:Contact:john.doe@acme.com"
```

This command can batch-update several targets at a time too:

```
$ emcli set_target_property
    -property_records=
        "oms1.acme.com:Contact:john.doe@acme.com;
        oms2.acme.com:Contact:john.doe@acme.com"
    -separator=property_records=";"
```

(Everything should be specified on a single line: It's spread out across multiple lines for clarity purposes only.)

A full description of all these EMCLI commands, including the new 10.2.0.5 ones, can be found in the Oracle documentation for the command-line tool: *Oracle Enterprise Manager Command Line Interface.*

Navigating the UI Console for Target Monitoring

While there have been clear opportunities to work with the Grid Control interface so far in this book, the overall principles that drive how you get around may not be entirely clear the minute you start poking around. It is worth taking the time to explicitly patrol the great expanse of the Grid Control Console web pages, and get a feel for how to navigate and utilize the Console for maximum benefit.

Locating the Target in the Console

If the entire environment only has a handful of targets, locating a single one will not be too difficult a task. But that story changes if there are thousands of Agents each monitoring several targets themselves. In those larger deployments, locating a single target in the entire enterprise is not as simple as just walking the list of all available targets and selecting the desired one. However, there are a few options in the Console to locate a target:

■ **Home page search**   On the very first page of Enterprise Manager, the Target Search area on the upper right of the screen is the first option (and usually also the best one) for any user to search and locate the right target. Any search can be done on either the entire set of targets, or limited to just one target type.

■ **All Targets search option**   A similar option is available from the All Targets page. This page is located as a subtab from the main Targets menu tab. Although it has the same search capabilities as the search on the main home page, it does offer one advantage: By clicking the hyperlink labeled Advanced Search, a user can search not just on name, but also on the fixed properties defined for each target.

■ **Grouping of targets** Besides the advantages in terms of standardizing the monitoring and maintenance, groups, if created effectively, can also help people narrow down the view of the enterprise to just the set of relevant targets and navigating a group hierarchy.

Once the target is located, the home page of that target is the main portal for all the monitoring and administration tasks an administrator can perform. This home page will be different based on the type of target you are monitoring, and the level of depth underneath it will also change.

Once you have drilled down to the home page, a couple of navigation truths will become immediately apparent. First, you will need to go back to the Target Type link from the tabs to back out of the specific target. Second, if you navigate from target to target within a target's home page (for example, you click the host link from a database page), the only way back to the previous target is to go up to Target Type again and drill back down again. In other words, there's a lot of clicking involved. Some pages give you a decent breadcrumb (that small text path of how you got to where you are, that shows up in the upper-left corner of the page), but it's based purely on a hierarchical page relationship (parent to child). You can't use it when links are making you hop all over the Grid Control Console.

Finding the Agent for a Target

But it's not always the target an Enterprise Administrator is interested in. Sometimes, the Agent for a given target is needed. Or, in environments where targets are running on clusters—meaning that targets can run on any of the nodes in a cluster—it's not always obvious to know which Agent is monitoring a target. To help with that, Grid Control has the option to find the monitoring Agent for a target. A special page is available (shown in Figure 7-4) to help locate the Agent:

```
https://<host>:<port>/em/console/admin/rep/emdConfig/emdFindAgent
```

Once on this page, you can search for any target to find the Agent monitoring it, and then review the Agent details from the Agent's home page, instead of the monitored target's home page.

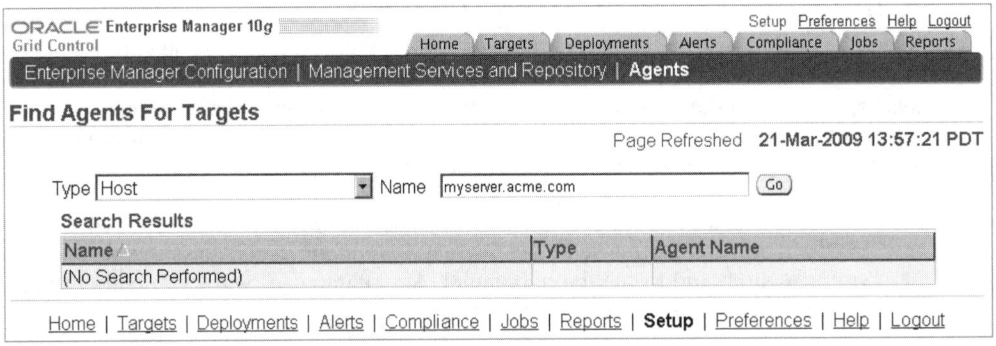

FIGURE 7-4. *Find Agents for Targets page*

Target State and Availability

Every target managed in Grid Control has an *availability* state defined. This availability is a vital part of the monitoring: It determines whether or not the target is operational and available for use. This availability is determined by a metric called Response, defined on each monitored target in the Console. The purpose of this metric is to report the operational state of the target. Although the metric is called Response, the Console will typically show this information as the Availability of the target, or the Status of the target.

Availability States

For straightforward targets (like databases, Application Servers, and so on), the availability of the target is evaluated at the Agent side, and uploaded to the OMS. For group and container targets, or targets running on multiple machines (like RAC databases), the availability of those targets is calculated by the repository itself, based on the availability of the members of that target. Based on the different result of that metric, the following states are possible for a target:

- **Up (1)**   This is the easiest state to describe. It means the target is up and running, and can be used by everyone requiring access to it. This is a definitive state: The Agent has determined the target is operational and ready for use.

- **Down (0)**   The metric concluded that the target is not available: No operations are possible on this target. This is a "clean" situation: No error or abnormal condition is reported. This is the only other definitive state: The Agent has determined that the target is not accessible. As such, no operational tasks and no administration tasks are possible for this target.

- **Metric Error (2)**   The Agent (or repository in case of a composite target) is unable to evaluate the state of the target. This can be due to a configuration error with the monitoring settings of the target (for example, wrong ORACLE_HOME specified), or an abnormal condition on the target preventing the Agent from getting the correct state (for example, Target not responding in time). The error message reported by the metric will have more detail as to what the cause of the error is. This state will continue until the error condition has been resolved.

- **Agent Down (3)**   The machine is reachable on the network, but the Agent is not running on the machine. Therefore, the exact condition of the target is not known, since there is no up-to-date information being collected by the Agent. This state is an historical state only. When an Agent is suspected to be down, it will be first marked as Unreachable (see the next status on the list). Later on when the Agent comes up, it informs the OMS that it was down for a given duration. That duration will then be marked as "Agent Down" in the availability history of the Agent target.

- **Unreachable (4)**   The OMS and the Agent are unable to communicate with each other. The exact condition of the target is not known, since there is no up-to-date information available in the repository. This can be a transient state, with the Agent happily collecting information, but not being able to upload all that data to the repository.

- **Blackout (5)**   A target can only be in blackout due to a User or Administrator intervention: A Grid Control user must define a blackout on a target first before the state of the target changes to Blackout. As long as the blackout is active, the state of the target will be forced to this state, regardless of the exact condition of the target. As soon as the blackout ends, the target will be first moved to the transient Pending state, and the Agent will be asked to re-evaluate the Response metric again, to send back the correct state of the target.

■ **Pending (6)** This is a temporary state. After a blackout ends, Grid Control does not know in what state the target really is. Therefore, the target is put in this transient state, to give the Agent time to re-evaluate the Response metric, and upload the correct state of the target. Only when the Agent reports back a definitive state (Up or Down) will this state be changed to the newly reported one. If the result of the Response metric is one of the unknown states (Metric Error, Agent Down, or Network Unavailable), the Pending state is kept in place.

NOTE
The availability information is available in the repository through a set of views. These views have the availability states already decoded into user-friendly strings. The underlying codes shown in the preceding list for each of the states are specified with each of the different availability states to allow administrators to write custom queries if needed using the internal state number.

To get an idea of the current availability states of all targets in the repository, use this query:

```
SELECT availability_status, COUNT(*) cnt
FROM   mgmt$availability_current
GROUP BY availability_status
```

Availability Grouping

The six availability states can be grouped together in the following conditions, for reporting purposes, and to display the condition of the target in the Console:

■ **Operational** Availability states used: Up (1)
This is the state you want all targets to be in: All is operational, ready for action, and showing up as that green part in the Availability pie chart in the Console.

■ **Unplanned downtime** Availability states used: Down (0)
This is the worst possible state. The target is not available. And no outages were planned for it. This is the red piece of the pie chart when you are looking at the Grid Control main page. It is the one color you do not want to see in the Console, and should actively pursue resolution whenever you see it.

■ **Planned downtime** Availability states used: Blackout (5)
Work is being done on these targets (also known as Maintenance mode). This is the black area of the pie chart—not quite green, but not really red either. Although this is technically not a *bad* state, you still want to keep the black area in that availability pie chart as small as possible.

■ **Unknown** Availability states used: Metric Error (2), Agent Down (3), Network Unavailable (4), Pending (6)
This is the *big unknown*, the grey area on the pie chart. Usually these states are the result of a configuration error or a network problem (that might not even be impacting the monitoring of the target at all). It is still a condition to avoid. These kinds of states should be resolved as soon as possible. If you cannot confirm it is up, how will you know if it goes down?

For the Enterprise Administrator, there is not much to do for the availability piece of the targets: As long as the targets are configured correctly (the right ORACLE_HOME, correct password, and so on), the Response metric will evaluate on the appointed schedule, and the availability calculations will run. But this metric is crucial in the monitoring and the management of the target. If a target is not in an Up state, the monitoring of the targets is undetermined, and not all the correct and necessary data might get collected. Also, tasks like jobs and configuration updates might not make it on those targets, making the administration of these targets very difficult.

To keep the Grid Control healthy, and keep a good operational overview of your enterprise, keep the number of targets in an Unplanned Downtime or Unknown state to the absolute minimum (preferably zero). The SQL query used in the previous example can be used again, but this time using the availability grouping:

```
SELECT availability_grouping, COUNT(*) cnt
FROM    (
        SELECT DECODE(availability_status,
                        'Target Up'   , 'Operational',
                        'Blackout'    , 'Planned Downtime',
                        'Target Down', 'Unplanned Downtime',
                        'Unknown') availability_grouping
        FROM    mgmt$availability_current
        )
GROUP BY availability_grouping
```

Summary

In this chapter, we provided a brief introduction to how Grid Control acts in relationship to the targets that you will want it to monitor and administer on your behalf. We discussed the monitoring setup that occurs for all targets, including credentials setup, monitoring properties, and user-defined target properties. We dove briefly into navigating the Grid Control Console to find targets, and conversely to find which agent is monitoring a target. Finally, we spent time showing the different states any target will be in, and how Grid Control groups the state of targets into availability groupings.

CHAPTER
8

Managing EM Users
and Audits

lan. Document. Audit.

All too often, people just start blindly adding new targets and creating new administrators, without any clear plan or any clear guideline on how to manage and maintain all of it.

And then of course, once the managerial questions surface, all hell breaks loose: Reports need to be generated for applications, accounts need to be synchronized and updated for Sarbanes-Oxley (SOX) compliance, and administrators need to be re-assigned to other projects or other applications to help out.

Without a clear strategy on how to classify, group, and organize the administrators and the targets in Grid Control, each of these tasks will be a grueling one, taking up quite some time, with a lot of not-so-nice verbal comments.

Defining Administrators

In order for people to see all the information stored in the repository, user accounts are needed to log in to Grid Control. And these accounts or the administrators should be able to see the information about the targets, and ideally, just those targets they are responsible for. There are three main groups of administrators (taking a little liberty here, but for simplicity's sake, we'll stick to these three main groups):

- **The regular user (the "mere mortal")**   The simplest and most common type of Grid Control user working in the enterprise. This user manages or maintains a finite set of targets (ranging from just one to a whole group or a Line Of Business (LOB) within a company. No special privileges are granted to this user, and only access to those targets he or she is responsible for is granted.

- **The overseer (the "big brother" users)**   Managers or users running reports on a regular basis typically need to see and have access to a lot of targets (potentially even all the targets in Grid Control). But their privileges on the individual targets are usually limited to "view only."

- **Super-users (the "gods" of Grid Control)**   Super-users are a special kind of user: They can do anything and see anything in Grid Control. This status should be reserved for the Enterprise Administrators only. Super-users bypass the whole privileges model, as they have all the privileges granted implicitly. Always have at least one more super-user available, besides SYSMAN. The repository owner is the Über-god, the user-that-shall-not-be-used in the day-to-day operations. This account should only be accessed for diagnostic reasons, or when running diagnostic tools like EMDIAG. On the other hand, the number of super-users should be kept pretty limited. Super-users have the capability to do anything in the system. An account like that could potentially create a lot of havoc in the wrong hands. It should be only given to those Enterprise Administrator users responsible for keeping Grid Control operational. All other users should be "mere mortals."

BEST PRACTICE
Avoid the creation of group accounts, or any type of account that is going to be shared by multiple people. With the shift of security awareness, and with all the security compliance in place, any kind of group account is not allowed for general purposes, since there is no accountability for these accounts.

Grid Control Privileges

In order to perform tasks in Grid Control, privileges are needed. These privileges form the basis for the security model, to prevent users from accessing or modifying certain targets. There are five sets of basic privileges present in Grid Control:

Job privileges	Control what a user can do and see for a specific Grid Control job. These privileges are granted at the job level, and cannot be assigned with the creation of a user or a role.
Report privileges	Control what a user can do and see for a specific report These privileges are granted at the report level, and cannot be assigned with the creation of a user or a role.
Target privileges	Control what a user can do and see for a specific target.
Template privileges	Control what a user can do and see for a specific monitoring template. These privileges are granted at the template level, and cannot be assigned with the creation of a user or a role.
System privileges	Control what a user can do and see at the overall enterprise level.

These privileges can then be grouped together in a role or a directory for a user. Working with roles, though, will make the whole user administration a lot easier, as it prevents having to grant each individual user new privileges each time a new target or a new job comes into the system.

Job Privileges

Job privileges are not defined at the role or user level. With the creation of a new job, either a newly running job, or a job in the job library, access to this job is defined to a role or an administrator.

Full	This is the highest level that can be granted: This grants full access to the job, to allow any change to be made to this job by the administrator or the role.
None	The lowest level that can be given, and the default for all jobs for a non-super-user administrator: The user or role is not allowed to see this job.
Owner	This is a special flavor of the `Full` privilege. The owner can always see and modify the job.
View	Administrator or role is allowed to see the job, but cannot make any changes.

Report Privileges

Report privileges are not defined at the role or user level. With the creation of a new report, access to the report is defined to a role or an administrator.

Publish	The administrator or role will be allowed to make changes to the publishing of a report.
Owner	This is an implicit privilege: The owner of a report can always make any change to the report.
View	The administrator or role will be allowed to see and use the report, but cannot make any changes.

Target Privileges

Every non-super-user account must be granted specific target privileges, in order to see or monitor targets in Grid Control.

`Add Target in Group`	Administrator or role can add a target in a specific group and grant privileges on a group.
`Clone From Target`	Ability to create a copy of an existing Grid Control target.
`Full`	This is the highest level that can be granted: This grants full access for both monitoring and administration of the target.
`Manage Target Group`	Administrator or role can add a target in a specific target group or delete a target from a specific target group.
`None`	The lowest level that can be given, and the default for all targets for a non-super-user administrator: The user or role is not allowed to see this target.
`Operator`	Administrator or role can see the target, and perform basic operator tasks like startup and shutdown on this target.
`View`	Administrator or role will be allowed to see the target and the configuration of the target, but cannot do any administration task.

Template Privileges

A monitoring template can only be created if an administrator has at least operator privileges on a target: Since a template changes the monitoring settings of a target, only an operator of that target can make those changes. Template privileges are not defined at the role or user level. With the creation of a new template, access to the template is defined to a role or an administrator.

`Full`	The administrator or role will be allowed to make changes to the monitoring template.
`Owner`	This is an implicit privilege: The owner of the template can always make any change to report.
`View`	The administrator or role will be allowed to see and use the template, but cannot make any changes.

System Privileges

System privileges define what an administrator will be able to do in the Console. Based on the settings and the privileges assigned to an account, the Administrator will be able to see certain tabs in the Console, and perform certain maintenance operations.

`ADD ANY TARGET`	Allows the administrator to discover new targets, add new targets to Agents, or create container targets (groups, systems, services)
`CREATE ANY ROLE`	Allows the administrator to create new roles
`DELETE ANY TARGET`	Allows the administrator to remove any targets from the Agent, or remove container targets (groups, systems, services)

`GRANT ANY REPORT VIEWER`	Allows administrator to grant privileges to any user to view a report
`MONITOR ENTERPRISE MANAGER`	Allows administrator access to view the infrastructure targets, used by the MTM (Monitor The Monitor) subsystem.
`USE ANY BEACON`	Use any beacon on any monitored host to monitor transactions, URLs, and network components.
`SUPER USER`	Ability to do any operation. By default this privilege is granted to the repository owner, that is, SYSMAN. This must be granted directly to a user and cannot be granted via a role.
`VIEW ANY TARGET`	View any discovered target in the Console. This privilege includes the `MONITOR ENTERPRISE MANAGER` privilege.
`VIEW ANY REPORT`	Ability to run any report defined in Grid Control, even reports the administrator has not created or defined.

Creating New Users

All of these privileges need to be assigned to a user in order to have an effect. Every user created in Grid Control has these basic attributes:

- **Name of the administrator**   The naming convention used for Grid Control users follows the same rules and restrictions as those for creating database users.

- **Password to log in to Grid Control**   Grid Control passwords follow the same rules (and therefore have the same restrictions) as passwords defined for database users: Any password that is valid for a database user can also be used as the password for the Grid Control administrator.

- **E-mail address**   This is an optional attribute, but should be used for all administrators. In order for this administrator to receive e-mail notifications, the e-mail address of the user definition should be filled in.

- **List of privileges and roles assigned to this user**   This can be specified during the creation of the user, or changed afterwards at any point in time.

Creating users should be well planned. Based on the various groups of targets, and the different divisions needing access to Grid Control, users, roles, and groups should be created. The best way to accomplish this task, is by working from the bottom up:

- Start by identifying the big groups or divisions that will have targets discovered in Grid Control.

- For each of these big groups, map the hierarchy of targets, grouping them together logically in smaller groups for manageability.

- Once the group structure is identified, map those groups to roles, with a role for each group of targets that need to be managed as a whole.

- With the groups and roles in place, now it's time to create the individual user accounts for the administrators managing these targets.

Modifying a User

Any logged-in user can only make updates to his or her account (like putting in a new or updated e-mail address, or changing the password). A super-user can do a lot more: Besides changing a password, he or she can also make changes to the roles and privileges granted to any account.

NOTE
A super-user can change the definition of another super-user, including changing the assigned roles and privileges, or even revoking the super-user privilege. This is another reason to keep the number of super-users limited in the system!

Deleting a User

Removing an account from the application is not something that should happen all the time. It's a necessary operation, and something that the SOX, Information Technology Infrastructure Library (ITIL), or any other compliance strategy mandates. Just to be complete, and maybe point out the obvious to some people, the restrictions on removing an account are as follows:

- Only super-users can remove accounts from the system (see Figure 8-1). Without this privilege, an administrator will not be able to delete any account in Grid Control.

- The SYSMAN user (repository owner) is protected, and cannot be removed.

- Any super-user can remove any other super-user. This is why it is prudent to keep the number of super-users limited to the deployment, to prevent rogue administrators from going on a "delete spree."

- If the administrator to be removed owns objects (like templates, jobs, reports, and so on), they will need to be reassigned to another valid account in Grid Control before the user gets deleted.

- If objects are found for the account, the Console will ask the Enterprise Administrator the action to take for these objects owned by the user-to-be-deleted.

ORACLE Enterprise Manager 10*g*
Grid Control

Setup Preferences Help Logout

Home Targets Deployments Alerts Compliance Jobs Reports

Enterprise Manager Configuration | Management Services and Repository | Agents

Delete administrator: DELETEME

Cancel View Objects OK

○ Delete Administrator Objects
  This will delete the administrator and all his or her associated Job Types, Jobs, Corrective Actions, Report Definitions, Reports and Templates. Blackouts will not be deleted.

⦿ Reassign Administrator Objects
  This will assign the administrator's objects to another administrator. The credentials belonging to the administrator will be deleted from the repository before any reassignment takes place.

New Owner [   ] ✎

Cancel View Objects OK

Home | Targets | Deployments | Alerts | Compliance | Jobs | Reports | **Setup** | Preferences | Help | Logout

---

FIGURE 8-1. *Removing a user*

Defining Roles and Assigning Privileges

Roles are a handy way of grouping privileges together into a manageable entity. As soon as a role is defined, granting access to a set of targets or giving specific privileges to a set of groups or templates becomes a lot easier to manage. Roles are therefore something that go hand in hand with grouping targets together into manageable entities, and breaking up the management and monitoring of targets into smaller groups of user and administrators.

BEST PRACTICE
Define a role for every logical group of targets in the enterprise. When a group role is available, adding (or removing) a new administrator to manage the targets of a specific group is just as easy as granting (or revoking) just the one role to that administrator, preventing Enterprise Administrators from having to go through a long set of individual privileges for the user each time.

Creating New Roles

Only super-users or administrator with the CREATE ANY ROLE privilege can create roles. When creating (or modifying) a role, the Console will guide you through a set of pages (called a *train* or a *wizard*) to provide the following grants:

- **Other roles**   A role can contain other roles.
- **System privileges**   The standard system privileges can be selected to be included in the role. Even if VIEW ANY TARGET is granted, you still have the option to select targets, and grant Operator or Full on targets.
- **Target privileges**   First the targets used by this role have to be selected from the list of all available targets. Next, the individual access to the selected targets can be defined.
- **Grant the role to administrators**   A set of administrators can already be granted access to this role.

Deleting a Role

A role is nothing more than a set of privileges. Removing a role is therefore just an update to the set of privileges users and administrators have. When a role is removed, it will have an immediate effect on all users, even the users logged in at that time. Handle the deleting of a role with care, to prevent angry calls from people working in the Console.

Set Up Centralized Authentication

The typical large data-center setups are using an identity management application for all the user and accounts. This allows the users to be centrally managed and maintained, while all other applications then simply reference the Lightweight Directory Access Protocol (LDAP) server for usernames, passwords, and account privileges.

GRID CONTROL WORKSHOP

Configuring Enterprise User Security (EUS)

Enterprise User Security (EUS) is a database option, which can be enabled to have the database use a central LDAP server with all the globally defined users. The main advantage of this database feature is the ability to centralize the user management, including the setup of the privileges for each user in one database. It also gives the added benefit to the users logged in to the Console of not having to log in any more to any database that is part of the same EUS deployment. Once the user is logged into Grid Control using EUS, any other database using the same LDAP server will automatically authenticate the user in that database too.

The following steps are needed to configure Grid Control with EUS:

Step 1. Configure the repository database to use EUS.

EUS is a database option that has to be enabled for each database participating in the centralized user management. Follow the instructions from the *Oracle Database Enterprise User Security Administrator's Guide* to set up the repository database to use EUS.

Step 2. Stop the OMS.

The authentication method needs to be changed. So all Management Servers have to be shut down for the update:

```
$ $ORACLE_HOME/opmn/bin/opmnctl stopall;
```

Step 3. Configure the Management Servers to use EUS.

On every Management Server, add this property in the emoms.properties file:

```
oracle.sysman.emSDK.sec.DirectoryAuthenticationType=EnterpriseUser
```

Step 4. Start OMS again.

Restart all the Management Servers again:

```
$ $ORACLE_HOME/opmn/bin/opmnctl startall;
```

Step 5. Create the appropriate users in the LDAP directory server.

All necessary accounts needed for Grid Control should be either already exist, or be created on the Oracle Internet Directory (OID) side.

Step 6. Create the EM accounts.

When a new account is created via Grid Control, the option will be available in the Console to specify whether to use LDAP server (enterprise user) or the local Grid Control repository (local user) for the authentication.

GRID CONTROL WORKSHOP

Configuring Single Sign-On (SSO)

Single Sign-On (SSO) is an option that can be used either in conjunction with EUS, or as a standalone option for Grid Control. It will require the same type of infrastructure EUS does (meaning a central repository of users to point to in order to get the authentication information). It provides the ability to hook up several enterprise-wide applications to the same SSO server: A user only has to log in once in order to access all the hooked-up applications.

NOTE
Both EUS and SSO can be configured at the same time, but Grid Control will only use one authentication method. If SSO is used as the authentication method, EUS will still be used for the user management in the repository database.

The following steps are needed to configure Grid Control with SSO:

Step 1.   Stop the OMS.

Since all authentication and authorization now has to go through the SSO server, all the Management Servers need to be shut down:

```
$ $ORACLE_HOME/opmn/bin/opmnctl stopall;
```

Step 2.   Configure the Management Servers to use SSO.

For every OMS, execute this command:

```
$ $ORACLE_HOME/bin/emctl config oms sso -host <sso_host>
    -port <ssoPort> -sid <ssoSid> -pass <orasso_password>
    -das <dasURL> -u <user that started http server>
```

Step 3.   Start OMS again.

Restart all the Management Servers again:

```
$ $ORACLE_HOME/opmn/bin/opmnctl startall;
```

Step 4.   Create the appropriate users in the LDAP directory server.

For the users to be able to log in to Grid Control, all necessary users should be either available, or need to get created on the LDAP server.

Step 5.   Create the EM accounts.

As with the EUS setup, all new accounts created via the Console will have the option to be defined locally (so only the Grid Control repository), or globally (user created in the LDAP server).

User Management

When EUS or SSO (or both) are enabled and operational, any new Grid Control user or administrator can be created in two ways:

- **A local user**   Local users are known only in the local repository, and will not use the central LDAP server to authenticate. SYSMAN will always be a local user, and can never be created as an enterprise user.

- **An enterprise user**   These types of users are defined on the OID side, and Grid control only has a reference to those users in the local repository. Without access to the OID server, these users will not be able to log in to Grid Control.

The recommendation is always to have at least one local user defined (besides the default SYSMAN), to be able to log in to the Console and perform basic tasks, even if the OID servers are not available.

NOTE
As soon as SSO is set up, whenever a user wants to log in to Grid Control, he or she will be redirected to the SSO login page, and be authenticated first before being redirected back to the Grid Control Console. There is always a way available to bypass the SSO login page for local users (non-SSO users) to log in to Grid Control: If the OID infrastructure is unavailable, administrators should still be able to get into the Grid Control Console and perform the necessary tasks, via Grid Control, to get everything operational again. To bypass the SSO login page, use this URL for all the local users:

```
https://<host>:<port>/em/console/logon/logon
```

Auditing

Accountability is a big thing in today's security world. All users logging in to the Console need to be identified, and actions need to be logged, to have a historical log of what happened when and by whom. Auditing can be enabled inside Grid Control to have a list of all operations (with their context) that were executed by the users.

Enabling Auditing

After the install of Grid Control, auditing is not enabled by default. An Enterprise Administrator has to enable the auditing in the system. This can be done in either of two ways:

- Enable global auditing for all modules and all actions:

```
BEGIN
  mgmt_audit_admin.set_audit(
    p_audit_mode => 0,
    p_audit_destination => null,
    p_audit_level => 1);
END;
```

The audit mode and destination should always be set to zero and NULL respectively, to store the audit information in the repository database. The audit level specifies the type of auditing that needs to happen:

0   Audit all operations
1   Audit only the specific ones that are enabled
2   Disable auditing for all operations

■   If specific auditing is required for selective operations, perform the following actions:

First enable the auditing framework, for selective operations only:

```
BEGIN
  mgmt_audit_admin.set_audit(
    p_audit_mode => 0,
    p_audit_destination => null,
    p_audit_level => 1);
END;
```

Next, specify the specific operations that need to be at audited. For 10.2.0.5 or higher, the routine uses the name of the operation as the key to turn the auditing on. For all 10*g*R2 releases prior to 10.2.0.4, the operation code was passed in as the parameter:

```
BEGIN
  mgmt_audit_admin.set_audit_on(<op_code>);
END;
```

Auditing can be disabled again for specific operations. This signature of this procedure follows the same rules: For 10.2.0.5 or higher, the name of the operation has to be passed to the routine. For all releases prior to 10.2.0.4, it's the operations code:

```
BEGIN
  mgmt_audit_admin.set_audit_off(<op_code>);
END;
```

The list of all available operation codes can be found in the *Oracle Enterprise Manager Advanced Configuration Guide*, Section 5.5. It can also be retrieved directly from the repository using this SQL statement:

```
SELECT op_code, operation_description
FROM   mgmt_operations_master
ORDER BY op_code
```

Audit Reporting

Starting from 10.2.0.5, the audit data can be viewed in the Console directly, with various filtering options to display just the records of interest.

```
https://<host>:<port>/em/console/sec/audit/auditData
```

The link is available on the Management Services and Repository page from the Audit section on the overview page. Once the auditing is enabled, the view MGMT$AUDIT_LOG can also be queried to get the details from the audited actions:

```
SELECT "USER NAME", operation, "OPERATION STATUS", "OPERATION TIMESTAMP"
FROM    mgmt$audit_log
ORDER BY "OPERATION TIMESTAMP", "USER NAME", operation
```

This view can then also be used to create reports in the reporting framework.
List all failed login attempts from yesterday:

```
SELECT a."USER NAME", a."CLIENT IP ADDRESS",
       p.target_name oms_host, a."OPERATION TIMESTAMP"
FROM    mgmt$audit_log a, mgmt$target_properties p
WHERE   a."OPERATION STATUS" != 'SUCCESS'
  AND   a."OPERATION"          = 'LOGIN'
  AND   a."OMS IP ADDRESS"     = p.property_value
  AND   p.property_name        = 'IP_address'
  AND   a."OPERATION TIMESTAMP"
          BETWEEN TRUNC(SYSDATE)-1 AND TRUNC(SYSDATE)
ORDER BY a."OPERATION TIMESTAMP", a."USER NAME"
```

Purging the Audit Data

The audit data is not purged by default to give control to the Enterprise Administrator to define the purge policy as required by the business. It is the responsibility of the Enterprise Administrator to define and run the purge policy. A special routine for the purging of the audit data is available:

```
BEGIN
   mgmt_audit_admin.audit_purge(<time>);
END;
```

Example:
Purge all data older than one year:

```
BEGIN
   mgmt_audit_admin.audit_purge(TRUNC(SYSDATE)-365);
END;
```

Starting from 10.2.0.5, instead of just purging the data from the audit tables, the data can be externalized to files. This way, all data older than a specified number of days will be exported in XML format to files in a directory, and then purged from the repository. To set up the externalization, use EMCLI:

```
$ emcli update_audit_setting -file_prefix=<prefix>
           -directory_name=<name> -file_size=<size>
           -data_retention_period=<days>
```

The directory name and the file prefix will determine the location and the file mask to use when creating the files. The size determines the maximum size per file.

Example:

Purge all audit data after one month, to the directory `/u01/backup/audit`, with files all starting with `gc_aud`. No file should be bigger than 10MB.

```
$ emcli update_audit_setting -file_prefix=gc_aud
        -directory_name="/u01/backup/audit" -file_size="10M"
        -data_retention_period=31
```

The files will be sequentially numbered using the specified prefix: `gc_aud00001.xml`, `gc_aud00002.xml`, and so on.

Summary

User and role management is a very important aspect of running enterprise management software. It is usually something that is either left alone or not really looked at during the rollout. This chapter has given you a set of features and possibilities within the Enterprise Manager product to use for defining user and privileges, and more importantly, setup auditing to keep track of who is doing what. With the increased auditing requirements, and the heightened security awareness of the last couple of years, it should be clear to anyone that there is a real need for having the right privileges and the right auditing in place for a global application. It goes beyond a clearly defined naming convention or naming standard: A set of groups and roles should be defined for any large deployment, to make the organization of the users and the privileges of these users easier to manage.

CHAPTER
9

Metrics and Notifications

n administrator might feel blind if nobody is getting alerts about a critical problem that happened on a server. Unattended problems do have a tendency to grow to such proportions that they can create problems and outages that could have been prevented. It's all about getting notified about what is happening in the enterprise: If some event has the ability to cripple an application or a machine, people need to know about it way before it reaches that danger level. And this is where notifications come into the picture. Based on rules defined by the administrator, messages can be sent out in response to an event that Enterprise Manager registered.

Maximizing the Power of Grid Control Metrics

Metrics are the cornerstone of all the information that is available for targets in Grid Control. Every bit of information, every data point shown in the Console for a given target was collected by some kind of metric for that target. Out of the box, the Agent collects a default set of metrics, and uploads that information to the OMS to be inserted into the repository. This set of information is always collected in the same way, using the same collection frequency and the same thresholds to report violations. These generic default settings are adequate for most targets. Managing these measurements and getting the units of measurement correct for your environment is a critical step to turn EM from a pesky chatterbox into the messenger of useful news (and, ultimately, into an automatic responder to that news). So, first we manage our measurement system so that we have a useful message, and then we need to work on message delivery. If a database event happens in a forest when no one is looking, does it make a noise? (Answer: no, but the users the next morning will.) Ensuring that a metric that generates an event gets the due attention is why notifications exist. They are your lifeline when it comes to managing the ever-growing and ever-sprawling ecosystems of the modern age. Getting notifications dialed in is a critical step. We group metrics and notifications together because deciding what is important (metrics) is the other side of the who/when (notifications) coin. Getting the most from Grid Control means tightening both of them down at the same time.

To truly utilize all the power of the metrics, you have to dig into the details. There's no way around it. But once you have an understanding of how Grid Control is handling metrics for a particular type of target, you owe it to yourself to standardize and apply your understanding to all targets in the same way. That level of standardization is not always possible (there are always exceptions, let's just face the facts), but it is a worthy goal. Particularly in a very large environment, getting 90 percent or more of your metrics configured from a single location is critical.

Reviewing Metrics in the GC Environment

First, it's important to understand how you can look at and review metrics for a particular target. As you are probably aware, many of the items in GC that you stare at on a constant basis are the result of a metric being collected, and an assessment of what that metric means being performed. As we said in Part I of this book, the Agent does the collection of facts from a target, but the Agent does no assessments whatsoever. It is not an intelligent Agent, with smarts built in to act on the facts. It is simply a collection utility on one end, and then a drone that can take instructions from GC and run them at the host machine to administer the target. First, let's spend time understanding the collection process. After that, we'll dive into the assessments of the facts that can be done at the OMS, and then acted upon.

Metric Collection by the Agent

The EM Agent is responsible for running scripts on an ongoing basis to check for interesting events that happen to a target. For instance, with a database, the Agent will periodically check to see if the database is up or down. It checks this by running a Perl script that resides in the Agent scripts library in the $AGENT_HOME/sysman/admin/scripts directory. Go have a look if you're curious about the script structure, but be cautioned: Manual update of these scripts is unsupported, and can cause you more harm than it's worth.

Clearly, there are some scripts that need to be run more often than others; it's good to know whether the database is up and operational on a more frequent basis than, say, knowing how full a tablespace's data files are. So, the collection scripts run at different times, and the frequency is known as the *collection schedule*. The collection schedule prescribes how often to run a particular Perl script. Here's the thing to remember, however: not every metric that is collected has an individual Perl script just for itself. For performance reasons, similar metrics are often grouped into a single script, so they must always run together, and they will always have the same collection schedule.

In addition, the collection schedule does not necessarily indicate how often you will have access to new facts for a particular metric. How often an Agent collects a metric has been separated from how often the Agent then uploads that information to the OMS. The frequency of uploads of a particular metric to the OMS is referred to as the *upload interval*. This is, again, a performance-related element. While we may need to capture a snapshot of how full the file system is for a host every 15 minutes, it may only make sense to upload this data after 24 or so collections, as this data is not necessarily prone to rapid changes.

Both the collection schedule and the upload interval can be modified to meet your needs, although this is not true for all metrics. Some metrics are only determined in real time, when a particular link is clicked. For instance, a list of top processes running on a host is not collected on a schedule, but if you click Top Processes from the Hosts page, the metric will gather the information and upload it for review. We will go through modifying the collection schedule and upload interval a little later in this chapter.

Metric Evaluation at the OMS

Once a fact has been collected and uploaded to the OMS, then something intelligent can be deduced, either by comparing the value of the metric against previous values of the same metric, or by comparing it to a known level that indicates the metric may be problematic and require intervention. These evaluations are governed by thresholds and policies, and result in alerts.

Metric Thresholds

There are two ways to view metrics: those with thresholds already set, and all metrics (with or without thresholds). There is a drop-down menu on the Metric and Policy Settings page to show you both. A *threshold* can best be understood as the point past which a metric is turned into an alert—it goes from being something that is of historical use to something that is immediately interesting to you. An *alert* is, of course, just a metric that has crossed a threshold. There are two thresholds for metrics: Warning and Critical, so that you can have different types of reactions for both.

Three main aspects can be tweaked for any metric:

- ■ **The metric itself** All the data that gets collected by the Agent has to serve a purpose. The default metrics are all providing useful data points for the monitoring and management of the target in general. For some specific targets, however (a development or test machine for instance), some metrics might not be relevant or needed. The sensible thing to do in this case is to simply disable the metric, to not get this useless data collected and uploaded in the repository.

- **The collection frequency**   The frequency of a metric will control how much data will get into Grid Control (and how much data needs to get rolled up). For critical machines, some metrics might need to be collected on a more frequent basis. On other machines (again, test and development machines come to mind here), the frequency of the metrics can be scaled back.

- **The threshold definitions**   The defaults the Agent is using are defined for average, general-purpose targets. Depending on the usage of the target, these default thresholds might not be strict enough. On others, they might be too strict, creating too many notifications and alerts.

Configuring Metrics in Grid Control

Understanding how to find metrics and configure them can be mystifying at first, but once you understand the logic you will get used to it: Metrics never appear in a single clearinghouse location for all of Grid Control. You won't find it in Setup or Preferences. Because the amount of configuration is so expansive, metrics configuration is always contextual by the particular type of target you are interested in.

For instance, let's look at database metrics again. To find them, you need to first navigate to the Targets tab, click on the Databases page, and then click on a specific database. Once you are looking at the home page for a database, you need to scroll to the bottom of the page and look under Related Links. Here, you will see a number of metric-related pages to use. There are five links of interest: Metric and Policy Settings, All Metrics, Metric Collection Errors, User-Defined Metrics, and Metric Baselines. If you navigate to a host page, however, you won't find all of these same metric-related links—Metric Baselines does not exist. Based on the level of capabilities surrounding the metric configurations of that target type, the links will change.

Metric and Policy Settings

The primary interface for dealing with the metric evaluations for a target is found on the Metric and Policy Settings page. This has two subpages: Metric Thresholds and Policies. We will discuss Policies in greater detail in a moment. For now, concentrate on the Metric Thresholds page, as seen in Figure 9-1. Notice that the "breadcrumb" under the Oracle logo and blue target-type bar shows you which target you are modifying (in this case, a host). Then, take a few moments and soak in the format of the page. You have the metric itself, the comparison operator, and then the value that is compared to get an evaluation of the value. After that, you have a bar for Corrective Actions (more on that later) and then the Collection Schedule and an Edit column.

Note that for some of the metrics, the pencil icon in the Edit column is a single pencil; in others, there are multiple pencils. This means that the metric applies to one or more item. For instance, the Filesystem Space Available (%) metric, if you click the Edit icon, allows you to then further configure the metric for multiple mount-points, if you want them evaluated separately. From this page, you can edit the thresholds, collection schedule, and other factors in how the metric is evaluated and then acted upon. The thresholds can be modified across all metrics from the single page by making all modifications, and then clicking the OK button in the upper-right corner. Alternatively, thresholds can be modified by clicking the Edit button. First, let's focus on the collection schedule modifications that can be made.

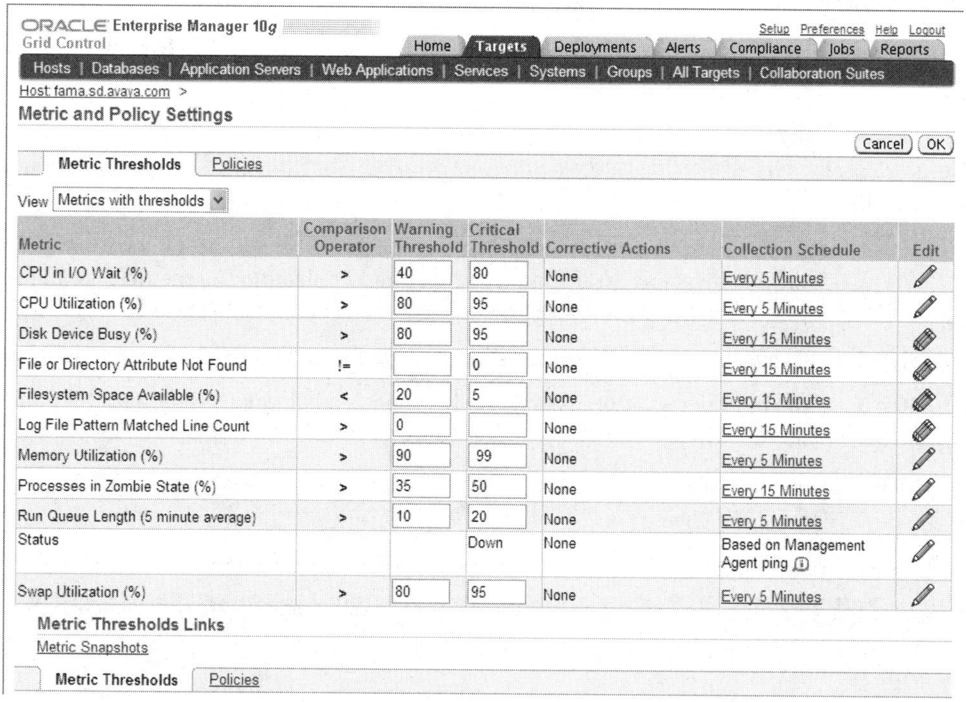

FIGURE 9-1.   *Metric and Policy Settings page*

Edit Collection Settings   By clicking on the link that displays the collection schedule, you can further modify the frequency of metric collection. The frequency of a metric should be changed for one of two reasons. First, the default collection frequency is not adequate for the usage of the target. On a mission-critical OLTP database, having to wait for 30 minutes by default to get alerted of failed logins might be too long. The frequency of that very same metric, on a development box, used to test software could well be scaled back to once every hour, or even once every day. The second reason to change the frequency is because the machine usage is preventing the metric from getting collected at the specified interval. If the execution of the metric takes longer than the frequency of the metric, the Agent will log a scheduling error in the Agent trace files.

Here's an example from the `emagent.trc` file:

```
SchedEntry{oracle_database:database:health_check} exceed next scheduletime,
delay=15
```

If the resource usage of the machine continues in the same way, preventing this metric from getting executed at the appointed interval, scale back the metric to a frequency that the machine will be capable of honoring.

GRID CONTROL WORKSHOP

Changing the Collection Schedule and Upload Interval for the Metric CPU Utilization (%)

Workshop Notes

Here, we give a very straightforward example of modifying the collection schedule for a host metric, CPU Utilization (%).

Step 1. Go to a host's target home page, and scroll to the bottom. Click the Metric and Policy Settings link. You should see the CPU Utilization (%) metric second from the top. Click the underlined value (the frequency) of the Collection Schedule column.

Step 2. Leave the frequency By Minutes, but change the value of Repeat Every to 10 Minutes.

Step 3. Note the Affected Metrics that will be impacted by a modification to this value (Figure 9-2).

Step 4. Click Continue.

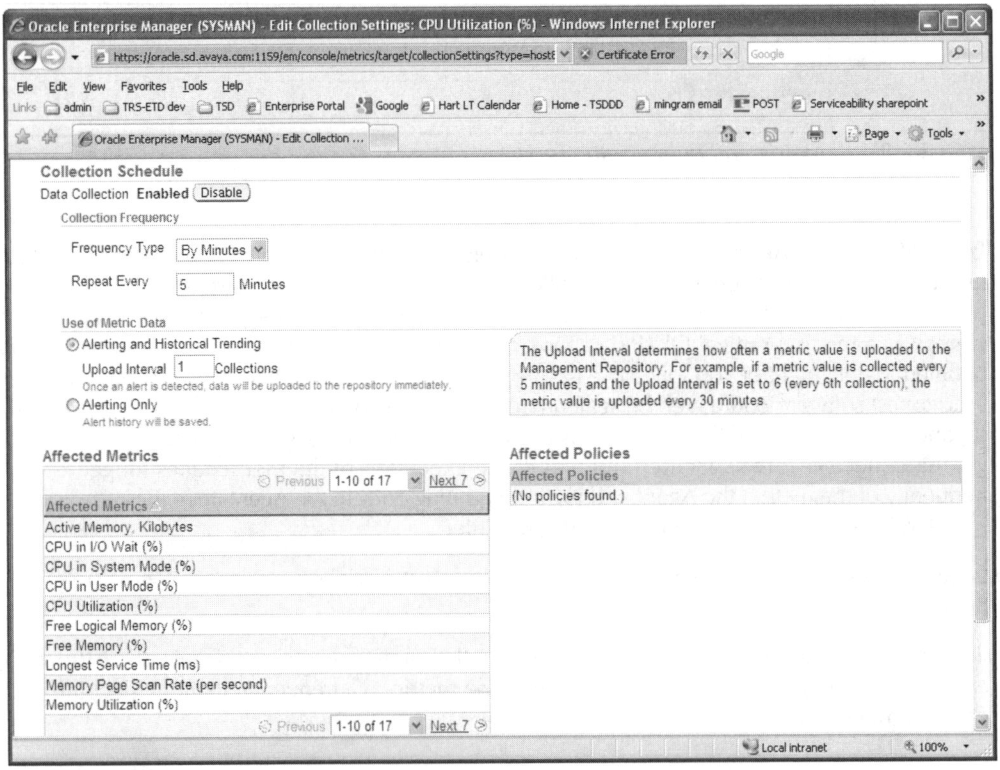

FIGURE 9-2. *Editing the collection schedule*

Disabling Metrics

Not all targets need all the metrics that are being collected by default. Some metrics might not be necessary, or they might even be irrelevant for a specific target. Metrics can be disabled, to prevent the gathering of the data at the Agent. A disabled metric will not load any data in the repository: Less data getting uploaded into the repository means less data to roll up, and less data to purge.

To disable a metric:

- On the target home page, click on the Metric and Policy Settings page.
- Click the frequency link of the Collection Schedule column.
- On the frequency page, shown in Figure 9-3, use the Disable button from the Collection Schedule section.

Note that the Response metric is the only metric that should never be disabled for a target. Without a Response metric, the Agent will not be able to determine the availability of the target. To see which metrics are disabled in the repository, run this SQL statement:

```
SELECT target_type, collection_name, COUNT(*)
FROM   mgmt$target_metric_collections
WHERE  is_enabled = 0
GROUP BY target_type, collection_name
```

Setting the Metric Thresholds

Before going into detail about the thresholds and the violations, let's review the different states a metric can be in. There are four states possible for every metric:

- **Clear**   This is the state most metrics *should* be in. The Agent had nothing to report about the metric data, and all data returned for the metric is well within the defined threshold limits.
- **Warning**   The data collected by the Agent has crossed the warning threshold, but has not yet crossed the critical threshold.

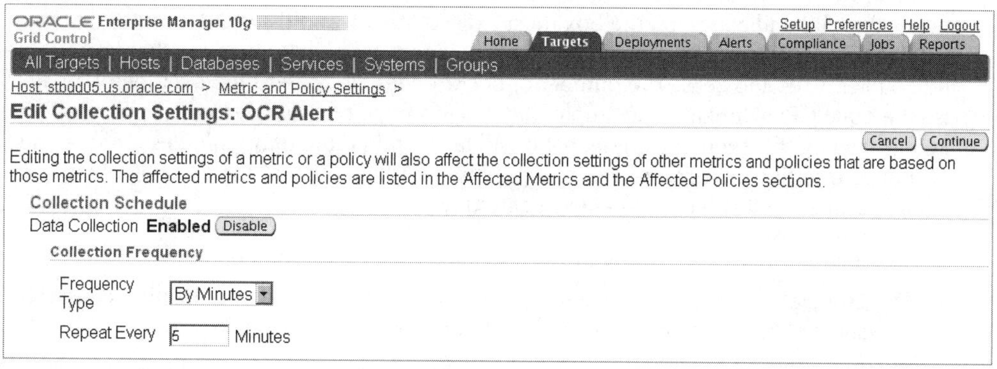

FIGURE 9-3.   *Disabling a metric*

- ■ **Critical** The data collected by the Agent has crossed the critical threshold.
- ■ **Error** The Agent was not able to collect the metric successfully. The error message will be uploaded as data to the repository, and the state of the metric will be shown as Error. As long as a metric is in an error state, no metric data is collected, and no data will be available in the repository for metric. This also means that for the hourly and daily rollups of this metric, no data will be available for the duration of the error condition.

With every evaluation of a metric, the Agent will compare the results against the defined thresholds. If the state of the metric changes, the Agent will generate and upload a new violation together with the metric data. If the state of the metric stays the same, the Agent will only upload the new data point. For the evaluation of the metric, the Agent simply compares the result of the metric with the defined warning and critical thresholds. For simple black-and-white metrics, the simple comparison with the thresholds is exactly what you want: If a disk on a machine starts to fill up, you definitely want to get alerted before it gets 100 percent full and starts creating problems.

For other metrics, though, a little more intelligence is needed. For CPU usage on a machine, for instance, an execution of a single command can cause a temporary spike in CPU for a couple of seconds. Triggering a new violation for this short-lived anomaly is not really what an Administrator wants: Getting woken up in the middle of the night because some command caused a spike in CPU usage, which is not even visible any more when the notification comes in, is the last thing any on-call operator wants to experience. To prevent these kinds of spurious notifications, a number of occurrences can be specified for the threshold: Only when the defined thresholds are crossed several consecutive evaluations in a row (defined by the number of occurrences) will the violation be triggered, and notifications will get sent out.

Here's an example of how to use this in an real-life example:

- ■ CPU Utilization (%) metric for a host
- ■ Metric defined to run every 5 minutes
- ■ Thresholds set to warning 80 percent and critical 90 percent
- ■ Number of occurrences set to 6

When the Agent collects the metric, and detects a threshold violation, it will keep track of the number of consecutive violations it has encountered. If the violation counter gets to 6, the violation will be triggered. With the collection frequency set to 5 minutes for this metric, this means the CPU utilization on the box must exceed the thresholds for 30 minutes in a row before a violation gets triggered. If a metric evaluation reports a value well below the defined thresholds, the counter is reset to zero. The number of occurrences also affects the clearing of an alert. If we use the same CPU Utilization example, the violation will only be cleared if six consecutive clears are reported by the Agent (meaning that it will take a minimum of 30 minutes for an alert to clear).

Because setting the occurrences affects both the triggering and the clearing of violations, the value specified for this has to be chosen carefully:

- ■ It needs to be high enough to avoid unnecessary triggering of alerts.
- ■ Especially for resource metrics, you want to avoid a spike in utilization caused by a short-lived command or operations to bother an administrator.
- ■ But it should not be set too high, to avoid an alert to remain outstanding in the Console, even though the actual condition on the box is already long-gone and resolved.

Using the Advanced Settings Page

When you click the pencil on the Edit Advanced Settings page, you can modify the Metric in key ways. First, you can add a Corrective Action for both the Warning and Critical thresholds. Corrective Actions are discussed in more detail later in this chapter.

From the Edit page, you can also change the Advanced Threshold settings. This allows you to make a further change from the main Metrics page: Not only can you change the value for Warning and Critical Thresholds, but you can also modify the Number of Occurrences.

Finally, notice that there is a radio button for Template Override. This button, when clicked, ensures that any modifications that are made for this metric, for this target, will be persistent, even if a monitoring template is later applied to the target.

Metric Collection Errors

If the gathering of the metric on the Agent side encounters an error, the Agent raises a metric error and sends it to the OMS server. For as long as the error condition continues, no metric data will be generated and uploaded for the metric. This also means that no alerts will be triggered for this metric for as long as the error persists. Some errors are transient errors, and can correct themselves over time (like a resource issue on a machine or the database). Other errors will persist, until an administrator intervenes and corrects the problem. Regardless of the cause of the error, each error should be analyzed, verified, and corrected, to prevent further interruptions of the metric data collections in the future. Once the error condition is resolved, the Agent will clear the error condition after the first successful completion of the metric collection.

GRID CONTROL WORKSHOP

Edit Collection Settings for CPU Utilization (%) Metric

Step 1. On the host target home page, click on the Metric and Policy settings page. On the main page, the warning and threshold settings can be changed directly.

Step 2. To change the number of occurrences, use the pencil icon in the Edit column to go to the Advanced Settings page (shown in Figure 9-4). This page allows a user to change not only the warning and threshold settings, but also to specify the number of occurrences for a metric.

Step 3. To check on the various thresholds of all the metric collections, the `mgmt$metric_collection` view can be used. Look for hosts that don't have warning and critical thresholds defined for the CPU Utilization metric:

```
SELECT target_name, warning_threshold, critical_threshold,
occurence_count
FROM    mgmt$metric_collection
WHERE   target_type   = 'host'
  AND   metric_name   = 'Load'
  AND   metric_column = 'cpuUtil'
  AND   (warning_threshold IS NULL OR critical_threshold IS NULL)
```

(continued)

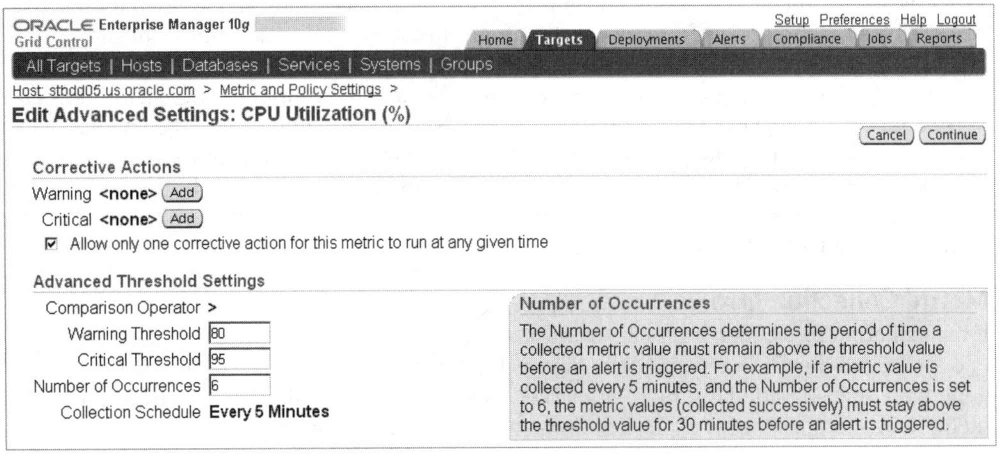

FIGURE 9-4.   *Metric Frequency settings*

Monitoring Templates

So far, all changes to the metrics have been confined to a single metric update for a single target. If it's just that single metric update, all of it can be quite easily done via the Console. But once you scale it up to hundreds of targets, and multiple metrics per target, doing the updates one by one in the Console is not really an option any more. And this is where templates come into the picture. The idea of a template is a reference setup or a gold image for a target: All the metric settings, including the frequencies, thresholds, corrective actions, and so on are captured into a single entity. These settings are grouped together into a template, given a name, and saved in the repository. Once a template is defined, it can be used to update the metric collection settings on any Agent, at any time, for all targets of the type the template was created for. A template can be edited again and updated to reflect any new changes, or additional tweaks made to the metric setup. Once all the updates are made to the template, it can be applied again to all targets requiring the changes.

BEST PRACTICE
For each type of target deployment (test, development, production, critical production, and so on), a template should be created, to be able to roll out a fixed set of metric collection settings on each target of that deployment type.

To create a new template, it always has to refer to a target to capture the state of the metrics from that target. This means that all tweaking and changes needed for the metrics will have to be done on at least one target manually, so a template can be created using that target as the image. When the template is created, it will capture all the settings from every metric known for that target. Metrics can be removed from the template definition, to keep just those metrics settings requiring changes. As a best practice, just keep those metrics in the template that require changed settings. All other metrics should be removed from the template definition, to allow the users responsible for those targets to update the settings, without having their changes overruled by the application of a template. The target settings over time will change, due to changes users and administrators make to the target, sometimes referred to as configuration drift. To make sure the metric settings used on the target are still the same as the ones from a template, a template comparison can be initiated in Grid Control, to verify the settings from one or more targets against those from the template. This operation will be submitted as a repository task inside the repository: It will run in the background, while the administrator can continue to work, and come back at a later time to see the results. Once the output is available, all the differences between the template and the settings on the targets will be highlighted. The administrator then has the option to reapply the template on one (or all) of the targets with differences, to make the monitoring consistent again across the board.

An additional feature regarding templates was added in 10.2.0.5: As soon as templates are defined in the system for specific target types, these templates can be used as the default template for each new target discovered into the system. This means that any new target of that type uploaded to the repository by an Agent will automatically have the metric settings of that template applied to it. This helps with the rollout of the basic monitoring settings for each newly discovered target of that type in the enterprise.

To set the default templates, go to the Monitoring Templates option from the Setup menu, and follow the Default Templates link to the page shown in Figure 9-5. Any template created for the given target type can be used as default template.

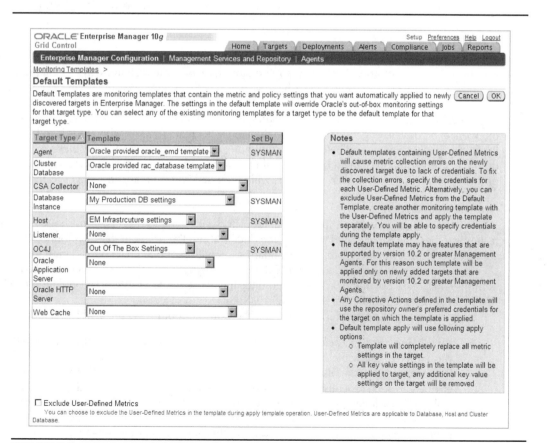

FIGURE 9-5. *Setting up default templates*

Metric Configuration Best Practices

When it comes to metric configurations, doing a one-off configuration for a single host as we did early in this chapter is fine for those situations where you have a unique target that deserves special attention. In general, however, stick with rolling out Monitoring Templates, which is a way to configure a set of metrics for a target type (such as Host), and then apply it to a large number of targets. This gives you ease of management from a metrics perspective—one change for all targets—but it also means you are getting an apples-to-apples level of comparison of metrics, if you need to compare behavior of one target to another. When it comes to setting thresholds, we would warn against getting too creative. Chances are that you already know what your system's tolerance levels are (or should be). First, stick with what you know and what you know the business will bear. Be mindful of the performance cost to setting very aggressive thresholds, as you will be making work for yourself to clear alerts and monitor systems. As for collection schedules, be mindful of the performance hit of setting a more frequent collection and upload interval. Every collection the Agent executes will consume CPU cycles on the machine. The more frequently a collection runs, the more CPU cycles it will consume. Changing all collections to run every minute might not be the monitoring solution you want to achieve: The overhead of running these collections at that frequency will be interfering with the regular work the box has to do. If you want proper monitoring of the system, pick a few key performance indicators, set them to an aggressive frequency, and tie those directly to your notification method.

Managing Alerts

Alerts are probably one of the most visible things in the Console, and something everyone, starting with administrators all the way up through the management chain, will pay attention to. The best way forward is to avoid them (the how-to for that was explained in the previous sections). But some alerts will be generated. And some alerts will appear in the Console. Once they are generated, an administrator will have to acknowledge the alert. And then of course we must do the work of actually fixing the condition so the alert will clear. The key with alerts is to handle them in a timely fashion, and before they start piling up in the Console. Twenty alerts is not a problem. Even a hundred might be manageable. But if you have a thousand or more to deal with, problems will be ignored and critical alerts will be missed with unplanned outages as the result.

Annotating Alerts

When the Agent (or repository, in case of a repository-side metric) detects a threshold violation, a standard message is generated to give some details about the problem that was found. These standard messages, however, are just a standard explanation of the threshold violation found, and do not contain any analysis, or any kind of details as to why this violation happened. When an administrator tracks down the problem, and finds the cause of the problem, the violation can be updated with the information of the analysis.

A violation can be updated in two ways in the Console (both ways are visible in Figure 9-6):

■ *An administrator can acknowledge a violation.* The acknowledgement is a feature that was added to allow the notification engine to repeat notifications for violations: As long as a user or administrator has not acknowledged the violation, the notification engine can send repetitive notifications for this alert. On the Alert Detail page of any violation, any logged-in user with operator privileges on the target can acknowledge the violation. For Grid Control this means that somebody is working on the problem and the notification engine will no longer consider this alert for sending repeating notifications.

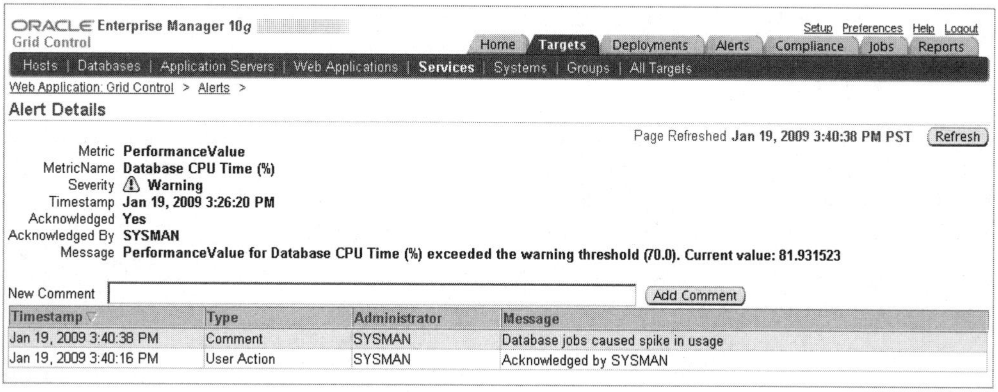

FIGURE 9-6. *Updating an outstanding alert*

■ *Add a comment to the violation.* Comments are just free-text messages, intended to document the work an administrator does to analyze and resolve the issue. There is no limit on how many comments a violation can have. Since all the comments are stored in the repository, administrators should show some constraint not to write an entire novel for every violation they work on.

Cleaning Up Stateless Alerts

Some metrics do not have a clearly defined sequence of states. A perfect example for this is the `alertlog` metric: The time the ORA-600 error was found in the `alertlog` is the time the violation will trigger. But when can this alert be considered as Clear? When does the error condition of the ORA-600 end? There is no way the Agent can detect this and generate a Clear state for this violation. An administrator will have to make a judgment call, and after debugging and analyzing the error, decide that the problem has been dealt with, and manually clear the outstanding alert. From the Alerts tab, for both the Critical and Warning type of errors, the stateless alerts can be selected and forced to Clear. An example of this is shown in Figure 9-7.

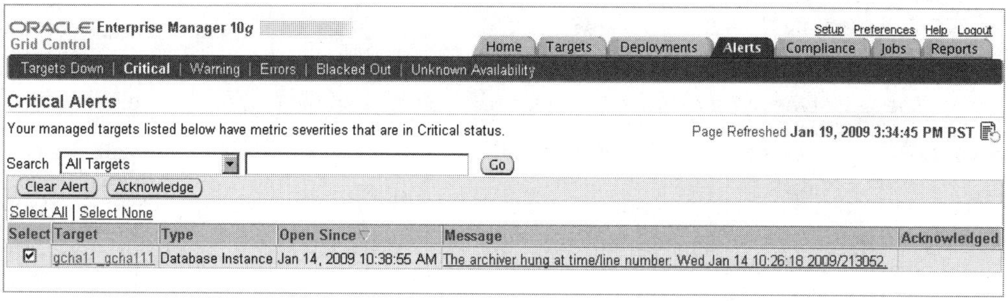

FIGURE 9-7. *Acknowledging a stateless alert*

NOTE
Errors cannot be forced to a Clear state, even for stateless metrics. The underlying error condition needs to be resolved to remove the error condition.

Even though the Console will allow multiple alerts to be updated at the same time, it is still limited to the context of the UI page, and will never be repository-wide. A special verb was added to EMCLI starting in version 10.2.0.5, to do a bulk update of stateless alerts on the command line, and close any open alerts older than a specified number of days:

```
$ emcli clear_stateless_alerts -older_than=<days>
        -target_type=<type> -target_name=<name>
        -metric_internal_name=<type>:<name>:<column>
        [-ignore_notifications] [-preview]
```

There are additional command-line options available for this verb, to add things like acknowledgements, or to drill down on member targets if a group or a service is specified as the target for the clear operation. The EMCLI help screen gives the full syntax of this verb, with all the explanation of all available command-line options:

```
$ emcli help clear_stateless_alerts
```

Normally, for every alert cleared, Grid Control will deliver notifications if administrators have registered an interest in receiving the alerts. For mass updates, however, flooding the mailbox (or pager) of a user is not always the smartest thing to do. To avoid generating this overflow of notifications, use the -ignore_notifications switch: Any update done to an outstanding alert will not be sent to the notification system, preventing the generation of notifications. If the additional option -preview is added to the command, EMCLI will run a simulation using the specified parameters, and will return the number of outstanding violations the command would potentially clear. Use this feature as a way to verify the impact of any mass update made to the stateless alerts.

The metric internal name looks pretty scary (and it is a little cryptic if you are not very familiar with the internal Grid Control nomenclature). But there are SQL statements and commands available to help determine the content of that internal name. One way to retrieve the metric internal name is to use this SQL statement:

```
SELECT DISTINCT target_type, metric_name, metric_column,
        metric_label ui_metric_name, column_label ui_column_name
FROM   mgmt_metrics
WHERE  statefull = 0
ORDER BY target_type, metric_name, metric_column
```

The same type of list can also be obtained via EMCLI on the command line:

```
$ emcli get_metrics_for_stateless_alerts -target_type=oracle_database
```

Let's finish this section by putting together all the information into one practical example: To clear up outstanding `alertlog` entries older than 60 days for the `orcl.world` database, the command to clear this is as follows:

```
$ emcli clear_stateless_alerts -older_than=60
        -target_type=oracle_database -target_name=orcl.world
        -metric_internal_name=oracle_database:alertLog:genericErrStack
```

Cleaning Up Alerts

As with policies, common sense has to prevail here. The best way to get rid of an alert is to resolve the underlying issue: no tricks, hacks, or sneaky ways to get rid of an alert. For instance, there is no point in trying to shove a Listener Down notification under the rug: Unless that listener is restarted, the problem will be there and cause potential connectivity problems for any user trying to use that listener to connect to a database. When the operator or the administrator of the target has taken the necessary steps to fix the issue, the alert will clear when the Agent runs the metric again for this target. But the alert will not clear if any of these conditions are still true:

■ If the target with the alert is down or in an error state, metrics will not run on the target, and therefore alerts will not clear. Of course, the same applies to the Agent: If the Agent is not running, metrics will not be evaluated either for any of the targets the Agent is monitoring.

■ If the metric has reported a metric error, no data points are collected, and, therefore, no thresholds can be evaluated to clear the alert. Before a normal metric collection can resume, the error condition must be fixed first. Tips and tricks on how to handle metrics errors are covered in Chapter 18 in the section "Agent Metric Debugging."

■ If the frequency of the metric includes a setting for the number of occurrences, it might take more than one collection cycle on the Agent side for the alert to clear. For example, if a metric is set to collect every 15 minutes, with the occurrences set to 3, it will take a minimum of three metric evaluations, or 45 minutes, for the metric to clear again after it has triggered an alert.

Another new feature in 10.2.0.5, demonstrated in Figure 9-8, can help with the clearing of alerts: Once an alert has triggered, and the user/operator has fixed the underlying problem, the metric can be re-evaluated again from the Console, to force a new collection to run on the Agent for that metric.

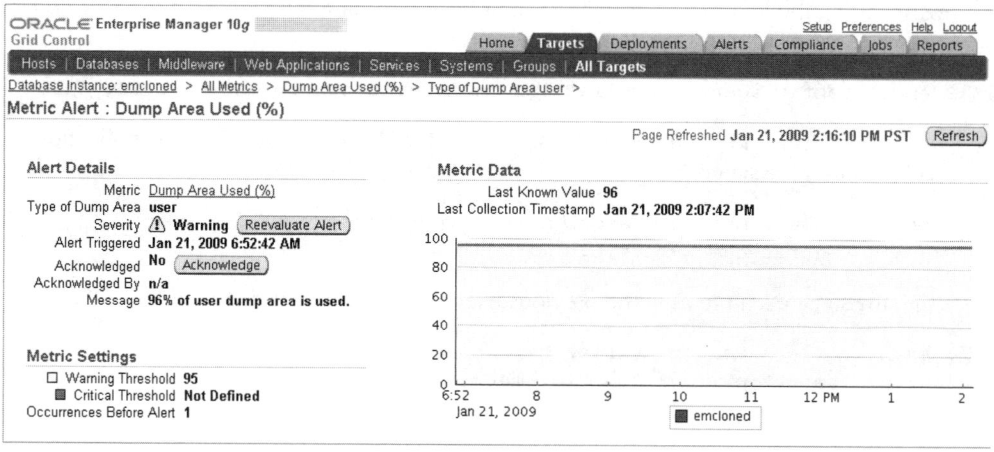

FIGURE 9-8. *Re-evaluating an outstanding alert*

Besides using the Console, there are also command-line possibilities to rerun collection. The Agent can be forced to rerun a metric on demand, and re-evaluate the conditions set on the metric:

```
$ emctl config agent runcollection <tgt name>:<tgt type> <collection>
```

The target name and the target type are the names of the target for which the collection has to be rerun.

The collection name of a metric will have to be retrieved from the repository. Using the example from the last picture (Dump Area Used % metric), running on a database called `orcl` `.world`, the SQL statement would look like this:

```
SELECT  c.coll_name collection_name
FROM    mgmt_coll_item_metrics c, mgmt_metrics m1, mgmt_metrics m2,
        mgmt_targets t
WHERE   t.target_name    = 'orcl.world'
  AND   t.target_type    = 'oracle_database'
  AND   m1.column_label  = 'Dump Area Used (%)'
  AND   t.target_type    = m1.target_type
  AND   t.type_meta_ver  = m1.type_meta_ver
  AND   (m1.category_prop_1=t.category_prop_1 OR m1.category_prop_1=' ')
  AND   (m1.category_prop_2=t.category_prop_2 OR m1.category_prop_2=' ')
  AND   (m1.category_prop_3=t.category_prop_3 OR m1.category_prop_3=' ')
  AND   (m1.category_prop_4=t.category_prop_4 OR m1.category_prop_4=' ')
  AND   (m1.category_prop_5=t.category_prop_5 OR m1.category_prop_5=' ')
  AND   m2.target_type    = m1.target_type
  AND   m2.type_meta_ver  = m1.type_meta_ver
  AND   m2.metric_name    = m1.metric_name
  AND   m2.metric_column  = ' '
  AND   c.target_type     = t.target_type
  AND   c.type_meta_ver   = t.type_meta_ver
  AND   c.metric_guid     = m2.metric_guid;
```

The output of this query is the collection name to use for this metric, in this case the `log_full` metric. Using the information from the example, and using the output from the SQL command, the EMCTL command becomes:

```
$ emctl config agent runcollection orcl.world:oracle_database log_full
```

In 10.2.0.5, an additional verb is also present for EMCLI to rerun a metric collection. For a regular metric, the syntax is:

```
$ emcli collect_metric -target_type=<type> -target_name=<name>
        -metric_name=<metric>
```

Using the same example as in the previous example, the command will look like this:

```
$ emcli collect_metric -target_type=oracle_database
        -target_name=orcl.world -metric_name=log_full
```

User-Defined Metrics

A user-defined metric (UDM) is an additional metric, added to a target by an administrator. The entire metric is custom-defined by the administrator, starting from the metric name and the commands the metric has to execute, to the frequency this metric should be collected with, and the critical and warning thresholds to be used to check for violations. UDMs are there to extend the current monitoring of targets in Grid Control. This should be used to add application-specific metrics, or to collect data points that are environment specific, and cannot be gathered or collected in a generic way. All the standard metric attributes can be added to this UDM:

- Every UDM has a unique name.
- Every UDM is tied to a specific type of target (Host, Database, and so on).
- Thresholds can be defined for a UDM, to generate violations and trigger notifications.
- A schedule can be specified, so that this new metric will be collected on a regular basis.

UDM Limitations

Even though a UDM is a regular metric as far as the Agent and repository are concerned, there are some limitations for UDMs:

- A UDM can only be defined on a host or a database (single instance or RAC) target. You can only register an OS script (for the host) or a SQL script (for the database).
- OS UDMs are limited to returning a single value. Any OS script defined as an UDM should only return one row with one value.
- SQL UDMs can either return the single row, with a single value, or return a table of multiple rows, with two columns: A key column (like a username, filename, and so on), followed by a value.

Dangers of a UDM

Writing an additional metric might seem like a simple and trivial task, but there are a couple of caveats and dangers lurking in the shadows. The first is simply redundancy. A lot of information is already being gathered by the Agents with the standard metrics. Before any new UDM is defined, always check the information currently available from the target, before adding a new metric. Chances are that the data point you are looking for is already there. Another danger is the error handling of the UDM. Errors should be reported in a consistent way, with more or less static error messages. Consider this example:

```
#!/bin/sh
out=`get_my_value`
if [ $? -ne 0 ];
then
    echo "em_error=${out}";
else
    echo "em_result=${out}";
fi
```

Although this looks like a perfectly valid and correct UDM definition, there is a very big problem with this script: The error message is completely random, and can therefore trigger a new error message with each invocation of this script. Since the Agent will always compare the last known error message with the current one, the danger exists that this script will generate a unique error message with each execution of the UDM. Over time, this can cause a performance problem on Grid Control, impacting all users and all targets, because of the overload of error messages this metric is generating. Especially if this UDM metric is rolled out to several targets, the error handling of the UDM script should be *very* explicit, capturing all known error messages in a standard and concise way.

Probably the biggest problem with UDMs is the number of notifications it will generate. It's easy to specify thresholds, and just wait for the alerts to come in. The trouble usually begins if users and administrators are getting flooded with notifications: If too many pointless alerts are generated, people will start to ignore them, and when a real problem surfaces for this metric, it will be discarded as just one more pointless one. A nice illustration of this problem is shown in the example of Figure 9-9. Granted, this example is using a metric specifically designed to exaggerate the problem, but the potential danger is there for each metric added to the system. And it's even not just relevant for UDM metrics: All metrics are suspect and need to be verified, to make sure they are not flooding the system (more about this coming up later on in this chapter).

A solution to combat the pointless notification generated by this sawtooth metric in the example is to set the number of occurrences: If the occurrences were changed from 1 to 2, no more alerts would be generated for this metric after approximately 10 P.M.

Credentials for UDM Metrics

Any defined UDM requires specific credentials to access the target and run the specified script. These credentials can be the same as the credentials used to monitor the target, but they have to be specified separately for the execution of the UDM. This means that any user or administrator who sets up or makes changes to an UDM must have a valid login to the target in order to work with the UDM definition.

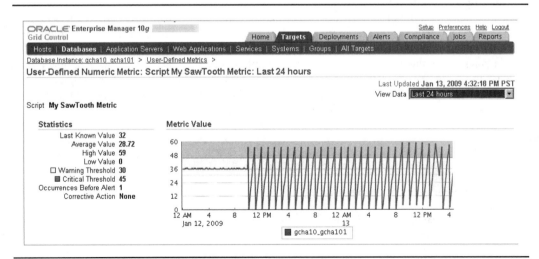

FIGURE 9-9. *UDM alert history example*

Policies in EM Grid Control

Policies are a special type of metric evaluated by the repository itself. They have a frequency to evaluate the policy rules, the thresholds are defined to be able to trigger alerts if needed, and policies can be disabled just like metrics. But they don't generate any new metric data. They use the data the standard metrics have collected and uploaded, and apply a business rule to validate and verify the data of the metric. If the rule reports a violation, the policy will trigger an alert, so administrators can be notified about the problem.

Anatomy of a Policy

The most important aspect of a policy is its state: the *condition* of the rule. A policy can have five distinct states:

- **Clear**   This is the state all policies should be in: Nothing to report. All is clear, and no violation was detected by the policy rule.

- **Informational**   These are the "nice to know" kinds of things: They won't pose a threat, or cause direct problems to the target, but these are things an administrator should be aware of.

- **Warning**   A violation was detected that should be looked at. Warnings are important and should be looked at, but these are not conditions that can cause fatal problems on the target.

- **Critical**   This state indicates a severe violation of the policy rule. These are conditions that need to be remedied immediately.

- **Error**   The policy evaluation failed. The most likely cause is incorrect data, or incomplete data. More information about the specific error can be found on the Errors section of the Compliance tab of Grid Control.

All policy rules can be put in any of the three different categories available:

- **Configuration**   The setup and configuration of a target is compared against the set of known problems and best practices.

- **Security**   All security violations and possible holes in access or permissions of files and objects are part of this category. There are well over 100 distinct policies in this category.

- **Storage**   This category contains checks for all space-related parameters, and the way the target is configured to use physical disc space.

Working with Policies

Each of the policy categories has its own library of defined business rules, and its own groups of policies defined. They evaluate on a defined schedule (24 hours by default), and can be changed and altered per target just like a metric. The policy settings can also be added to a template, so that all the tweaks and changes made on one target can be replicated to all similar targets in the enterprise. These policy states are used to calculate the compliance score of every target: With every evaluation cycle of the policies, every violation reported will be discounted against the compliance score. Once the compliance score is calculated, the trend of how this score is evolving can be viewed on the Policy Trend Overview page shown in Figure 9-10. This page gives the history of how the compliance of this target has evolved, and which policies have triggered a violation and require attention from an administrator.

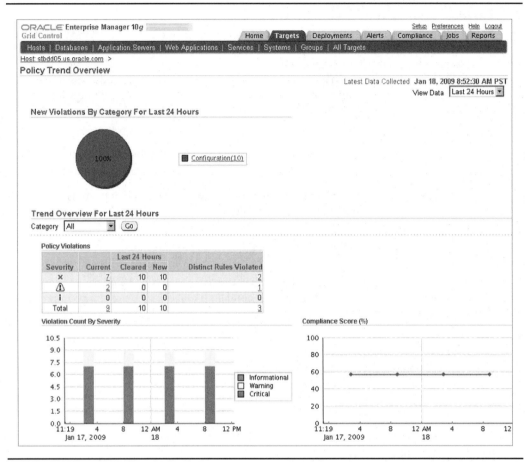

FIGURE 9-10. *Policy Trend Overview page*

Cleaning Up Policy Alerts

Any policy alert can be cleaned up and resolved in three ways. First, resolve the underlying problem. This is just common sense, but if a configuration setting is not correct, or can cause potential trouble in a production environment, the first thing any administrator should be doing is to *fix* the problem. This is (and should be) the most common way of clearing policy violations. Take the following, for example: for database security purposes, the execute privileges on DBMS_LOB, DBMS_JOB, UTL_FILE, UTL_HTTP, and UTL_TCP should be revoked from the PUBLIC role, preventing anyone logged in to the database from being able to run rogue PL/SQL code. These are real security threats that should get resolved in any production database. Suppressing or disabling these policies is not a wise decision, especially if security audits of these databases will happen.

The second way to clean up policy alerts is to simply disable those that you do not want to know about. On test machines, with developers working on a database, and installing and deinstalling it all the time, there is little point in checking for a default password, or requiring strict password complexity. For development machines, these rules can be disabled. However, policies cannot be disabled on a global level: They have to be disabled on a per-target basis.

BEST PRACTICE
*Update all the policies for one representative target in the enterprise,
and create a template from all the policy changes. This template can
then be rolled out to all similar targets, to update the policy settings
on all the affected targets.*

The third way to clean up policy alerts is to suppress the violation. This is, in a way, sweeping the problem under the rug—not exactly something that you want to do with every policy violation. This is only to be used in an exception case, where the rule is valid, but there is a specific business reason to remove a single violation from the rule. Suppressing can also be done on a more fine-grained level: Instead of disabling the entire policy rule, only a specific violation for the rule can be suppressed. For example, on a production machine, the Open Ports rule will complain about port 22 being open and accessible. Port 22 is the port SSH uses to connect to a system. Since SSH is a secure protocol, and *some* form of access to the machine will be needed to let administrators do their work, this violation can be suppressed. Completely disabling the Open Port policy rule is not a good solution, as valid complaints for some nonsecure protocols in use might still trigger on this box, and generate a violation.

When suppressing violations, always specify a clear comment, so anybody auditing or verifying the policy violations will know why that particular violation was suppressed. As with disabling policies, suppressing policy violations cannot be done on a global basis. Individual violations per target have to be suppressed. Templates also cannot be used to suppress violations.

BEST PRACTICE
*If a certain policy rule has a well-known exception (like port 22
for the Open Port policy), the policy can be updated to have that
exception excluded from the values to check for. This approach is the
recommended way to suppress a violation: It's better to prevent alerts
than to deal with them and ignore them. These exclusions can also be
stored in templates, and rolled out to all the targets in the enterprise.*

Suspend Monitoring with Blackouts

The best medicine is prevention. And that goes for alerts and violations, too. This has already been mentioned before, but it's such an important statement to make that repeating it again is not a waste of valuable pages in this book. Every alert that the Agent does not generate will not have to be uploaded to the OMS, will not have to be processed and put in the notification queue to alert administrators about the condition. An important feature any administrator has available in Grid Control to prevent alerts from getting in, is defining a blackout on a target: A *blackout* is just a period of time for which no metric collections will happen on the specified target. And if there are no metric collections, no metric data is gathered, and no alerts can therefore be triggered. This ability to black out a target is necessary to allow maintenance to be done on targets. If there is downtime of an application because of a hardware upgrade, or a software patch to be applied, there is no need to generate all kinds of alerts and violations about the changes happening on the machine during those operations. It was well known in advance, so the fact that the application is down, or the CPU is spiking because a bunch of programs have to be recompiled because of an OS patch, and so on, should come as no surprise to anyone responsible for this target.

Types of Blackouts

An administrator can create two types of blackouts: console blackouts, and agent blackouts. Let's discuss console blackouts first.

Console blackouts are initiated via the Console. These blackouts can be created on multiple targets at once, even across multiple Agents. Any Console blackout can be modified and edited in the Console, but no EMCTL commands executed by the Agent can modify this type of blackout. The blackout page in the Console can be reached via the Setup menu, or by directly typing in the URL:

```
https://<oms>:<port>/em/console/admin/rep/blackout/blackoutsMain
```

There is also a set of EMCLI verbs available to perform blackout operations.

```
$ emcli create_blackout -name="<name>" -add_targets=<list>
        [-propagate_targets] -schedule="<schedule>" -reason="<text>"
$ emcli delete_blackout -name="<name>"
$ emcli get_blackouts
```

All blackouts created by EMCLI will be considered Console blackouts, and can be modified in the Console by administrators.

The second kind of blackouts is *agent blackouts*, created with the EMCTL command. EMCTL can only black out those targets the particular Agent is monitoring. It cannot black out targets from another Agent. Modifications are not possible with the EMCTL command: it can only create or remove a blackout. The Console, however, can force an Agent blackout to be stopped. It will not be able to modify the blackout, or change the targets the blackout was registered on, but it will be able to force the blackout to end.

On the Agent side, the EMCTL command has options to create and remove blackouts from targets:

```
$ emctl start blackout <name> [-nodeLevel]
            [<Target_name>[:<Target_Type>]].... [-d <Duration>]
$ emctl status blackout [<Target_name>[:<Target_Type>]]
$ emctl stop blackout <Blackoutname>
```

Indefinite Blackouts

A blackout can also be defined with no end-date. Practically speaking, this means that this target is defined in Grid Control, but with no monitoring, and no metric collections will happen on this target until the blackout is stopped. These indefinite blackouts can be practical in a setup phase, when a set of machines is getting rolled out, but the setup and configuration has not completed yet. But for each blackout that remains in effect for a prolonged period of time, an Enterprise Administrator has to ask him- or herself this question: If nobody cares about this target (since it's blacked out), why does it need to be a part of the Grid Control deployment?

There might be valid reasons to keep a target blacked out for a (hopefully short) period of time, but in general, any indefinite blackout defined by users and administrators should be questioned, and where possible, removed from Grid Control. To locate these blackouts, run this SQL query:

```
SELECT b.blackout_name, b.created_by, w.start_time
FROM   mgmt_blackout_windows w, mgmt_blackouts b
WHERE  b.blackout_guid = w.blackout_guid
  AND  w.end_time IS NULL
```

Corrective Actions

Having thresholds on metrics, and sending notifications if a threshold gets violated, is only half of the battle. As soon as a violation is reported, an Administrator or Operator will have to analyze the notification, take an action to fix the problem, and get the reported condition back to normal. For most metrics, resolving the issue will require some detailed information about the environment, and the specific setup of the machine to resolve the issue. Automating these kinds of steps is pretty hard. But in some cases, a fix for a specific condition can be automated, and can be scripted. And these scripts can be specified as a Corrective Action or a Response Action in Grid Control.

NOTE
The textbook example for this is a Listener Down condition. If the listener is found down, the solution is as simple as restarting it like this:

```
$ lsnrctl start listener
```

This startup command can be entered as a fix routine, to be run automatically when the Agent detects the Target Down condition.

Corrective Actions can be specified for both warning and critical threshold violations. They are implemented as Grid Control jobs, stored in the repository, and executed by the OMS when the Agent uploads the violation. Since a Corrective Action is a job, the status of this job can be tracked by user and administrators, and notifications can be sent out for the Corrective Action itself, to keep up to date on the progress of the fix routine. A *Response Action* is a special kind of Corrective Action that can be specified for a metric to execute an OS command if the target is found to be not available. The main difference between a Corrective Action and a Response Action is that a CA is initiated from the OMS server in case of a threshold violation, while the Agent executes the Response Action immediately as soon as the metric reports a violation. The Agent is not tracking the execution of the Response Action, and will not send an update on the execution of the script. Any kind of notification of tracking the script needs to do must be incorporated into the Response Action itself.

To set up a fix routine to be executed in case of a violation:

- On the target home page, click on the Metric and Policy settings page.
- For any of the metrics, click the pencil icon of the Edit column (see Figure 9-3).
- Add a critical (or warning if applicable) Corrective Action.
- From the drop-down list, select the appropriate action to take.
- Specify the details of the fix routine.
- For Corrective Actions, this will be the definition on how Grid Control has to execute the job.
- For a Response Action, specify the OS script that has to be executed.

Getting the Most (or Should We Say Least) Out of Notifications

To make sure notifications are working for you, and not against you, is to be sure that your notifications are only telling you things you actually care about. The first step, obviously, is getting your metrics right, so the important things are knowable at the right level of criticality.

The second step is to properly configure the notifications mechanism in Grid Control to only notify who needs to know, when they need to know, and how they want to know. The How is referred to as *methods*, the Why is covered by *rules*, and Who and When are covered by *schedules*. These three mechanisms work in unison to ensure that you can flexibly and quickly make changes to notifications without making specific rules per user or administrator.

Notifications are not sent by the repository or the Agents. The OMS machines will distribute the notifications to their destination. Any of the available Management Servers can send out notifications. All notification methods should be callable from each of the servers in the infrastructure. While alerts can come only from Metrics and Policies, notifications can also come from other operations in EM, such as jobs.

Understanding and Utilizing Methods Effectively

In order for the OMS to know how to send an alert to the administrators, a notification method is defined. This will let the OMS server know what to do in case a notification of that type has to be sent out. There are four notification methods available in Grid Control: SMTP (e-mail), OS command, SNMP trap, and PL/SQL procedure.

- **SMTP (e-mail)**   Send e-mail to a specified e-mail address. With the current forwarding capabilities service providers offer, an e-mail can even be forwarded to a phone or a pager.

   For a *real* e-mail address the long format can be selected. This means a full e-mail with all the details about the alert and the context of the alert.

   For pagers and phones, the short format has to be selected. In this case an abbreviated e-mail will be sent that contains just the basic information.

   For any e-mail to be sent, the outgoing e-mail servers (the SMTP servers) need to be configured first. This is done at a global level only once, and all the OMS servers will use the same configuration to send the e-mail.

- **OS command**   Execute a script or an OS command. Each OMS machine has to be able to execute that same command in the same way.

- **SNMP trap**   Send out an SNMP trap with the notification details.

- **PL/SQL procedure**   Execute a PL/SQL procedure in the repository.

NOTE
In the Console, information may be shown about a Java Callback notification type. This is an internal type, which the Connectors use to communicate with external third-party software.

Setting Up E-mail Notifications

E-mail is perhaps the easiest of the notification methods to set up. Setting up the server for sending e-mail messages is something that should have been done during the setup of the OMS machines (see Chapter 2). If the Enterprise Administrators have done their work properly, and finished the OMS install, the e-mail setup is already done and operational.

Each administrator defined in Grid Control also has an e-mail address associated with the user account. When a user subscribes to a certain alert, this e-mail address is used to distribute the e-mail notification. While adding an e-mail address in Grid Control, the user will have the choice to specify either long or short as the e-mail notification type to be used for that e-mail address.

- **Long messages**   These types of notifications are intended for use with regular e-mail addresses. The full details of the alert will be shown in the notification. The subject of the e-mail will contain the target name and the alert message. The body of a long e-mail will have all the details of the alert that triggered the notification.

- **Short messages**   The short e-mail format is intended for SMS text messages, or e-mail addresses used to forward to pagers. Short e-mail messages have a limited length. This length (155 bytes by default) is specified to allow short e-mail notifications to be sent as text messages to cell phones.

  ```
  em.notification.short_format_length=155
  ```

NOTE
Do not increase the length of the short e-mail messages if notifications need to be sent as text messages to cell phone. The maximum size that can be transmitted as a text message is 155 bytes.

Setting Up OS Command Notifications

Any OMS server can execute an OS command notification, and there is no way to prevent a certain Management Server from delivering a notification. Before any scripts can be used as an OS notification method, the script has to be copied over to all OMS servers using the same location. The user owning the OMS software has to be capable of executing the OS command. Table 9-1 shows the variables containing the details of the notifications that are available to use in OS scripts. Each of these variables can be used in the OS scripts. The values will be set as environment variables, with the name *ENV_<name of the variable>*.

Environment Variable	Description
TARGET_NAME	Name of the target on which the violation occurred
TARGET_TYPE	Type of target on which the violation occurred
HOST	Name of the machine on which the target resides
METRIC	The metric that has generated the violation
METRIC_VALUE	The value of the metric when the violation was recorded. Not set for policy violations
POLICY_RULE	The name of the policy that triggered the violation. Not set for metric severities
KEY_VALUE_NAME	Name of the key value
KEY_VALUE	The key of the metric that triggered the alert
VIOLATION_CONTEXT	A comma-separated list of name-value pairs that show the alert context

TABLE 9-1.   *OS Command Variables (continued)*

Environment Variable	Description
TIMESTAMP	Time when the severity occurred, formatted using the locale settings of the Management Server
SEVERITY	Type of violation
MESSAGE	Message for the alert that provides details about what triggered the condition
RULE_NAME	Name of the notification rule that resulted in the severity
RULE_OWNER	Name of the Enterprise Manager administrator who owns the rule

TABLE 9-1. *OS Command Variables*

GRID CONTROL WORKSHOP

Setting Up an OS Command for Notifications

Workshop Notes

The simplest form for a notification handler is the ability to write the alert information to a file. This file can then be parsed or manipulated by a third-party tool for further analysis. The following example simply dumps all available alert information to a file.

> **Step 1.** Create the OS script. Create a shell script called `gc_notif_demo.sh` with the following content:

```
#!/bin/sh
#
echo "----------------------------------------" >> /u01/notification.log
date                                            >> /u01/notification.log
echo "----------------------------------------" >> /u01/notification.log
echo "TARGET_NAME       = ${ENV_TARGET_NAME}"   >> /u01/notification.log
echo "TARGET_TYPE       = ${ENV_TARGET_TYPE}"   >> /u01/notification.log
echo "HOST              = ${ENV_HOST}"          >> /u01/notification.log
echo "METRIC            = ${ENV_METRIC}"        >> /u01/notification.log
echo "METRIC_VALUE      = ${ENV_METRIC_VALUE}"  >> /u01/notification.log
echo "POLICY_RULE       = ${ENV_POLICY_RULE}"   >> /u01/notification.log
echo "KEY_VALUE_NAME    = ${ENV_KEY_VALUE_NAME}" >> /u01/notification.log
echo "KEY_VALUE         = ${ENV_KEY_VALUE}"     >> /u01/notification.log
echo "VIOLATION_CONTEXT = ${ENV_VIOLATION_CONTEXT}" >> /u01/notification.log
echo "TIMESTAMP         = ${ENV_TIMESTAMP}"     >> /u01/notification.log
echo "SEVERITY          = ${ENV_SEVERITY}"      >> /u01/notification.log
echo "MESSAGE           = ${ENV_MESSAGE}"       >> /u01/notification.log
echo "RULE_NAME         = ${ENV_RULE_NAME}"     >> /u01/notification.log
echo "RULE_OWNER        = ${ENV_RULE_OWNER}"    >> /u01/notification.log
#
# ----- eof: gc_notif_demo.sh ----- #
```

Step 2. Define the notification method.

■ Copy the file `gc_notif_demo.sh` to the same location on every OMS.

■ From the Setup menu, select the Notification Methods item.

■ In the Scripts and SNMP Traps section, select OS Command.

■ On the next screen:

Name: Enter the name for this method (make it user-friendly so you know what you are referring to).

Description: Free-text description for this OS script.

OS Script: Enter the absolute location of the demo script. Example: `<ORACLE_HOME>/sysman/bin/gc_notif_demo.sh`

■ Use the Test OS Command button to make sure everything is entered correctly.

■ Finish the setup by clicking the OK button.

Step 3. Set up the notification rule. With the OS script defined, we can now set up the rules to specify when to call this OS script:

■ Go to the Preferences | Notification Rules menu.

■ Click the Create button. This will launch a page with multiple tabs to define the notification rule.

■ On the first General tab of this create page, enter a (user-friendly) name, the descriptions, and the default list of targets this rule is going to get used for.

■ If you want everybody to be able to use and see this rule, you can click the Make Public option.

■ On the Availability tab, you have control over when this rule is going to get triggered in case of system errors or blackouts defined on the targets.

■ On the Metrics tab, select all the metric this rule applies to. Specify the specific metric states that will trigger the notification. And if there are Corrective Actions defined, they can be specified as well.

■ On this last tab named Methods, locate the notification method defined for the OS script, and select that method by checking the Assign Method To Rule column.

■ After you wrap up the creation of the rule with the Finish button, the rule will be in effect, and be used immediately by Grid Control for any new violation coming in.

Setting Up SNMP Trap Notifications

Another form of notification is to send SNMP traps to a third-party tool. The setup of this is very straightforward: specify the trap server, the port, and community to use, and that is all there is to do. Currently, only SNMPv1 is supported. Any trap the OMS sends will have the information in Table 9-2. Details of the SNMP trap can be found in the trap definition. This file is installed in the OMS home:

`<ORACLE_HOME>/network/doc/omstrap.v1`

SNMP Object ID	Description
oraEM4AlertEntry	Information about a particular Enterprise Manager alert
oraEM4AlertIndex	Index of a particular alert, unique only at the moment an alert is generated
oraEM4AlertTargetName	The name of the target to which this alert applies
oraEM4AlertTargetType	The type of the target to which this alert applies
oraEM4AlertHostName	The name of the host on which this alert originated
oraEM4AlertMetricName	The name of the EM metric or policy that generated this alert
oraEM4AlertKeyValue	The value of the key column, if present, for the EM metric that generated this alert
oraEM4AlertTimeStamp	The time at which this alert was generated
oraEM4AlertSeverity	Depending on the metric, this can be Critical, Warning, Clear, Up, Down/Agent Unreachable, Agent Unreachable Clear, Blackout Start, or Blackout End
oraEM4AlertMessage	The message generated by EM for this alert
oraEM4AlertRuleName	The name of the notification rule that caused this notification
oraEM4AlertRuleOwner	The owner of the notification rule that caused this notification

TABLE 9-2. *SNMP Trap Information*

Setting Up PL/SQL Notifications

The PL/SQL type of method requires a PL/SQL routine that the OMS server will call, run as the repository owner. Any routine specified must pass the following prerequisites:

- The signature of the routine is fixed. It must be a procedure, either a standalone one, or one part of a package, that accepts a single parameter of the type MGMT_NOTIFY_SEVERITY.

- The repository owner (SYSMAN) needs to have explicit execute privileges on the package or procedure to run the PL/SQL routine.

When defining the notification method, always fully qualify the PL/SQL routine with the name of the owner of the PL/SQL routine; and always use the Test PL/SQL Procedure to validate the definition of the PL/SQL method.

NOTE
Since the PL/SQL procedure will be executed while all the other repository tasks are running, the impact of this routine should be minimal. The performance and work done should be carefully examined before a PL/SQL notification routine is put in production. Even an elapsed time of 2 seconds on average for the execution of the notification routine can be too much if there are more than 60 notifications triggered a minute for this method.

GRID CONTROL WORKSHOP

Setting Up a PL/SQL Command for Notifications

Workshop Notes

For the PL/SQL workshop, let's do a simple example to store all alert notifications coming in. This is just meant as an example, which can be tailored and adjusted to the specific needs of the Grid Control infrastructure it is running in.

Step 1. Create the table that will hold the notification data. Create the table used to store the notification details:

```
CREATE TABLE em_notification_table (
  rule_owner            VARCHAR2(64),
  rule_name             VARCHAR2(132),
  target_name           VARCHAR2(64),
  target_type           VARCHAR2(64),
  timezone              VARCHAR2(64),
  host_name             VARCHAR2(128),
  metric_name           VARCHAR2(64),
  metric_description    VARCHAR2(128),
  metric_column         VARCHAR2(64),
  metric_value          VARCHAR2(1024),
  key_value_name        VARCHAR2(512),
  key_value             VARCHAR2(256),
  key_value_guid        VARCHAR2(256),
  collection_timestamp  DATE,
  severity_code         NUMBER,
  message               VARCHAR2(4000),
  severity_guid         RAW(16),
  target_guid           RAW(16),
  metric_guid           RAW(16)
);
```

Step 2. Create the PL/SQL package that will be called for the notification. A simple PL/SQL package, with just the definition to store the notification object in the table created for this purpose:

```
-- ---------------------------------------------------------------- --
-- EM_NOTIFICATION_DEMO: Package
-- ---------------------------------------------------------------- --

CREATE OR REPLACE PACKAGE em_notification_demo AS

  PROCEDURE InsertTable (e IN MGMT_NOTIFY_SEVERITY);

END em_notification_demo;
/
```

(continued)

```
-- ---------------------------------------------------------- --
-- EM_NOTIFICATION_DEMO: Package Body
-- ---------------------------------------------------------- --

CREATE OR REPLACE PACKAGE BODY em_notification_demo AS

  PROCEDURE InsertTable (e IN MGMT_NOTIFY_SEVERITY) IS
  BEGIN
    INSERT INTO em_notification_table
      (rule_owner, rule_name, target_name, target_type, timezone,
       host_name, metric_name, metric_description, metric_column,
       metric_value, key_value_name, key_value, key_value_guid,
       collection_timestamp, severity_code, message, severity_guid,
       target_guid, metric_guid)
    VALUES
      (e.rule_owner, e.rule_name, e.target_name, e.target_type,
       e.timezone, e.host_name, e.metric_name, e.metric_description,
       e.metric_column, e.metric_value, e.key_value_name, e.key_value,
       e.key_value_guid, e.collection_timestamp, e.severity_code,
       e.message, e.severity_guid, e.target_guid, e.metric_guid);
    COMMIT;
  END InsertTable;

END em_notification_demo;
/
```

Step 3.   Define the notification method. We first need to define the PL/SQL interface in the system, so it can be used and referenced when handling severities.

- From the Setup menu, select the Notification Methods item.
- In the Scripts and SNMP Traps section, select Add PL/SQL Procedure.
- On the next screen:

   Name: Enter the user-friendly name for this method.

   Description: Free-text description for this PL/SQL routine.

   PLSQL Procedure: Enter the full name of the procedure, including the owner of the PL/SQL procedure: `sysman.em_notification_demo.InsertTable`
- Use the Test Procedure button to make sure everything is entered correctly
- Finish the setup by clicking the OK button.

Step 4.   Set up the notification rule. Now that there is a mechanism to deliver the notification, we need to set up the rules on when to call this method:

- Go to the Preferences | Notification Rules menu.
- Click the Create button, to get the same page with all the tabs for the creation of the notification rule.

- On the General tab, fill in the user-friendly name, and the description of the rule. Specify the type of targets this rule is used for, and if needed specify the subset of targets to be used for this rule.

- On the Metrics tab, select all the metrics that will be using this rule, including the various metric states and corrective actions if needed.

- On this last screen, you can select which notification method you want to use to handle the reported severity. On the top of the screen, you can select whether you want to send an e-mail to a particular user or users, on top of any methods you might select on the bottom of the screen. Select the previously defined PL/SQL method.

- Use the Finish button to save the notification rule.

Notification Rules

We've spent considerable time going over the methods. Notification rules set the conditions for which we would send a notification: perhaps a target is down, or CPU utilization is above a critical threshold. These are straightforward, and relate to alerts; however, a rule could also be a failing job, or a failing corrective action. Basically, the Notification Rules can be thought of as a list of events that different administrators might find interesting.

You can take a look at default, out-of-box rules by going to Preferences | Notification | Rules in EM. From this list, you can get a sense of the typical events that warrant notification. (Note: If you are logged in .... as an administrator other than SYSMAN, you may not see all existing rules.) Some of these are aggregate notifications; that is, there are multiple conditions that will trigger a single rule. That way, you can subscribe to a single rule to get multiple notifications. For instance, take Host Availability and Critical States: This monitors a slew of host metrics that would be of interest to a system administrator, and creates a single rule for them. As you can see in Figure 9-11, by clicking on the Rule name, you get more details, such as which targets the rule is set for, and which metrics are being evaluated as triggering events for the notification.

Building Rules

Building rules is done from the same screen as in Figure 9-11 for viewing them. There are buttons to create like, edit, delete, and create rules. When you are creating a rule, you need to define what target type the rule will be for, and of those targets is this a rule for all targets, or a subset. You can then set availability conditions for the rule, along with metric and policy violations you want to monitor with the rule. There is also a Jobs tab for specifying a rule based on a job or action.

Preferences

Notification Rules >

View Notification Rule: Host Availability and Critical States

This summarizes how and when Enterprise Manager will send notifications for this rule.

General

Owner SYSMAN
Description System-generated notification rule for monitoring Hosts' availability and critical metric statuses.
Public Yes
Target Type Host

Targets

All targets of type **Host**

Availability

Agent Unreachable Yes
Agent Unreachable Resolved Yes
Blackout Started No
Blackout Ended No

Metrics

Metric	Objects	Severity States	Corrective Action States	
			On Critical	On Warning
CPU Utilization (%)	n/a	Critical		
Average Disk I/O Service Time (ms)	All Objects	Critical		
CPU in I/O Wait (%)	%,%,%	Critical		
Disk Device Busy (%)	%,%,%,%	Critical		
Swap Utilization (%)	n/a	Critical		
Network Interface Combined Utilization (%)	All Objects	Critical		
Memory Utilization (%)	n/a	Critical		
Filesystem Space Available (%)	All Objects	Critical		
Average Disk I/O Wait Time (ms)	All Objects	Critical		

FIGURE 9-11. *View Notification Rule page*

NOTE
While you can build a single rule to, um, rule them all, this is probably not the best idea. Instead, have availability rules, policy violation rules, and job rules as separate sets so you can mix and match to meet your particular needs. In some cases, it might be worth a mix and match, but apply critical thinking ahead of time. The flexibility can be maddening, but it allows you to scale. And scaling is what this entire book is about.

The final tab when you are creating a rule is the Actions tab, which is where you specify what action the rule should take when it has discovered the event you have configured. For instance, we have created a rule that will send a notification if any tablespace space available in any database hits a critical threshold. When I go to the Actions tab, I can choose to get an e-mail notification (the most straightforward), or if I have configured any other methods, I can choose those.

On the Actions tab, note that you have an important decision to make: Should you send repeat notifications for every stateful event you have configured in the rule? That is, should you spam yourself until you respond and rectify the condition, or will a single e-mail be enough the first time it occurs? Be careful with this question; it is easy to simply say no to spam and be done with that. However, repeat notifications give you a sense of when something occurred, and the ongoing duration. In the end, this is all about your working style, so think it through and make the call. We prefer a single notification, because it ensures we are paying close attention to the e-mails coming in, instead of simply growing numb to the barrage.

What Are Schedules?

Schedules are the mechanisms by which each administrator is assigned a time, and a particular e-mail address, for receiving notifications. By default, every administrator has a schedule that sends e-mails to the default e-mail address of that user 24/7, every day of the year. However, if business rules and schedules dictate that you have different people watching the shop at night than during the day, you can essentially configure your schedule to stop sending notifications for different periods—by the hour or by the day of the week.

You can also change the e-mail address that is utilized for a notification, based on time of day or day of week. If the administrator has configured more than one e-mail address as part of the Preferences | General page, then when you go to the button Edit Schedule Definition you can select a different e-mail address.

> **NOTE**
> *As we've stated in other places in this book, but we will state again: do not share administrator logins. While you can have a single admin login, and then change the schedule to send e-mails to different users, based on everyone's schedule, it goes without saying that this is a bad idea, not just because of security problems, but also from the mess of trying to keep it all up to date. Instead, ensure that everyone logs in as themselves, and then keeps their own schedule in EM up to date according to their own needs. Self-service is the only way to make this work.*

Building an Effective Schedule

Ensuring that you get the e-mails you want, when you want them, is perhaps not as straightforward as you would expect. To modify your schedule, first ensure that you have gone to the Preferences | General page and added any rows for additional e-mail addresses you want to employ. Then, go to Preferences | Notification | Schedule. If you are managing a schedule for yourself, it should appear in front of you immediately. If you creating a schedule for someone else, you will need to click the flashlight icon next to the name, and then click the Change button.

To modify the schedule, click the Edit Schedule Definition button. First, you modify your Rotation Frequency. This allows you to have a weekly schedule, for instance, or set a schedule that has multiweek details, and then repeats. That allows you to have multiweek variations before it repeats.

Note that you can edit the existing schedule, if it is mostly right, or replace it entirely with a new one. You cannot have multiple saved schedules.

When you click Continue, you will be presented with a screen where you can do a batch-fill of segments of time, as seen in Figure 9-12. The time is sliced into hours, and then by days. If you specified a multiweek rotation, you can change the view to each week in the rotation and change it independently. Filling this in can be done one hour at a time by clicking in the text field for each hour of the week. Ugh. Alternatively, you can use the batch fill section to apply a few quick rules to get it right. For instance, by setting Start time to 12 A.M., and End time to 12 A.M., clicking radio buttons for Saturday and Sunday, removing the e-mail address entirely, and then clicking the Batch Fill-in button, you eliminate any e-mails from coming to you during the weekend (nice).

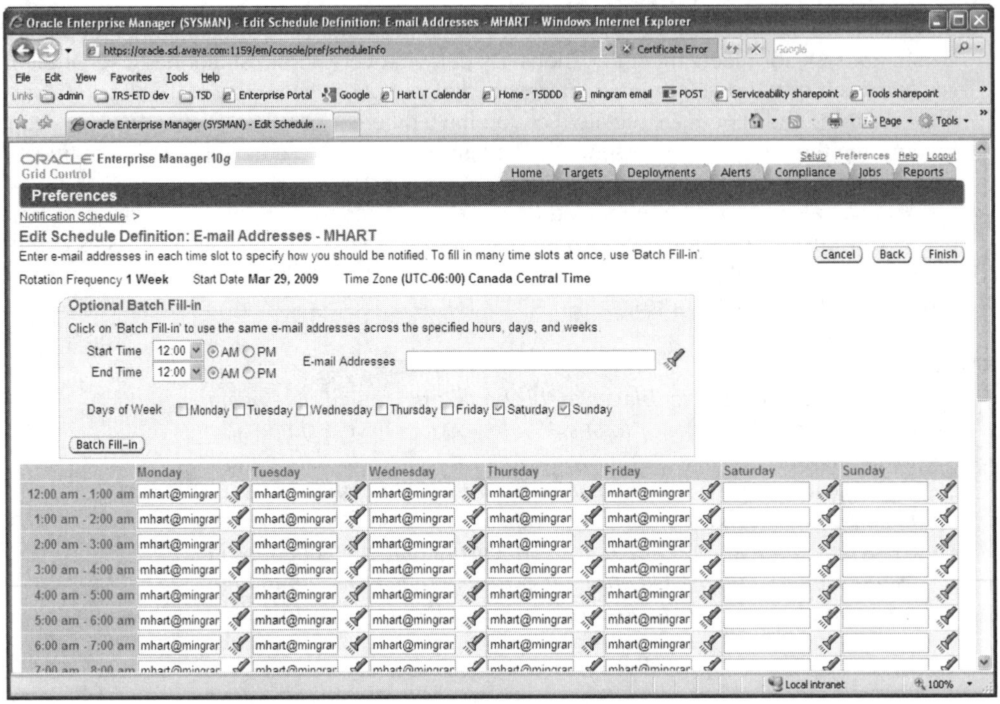

FIGURE 9-12. *Edit Notification Schedule page*

Summary

In this chapter, we went into the details of what Grid Control metrics are, how they are generated, and how to get the most from them. We discussed the difference between a metric, which is a collected fact, and a threshold, which is the fact compared to a baseline of acceptable behavior. We covered guidelines for good metrics and thresholds, how to configure them to meet your needs, and how to disable them outright. Then, we discussed managing Alerts—the flags that show up when a metric crosses its threshold. Then we walked you through User-Defined Metrics, how to configure them, and easy pitfalls to avoid if you use them. We touched on using Blackouts to temporarily suspend metrics and notifications from being generated. Finally, we discussed how to set up notifications for users, how to create methods for pushing notifications to your users, and how to create schedules for those notifications.

CHAPTER
10

Jobs and Task
Automation

ractically all platform strategies rely on some form of automated process to drive business continuity. Database backups, Application Server replications, log rotations, ETL batches—all look to task automation as a means of consistent and repeatable execution. And these tasks are increasingly becoming intertwined and complicated. Certain tasks rely on the successful completion of other tasks before they can run. Certain files need to be available to avoid exceptions in the workflow. Some days, the previous job will run longer than you expected, allowing your next job to start before the previous one even completes. As a professional you can make an educated guess on the dependencies and timing of these tasks, but getting it right is typically a labor-intensive, trial-and-error process. Even when the dependencies are met, and there are enough buffers built into the schedule to avoid overlap, this practice reinforces inefficient and poor resource utilization. And with the growing complexity of these processes, the sophistication of the automation system in your toolkit has to keep pace. The Oracle Management Agent provides the most effective way to execute these tasks end-to-end as Grid Control jobs so they run according to the schedule and standards you set in place.

Jobs

To capture the essence of a job is to understand how Oracle approaches task automation for internal and external consumption. First, jobs serve as the backbone of Grid Control when it comes to self-maintaining by performing administrative and cleanup operations against itself. All patching and provisioning frameworks used within Grid Control leverage jobs to execute complex install and configuration tasks. Externally, Grid Control enables system administrators to create jobs for commonly run tasks, thereby mitigating human errors associated with system maintenance. Second, understand that Oracle defines a job as a unit of work. A unit of work consists of a single task or a series of tasks that can be scheduled through the job system to be executed immediately or take place at a later date and time. The frequency of execution can be set to occur just once or over specific intervals based on pre-established conditions. Finally, Oracle designed a system to carry out and send notifications for all defined jobs. Oracle's approach to automation is truly a striking design that finds itself at the juncture of form and function and, like all quality software, expresses the product's intent for effectiveness, reliability, and consistency. It is when all these aspects are combined with the demanding forces of the business world that job automation evokes a much larger and deeper concept. Welcome to the backbone of Grid Control.

Anatomy of a Job

At a high level, the genetic makeup of a job requires the following when defined:

- **Job owner**   Who owns this job? This designation is automatically assigned to the administrator who is creating the job.

- **Classification of job**   What specific tasks should be run? Based on the type of job, whether it's something like an OS command, SQL script, or RMAN backup, additional options are made available when outlining the task(s).

- **Schedule**   When should this job run?

- ■ **Intended target**   What managed target is the job intended for?
- ■ **Privileges**   Who can see and edit the job? By default, the job owner has all privileges and is the only one who can grant `view` and `full` privileges to other Enterprise Manager users.

Managed Targets to Execute Jobs Against

Enterprise Manager allows administrators to define jobs to be executed against a single target or group of targets. A single target can be a local database, operating system, or a logical grouping of targets, such as the West Coast Datacenter, which we will outline with greater detail in later chapters. The functionality of jobs is not restricted to only the Jobs tab, either; you will find job functionality is conveniently available while you are working on things such as host provisioning or deployments. For instance, on the Deployments page you can create a job to clone a database, and under the Provisioning subtab, you can create a job to provision the OS to a physical server.

GRID CONTROL WORKSHOP

Creating Jobs and Notifications for a Managed Host

Jobs are the automation framework for Enterprise Manager that produces consistent results for driving standardization into your organization. Create jobs for commonly run tasks and use built-in notifications to keep track of its progress as you look toward other aspects of managing your enterprise.

Workshop Notes

In this workshop, we will walk through the steps required to create a single-task job and set up e-mail notifications around the status of the job execution.

Step 1.   Click the Jobs tab from the Oracle Enterprise Manager 10g Grid Control home page.

Step 2.   Select the Startup Database option from the Create Job drop-down list. Click Go, as shown in the following illustration.

Step 3.   Enter the name and description of the task. Click the Add button to add database targets, as shown in the following illustration.

(continued)

Step 4. Select your database targets and click the appropriate Select check boxes.

Step 5. Click the Parameters subtab.

Step 6. Select the appropriate Startup Mode, Initialization Parameters, and click the Credentials subtab.

Step 7. Select Override Preferred Credentials and enter the appropriate values. Click the Schedule subtab, as shown in the following illustration.

Step 8. If you do not set a schedule before submitting a job, Enterprise Manager will execute the job immediately with an indefinite grace period. A *grace period* is the maximum permissible delay allowed when attempting to execute a job. If Enterprise Manager is unable to execute a job within the grace period, the job will be skipped. One Time (Immediately) is selected by default to run the job once, as shown in the following illustration. Schedule the task and click the Access tab.

ORACLE Enterprise Manager 10*g*
Grid Control

Setup Preferences Help Logout

Home | Targets | Deployments | Alerts | Compliance | **Jobs** | Reports

Job Activity | Job Library

Create 'Startup Database' Job

Cancel | Save to Library | Submit

General | Parameters | Credentials | Schedule | Access

Type ○ One Time (Immediately) ● One Time (Later) ○ Repeating

Time Zone (UTC-08:00) US Pacific Time (PST)

Start Date Dec 25, 2009

Start Time 5 : 19 ● AM ○ PM

Grace Period ○ Indefinite
● End After   Hours 43 Minutes

General | Parameters | Credentials | Schedule | Access

Cancel | Save to Library | Submit

Home | Targets | Deployments | Alerts | Compliance | **Jobs** | Reports | Setup | Preferences | Help | Logout

Step 9. The Access tab allows administrators to set privileges on jobs in an effort to mitigate the painstaking effort that would be involved if every administrator were required to define jobs that performed duplicate tasks. With privileges, you can:

- View access to the administrators who need to see the results of the job
- Give full access to the administrators who may need to edit the job definition or share the job

These privileges can be granted on an as-needed basis. Also on the Access tab, notifications can be set based on status values (criteria) that will be sent to the job owner, as shown in the following illustration. Notifications are entirely dependent on these criteria and the notification schedule of the job owner.

ORACLE Enterprise Manager 10*g*
Grid Control

Setup Preferences Help Logout

Home | Targets | Deployments | Alerts | Compliance | **Jobs** | Reports

Job Activity | Job Library

Create 'Startup Database' Job

Cancel | Save to Library | Submit

General | Parameters | Credentials | Schedule | Access

This table contains Administrators and Roles that have access to this job.

Add

Name	Type	Access Level	Remove
MHART	Super Administrator	View	
SYS	Super Administrator	View	
SYSMAN	Super Administrator	Owner	
SYSTEM	Super Administrator	View	

E-Mail Notification for Owner

A Notification rule may be used by any Administrator to receive notifications about this job. The owner may choose to receive e-mail notifications based on any of the selected status values below. E-mail will be sent based on the Owner's notification schedule.

☑ Scheduled ☐ Running ☑ Suspended ☑ Succeeded ☑ Problems ☐ Action Required

General | Parameters | Credentials | Schedule | Access

Cancel | Save to Library | Submit

Home | Targets | Deployments | Alerts | Compliance | **Jobs** | Reports | Setup | Preferences | Help | Logout

Step 10. To execute the job, click Submit.

Further Classification of Jobs, Job Executions, and Job Runs

To be clear about existing text on jobs, the terms *job execution* and *job run* are simply associated to a matter of volume and repetition. Job executions are usually associated with one target, for example, a backup job on a single database instance. Even when a job is run against more than one database, behind the scenes, you will have multiple executions taking place, one execution occurring per database. With that said, job executions are not always a one-to-one mapping to a target. Some executions have multiple targets, for example, when comparing host configurations. Other executions have no targets, for example, when downloading alerts and updates from My Oracle Support. When you scale the volume of your targets and the jobs tied to them, it would become a tedious endeavor to examine the status of each and every execution on any given day. The ability to have a dashboard view on the status of these executions is what Enterprise Manager refers to as a Job Run. Therefore, a Job Run is simply the sum of all job executions of a specific job that ran on a specific date.

Let's take an example of our junior DBA Illiana, who is responsible for executing weekly backup jobs against hundreds of databases over a period of the past several years. Carrying on with the scenario of weekly backups for these databases, the following can be derived:

- A week's run will have a full set of executions for all production databases. So a *run* boils down to a single iteration of a repeating job.

- The *execution* is just—as the word suggests—the *execution* of the task for one or more managed targets. So the *execution* of the weekly run will be the backup of the database.

- Each execution can have a growing addition of *steps*. In the case of a backup, the steps for a database backup would be as follows:
  - Place the tablespace in backup mode.
  - Create an RMAN backup.
  - Take the tablespace out of backup mode.

  Each of these steps is carried out in sequence and strung together as one execution. Illiana could add additional steps where she felt necessary, such as executing an OS command to rotate alert logs or sending a notification to all application developers once the databases are back online.

  - Every step has an output. This is the output that the command or task generated.

The Job System

By now, there have been several references to the Enterprise Manager Job System, so you might find a detailed explanation useful. The Job System when broken down has a dual purpose within Grid Control:

- It performs the processing of all the jobs that you throw against the environment, for example, backup, cloning, and patching of specific targets.

- It serves as the portal from which administrators create their own jobs using their own custom OS and SQL scripts or leverage predefined jobs provided by Oracle.

All job processing is done at the OMS level. The OMS will identify what work needs to be done, gather the details surrounding the work, and then communicate the information to the Management Agents for execution. All jobs are broken down into two phases:

■ The *dispatcher* checks to see what tasks are placed into scheduled mode and ready to be executed.

■ Once a task is picked up by the dispatcher, it is handed off to a *job worker*, who will then communicate with the Management Agents to execute and report on the results.

GRID CONTROL WORKSHOP

Selecting Out-of-Box Jobs in Grid Control

With every installation of Grid Control, there is a listing of jobs that come as part of an out-of-box experience.

Workshop Notes

As SYSMAN, use the following query to determine what jobs are available with every Grid Control release.

```
SQL> SELECT job_id, job_name, job_type
  2   FROM mgmt_job
  3   WHERE job_owner='SYSMAN'
  4   AND job_description LIKE '%Out Of The Box%'
  5   /
```

In Linux environments, jobs are ready to be executed immediately once a Managed Agent is brought online. For environments running Microsoft Windows, some postinstallation tasks are required for jobs to successfully complete. The next exercise will walk you through setting the correct credentials for environments running on Microsoft Windows.

GRID CONTROL WORKSHOP

Setting Credentials for the Job System to Work with Enterprise Manager in Microsoft Windows Environments

Windows systems require that you set the correct credentials for the Jobs system to work properly in Grid Control. By default, the Management Agent service is installed as a LocalSystem user. When submitting jobs, such as stopping or starting the database, the user submitting the job must have the Log on as a batch job privilege enabled.

(continued)

Workshop Notes

Perform the following steps to establish that privilege for any operating system user who needs to submit an Enterprise Manager Job.

Step 1.   Start the Local Security Policy tool:

- **Windows 2000**   From the Start menu, select Control Panel | Administrative Tools | Local Security Policy.

- **Windows 2003**   From the Start menu, select Administrative Tools | Local Security Policy.

- **Windows XP**   From the Start menu, select Control Panel | Administrative Tools | Local Security Policy.

- **Windows Vista**   From the Vista Icon menu, select Control Panel | System and Maintenance | Administrative Tools, and click the Local Security Policy.

Step 2.   Under the Security Settings list, expand the list to Local Policies.

Step 3.   Under Local Policies, double-click User Rights Assignment.

Step 4.   Under Policy, search for the Log On as a Batch Job policy. If the Management Agent service is installed as any other user (that is, not LocalSystem), then, in addition to granting the `Log on as a batch job` privilege, you must grant the Windows service user the following three privileges:

- Act as part of the operating system

- Adjust memory quotas for a process

- Replace a process level token

Step 5.   With each policy, perform the following steps:

- Double-click the policy name.

- In the Properties dialog box, click Add User or Group.

- In the Select Users or Groups dialog box, enter the name of the user (for example, **dxnguyen**, **kennedy**, **administrator**, and so on).

Click Check Names to check that you've entered the name correctly.
Click OK.

Step 6.   Click OK to exit the Properties dialog box, then exit Local Security Settings and Administrative Tools.

Step 7.   Restart your computer.

It is worth noting that if a user exists both locally and at the domain level, Windows gives precedence to the local user. To use the domain user, qualify the username with the domain name. For example, to use the user kennedy in the ACCOUNTS domain, specify the username as ACCOUNTS\kennedy.

Moving forward, you should now be able to complete all workshops regardless of platform. Even though most of the workshops have been specifically tailored for Linux, they have been proven to work with minor adjustments to areas such as code references to directory structure for environments running on Microsoft Windows.

GRID CONTROL WORKSHOP

Leveraging the Job System to Run OS Commands for a Specific Host

Oracle's alert logs chronologically record messages and errors arising from daily database operations. Within Oracle, it is perfectly possible to delete, or rename, the alert log, if desired (for example, if it reaches a certain size). Oracle simply re-creates a new alert log the next time it writes to it.

Workshop Notes

Create an OS job to rotate the `alert.log` for a database running on a targeted host.

Step 1. Click the Jobs tab from the Oracle Enterprise Manager 10*g* Grid Control home page.

Step 2. Select the OS Command option from the Create Job drop-down list. Click Go.

Step 3. Enter the name and description of the task. Select Database Instance from the Target Type drop-down menu and click the Add button to select Database Instances, as shown in the following illustration.

Step 4. Select your targets and click the appropriate Select check boxes.

Step 5. Click the Parameters subtab. Change the Command Type to **Script**.

(continued)

Step 6. Enter the following segment of code:

```
LOG_DATE=$(date +"%%d_%%m_%%Y_%%T"); export LOG_DATE
cd %OracleHome%/../../diag/rdbms/%SID%/%SID%/trace/
echo "Verifying existing content:"
ls -la | grep *.log
mv alert_%SID%.log /home/oracle/logs/alert_%SID%-$LOG_DATE.bak
echo "Verifying backup content:"
ls -ls /home/oracle/logs/*.bak
```

Step 7. Click the Credentials subtab and select Override Preferred Credentials. After entering the appropriate values, click the Schedule subtab.

Step 8. Schedule the task and click the Access tab.

Step 9. Click Submit to kick off the job and direct you to the Job Activity page. Every successful creation of a job will result in a confirmation message and a hyperlink to view the activity details for the newly created job.

Step 10. The status of each execution within the job is displayed in a summary format as shown in the following illustration.

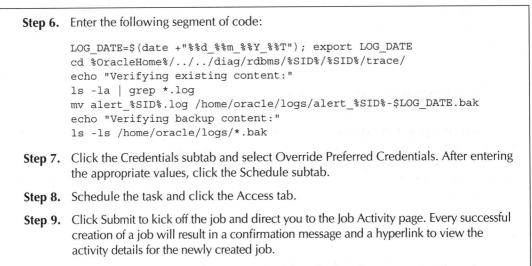

NOTE
The path to the alert log's location varies between database releases, and the path in which you store the archived logs should be tailored to fit standards within your organization. Adjust the script's contents to accommodate both factors when working through this exercise.

In addition to supporting the standard job operations of `create`, `edit`, `create like`, and `delete`, the Job System is repository-based, so it allows you to suspend and resume jobs, as well as retry failed executions. For example, you may need to suspend a job if a needed resource was not available or the job needs to be postponed. Once you suspend a job, any scheduled executions will not occur until you decide to resume the job.

When you're analyzing a failed execution, it is useful to be able to retry a failed execution once the cause of the problem has been determined. This alleviates the need to create a new job for that failed execution. When you use the Retry operation in the Job System, Enterprise Manager provides links from the failed execution to the retried execution and vice versa, should it become useful to retroactively examine the causes of the failed executions.

GRID CONTROL WORKSHOP

Modifying Job Purge Policies of the Job System

The default policy of the Job System is to purge completed jobs older than 30 days. If the standards you set in place within your company dictate otherwise, the option to change this policy should be made available. Unfortunately, the Grid Control Console does not allow you to change this policy, but you can change it from within SQL*Plus.

Workshop Notes

Use the following steps to adjust the frequency with which the Job System purges the history of completed jobs.

Step 1. As SYSMAN, log in to SQL*Plus and issue the following statement to check the current values for the purge policies:

```
SQL> select * from mgmt_job_purge_policies;
POLICY_NAME                        TIME_FRAME
---------------------------------- ----------
SYSPURGE_POLICY                            30
REFRESHFROMMETALINKPURGEPOLICY              7
FIXINVENTORYPURGEPOLICY                     7
OPATCHPATCHUPDATE_PAPURGEPOLICY             7
```

The purge policy responsible for the job deletion is called SYSPURGE_POLICY. As seen in the code for Step 1, the default value is set to 30 days. The actual purging of completed job history is implemented via a DBMS job that runs once a day in the repository database. When the job runs, it looks for finished jobs that are *n* number of days older than the current time (value of `sysdate` in the repository database) and deletes these jobs.

(continued)

Step 2. To change the time period, you must drop and re-create the policy with a different time frame. Perform the following procedures to change the default policy:

```
SQL> execute MGMT_JOBS.drop_purge_policy('SYSPURGE_POLICY');
PL/SQL procedure successfully completed.
SQL> execute MGMT_JOBS.register_purge_policy('SYSPURGE_POLICY', 60,
null);
PL/SQL procedure successfully completed.
SQL> COMMIT;
Commit complete.
```

Step 3. Finally, verify that the change was committed by issuing the following statement:

```
SQL> select * from mgmt_job_purge_policies;
POLICY_NAME                        TIME_FRAME
---------------------------------- ----------
SYSPURGE_POLICY                            60
```

The preceding statement reveals the increase to the retention period from 30 to 60 days. Obviously, the timeframe can also be reduced below 30 days, depending on the standards you want to set in place for your organization.

Step 4. You can check when the purge job will be executed next. The actual time that the job runs may vary with each Enterprise Manager installation. To determine this, issue the following statement:

```
SQL> alter session set nls_date_format='mm/dd/yy hh:mi:ss pm';
Session altered.
SQL> select what, next_date from user_jobs where what like '%JOB_
ENGINE%';
WHAT                                 NEXT_DATE
-----------------                    -------------------
MGMT_JOB_ENGINE.apply_purge_policies(); 06/07/09 01:21:13 am
```

In this example, the purge policy DBMS job will run every day at 01:21:13 A.M., repository time.

Using and Defining Jobs

With the installation of Enterprise Manager, some predefined job tasks are available for targets and deployments. Oracle defines job tasks as unchangeable logic such as patching your applications, backing up a database, and so on. The predefined database jobs include backup, export, and import. The predefined jobs associated with deployments include patching and cloning Oracle homes and databases. In addition, Oracle extends the job system to allow you to define your own job tasks by writing code to be included in scripts at the OS or database level. The advantages of using these scripts include:

■ When defining jobs, you can use properties specific to that target like host environment variables.

■ You can submit the jobs against many targets or a group. The job automatically keeps up with the group membership.

■ For host command jobs, you can submit to a cluster.

■ For SQL jobs, you can submit to a Real Application Cluster.

Combined with the Job System, you can create and execute from a sampling of some of the most common jobs:

■ **Clone Home**   Copies the known state of an Oracle home. For example, after you have an Oracle home in a known state (you have chosen particular install options for it, applied required patches to it, and tested it), you may want to clone that Oracle home to one or more hosts.

■ **OS Command**   Executes a user-defined OS script on a host.

■ **OPatch Update**   Finds a patch and then applies that patch.

■ **Refresh from MetaLink**   Notifies you of critical patch advisories by Oracle's self-service support site.

■ **SQL script**   Executes a user-defined SQL script for database instances.

GRID CONTROL WORKSHOP

Creating and Scheduling a Multitask Job

Grid Control makes the distinction between single-task and multitask jobs. The differences between the two jobs are that single-tasks encapsulate one task as a scheduled unit of work, whereas multitask jobs represent several tasks in the same unit of work. You can create a multitask job consisting of two tasks, each a different job type, operating on two separate (and different) target types, for example:

■ The first task is an OS command job type and performs an operation on the first host.

■ If the first task is successful, run the second task (SQL script job type) against the database.

If there are any exceptions while kicking off subsequent tasks on the list, the Initialization Error Handling task can be created to handle the exception.

Workshop Notes

In this exercise, you will create a multitask job against a database and the host that it resides on. We are carrying on from the previous exercise by shutting down a database, rotating database alert logs, and bringing the database back online.

Step 1.   Click the Jobs tab from the Oracle Enterprise Manager 10*g* Grid Control home page.

Step 2.   By default, the Job Activity subtab is selected. From the Create Job drop-down list, select Multitask and click the Go button.

Step 3.   The Create Multi-Task page is displayed. Click the General subtab to enter job-related information. Enter a name for the job and a description. In the Targets drop-down list, you see two options: Same Targets for All Tasks and Different Targets for

(continued)

Different Tasks. Respectively, the difference between each is that the first option enables you to create multitask jobs against targets of a similar type, while the other option allows you to operate on two separate (and different) target types. Here, we are going to go with the first option, Same Targets for All Tasks, and from the Target Type drop-down list, select Database Instance.

Step 4. In the Targets section, click the Add button, select a Database Instance, and click the Select button. Note: You can select multiple database instances here if you so choose.

Step 5. Select the database under the Target section, and click the Tasks subtab.

Step 6. Under the Type drop-down list, select Shutdown Database and click the Add button.

Step 7. The Add "Shutdown Database" Task page is displayed. On the General subtabbed page, specify a name for the job in the Name field. Click the Parameters subtab.

Step 8. You will be presented with four (4) database shutdown modes. The one we are interested in is Immediate: No new connections are allowed to the database and all uncommitted transactions are rolled back. Click the Credentials subtab.

Step 9. Under Credentials, you can either use the preferred credentials or override them. Here, select Override Preferred Credentials and enter the appropriate information, making sure that under SYSDBA Database Credentials, from the Role drop-down list, you select SYSDBA. Click Continue.

Step 10. The Tasks page is displayed again. You can select the second task here. Select OS Command from the Type drop-down list and click the Add button.

Step 11. From here, you will follow the steps outlined in the previous workshop, "Leveraging the Job System to Run OS Commands for a Specific Host." There are two things worth noting:

- Make sure the path to the alert logs and backup directory for the rotated logs reflects your environment and database version.
- Provide a different name for the job, to avoid any conflicts.

Step 12. The Tasks page is displayed again. You can select the final task here. Select Startup Database from the drop-down list and click the Add button.

Step 13. Specify a name for the task and click the Parameters tab.

Step 14. In the Startup mode section, select Open the Database. This will start the instance, mount, and open the database. Click the Credentials subtab.

Step 15. Under Credentials, you can either use the preferred credentials or override them. Here, select Override Preferred Credentials and enter the appropriate information, making sure that under SYSDBA Database Credentials, from the Role drop-down list, you select SYSDBA. Click Continue.

Step 16. On the Tasks page, you can set task conditions and dependency logic. You can also add a task initialization errors handling process. Task conditions define states in which the task will be executed:

- **Always** Task is executed each time the job is run.
- **On Success** Task execution depends on the successful execution of another task.
- **On Failure** Task execution depends on the execution failure of another task.

In the Condition column, specify the condition for the OS command and Database Startup job as On Success, as shown in the following illustration.

Step 17. In the Depends On column, make sure each job reflects the following order of dependence: Shutdown Database, and OS Command. Click the Schedule tab.

Step 18. Schedule the task and click the Access subtab.

Step 19. Add any necessary administrators, grant permissions, and select notification values.

Step 20. Click the Submit button to create the job.

Step 21. You have successfully created a multitask job!

As this workshop clearly shows, you now have an end-to-end solution using the Job System to drive task automation by stringing together an infinite number of steps. Imagine if you will, the possibility of adding an RMAN script to this workshop to back up a database, or sending PL/SQL e-mail notifications to development teams across the globe that their databases are going to be online/offline, or even executing cleanup scripts to critical directories once the backup jobs are complete. More appealing, the results are, in part, quite predictable once set in motion, saving you time and money. Oracle has even gone to the length of understanding that once you have taken the time to build up such a massive job, the idea of having anyone re-create it from scratch is a painful aspect to imagine. For this reason, Enterprise Manager opens up the repository as a mechanism for storing frequently used jobs or the basic definition of a job, so that your administrative team can choose to reuse and build upon them. This by all accounts is a library, not of books, but jobs.

Job Library

Once you have defined jobs, you can save these jobs to the Job Library, leveraging it as a repository for frequently used jobs. As with active jobs, you can grant `View` or `Full` access to specific administrators to prevent the creation of similar tasks. In addition, the benefits for using the Job Library as a repository for stored jobs are:

- Basic definitions of jobs can be retrieved and then targets and other custom settings can be added before submitting the newly customized job.

- Stored jobs are for both your own reuse or to share with others. You can share jobs using views or giving full access to these jobs.

You will find the Job Library extremely beneficial, especially for complex repeating jobs with a multitude of steps, such as multitask jobs.

GRID CONTROL WORKSHOP

Querying the Job Library for All Stored Jobs
A command-line interface for retrieving all jobs from the Job Library stored in the repository using SQL.

Workshop Notes
Use the following procedures to query the Job Library for all jobs stored in Repository.

Step 1. As SYSMAN, issue the following SQL statement in SQL*Plus:

```
SQL> SELECT job_id, job_name, job_owner, job_type, job_description
  2  FROM mgmt_job j
  3  WHERE is_library =1
  4  AND nested = 0
  5  AND system_job = 0
  6  AND is_corrective_action = 0
  7  /
```

GRID CONTROL WORKSHOP

Creating and Saving a Job to the Job Library

The Job Library enables you to share and reuse jobs that have been created.

Workshop Notes

In this exercise we will take an existing multitask job and save it to the Job Library.

Step 1. From the Job Activity subtab, query the Name of the most recent multitask job you submitted and click Go.

Step 2. Here, you see the multitask job that you created. You add this job to the Job Library.

Step 3. Select the job that you just submitted. Click the Copy To Library button.

Step 4. Provide a different name for the job to avoid any conflicts. Select the database against which you want to create the job.

Step 5. Click the Save To Library button.

Step 6. You have successfully saved the job to the library.

Step 7. You can see the saved job under the Job Library tab.

You now know how to save a job in the Job Library so you can have a platform to kick off commonly run jobs and promote reuse where possible. When you submit jobs from the Job Library, Enterprise Manager will spawn a child job using all the details outlined from the parent. This gives you the ability to customize stored jobs based on your organizational needs without altering the original format. You can reference this job and any others by using the Job Library page to display and manage jobs in the Enterprise Manager Job Library.

A Note on Enterprise Manager Command-Line Interface and Jobs

The Enterprise Manager Command Line Interface (EMCLI) allows for the execution of a subset of the Grid Control functionality from text-based consoles. This feature allows functionality to be integrated into various self-written programs and scripts. The command-line interface can be installed on any client; no additional Oracle Software is needed, other than Java, which has to be installed and part of the *PATH* variable. The command-line interface supports approximately 160 commands in 27 verb groups; however, it does not extend the ability to create jobs from scratch—jobs must already be part of the library in order to be submitted. Although far from complete, here is a sampling of possibilities EMCLI provides:

- Integrates with third-party or custom software through scripting. Actions (such as adding/deleting targets, submitting/deleting jobs, creating/deleting users) that are part of a customer's business model can be performed through scripting.

- Every day, send an e-mail list of backup jobs that were still running after 6 A.M.

- Every week, write pertinent information about failed Enterprise Manager jobs to a file and then purge the Enterprise Manager job history.

GRID CONTROL WORKSHOP

Executing Jobs Using the Enterprise Manager Command-Line Interface

EMCLI enables you to submit defined jobs stored in the Job Library or execute simple commands interactively from an OS shell.

Workshop Notes

In this exercise we retrieve a stored SQL job from the Job Library and submit it. We will continue the use of EMCLI to submit simple SQL and OS commands interactively from a text-based console.

Step 1. Log in to the EMCLI utility as the repository owner:

```
[oracle@oms ~]$ emcli login -username="sysman"
Enter password : ********
Login Successful
```

Step 2. Assuming you've stored the job created from the first workshop, we will submit the task using the following command:

```
[oracle@oms ~]$ emcli submit_job -job="STARTUP_XE_
DATABASES:SQLScript" -targets="XE.acme.com:oracle_data-
base" -parameters="db_username:sys;db_password:password;db_
role:sysdba;host_username:oracle;host_password:password;"

Job ID                            Execution ID
681C1B0285D9B32EE0407A87BE2242E2  681C1B0285DBB32EE0407A87BE2242E2
```

Generic form:

```
emcli submit_job -job="name:type" -targets="databaseSID:oracle_
database" -parameters="db_username:login;db_password:password;
db_role:role;host_username:login;host_password:password;"
```

where:

- **job**   *name* represents the name for the submitted job. *type* represents the supported type of the submitted job, either OSCommand or SQLScript, which are already predefined in the EM job system. The specified job type determines which targets and which parameters can be specified for the targets and parameters arguments.

- **targets**   A list of target name, target type pairs. The OSCommand jobs are allowed to be submitted against targets of type host, oracle_database, and group (if it contains host targets). The SQLScript jobs are allowed to be submitted against targets of type oracle_database and group (if it contains database targets).

- **parameters**   The SQLScript jobs support the parameters named sql_script, db_username, db_password, db_role, host_username, host_password, and credential_set_name. For the SQLScript type, in order to appropriately override credentials, the parameters db_username, db_password, db_role, host_username, and host_password must be present.

Step 3. Retrieve the results from the job recently executed:

```
[oracle@oms ~]$ emcli get_jobs -job="681C1B0285D9B32EE0407A87BE2242E2"
```

Generic form:

```
emcli get_jobs -job="job_id"
```

Alternatively, you can interact with any text-based console to execute OS commands:

```
[oracle@oms ~]$ emcli execute_hostcmd -cmd="ls -la /home/
oracle" -targets="stylesofnone.acme.com:host" -credential_set_
name="HostCredsPriv"
```

Generic form:

```
emcli execute_hostcmd -cmd="OScommand" -targets="hostname
.domain:host" -credential_set_name="name"
```

There is also the option to issue EMCLI commands to execute SQL statements:

```
[oracle@repodb ~]$ emcli execute_sql -sql="select * from dual;"
-targets="repodb.acme.com:oracle_database" -credential_set_
name="DBCredsSYSDBA"
```

Generic form:

```
emcli execute_sql -sql="command" -targets="databaseSID:oracle_data-
base" -credential_set_name="name"
```

Step 4. To prevent session management issues, log out of EMCLI:

```
[oracle@oms ~]$ emcli logout
```

For a more descriptive outline of the product and its capabilities, reference the *Oracle Enterprise Manager Command Line Interface* 10*g* Release 5 (10.2.0.5) from the Oracle Technology Network.

Jobs and Groups

In addition to submitting jobs to individual targets, you can submit jobs against a group of targets. Any job that you submit to a group is automatically extended to all its member targets and takes into account the membership of the group as it changes. For example, if a Human Resources OS job is submitted to the Payroll group, then if a new host is added to this group, the host will automatically be part of the Human Resources job. In addition, if the Payroll group is composed of diverse targets, for example, databases, hosts, and application servers, then the job will only run against applicable targets in the group. By accessing the Groups home page, you can analyze the job activity for that group. Look to Chapter 13 for further discussion and detailed explanations of Groups.

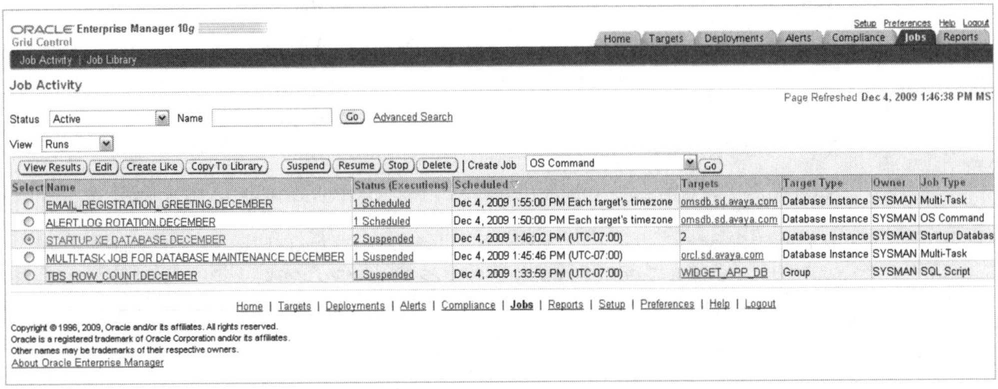

FIGURE 10-1. *A sample listing of all jobs scheduled in the enterprise*

Analyzing, Diagnosing, and Troubleshooting Jobs

After you submit jobs, the status of all job executions across all targets is automatically rolled up and available for review on the Grid Control home page. Figure 10-1 shows the All Targets Jobs information on the Grid Control home page. This information is particularly important when you are examining jobs that execute against several, if not hundreds, of systems. By clicking the number associated with a particular execution, you can drill down to study the details of the failed job.

The status of a job changes several times during its lifecycle. Oracle encapsulates the status of these jobs to the following states:

- **Scheduled** The job is created and will run at the specified time.
- **Running** The job is being executed and currently is in progress.
- **Initialization Error** The job or step could not be run successfully. If a step in a job fails initialization, the job status is Initialization Error.
- **Failed** The job was executed, but the results indicate some failure.
- **Succeeded** The job was executed, completely.
- **Stopped** The job owner has canceled the completion of the job.
- **Stop Pending** The job owner has stopped the job. The already running steps are completing execution.
- **Suspended** This indicates that the execution of the job is deferred to some later point.
- **Inactive** This status indicates that the target is no longer part of the grid.
- **Reassigned** The owner of the job has changed.
- **Skipped** The job was not executed at the specified time and has been omitted.

The progress of such jobs and the status change as each job cycles through its lifecycle can be seen by participating in the next workshop.

GRID CONTROL WORKSHOP

Monitoring the Results of a Multitask Job

After a job is submitted, executions across all targets are automatically rolled up and available for review on the Grid Control home page.

Workshop Notes

Perform the following steps to monitor the results of a multitask job.

Step 1. Click the Jobs tab, and then the Job Activity subtab. Click the multitask job that you have recently submitted.

Step 2. You can see that the job is running. For this particular workshop, both the database shutdown and log rotation tasks show completed, as shown in the following illustration. You can see that the database startup task is now in progress.

Step 3. You can drill down the Database Startup step to see the progress of the job. Click the Task: DATABASE STARTUP link.

Step 4. The step has completed successfully, as shown in the following illustration.

(continued)

Step 5. You can drill down further to see the process. Click Step: Command to see the steps.

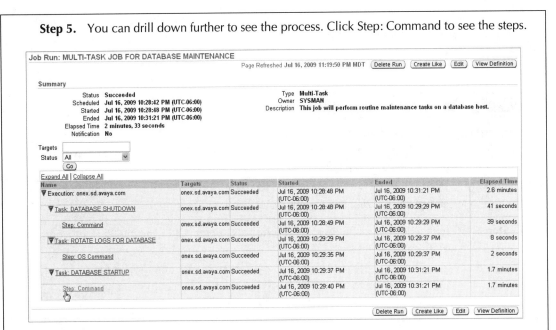

Step 6. In the following illustration, you see the complete information about the progress of the job.

Step 7. The home page shows you that all the steps of this job are now complete.

Alternatively, if you want to monitor the end result of a submitted job using SQL, you can perform the following steps outlined in the next workshop.

GRID CONTROL WORKSHOP

Retrieve the Results from a Job Using SQL

After a job is submitted, execution results across all targets are automatically stored in the repository for retrieval by the Grid Control Console.

Workshop Notes

Perform the following steps to retrieve the status of a submitted job using SQL.

Step 1. As SYSMAN, execute the following query from any SQL*Plus console:

```
SELECT DECODE(status, 1, 'SCHEDULED', 2, 'RUNNING', 3, 'FAILED
INIT', 4, 'FAILED', 5, 'SUCCEEDED', 6, 'SUSPENDED', 7, 'AGENT
DOWN', 8, 'STOPPED', 9, 'SUSPENDED/LOCK', 10, 'SUSPENDED/EVENT',
11, 'SUSPENDED/BLACKOUT', 12, 'STOP PENDING', 13, 'SUSPEND PEND-
ING', 14, 'INACTIVE', 15, 'QUEUED', 16, 'FAILED/RETRIED', 17,
'WAITING', 18, 'SKIPPED', status) "JOB_STATUS", status_detail FROM
MGMT_JOB_EXEC_SUMMARY WHERE JOB_ID IN (SELECT job_id FROM MGMT_JOB
WHERE job_name like '%');
```

Careful inspection of the query shows that the % is a wildcard character and can be replaced with the job name or a variation of the name using a combination of wildcard characters and portions of the job name. All status results are numerical requiring a decoder ring (that is, a lengthy syntax) to appropriately interpret the results. This is the same approach the Enterprise Manager uses behind the scenes to render results to the Grid Control Console.

Step 2. Additionally, we can build from the previous workshops and utilize EMCLI to pass the SQL command should avoiding SQL*Plus altogether.

```
[oracle@oms ~]$ emcli execute_sql -sql="SELECT DECODE(status, 1,
'SCHEDULED', 2, 'RUNNING', 3, 'FAILED INIT', 4, 'FAILED', 5,
'SUCCEEDED', 6, 'SUSPENDED', 7, 'AGENT DOWN', 8, 'STOPPED', 9,
'SUSPENDED/LOCK', 10, 'SUSPENDED/EVENT', 11, 'SUSPENDED/BLACK-
OUT', 12, 'STOP PENDING', 13, 'SUSPEND PENDING', 14, 'INACTIVE',
15, 'QUEUED', 16, 'FAILED/RETRIED', 17, 'WAITING', 18, 'SKIPPED',
status) "JOB_STATUS", status_detail FROM MGMT_JOB_EXEC_SUMMARY
WHERE JOB_ID IN (SELECT job_id FROM MGMT_JOB WHERE job_name like
'%%');" -targets="repodb.acme.com:oracle_database" -credential_set_
name="DBCredsSYSDBA"
```

For EMCLI, you will have to escape % by using %% to avoid having the tool render the syntax as a literal. Also, make sure both target and login credentials reflect the repository that is storing the jobs.

Searching Jobs

By default, Enterprise Manager enables you to search by job name and status. To search for jobs using more specific job criteria, there is a link to the Advanced Search option from the Job Activity Page. On the Advanced Search page, select values for the options you want to search for. After you have filtered the jobs you want to display, you can view job information in the Results table either by job Executions or by job Runs. You can display jobs using the search filters displayed on the page. All search criteria specified are combined using the logical AND. In all cases, if the search filters result in more than 500 rows in the job results table, only the first 500 results are shown, so you should refine the search filters as needed. Here are some interesting analytical tricks worth noting on these particular fields:

- **Name and Target Name** When conducting searches, you can specify wildcard characters (such as % or *). For example, if you specify %OS% in the Name field, a case-insensitive search begins for all jobs that have the string "OS", "Os", "os", or "oS" in them. You could also conduct the same search by specifying %OS in the Name field, because Enterprise Manager implicitly adds the wildcard character at the end of the specified search string. To perform an exact search, specify the search string in double quotes. For example, if you specify "ROTATE ALERT LOGS" in the Name field, it returns only jobs whose name is ROTATE ALERT LOGS.

- The same semantics apply to the Target Name field, except the search is case-sensitive. You need to be sure you enter the appropriate case when specifying the Target Name. Finally, when you specify a group in the Target Name field, be sure you choose the accompanying type (such as group, services, web applications) in the Target Type search field.

- **Status** When investigating job status, take note of the different varieties of the Suspended status. The Problems status is not specifically a job status, but a logical combination of the following different job statuses that indicate some type of problem: Failed, Error, Skipped, Reassigned, Stopped, Inactive, and Credentials Missing.

- **Scheduled Start** This time filter enables you to select jobs that were scheduled to start at the selected time period and later. For example, if Last 7 Days was chosen, these will show jobs whose scheduled start date was at most seven days ago (that is, seven days ago until the future).

- **Target Type** Most of the parameters are self-explanatory except `Targetless`. The `Targetless` target type applies to Enterprise Manager jobs that are not associated with any target—`RefreshFromMetalink` is the classic example. The option All Member Targets of Target Named Below must be used in conjunction with the Target Name field, specifically, when you want to find jobs that were submitted to a composite entity (for example, group, database cluster, host cluster, application server, and so forth) as well as to any member of the composite entity. For example, if you specify your target type to be All Member Targets of the Target Named Below and your target name was DB_GROUP, and the DB_GROUP was composed of databases DEV and PROD, expect your results to include all jobs that were either submitted to the DB_GROUP directly, submitted to database DEV, submitted to database PROD, or any combination of the three.

Maintaining the Job System

The job system can scale hundreds if not thousands of executions for multiple targets, but only if you are diligent about keeping up with the Grid Control infrastructure that all deployments of jobs are passing through. Such maintenance is necessary regardless of the workload or size of the Grid Control site. The cornerstone of maintenance for the job system includes routinely doing the following before submitting any jobs:

- **Clear OMS and OMR system errors** Reviewing the Errors Page reported by the Management Services and Repository subsystems on a weekly basis helps identify errors logged into their respective log files. Some errors may be due to misconfigured targets and other errors may results in reported bugs. To check for a page listing of possible errors, click Setup, Management Services and Repository, and then the Errors Page.

■ **Clearing any Critical and Warning alerts** Additionally, Critical and Warning subtabs are displayed for recent targets alerts and should be addressed. Most alerts that are automatically cleared from these subtabs, but what remains are those that cannot automatically clear because there is an underlying issue that Grid Control cannot address. Some alerts may just need to be manually cleared, while others are legitimate alerts that require attention on your part before being cleared. Without being addressed, these alerts will repeatedly fire and waste OMS resources and can cause a backlog in notification delivery or metric data uploads.

■ With a Metalink support account, keep up to date with all Enterprise Manager bugs and recommended patches using the following documents:

  ■ 759579.1: JOB SYSTEM 10.2.0.3 GRIDCONTROL RECOMMENDED PATCHES

  ■ 736150.1: JOB SYSTEM 10.2.0.4 GRIDCONTROL RECOMMENDED PATCHES

  ■ 837859.1: JOB SYSTEM 10.2.0.5 GRIDCONTROL RECOMMENDED PATCHES

■ Chapter 6 also highlights additional information for maintaining the infrastructure especially if the infrastructure as a whole is evolving.

Sometimes, software gremlins rear their ugly heads and in-depth diagnosis on your part is required to uncover a root cause. When traditional troubleshooting methods seem to fail, our recommendation is to reach out to the Oracle community using the OTN forums or seek professional guidance from Oracle Support Services. To date, the most prevalent occurrence with the job system seems to be when a job is stuck displaying an incorrect status even after attempts to stop (and delete) a job from the Grid Control Console has failed. The next workshop walks you through the necessary steps to forcefully persuade the job system to release the job.

GRID CONTROL WORKSHOP

Removing Jobs Stuck in a Status of SUSPEND

You may find that you are unable to remove jobs that report an incorrect status, such as SUSPEND, using traditional methods offered by the Grid Control Console.

Workshop Notes

Follow these steps to remove jobs that display the following messages when performing certain Grid Control Console actions:

■ Trying to suspend or stop a job results in the following message: All executions of the job were stopped successfully. Currently running steps will not be stopped.

■ Trying to stop job executions in a Stop Pending status results in the following message: The specified job, job run, or execution is still active. It must finish running, or be stopped before it can be deleted. Filter on status Active to see active executions.

■ The resubmission of a job results in the following message: The specified job cannot be resubmitted. It either has active executions, or it has no failed executions.

Note that these steps should be followed only when all traditional means have resulted in limited success.

Step 1. From the Job Run Details page, copy the URL to the job that is in a questionable status and paste the contents to an external text file. For example

```
https://oms.acme.com:1159/em/console/jobs/runDetails?execId=6BF8C7D
9A7314490E0407A87BE224937
```

Step 2. As SYSMAN, log in to the EM repository database and gather information about the job:

```
select job_id, job_name, job_owner from mgmt_job where job_
name like '%<name of job as seen in the console>%';
```

Step 3. Stop all the executions and job runs of this particular job:

```
SQL> exec mgmt_diag.stopcurrentjobexec('<job_ID
returned by above query>');
```

or

```
SQL> exec mgmt_job_engine.stop_all_executions_with_id('<job_ID
returned by above query>',TRUE);
```

Step 4. The next procedure allows for the deletion of the troublesome job:

```
SQL> exec mgmt_job_engine.delete_job('<job_name
returned by above query >','<job_owner returned by above query>');
```

Step 5. If the previous step produced an undesirable result, proceed to make changes to the mgmt_job_exec_summary table and forcefully update the suspended or scheduled records using the following command:

```
SQL> UPDATE mgmt_job_exec_summary SET status = 8, end_time =
(sysdate - 1) WHERE job_id ='<job ID as returned by above query>';
```

If no errors are reported, issue the command:

```
SQL> commit;
```

Otherwise revert by issuing the command:

```
SQL> rollback;
```

If you are uncomfortable altering the repository, we suggest shutting down the OMS and taking necessary backups of the repository or seeking the professional guidance of Oracle Support Services.

Step 6. Once this update occurs, the possibility of deleting the job from the Grid Control Console is tipped in your favor, and should complete without any further complications. If that is not the case (or the job is no longer displayed), take the previously stored link from the text editor and directly visit that page, where the opportunity to delete the job is clearly presented as an option.

Summary

In this Jobs chapter, we wanted to orient you to the sophisticated task automation system built into Grid Control, and highlight the mechanisms for configuring and using it effectively to help you decrease your guesswork when it comes to understanding the dependencies, timing, and output of your companies automated business jobs. At first glance, the Job System might appear to devalue the Herculean efforts made by you and your IT colleagues. But recall, if you will, that what were once single-server cron jobs are now a global rollout of patches. This progression is unavoidable: Automation has evolved to play just as an important role in the global economy as it does with our daily experience. In every business process, the results of automating manual-intensive tasks will lead to a more efficient enterprise of increased productivity, improved reliability, predictable results, and so on. This makes effective, rapid, error-free automation planning a critical element of your business's daily operation.

On the same note, we should not mistake automation as a single discrete thing, but rather, a word used to describe an almost impossibly varied and complicated set of behaviors that differs from organization to organization. It is therefore important to leverage tools that have scope and capabilities across different systems, platforms, and data centers so that jobs can be coordinated, reused, and leveraged by different interdependent teams.

CHAPTER
11

Reporting and Dashboards

oday we are operating in a self-service world, where users have high expectations for applications that are both functionally complete as well as highly available. The ubiquity of web-based applications has driven these expectations even further because the user community is much larger, geographically dispersed, demanding, and highly dependent on the applications and services provided. For some companies, web applications have become the face of the business and, thus, have a far-reaching and direct impact on the failure and success of the business itself. In order to create a functionally complete application, developers spend much of their time bridging traditional IT systems with new applications running on middleware servers and exposing functionality as services for other lines of business to consume. And as the previous chapter demonstrated, traditional IT shops are leveraging the power of task automation, making IT operations inherently linked to the success or failure of the business itself.

The criticality and complexity of modern-day business applications have made it a stronger case for data centers to manage and report on the quality of their services as they aim for higher standards of availability. To deliver, you and your administrative team need to quickly understand the IT infrastructure that runs the applications and the interactions that take place between them. You need to keep informed proactively of problems and their potential impact, quickly diagnose the root cause, and resolve all issues in order to be aligned with the expectations set out by the user community. You will need to constantly monitor and understand the end-user experience. Finally, you will need a reporting solution that is embedded with all aspects of your business and intrinsically provides reliable information. Grid Control's approach embeds a comprehensive reporting solution that quickly enables the aggregation of information so decisions can be made by key stakeholders.

Reports

The collection and gathering of information is naturally the first step. But what do you do once you have obtained it? How do you quickly ensure that other critical stakeholders can consume and continue to share in the wealth of knowledge and data that's been made available? The purpose of the reporting features of Grid Control is just that: to roll up the data in a way that makes it easier for people to understand, or to provide the necessary data to back up simple inquiries about the business; like, just how many physical machines do I have running on my data center floor? In the end, it all boils down to representing the existing data in a new way, a way that is not present in the product by default, but is capable of representing the very nature of what is taking place in your business today.

The one hesitation administrators typically face when first utilizing the reporting features of Grid Control is the false expectation that it provides a full-featured suite of reporting utilities that they must be acquainted with prior to use—when that is not the case. What the reporting capability provides is a way to represent the data from the repository in a similar manner as the product sees it. It does not have all the features, reporting objects, and widgets of a traditional reporting framework: only the basic constructs to represent the data, tables, and graphs—outlined in a manner for immediate use with minimal setup.

Common Uses for Reports

In its simplest form, a report is a graphical representation of a simple question. It is a way to answer a question from an administrator, an Enterprise Administrator, or from upper management about the state and condition of the business. Some questions are pretty simple and straightforward. Others may not be as easy, and may require the correlation of several pieces of data. As an example, some of the questions the reporting framework can answer are:

■   How many machines, running which OS, on what type of physical hardware do I have in my environment?

■   Which databases were down for more than 10 minutes in the last month, and why?

■   Which administrator is submitting the most jobs against a particular managed target?

■   Which Line of Business/Group has the most outstanding alerts and violations?

■   Which machines are about to max out on CPU capacity?

■   How much disk consumption have my databases been experiencing in the past six months?

The beauty of the reporting framework is that of all the data that is present in the repository, from target information to out-of-box templates, is at the disposal of an administrator and can be further mined to generate unique reports. By interchanging pieces of information—like group definitions, or custom-added data like line of business, point of contact, and so on—environment-specific questions can be modeled. For example:

■   What is the status and resource consumption of all firewalls in the DMZ that is facing the Internet?

■   What is the response time of the company's website for the last quarter?

■   Provide a listing of the most common alertlog messages for 10.2.0.4.0 databases running on Linux 64-bit.

■   What is the disk consumption of all SAN storage of the finance division?

How to Get a Report

There are three distinct methods for retrieving a report: from the Grid Control console, accessing a publicly exposed URL, or based on a defined schedule.

Grid Control Console

For on-demand access of any predefined, customized, or out-of-box reports, click the Reports tab from the main page of the Grid Control Console. These reports are generated every time an administrator clicks on a hyperlinked report from the console.

Public Reports

A report can be defined as "public." This means it is pregenerated and can be accessed from a well-known URL:

```
https://<hostname>:<port>/em/public/reports
```

Only super-users or administrators that have the privilege GRANT ANY REPORT VIEWER can create a public report. Once the reports become public, no authentication is made available for these reports, so any user who can access the public reports folder on the Grid Control website can view the public reports.

Scheduled Reports

Any report created in Grid Control can be scheduled to be emailed to individuals, or a copy of the report can be saved based on a specified timeline (one-time immediately, one-time later, or at specified intervals). A job is submitted when you schedule the report and is executed using the target privileges of the report owner.

The Anatomy of a Report

Every report has several different attributes and characteristics:

- **Report definition**   The main thing, of course, is the title and the description for the report. The report also includes the category and subcategory, to further classify the report. A set of standard categories will be present with the initial rollout of Grid Control. These are the categories used by all of the out-of-box reports. When you are adding custom reports, you can add new categories and subcategories, to represent environment-specific groups, or a customized category of reports.

  The default out-of-box categories and definitions are:

  - **Deployment and Configuration**   Setup and configuration of the discovered targets
  - **Enterprise Manager Setup**   Grid Control infrastructure reports
  - **Monitoring**   Target monitoring, including alerts and notifications
  - **Security**   Target security settings, and security policy overviews
  - **Storage**   Target storage overview reports

- **Targets list for the report**   A report can be defined to run against a specific target, against all targets of a certain target type (one at a time), or it can be run against the repository itself (by either specifying the OMS and Repository Target or leaving the target details blank). When a target type is selected for a report, the administrator will have to specify a target of that type when running the report.

- **Privileges**   There are three types of privilege modes for a report:

  - *Viewer* **privileges**   This is the default setting when a new report is created. This means that the administrator requesting the report defines the privileges that govern what type of information is available. The generated report will only contain information that the requestor has access to.

  - *Creator* **privileges**   This is a privilege that can be specified during the creation of a report. In this case, the administrator that created the report determines what information is available. The requestor will see the same thing the creator does, even if certain targets or jobs are not available to the administrator requesting the report.

  - *Public* **reports**   No authentication is required for these reports. Any user can access these. This is actually a subset of the Creator category. If, during the creation of the report, the owner selected the Allow Viewing Without Logging In to Enterprise Manager option, anyone will be able to view the report directly from the public report URL (`/em/public/reports`). The report will be generated with the privileges of the owner of the report.

- **Time period**   For reports dealing with metric data, or historical alert and notification information, a time period can be set for this report. This can be a fixed one (like last week, this month, or a custom time period), or the administrator can specify a time period when running the report.

- **Visual Style**   There are only two style types available: One is the standard Grid Control UI page style, which renders the page in the same way, using the same style elements as the rest of the Grid Control console. The other is the Dashboard style, which is visually intended for depicting real-time and summary-like reports.

- **Elements**   Every report will have at least one reporting element. That element will have some attributes of its own and has a layout definition associated with it.

    These elements include:

    - **Table from SQL**   Report the information returned by a SQL statement in a table.
    - **Chart from SQL**   Render the information graphically from the results returned within a SQL statement. These are typically rendered as pie charts, bar charts, or a time-series line graph.
    - **Images**   Add any image to your report.
    - **Custom Texts**   Styled text that can be added to the report.
    - **Predefined Elements**   These are complex widget-like elements, which are target-type–specific; they provide details about a specific aspect of that target, like displaying HTTP traffic information for a website, metric details, and so on.

For any of the SQL statements, variables can be inserted, which will be replaced at runtime with the specified values provided by the user running or using the report. The available variables are:

%%EMIP_BIND_END_DATE%%	The endpoint of the time period to use for the report. This variable is used for reports with a custom time period.
%%EMIP_BIND_START_DATE%%	The start point of the time period to use for the report. This variable is used for reports with a custom time period.
%%EMIP_BIND_TARGET_GUID%%	The target this report is to be run against. This variable will be used in the case of a report defined against a specific target type (or all targets, for that matter).

Creating a New Report

Any administrator can create a report. And any target can be used to report on, as long as the administrator has at least View privileges on the target. All data represented in the reports must be constructed from SQL statements against the repository, using views.

The reason views are used, and not the base tables, is twofold:

- **Data security**   By forcing people to use views, the security policies and security restrictions will be imposed on the users by default, with no way of circumventing the defined security model.

■ **Layer of abstraction**   It allows for abstraction of the underlying physical schema of the repository. After an upgrade, or with the release of a new feature or plug-in, the underlying schema might have changed, but the views will still represent the data in the same way, allowing the reports to continue to work, even after (sometimes radical) repository schema changes.

A wizard will guide the user through the process of creating the report, starting with the basic definition of the report, the various elements and SQL statements this report needs to run and the layout of these elements in the report, the schedule if any, and finally the access controls for administrators.

NOTE
Only custom reports added to the system can be edited. The out-of-the-box reports cannot be modified or edited by any user. The only thing allowed for out-of-box reports is to perform a Create Like *operation, which enables the administrator to customize a copy of the original report.*

GRID CONTROL WORKSHOP

Create a Diagnostics Report on Your Management Agent's Health

Workshop Notes

Using the tidbits of knowledge outlined so far in the chapter, let's create a useful diagnostics report of all the Management Agents deployed into the enterprise. The report will contain the following information:

■ Pie chart with a breakdown of the availability of all the Management Agents

■ A table with the count of Management Agents by OS and version

■ A count of target data not being uploaded by each Management Agent

■ A list with a count of open errors and alerts reported by each Management Agent

This report is pretty simple and straightforward. To get things started, we will use the default settings for the individual elements unless otherwise noted. These settings can always be changed at some later point.

Step 1.   Outline the details of the report.

To access all the reports that exist in your environment, click the Reports tab from the Grid Control Console. Click the Create button to create a new Report Definition and provide the following details, as shown in Figure 11-1.
First, the title and a descriptor of the report:

Title: **Overview of the Management Agent's Health**
Description: **Health Check overview of all Management Agents deployed into the enterprise**.

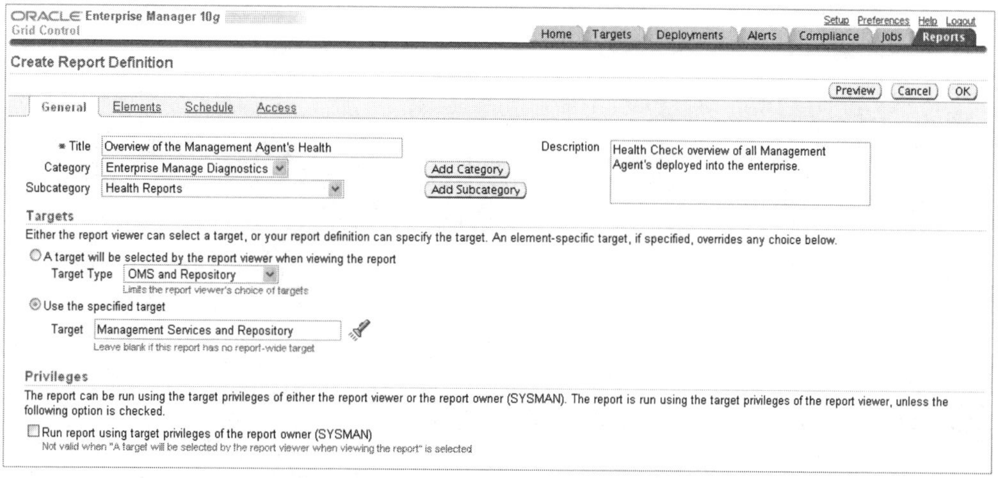

FIGURE 11-1. *General report information*

Since this is a diagnostics report, doing some basic health-checks, we'll create a new category and subcategory for this report:

Category: **Enterprise Manager Diagnostics**
Subcategory: **Health Reports**

There is no immediate need to specify a target with this report. However, to ensure that this report is not running against some randomized target, specify the Management Services and Repository option.

Step 2. Create the elements that will make up the report.

From the Elements subtab, click the Add button to launch the listing of all possible elements available to report. We will need to add four (4) elements for the information we intend to display, as shown in Figure 11-2:

- Chart from SQL (one object): A pie chart used to display the agent's availability.

- Table from SQL (three objects): Three table objects, to list the number of Management Agents by OS and version, the count of targets not uploading data per agent, and the total count of errors and alerts reported by the agents.

The element Type can easily be queried using the search widget supplied by Grid Control. Essentially, the query you can pass to quickly search and add the four elements would be:

Type: %SQL%
Applicable Target Type: Any

Once the query is complete, the details can be systematically specified for each of these elements by clicking the Set Parameters icon.

(continued)

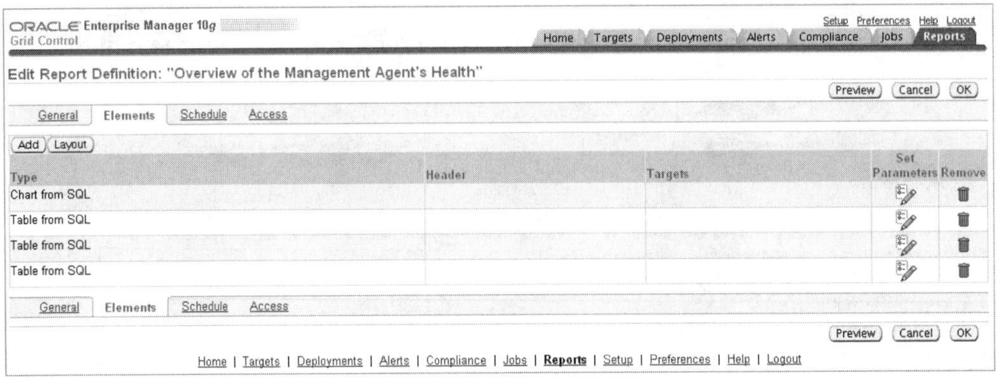

FIGURE 11-2. *Reporting elements prior to setting specific parameters*

Step 3. Customize the first element: A pie chart listing the Management Agent's availability.

Click the Set Parameters icon for the first element and enter the following parameters:
Header: **Availability of all Management Agents**
Chart Type: **Pie Chart**
Enter the following SQL statement:

```
SELECT availability_status, COUNT(*) cnt
FROM   sysman.mgmt$availability_current
WHERE  target_type = 'oracle_emd'
GROUP BY availability_status
```

Click Continue.

Step 4. Customize the second element: List of Management Agents by OS and version.

Click the Set Parameters icon for the second element and enter the following parameters:
Header: **List of Management Agents by OS and version**
Enter the following SQL statement:

```
SELECT t.type_qualifier1 "OS", p.property_value "Version",
COUNT(*) "Total"
FROM   sysman.mgmt$target t, sysman.mgmt$target_properties p
WHERE  t.target_type = 'oracle_emd'
AND  t.target_guid = p.target_guid
AND  p.property_name = 'Version'
GROUP BY t.type_qualifier1, p.property_value
ORDER BY p.property_value, t.type_qualifier1
```

Click Continue.

Step 5. Customize the third element: Outline all targets not uploading target data.

Click the Set Parameters icon for the third element and enter the following parameters:
Header: **A count of target data not being uploaded by each Management Agent**
Enter the following SQL statement:

```
SELECT target_name, collection_timestamp, message
FROM   sysman.mgmt$alert_current
WHERE  metric_name = 'Targets_not_uploading'
ORDER BY collection_timestamp
```

Click Continue.

Step 6.   Customize the fourth element: Outline all alerts and errors reported by the Management Agents.

Click the Set Parameters icon for the fourth element and enter the following parameters:
Header: **Overview of errors and alerts issued by each Management Agent**
Enter the following SQL statement:

```
SELECT t.host_name "Host", SUM(NVL(e.cnt_err,0)) "Errors",
SUM(NVL(a.cnt_warn,0)) "Warnings",
SUM(NVL(a.cnt_crit,0)) "Critical"
FROM   mgmt$target t,(SELECT target_guid, COUNT(*) cnt_err
FROM   sysman.mgmt$metric_error_current
GROUP BY target_guid) e,
(SELECT target_guid, SUM(DECODE(violation_level,20,1,0)) cnt_warn,
SUM(DECODE(violation_level,25,1,0)) cnt_crit
FROM sysman.mgmt$alert_current
GROUP BY target_guid) a
WHERE  t.target_guid = e.target_guid (+)
AND  t.target_guid = a.target_guid (+)
AND  t.emd_url IS NOT NULL
AND  NVL(e.cnt_err,0)+NVL(cnt_warn,0)+NVL(cnt_crit,0) > 0
GROUP BY t.host_name
ORDER BY SUM(NVL(e.cnt_err,0))+SUM(NVL(a.cnt_warn,0))+
SUM(NVL(a.cnt_crit,0)) DESC
```

Click Continue.

Step 7.   Arranging the layout of the report.

For presentation purposes, the remaining step is to align the pie chart and the three tables by row. From the list of element types, select the button labeled Layout. From here you can select each element and click the Move Up or Move Down icon based on your preference.

In this particular example, as shown in Figure 11-3, we chose to display the pie chart and the first table in the same row, followed by the remaining tables in their own respective rows. As all the elements are moved up, the last row (4) will be *empty*. Click Continue to save the layout. When the layout is saved, this empty row is automatically removed, keeping only the rows that actually contain some reporting element.

(continued)

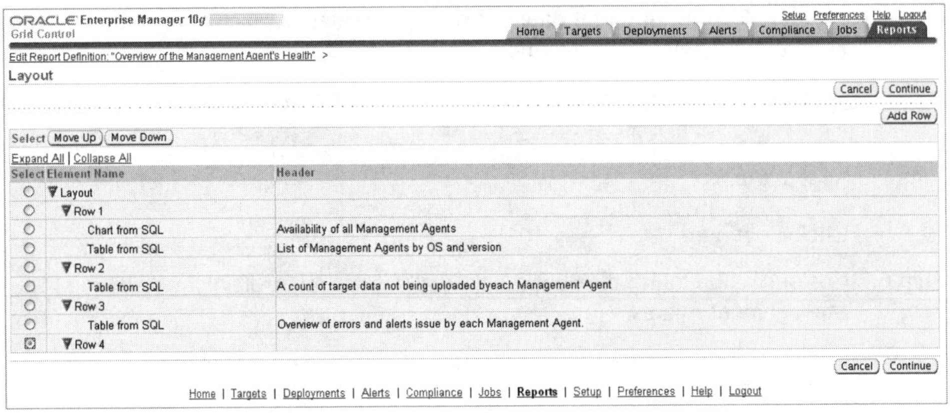

FIGURE 11-3. *Layout of the diagnostics report*

Step 8. Schedule and Access.

To keep things simple and straightforward, we will accept the defaults and make no notable changes to these two subtabs. These settings can always be changed afterwards if you want to email copies of the report, alter the reporting schedule, mark it as a public report, and so forth.

Step 9. Finalize and save the report.

When this new report is saved, the new category and subcategory will now be part of the reporting tree, as shown in Figure 11-4, and the report will be available for administrators to use.

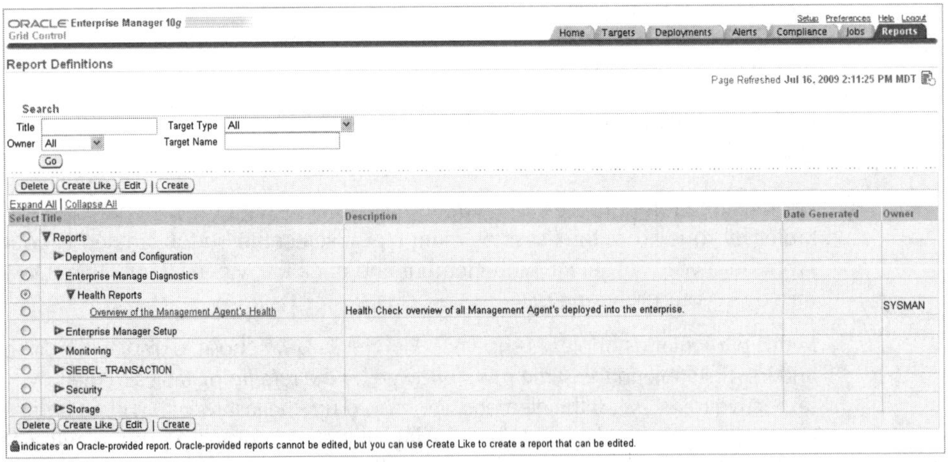

FIGURE 11-4. *Defined reports in the framework*

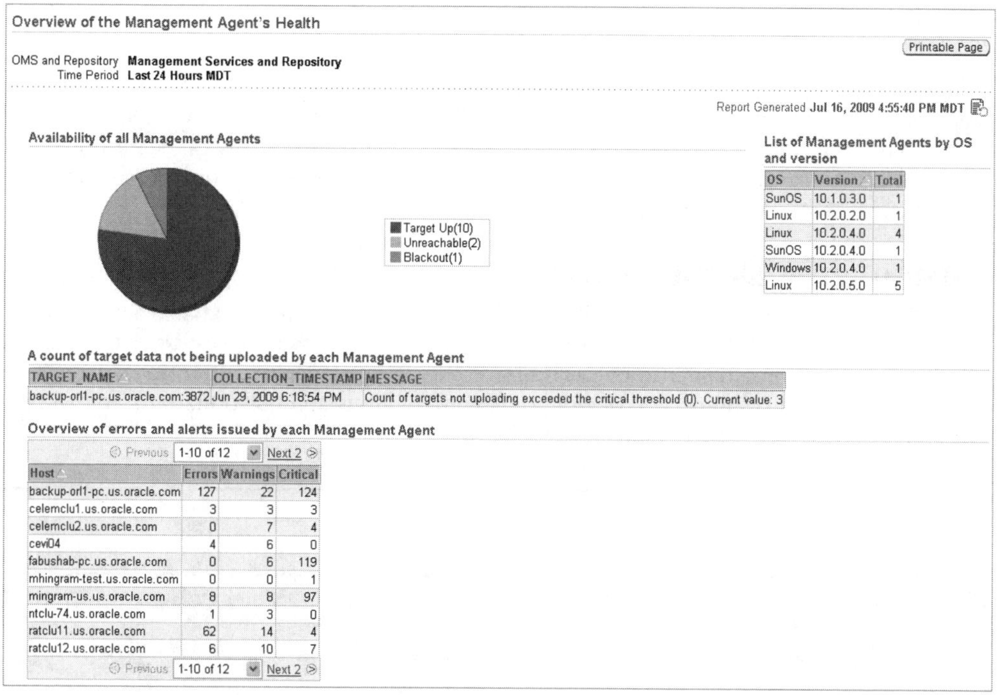

Overview of the Management Agent's Health

OMS and Repository **Management Services and Repository**
Time Period **Last 24 Hours MDT**

Report Generated **Jul 16, 2009 4:55:40 PM MDT**

Availability of all Management Agents

■ Target Up(10)
■ Unreachable(2)
■ Blackout(1)

List of Management Agents by OS and version

OS	Version	Total
SunOS	10.1.0.3.0	1
Linux	10.2.0.2.0	1
Linux	10.2.0.4.0	4
SunOS	10.2.0.4.0	1
Windows	10.2.0.4.0	1
Linux	10.2.0.5.0	5

A count of target data not being uploaded by each Management Agent

TARGET_NAME	COLLECTION_TIMESTAMP	MESSAGE
backup-orl1-pc.us.oracle.com:3872	Jun 29, 2009 6:18:54 PM	Count of targets not uploading exceeded the critical threshold (0). Current value: 3

Overview of errors and alerts issued by each Management Agent

Previous 1-10 of 12 Next 2

Host	Errors	Warnings	Critical
backup-orl1-pc.us.oracle.com	127	22	124
celemclu1.us.oracle.com	3	3	3
celemclu2.us.oracle.com	0	7	4
cevi04	4	6	0
fabushab-pc.us.oracle.com	0	6	119
rhingram-test.us.oracle.com	0	0	1
mingram-us.us.oracle.com	8	8	97
ntclu-74.us.oracle.com	1	3	0
ratclu11.us.oracle.com	62	14	4
ratclu12.us.oracle.com	6	10	7

Previous 1-10 of 12 Next 2

FIGURE 11-5. *The results from the report "An Overview of the Management Agent's Health"*

Step 10. Execute and verify the report.

By clicking the hyperlinked title of the report, you will be able to see the report executed using the most recent data stored in the repository, as shown in Figure 11-5. Now that's business intelligence at your fingertips!

Dashboards

So why the need for dashboards instead of relying on just conventional reporting? Traditionally, as a general rule, businesses employed a *siloed* approach toward system monitoring, which results in the reporting of only the IT infrastructure itself. In other words, the individual components that make up the ecosystem (for example, network, physical hardware, databases, deployed applications, and so on) were used to determine the overall health of the environment, all the while neglecting the experiences of the end user. Therefore, conventional reporting techniques sought a new maturity—no longer should aggregation of critical information be left to which monitored pieces "alarmed" the loudest. This was crude at best and the success of this approach relied heavily on the communication practices that were used by individuals within the business units. Because of the disjointed nature of these silos, it was not easy to offer a centralized view of the way the actual business was running at any given moment.

The advent of Grid Control's Dashboard makes such a view feasible, and creates a means of immediately gauging the status of the overall health and performance of your entire ecosystem. Most dashboards are intuitive and illustrate the availability and status of each component, performance and usage data, as well as any service-level statistics. In short, while reporting in Grid Control is just a representation of data in the repository, a dashboard's focus is to roll up state information in an executive-style manner (following the "manage many as one" mantra) for a set or group of targets, as shown in Figure 11-6. To get a glimpse of any of the dashboards, click the rightmost button, labeled Launch Dashboard, from the home page of any of the containers (such as Services, Systems, or Groups).

Customizing Dashboards

Since dashboards are really a representation of information about recent changes to the business, the data and the type of rollups can never be changed. Only a few things, such as the way the dashboard is being presented, can be customized. A hyperlink labeled Customize is made available with every dashboard should you decide to view the options and customize. As an example,

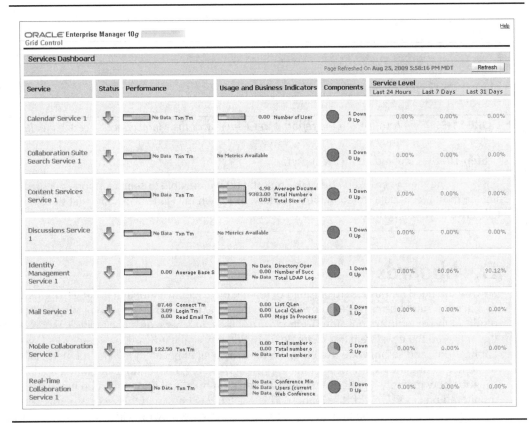

FIGURE 11-6. *This System Dashboard gives administrators a near–real-time view of key performance indicators.*

for normal reports rendered in a web browser, the names and headers of columns can be long and descriptive. For dashboards, however, which can be rendered on much smaller screens like the ones found on mobile devices, the column labels need to be abbreviated. This can be done on the Columns tab of the target definition page, as shown in Figure 11-7.

For heterogeneous groups, the rollup of the report can either happen on a per-target or per-n-target type basis.

NOTE
If the dashboard is defined to Group by Target Type, the columns defined per target will not be used, and only rollup metrics, such as Alerts, will be shown in the dashboard.

Writing Your Own Dashboards

As you know, all dashboards launched from the container targets cannot be fully customized or re-created. What is possible though, is to create custom reports, and give them the dashboard look-and-feel. During the creation of any new report, the user has the option to specify either the normal report layout or the dashboard style. You can select this style change from the Options section at the bottom of the General tab while creating a report.

Functionally, there is no difference between the *classic* style (shown in Figure 11-8) or the *dashboard* style (shown in Figure 11-9). All features of the reporting framework are available for both styles of reports. The only thing that will be different is the way the reports are finally presented in the console.

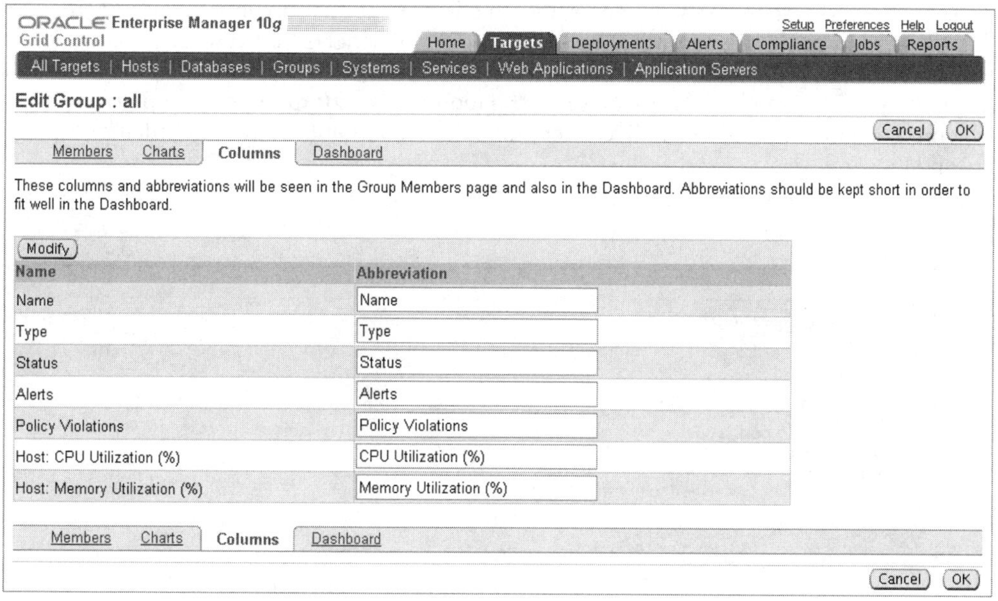

FIGURE 11-7. *Setting up the dashboard columns*

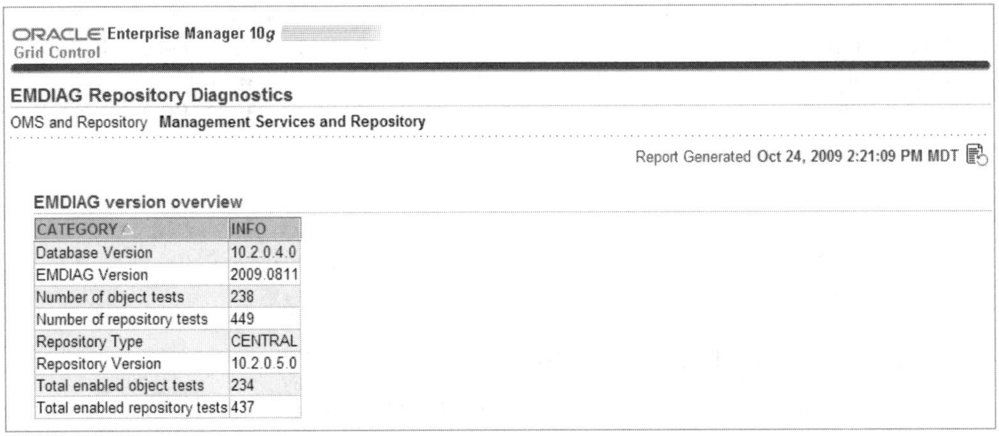
ORACLE Enterprise Manager 10*g*
Grid Control

EMDIAG Repository Diagnostics

OMS and Repository **Management Services and Repository**

Report Generated Oct 24, 2009 2:21:09 PM MDT

EMDIAG version overview

CATEGORY	INFO
Database Version	10.2.0.4.0
EMDIAG Version	2009.0811
Number of object tests	238
Number of repository tests	449
Repository Type	CENTRAL
Repository Version	10.2.0.5.0
Total enabled object tests	234
Total enabled repository tests	437

FIGURE 11-8. *Sample of the Classic Report layout*

An End-to-End View of Deployed Applications: Topology Viewer

For applications, Grid Control offers a topology viewer that serves as a graphical representation of all deployed applications in your enterprise. The topology viewer maps all the components of an application, depicting the relationships that the application has to other applications, services, and system hardware and software components, as shown in Figure 11-10. The data is valuable for providing an understanding of the dependencies that your application has, and if problems arise, you have a navigation mechanism as you traverse from the bottom to the top of the stack in search of the root cause. The requirement for running the topology viewer is the combination of the Adobe SVG Viewer plug-in and Internet Explorer 5.5 or later version running on Windows.

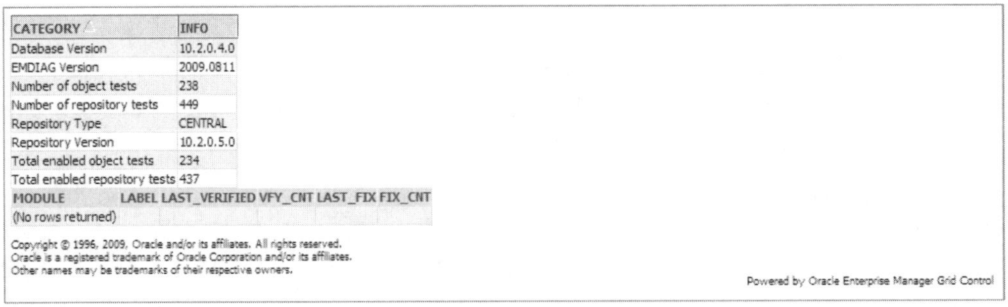
CATEGORY	INFO
Database Version	10.2.0.4.0
EMDIAG Version	2009.0811
Number of object tests	238
Number of repository tests	449
Repository Type	CENTRAL
Repository Version	10.2.0.5.0
Total enabled object tests	234
Total enabled repository tests	437

MODULE	LABEL	LAST_VERIFIED	VFY_CNT	LAST_FIX	FIX_CNT
(No rows returned)					

Copyright © 1996, 2009, Oracle and/or its affiliates. All rights reserved.
Oracle is a registered trademark of Oracle Corporation and/or its affiliates.
Other names may be trademarks of their respective owners.

Powered by Oracle Enterprise Manager Grid Control

FIGURE 11-9. *Sample of Dashboard Style layout*

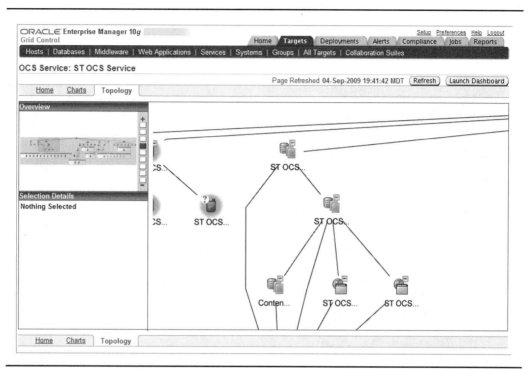

FIGURE 11-10. *An applications topology viewer*

Summary

As your management continually looks to your IT data centers as a means to run their business, critical processes and applications become vulnerable to your infrastructure's ability to service their needs. Given such demands and the complexities that are inherent in modern-day deployments, there is an enormous challenge when it comes to understanding the relationship of every deployment while providing meaningful feedback to those who have a vested interest in your success. If leveraged, Grid Control's reporting and dashboard mechanisms—with the over 100 out-of-box reports—should be one of the biggest arsenals you have to deliver the level of service that everyone will come to expect.

PART
III

Enterprise Manager
Power User's Guide

CHAPTER
12

Host Management

s the size and complexity of heterogeneous systems increase and with the growing dependency of the distributed applications that can run on such systems, the task of managing these resources can quickly become overwhelming to any system administration team. Become the hero that you are by restoring order and time to your team's busy schedule, using Grid Control to automate those repetitive and time-consuming tasks!

Hosts

The first approach to unraveling the evil layers of IT complexity begins by taking a look at the current administration practice behind the lifecycle management of hosts. Ineffective methods of controlling hosts erode the value of any technology investments that ride on top of the host system. Restore value by identifying and automating the repetitive and tiresome aspects that come with host management, so that a system administrator can focus his or her attention on delivering more value-adding services to the business, like trend analysis, instead of tackling the problems that surface when these tasks are done piecemeal.

As you already know, Enterprise Manager is more than a simple host-status-monitoring tool. The tools that Enterprise Manager Grid Control provides with respect to host management can be summed up into three parts:

- Deploying new target hosts using the provisioning facility
- Evaluating and comparing host configurations
- Performing automated tasks to effectively manage your ecosystem

These are parts of a larger whole that, when combined, allow you to manage hosts across their entire lifecycle. The workshops outlined in this chapter ensure the validity of this approach by incrementally deepening your Grid Control experience to develop a plug-and-play approach to the provisioning, patching, auditing, monitoring, and administering of Linux, Unix, and Windows environments. As you move through each workshop, note that the authors have made every attempt to attach a human perspective to the process, so you can immediately begin identifying an alignment between the actual needs of your business and the efforts required by these exercises.

Provisioning Hosts

The provisioning feature of Enterprise Manager is the first step toward an automated lifecycle management of hosts in the enterprise. This feature enables you to provision and patch the entire software stack, which includes the operating system, middleware, database, third-party software, and applications supplemented by a management agent for immediate communication back to a Management Server. All this would of itself be enough to warrant another book, but we feel it appropriate to provide a general overview of concept and functionality here. For more information, please review the chapter "Lifecycle Management" from the *Oracle Enterprise Manager Core Concepts Guide* and the published Oracle white paper, *Best Practices for Bare Metal Provisioning of Linux using Oracle Enterprise Manager 10g.*

As shown in Figure 12-1, Enterprise Manager begins its comprehensive lifecycle management through the deployment of referenced hosts, followed by the mass unattended deployments of new hosts once the original deployment is crowned a "gold image." From here, Grid Control is

FIGURE 12-1. *Comprehensive lifecycle management*

leveraged as part of an overall change management practice; first, through the notification of critical patches and vulnerabilities for the entire technology stack. Second, any necessary patches are automatically acquired and mass deployment across the enterprise is initiated. Third, administrators are allowed to build automated verification processes to ensure the successful implementation of any patch installations. Finally, Grid Control allows for decommissioning of resources so the administrator could deactivate and reallocate for different purposes.

Provisioning of software or applications can be broken into three parts:

■ Bare metal provisioning

■ Grid Control software libraries

■ Cloning

Operating system provisioning is the simplest way to deploy cost-effective systems in a consistent manner. Grid Control provides provisioning on "bare metal" systems of the Linux operating system using a standardized PXE booting process. The same provisioning mechanism later facilitates the deployment of additional software on top of the operating system. Grid Control is extensible so vendors can provide scripts to provision third-party hardware, such as storage disks or load balancers.

Next, provisioning can be done from a Grid Control Software Library. The Software Library is a centralized repository of software images and scripts that, when combined, provide the ability to automate a "change and release management" practice. A sample scenario of use is to use the provisioning application to create a default image with a minimum set of software packages required to provision on bare metal systems. The provisioning application will in turn use the Grid Control Job System to stage the image onto the staging server in preparation for installation. When the new machine is plugged in to the network, the boot server directs the machine to install the specified default image, which includes the operating system, networking information, and deployed Management Agent that would communicate back to the Management Service. A sample scenario of practice, in the context of development, staging, and production environments, is to take these images and have them versioned at different maturity levels, so that when you find yourself at the point where your environments are ready to be promoted, it can be rolled out in a consistent manner.

Finally, cloning is the mechanism to deploy tested and approved software (for example, gold images) imaged from either a reference host or the Grid Control Software Library to multiple hosts in a repeated fashion. You can use cloning to standardize the deployment of Oracle Database and Oracle Application Server instances. We will work through a couple of in-depth cloning workshops as part of a larger discussion of Application Monitoring in Chapter 17.

Viewing Host Configuration

As soon as a Management Agent is deployed to the host, Enterprise Manager automatically starts monitoring availability, performance, and configuration information for that managed target. As noted earlier in this book, the continual stream of information may come across as overwhelming until you make sense of its purpose. Anyone who requires host information, such as DBAs who manage databases on these hosts, will benefit from Grid Control's out-of-box host management features. So let's begin by taking a look at a working configuration of a host to make sense of what the agent is trying to tell us.

GRID CONTROL WORKSHOP

Evaluating a Sample Host

Workshop Notes

This workshop will guide you through answering some of the questions commonly asked of an administrator when a target is actively being managed.

Step 1. To access details of a managed host, click the Targets tab from the home page of the Grid Control Console. By default, you will be navigating the Hosts page.

Step 2. From the list of managed hosts, select any one of them, as shown in the following illustration. Congratulations, you are now looking at the home page of your first managed target!

Step 3. As you can see in the following illustration, Enterprise Manager consolidates the relevant host information into a convenient single-screen home page. You can see the availability, key configuration information, and outstanding alerts, as well as other pertinent information about the host.

Here is a sampling of what to expect as you cycle through each of the subtabs:

- From the Home page, you can glean the data provided and come up with some general information on the state of this host. Broken up, each of the sections gives you a dashboard approach in determining whether this target is available for your intended use.

- From the Performance page, you can see indicators and health statistics, specifically concerning CPU, Memory, and Disk I/O utilization of the host. By analyzing current and historic trending, you can easily determine how responsive the target is expected to be.

- From the Administration page, you can ensure that the target is working properly by leveraging a pool of common utilities to configure and maintain the host. Currently, this feature is only available for Linux-based systems and requires the installation of YAST and EM Wrapper Scripts from `http://oss.oracle.com/projects/yast`.

- From the Targets page, there is a listing of managed targets (both Oracle- and non-Oracle-specific), such as databases, application servers, and listeners that were previously installed on the host and auto-discovered by the Management Agent. It's worth noting that auto-discovery occurs the first time the agent is installed and started on the server, not every time it starts. Therefore, after the agent's initial run, in order for new targets to be managed, they must be manually discovered in Grid Control.

- From the Configuration page, you will see pertinent information describing the genetic makeup of the host, such as hardware, operating system, and software details. In addition, from this page you can view the configuration history of this host, take configuration snapshots, and compare the configuration of this host to the configuration of one or more other hosts. These capabilities will propel you far beyond the reaches of singular host management to the automation of tasks required to successfully manage a full fleet of hosts in the enterprise.

Although this exercise is a useful introduction to GC's reporting capabilities, it would not be an ideal approach for evaluating a large number of managed hosts. To evolve into a power user, you can start by automating tasks such as system comparisons in an effort to limit *system differentiation* in the environment. After all, as in peer-to-peer computing, a successful grid strategy requires accessibility to all shared resources, and system differentiation is the first misstep toward system-wide unavailability.

What Do You Really Know about Your Hosts?

Before Grid Control, there were few means of obtaining, synthesizing, and tracking information of hosts once deployed into the enterprise. If obtained, pieces of information were saved off to disparate locations (that is, spreadsheets) and knowledge of their whereabouts siloed to one or two key individuals. This practice contributed to delays and costs when maintaining the infrastructure and is what we commonly refer to as *information sprawl*.

The next couple of workshops attempt to mitigate such a practice by using Grid Control not only to view detailed configuration information of hosts, but also to manage the relationships that exist between them. By auditing these relationships in search of specific configurations of software installations, comparing host configurations, and identifying hardware and operating system differences, you will quickly come to informed decisions backed up with substantial data.

GRID CONTROL WORKSHOP

Evaluating Host Configuration History

Enterprise Manager automatically tracks all changes to the host configuration, allowing you to identify what has changed and when the change was made to your host. This can also be used as part of a larger process for managing physical assets in the enterprise.

Workshop Notes

In this scenario, Carl Compton the Comptroller has agreed to procure and distribute memory for physical systems in two data centers throughout the country. Perform the following steps to view the host configuration history and ensure that the upgrade went successfully:

Step 1. To view the configuration history of the host, as shown in the following illustration, click the Configuration subtab and then click the History button.

Host: hobgoblin.sd.avaya.com

Latest Data Collected From Target Apr 13, 2009 12:07:22 PM MDT (Refresh)

Home   Performance   Administration   Targets   Configuration

(Save) (History) (Compare Configuration) (Compare to Multiple Configurations(Job))

Hardware

		Operating System	
System Configuration	x86_64	Operating System	Red Hat Enterprise Linux Server release 5.3 (Tikanga) 2.6.18 128.el5 (64-bit)
Hardware Provider	Intel Based Hardware	Packages	1020
Number of CPUs	2	Related Link	Operating System Details
Memory Size (MB)	3775		
Related Link	Hardware Details		

ORACLE Enterprise Manager 10g

Grid Control

Setup Preferences Help Logout

Home   Targets   Deployments   Alerts   Compliance   Jobs   Reports

General | Provisioning

Configuration History

Enterprise Manager automatically collects configuration information for targets such as hosts and databases.   Page Refreshed Apr 3, 2009 4:39:24 PM MDT (Search Using SQL)
Changes to these configurations are recorded and may be viewed from this page.

Category [Host   ▼]
         Changing the category clears any existing results.

▼ **Search**

Target Name	is exactly ▼	hobgoblin.sd.avaya.com		Change Discovered after	3/27/09 ▦
Target Property	Deployment Type ▼				(Example: 12/15/02)
Member Of	contains ▼				01 ▼ 43 ▼ ⊙ AM ○ PM
Type of Change	is	All ▼		Change Discovered before	uyen
	(Go) (Clear)				(Example: 12/15/02)
					12 ▼ 00 ▼ ⊙ AM ○ PM

View History Records [Show All ▼]   (Save to File)

⊙ Previous [Show All 157 ▼] Next ⊙

Change Discovered ▽	Target Name	Category	Descriptor Key	Value	Type of Change	Attribute	New Value	Old Value	Details
Apr 3, 2009 11:40:18 AM MDT	hobgoblin.sd.avaya.com	Host: Hardware: Hardware (Summary)			Change	Local Disk Space (GB)	5.96	6.01	∞Q
Apr 3, 2009	hobgoblin.sd.avaya.com	Host:			Change	Local Disk	6.01	5.96	∞Q

Step 2. By default, this page displays all the configuration changes that occurred on the host during the last seven days, as shown in the following illustration.

ORACLE Enterprise Manager 10g

Grid Control

Setup Preferences Help Logout

Home   Targets   Deployments   Alerts   Compliance   Jobs   Reports

General | Provisioning

Configuration History

Enterprise Manager automatically collects configuration information for targets such as hosts and databases.   Page Refreshed Apr 3, 2009 5:19:04 PM MDT (Search Using SQL)
Changes to these configurations are recorded and may be viewed from this page.

Category [Hardware (Summary)   ▼]
         Changing the category clears any existing results.

▼ **Search**

Target Name	contains ▼	hobgoblin.sd.avaya.com		Change Discovered after	3/27/09 ▦
Target Property	Deployment Type ▼				(Example: 12/15/02)
Member Of	contains ▼				08 ▼ 00 ▼ ⊙ AM ○ PM
Type of Change	is	Change ▼		Change Discovered before	4/3/09 ▦
					(Example: 12/15/02)
					07 ▼ 00 ▼ ⊙ AM ○ PM

Category-Specific Filters

Attribute	is	Memory Size (MB) ▼		New Value	contains ▼	
	(Go) (Clear)			Old Value	contains ▼	

View History Records [Grouped ▼]   (Save to File)

Change Discovered ▽	Target Name	History Records
Mar 28, 2009 12:01:57 PM MDT	hobgoblin.sd.avaya.com	1

(continued)

Step 3. For this exercise, change the search criteria as follows:

- The Category drop-down menu is Hardware (Summary).
- The Target Name drop-down menu Is Contains, with a sample value like **hobgoblin.sd.avaya.com**.
- The Type of Change drop-down menu is Change.
- Alter the date parameters Change Discovered After and Change Discovered Before, to view changes over a longer period of seven days.
- Click Go.

As you will see, the results indicate that a change was discovered. As the following illustration confirms, the on-premise technician successfully upgraded the memory.

Step 4. Click Save to File to archive the results as part of your asset management practice, and click the browser's Back button to navigate back to the host configuration page.

As all collected information is done by the Management Agent and stored in the Oracle Management Repository, this same query can be done via SQL using the following lengthy syntax:

```
SELECT * FROM (SELECT LBL_DELTATIME,LBL_TIMEZONE,LBL_TARGETNAME,LBL_
TARGETTYPE,LBL_HOSTNAME,LBL_CATEGORY,LBL_OPERATION,LBL_ATTRIBUTE,LBL_
NEWVALUE,LBL_OLDVALUE,LBL_DELTAGUID FROM (SELECT /*+FIRST_ROWS(2000)*/
DELTATIME as LBL_DELTATIME,TIMEZONE as LBL_TIMEZONE,TARGET_NAME
as LBL_TARGETNAME,TARGET_TYPE as LBL_TARGETTYPE,HOSTNAME as LBL_
HOSTNAME,CATEGORY as LBL_CATEGORY,DELTAGUID as LBL_DELTAGUID,OPERATION
as LBL_OPERATION,ATTRIBUTE as LBL_ATTRIBUTE,NEWVALUE as LBL_
NEWVALUE,OLDVALUE as LBL_OLDVALUE FROM MGMT$ECM_CONFIG_HISTORY WHERE
```

```
(TARGET_TYPE = 'host') AND (SNAPSHOTTYPE = 'host_configuration') AND
(COLLECTIONTYPE = 'ECM$HIST_HARDWARE') ORDER BY DELTATIME DESC,TARGET_
NAME,CATEGORY,DELTAGUID) WHERE (LBL_TARGETNAME = 'hobgoblin.acme.com')
AND (LBL_OPERATION = 'UPDATE') AND (LBL_ATTRIBUTE = 'MEMORY_SIZE_IN_MB')
AND (LBL_DELTATIME >= TO_DATE('3/28/09 12:01:57','MM/DD/YY HH24:MI:SS'))
AND (LBL_DELTATIME <= TO_DATE('3/28/09 12:01:57','MM/DD/YY HH24:MI:SS'))
) ORDER BY LBL_DELTATIME DESC,LBL_TARGETNAME,LBL_CATEGORY,LBL_DELTAGUID;
```

Which method would you prefer to use?

Grid Control also tracks historical changes to configurations for databases and applications servers, something you will find especially useful in helping you diagnose problems. Targets interact with each other, and changes in one target may affect the behavior of other related targets. Tracking historical changes can be very important when trying to determine a root cause as it provides clues as to which changes might have affected it. Hence, Oracle felt it necessary to be able to see historical changes for a number of related targets other than just hosts.

For scenarios where you already have in mind what you are looking for, you can use Grid Control to search your configurations stored in the Management Repository. When you perform a search of your configurations, the search query accesses the enterprise configuration management views in the Management Repository. The next workshop will aim to search host configuration details stored in the Management Repository.

GRID CONTROL WORKSHOP

Searching Host Configurations

Workshop Notes

In this scenario, Vivien's manager has informed her that a security advisory has been issued for a browser issue experienced by clients deployed throughout her call centers. Vivien needs to quickly identify which of these clients are running the software addressed by this advisory and formulate an upgrade plan with minimal business impact. Follow these steps to search configuration details stored in the Management Repository:

Step 1. Click the Deployments tab.

Step 2. Click Search in the Configuration section.

Step 3. Click Search Operating Systems Components Installed on Hosts, in the Search Operating System Configuration Data section.

Step 4. In the Operating System drop-down menu, select Contains and type **%Linux%**.

Step 5. In the Component Type drop-down menu, select Contains and type **Package**.

Step 6. In the Component drop down menu, select Contains and type **%firefox 0:1.5.0 %**.

Step 7. Click Go.

(continued)

As the following illustration shows, a table is returned showing the Host Name, Operating System, Component, and Description of the package queried. Vivien can now quickly prioritize and deal with vulnerable clients mitigating the impact on her line of business.

With grid computing, organizations align information and computing resources by pooling and sharing them across networks. Confidence in this approach dwindles when there are unintended differences host to host. Enterprise Manager lets you compare existing configurations and determine differences between two or more hosts.

GRID CONTROL WORKSHOP

Comparing Configurations

Workshop Notes

Perform the following steps to compare two host configurations.

Step 1. Click the Deployments tab.

Step 2. Click Compare Configurations in the Configuration section to launch the Comparison Wizard.

Step 3. Select the first host from the menu and select the Continue button.

Step 4. Select the second host and click the Compare button.

Step 5. The following illustration shows the results from the host comparison wizard. You can view the summary of the comparison results on this page, and you can navigate to more detailed information about the differences in the comparison items. Click the first Different link in the Hardware & Operating System section.

Step 6. The following illustration shows detailed results of hardware comparisons for two host configurations. At the very top of the page, you will see the names of the first and second selected hosts involved in the comparison and a timestamp when each host configuration was collected. The remaining tables provide additional details on comparisons of CPU, I/O, and Network Interfaces for the two hosts. Click the OK button to go back to the Comparison Results Summary.

(continued)

Step 7. Click the second Different link in the Hardware & Operating System section.

Step 8. The following illustration reveals in detail the results of the operating system comparison between two host configurations. The Comparison Summary table describes information about the properties, file systems, packages, and patches of the two hosts that were compared. The General Information table displays the comparison summary of the operating systems for the two hosts. The Operating System Properties table displays the comparison of any operating system properties for the two hosts.

Comparison Results: Operating System Software

First Host	hobgoblin.sd.avaya.com	Second Host	fama.sd.avaya.com
Date	Apr 3, 2009 2:36:44 PM MDT	Date	Apr 4, 2009 2:35:54 AM MDT
Operating System	Red Hat Enterprise Linux Server release 5.3 (Tikanga) 2.6.18 128.el5 (64-bit)	Operating System	Enterprise Linux Enterprise Linux AS release 4 78.0.0.0.1.ELhugemem (32-bit)

General   File Systems   Packages

Comparison Summary

	Different	Only on hobgoblin.sd.avaya.com	Only on fama.sd.avaya.com
File Systems	0	2	4
OS Properties	38	99	30
Package(s)	565	454	222
Patches	0	0	0

General Information

Comparison Result	hobgoblin.sd.avaya.com	fama.sd.avaya.com
⇌	Red Hat Enterprise Linux Server release 5.3 (Tikanga) 2.6.18 128.el5 (64-bit) 3999.99 MB Maximum Swap Space	Enterprise Linux Enterprise Linux AS release 4 (October Update 7) 2.6.9 78.0.0.0.1.ELhugemem (32-bit) 4095.99 MB Maximum Swap Space

Operating System Properties

Previous 1-10 of 167 ▾ Next 10 ⊗

Comparison Result	Source	Name	hobgoblin.sd.avaya.com	fama.sd.avaya.com
⇌	/sbin/sysctl	Maximum Swap Space (MB)	3999.99	4095.99
⇌	/sbin/sysctl	dev.parport.parport0.base-addr	888 0	888 1912
⇌	/sbin/sysctl	dev.parport.parport0.irq	7	-1

If the hosts meet a certain criteria, you can then save the configuration as an ideal image and store it as a local file on the filesystem or as an entry in the repository to be used for future comparisons against current/saved configurations.

Now that comparisons between one or more hosts can quickly be assessed by your system administration team, you can include an addition to the practice by taking some out-of-box security policies and use Grid Control to drive automated security assessments against your hosts. The results from these exercises not only aid in the early detection of critical vulnerabilities, but they can also help in determining the thresholds that both your organization and applications are willing to accept.

GRID CONTROL WORKSHOP

Monitoring Policy Violations and Host Compliance Scores

Policy violations consist of the summary of all the policy rule violations of hosts in your enterprise. Viewing the policy violations allows you to prioritize so you can deal with the most critical policy violations or those that have the biggest impact on your line of business.

Workshop Notes

This workshop will guide you through the steps to manage policy violations.

Step 1. Click the Compliance tab.

Step 2. By default, you will be navigating the Policy Violations page. Click the number value under the Violation Count column for the Open Ports policy violation, as shown in the following illustration.

Step 3. The details from the Policy Violation page provide information about this specific policy rule, as shown in the following illustration. This page includes a detailed

(continued)

view of the violation, including how many objects were in violation, the potential impact, recommendations about repairs, and additional details.

Step 4. Scroll down to the Related Links section and click the Edit Policy Settings link.

Step 5. Once a policy has been associated with a target, circumstances may dictate that the settings for the policy be updated. The Edit Policy Rule Settings page gives you the opportunity to change the settings to reflect the thresholds set out by your organization or the applications that represent it. From this page, as shown in the following illustration, you can do the following:

■ Select Policy Evaluation: Enabled or Disabled.

■ Modify Importance settings.

■ Change parameter rules such as which ports to test and which to exclude.

■ Add a corrective action. *Corrective actions* are automatically crafted responses to alerts or policy violations.

■ Select if (another) metric can override these settings.

Click Continue to save any changes to the policy.

Step 6. Click the OK button to save and confirm the changes.

Step 7. To apply address compliance scores, click the Compliance tab, and click the Compliance Score (%) column heading to determine the target with the lowest score, as shown in the following illustration.

You can now address the targets that pose the greatest risk to your infrastructure. It's important to note that policy rules exist for different target types, such as Oracle databases, application servers, and listeners. All policies are stored in the Policy Rule Library, which you can navigate by clicking the Library subtab from the Compliance page.

If we were to compare the meaning of the term *utility computing* to the operation of your local electrical utilities company, then your applications rely on a grid infrastructure just as appliances rely on electricity from outlets. Much like charging your mobile phone in an outlet with questionable output, inconsistencies in the infrastructure could lead to unmanageable results of your applications. A successful grid strategy relies heavily on the fact that you can quickly pinpoint inconsistencies and avoid issues by determining the thresholds that your applications can sustain when running in a heterogeneous environment.

Oracle, What Are My Agents Monitoring?

Now that there is a level of predictability in our infrastructure practice, we can look at introducing some of the system monitoring features specific to host management when using Oracle Enterprise Manager. The objective of this setting is to introduce familiarity with system monitoring features that generically apply to any managed target such as hosts, databases, and applications servers. Monitoring features that are specific to those components are covered in their respective chapters.

GRID CONTROL WORKSHOP

Monitoring Log Files as Part of a Linux Security Administration Practice

In order to determine if an intruder has violated your system, you should be familiar with the normal system administration tools, and be able to use them to find the "footprint" that a cracker may have left behind. This procedure can be relatively simple, or practically impossible, depending on how much preparation was done on the system, at which stage you've detected an intrusion, and how skilled the actual intruder is. Since many business-critical applications are deployed on Linux hosts, and Linux maintains a very good framework for logging system events, which in turn can be helpful for tracking connections to these systems, it comes as no surprise that log file analysis is often suggested as a best practice.

Workshop Notes

Let's use the Log File Monitoring functionality in Enterprise Manager to monitor specific logs for potential intrusions and generate notifications whenever specific messages are generated in these log files.

Step 1.   Navigate to the Host home page by clicking the Targets tab.

Step 2.   Scroll down to the Related Links section and click the Metric and Policy Settings link.

Step 3.   Find the metric Log File Pattern Matched Line Count in the metric list and click the Edit icon for this metric, as shown in the following illustration.

Metric and Policy Settings

Cancel   OK

Metric Thresholds   Policies

View Metrics with thresholds ▾

Metric	Comparison Operator	Warning Threshold	Critical Threshold	Corrective Actions	Collection Schedule	Edit
CPU in I/O Wait (%)	>	40	80	None	Every 5 Minutes	✎
CPU Utilization (%)	>	80	95	None	Every 5 Minutes	✎
Disk Device Busy (%)	>	80	95	None	Every 15 Minutes	✎
File or Directory Attribute Not Found	!=		0	None	Every 15 Minutes	✎
Filesystem Space Available (%)	<	20	5	None	Every 15 Minutes	✎
Log File Pattern Matched Line Count	>	0		None	Every 15 Minutes	✎
Memory Utilization (%)	>	80	95	None	Every 5 Minutes	✎
Processes in Zombie State (%)	>	35	50	None	Every 15 Minutes	✎
Run Queue Length (5 minute average)	>	10	20	None	Every 5 Minutes	✎
Status			Down	None	Based on Management Agent ping	✎
Swap Utilization (%)	>	80	95	None	Every 5 Minutes	✎

✓ TIP Empty Thresholds will disable alerts for that metric.

Metric Thresholds Links
Metric Snapshots

Metric Thresholds   Policies

Step 4.   Click the Add button to set up a monitoring preference for the intrusion message. To add some context, the Linux operating system, as part of its default system administration tools, logs all system login events in the /var/log/secure log. It is this log file that we will instruct Enterprise Manager to actively monitor. Depending on the particular distribution of Linux, the /var/log/secure file may only have read-permissions for the root user. This poses a problem for the Management Agent as metric collection permissions extend only to the user that installed the software. To address this issue, change the permissions to allow a minimum of read access to the file:

```
[root@i187ucanu5] chmod 744 /var/log/secure
```

Note that for the purposes of this exercise, we are allowing this file to be read by anyone. The ideal security practice would be establishing sudo privileges using the built-in Enterprise Manager Preferred Credentials capability (see Chapter 7).

Step 5.   Specify the Log File Name as **/var/log/secure** and Match Pattern as **session opened for user root by**, Warning Threshold as **2**. This will ensure that a warning alert is generated every time there are at least three occurrences of the warning message. Click the Add button again to set up monitoring for the critical message.

Step 6.   Again, specify the Log File Name as **/var/log/secure** and Match Pattern as, **Failed password for root from**, Critical Threshold as **0**. This will ensure that a critical alert gets generated every time there is at least one occurrence of this critical message.

(continued)

Click the Continue button to return to the Metric and Policy Settings page, as shown in the following illustration.

Step 7. Your changes will be reflected in the metrics table. Click the OK button to save and confirm your changes.

Step 8. From a remote console, log in using a non-privileged user (for example, dxnguyen) via SSH and su to root. The following entry will be logged in the /var/log/secure file:

```
Nov 7 19:07:09 hobgoblin su: pam_unix(su:session): session opened
for user root by dxnguyen(uid=666)
```

Step 9. Repeat step 8 to ensure that three entries are logged in order to trigger a warning alert.

Step 10. From a remote console, perform a failed login using an incorrect password as the privileged user, root via SSH. The following entry will be logged in the /var/log/secure file and will trigger a critical alert:

```
Dec 25 19:08:20 hobgoblin sshd[6267]: Failed password for root from
135.148.283.54 port 2716 ssh2
```

After the default 15-minute collection schedule occurs, you should see alerts raised from the Home page of the targeted host as shown in the following illustration.

Creating and Enforcing Standards for Host Management

The notoriety and creation of standards can range from common practice throughout the industry to an agreement between two departmental colleagues. In light of this fact, most departments find that the biggest deterrence from exerting any effort is not because of standards, rather because of the difficulty that comes with standardizing into an existing environment. The benefits of using Enterprise Manager as a mechanism for standardization are a game changer. It drives predictability into the picture and develops a system that allows task automation to be used as a standards creator.

Now that we have covered most of the critical aspects of host management, it is time to combine these experiences to conceive standards that can be plugged back into the Enterprise Manager system for enforcement.

GRID CONTROL WORKSHOP

Tracking Storage Resources

Tracking usage and storage resource allocation is essential when aligning computing resources across large IT departments. Unallocated and underutilized storage can be put to better use. In addition, administrators often need to understand historical trends at a business entity-level in order to effectively plan and justify future growth.

(continued)

Workshop Notes
Perform the following steps to view storage resource utilization:

Step 1. Navigate to the Host home page by clicking the Targets tab.

Step 2. Scroll down to the Related Links section and click the Storage Details link.

Step 3. The Storage Details page provides detailed storage resource allocation and usage information for your host. The Storage Details page provides the following information:

- **Overall Utilization** Shows summary attributes that provide a system-level view of storage resource utilization.

- **Provisioning Summary** Shows allocation-related summary attributes for File Systems, ASM, Volumes, and Disks for the associated hosts.

- **Consumption Summary** Shows usage-related summary attributes for Databases and File Systems. In addition, details are provided for each storage layer, such as Disks, File Systems, ASM, and so on, as shown in the following illustration.

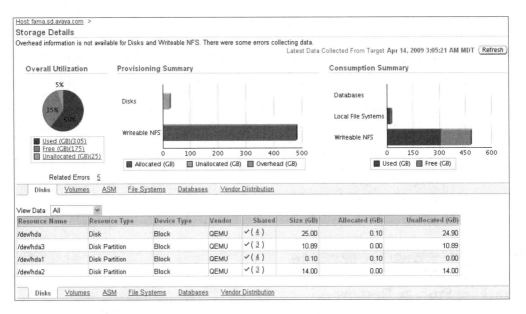

Click the Storage History link in the Related Links section.

Step 4. The Storage History page provides a quick glimpse of the history of the storage usage for the choice selected in the View drop-down list, as shown in the following illustration. Using this page, you can view the Storage History at a host level, as well as the storage history for databases, local file systems, local disks, volumes, and writable NFS statistics. In addition, Enterprise Manager provides Storage Reports at a group level. The topic of groups will be covered extensively in the next chapter, but this is where you can quickly analyze the storage utilization across all the hosts managed by as a group.

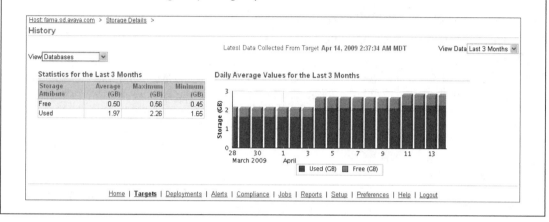

Using the historical trends presented by the previous exercise, you can analyze usage trends and predict how much storage your organization may need in the future. There may come a time when trending comes across as suspect or additional diagnostics must take place to collaborate the reporting. The next couple of exercises serve as an example to show how you can plug in the monitoring and auditing capabilities of Enterprise Manage to help diagnose such problems.

GRID CONTROL WORKSHOP

Monitoring Files and Directories

In certain cases, historical trending of disk storage may appear erratic and require additional diagnostics. Even with the continuous drop in price for storage, administrators are constantly tasked to keep an eye on disk usage to ensure that the system is not overloaded.

In the following two-part exercise, you will deepen Enterprise Manager's capabilities to monitor files and directories. In this case, you will ensure that the directory set aside for file storage does not exceed a critical threshold of 512MB. In the event that it has crossed a warning threshold of 256MB, you will trigger a corrective action to audit and ascertain the disk usage of all the subdirectories, and report the top five or ten users therein.

(continued)

Workshop Notes

Perform the following steps to configure file and directory monitoring.

Step 1. Navigate to the Host home page by clicking the Target tab.

Step 2. Scroll down to the Related Links section and click the Metric and Policy Settings link.

Step 3. Select All Metrics from the View drop-down list.

Step 4. You will see four metrics that are specific for file and directory monitoring, such as File or Directory Permissions, File or Directory Size (MB), and so on, as shown in the following illustration. Click the Edit icon for the File or Directory Size (MB) metric.

Metric and Policy Settings

Cancel OK

Metric Thresholds Policies

View All metrics

Metric	Comparison Operator	Warning Threshold	Critical Threshold	Corrective Actions	Collection Schedule	Edit
Active Memory, Kilobytes	>			None	Every 5 Minutes	
Available (MB)	<			None	Every 15 Minutes	
Average Disk I/O Service Time (ms)	>			None	Every 15 Minutes	
Buffer Cache Read Hit Ratio (%)	>			None	Disabled	
Buffer Cache Write Hit Ratio (%)	>			None	Disabled	
CPU in I/O Wait (%)	>	40	80	None	Every 5 Minutes	
CPU in System Mode (%)	>			None	Every 5 Minutes	
CPU in User Mode (%)	>			None	Every 5 Minutes	
CPU Utilization (%)	>	80	95	None	Every 5 Minutes	
Disk Device Busy (%)	>	80	95	None	Every 15 Minutes	
File or Directory Attribute Not Found	!=		0	None	Every 15 Minutes	
File or Directory Permissions	!=			None	Every 15 Minutes	
File or Directory Size (MB)	>			None	Every 15 Minutes	
File or Directory Size Change Rate (KB/minute)	>			None	Every 15 Minutes	

Step 5. The table lists all File or Directory Name objects monitored for this metric. You can specify different threshold settings for each File or Directory Name object. Click the Add button to set up monitoring for a sample directory, such as /stage.

Step 6. Specify the File or Directory Name as **/stage**, Warning Threshold as **256MB**, and Critical Threshold as **512MB**, as shown in the following illustration. Click the Continue button to return to the Metric and Policy Settings page.

Host: argus.sd.avaya.com > Metric and Policy Settings >
Edit Advanced Settings: File or Directory Size (MB)

(Cancel) (Continue)

Monitored Objects

The table lists all File or Directory Name objects monitored for this metric. You can specify different threshold settings for each File or Directory Name object.

(Add) (Reorder)

(Edit) (Remove)

Select File or Directory Name	Comparison Operator	Warning Threshold	Critical Threshold	Corrective Action
⦿ /stage	>	256	512	None
○ All others	>			None

✎ TIP Empty Thresholds will disable alerts for that metric.
✎ TIP You can optionally use "%" wildcard character to represent multiple objects. (Example: /u1% represents /u11, /u12 etc)
✎ TIP If the object name contains "%" or "\", specify it as "\%" or "\\" (Example: 'c:\temp' needs to be entered as 'c:\\temp')

(Cancel) (Continue)

ⓘ **Information**

The settings have been modified but not saved to the repository. You can make further changes to the settings and click on the OK button to save the data.

Metric and Policy Settings

(Cancel) (OK)

Metric Thresholds | Policies

View [All metrics ▾]

Metric	Comparison Operator	Warning Threshold	Critical Threshold	Corrective Actions	Collection Schedule	Edit
Active Memory, Kilobytes	>			None	Every 5 Minutes	✎
Available (MB)	<			None	Every 15 Minutes	✎
Average Disk I/O Service Time (ms)	>			None	Every 15 Minutes	✎
Buffer Cache Read Hit Ratio (%)	>			None	Disabled	✎
Buffer Cache Write Hit Ratio (%)	>			None	Disabled	✎
CPU in I/O Wait (%)	>	40	80	None	Every 5 Minutes	✎
CPU in System Mode (%)	>			None	Every 5 Minutes	✎
CPU in User Mode (%)	>			None	Every 5 Minutes	✎
CPU Utilization (%)	>	80	95	None	Every 5 Minutes	✎
Disk Device Busy (%)	>	80	95	None	Every 15 Minutes	✎
File or Directory Attribute Not Found	!=		0	None	Every 15 Minutes	✎
File or Directory Permissions	!=			None	Every 15 Minutes	✎
File or Directory Size (MB)						✎
/stage	>	256	512	None	Every 15 Minutes	✎

Step 7. Your changes will be reflected in the metrics table. Click OK to save your changes.

Step 8. Log in to the targeted host via SFTP and incrementally add files to `/stage`, as shown in the following illustration. After the threshold of 256MB has been passed, an alert will be triggered in the Host home page. Continue to incrementally add files until you breach the critical threshold of 512MB to trigger the final alert.

(continued)

Note that alerts will be raised based on the timing of the Management Agent's collection schedule, defaulted to 15-minute intervals.

Now that we have successfully set thresholds in place to monitor the activity of files and directories, we are going to expand on this workshop to define a set of corrective actions and trigger them when certain thresholds have been violated.

GRID CONTROL WORKSHOP

Issuing Corrective Actions When Thresholds Are Violated

Step 1. To access the general Enterprise Manager configuration and system monitoring functions, click the Setup link.

Step 2. Scroll down the menu section on the left and click the Corrective Action Library link.

Step 3. From the Create Library Corrective Action drop-down list, select OS Command and click Go, as shown in the following illustration.

Step 4. Under the General listing, populate the fields Name, Description, and Target Type with the following data:

- Name: **SNAPSHOT OF DISK USAGE**
- Description: **Corrective action to ascertain disk usage of all subdirectories, and report the top resource intensive users**.
- Target Type: **Host**

Step 5. Under the Parameters listing, select Script from the Command Type drop-down list.

Step 6. In the OS script box, we are going to insert the following snippet of code:

```
#!/bin/bash
# Disk usage analysis script for Linux

DISKQUOTA=1024
# Disk quota allocated per user in MB.
for handle in $(cut -d: -f1,3 /etc/passwd | awk -F: '$2 > 99 {print
$1}')
# Assuming that all user accounts are >=100
do
    echo -n "User $handle has exceeded expected disk usage. Disk
consumption is: "
    # You might need to modify the following list of directories to
match the
    # layout of your disk.
    find / /usr /var /home /u01 /tmp /stage -xdev -user $handle
-type f -ls | \
```

(continued)

```
        awk '{ sum += $7 } END { print sum / (1024*1024) " MB" }'
done | awk "\$9 > $DISKQUOTA { print \$0 }"
exit 0
```

Guidance about the modification to this and other shell scripts is beyond the scope of this chapter, but, if you would like access to other wicked shell scripts, I recommend the book *Wicked Cool Shell Scripts* by Dave Taylor (`http://www` `.intuitive.com/wicked`) as a very useful resource.

Step 7. Under the Credentials listing, select the Override Preferred Credentials radio button and provide the necessary credentials to parse the entire filesystem, as shown in the following illustration.

Step 8. Click Save To Library. The following illustration shows confirmation of the newly created and stored job.

Step 9. Navigating back to the Metric and Policy Settings from the host, we are going to select the Edit icon of the `/stage` object of the File or Directory Size (MB) metric.

Step 10. In the Corrective Actions section, click the Add button to address Warning Thresholds.

Step 11. Select From Library from the drop-down menu and click Continue, as shown in the
following illustration.

Step 12. Select the corrective action named SNAPSHOT OF DISK USAGE and click
Continue, as shown in the following illustration.

Step 13. Specify a descriptive name, **SNAPSHOT OF DISK USAGE FOR <HOST>**, where
<HOST> is the hostname of your managed target. Click Continue, as shown in the
following illustration.

Step 14. For the Advanced Threshold Settings section, we will keep the remaining values for
validating the exercise, but we suggest that you adjust the parameters to better align
with the needs of your business. For instance, set Warning Threshold to 102400 (MB),
Critical Threshold to 128000 (MB), and Number of Occurrences to 360 (24 hours

(continued)

collected successfully on a 15-minute collection schedule). Click Continue, as shown in the following illustration.

Host:yeti.sd.avaya.com > Metric and Policy Settings >
Edit Advanced Settings: File or Directory Size (MB)

Cancel | Continue

File or Directory Name **/stage**

Corrective Actions

Warning SNAPSHOT OF DISK USAGE FOR HOST (Remove)

Critical **<none>** (Add)

☑ Allow only one corrective action for this metric to run at any given time

Advanced Threshold Settings

Comparison Operator **>**	
Warning Threshold	256
Critical Threshold	512
Number of Occurrences	1
Collection Schedule **Every 15 Minutes**	

Number of Occurrences

To prevent false alerts due to spikes in metric values, the Number of Occurrences determines the period of time a collected metric value must remain above or below the threshold value before an alert is triggered or cleared. For example, if a metric value is collected every 5 minutes, and the Number of Occurrences is set to 6, the metric values (collected successfully) must stay above the threshold value for 30 minutes before an alert is triggered. Likewise, once the alert is triggered, the same metric value must stay below its threshold for 6 consecutive occurrences (30 minutes) before it is cleared.

☑ TIP Empty Thresholds will disable alerts for that metric.

Template Override

☐ Prevent metric settings on this page from being changed when a monitoring template is applied to the target

Cancel | Continue

Home | **Targets** | Deployments | Alerts | Compliance | Jobs | Reports | Setup | Preferences | Help | Logout

Step 15. Click OK twice to save and commit the metric changes to the repository.

Step 16. The next time the warning threshold is breached, a corrective action will be triggered, and the results made available in the Alerts section of the Hosts home page.

Step 17. To see details including the results of the corrective action, visit the host's home page, and click the value in the Message column of the Alerts section, followed by a final click of the value in the Message column of the Updates section for the corrective action.

Metric Alert : File or Directory Size (MB)

Page Refreshed Apr 15, 2009 5:30:05 AM MDT (Refresh)

Alert Details

Metric	File or Directory Size (MB)
File or Directory Name	**/stage**
Severity	⚠ **Warning** (Reevaluate Alert)
Alert Triggered	**Apr 14, 2009 5:48:00 PM**
Last Updated	**Apr 15, 2009 10:04:21 PM**
Acknowledged	**No** (Acknowledge)
Acknowledged By	**n/a**
Message	**Size of /stage is 295.58 MB, crossed warning (256) or critical (512) threshold.**

Metric Data

Last Known Value **342.56**
Last Collection Timestamp **Apr 14, 2009 6:33:09 PM**

Actions

Edit Thresholds

Metric Settings

☐ Warning Threshold 256
■ Critical Threshold 512
Occurrences Before Alert 1

Updates

New Comment _____ (Add Comment)

Timestamp	Type	Administrator	Message
Apr 15, 2009 10:04:21 PM	Corrective Action	<SYSTEM>	Execution created for Corrective Action SNAPSHOT OF DISK USAGE FOR HOST Corrective Action status 'Succeeded'.
Apr 14, 2009 5:48:00 PM	⚠	<SYSTEM>	Size of /stage is 295.58 MB, crossed warning (256) or critical (512) threshold.

The details of the corrective action include the output of the script, as shown in the preceding illustration. As you can see, we've rounded up quite a few consumption bandits!

The most common monitoring technique is to manually navigate to the /users or /home directory, and evaluate the results from the command du. Other than being manually intensive, the problem with this approach is that it does not take into account space usage elsewhere on the hard disk(s). Users who have additional archive space usage elsewhere on a second drive or sneaky types who keep MP3s in a dot directory of a shared FTP or disk mount will escape undetected. A complete standard of this nature should include some sort of automated notification such as an e-mail to warn users when they've exceeded standard disk space, as shown in the following illustration.

Hopefully, by now, we have shown that the common theme of these workshops is that the most effective means of standardization is one of a cyclic and automated nature: the auditing, monitoring, correction, and notification of tasks.

Summary

There is no simpler pursuit that gives greater pleasure for any system administration team than simplifying labor-intensive tasks that would generally take days and still result in a reduction of deployment risks to the ecosystem. Today's IT ecosystems have evolved to include a variety of platforms from a wide array of vendors. A typical enterprise also contains hardware components and applications from a number of internal and external suppliers. In this chapter, we have journeyed to the other side of the same coin, by addressing how one would manage such rich deployments and still have an effective grid capable of delivering on-demand applications as utilities. The workshops established means to automate tiresome aspects of host management, thereby, shifting the attention on delivering practices with more added value and suffering from a nice side effect of less work!

In the next chapter, we move on to three important aggregated target types: Systems, Services, and Groups. To set up a Service, we must create a System, organize targets into logical sets called Groups, and then build on them to configure one industry-defining service type in particular: an e-commerce application!

CHAPTER
13

Systems, Services,
and Groups

nce a lot of Agents and targets on those Agents have been added to the Console, a new problem will arise: How do you manage all these targets?

Container targets, like groups, systems and services, are a way to logically group targets into *entities*, which make sense for the environment they are running in. These entities can be a Line-Of-Business (LOB), a group of DBAs, all targets for a specific application, or even targets grouped per location. By grouping these targets together, an Administrator can get a bird's-eye view of that set of targets, and perform administrative tasks on the whole set of targets in that group (the "manage as one" paradigm).

You have likely already seen the terms "System," "Services," and "Groups" in tabs and headers, and they have been spoken of briefly in the installation and configuration guide. You probably have a fairly good idea what is meant by them from your own ecosystem management activities. However, it is worth discussing the specific meaning these terms have within Grid Control, and then spending some time configuring them for optimal use. We will start with Systems, how to build and use them, as well as best practices, and then follow with similar discussions about Services and Groups. These three logical units serve similar functions, but it is important to know when to use each of them, and how to use them together for a power GC experience.

Systems, Services, and Groups all are discussed in the same chapter together because they are different interpretations of the same need: a logical grouping of targets. Which makes which, and therefore how we can assign attributes to them, depends largely on the intended audience.

Systems

A *System*, in Grid Control, refers to a specific target type that warrants its own tab at the top of the web console, and can roughly be defined as a logical grouping of targets that support a specific function. The System is the physical representation of that group of targets. Its main purpose is to provide a global overview of all the machines involved, and to allow administrative tasks to be run on the complete system in a simple way. Administrators can customize the way this rollup is represented, by identifying some key metrics to identify performance and usage of the system. This information is then also shown in the system dashboard, to give administrators and management a one-page rollup of the state of all targets in this System.

The function could further be defined in your ecosystem more specifically as a Service. A specific System might support multiple Services (although a Service will only be supported by a single System).

Think of it this way: You are running your e-commerce web site in your ecosystem. For that function to be served, you need an application server and a database. These reside on physical boxes. There you have four independent targets in Grid Control to be managed. So they can be grouped together as a System, named "E-commerce."

Now, you planned ahead, in this theoretical instance, and you have plenty of resource availability on these two physical boxes. So when it comes time to deploy your human resources application, you utilize the same servers, including the same application server and database. So you have the same System, but you will use it for another function. Dang, why'd we name it "E-commerce?" So we tear it down, and rebuild it as a more generic System, perhaps "InfrastructureWest." This is depicted in Figure 13-1.

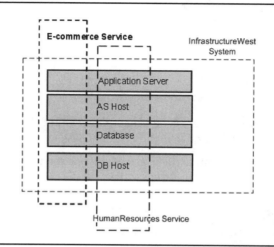

FIGURE 13-1. *Using the same system for multiple services*

Then, you create two Services: E-commerce and HumanResources, which utilize the same system, InfrastructureWest. Now you are cooking with butter, and starting to deploy the principles behind the Grid Control architecture.

When all the necessary targets for this system are put together, dependencies can be defined between the various components. These dependencies serve a dual purpose: They help visualize the flow of the system components, but the RCA engine also uses those dependencies to determine the state and condition of the system.

Building a System

Now it is time to start tinkering with Systems themselves, and building them to match the needs of your ecosystem. But first, a quick note on studying how systems are used. As you may have noticed, Grid Control comes to you with a System already built for you that you can use to review the "out-of-box" principles of System building. That System is the Enterprise Manager system, and represents the targets required to bring you the EM Grid Control functionality itself. It is worth a quick look to see how Oracle organizes these things.

When you get to the Systems page of the Targets tab, you will see the EM Website System, and above that, the now-ubiquitous Add line. If you choose the drop-down, you will see that Oracle provides default types of systems. The specific options for systems have to do with specific technologies that Oracle offers for access and identity management, and won't be covered here. For the sake of this exercise, we will create a generic System.

It is worth noting at this point that you will get better results with some of the elements discussed in this chapter when you are accessing the console from Internet Explorer instead of another browser, such as Firefox.

GRID CONTROL WORKSHOP

Creating a System in Grid Control

Workshop Notes

This workshop will create a generic system with multiple targets required to sustain a web application designed for running an ecommerce website.

Step 1. Go to the Systems page of the Targets tab in Grid Control. From the Add menu, ensure that the drop-down option box has System displayed, and click Go.

Step 2. Name the System **InfrastructureDenver1**, and then click the Add button that is just below the Components menu, as shown in the following illustration.

Step 3. A pop-up window appears that provides you with a list of all targets, including a search box, as shown in the following illustration. Select the target items that make up this system by clicking the radio button next to the target. When you have finished selecting all of the items, use the Select link at the top to go back to EM Console.

After you click Select, you are returned to the Create System page, with your targets showing. You can add more targets, or remove any mistakes at this stage.

(continued)

Step 4. Click the Topology tab. (This is a good opportunity to download and install the Adobe SVG Viewer plug-in if you haven't already.) Utilize the instructions provided to create associations, as shown in the following illustration. SHIFT-click Listeners and Databases and then right-click and choose Add Association, for example, to show an association between these two target types.

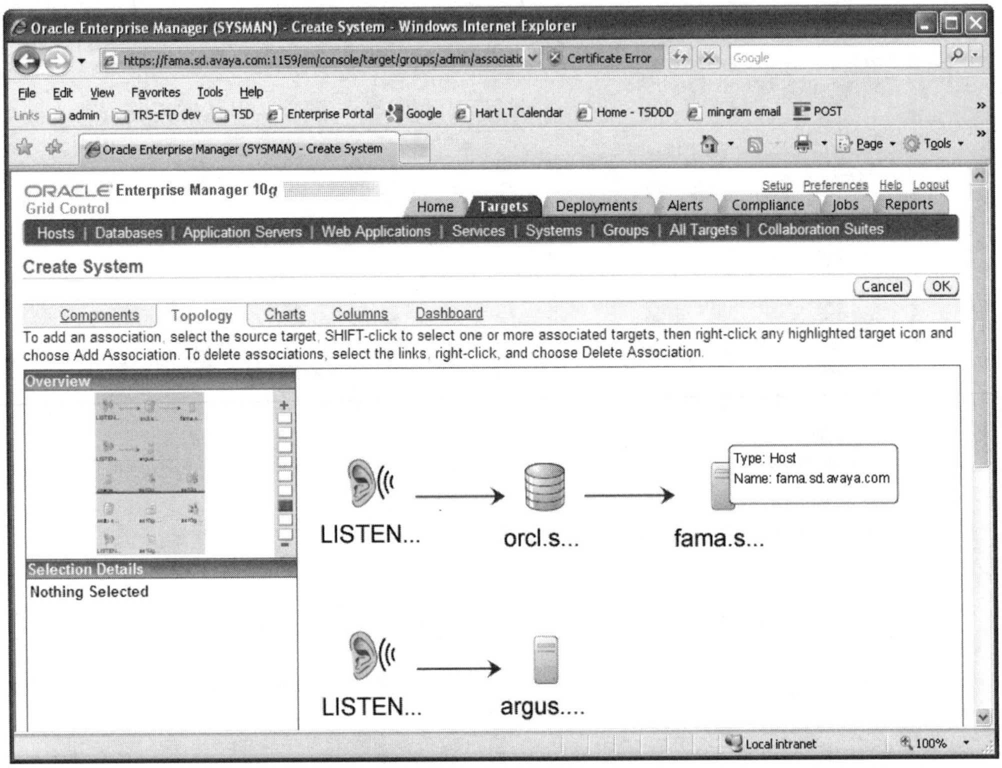

Step 5. Choose the charts you want to see by default when you visit the System's Charts page. Defaults are provided, and you can also choose the Add button to select other available charts.

Step 6. Review the columns that will appear in the Systems Components page. These can be modified if they are not to your satisfaction; here, we take the defaults.

Step 7. Finalize your dashboard options, including refresh frequency, and how to organize the targets on the page when you review the dashboard, as shown in the following illustration. When you are done here, click the OK button to finalize the creation of the new System.

(continued)

Step 8. Review the system from the Systems tab to ensure that it meets your needs. You can use the Configure or Remove buttons here to fix or delete the new System, or click the link named System itself to review your results, as shown in the following illustration.

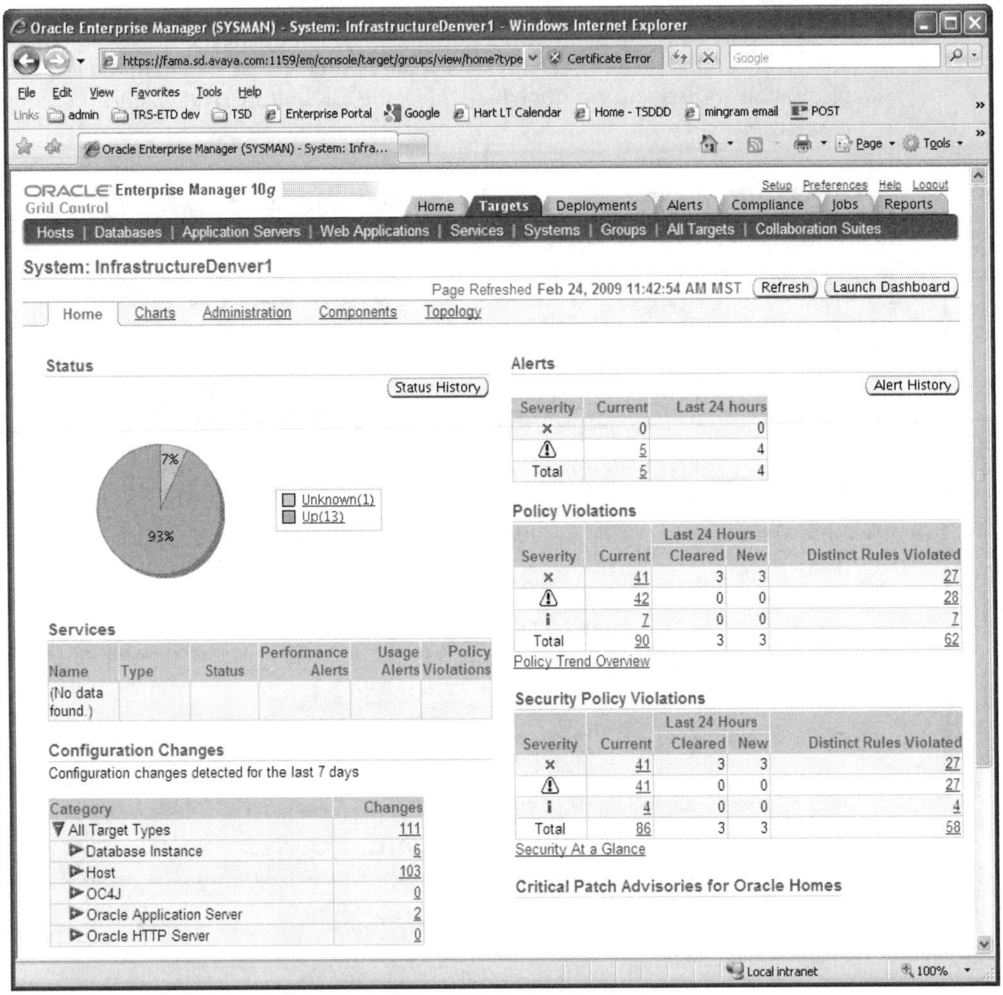

Best Practices for Using Systems

Use Systems for functionally grouped pieces of the infrastructure, not for logical groups for organizational purposes—that's what Groups are for. Stay disciplined.

Which came first, the system or the service? It's a chicken-or-egg question. You will be modifying both to ensure that you have them correctly organized. Typically, you should be function-driven, but system-minded: Understanding the reusability of systems allows you to better take advantage of existing capabilities, resources, and monitored pages.

Services

Services are closely linked to Systems in Grid Control. In fact, to define a Service, you must first create its corresponding System. So why do you need a Service, if you already have the System? The Service represents a logical understanding of how a function is being delivered into the business. To go any further requires us to brush up on our Service-Oriented Architecture (SOA) nomenclature.

Now, we're not going to get down and dirty in the semantic battles over what constitutes a "real" SOA environment. But the overall philosophy is critical to understanding how to use Services in Grid Control. And that philosophy holds that a Service is always an *end-user–defined function* that is delivered to the business via technology. It is critical to bring attention to the fact that the function is defined by the end user. In other words, a Service in this sense is never "the database storage function" or the "load balancing function." Instead, the Service is likely to be "the e-commerce web site."

As such, a Service is also most likely to be a vertical slice across multiple horizontal technology components. This is shown in Figure 13-2. In this example, you see the challenge of the modern technologist to keep functions being delivered to the satisfaction of an end user who doesn't care about the complexity, and just wants the function to be delivered as a utility. From this comes the term "utility computing," which is often synonymous with "grid computing," and has led us to the capabilities of "cloud computing" (a topic for a different book!).

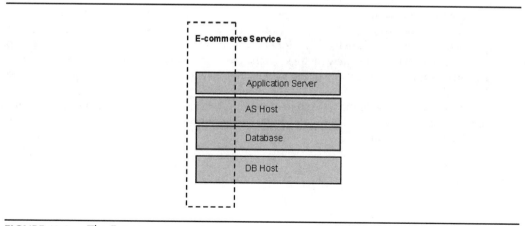

FIGURE 13-2. *The E-commerce service rests on multiple technologies.*

What does this mean for Grid Control's Services? A Service is defined as the overall function provided by the technology components, and it requires a System that represents the group of horizontal technologies, as depicted in the section on Systems in Figure 13-1. Multiple Services may use the same System, or components of one System may be in another System. But defining and monitoring Services will bring you one step closer to understanding the overall ecosystem in terms the end users understand.

Think about it this way: Let's say you are responsible for maintaining the data center systems that deliver CRM functionality to your company. That function requires a database, multiple application servers, host systems, and so on. In a traditional world, when a user calls you to complain that CRM is down, how do you go about trying to figure out which technology component is at fault? Do you always start with the database? With the application servers? Host disk space? It is essentially a hunt group: Start with one, then move to the next, until you find the culprit. But if you define CRM as a Service in Grid Control, you have a vertical view of all components that deliver that Service, and you can quickly see the status of all the components and begin a rapid triage response.

Before we move to the topic of building and using Services, we should make another point on Services in Grid Control: Services are the mechanism by which Application Service Level Monitoring and End User Performance Monitoring are configured. We won't be diving into that topic here, but rather circling back around to Application Monitoring in Chapter 17.

Web Application

A web application is a special kind of *service*. It behaves the same way as a service (meaning it should be based on a system), and has the same capabilities for defining aggregate metrics and defining availability. The only difference is that this type of service is monitored via web transactions. A special Grid Control target (called a *beacon*) executes these transactions to monitor the web application.

Building a Service

Although it is possible to specify targets directly for the service definition, it is advisable to first define a system, and use the system definition as the basis for the service. If a system is used, the dependencies defined at the system level of the various components can help narrow down alerts and notifications for the application.

A service can also define some key metrics to identify load and performance of the application. These metrics can be aggregated from any of the components, and will be evaluated based on the specified schedule directly in the repository, based on the metric data the components have reported.

Since we have defined *new* metrics, all the functionality of the metrics framework is now available, from setting the value of thresholds, to receiving alerts based on violations of those thresholds.

On top of these performance and load metrics, Service Levels can be defined. These SLAs are also evaluated at regular intervals, and alerts will be triggered if any of the service levels have violated their threshold.

GRID CONTROL WORKSHOP

Creating a Generic Service

Workshop Notes

Here we create a generic service that will have its availability based on its System's key component's uptime. We will not create this as an aggregate Service.

Step 1. Go to the Services page of the Targets tab, and review the EM Web Service for its key components and make-up. Then, choose Create a Generic Service from the list. This will take you to the Create Service Wizard, Step 1 of 7. Name the Service, and provide a time zone. We will use the System Time Zone for this example.

Step 2. Select the System that will host this service. We will use the InfrastructureDenver1 system, as shown in the following illustration. Once you have added the system, you will need to select those components (targets) that are key to this service, and therefore monitored for uptime. Be sure to look at the selection process: Only ten targets show up at a time!

(continued)

Step 3. Choose the type of availability you want monitored for this Service. This can be based on a Service Test using a beacon (more in Chapter 15), or using the uptime of key System components. For this example, we define availability based on System from the drop-down. Once you have made the choice, you must indicate whether all components must be up, or just one component. Choose All Key Components Are Up.

Step 4. Create performance metrics for the Service. For the sake of simplicity, we will only be configuring a single metric here for performance monitoring of the Service: Filesystem Space Available (%).

First, on the line that states Add "Based on System," click Go.

Then, change Target Type on the next screen to Host, and the Metric to Filesystem Space Available (%).

For the system components that match the target type, there are two ways to monitor: set up a metric per host, or aggregate for all hosts. For file space metrics, it is difficult to get a good metric that doesn't impair you from knowing an interesting event per host, but we will use an Aggregate Function of Average for all three hosts in our configuration, as shown in the following illustration.

Be sure to search for the object to be monitored, here we use the /u01 file system.

Click Continue. Note: You cannot repeat this for multiple hosts in the system that you are concerned with—there can be only one metric of a given Metric Name per Service. You will also need to set Warning and Critical thresholds. Here, because we are dealing with a percentage, we answer in terms of percent full, and we actually set a lower threshold than on a single system, because this is an average of three: Warning Threshold 75, Critical Threshold 85.

(continued)

Step 5. Click Next. We will skip Usage Metrics for this exercise. Click Next. This should take you to a Review step so that you can take a look at your progress and go back and make any changes that you require. If you are satisfied, click Finish.

Congratulations! You have created a Service that will show you the availability of an ecommerce application that includes the OC4J container, the Application Server, the Listener, the Database, and the Hosts for all of the components as shown in the following illustration. The availability here is (sheepishly) defined by available hard drive space, but you see the point, hopefully. You can go in and add any number of other availability metrics now that the Service has been created.

Best Practices for Using Services

Utilize services to give you a rapid response and fault diagnosis methodology for availability and performance issues that arise from your ecosystem. There are mechanisms to ensure that you have your horizontal technology slices taken care of, and that's important too—if you have a strong database practice in your business, you should utilize that to keep your databases up and running. But Services allow you to approach the overall technology stack holistically, and you should try it out. It's a game changer.

We've spoken here mostly about Services in terms of business functions, but we understand and want to note that sometimes the business function is delivering technology functionality itself to a consumer of your goods. If you are in the business of supplying technology environments to developers, for instance, it could very well be that your service is simply that—the technology environment. It's still useful to configure the Service so that you can put metrics around the vertical slice.

You're not done with utilizing Services until you've accurately set up required metrics of interest for it (such as the Filesystem Space Available example earlier). Setting up services is taking you beyond the out-of-box experience, and it requires you to tighten up your expectations. Know what you want to measure, and know what you want to see raise an alert!

You're *really* not done with Services until you create a Notification Rule for the Service that allows you to go from getting an alarm raised to getting that alarm dumped in your inbox so you know to react. Without closing that loop, you're simply not leveraging the Service for what it's for. We'll go into notifications and metrics in more detail in the next chapter.

Groups

Unlike Systems and Services, a Group does not have a predefined set of characteristics or audiences. Building a group allows you to define your own subset of any number of targets within Grid Control to meet your own needs. This could be a set of targets of all the databases, for a particular DBA function within your business. Or it could be all hosts, for system administrators. This kind of horizontal slicing is common, but it is not the only way to use groups. It could be regionally or geographically oriented, based on accountability to a certain organization for monitoring and keeping those items up and operational. A group can also be a temporary grouping built to enable a certain team to monitor a specific aspect of the ecosystem, such as the impact of an application upgrade, or the change in workforce hours to overall throughput.

Another critical use, and the one that doubles as best practice, is to use groups in association with users and roles to protect authorization to specific systems, services, and targets. By building a specific group with allowed targets, you can then utilize role-based access to ensure that no EM user has access to target elements they don't need to know about.

Groups can contain other groups, making it possible to build a hierarchy of targets, modeling the use and distribution of all machines in the enterprise. The Agents will not be aware of any of the groups, or know which targets are in what groups. Group definitions are only kept in the repository.

BEST PRACTICE
Although there is no restriction on the number of targets that can be put in a group, there is still the usability factor for the Administrators in the Console. If a group contains more than a thousand targets, navigating though all those targets in the group will be a challenge. If there are cases where a large number of targets are needed in a logical group, like groups for an LOB, or physical data center locations, the overall group can contain smaller groups, building a hierarchy of groups and targets.

Redundancy Groups

This is a special type of group: If a set of targets, all of the same type, are providing the same service, or providing the same functionality, they can be put in a Redundancy Group. This group behaves like a normal group, except that it has an availability state, which is calculated as follows:

- As long as one member of the group is up and running, the status of the redundancy group is considered up.
- If all members are down, the group will also be marked as down.

For certain types of targets, the concept of a Redundancy Group is already present in Grid Control in another way:

- RAC databases, and database instances. A RAC database is in fact a specialized redundancy group of the database instances of that database.
- For Apache HTTP Servers, and OC4J applications, there is already the HA Group functionality available at the Application Server level, which provides the same functionality as the Redundancy Group.

Building a Group

The first step in building the group is to decide on your grouping criteria. Common grouping criteria include:

- Geographic or regional cohesiveness
- Business unit
- Responsible administrators
- Security and access control
- Target type (database, application server, physical hosts, and so on)

When you determine which group types you need, then you are ready to get into the UI and get the group built.

GRID CONTROL WORKSHOP

Creating a Group

Workshop Notes

In this workshop, we will create a target type group of multiple physical hosts in the environment, and then go into User and Role Preferences to ensure that user agupta will only have access to the databases when he logs in to Enterprise Manager.

Step 1. From the Targets tab, click Groups. Unless you've already been experimenting here, there should be no default groups. Click the Add button. This takes you to the Create Group page.

Step 2.   Name the group **Denver Servers**, and click the Add button under the Members heading. This provides a pop-up for searching for targets (which should be familiar from the Create System Workshop earlier in this chapter). Use the Search function to limit your search to the Target Type of Host. Choose the hosts for this group, and then click Select.

Step 3.   Specify a time zone that will identify this group. By default, you are on the Members tab of this page. Notice that you can also modify the Charts, Columns, and Dashboard available for this group, just as you can with Systems and Services. This is where you can further customize how you understand the details of these systems. However, in our case, we are setting up a group for our System Administrator, and will be delegating the details to him. For now, we leave the defaults, as shown in the following illustration, and click OK.

Congratulations, you have created a Group. While that is all there is to it, for our example, we're not done yet. Now we need to ensure that user agupta only has access to this group, instead of wider access to other targets within Grid Control.

Step 4.   Click Setup in the upper-right corner of Grid Control. Then, click Roles. Create a new Role called **DenSysAdmin**. Skip the Roles and System Privileges pages and stop at Targets, as shown in the following illustration. From the drop-drown at

(continued)

Available Targets, choose Type of Group. Select the Denver Servers(Group) from the list and click the Move button in the middle of the page. Then click Next.

Step 5. You need to assign target privileges on Denver Servers to the Role. Over to the right from Denver Servers under Privilege, change the drop-down from View to Full. Then click Next.

Step 6. Now you can select the administrator. We've already created user agupta, so we can move him to Selected Administrators and click Next. (If you haven't created any non-default administrators yet, don't worry; just click Next anyway. You can add this Role to the user as part of the Create Administrator steps.)

Step 7. Review your options, and then click Finish. Now you have created the Role, and assigned it to the administrator.

Step 8. To confirm the desired results, log out and log back in to EM as the user (agupta in this case). When you log in, you will notice that agupta's home page is identical to the group page for Denver Servers, as shown in the following illustration. We've restricted Anil Gupta to viewing just the five hosts that are his responsibility.

Best Practices for Using Groups

Groups are a powerful tool in your tool belt, when it comes to taming the wilds of two kinds of sprawl: data center sprawl and administrator privs sprawl. So here are your words to live by when it comes to using Groups in Grid Control:

Always use Groups in conjunction with Roles to ensure that you have a grasp on user access. As with root on your servers, stop logging in to EM as SYSMAN. Create your own administrator, and then administrators for all other users. Then, assign the group to a role so you always have a straightforward way to manage access.

Delegate the specifics of the Group administration to an administrator who is primarily responsible for that Group's care and feeding. Don't get caught up in doing other people's dirty work in EM. If Anil Gupta is responsible for the Denver servers, then he's also responsible for configuring the metrics, charts, and dashboard that are of interest to him. (Note: This is not always possible to delegate. If you are the EM guru, you will suffer from that aspect of human nature that resists delegation when it comes to menial tasks. We can help little with that, other than to say, try, always try.)

Other than Super Administrators, everyone should be seeing only a group when they log in to Grid Control. This is simply good organizational practice to save you from mistaken access to new targets that come online, or unnecessary information deluge to the wrong users.

Don't get too creative with your Grouping types. Best move is to pick a few simple ways to cut the pie and leave it at that. And to make things simpler to understand, use the Group Description tag to always describe what type of group it is: geographic, functional accountability, business unit, and so on.

Defining the EM System and Service

Since Grid Control itself is an *application*, providing the service of *enterprise management*, we can use these features to model the management infrastructure. This provides us with a straightforward, and essential, practice exercise for using aggregate target types: defining the EM System and Service.

In order to model the entire infrastructure, we need the following targets to be present:

- All OMS servers must be discovered in Grid Control.

- If available, discover the additional network devices, like load balancers, proxy servers, and firewalls used in the Grid Control rollout.

- Discover the repository database (or RAC with all the instances), including any data guard instance that might be used.

Once all the infrastructure pieces are present in the console, we can create the system and the service:

- First create the system, to represent the physical targets.

- Then define the service, using the system as a reference for all the components.

Setting Up the Grid Control System

Defining a Grid Control system will not only help with the management and administration of the infrastructure; it will also highlight the benefits and the ease of use of monitoring an application from a single entry point. By setting this up for the infrastructure itself, all Enterprise Administrators can leverage that knowledge and expertise to start managing the specific systems and applications, for which they are responsible.

GRID CONTROL WORKSHOP

Creating a Grid Control System

Workshop Notes

In this workshop, we will utilize the Grid Control infrastructure that was built in the first part of this book to build a comprehensive EM System for Grid Control.

- Log in to Grid Control as SYSMAN or a super user.

- On the Targets tab, select the Systems subtab.

- On the drop-down list, select System, and click Go.

■ On the first tab of the Create System page, all the infrastructure information can be added:

■ **Name of the system** This is a free-text field, so you can enter any name. For simplicity's sake, we can just call it Grid Control.

■ **Time Zone** Every system needs to have a time zone defined. This time zone will be used to display and compare the data for all the member targets.

As a best practice, use the time zone of the repository database for the system.

■ **Components** These are all the targets that will be part of the system. From the target selection list box, select the following targets:

■ The repository database, the associated listener, and the host the database is running on.

In the case of RAC, select all database instances, all hosts, and all listeners of the cluster database.

■ For every OMS, select the host the OMS is running on, the OC4J_EM OC4J_EMPROV applications, the HTTP Server, and the Application Server itself.

■ The OMS and Repository Target, which is typically installed and configured on the first OMS machine.

■ To define a new system, this is all it takes. After you click the OK button, the system will be available in Grid Control, and ready to be used, as shown in the following illustration.

Using the EM System

With the system defined, it is now visible in the console as a first-class target. Systems have a specific home page, designed to give rollup information about all the components (members) that are part of the system, as illustrated in Figure 13-3.

With the new target now available in the Console, go to the Grid Control systems home page, to get an overview of all the information:

■ **Charts tab** This tab gives a series of graphs and charts of all the key statistics of this service, to get an idea of the operational availability and the performance of the system.

The main thing is to *not* have too many graphs defined on this page: An overload of information will not only be very difficult to assimilate, but it will also take a long amount of time to generate once significant history about all the metrics becomes available in the repository.

Depending on the complexity of the environment, the need for certain charts might be there. But for starters, you should only report on a couple of key things that are absolutely critical to the infrastructure.

The charts can be modified and updated by either using the Customize Charts button on the charts tab itself, or by editing the system and changing the charts settings there.

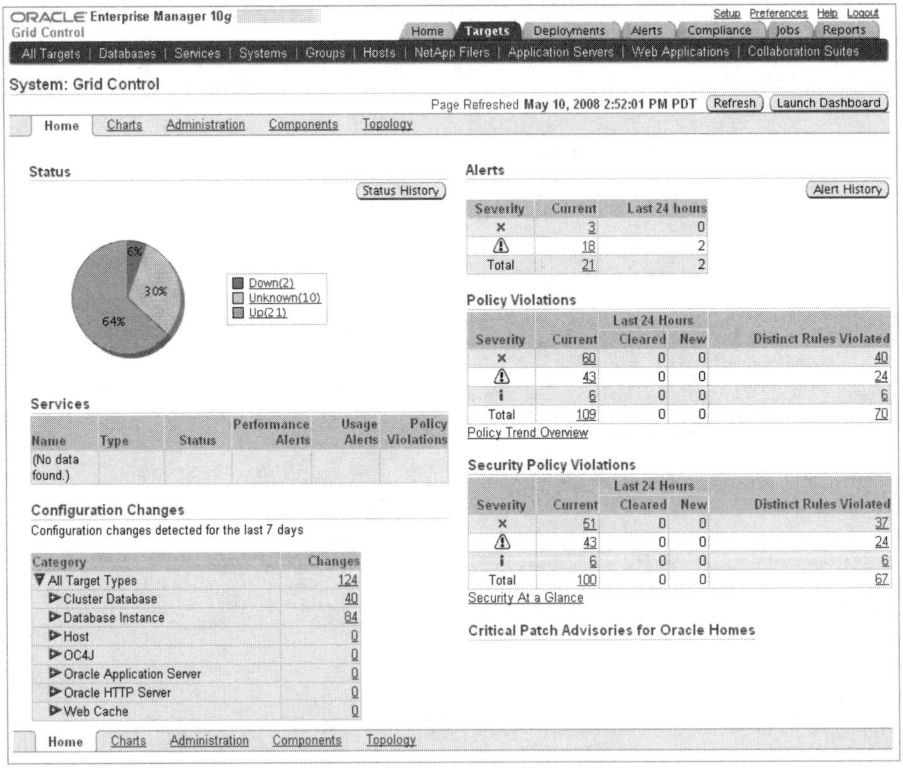

FIGURE 13-3. *The system home page*

■ **Administration tab**   Maintenance tasks and operations relevant to the entire system will be listed on this page. Operations like submitting new jobs, creating blackouts, and performing a search on the known configuration of the members can be launched from this page.

■ **Components tab**   Each time a change is made in the infrastructure of Grid Control (like adding an OMS, or changing a RAC instance), the components of the system will need to be modified as well.

Use the Edit System link from the Related Links section at the bottom of the page to add or remove members.

■ **Topology tab**   On this page the associations can be defined between the various components. These associations will be used to do Root Cause Analysis, and roll up failures to the appropriate levels when encountered.

The topology layout and the associations between the members of the system can only be changed when editing the system.

Customizing the Topology Map

Changes to the topology map can only be made when editing the system. On the topology page, the default layout will always be set to the automatic layout Grid Control provides. It is possible, however, to create your own custom layout, and organize all the targets manually.

Besides rearranging the layout, you can make associations between the various members. These associations can make it easier for people to understand the flow of operations between all the members. But it is also an essential piece that the RCA (Root Cause Analysis) engine will use to determine outages, and determine the extent of that outage in the system (and associated services if defined). Based on alerts and violations reported by Grid Control, the RCA engine will use the system definition, with the defined associations, to determine the impact of each alert, as shown in the following illustration.

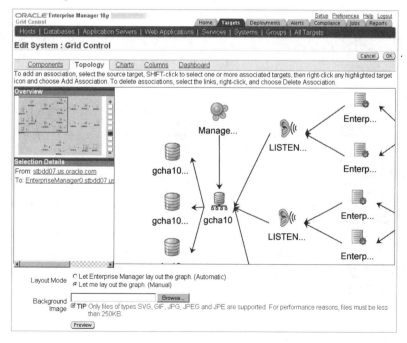

Modifying the Dashboard Settings

Dashboards are a kind of rollup report, designed to give an overview of the overall health and performance of a group of targets. The overall settings of the dashboard report, like the refresh rate, can be changed on the Dashboard tab, while editing the system.

- The refresh rate is set to 3 minutes by default. It controls what interval will be used to automatically refresh the page.

- For small systems, with a limited number of members, details about each individual member can be displayed on the dashboard directly. When there are too many targets as part of the system, the default view can be switched to Group by Target Type: All targets of the same type will be shown when the dashboard is launched, with the ability to drill down into a specific type of target to see the details.

- The final option to tweak is the ability to show the alert detail. For a system that is correctly set up, with the users and administrators all doing their work, and responding to the alerts in a timely manner, the list of open alerts should be small enough to make it possible to show the details in the dashboard by default.

As with the Charts page of the system, the columns used in the dashboard can also be changed: All the columns selected will be used to show the target details.

- If the dashboard view is set to Group by Target Type, the first page of the dashboard will only contain the availability status and the alert details. All specified columns are only used on target detail pages.

- Columns specific to a given type will only be used on the details page of that particular target type, as shown in the following illustration.

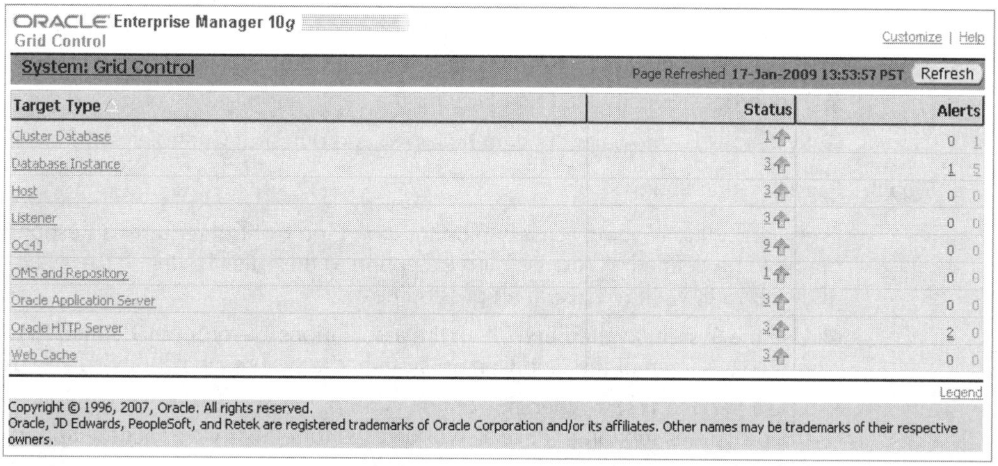

ORACLE Enterprise Manager 10*g*
Grid Control

Customize | Help

System: Grid Control

Page Refreshed **17-Jan-2009 13:53:57 PST** Refresh

Target Type △	Status	Alerts	
Cluster Database	1 ⬆	0	1
Database Instance	3 ⬆	1	5
Host	3 ⬆	0	0
Listener	3 ⬆	0	0
OC4J	2 ⬆	0	0
OMS and Repository	1 ⬆	0	0
Oracle Application Server	3 ⬆	0	0
Oracle HTTP Server	3 ⬆	2	0
Web Cache	3 ⬆	0	0

Legend

FIGURE 13-4. *System dashboard example*

After customizing all the settings for the system, the dashboard is ready to go. With the target grouping enabled, it will look something like Figure 13-4.

GRID CONTROL WORKSHOP

Setting Up the Grid Control Service

Workshop Notes

Now that the system is defined (which controls the physical definition of the targets), it's time to define the Grid Control application.

Step 1. To create any web-based application service, follow these links in the Console:

- From the Targets tab, select the Services subtab.
- Select Web Application from the Add drop-down list.

The creation process for a service is in the form of a discovery wizard that will guide the user through all the steps needed to add the application. In this wizard, there are seven pages in total to walk through to define all the settings for the service.

Step 2. Page 1 - General

The first page is just the main properties of the service, to correctly identify the service, and give it the right overall properties.

- **Name of the service**   To keep it consistent, just name this one Grid Control too.
- **Time zone**   Like a system, a service needs a time zone to be used as the point of reference.

(continued)

Since we have a Grid Control system defined, we can now use that definition, and the time zone of the system as our point of reference for the service: Keep the Use System Time Zone option selected for this.

- **Properties**   Specify the login URL for the application.
- **System**   Use the Select System button to add our Grid Control system.

Step 3.   Page 2 – Availability

Every target that is being actively monitored in Grid Control requires a Response metric to be defined. A service is no exception to this rule. To define the availability of the service, we have two main possibilities:

- **Use the System availability**   If all the associations are properly defined in the topology screen of the Grid Control system, the system availability *can* be used.
- **Use a Service Test**   When this option is used, the application URL (defined in the properties section of Page 1) will be used to regularly contact the application to make sure it is still responding.

For web applications (like Grid Control), it actually makes more sense to use the Service Test option to mimic the behavior of an end user and try to get to the login page of the application.

Step 4.   Page 3 – Service Test

This page is only available if the Service Test option was chosen on Page 2, to use the application login as the Response metric.

On this page, you can define the actions to take to determine if the web application is up and running.

- **Name of the service test**   This can be anything. To keep it simple, use something like EM login.
- **Collection frequency**   The default frequency set for an application test is always set to 5 minutes. Based on the criticality of the Grid Control application, the frequency of this test can be changed.
- **Transaction**   To keep it simple, we'll stick with the Basic URL. The value for this will be already filled in (the application URL specified on Page 1).

Step 5.   Page 4 – Beacons

The login URL needs to be played back from a specific point on the network. These network points should be representative locations in the enterprise from which users will be logging in to Grid Control.

For setting up the initial service, simply start with one of the OMS machines as the beacon to do the login. This can always be changed afterwards when the infrastructure has grown to include additional locations, or it can be changed to a more representative location in the network:

- Use the Create button to add a beacon.
- Search for an Agent on one of the OMS machines.

- Choose a representative name for that beacon (like OMS or something like that).

- Since we're working on the OMS machines, no proxy information should be needed to do the login. However, if other beacons are added later on, located in different areas in the network, proxy information might need to be filled in.

- Make the new beacon on the OMS machine the local beacon. The *local* beacon is the main beacon that is used to determine the state of the application. This should always be a beacon that is close to the application, and is not affected by the availability of network components while trying to connect to the application. With the newly created beacon defined on the OMS machines themselves, it is a textbook example of a local beacon.

In case Grid Control has been secured, and the access to the Console is via HTTPS, the EM certificate data will have to be added to the b64 certificate file of the Agent with the local beacon.

Step 6. Page 5 – Performance Metrics

On this page, the threshold definitions are specified for the availability test. These are the values the beacon will use to determine whether or not to trigger an alert on the response time of the login URL. The default of 6 seconds (warning) and 12 seconds (critical) are *starting point* values. They are conservative numbers for the typical web application. Based on the criticality and the size of the Grid Control environment, these values might need some tweaking.

Step 7. Page 6 – Usage Metrics

This is another way to customize and tweak the service definition. Usage metrics can calculate aggregate values for certain metrics across all components used in the service. This can be useful for defining metrics like

- The average Error Rate % of all the HTTP servers

- The total Active HTTP Connection of all the HTTP servers

Step 8. Page 7 – Review

This page gives an overview of all the settings. It's your last chance to review all the parameters specified on the previous pages before actually submitting the definition to the repository database.

If there are things that require a change in the definition, the Back button of the web browser can be used to go back to the appropriate page of the wizard to correct the values.

Once the Finish button is used, the settings will be confirmed, and the Grid Control service will be ready for action.

Note that if the OMS goes down, notifications by default cannot be sent for any metric violation or alarming event. There are two ways around this: having multiple OMS instances in your Grid Control environment (as described in Chapter 3), or by using Out-of-Band notifications as described in Chapter 4.

Additional Changes for the Grid Control Service

The various pages of the setup wizard for a service already give enough possibilities to monitor any kind of service right after creation. But as with everything else in a data center, an application will evolve and change, and changes will be needed down the line. Any system or service defined in Grid Control can be edited to add targets, change the beacon tests to check the application, and so on.

Adding Performance Metrics

With the definition of the Service, there will always be at least one performance metric (the one measuring the response time of the application). Additional performance metrics can be added to the Service definition based on the usage and specific requirements of the deployment. These performance metrics can be from any of the targets that are part of the service.

The two obvious ones to have as performance metrics for Grid Control are the Database CPU Time (%) of the repository and the Loader Throughput metric of the repository target, as shown in the following illustration. But other metrics can be added to reflect the performance of components like the HTTP Server, the OC4J application, or even the Server Load Balancer if the target is discovered in Grid Control.

Service Management

With the system and service both defined, and the overall performance and availability data being available, we can use this data now to define a Service Level. Based on the Performance metrics and thresholds defined during the creation of the service, an *expected service level* can be set. This expected service level is a percentage specifying how much time the application should be operating within the range of all specified thresholds: Any violation reported for the Performance metrics will be discounted against the service level.

Using the Beacon

The local beacon defined for the Grid Control application is just monitoring the application from one point in the network. (For a full discussion on what beacons are, and how to use them, jump ahead to Chapter 17.) As the Grid Control infrastructure grows, additional beacons can be added to the Service definition: This could be location-driven (like a beacon per data center that has Agents installed), or even per geographical regions (like one per continent). This beacon can also be used to perform other tasks:

■ Grid Control will periodically (typically every 24 hours) connect to My Oracle Support and retrieve the latest information on CPUs and other critical patches.

■ To make sure the OMS can reach that server to retrieve the information, a watch list entry can be added to the beacon to check the connectivity. Both of the watch list mechanisms the Beacon has can be used to validate the server `updates.oracle.com`.

■ If an SLB or a Proxy Server is used for web traffic, these devices can also be checked by a beacon with a watch list.

Summary

Systems, Services, and Groups share many characteristics, and have many of the same attributes that require attention both during creation and ongoing administration. However, all three are used in very different ways. Systems are a logical grouping of targets that provide a specific function, and are required to define a cohesive end-to-end technology stack before creating a Service. A Service is a more nuanced type of target that attempts to put a horizontal slice across multiple pieces of technology in the System. Services allow for user-defined metrics to be placed around availability and performance, and aid significantly in rapid troubleshooting during problems experienced by an end user. Groups are a more fluid version of a logical selection of targets, and can be used to serve different business purposes defined by the Grid Control administrator. Groups are extremely valuable in defining and controlling access and privileges to groups of targets that can be defined by the business.

CHAPTER
14

Database Management
in Grid Control

nterprise Manager Grid Control is a comprehensive monitoring, managing, and administration suite built to provide complete coverage of a data center ecosystem. The patterns have been normalized, and assumptions made that GC will be a single source of truth in the environment in which it resides.

Or, you can use it to manage your databases. It is very good at this, too.

The last time we did an informal hand-raising test of people who were utilizing Grid Control, they were still primarily using it for database activities. Managing the middle tier and applications, they assure us, will be next. But first and foremost, it needs to do some table stakes activities for my database ecosystem. Maybe, just maybe, after that we'll talk ecosystem.

We don't know if you are in this boat, and we've written plenty of pages here ensuring that you can use all of Grid Control's functionality. But this chapter concentrates on managing your databases. In the next two chapters, we will go into RAC and cluster management, and then Data Guard (standby) management as well. But first, to the database we go.

Enterprise Manager Database Control

Before we go any further, it is critical to explain the difference between two items in your ecosystem that look very similar, but act very differently. Here, we are talking about Enterprise Manager Grid Control (what this book is about) and Enterprise Manager Database Control (emdbc, or sometimes emdb console).

DB Control: What's Different?

So what is different? For starters, the scope is different between Database Control and Grid Control, and we're not just talking here about the difference between monitoring a database and monitoring the database, host, middle-tier, OS, and so on. In fact, Database Control is limited not just to database management, but to the management of a single database. If you want to monitor more than one database from a single console, you must use Grid Control. It's that simple. DB Control gives you a subset of Grid Control functionality, limited to the single Oracle database that it came installed with.

Database Control Architecture

Architecturally, DB Control looks similar to Grid Control. It requires an GC repository, just as Grid Control does, but instead of externalizing this somewhere in your environment, the repository for DB Control resides within the database it is monitoring. A SYSMAN user is created, and this user houses the repository. There are a couple of immediate things to point out because of this:

- From 10g on, you will likely find a SYSMAN user in most databases built using an Oracle Database Configuration Assistant (DBCA).

- Because Grid Control requires the user SYSMAN, DB Control is incompatible with Grid Control in the same database—that is, you can't install Grid Control into a database that you may also want to monitor with DB Control.

As you remember, Grid Control deploys both an OMS application in an OC4J container, and then independently deploys the agent to all monitored systems. DB Control doesn't need to monitor anything outside of itself: The OMS and Agent are configured and deployed at the same time from the same database home, when you configure DB Control. This deployment also includes the HTTP server for the DB Control UI console that you log in to to access DB Control.

Don't be fooled, either, by the idea that you may have multiple databases running on a single server, and you should at least be able to utilize DB Control for all the databases in a single server. Not so. A separate DB Control application (including OMS, Agent, and HTTP server) will be running for each database on the server, and will employ a different HTTPS port that increments up with each additional DB Control that you deploy.

DB Control runs its software out of the *ORACLE_HOME* that also runs the database. For each database that runs DB Control, you will get an additional directory in your *ORACLE_HOME* with the naming convention of:

```
$ORACLE_HOME/host_sid/
```

> **NOTE**
> *If you run multiple DB Control instances for each of your databases on a single host, you will have a separate URL for each DB Control console you need to log in to. Furthermore, these URLs will not be readily differentiated by the human eye. For instance, the first DB Control URL may be* https://hobgoblin.acme.com:1153/ *em, which corresponds to the database named TEST. The second DB Control URL will be* https://hobgoblin.acme.com:1154/em, *corresponding to the database named PROD. To the naked eye, the only differentiation is the port number!*
> *To properly differentiate, be sure to bookmark your URLs, and then name them to correspond to the right database. (Better yet—use Grid Control!)*

Database Control: Installation and Configuration

From a software installation perspective, there is no work required on your part: DB Control software is installed by default along with any 10*g* or 11*g* database software installation. You would have to go out of your way to *not* install it.

As we mentioned briefly before, DB Control is configured by default for most databases that are created using DBCA (Database Configuration Assistant). As part of that wizard, you can choose to install or not install. When you create a new database, DBCA will also provide default configuration tasks, as seen in Figure 14-1. In addition, you can always engage DBCA to add DB Control to an existing database.

In addition to using DBCA, you can utilize a command-line tool called Enterprise Manager Configuration Assistant (emca) to perform DB Control config tasks. Emca is called from the command line, after setting the *ORACLE_HOME* and *ORACLE_SID* for the database you want to configure, and is used for:

- Building a new dbconsole where one did not exist:
  ```
  export ORACLE_SID=V102
  emca -config dbcontrol db -repos create
  ```
- Removing an existing dbconsole configuration:
  ```
  emca -deconfig dbcontrol db -repos drop
  ```

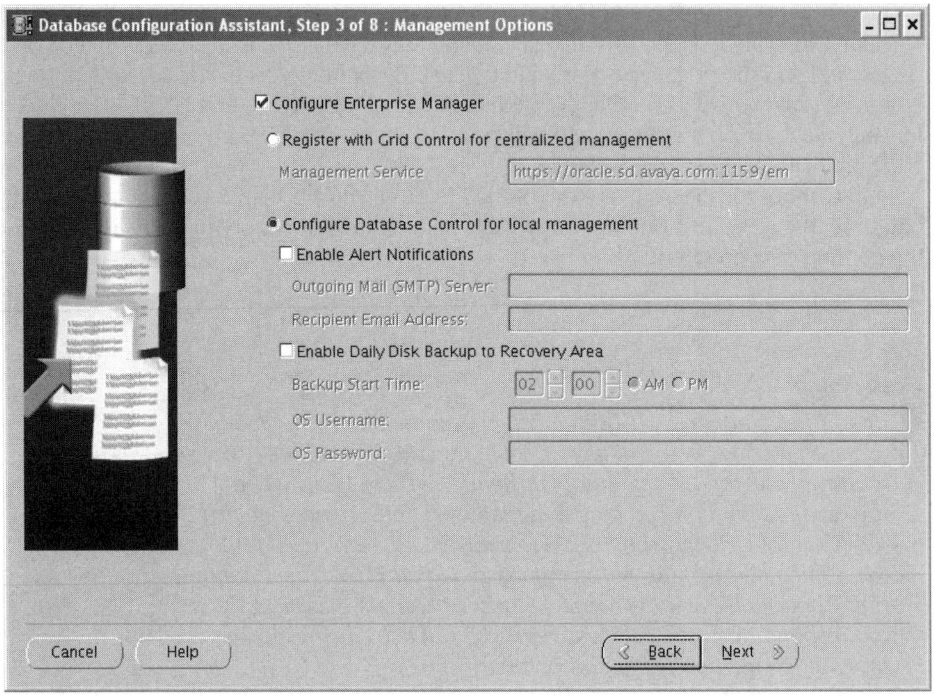

FIGURE 14-1. *Database Configuration Assistant (DBCA)*

- Configuring dbconsole for asm:

  ```
  emca -config dbcontrol asm
  ```
- Configuring dbconsole for RAC databases:

  ```
  emca -config dbcontrol db -repos create -cluster
  ```

Controlling Database Control

External control of DB Control utilizes the emctl utility, although it is not used in the same ways as the same-named utility in Grid Control. Emctl is called from the command line, and it stops, starts, and checks status on DB Control:

```
emctl start dbconsole
emctl stop dbconsole
emctl status dbconsole
```

On a Windows-based system, you can utilize emctl, but it makes more sense there to utilize the Windows Service OracleHomeNamedbconsoleSID, which can be stopped and started from the Services control panel.

Caution: Running DB Control and Grid Control on the Same System

Be very careful about running dbconsole for a database on a system where you also have a Grid Control agent running. The most common mistake comes from starting or stopping either the agent or DB Control using emctl.

EMCTL is a common name for the command-line tool used in both the *AGENT_HOME* and the *ORACLE_HOME* for the database; this can lead to confusion if you have your *$ORACLE_HOME* or *$PATH* variables set incorrectly. For example, let's assume you mean to shut down the grid control agent, so you issue the command:

```
emctl stop agent
```

This command completes successfully. However, because the *$ORACLE_HOME* is currently set for your database, this does not stop the Grid Control Agent; it shuts down the Agent inside the DB Control application!

Typically, the biggest problem comes from the opposite situation: You see in Grid Control that your Agent is down on a server, say hobgoblin.acme.com. So you go to this server and type

```
emctl start agent
Agent already started
```

That's confusing. But then you notice your *$PATH* points to your database *ORACLE_HOME*. No problem, you think, and you CD into the exact AGENT_HOME/bin directory, and run the emctl start agent command again, but you still see the "agent already started" message. This is when you realize that you're in the bash shell, which overrides current location with $PATH variables. A which command will reveal this:

```
which emctl
/u01/app/oracle/product/db_1/bin/emctl
```

The moral of the story is to always know where you are, and if you are seeing fishy emctl output, do a which command and see which version of this executable you are using.

DB Control Limitations

As you may be starting to suspect, there are significant restraints on DB Control that don't exist with Grid Control:

■ There is a "single source of failure" problem that you will encounter if you depend on DB Control. It runs its software from the same location as the database, meaning that software corruption has a larger impact.

■ DB Control utilizes the database it monitors for its repository; meaning that if you are in a recovery situation for the database, DB Control is also in a recovery situation.

■ The repository is generating records, so even an idle database will generate significant daily archivelogs, if you are running in archivelog mode, based purely on the DB Control's normal operations. This also means the tablespace housing the SYSMAN schema is taking up disk space as well.

■ You are exposed to HTTP server (and corresponding URL) sprawl if you utilize DB Control for multiple databases on the same server.

Configuring Databases in Grid Control

Now that we've put DB Control out of our minds for the moment, it's time to concentrate on setting up Grid Control to manage all of our databases. To manage databases, Grid Control must first know about the database. This means you need to have an Agent installed and running on the server where the database is housed, and that the database has been discovered by that agent.

Database Discovery

Database discovery can occur in a couple of different ways, depending on the order in which the Agent or the database exists. For systems on which the database already exists, and then the Grid Agent is installed, the Agent will run a discovery process to determine if there are any databases to be managed.

This auto-discovery requires the database to be located in the OraTab file (or the Windows Registry). There, it finds the SID and then it utilizes that to look for a listener that it can use to connect to that SID. The listener must have that SID registered, and currently be listening for it, for auto-discovery by the agent to succeed.

If the listener is down, or the OraTab file does not contain a particular database, you can rectify these situations and then manually run a discovery process from the Grid Control console. Whereas the auto-discovery process that runs at Agent install will ignore databases that it cannot connect to, the manually run discovery process will identify these databases, and then ask for connectivity remediation from the user.

To complete the discovery and database registration process, and for the ongoing monitoring of the database, Grid Control connects to the database as user dbsnmp. By default, Grid Control will not know the password for dbsnmp, so you will have to provide this. This shows up as a metric collection error in Grid Control. The user dbsnmp is a default database user in all databases that are created using the Database Configuration Assistant (DBCA), and the password is defaulted to the same as SYS and SYSTEM unless you specify otherwise in DBCA. Even if discovery fails, you can still manually add a database to the Agent, using the Agent home page.

Duplicate Database Targets

Many database environments do not have unique database naming controls in place (how many databases named ORCL do *you* have?). While this is not a deal-breaker, it does cause problems for Grid Control, which expects every database to be uniquely identified before it can manage them properly. This will show up as a duplicate target from the home page if db_unique_name is set to the same value for both databases. You will need to utilize the Listener Configuration Assistant to add a fully qualified name to the database in order for the host to differentiate databases with the same SID across the enterprise. If db_unique_name is not set, Grid Control should concatenate the hostname and SID to ensure uniqueness.

Preferred Credentials for Database Activities

As we mentioned previously, Grid Control will monitor your database utilizing the dbsnmp user. The agent uses dbsnmp to log in locally to get default database metrics for monitoring purposes. For example, the database home page, shown in Figure 14-2, contains data that is grabbed via dbsnmp: host CPU utilization, active sessions, SQL response time, and elements such as a space summary and high-availability information (and, of course, the handy green arrow showing you that the database is, in fact, up and running).

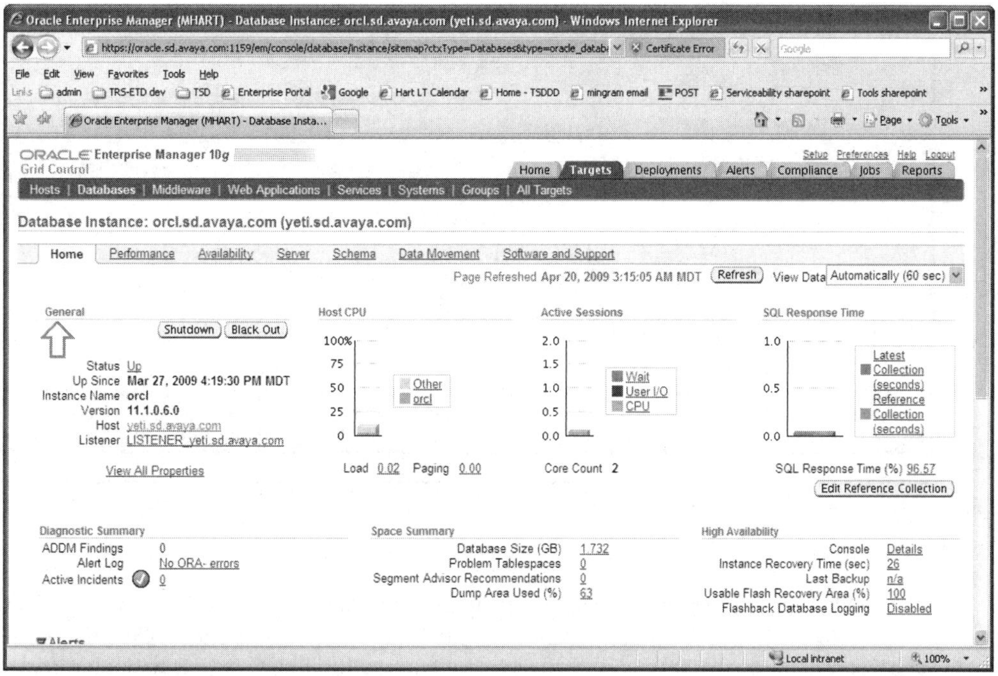

FIGURE 14-2. *Database home page*

However, move to any other tab, and you will be prompted for a username and password to log in to the database. For understanding performance, or availability, or schema information, you will need to pass your credentials to Grid Control so the OMS can proxy a connection directly into the database. When you first click a tab that requires such a connection, you will be prompted to provide credentials. When you do so, you can choose to log in as NORMAL, SYSOPER, or SYSDBA. This login will keep you logged in for the remainder of your Grid Control session, and allow you to view the database tabs and perform database operations, based on your level of privilege (NORMAL, SYSDBA, and so on).

If an operation requires SYSDBA privileges, that operation will be greyed out if you are logged in as NORMAL, so don't let it confuse you. If you want to perform such an operation, you will need to log out and log back in. This operation is not exactly intuitive, either. The Logout link is in the upper-right corner (or the lower-right corner)—the logout that takes you completely out of Grid Control. However, if you are also logged in to a database, this Logout link works double duty. After you click it, it will ask you what you want to log out of, as shown in Figure 14-3. Here, you can log out of just the database, with an option to display the login for that database again (should you be attempting to log in with a different set of privileges). You can also use the second radio button, and log out of all targets and Grid Control.

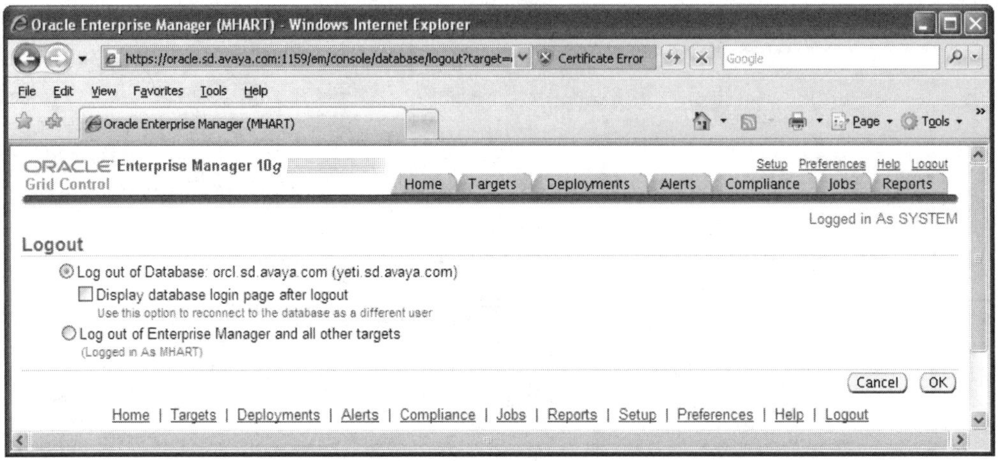

FIGURE 14-3. *Logging out of database*

You will also notice, when you are logging in to a database, that there is a small selection box below the login labeled "Save as Preferred Credential." The term "Preferred Credentials" refers to a set of Grid Control–managed credentials that are saved for all GC targets that a particular user has access to via Grid Control. If they are not set already, you can log in here as a user, click the Save as Preferred Credential box, and then these logins will be saved for you when you come to this database login screen. After this time, when you come back, the username and password will be prepopulated so that you will not have to provide them again.

Preferred Credentials are centrally managed for all targets from the Preferences link in the upper-right corner. Click on the left-side link Preferred Credentials. This shows you all target types, and how many targets have credentials set. For database credentials, you can go to the database instance target type, and click the icon for Set Credentials. This will reveal all databases and the corresponding credentials that have been set. There are three types of credentials to be set, in two different ways:

- Default Credentials are a set of credentials for Grid Control to always try, if there are not more explicit credentials set at the individual target level. In highly standardized environments, where administrators typically keep credentials normalized across an environment, these can be set to provide a first best attempt.

- Target Credentials are set for individual database targets and will always be used for that particular target database, and no other.

- NORMAL username and password are for typical database logins.

- SYSDBA credentials are for privileged database activities, such as startup and shutdown.

- Host credentials on this page refer to the user that should be utilized when Grid Control needs to operate at the host level to perform a database operation, such as database backup and recovery operations.

NOTE
Preferred Credentials are set per user. This means that every administrator that logs into GC has their own set of privileges to care for. From a security perspective, this once again means it is absolutely critical that you ensure all users, no matter their level of access, log in to Grid Control as themselves, and not as a shared user (such as SYSMAN). If you have a shared user in GC, and that shared user has set Preferred Credentials, then all the people who share the GC user also share the users set in GC: host credentials, middle-tier credentials, and database credentials.

Database Administration in Grid Control

As with all target types, Grid Control is most useful when it is utilized across the entire ecosystem and this is nowhere more true than with database management. However, before we get into multiple-database management, we want to start with the tools that GC makes available to the DBA from a per-database perspective. As you will see, there is plenty to be exposed to, as Oracle continues its endeavor of making GC a one-stop shop for all DBA activities.

Database Monitoring

There is a large amount of default database monitoring that occurs out of the box by Grid Control when an agent discovers the database. The agent immediately begins running its database-specific Perl scripts that execute SQL and PL/SQL against the database to collect metric facts. These metrics are returned to the OMS, which determines whether a threshold has been passed and whether an alert needs to be generated.

To understand the full portfolio of metrics that are collected for a database, you can simply start to poke around the All Metrics link from the Related Links at the bottom of any particular database target home page. Be sure to click the Expand All button so the nested metrics are all apparent. There are hundreds of data points that Grid Control is capable of collecting. There are the important ones, such as reporting data block corruption and deadlocks, to the obscure ones like Streams Apply – (%) Spilled Messages.

In many places in this book so far, we've set the Tablespace Space Used (%) metric to be used as an example of working with metrics (see Chapter 9). We won't belabor the point here, but setting appropriate thresholds for the metrics that are of a critical nature to the database will ensure success. We'll get to that later.

Database Administration

As we mentioned previously, all proactive administration of the database, or any activity that requires real-time access to database information, will require you to submit database credentials. For some jobs, you will also require host credentials. Once logged in, you can perform nearly all common database administration activities:

- Configuration management
- Performance monitoring
- Administration and maintenance

The Database Home Page

Orienting yourself to the home page is an important first step. It is from here that you get your shorthand for the database you are managing. In an environment where there can be dozens or hundreds of databases, it's important to have rollup information that can reorient you quickly to the particulars.

- **General** Status, name, version, and host: the basic necessities.
- **Host CPU, Active Sessions, SQL Response Time** This is the critical heartbeat monitor of the database, boiled down to three critical metrics.
- **Diagnostic Summary** Anything wrong? Automatic Database Diagnostic Monitoring (ADDM) or the Alert log will be displayed here.
- **Space Summary** Critical view of any space issues related to this database.
- **High Availability** Get a sense of your instance recovery time and your last backup here.
- **Alerts** Any warning or critical thresholds that have been passed will be displayed here for review.
- **Job Activity** All jobs in the past seven days will show their status here.

The Related Links Section of the Page

At the bottom of each Grid Control page, you find the Related Links section. This section for the database has crucial links to common database functions. As you may have already noticed, the related links are context-specific. Related links provide access to critical components of Grid Control that are not accessible directly anywhere else. When you are viewing a database target, the same 23 links will appear when you are using any of the tabs across the top of the page. Table 14-1 gives a brief description, which is useful for understanding the vast array of activities that GC can assist you with.

Another way to understand Related Links is as a consolidated, cross-reference view of all the different nooks and crannies within Grid Control where you can do useful stuff on behalf of your database, but may not know about if you didn't see it linked directly from the database home page. For instance, you can go directly to the Deployments tab at the top of GC, scroll down to the Patching section, and click Patching Through Deployment Procedures, and you will find the means for applying a patch to a database, halfway down the list, buried underneath the section for patching Linux. Or, you can go to the Related Links section of the database you are actually interested in, and click Apply Patch. Both of these routes take you to the same place in Grid Control.

A quick warning: some of these links go in a single direction—they take you to places in Grid Control that don't have a record of where you came from, so you may have to go up to Targets | Databases | Database Home Page to get back to where you started. I refer to these as "shortcut links," as you aren't left with a breadcrumb at the top of the page to take you back to your database home page.

After you have reviewed the general overview of the database provided on the home page, and oriented yourself to the options in the Related Links section that will be common across all tabs, it is time to dig deeper into the six remaining tabs that sit across the top of the Database Instance home page, and roughly group the DBA's activities for any given database: Performance, Availability, Server, Schema, Data Movement, and Software and Support. But first, there are a few fairly important tasks from the home page to look out for.

Related Link Name	Link function
Access	Assign Grid Control administrator access to this database target.
Advisor Central	Centralized location for accessing all database advisor utilities.
Alert History	Overview of all alerts for the target based on 24 hours, 7 days, or 31 days.
Alert Log Contents	Link to a page that provides a mechanism for retrieving text from the alert log.
All Metrics	Overview of all available metrics for the database target type. This is not the location to set thresholds or make changes to upload or collection intervals.
Apply Patch	Shortcut link to the Deployments tab of Grid Control for viewing the database patch procedure.
Archive/Purge Alert Log	Page to archive or purge the alert log.
Baseline Metric Thresholds	Begin the process of understanding this particular database's metric baselines from a trending perspective.
Blackouts	Shortcut Link to the Setup I Blackouts page, prefiltered for the database you are currently looking at.
Deployments	Shortcut link that takes Apply Patch one step further by landing you on the Deployments page for actually scheduling a software update.
Execute SQL	Pops up a new window for viewing all the SQL that GC is running on your behalf against this database.
GC SQL History	Run a SQL or PL/SQL command manually against this database.
Jobs	Shortcut Link to the Jobs Activity tab, prefiltered for the database you are looking at.
Metric And Policy Settings	Location for modifying the metric settings for the database (thresholds, corrective actions, and collection schedule; see Chapter 9 for more information).
Metric Collection Errors	View any errors that the agent is reporting based on an inability to gather any metrics for this database.
Monitoring Configuration	Change the dbsmp password or listener configuration settings for the agent to connect to this database.
Monitor in Memory Access Mode	Switch GC monitoring to direct SGA system-level calls instead of using SQL; useful for severe performance degradation troubleshooting.
Reports	Shortcut link to the Reports tab, pre-filtered to database reports for the database you are looking at.
Scheduler Central	Manage all jobs running against the database, by GC or by the database itself.
SQL Worksheet	Pop up a new window for utilizing a worksheet approach to multiple SQL command sessions with the database.
Target Properties	Manually added database properties used by an IT dept to keep additional details, such as the primary contact person or line of business.
Trace Files	Gather bdump and udump trace files for review, or purge existing ones.
User-Defined Metrics	Manage user-defined metrics (see Chapter 9).

TABLE 14-1. *Related Links for Databases*

Reviewing the Alert Log

For 10*g* and lower databases, you can extract ASCII text from the alert log and display it in the Grid Control console for troubleshooting problems. The interface enables you to specify a date range in which to contain your query. Simply clicking the Go button will attempt to pull the last 100,000 bytes of the file.

However, this works slightly differently for 11*g* databases, where Automatic Diagnostic Repository (ADR) is used. When ADR is in use, the alert log now comes with XML tags, and the diagnostic information can be viewed as separated records. In this situation, you can utilize the View Alert Log Contents link as a tail showing the most recent 50, 100, 500, 1000, or 2000 entries.

Starting Up and Shutting Down a DB

From the home page, on the left next to the big green arrow pointing up, there is a button for shutting down the database (next to the Blackout button; we'll get to this in a second). When you click Shutdown, you are then asked for Host Credentials and Database Credentials.

You must provide Host Credentials because a shutdown or startup command must be run as an OS job, and therefore it needs host credentials that have privileges to run such a database command. If you have set up Preferred Credentials for this database, they will be supplied here automatically. Note, of course, that SYSDBA or SYSOPER privileges are required for this activity. Once you click OK, the database will ask for one more confirmation, and then perform the operation. Note that Grid Control will confirm credentials at this stage, instead of waiting for the job to fail.

You may note that after the shutdown, the status still shows the database as up. There will be a lag in the OMS status and the actual database status, based on the timing of information uploaded from the agent. When it finally refreshes the current status, you will see the information, as shown in Figure 14-4.

Note that from the database home page, there are no other tabs available, just the home page. And you have two new buttons: Startup, and Perform Recovery. We will talk more about backup and recovery a bit later.

Setting a Database Blackout

There is one final activity to hit upon from the home page. As you have seen, right next to the Shutdown button on the home page is the Blackout button. This serves as a good reminder that if you are going to take the database down on purpose, you should inform Grid Control that there is a scheduled or purposeful outage coming, and set a blackout. This will inform the Agent on that system to suppress any metric failures for this particular target, and therefore any unnecessary nag-mail from the system.

The Blackout button is another shortcut link: it takes you to the Setup | Blackouts | Create page, and prepopulates the Add Targets section with the database you are linking from. It will allow you to schedule a start time (defaulted to immediate), and a duration.

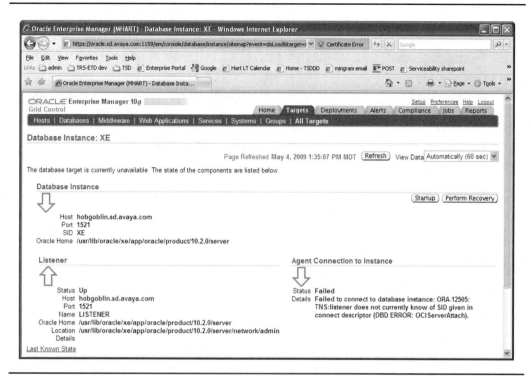

FIGURE 14-4. *Grid Control status after database shutdown*

Performance

So, enough with the home page. Let's turn our eyes to the first tab of useful stuff, the Performance page. The first thing you will note is that you must log in to the database to gain access to the performance page—this is because you need a JDBC connection to be established directly to the database. We won't be relying on the OMS repository for this information, but rather gathering it in real time from the database.

The second thing you'll notice is that you have some charts to interpret—loads and loads of data.

Performance, Tuning, and GC

So, let's separate out the performance monitoring component of your day from the part where you do anything about it. From a gathering perspective, there is no shortage of data that is being displayed for you in Grid Control. By default, you get a view of CPU utilization (as a percentage),

Average Active Sessions, and then tabbed graphs for throughput, IO, Parallel execution, and Services performance, as shown in the following illustration.

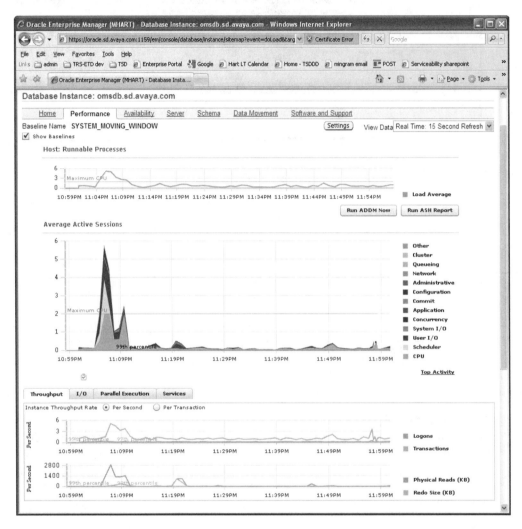

There is a button below the Average Active Sessions section for a view of Top Activity. Top Activity provides a chart to understand the activity makeup of the database minute by minute. This is essentially a real-time dashboard of current database activity by activity type. It allows you to then pick a particular 5-minute interval (by dragging the grey box) and pull up the top

SQL and top sessions for that period, which are then displayed below the graph, as shown in the following illustration.

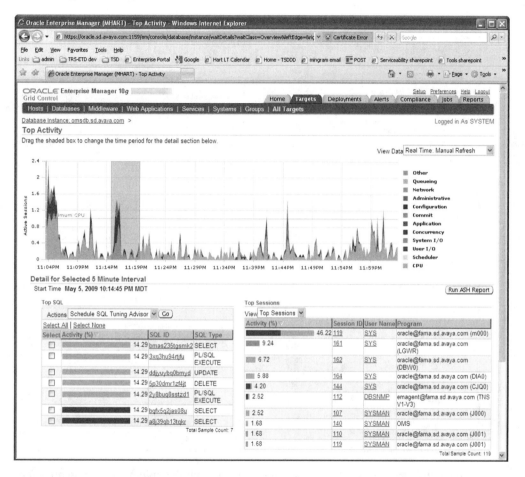

This allows you to drill down further into a particular piece of SQL. You can view the SQL statement by clicking on the SQL ID of the SQL statement. This takes you deeper down the rabbit hole, and provides not just the SQL text, but statistics, the explain plan, plan control, and tuning history elements for this particular statement, as shown in the following illustration.

This is just one very simplistic example of how to drill down into the performance data that is made available by Grid Control. It is beyond the scope of this book to provide you with the framework for accurately understanding all the details of the bottlenecks and opportunities in your database.

Additional Monitoring Links

You should now see that in addition to the default Related Links that will always be at the bottom of each database page, the Performance tab comes with an additional set of links, Additional Monitoring Links. These provide access to the tools and activities that will consume your time as you work to tune your database or diagnose a performance bottleneck. Table 14-2 breaks these links down for you.

Where Do Grid Control's Performance Functions Come From?

Remember how we told you that you needed to log in to the monitored database to get access to the performance data? There's an explanation for this behavior. Basically, it boils down to how much work Grid Control is actually putting into database performance monitoring. The answer is: very little.

The bulk of the performance monitoring and administrative work that you can access via Grid Control is not the native features of Grid Control, but rather a user interface layer on top of the base functionality that resides within the database itself. This goes for Database Control as well—which is why the UIs for Grid Control and Database Control are so close to identical.

This goes for data that is captured, but also for some of the tools and analyzers we will discuss later in this chapter. For instance, ADDM is an inherent functionality of the database, as is the Active Session History (ASH) report. You can access these performance monitoring tools from SQL*Plus, with a touch of PL/SQL help. Grid Control provides a GUI mechanism that sure beats doing the legwork manually.

Additional Monitoring Link Name	Link Function
Top Activity	Access point to understanding top SQL and sessions in real time (15-second refresh).
Top Consumers	Understanding database performance from a resource consumer point of view: top services, modules, clients, and actions.
Duplicate SQL	This tool helps identify candidates for SQL sharing through bind variable and SQL coding convention standardization.
Blocking Sessions	Diagnose blocking sessions for the database.
Hang Analysis	Provides a graphic view of any database hang conditions that are currently taking place, organization by session IDs (SID). Requires SYSDBA login.
Instance Locks	View all database locks, blocking or otherwise, and quickly kill the session or investigate the session details further.
Instance Activity	Real time, per-second view of cursors, transactions, session, and I/O metrics.
Search Sessions	Search for a particular session using common criteria such as SID, DB user, OS user, and so on.
Search SQL	Find a particular SQL statement via data source and filter conditions, then save that SQL to a Tuning Set.
Snapshots	Automatic Workload Repository (AWR) snapshots can be viewed, deleted, created, or compared from this shortcut link to the AWR page.
AWR Baselines	Shortcut link to the AWR page that allows you to manage AWR baselines.
SQL Tuning Sets	Create and manage SQL tuning sets that can be used for tuning operations.
SQL Performance Analyzer	Test and analyze the performance of SQL statements by running tuning experiments on possible SQL changes.
SQL Monitoring	Diagnostic tool that displays the status of any SQL code that has been executing for more than 5 seconds.

TABLE 14-2. *Additional Monitoring Links from the Performance Tab*

Automatic Database Diagnostic Monitoring (ADDM)

When you are pursuing a performance-related workstream, sometimes you know where to start, and you have a particular SQL statement or PL/SQL block that you want to get performance improvements from. However, identifying where to start looking for performance bottlenecks is the bulk of the battle—you have a haystack, and you need a needle. And finding the needle in the database haystack often means trying to determine where and when to begin collecting monitoring data.

Automatic Database Diagnostic Monitoring (ADDM) was introduced in Oracle Database 10g to help with this. ADDM is a tool that will look at the haystack of performance data and suggest where the needles are, or where they are most likely to be.

The data that ADDM looks at is housed in the Automatic Workload Repository or AWR for short. AWR is a data dictionary collection of performance information that takes active session information and builds a snapshot of data at specific intervals. The interval is once per hour by default, and AWR keeps this information for a week before it begins to remove the data. Both the retention period and the collection interval can be modified.

Once AWR has collected the data, you can run ADDM to give you suggestions on what you should do next, effectively shortening the investigation time for performance issues. Because ADDM is a suggestion-generating tool, it falls into the tool suite that Grid Control clumps together as Advisors in the Advisor Central section of the Database pages.

Active Session History (ASH)

Closely related to ADDM is ASH, or Active Session History. This is a report (not an Advisor) that allows you to pick two points in time between AWR runs to help you troubleshoot a smaller window of time than ADDM.

ASH provides a view of top events, top SQL, and so on within a smaller timeframe, that is, a timeframe in which the top event may have had a large impact, but that impact is squashed flat when averaged across an hour or a day. This provides a mechanism for understanding and diagnosing performance issues that were time dependent.

ASH reports can be run for any period of time within the retention period of the AWR snapshots. Grid Control does not do a whole lot of work here; it acts instead as simplifying mechanism for running an ASH report, and then reading the results.

The SQL Advisors

From the Related Links, you can select Advisor Central and then SQL Advisors to take you to the centralized location for evaluating, tuning, and fixing SQL within the database.

The first Advisor is the SQL Access Advisor. This tool enables you to verify that existing access structures such as indexes are being used correctly by the SQL that is meant to benefit from them. In addition, it can then recommend new access structures, such as indexes, materialized views and partitions, based on the SQL being run and the base tables it is accessing.

The SQL Tuning Advisor analyzes individual SQL statements and recommends actions for optimizing the statement for best possible performance. This analysis can be performed on demand, given a particular SQL statement, or you can take advantage of the results that the Oracle database collects automatically for the heavy-hitter SQL that has already been identified in the system.

Finally there is the SQL Repair Advisor, which is not kicked off from any one place, but rather is a piece of logic that runs in the background when you are in the Support Workbench or SQL Worksheet sections of Grid Control. When a SQL incident is reported to the Support Workbench, the SQL Repair Advisor will attempt to suggest a possible fix to a broken SQL Statement. Likewise, from within SQL Worksheet, the Repair Advisor will attempt to help out if a broken SQL statement is attempted.

Availability

From the Database Availability tab, you have access to all of Grid Control's tools and screens for managing the overall availability of the database, from backup and recovery to Data Guard configurations. We'll cover Data Guard later in Chapter 16, so we'll leave that alone here. Instead, we will focus on backup and recovery settings and utilization within Grid Control. But first, there are two links at the top of the page that should grab our attention.

High Availability Console

The HA Console provides a consolidated view of availability monitoring information, as shown in the following illustration. This includes overall uptime, backup/recovery summary, and Flash Recovery Area statistics. This information has some redundancy with the home page, but provides a more focused view of just the HA information.

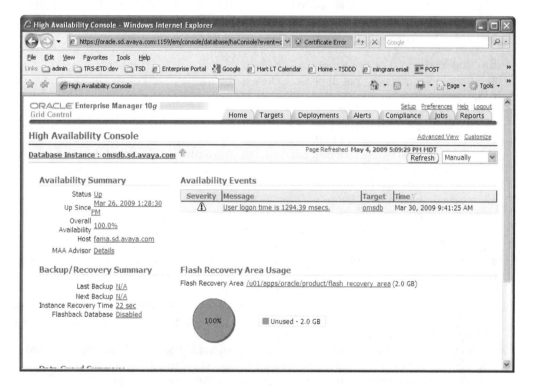

Maximum Availability Architecture Advisor

The MAA Advisor is really more of a checklist of all the things you need to configure and manage in order to comply with the Oracle-suggested availability architecture. This architecture is tested and confirmed to provide maximum uptime for a database and protect against all different categories of downtime: computer failures, human errors, storage failures, data corruption, and site failures.

The MAA page provides the checklist, and then shortcut links to the locations in Grid Control where you can make the configuration changes required to comply with each item. For instance, to configure archivelog mode, you can follow the link from the MAA advisor to the Recovery Settings page of the Availability tab, where you can click a radio button, reboot the database, and go into archivelog mode.

This is an extremely useful cheat sheet for availability, and we suggest going through each item and using this to guide your compliance for ultimate availability. Your database needs may not require five nines of availability (99.999 percent uptime), but at least you'll be able to quickly check which items you have done, and which ones remain options should your HA needs change. Note, of course, that some of these checklist items, such as Oracle Streams, can take significant configuration time, and may not be the best solution for your database, so proceed with caution.

Backup and Recovery

From the Availability tab, under the MAA Advisor link, the page is divided into two sections, Backup/Recovery and Data Guard. The Backup/Recovery section is further divided into Setup and Manage. Let's first look at the Backup Settings page.

Backup Settings

The Backup Settings page has three tabs: Device, Backup Set, and Policy. Let's look at the three pages separately.

Device Configuration From the Device tab, you will be able to set up both disk and tape settings. These settings are not there to set the default device, but rather individual settings for all channels on these devices. For disk backups, you set parallelism, backup location, and type of backup (backup set or image copy). This is also where you would turn compression on, if you want to use it. For tape backups, you tell GC how many tape devices will be employed, and the tape backup type (compressed or non-compressed). In addition, for tapes, you can provide any environment settings that are required for the tape backup software to operate.

Note that on the Device tab, at the bottom of the tab is a place for host credentials. These are required in order for GC to submit a job to make the desired changes on the target database. This same requirement will be placed at the bottom of each tab in the Configure Backup Settings page.

Backup Set Configuration After you have made device configuration decisions, the next tab, Backup Set, allows permanent configuration settings for how the backup sets will be generated. Remember, this only applies to those backups that use backup sets, instead of image copies (disk backups can be either; tape backups are always backup sets).

If you are using disk backups, there is only one thing to configure here: the maximum size of your backup pieces. If you will be backing up to tape, you can set up how many copies of each datafile backup set you will create on the tape devices, and the number of copies of each archivelog backup to create.

Policy Settings The Policy tab allows for configuration of those settings that relate to your own business backup policy. This includes turning on autobackups of the control file and spfile, and where the autobackups will be located (if disk backups are used). Multiple backup rules and configuration changes are made on this page, from backup optimization to block change tracking to tablespace exclusion rules. Finally, here is where you configure your retention policy, for both backups and archivelogs after you have backed them up.

GRID CONTROL WORKSHOP

Configure Backup Settings in Grid Control

Workshop Notes

In this workshop, we assume you have an Oracle 11g database and want to configure it to back up to a disk location other than the Flash Recovery Area (FRA) with two channels, that you want `filesperset` to be 2, and that you want a recovery window of seven days.

Step 1. Set up the disk backup settings. Click on the database you want to configure, and then click the Availability tab. Then click the link Backup Settings. The default page is the Device tab. Change Parallelism to **2**, and Disk backup location to **/u01/ backup**. Click the Test Disk Backup Button to the right to confirm that the location you have specified exists.

Step 2. Click the Backup Set tab. Change Backup Piece (File) Size to 500MB.

Step 3. Click the Policy tab. Click the box labeled Automatically Back Up the Control File and Server Parameter File. Set the Autobackup disk location to **u01/backup** (same location as the backups in step 1).

Step 4. Under the header Retention Policy, change the policy to Retain Backups That Are Necessary for a Recovery to Any Time Within the Specified Number of Days. Set the value to 7 days.

Step 5. From this last tab, set the host server username and password to the user that installed your database software. Then, click OK.

Step 6. Confirm that the changes have taken effect for this database. Connect to the host server where this database resides:

```
Export ORACLE_SID=ORCL
rman target /
RMAN> show all;
using target database control file instead of recovery catalog
RMAN configuration parameters are:
CONFIGURE RETENTION POLICY TO RECOVERY WINDOW OF 7 DAYS;
CONFIGURE CONTROLFILE AUTOBACKUP ON;
...
CONFIGURE CONTROLFILE AUTOBACKUP FORMAT FOR DEVICE TYPE DISK TO
'/u01/backup/%F';
...
CONFIGURE DEVICE TYPE DISK PARALLELISM 2 BACKUP TYPE TO BACKUPSET;
CONFIGURE CHANNEL DEVICE TYPE DISK FORMAT   '/u01/backup/%U'
MAXPIECESIZE 500 M;
...
CONFIGURE CHANNEL DEVICE TYPE 'SBT_TAPE' MAXPIECESIZE 500 M;
...
```

Configuring Recovery Settings

After you have configured the backup settings, Grid Control provides the page for configuring recovery settings. This page is linked from the main Availability tab of the database target. Configuring the recovery settings actually covers a wide scope of different options. GC further divides the recovery settings into three types of recovery: Instance Recovery, Media Recovery, and Flash Recovery.

Instance Recovery   There is only one setting that refers to instance recovery: FAST_START_ MTTR_TARGET. This is an initialization parameter that determines a target value, in seconds, that you are interested in hitting when instance recovery is initiated on the database. MTTR stands for Mean Time To Recovery, and is a common name for exactly how long it takes for a database to be operational again after it has crashed for some reason.

FAST_START_MTTR_TARGET is a combination of a number of changes that are made internally to facilitate the speedy recovery of your instance, and is also referred to as automatic checkpoint tuning. This parameter made log_checkpoint_timeout and log_checkpoint_interval obsolete. From GC you can specify this value in seconds. The valid range is 0–3600 seconds (60 minutes).

Media Recovery   This section is where you set up archivelog mode for the database. It shows up here as a simple radio button, but do not think that GC has changed the Oracle RDBMS: A reboot is still required before this will take effect. In fact GC will submit a job to the OS to perform the change.

In addition to enabling archivelog mode, you can specify your log_archive_dest parameters here. As you can see, the tenth slot is filled by default with USE_DB_RECOVERY_FILE_DEST, aka the Flash Recovery Area (FRA).

Flash Recovery   Under the heading Flash Recovery you can configure your Flash Recovery Area, providing both an FRA destination as well as size. More useful is an excellent pie graph displaying current used space in the FRA, broken down by file type—this is the same pie chart on the HA Console page.

In addition to configuring the FRA, here is where you can turn Flashback Database on. Flashback Database is a new functionality from 10*g* onward that can radically reduce point-in-time recovery by rewinding the database (literally). Like archivelog mode, turning on Flashback Database will require a database reboot; we suggest that you do them both at the same time to save yourself a bit of hassle. Along with turning Flashback Database on, you can set your flashback target value, in hours.

GRID CONTROL WORKSHOP

Configure Recovery Settings in Grid Control

Workshop Notes

This workshop will make changes that set a second archive destination in addition to the FRA, add more space to the FRA, and enable Flashback Database. This workshop assumes you are already in archivelog mode.

Step 1.   Log in to Grid Control as user SYS with role SYSDBA. If you are not logged in as SYS, the options on the Recovery Settings page will be greyed out.

(continued)

Step 2. Navigate to the Database | Availability | Recovery Settings page.

Step 3. Set a new archivelog destination to **/u01/backup**.

Step 4. Change Flash Recovery Area to **4GB**.

Step 5. Click the radio button to enable Flashback Database. Set the Flashback Retention Time to **24** hours.

Step 6. Click the Apply button. This will prompt you to shut down the database. Choose Yes. You will then need to provide host and database credentials for the shutdown.

Step 7. After the database is restarted, navigate back to Recovery Settings page to confirm the changes.

Database Backups from Grid Control

Now that you have configured your database for backups from the GC interface, you can get to the nitty-gritty of actually taking a backup. From the GC console, after you have selected your database and clicked the Availability tab, you will see a link labeled Schedule a Backup. From the Schedule Backup page, you are given two options: Select the Oracle-Suggested Backup, or Schedule a Customized Backup.

The Oracle-Suggested Backup

Starting with 10g, Oracle has put together a full backup strategy that is "ready to wear" straight from the rack. This is available only via Enterprise Manager (in both Grid Control and Database Control), and it requires the existence of the Flash Recovery Area. The suggested strategy will check the settings you've configured for your database, and it will draw conclusions about whether you want a disk-only backup, a tape-only backup, or a combined disk and tape backup.

The Disk-Only Backup Strategy   The disk-only strategy suggested is the most straightforward. It utilizes the Incremental Apply to Database Copy functionality to create a backup strategy that is self-cleaning. Here's how it works. In this example we start the Oracle-suggested strategy on a Monday evening at 10 P.M. The database is running in archivelog mode, has automatic controlfile and spfile backups enabled, and uses a Flash Recovery Area.

■ Monday night: A full image copy of every datafile is taken for the database. This backup is stored in the Flash Recovery Area.

■ Tuesday night: A Level 1 incremental backup set is created. All blocks that have changed since Monday night at 10 P.M. are backed up.

■ Wednesday night: First, RMAN applies the Tuesday night incremental backup to the Monday night image copy. Now, the full image copy backup is a current copy of the database as it looked Tuesday night at 10 P.M. After that is complete, RMAN takes a new Level 1 backup.

■ Thursday night: RMAN applies the Wednesday night incremental backup to the image copy; now, our database backup is current as of Wednesday night at 10 P.M. Then, a new incremental Level 1 backup is taken, with all changes since Wednesday night.

■ Friday night: and so on.

A few things to notice about this backup strategy: first, a full database backup is only taken once. After that, RMAN only takes Level 1 incremental backups. Then, nightly, the previous night's incremental is applied. Second, this strategy ensures that the database backup is at least 24 hours behind the current point in time. This allows for a point-in-time recovery to any point in the previous 24 hours, but nothing earlier than that. At most, the database backup is 48 hours behind the current time, so recovery is never that far behind.

There are limitations to this strategy, but that's one of the drawbacks to a "one-size-fits-all" approach to backups.

Tape-Only Suggested Strategy   A tape-only strategy differs in many ways from the disk-only suggested strategy. First, no backup will ever be created in the FRA. Sure, archivelogs will accumulate there, but all backups will go directly to the tape device. In addition, the tape-only strategy cannot take advantage of the incremental apply feature. Remember, an image copy backup cannot be taken to tape. All backups to tape will be of type backup set.

When you schedule an Oracle-suggested tape-only backup, there are two RMAN scripts that are generated: a daily backup, and a weekly backup. First, the weekly script is run. This creates a full database backup, including all archivelogs. Then, the daily script is run. The daily backup does an incremental backup of only changed blocks, along with all archivelogs not already backed up. Then, once a week, the full database backup runs again.

During the wizard for the tape-only backup, if you have not specified a retention policy, GC will ask you to specify one. Then, as part of the daily backup, your retention policy will be enforced on the tape channel.

Disk and Tape Suggested Strategy   When you combine disk backups with tape backups, the hybrid solution demands more input from you than either of the previous suggested strategies. And, for the first time, a decision must be made.

First, the disk part of the strategy. The disk-based strategy is identical in the disk-tape approach as it is in disk-only: a full image copy in the Flash Recovery Area, and then incremental backups each night that are then applied to the image copy.

As far as the tape part of the strategy, there is a decision to be made: How much do you want backed up to tape on a daily basis? On a weekly basis, the suggested strategy will back up all recovery-related files (with the `backup recovery files` command in RMAN). But, you must choose how much to back up daily: nothing, archivelogs only, archivelogs and incrementals, or archivelogs and the full database copy.

Scheduling Customized Backup Jobs

From the same page where you can schedule an Oracle-Suggested Backup strategy, you can also build your own customized backup job. This is a wizard-driven process that steps you through the different choices to be made about the backup. When the wizard is finished, you can run it as a one-time backup immediately, schedule it for later, or set it up to repeat continually every so often.

It is important to take the time to develop a full backup strategy ahead of time, but GC will provide some guidance on how to develop that strategy. These little tips appear as small-font hints underlying some of the decisions you will make in the backup scheduling wizard.

RMAN Script Job vs. Scheduled Backup Wizard

There is another way to use Grid Control to schedule and run RMAN backups of a target database. If you go to the Jobs tab in Grid Control (or the Jobs link under Related Links in Database Control), and look at the drop-down list of possible job types to create, you will see RMAN Script. This is a specific type of job specification that allows you to use GC to execute an RMAN script that already exists at the target server.

So what is different from an RMAN Script job and a Host Command job? If you choose an RMAN Script job, GC will use its built-in mechanisms to ensure that the environment is properly configured for your target database before running the script. This is a very nice feature, which you know if you have ever run into the dreaded compatibility matrix of RMAN executables versus target databases (see Chapter 3, if you dare).

GRID CONTROL WORKSHOP

Create an RMAN Script Job in Grid Control

Workshop Notes

This workshop will use Grid Control to schedule an RMAN backup. However, the backup will be specified by an RMAN script that already exists as a file on the Linux machine where database ORCL exists. This script exists in /home/oracle/scripts, named rmanback.rcv, and contains the following code:

```
backup incremental level 1 cumulative device type disk filesperset = 2
database;
backup device type disk filesperset = 2 archivelog all not backed up
delete all input;
delete noprompt obsolete device type disk;
```

Step 1. Go to the jobs page of GC. From Grid Control, there is a tab along the upper-right side. In Database Control, go to the bottom under Related Links to find the Jobs link.

Step 2. Create a new job of type RMAN Script.

Step 3. On the General tab, give the job the name **RMAN_BACK_INC_1_ARCH_DELETE_ OBS**. From this tab, you also need to add the targets (for Grid Control). Choose the Add button and select your desired database.

Step 3. Click the Parameters tab. In the box, provide the full path and name to your backup script you created on the target server.

Step 4. On the Credentials page, ensure that you have provided SYSDBA Database Credentials, as this is required by RMAN.

Step 5. Set a schedule for the job. This can be a one-time (immediately), one-time later, or a repeating job.

Step 6. Click the Submit button to send the job to the active jobs page. Alternatively, you can save the job to the library, or submit the job now and save it to the library.

Performing Recovery in Grid Control

After all the backing up that can be done from GC, it should come as no surprise that you can also perform recovery from GC. If you have made yourself aware of how GC Recovery works, you will have noticed that it has the capabilities to lead you toward the flashback technologies.Flashback technologies provide a whole new arsenal against downtime, particularly when it comes to user-induced trauma. So, if it is control you seek, it must be stated that you are not in complete control of your recovery situation until you have explored your flashback options.

Whole Database Recovery

When the database is still open, you can get to the recovery system within Enterprise Manager from the same Availability page that you use to configure backup/recovery settings, or schedule backups. The Perform Recovery link opens a page that provides you with two options: The first is to perform whole database recovery. Whole database recovery is displayed as a multiple-choice quiz: Recover to the current point in time, or to some previous point in time; restore all datafiles; and recover from previously restored datafiles.

Recover to Current Time or Previous Point in Time   The first option is the one that will do what you expect: restore datafiles and recover them using archivelogs. The only option you decide is the time at which you want the database to be opened. In fact, if you walk through this wizard, you will find that the generated RMAN script is this (click the Edit RMAN Script button to see the output):

```
run {
restore database;
recover database;
}
```

The other option is to perform Point-In-Time Recovery (PITR).You can specify the point in time you want to recover to as—well, a point in time—but also as a log sequence number, a system change number (SCN), or a Restore Point. Note that when you do a point-in-time recovery, and you have Flashback Database turned on, you see a blue-font tip telling you to consider Flashback Database. You can click Next to choose this. When you specify your time (or SCN or log), GC evaluates whether this point falls within the timeframe that is available for Flashback Database, and offers you the choice: Flashback or traditional PITR? Choosing Flashback takes you to the flashback wizard, and choosing Traditional carries you through this wizard.

Restore All Datafiles   From the main Perform Recovery page, the second option is to Restore All Files. Choosing this option will initiate a datafile restore that does not also perform a recovery. As you may have guessed, following this through to the end of the wizard, and selecting Edit RMAN Script, will show the following:

```
run {
restore database;
}
```

Recovery from Previously Restored Datafiles   Finally, you can choose to recover the database from previously restored datafiles. This simply means that if you choose this option, only a recover command will be issued in RMAN. This does *not* mean that if you chose to restore datafiles to a different location, that you can then specify those files in this wizard.

This is a recover only. It will rely completely on the control file's v$datafile list to determine which files to restore.

There is a check box at the bottom that lets GC open the database in read-only mode after the recovery so you can validate the database. This option allows you to confirm that the point in time you specified was correct.

GRID CONTROL WORKSHOP

Perform Database Recovery from Grid Control

Workshop Notes

In this workshop, we will perform a point-in-time recovery to a point in the past, using the backups taken previously in this chapter with GC. This workshop utilizes Grid Control to perform the recovery, which allows us to monitor the recovery job while it is in progress. Recovery from Database Control will be slightly different than what is detailed here.

Step 1. Go to the Database Home Page | Availability | Perform Recovery page. Choose Recover to the Current Time or a Previous Point in Time, and then click the Perform Whole Database Recovery button.

Step 2. Select the option to recover to a prior point in time. We will set this with a date in this example. Click Next.

Step 3. If you have turned on Flashback Database, and your point in time falls within the flashback window, you will get a screen asking if you would like to use Flashback Database. Choose No, Use Traditional Point-in-Time Recovery. Click Next.

Step 4. Choose to restore the files to the default location. Click Next. This will take you to the Schedule page, but all recovery jobs run immediately. Click Next.

Step 5. Click the button Edit RMAN Script to look at what RMAN will be running. Click Cancel after you review. Then, click Submit Job.

Step 6. GC will provide a screen saying "The job has been successfully submitted." Click the View Job button. The job page shows the history of each job step, known as an *execution*. You can refresh your browser to get up-to-date step and elapsed time values.

Step 7. Click the Step:Recovery link under Executions. This allows you to monitor the progress of the RMAN job.

Object-Level Recovery

Object-level recovery can be a bit misleading. Situated below the Whole Database Recovery option after you click the main Perform Recovery link, this is ostensibly the place for doing any kind of recovery that is some smaller subset of the database. The misleading bit concerns what is meant by "object." The answer: anything that is not the whole database: tablespaces, datafiles, tables. On anything below the entire database in granularity, you perform recovery from here.

This means that "object-level recovery" refers to both logical objects and physical objects. Some logical objects, such as tablespaces, still require a physical media restore/recovery operation. Other logical objects, such as tables, when selected, actually take you into the flashback technologies world, which is completely different from media recovery. Physical objects are straightforward: If you want to recover a single datafile, that would be a restore and recover. You also have the ability to perform block media recovery from the Object Level menu.

Oracle has done a good job of providing a complete set of recovery options within Grid Control, so it would be impossible in this single chapter to review the wizard steps that you walk through based on each type of object-level recovery. Such a chapter would be as long as the rest of this book. We encourage you to go through each of the different types of GC recovery, to familiarize yourself with the language Oracle is using within GC for each type of recovery.

Backup Management and Reporting

It is perhaps in the arena of managing your backups that GC really proves its worth. Running backups and recoveries from the command line is one thing; but reading the output of report and list commands from a terminal is something else completely. From GC, managing existing backups is considerably friendlier. The management is divided into three types: managing current backups, managing restore points, and creating backup reports.

Manage Current Backups

Directly below the Schedule Backup and Perform Recovery links on the Database Maintenance page, you will find the Manage Current Backups link. This takes you to the page where you can perform common management activities: crosschecks, delete obsolete, delete expired, and so on.

Across the top, you will see some quick link type buttons for common tasks: Catalog Additional Files, Crosscheck All, Delete All Obsolete, and Delete All Expired. These buttons all do just what they say they do, and you can read about these options in your handy RMAN Backup and Recovery book.

Manage Restore Points

From Manage Restore Points, you can create new restore points, view existing restore point information, or delete existing restore points. From GC, you can look at the restore point creation time, the amount of storage required, and the creation SCN. If you notice that the Guaranteed Restore Point is greyed out, this is because you are logged into the target database with NORMAL privileges, and SYSDBA privileges are required for creation of Guaranteed Restore Points. In addition, the ability to find the Recover Whole Database To button depends on being logged in as SYSDBA user. Clicking this button will bring up a confirmation screen and then take you to the Perform Whole Database Recovery page.

View and Manage Transactions

This handy little section is where the Grid Control implementation of LogMiner is buried. If you haven't worked with LogMiner in the past, lucky you! From this link you can view transactions in the archive redo logs and even flash back a transaction that has been harmful to the database. This is an extremely useful diagnostic tool, not to mention a time saver when it comes to backing away from damaging human error without restoring the entire database to a point in the past.

The Server

The Server tab is where the bulk of the day-to-day DBA activities are located. This is the one-stop shop for system-side database activities, the care and feeding of the ongoing production database. There is literally too much to cover here, so we are going to breeze across the surface and then dive into the particularly interesting value-add items that Grid Control brings to the party.

Storage

The links under the Storage header all provide you with detailed information about specific storage objects: Control Files, Permanent and Temporary Tablespaces, Datafiles, Rollback Segments, and Redo and Archive Logs. This is an excellent location to come to browse for specific information that typically you look for in the v$views; for instance, the Control Files link, under the Advanced Tab, will show you the DBID, the current system change number, the logfile sequence number, and so on.

Tablespace management, particularly, is quite handy from Grid Control. You get an overview of allocated and used space in the tablespace, along with a grid of pertinent information, as shown in Figure 14-5.

Furthermore, the actions you can take from the Tablespace Actions button provides a wealth of easy visual clues that can help you plan, diagnose, and execute constantly improving space strategies. A good example of this is to choose View Tablespace Contents. This takes a few seconds, then provides a look at the Segments and the Extent Map inside the tablespace you are looking at. When you are looking at the Extent Map, it automatically highlights in yellow the

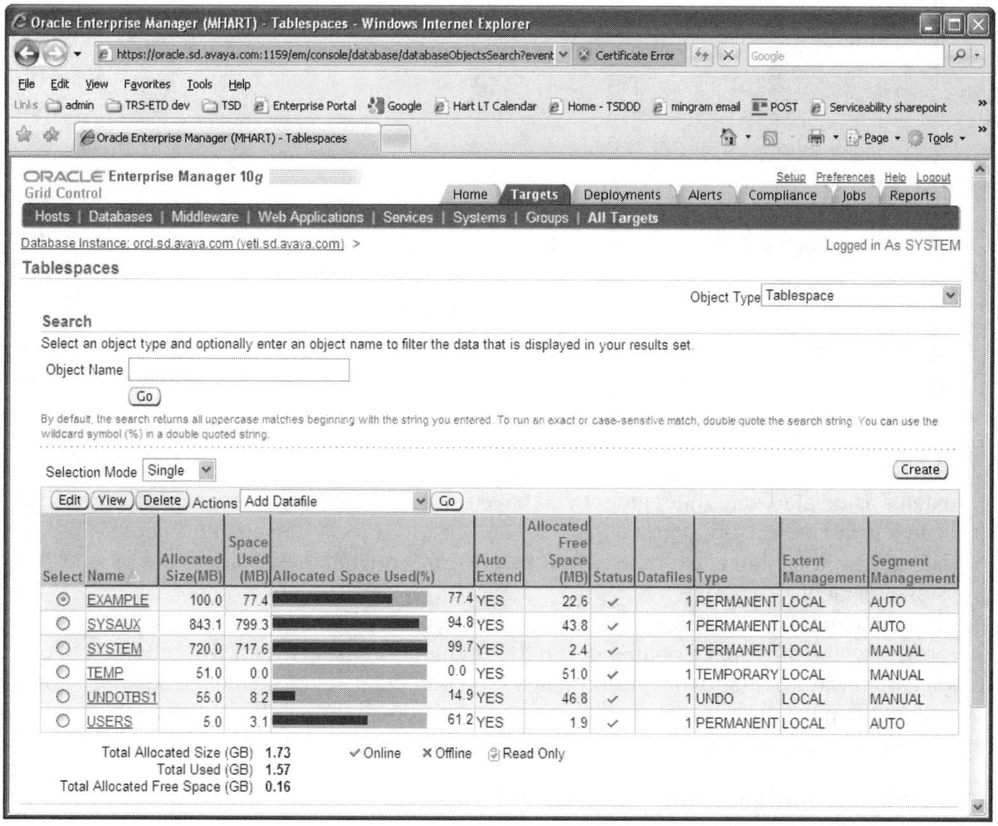

FIGURE 14-5. *Tablespace view*

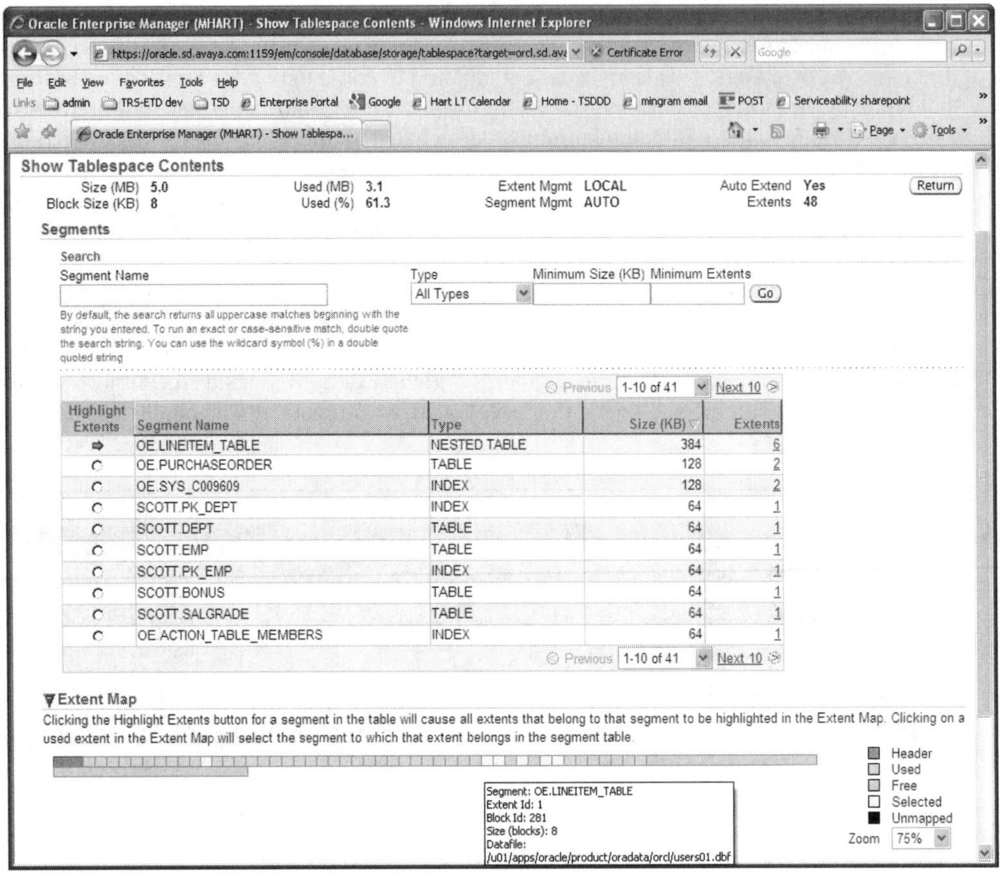

FIGURE 14-6. *Segment and extent mapping in Grid Control*

extents associated with the segment you have selected in the Segments section above. For instance, in Figure 14-6, you see that OE.LINEITGC_TABLE is selected in segments. Below, in the Extent Map, if we hover over the yellow extents, we see that these map to the OE.LINEITGC_TABLE segment.

Furthermore, you can see that from the Tablespace page, you can also issue a command to reorganize the tablespace online, or run the Segment Advisor, which will provide Oracle-suggested ways of improving performance for a particular set of segments. Segment Advisor uses automatic space metrics collected to determine historical growth trends for a tablespace, and then provide advice on shrinking or reorganizing segments to free up space.

Database Configuration Management

Configuration management in this context refers to instance parameters that control the overall functionality of the database. The Memory Advisor provides mechanisms for monitoring memory and gathering statistics so that the system can provide advice on memory settings for the database, from PGA to SGA settings, and the contents (by type) in each, as shown in the following illustration. This includes PGA Memory Usage Details as a separate window that pops up after you click the PGA tab halfway down the page, then the PGA Memory Usage Details button.

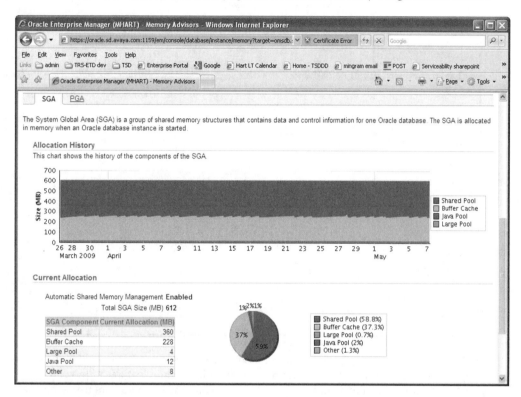

Automatic Undo Segment allows you to manage the configuration of Undo in the database, from changing the undo tablespace to getting advice from the Undo Advisor on what an optimal size would be for the Undo Tablespace given the amount of time you want to keep transactions available for Flashback and other undo operations.

Initialization Parameters is the location where you can modify all initialization parameters for the database. In an 11g database, there are 290 possible parameters (not including hidden, or "underscore" parameters, such as _b_tree_bitmap_plans, which you have to set to FALSE in order to use an 11g database for your Grid Control Repository), so Grid Control provides a search function for you to use to get directly to the init parameter of most interest to you.

Notice, here, as with the Memory Advisor, that there is a button labeled Execute on Multiple Databases, as shown in the following illustration. This function allows you to take advantage of the fact that you have Grid Control, not Database Control, and thus can standardize changes you make by applying an init parameter change to all databases that require standardization. We'll discuss a little later how to use Compare Configurations to compare two or more databases with each other to get a delta on differences. But be sure to remember this button—it can save you time and energy down the road.

View Database Feature Usage is an excellent and curious page, showing that the Oracle database is now tracking how often and when you utilize certain features of the particular database under review. I'm assuming this is to show you how often you are using the excellent and cool stuff that Oracle crams into each database release, and, with a little curiosity on your part, can show you the things you aren't using. Are you paying too much for an Enterprise Edition license? A little investigation might help.

Security

Database Users, Roles, and Profiles are handled from the Security section of the Server tab. Managing Users is a straightforward, grid-oriented view where you can select either a single or multiple users and perform actions against them: Edit, View, Delete, Create (and Create Like), Expire Password, Generate DDL, and Lock/Unlock the User. The Generate DDL shows you the DDL required to rebuild the user. When you choose Edit or Create a User from Grid Control, you have the option to do so on multiple databases at the same time using Execute on Multiple Databases.

The Roles tab allows you to utilize the GUI to add Roles to Roles, edit System and Object Privileges, as well as Consumer Group Privileges. This has a Show SQL button, and—importantly—you find here the Execute on Multiple Databases button. So when you modify a role in Grid Control, you can execute the command on more than one database to save yourself repetitive stress syndrome.

Profile creation and editing works in the same way as Users and Roles: you can make all necessary changes, and apply to just this one database, or multiple databases.

In addition to standard user management, the Security section also allows you to configure more advanced Security settings: Audits, Data Encryption, Virtual Private Database Policies, and Application Contexts. These topics are well beyond the scope of this book to discuss, but Grid Control has comprehensively built interfaces for these different functions.

Other Server Topics

There are six other topics on the Server tab, but we will not go into depth on these subjects. The following brief table discusses what these links provide you.

Server Tab Links	Brief Description of Function
Oracle Scheduler	Job scheduling, chaining, and classifying can be managed from this set of links. These are not to be confused with Grid Control Jobs; these are jobs run inside the particular database. As with most operations from this page, you can make changes and apply them to multiple databases.
Statistics Management	Manage the Automatic Workload Repository (AWR) that was discussed at greater length in our earlier discussion on Performance.
Resource Manager	These links provide mechanisms for managing Consumer Groups, used for setting consumption priorities for different classes of users and objects.
Query Optimizer	Managing how the RDBMS builds and follows SQL Explain plans can be a full-time job, particularly with older applications built for previous database versions, or with databases with highly variable row counts. This section helps you manage how the Optimizer makes plan decisions based on table statistics.
Change Database	This set of links helps you change a database to a clustered (RAC) database, add instances, or delete instances from a RAC cluster.

Schema Monitoring and Management

From a day-to-day perspective, the Schema tab is going to be the place where a DBA will spend plenty of time managing the database. This is where database objects and database code are managed. This is the meat on the skeleton that is built everywhere else in the management system: Here are the tables, indexes, views, PL/SQL packages, and functions that make up the logic and structure data that your business relies on.

Database Objects

Managing objects from within Grid Control is... not bad. When you search for a table from the Table link, you can do a view and see all metadata about that table in a single web page. This is useful. When you want to see the data in the table itself, there is an option to select View Data and then click Go. This provides the table in a spreadsheet format. However, it needs to be pointed out that

Grid Control in this iteration is no entity relationship (E/R) modeling or relationship management tool. If you are used to the more sophisticated desktop applications that perform these same types of tasks, this is going to feel a bit clunky. Don't get us wrong; Grid Control is a critical tool in your tool belt for managing a group of databases. But you may still need your desktop-based, thick-client E/R tools as well. There is simply no way to get that bird's-eye view of the relationships between tables and code here.

You will notice that below Database Objects there are multiple links to different object types. However, the first six links take you to a similar object page that you can then use to get to any object type beyond these six—they simply represent the six most common objects you will want to manage. Figure 14-7 shows you the Object Type drop-down list of all objects you can manage from this page. While the focus shows you this is a Tables page, the drop-down list on the right shows you a massive number of objects.

Note that the drop-down from the Object page consists of the entirety of the top three sets of links on the Schema Page: Database Objects, Programs, and Materialized Views. In addition, there are links for User Defined Types (Array, Object, and Table Types), and XML Schema from the XML Database topic as well. So, there are two ways to get to where you need to go: straight from a link on the Server page, or once you are in the Object view, you can use this drop-down.

There are two exceptions from the Database Objects topic: Directory Objects and Reorganize Objects. Directory Objects is broken out because directories work in a different fashion,

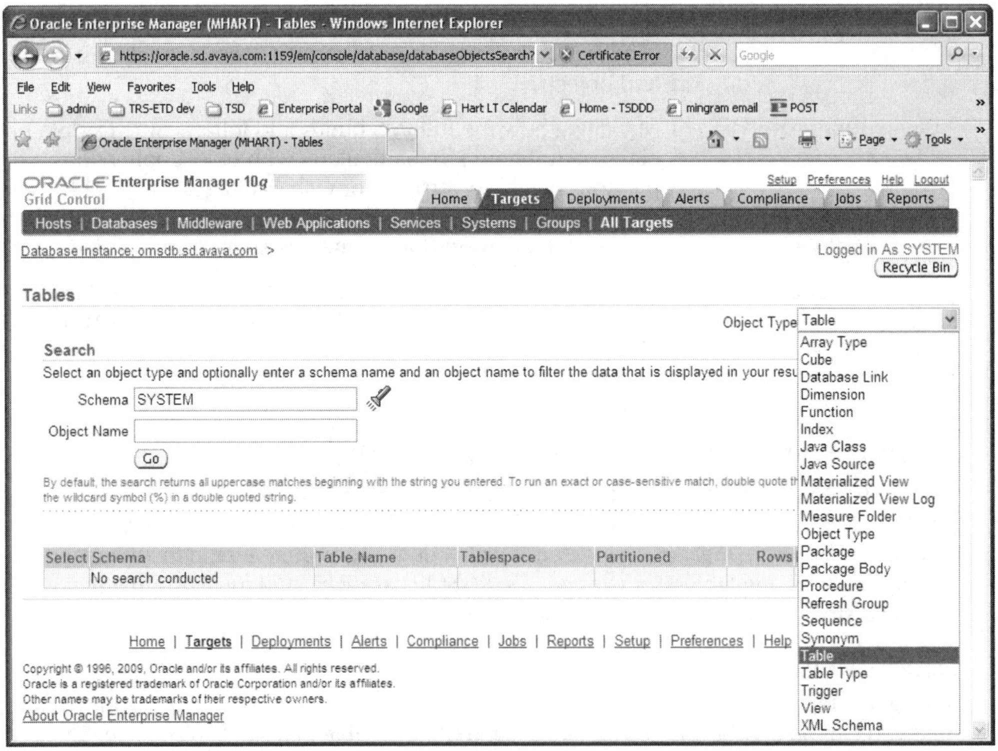

FIGURE 14-7. *Object management in Grid Control*

and therefore need a different logic for managing. Managing Directory Objects from Grid Control is much preferable to doing it manually, so we suggest you familiarize yourself with this link.

Reorganizing database objects can also be a laborious process that Grid Control can help with. The link from the Server tab opens a wizard that walks you through a reorganization activity on the database. This reorganization allows you to select a specific object, an entire schema, or a tablespace. It allows you to choose to do the reorganization online or offline, and allows you to set the scratch tablespace that will be used during the reorganization. After you have built the script, Grid Control programmatically checks for sufficient space and quota for the schema in question to ensure, as much as possible, that your reorganization will be successful before you start it. This alone is worth using Grid Control.

At this time, reorganization is something you are proactively doing from your own knowledge, or because you are reacting to a performance or space issue. There is no reorganization advisor yet that can point out good candidates for this activity.

Other Database Options from the Schema Tab

Beyond database object management, the Schema tab allows for management of other schema elements that may be used in your database environment.

- **Change Management** is available when you purchase the Change Management Pack for Grid Control, and allows you to baseline the data dictionary definitions for a database, and then use them to run comparisons to watch for dictionary drift or to make rectifications through a dictionary synchronization process.

- **Data Masking** allows for creating masking formats and saving them to the Format Library. Masking is the process of obfuscating sensitive data in the database from the eyes of administrators, developers, and testers in non-production environments. The Format Library provides a set of prebuilt masking formats that you can utilize out of the box.

- **XML Database** provides a mechanism for specifically configuring, managing, and extending the XDB functionality of the Oracle Database. If you are utilizing Oracle to store and retrieve XML structured schemas, this is where you can utilize that feature set.

- **Workspace Manager** allows you to manage the feature of Oracle RDBMS called Workspaces, which is a mechanism for sharing versions of table rows with small subsets of database users for testing and development purposes. This allows for persistence of versions and version control hierarchies.

- **Text Manager** allows you to manage Oracle Text, a specific feature set in Oracle for indexing and managing external document types such as Microsoft Word, PDF, and plain text. Configuring Text does not occur from within Grid Control; the function here is just the management of indexes created after the initial configuration is done.

Data Movement

Data Movement refers to the different ways that RDBMS structured data can be moved from physical location to physical location. This makes up a significant portion of the work a DBA does, so it makes sense to aggregate all of these activities to one page. In fact, there have been innovations in this space over the past few releases, and one of the true benefits of using Grid Control is that you have happy accidents when you are looking for a tried-and-true performer, such as Export, and you discover yourself staring at a Clone Database link and wondering if that is a better option for your activity than using a logical export.

Move Row Data

Row data movement can come in one of three formats: using the new Data Pump (replaces the traditional import/export tools of years gone by), using SQL*Loader, or using a direct database link to another database.

Import/Export is relatively straightforward. The link Export to Export Files defines an export job, and the link Import from Export Files defines an import job. Import from Database refers to a direct, DB Link connection to another database known to this database, and allows you to select objects that the dblink has access to and use straight SQL to move them over to this database.

To utilize SQL*Loader, you need to select the link Load Data from User Files. This will ask you to create or use a control file—don't confuse this with a database control file; this is a SQL*Loader control file that controls how to manage the data from the user file into the target database files.

Move Database Files

Database Cloning has been discussed earlier in the discussion on High Availability , so we won't revisit that topic here—it's just another shortcut to the same wizard. Transport Tablespaces is an excellent function that's been around since Oracle 8*i*, and allows you to move entire tablespaces from one database to another. The Grid Control Wizard provides a straightforward mechanism for either generating a set of tablespaces to move to another database, or to integrate a set of tablespaces that were generated from another database. If you have ever gone through this process manually in previous versions, then you will understand the benefit of utilizing all the Grid Control information already at your fingertips to make this process go smoothly.

Streams and Replication

Streams and Replication are specific database options that are utilized for moving records from one database to the next in (close to) real time. Both of these options are similar in function, although you could roughly refer to Streams as *log-based replication* (it utilizes redo and archive logs to mine records and apply them at another database) and Advanced Replication as *trigger-based replication* (it utilizes database triggers to create secondary clone records and then applies them automatically to another database via database links).

Both of these subjects could not be covered in this chapter. It is worth noting that both of these options have typically been controlled in the past through thick-client management applications, so it is beneficial over the past few releases of Grid Control to see the management become integrated with overall database management. Now, you can set up and manage full replication environments utilizing the database discovery and levers that are already patterned in Grid Control.

We will hold off on discussing the Software and Support link, as this is an important section that will be discussed in the next section on ecosystem management.

Grid Control and Managing the Production Database Ecosystem

Nearly everything we've discussed so far, as it pertains to database management, has consisted of activities that occurred on a per-database level. In other words, these are mainly all tasks that occur when you are looking at just one database, and therefore are tasks that will look the same whether you are in Grid Control or Database Control. So does Grid Control give us better capabilities? Let's spend a few moments to discuss the benefits.

- **Centralized URL management**   All right, so it sounds like a small benefit, but having a single location for managing multiple databases will make your life simpler, particularly as the number of databases you manage increases.

- **Service-level fault reporting**   As you learned in Chapter 13, everyone in the information supply chain benefits when end-to-end fault analysis is utilized to determine where an issue is isolated.

- **Consolidated targets for data rollup**   By utilizing groups, we gain the efficiency of having multiple ways of differentiating monitoring tasks and viewing metric alarms.

- **Single Job Library**   Sharing jobs across multiple databases makes scripting and executing similar operations against multiple databases just about as easy as it can possibly get.

- **Database change management**   Having a consolidated view into the entire database lifecycle (from development to test to production) allows for better change management as the hand-off to each environment takes place. And after a database goes into production, you can monitor drift across targets and keep better tabs on your enterprise-wide standards.

Databases and Consolidated Targets (Groups, Systems, Services)

Consolidated targets, such as Groups, can provide excellent power when it comes to database management. By grouping databases together into a single viewable target, you can quickly and easily perform actions against the entire group, instead of against each database in turn.

A good example is a SQL script that you need to run against your application schema to track the number of new rows created each day. Because you have deployed the application in multiple production environments at each of your plants, you can use row creation as a sign of forthcoming impact to the overall growth and access paths you may need to be putting into place.

Using Grid Control, you can create a group that is made up of all databases that house the particular application you need to reference. Then, you can create a SQL Script type job in the Job Library. After setting the script, the credentials, and the schedule, you add your new database group to the Target list, and you are done. The additional benefit is that you don't have to then

GRID CONTROL WORKSHOP

Run a SQL Script Against Multiple Databases

Workshop Notes

We will create a SQL script that counts rows in a table, and then use Groups and the Job Library to submit to all databases at once. For the sake of simplicity, we will run our statement against v$tablespace, as user system, on two databases.

Step 1.   Create a database group. Go to Targets | Groups, and next to the Create Group option, click Go. Name the group appropriately, and then click Search for Members. In the pop-up window, filter on Database Instance, and choose the databases that have the correct table we want to count. Then click OK.

(continued)

Step 2. Create a SQL Script job in the Job Library. Click the Jobs tab, then Job Library. Next to Create Library Job, choose SQL Script and click Go.

Give the new job a name and description, then click Add to add your group from above. By default the target type is Database Instance, as shown in the following illustration. You will need to change that from the drop-down to Group.

NOTE
You will need to set Preferred Credentials for each database instance in the group before you proceed with submitting your job. This includes host credentials, as SQL*Plus will be invoked for this job.

Step 3. Create the SQL statement in the Parameters tab. You can take the defaults for Credentials (given that you have Preferred Credentials set) and the default for schedule (run on demand). Then click Save to Library. You will see the job in the Library.

Step 4. Submit the job. You will be given one more chance to change targets or other parameters for this run. Click Submit. Then click the link to the specific job run in the Confirmation Message to review the progress and the results, as shown in the following illustration.

```
Show All Details | Hide All Details
Select Details Targets         Status          Started                          Ended                            Elapsed Time
   ⊗  ▼Hide XE                Succeeded       May 6, 2009 6:39:50 PM (UTC-06:00)   May 6, 2009 6:40:09 PM (UTC-06:00)   18 seconds
      Output Log


SQL*Plus: Release 10.2.0.1.0 - Production on Mon May 4 07:51:24 2009

Copyright (c) 1982, 2005, Oracle.  All rights reserved.

SQL> SQL> SQL> SQL> Connected.
SQL> SQL> SQL> SQL> SQL>
  COUNT(*)
----------
        5

SQL> SQL> SQL> Disconnected from Oracle Database 10g Express Edition Release 10.2.0.1.0 - Production

View Complete Log...
   ○  ▼Hide orcl.sd.avaya.com   Succeeded    May 6, 2009 6:39:50 PM (UTC-06:00)   May 6, 2009 6:39:52 PM (UTC-06:00)   2 seconds
              (yeti.sd.avaya.com)
      Output Log


SQL*Plus: Release 11.1.0.6.0 - Production on Mon May 4 07:51:24 2009

Copyright (c) 1982, 2007, Oracle.  All rights reserved.

SQL> SQL> SQL> SQL> Connected.
SQL> SQL> SQL> SQL> SQL>
  COUNT(*)
----------
        6

SQL> SQL> SQL> Disconnected from Oracle Database 11g Enterprise Edition Release 11.1.0.6.0 - Production
With the Partitioning, OLAP, Data Mining and Real Application Testing options

View Complete Log...
```

You can click the blue (+) triangle to show the logged results of the job.

manage the job per database. If you add or remove a database from the group, the SQL script is attached to the group definition, not the database.

Database Change Management

Beyond the benefits of grouping and consolidating jobs, database change management plays a big part in the overall power of Grid Control. Again, there is a component of change management that is inherent within a single database, but leveraging Grid Control to deploy and maintain enterprise standards will make your life easier, once you get it set up.

Comparing Configurations

We stated earlier that we would return to the Software and Support tab of the database pages in Grid Control. We wanted to hold off because the Configuration section of this section of Grid Control demonstrates the power of having a centralized repository of information about all databases and systems in your environment. First, let's discuss how to compare configurations.

Comparing configurations allows you to utilize the information in the Grid Control repository to compare multiple databases to each other and generate a delta. This delta can then be used to understand drift in database parameters, SGA size, space and disk usage, and other elements about the database that may be of interest.

Saved Configurations   You can compare configurations between two current state databases, or you can utilize a saved configuration. A saved configuration is useful when you reach a baseline point in a database build, and have created what you believe to be the gold image of what your database should look like. When you save it, you take a snapshot of a point in time, and then can use that to compare the database to itself over time.

This latter function has proven to be extremely useful to us in our application lifecycle management. Given that a database, once put into a development environment, may become modified over time by developers, it is important to understand what those changes are so they can be transferred to the testing environment when the hand-off to the testing team takes place. And the same goes for the move to production from test—it is critical to understand any differences that exist. Prior to Grid Control, this can be an extremely manual, error-prone process.

The opposite can also be true: As opposed to ensuring that you can move all necessary development changes forward, you will also find that you need to move production requirements deeper into the test and even development environments. For example, some configuration elements of the database may be mandated by the enterprise production environment standards. These can cause problems if they are not accounted for early in the development process, and can lead to a long list of bugs that could have been avoided—and insert delay into precious deployment cycles. Instead, by comparing the production database environment, either a live one or a saved configuration, to the test environment, you can create as real a test as possible and identify problems early in the application lifecycle.

Saving the configuration must be done manually, and the best place to go to save the current configuration is to follow the link from Database | Software and Support | Last Collected Configuration. This shows you the last collected configuration in the OMS for the current target, and there is a Save button at the top that allows you to give a description and then save the configuration to the OMS, or to a file, as shown in the following illustration. Saving to a file allows you to import the configuration into a different Grid Control environment, if you are trying to troubleshoot an issue, or want to share a configuration with another GC environment for comparisons.

Comparing Hosts   When you have a comparison of two databases up on the screen in Grid Control, there is a button in the far-right corner that allows you to quickly compare the hosts for the two databases as well. Host configuration plays a critical role in database success, so this comparison can help you further ensure that you have as standard a view as possible between the two environments.

Comparing Multiple Configurations   If you are telling yourself right now that it is overly simplistic to be doing one-to-one comparisons of environments, Grid Control can account for that by offering you the multiple comparison option. This will allow you to specify multiple configurations to compare your database to—which can be a series of saved versions of it, saved versions from a different database, or multiple other live databases.

Because of the iterative nature of a multiple-target comparison, this must be run as a job, and therefore the job must be built and scheduled a bit differently. When you complete the job, you can look at the Results section of the job in the Job Activity screen (be sure to change the default view from Running to Succeeded to see the job if it is complete) to see the high level of the multiple comparison.

Database Patching

Grid Control provides the mechanisms for uploading patches that you need to roll out across your environment, or that are downloaded automatically from Oracle's support site. These are stored on the OMS server in a central repository location. Once the patch is in this location, you can then check the patch prerequisites, and create a provisioning job that will apply the patch to one or more database.

ORACLE_HOME Cloning

In addition to database cloning operations, you can also use Grid Control to clone an *ORACLE_HOME* to another location on the same host, or to a location on a new host.

Summary

In this chapter, we went into the specifics of using Grid Control to manage an ecosystem of Oracle databases. We started by describing the differences between Grid Control and Database Control, as well as introducing how to use Database Control. We then provided an overview of the level of functionality available in Grid Control to cover database administration, performance management, backup and recovery, and other critical database functions.

CHAPTER
15

RAC and Cluster Management

racle Real Application Clusters (RAC) is a robust feature of the Oracle RDBMS engine that allows you to access the same database from multiple servers simultaneously. This provides high availability and scalability to the Oracle database service.

Whenever you hear "clusters" you think of highly available systems with multiple servers. There are a number of ways to run services on Clusters, the most common being Cold Failover Clusters (CFC). This is a low-cost solution to host a service and make it highly available by means of enabling the service to run as an independent package within the cluster. While taking advantage of the power of each cluster member and the resources available to the cluster, this service can run on any host in the cluster as needed. We will concentrate on RAC clusters in this chapter and begin by outlining the primary advantages of Oracle RAC.

Simply, an Oracle database can be divided into two major components; files on disk (such as control files, redo logs, data files, and binaries) and memory-resident processes (SGA, cache, and various daemons: pmon, smon, arch, dbwr, lgwr). The memory-resident objects are the instantiation of the disk-resident files, hence the Oracle instance. To take advantage of the merits of a cluster, RAC facilitates instantiation of an instance of a database on each node in the cluster. In doing so, Oracle is extending the database and providing both redundancy and availability to a single database. This concept is naturally coupled with powerful facilitation software, which enables the database to instantiate multiple instances.

Oracle Clusterware is software that enables servers to operate together as if they are one server entity. It is composed of a native Oracle clusterware stack, RDBMS engine, advanced networking topology, and optional storage management features. There can be only one instance of clusterware running on each node in the cluster and one ASM instance, but you can have as many RAC databases or single instances as you want on each node.

Managing RAC Clusters in Grid Control

To manage RAC clusters in Grid Control you must have a resident Grid Control agent process running and reporting to the OMS on each cluster member. The following section provides a workshop on how to install these agents on the cluster from the Grid Control Console. This is one way to install the agent on candidate-managed nodes.

GRID CONTROL WORKSHOP

Installing the Agent on Cluster Nodes

Workshop Notes

In this workshop, we will utilize the Grid Control Deployments capabilities to install agents on cluster nodes. Begin at the Deployments tab from Grid Control and locate the Agent Installation section. You have three options available to deploy agent software to managed nodes. We recommend using the first option for RAC agents instead of deploying the agent from an existing shared agent home.

On the Installation Details page, in the Hosts section, enter each hostname in the cluster separated by a comma as shown in the following illustration.

The cluster name is essential here. You want to use a unique name that identifies this RAC cluster. In a multicluster deployment environment, ensure that you don't use the default "CRS" cluster name for your clusters. If you don't know the cluster name before you install the agent, you can run the following command from the CRS home /bin directory on any cluster member target to find the cluster name that was given to this cluster when CRS was installed:

```
cemutlo -n
```

(continued)

If the cluster name is "CRS" you can still override this on the Agent Deployment screen (see the following illustration). This will not change the cluster name on the cluster nodes, but it will help you to identify this cluster in Grid Control Console uniquely.

When you "push" agents to target clustered nodes, the OC4J EM_PROV process is invoked on the OMS host and runs the installer in Cluster mode on the first node listed in the node list you provide. This requires SSH connectivity equivalence between the OMS node and the cluster target. This requirement is needed to run remote operations without having to actually involve a user shell session. Generally, your cluster nodes were initially configured to have this requirement among all cluster nodes. Ensure that this is still the case and a sys admin has not removed this connectivity equivalence configuration among these cluster members.

One of the easiest ways to verify this requirement is to run a simple remote command from the first cluster node to each cluster node. Example:

```
Node1>  ssh node2 hostname
```

This should return *only* the hostname of the node2. No other prompts or banners should be displayed, as that will cause connectivity problems during the agent deployment.

Remember to run `root.sh` after the agent is installed on each node. This is a must-do step as it ensures that the installer establishes proper permissions to the agent executables for future metric collection calls. A couple more things to keep in mind when you provision agents to targets from the Grid Control Console are

- The use of a Server Load Balancer (SLB) when multiple OMS servers are used
- The location of Oracle inventory

Provide the SLB service name and port for agent registration with the OMS, and ensure that agent software is accessible to all management services, since we don't know which OMS will be selected for this provisioning task. The following illustration shows the fields you will see in the Console and examples for filling in required fields.

Load Balancer Host and Port

Load Balancer Host, Port parameters can be provided here. Please make sure that agent source software is available on all the Oracle Management Server for the platform and version selected.

Load Balancer Host `appslab213.us.oracle.com`
This is the Load Balancer host name; must be specified with Load Balancer port. Example: slbhost.mydomain.com.

Load Balancer Port `4889`
This port should be available over firewall, if any. Agent will use this port to start communication with Management Server over HTTP, it must be specified with Load Balancer host. Example: 80

Additional Parameters

Additional parameter to agent installation can be provided here.

Additional Parameters [   ]
Example: -i /home/oraInst.loc (to use a non-default oracle inventory location)

Management Server Security

If you want to secure communications to the Management Server, specify the registration password here, or get the approval of a super administrator to add new agents to Enterprise Manager after the installation is complete.

Management Server Registration Password `*******`
Confirm Password `*******`

Additional Scripts

Optionally, you can choose to execute additional scripts before the installation is initiated, and after it is completed.

Pre-Installation Script File [   ]
Note that the script specified here needs to be present on all the remote hosts in the path specified.

☐ Run as Superuser.
User should be enabled for

When the agent deployment is completed successfully, you will see your new targets in the Console—probably in a pending status. This is normal in most environments since it is impossible for the installer to "guess" the monitoring database user password that the agent will use for metric collections.

We're not done just yet. We still have to configure our Cluster targets for proper monitoring. The next section will walk you through configuring your cluster targets.

Configure the Cluster Components in Grid Control

Once your agent is installed, the target cluster components will be displayed in the Console, but their status may not be shown accurately. You must configure each discovered RAC database as well as all ASM instances (if any) individually and specify monitoring properties. On the Cluster Database Configuration page (see the following illustration), provide the DBSNMP monitoring user's password. This is at the cluster database level. Inspect the connect descriptor and edit if needed.

You should also view the instances at the bottom of the same page and edit any instance to ensure that the listener's VIP name and proper port has been discovered and used to access each instance, as seen in the following illustration.

If you edit individual instances, notice that you cannot change the DBSNMP password at the instance level, obviously since it has been set for all instances at the cluster database level. You will be able, however, to edit connect descriptors and listener hostname and port for each instance, as shown in the following illustration.

The first thing a RAC administrator should do is to go to the Cluster target home page. From that page we can find the following info about the cluster:

- The number of nodes in the cluster
- The number of RAC databases running on this cluster

While you're on the Cluster home page, look for alerts and do try to fix them, as they are costly in terms of repository performance and consequently console performance. Also you can see the collective status of the nodes in your cluster. This is a bird's-eye view of either up or down, as seen in the following illustration.

A quick look at the hardware configuration of the cluster members is displayed on the home page, but you can see a bit more detail by clicking the View All Properties link, which takes you to the master node's home page, and then you can click the Hardware Platform CPU link. See the following illustration.

Hostname	**fabushab-sunclu1.us.oracle.com**		Local Disk Capacity (GB)	**208.21**	History
System Configuration	**i686**		Clock Frequency (MHz)		
Machine Architecture	**GenuineIntel i686**		Number of CPUs	**1**	
Hardware Provider	**Intel Based Hardware**		Number of CPU boards	**1**	
Memory Size (MB)	**3280**		Number of IO devices	**16**	

CPUs

CPU speed (MHZ)	Vendor	PROM Revision	ECACHE (MB)	CPU Implementation	Mask
2128	GenuineIntel	15	2	Intel(R) Core(TM)2 CPU 6400 @ 2.13GHz	6

IO Devices

Name	Vendor	Bus Type	Frequency (MHZ)	PROM Revision
00:00.0 Host bridge	Dell OptiPlex 745	PCI	66	02
00:02.0 VGA compatible controller	Dell Unknown device 01da	PCI	66	02
00:02.1 Display controller	Dell Unknown device 01da	PCI	66	02
00:1a.0 USB Controller	Dell OptiPlex 745	PCI	66	02
00:1a.1 USB Controller	Dell OptiPlex 745	PCI	66	02
00:1a.7 USB Controller	Dell OptiPlex 745	PCI	66	02
00:1b.0 Audio device	Dell OptiPlex 745	PCI	66	02
00:1d.0 USB Controller	Dell OptiPlex 745	PCI	66	02
00:1d.1 USB Controller	Dell OptiPlex 745	PCI	66	02
00:1d.2 USB Controller	Dell OptiPlex 745	PCI	66	02
00:1d.7 USB Controller	Dell OptiPlex 745	PCI	66	02
00:1f.2 IDE interface	Dell OptiPlex 745	PCI	66	02
00:1f.3 SMBus	Dell OptiPlex 745	PCI	66	02
00:1f.5 IDE interface	Dell OptiPlex 745	PCI	66	02
03:00.0 Ethernet controller	Dell Unknown device 01da	PCI	66	02
04:02.0 Ethernet controller	ADMtek Unknown device 0570	PCI	66	11

Network Interfaces

Name	INET Address	Maximum Transfer Unit	Broadcast Address	Mask	Flags	MAC Address	Hostname Aliases
eth0	10.148.60.238	1500	10.148.63.255	255.255.252.0	BROADCAST,MULTICAST,RUNNING,UP	00:1E:E5:D7:90:8F	fabushab-sunclu1.us.oracl
eth0:1	10.148.60.239	1500	10.148.63.255	255.255.252.0	BROADCAST,MULTICAST,RUNNING,UP	00:1E:E5:D7:90:8F	fabushab-sunclu1-v.us.ora
eth1	192.168.50.1	1500	192.168.50.255	255.255.255.0	BROADCAST,MULTICAST,RUNNING,UP	00:1E:4F:95:6C:0A	fabushab-sunclu1-i

After verifying and fixing all alerts, the administrator will typically go to the Interconnect page in the cluster home page and look for the interconnect statistics. Interconnect is an essential and vital part of the Cluster, and its performance affects the cluster performance to a great degree. Click the Interconnects tab from the home page, as shown in the following illustration. This will reveal information that will help in monitoring and administering this critical component.

One of the most important statistics to monitor is the "Private Interconnect Transfer Rate (MB/Sec)." Make sure that the transfer rate is not close to the limit of transfer rate imposed by the network cards used for the Interconnect (1 Gig E, InfiniBand, and so on). For example, if we are using a 1 Gig E card, the theoretical transfer rate is approximately 125 MB/sec. Now, the practical transfer rate is around ~70 to 80 percent of that number, which will bring this rate down to approximately 87 MB/sec.

Other statistics to monitor are "Total I/O Rate in MB/Sec (Last 5 Minutes)" and the "Total Error Rate (%) (Last 5 Minutes)."

The first metric represents the total I/O rate on the network interface. It is measured as the sum of Network Interface Read (MB/s) and Network Interface Write (MB/s). The second metric represents the number of total errors per second encountered on the network interface. This is the rate of read and write errors encountered on the network interface. A zero value is desired here, of course.

If you've just inherited monitoring a new cluster and would like to see the IP address for the Private interconnect (or even Public and VIP), you can click on the interface name for any host and you should see more details about the host machine in general and information about network interfaces specifically, as demonstrated in the next few illustrations.

An important thing to note at the bottom of the hardware configuration page is the Maximum Transfer Unit (MTU) for the interconnect interface. The standard MTU is 1500 Bytes and has to be the same on all nodes and also in the Private network switch. A setting of 1500 is good for most systems, but in certain cases (mostly with data warehouse–like DBs and applications) we recommend using jumbo frames. When you're using jumbo frames, the MTU size is 9000 Bytes, and it's very important that for all Interconnect network cards, the MTU size should be set to the exact same value and the Network Switch ports used for the interconnect should be set to 9000. Otherwise, the Interconnect performance will degrade greatly and the performance of RAC databases will degrade accordingly.

In RAC environments, the RDBMS engine gathers global cache workload statistics, which are reported in STATSPACK, AWRs. Global cache lost blocks statistics ("gc cr block lost" and/or "gc current block lost") for each node in the cluster as well as aggregate statistics for the cluster indicate problems or inefficiencies in packet processing for the interconnect traffic. Look for these graphs under the Performance tab in the illustration of the Performance page. These statistics should be monitored and evaluated regularly to guarantee efficient interconnect Global Cache and Enqueue Service (GCS/GES) and cluster processing. Any block loss indicates a problem in network packet processing and should be investigated.

Navigating Through the Cluster Resources

From the main cluster page, you can click on the Targets tab to see all monitored targets that belong to this cluster, as shown in the following illustration. This page is the easiest way to navigate between all monitored targets and a definitive source of reference for the status and alerts of all resources in a cluster.

From the main cluster page, you can also click on each host and review the host info and OS-specific statistics. Useful statistics to keep an eye on for any cluster and RAC DB are CPU Utilization and Disk IO Utilization. First, you navigate to the host page for the cluster node, as you would for any typical (non-cluster) host, and then click on the Performance tab to see more detailed information about CPU and Disk IO Utilization.

After reviewing the cluster statistics and host statistics, you can navigate to your RAC DB targets hosted by this cluster. To navigate to your cluster DB page, you can click on the RAC DB link under the Cluster Database section and it will take you to that RAC DB home page. In this page you get general information about this RAC DB like the number of instances, brief statistics about each instance, alerts specific to this RAC DB (on all instances), and links to ASM instances on each node.

Then you can navigate to the performance page (shown in the following illustration) by clicking on the Performance tab in the home page. Among the important pieces of information in this page is the Global Cache Block Access Latency chart, which shows the end-to-end elapsed time or latency for a block request.

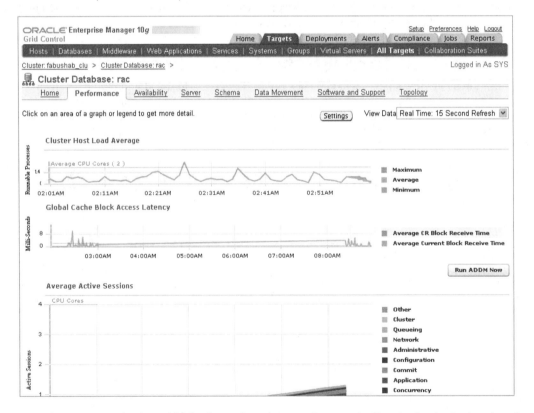

If accessing a database block of any class does not locate a buffered copy in the local cache, a global cache operation is initiated. Before reading a block from disk, an attempt is made to find the block in the buffer cache of another instance. If the block is present in another instance, a version of the block may be shipped. Two different kinds of blocks are distinguished: current and consistent read blocks. The average block receive time represents the end-to-end elapsed time or latency for a block request. Long latencies can be caused by

- A high number of requests caused by SQL statements that are not tuned.
- A large number of processes in the run queue waiting for CPU (scheduling delays).
- Slow, busy, or faulty interconnects. In these cases, look for dropped packets, retransmits, or cyclic redundancy check (CRC) errors. Ensure that the network is private and that inter-instance traffic is not routed through a public network. You can access the Cluster Interconnects page from the Cluster Cache Coherency page to monitor the transfer and related statistics for interconnects.

You can access more specific statistics by clicking on either Average Current Block Receive Time or Average CR Block Receive Time, as shown in the following illustration.

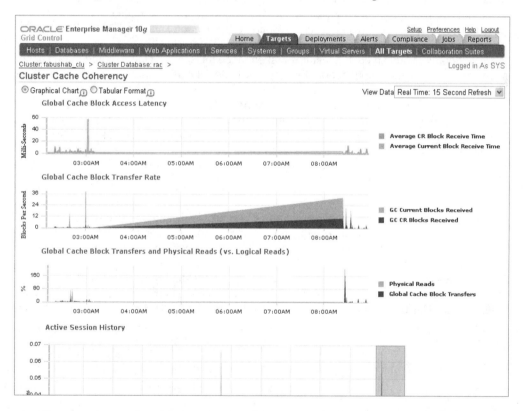

These graphs are showing Statistics for all instances. If you want to see statistics for each instance, you need to go to that instance's performance page or choose to view the data in tabular format and then click View Data by Instance.

Cluster-Managed Database Services

With respect to perceived availability and load balancing of client/application connections to the cluster database, it is necessary to have the ability to selectively control access to each instance. Cluster database services are a powerful way for the DBA to control application connectivity access to database instances. You can monitor, edit, and control cluster database services directly from the Console and propagate changes to the local `tnsnames.ora` file.

To illustrate the benefits of defining cluster database services, consider having an eight-node RAC cluster that services a RAC database with an instance on each node. By default, each instance has an equal role in accepting connections from client applications. When you have multiple applications accessing the same database, Oracle offers you the flexibility to assign certain instances dedicated to provide database services to certain applications. For example, you can group two instances and dedicate them to service a small application, and group the other six instances to service your larger and more resource-intensive business suite application. Grid Control offers you a user-friendly GUI that allows you to define new services and select each instance's service policy. It also covers Transparent Application Failover (TAF) Policy properties as well as the option to enable Distributed Transaction Processing.

Additionally, you can enable features that enhance the speed of failover and load balancing such as Fast Application Notification (FAN) for OCI and ODP.NET applications. You can specify Warning and Critical thresholds to publish alerts when the service elapsed response time and/or CPU time (both in milliseconds) exceed the threshold. There are still more features that you can view, create, edit, and control than you can imagine. If you follow the link to Consumer Group Mappings, you can define rules that enable the resource manager to automatically assign sessions to consumer groups and set each priority accordingly. If you really like the current rules, you can propagate those rules to multiple databases managed by Grid Control.

Listener Information

Listeners play an important role in instrumenting and providing each service with their availability and fast application notification. You can go to the main cluster page to check the status of listeners on each node. Click Targets and then click the Listener link on the node you are interested in.

From this page you can get a good idea about the status/state of the listener plus some basic statistics. To get more performance statistics, you can click the Performance tab in the main listener page. This provides a quick view of overall connection statistics.

To see which RAC DBs are serviced by this listener, you can click the Serviced Databases link, as shown in the following illustration.

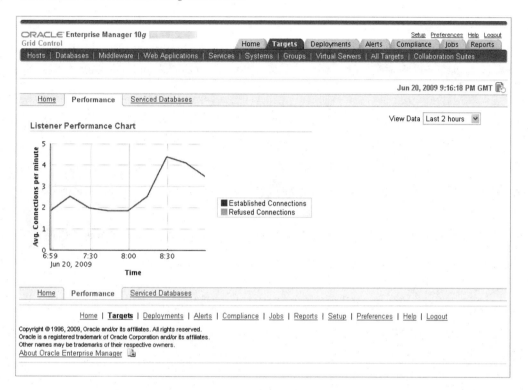

ASM Monitoring

Another resource that is highly recommended in a RAC environment is the Automatic Storage Manager (ASM) instances on each node in the cluster. ASM is a volume manager utility provided by Oracle that allows for out-of-box-shared access to disk resources by multiple database instances. To navigate to the ASM resource, you can go to the Targets tab in the cluster home page and click on any ASM instance. This page shows some important information about the ASM instance on that node and some basic disk group statistics, as shown in the following illustration.

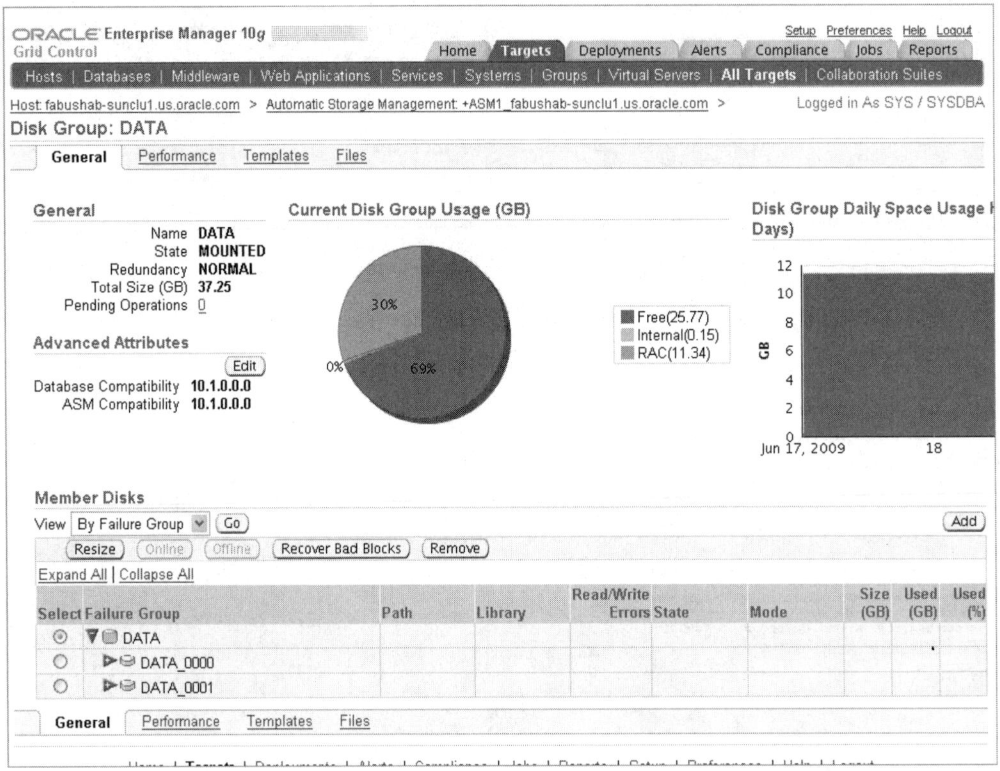

To get more detailed performance statistics, you can click the Performance tab. If you want to see Disk I/O Cumulative Statistics, you can click the Disk Group I/O Cumulative Statistics link under the Additional Monitoring links and you will see more detailed IO Statistics, as shown in the following illustration.

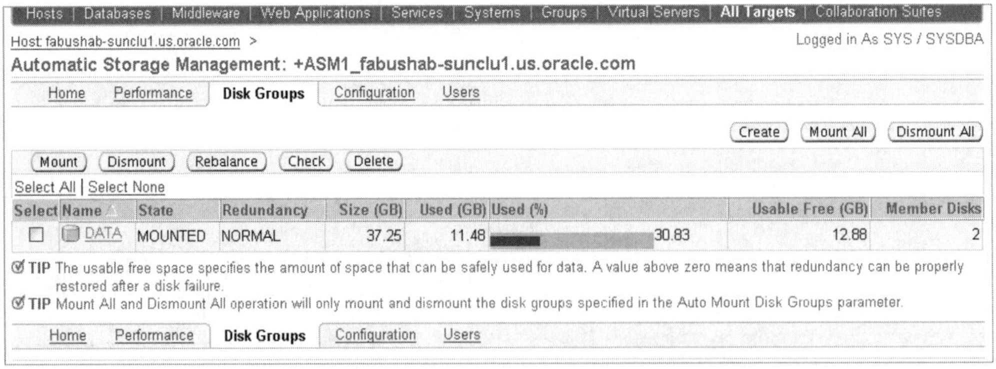

To add or delete a disk group, go to the Disk Groups subtab under the main ASM page. From this page you can see the current space utilization in this disk group plus the number of Disks or LUNs used to create this disk group, as shown in the following illustration. You can also add a disk group, drop a disk group, or mount and unmount a diskgroup. Also, if you have pending operations on a disk group, you can initiate a rebalance action on that disk group.

By clicking on the disk group, you will see more detailed status and stats about this specific Disk Group and space allocation per DB using this disk group. This is where you can find detailed disk (DATA_000 and DATA_001) information and devices used for each disk, along with space utilization views.

From this page, you can add or remove disks to this disk group. Also you can resize an existing disk. Keep in mind that before you resize the ASM disk from ASM, you need to physically resize the disk by adding storage to it, and then you can reflect this inside ASM.

For a more detailed view of each disk, click the Disk link (DATA_0000). The Member Disk screen (shown in the following illustration) includes I/O response time, throughput, and general disk attributes that are kept available to you at all times.

For cluster-wide performance statistics for ASM operations, click the Performance tab on the Disk Group page, as shown in the following illustration.

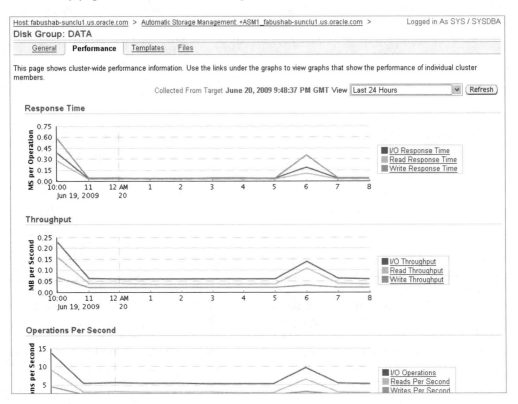

ASM File Type Templates

ASM supports most file types required by the database (control files, redo logs, data files, and so on), and we have a system default template that provides the attributes for file creation. These templates allow you to control how a file is generated so that it does not have to be specified on each creation. For instance, you can specify that an archivelog should always be mirrored when it is created within the ASM disk group. Thereafter, whenever an archivelog is created, a mirrored copy will always be generated automatically.

To manage those templates and add or delete templates, you can click on the template page in the Disk Group page. To change attributes of certain templates, you can just click on the template and change it accordingly.

Viewing Files within an ASM Disk Group

You can view files stored in the ASM Disk group: files such as ControlFiles, DataFiles, ArchiveLogs, Pfile/Spfile, and Tempfiles. Click the Files tab on the Disk Group page, as shown in the following illustration.

Notice here that while you navigate under the Disk group, you can select the RAC-specific database in which you are interested and then expand it to see the files stored in this Disk Group. If you're interested in specific file types, for example, data files, you can expand that type by clicking the triangle next to the type.

To get more information about a specific file, you can click the file and you will get more information about it. For example, with a data file selected, you will be able to view its redundancy level, block size, number of blocks, logical size, striped type, and creation date.

You can also create custom directories under the Files page. If files don't belong to any database, you can manually delete/remove them from the ASM Disk Group so you can reuse the space.

Lastly, it is worth mentioning that if you want to change some of the `init` parameters (or configuration parameters) for the ASM instance, you can click the Configuration tab. From there, you can change the `DISCOVERY_STRING`, the disk groups you want ASM to mount automatically when the ASM instance starts up, or the default rebalance power (see the following illustration).

Remember, this change is made to the `init` parameters for the ASM instance itself and does not impact or make changes to `init` parameters of any database that resides within the ASM diskgroups.

Summary

Monitoring complex environments, such as Oracle RAC clusters, require equally advanced and feature-rich tools that offer the functionality you need to get your arms around your servers. Grid Control clearly stands head-and-shoulders above any available management consoles when it comes to viewing, diagnosing, configuring, and deploying changes in your RAC environments. You need solid facts about your RAC cluster before making decisions to add hardware or tweak parameters. Investigate bottlenecks live during your application's high volume periods and drill down cluster-component levels quickly to identify and schedule your most critical maintenance tasks. Oracle Enterprise Manger Grid Control simplifies management tasks by providing cluster-wide performance statistics, key component metrics, advanced configuration tools, and dashboards, and tops it off with customizable reporting capabilities to ease your administration responsibilities.

CHAPTER
16

Data Guard Management

hen it comes to managing your highly available database, there's nothing more important than being able to visually see every aspect of your environment in one console. Grid Control gives you the ability to focus on data management with respect to logical items, such as tables and tablespaces, and physical items such as archived logs, backup sets, and cluster nodes. When it comes to disaster recovery, Grid Control maintains the ability to visually organize complex information from multiple sources and provide mechanisms to monitor and administer the Oracle disaster recovery solution, Data Guard. In its early stages, Grid Control had only a skeleton of Data Guard capabilities. But as it has evolved, it has included more and more capabilities, making it the default location for Data Guard configuration, monitoring, and administration.

The High Availability Console

So, what's in Grid Control for Data Guard management? The latest version of Grid Control allows you to get to the Data Guard home page via a quick Details link under the High Availability section on the Database target's home page. This takes you to the one-stop-shop High Availability Console page of this target database. On this page, you will see a Summary of this target database's availability such as Current Status, last start "Up Since" date and time, Overall Availability percentage since this target database was discovered in Grid Control, the current hosting server name, and last but not least, an MAA Advisor link. The MAA Advisor gives you expert advice on best-practice solutions for a list of outage categories and the level of recommendation (see the following illustration).

ORACLE Enterprise Manager 10*g*
Grid Control

Setup   Preferences   Help   Logout
Home   Targets   Deployments   Alerts   Compliance   Jobs   Reports

Maximum Availability Architecture (MAA) Advisor (ten2 - Primary Database)

Refresh   OK

Maximum Availability Architecture (MAA) is Oracle's High Availability (HA) blueprint. MAA provides a fully integrated and validated HA architecture with operational and configuration best practices that eliminate or reduce downtime. This table describes the configuration status and Enterprise Manager link for various HA solutions for each outage type.

MAA Summary   **This configuration is not protected for some outage types: Data Corruptions**
Recommendation   **Configure at least one recommended solution for each outage type to ensure maximum availability**

Outage Type	Oracle Solution	Recommendation Level	Configuration Status	Benefits
All Failures	Schedule Backups		✓	Fully managed database recovery and disk-based backups.
All Failures	Configure ARCHIVELOG Mode		✓	Enables online database backup and is necessary to recover the database to a point in time later than what has already been restored. Features such as Oracle Data Guard require that the production database run in ARCHIVELOG mode.
Computer Failures	Configure Oracle Data Guard			Fast-start Failover and fast application notification with integrated Oracle clients.
Computer Failures	Configure Oracle Real Application Clusters and Oracle Clusterware		-	Automatic recovery of failed nodes and instances. Fast application notification with integrated Oracle client failover.
Computer Failures	Configure Oracle Streams			Online replica database resumes processing. Whole database replication is recommended for protection.
Human Errors - Erroneous Transactions	Configure Flashback Query or Flashback Table		✓	Fine-grained query or rewind of specific tables.
Human Errors - Accidentally Dropped Tables	Configure Flashback Drop			Ability to quickly restore a dropped table.
Human Errors - Database Wide Impact	Configure Flashback Database		✓	Database-wide rewind to a point-in-time in the past.
Storage Failures	Configure Oracle Data Guard		✓	Fast-start Failover and fast application notification with integrated Oracle clients.
Storage Failures	Migrate Storage to Automatic Storage Management		-	ASM redundancy allows for redundant copies of the data in separate failure groups spanning different disk, controllers or storage arrays. Automatic, online rebalancing provides zero downtime.
Storage Failures	Configure Oracle Streams			Online replica database resumes processing. Whole database replication is recommended for protection.
Data Corruptions	Configure DB_BLOCK_CHECKING and DB_BLOCK_CHECKSUM Initialization Parameters	High	-	Comprehensive database block corruption prevention and detection.
Site Failures	Configure Oracle Data Guard		✓	Fast-start Failover and fast application notification with integrated Oracle clients.

NOTE
When prompted to log in to the database, use a SYSDBA privileged user. If you log in as a user with SYSDBA privileges, you will have access to all Data Guard functionality, including all monitoring and management features. If you log in as a non-SYSDBA user, you will have access to monitoring functions only; features such as standby creation, switchover, and failover will not be available.

The HA Console also lists a similar Summary for the Data Guard instance, as shown in the following illustration. It includes current status, hosting server, Data Guard Alerts, and Primary Redo Rate in KB per second. You can also set the refresh rate of this HA Console home page from Manual refresh to 5- or 60-second intervals.

Check out the Advanced View of this HA Console for graphical charts of the Availability History, aggregated by Day, Week, and Month; Used Flash Recovery Area (FRA) percentage, and Redo Rate for the last two hours. You can also customize this page's appearance, refresh options, chart duration period, and Cluster Services chart view.

After you have oriented yourself to the HA Console, you can select your main view through a toggle Switch To list of available views. For example, if the current view shows the primary database High Availability Console, then you can switch to the standby database view.

Data Guard Overview

Many DBAs are already familiar with the functionality known as Oracle Standby Database. It is an architectural feature that adds a little functionality to operations that already take place on your system: the archiving of every single change that happens on a database. The Standby

Database was a simple concept, in the beginning, and even though the overall architecture is now referred to as Data Guard, the foundation is still simple: take the archive logs from your production database, move them to another computer that has a copy of that database, and apply the archive logs to the copy as often, and as quickly as you can. In such a way, Data Guard is able to provide an efficient disaster recovery solution by maintaining transactionally consistent copies of the production database at a remote site. These copies, or standbys, can be one of two types, physical or logical. Which one you choose to include in your Data Guard configuration depends on what business needs you are trying to satisfy.

Over time, the Data Guard infrastructure has grown in power and flexibility so that it now represents a fully actualized disaster recovery solution for your Oracle databases—both single instance and RAC clusters. It has slowly built up a full infrastructure to ship archive logs, find archive gaps, and automatically fail over to a standby database should a disaster occur. Failing back to the first primary is now built in, along with the ability to guarantee different degrees of consistency or lag with the primary database—depending on your business rules.

Data Guard uses a "Broker" feature, which is a distributed management framework that automates and centralizes the creation, maintenance, and monitoring of Data Guard configurations. Some advantages of using a Data Guard broker include:

- Integrated support for RAC
- Easy creation and management of physical and logical standby databases
- Built-in monitoring and management
- Automated failover operations

You also have the "Observer" process that enables Fast-Start-Failover feature to determine the conditions that warrant a failover. You can invoke the Fast-Start Failover wizard from the Data Guard Overview page by clicking the Disabled link. Configuring Fast-Start Failover is covered in the third workshop in this chapter, "Configure a Physical Standby for RAC."

Obviously, this book is about Grid Control and not Data Guard, and going into significant detail here would be too much for our page count. From here on out in this chapter, we assume that you are familiar with the basics of Data Guard and are ready to see how Grid Control can help you manage the DG environment.

Creating a Physical Standby Database in Grid Control

You can configure a single-instance database and set up a physical standby instance on another managed host directly from the Grid Control Console. If the database is in NOARCHIVE LOG mode, the Console gives you the opportunity to configure the database in this mode, restart it, and perform a full cold backup afterwards. Obviously, to ship logs to another database, you need to be in archivelog mode.

Once you enable ARCHIVE LOG mode and restart the database, you will also be able to choose to use Fast-Start instance recovery time (as shown in the following illustration). The Fast-Start checkpointing feature is enabled by specifying a nonzero desired Mean Time To Recover (MTTR) value, which will be used to set the FAST_START_MTTR_TARGET initialization parameter. This parameter controls the amount of time the database takes to perform crash recovery for a single instance. When fast-start checkpointing is enabled, Oracle automatically maintains the speed of checkpointing so that the requested MTTR is achieved. Setting the value to 0 will disable this functionality (by default, the value of `FAST_START_MTTR_TARGET` is zero). An estimated value will be given on the Console screen for your info.

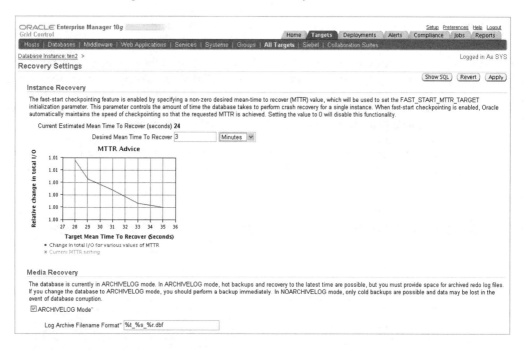

While creating a Physical Data Guard instance on a remote host, the DG Wizard walks you through all steps required to complete this task. One thing to note, however, is that the default monitoring credentials for the standby database instance are non-SYSDBA. If that option is chosen, you must provide username and password. We highly recommend using a SYSDBA user. If non-SYSDBA monitoring credentials are used, Data Guard performance monitoring will not be available for a mounted physical standby database.

GRID CONTROL WORKSHOP

Creating a Physical Standby

Workshop Notes

This workshop will walk through the creation of a physical standby database. The standby database creation process runs as an Enterprise Manager job.

Step 1. Put the database in archivelog mode. From the database home page, go to Availability | Recovery Options. Be sure you are logged in to the database with SYSDBA privileges, and then click the radio button to Enable Archivelog Mode. A database reboot is required.

Step 2. From the database home page, go to the High Availability section in the lower right and click on Console | Details. This puts you in the HA Console page. Click on the Add Standby Database link under Data Guard Summary.

Step 3. From the wizard's first page, choose the option Create a New Physical Standby Database and click Continue.

Step 4. Select a backup type to utilize for the instantiation of the new standby database. You can create a new online backup using RMAN, or utilize a staging area for the backups, as shown in the following illustration. Alternatively, you can utilize an existing RMAN backup, which will skip the need to create a new backup. However, this RMAN backup would need to have been created when your database was already in archivelog mode, and you must have all the archivelogs available to RMAN extending back to the backup time (for more on utilizing EM to make RMAN backups, refer to Chapter 14). For this exercise, we are creating a new RMAN backup.

Step 5. Specify the backup options. As shown in the following illustration, you need to tell the wizard how many file copy processes will be run in parallel for the backup; provide the host credentials for the RMAN job; and specify the options for the DG standby redo logs.

Step 6. Specify details of the standby database name and location. Here, we call the instance `ten2pdg`, storage is on the File System, and we are creating the standby database on the same host as the primary.

Step 7. On the wizard step for specifying file locations, choose the defaults, which will create the files in the OFA format familiar to all DBAs. Click Next.

Step 8. On the final Configuration step, you need to ensure you get a unique name for the database, the location for the standby archivelogs, and specify the Standby Database monitoring credentials. Note that the monitoring credentials for a Standby Database are different than for a standard database—because the database will typically run in a mount mode, monitoring cannot occur unless the credentials have SYSDBA privileges. Choose SYSDBA credentials. Be sure to leave Use Data Guard Broker selected at the bottom.

Also, note at the bottom the DG connect identifiers can be changed. By default, it utilizes the connection information that is provided by Enterprise Manager.

Once you are satisfied with the selections, click Next.

(continued)

Step 9. Review the final configuration elements. Once you are comfortable with the configuration, click on Finish. This will take some time to complete.

Once you submit this job, you cannot cancel it at this stage. After all steps are complete, you will be returned to the Data Guard overview page, and you will be able to see the new Physical Standby database as shown in the following illustration.

Step 10. When you are finished, the standby database instance is *not* automatically added to Grid Control. You will have to perform a discovery against the standby host to complete the circle. Once discovery is initiated and your newly discovered targets on the standby node are listed, click the Configure icon to edit monitoring properties.

At this screen, you can provide a unique target name for this standby instance. But for a standby instance, no users are allowed to log in to the database. So, you will have to use the SYS user or a user with SYSDBA privileges to allow the agent access for metric collections. Notice that the Monitor Username field is not editable as shown in the following illustration. However, when you select a SYSDBA role from the drop-down list, the Monitor Username field will become editable and you can specify SYS.

Step 11. You're not finished just yet. Remember to uncheck all discovered targets that you don't want to monitor via this agent, as shown in the following illustration, and then click OK to finish adding this target standby database to the agent's list of targets.

When you click OK in Step 11, all selected targets along with their configurations will be sent to the management agent to finalize the discovery process and instruct

(continued)

the agent to start monitoring those new targets. You should make sure this step has successfully completed. Once it completes, you will see a confirmation page as shown in the following illustration.

One final thing to keep in mind here: it will take the agent a few minutes to identify this new database instance as a Physical Standby database instance. So, don't rush and try to look for problems, or remove it from the Console in an effort to fix this view.

Data Guard Management Operations: An Overview

Now that you have a physical standby database, your Data Guard environment is ready for use. Here is a brief look at the top features for maintaining a Data Guard in Grid Control that make your life a whole lot easier when it comes to managing this aspect of your data center.

Change Database Role

You can change the role of the database. You can go from primary to standby in seconds directly from the HA Console links. You can also look at configuration, that is, time of lag for standby.

Validate Your Current Setup Against Oracle Best Practices

Check current setup against recommendations primarily for standby redo log files. First, go to the HA Console | MAA Advisor Details link. You can also go to the High Availability Operations links at the bottom of the HA Console page, and then click the Verify Configuration link.

Manage Standby Redo Logs

There is also an option to manage standby redo logs (SRL) such as drop/add or rename and so on. SRL management is automatic when managing DG through EM. The correct number of SRLs is added automatically to all databases when you create a standby, upgrade protection mode, or enable FSFO. Additionally, you can run Verify to check for (and add) the correct number of SRLs at any time.

Change Configuration Options to the DG Environment

Maintenance of DG configuration needs expansion to include additional options for log transport such as timeout, `max_failures`, and so on (attributes in `log_archive_dest_X`). You can change Net Timeout and other DG parameters from the Primary/Standby/Common Properties pages off the Data Guard overview. So, again, click the HA Console | High Availability Operations links at the bottom and then click Setup and Manage.

Turn Off Log Apply at the Standby Database

Turn off applying logs by changing the state of a database. Simply click Edit after selecting the radio button next to the standby instance, and select Log Apply Off. Apply and you are done. This is especially handy when you perform maintenance on the database and do not want to keep applying logs.

Test the Log Transport Mechanism

Testing the log transport—this is nice when setting up DG to know whether primary will be able to send archive logs to the standby or there is a problem. To do this, run the Verify operation from the Data Guard overview page, which will test log transport (among other things). You can also run the Test Application from the Data Guard Performance page. Of course, even if you don't do this, you will be notified of any problems with log shipping via the Data Guard status alert, as well as seeing a non-normal status in the db home page and DG overview.

Monitor HA Overall Performance

Use the HA Console Performance metric chart and look at each sequence sent by the primary and sequences received and applied by the standby database. If Apply Lags exceed your set thresholds, you can force apply directly from the same page. Too much lag may be due to stuck arch processes.

Move Archivelogs Across Servers When a Gap Occurs

You can move archivelog files from one machine to the other (when there is a gap). This is especially useful when either side is using ASM. Doing it manually is not usually an easy task. All gaps are done automatically via Fetch Apply Log (FAL). If any files are missing, this operation can fail. Gaps are not explicitly managed via metrics; they are implicitly handled via the Transport or Apply Lag metrics.

While it would be nice to see some automatic fix-it for log gaps added in a future release of Grid Control, such as when a hung archiving process causes lags in log shipping, no such functionality exists yet. For now, you will have to set up Corrective Actions manually for such operations.

Review the DG Performance Metric

The Data Guard Performance Metric is a group of four metrics, which also shows up in the HA Console. This metric helps in Gap detection for true log gaps (v$archive_gap), need alerts, and the fix-it feature. I think right now the user has to write fix-it scripts or there's no automatic way to resolve log gap. Performance statistics on log shipping are a common problem for users about lags in log shipping.

Change the Standby to Fast-Start Failover

Fast-Start Failover (FSFO) allows the DG processes to automatically initiate a failover under conditions of failure in the primary database that Data Guard can detect. Before you enable FSFO, the following prerequisites must be met so that the broker can allow you to enable FSFO:

- Ensure that the broker configuration is running in maximum availability mode. This includes configuring the protection mode, standby redo logs, and the LogXptMode property.

- Enable Flashback Database and set up a flash recovery area on both the primary database and the target standby database.

- Install the DGMGRL command-line interface on the observer computer.

- Configure the TNSNAMES.ORA file on the observer system so that the observer is able to connect to the primary database and the preselected target standby database.

GRID CONTROL WORKSHOP

Configuring Fast-Start Failover

Workshop Notes

When you use Grid Control to configure FSFO, all you need to do is use the Fast-Start Failover wizard.

Step 1. Go to the Data Guard Overview page and look for the Fast-Start Failover status field.

Step 2. Click the Disabled link to invoke the Fast-Start Failover Page.

Step 3. From the Fast-Start Failover Change Mode page, click Enabled.

This tells the broker to start the observer and change the configuration's protection mode to maximum availability as needed. Then, on the Fast-Start Failover Configure page, as shown in the following illustration, select the standby database that should be the target of a failover.

Step 4. If the Observer is not configured, you can configure it by clicking the Configure Observer button. On the Fast-Start Failover: Configure Observer screen, find a suitable managed host, Observer Oracle Home, and optionally an alternate or additional Observer Host as shown in the following illustration.

The Observer host can be any managed host in Grid Control. Select from a list of hosts by clicking the flashlight icon. You can also specify an alternate observer host the same way. The location of Oracle home binaries for the observer on the host is automatically filled in for you once you select the observer host. Your Observer host will be registered with the DataGuard Broker, and the primary target database will be updated. All operations are summarized in the screen as shown in the following illustration.

Step 5. Enable Flash-Back logging for each database, primary and standby and select how far back the database can be flashed back.

Data Guard Monitoring and Metrics

Data Guard–specific metrics are available out of the box for database targets. You can edit or change Data Guard metrics by going to the Metrics and Policy Settings page from either the primary or standby database target's home page.

Data Guard Fast-Start Failover

When Fast-Start Failover is enabled, these metrics will generate a critical alert on the new primary database (old standby) if a fast-start failover occurs:

■ **Fast-Start Failover Occurred**   Indicates that a fast-start failover has occurred. The value is 0 if fast-start failover has not occurred and 1 if fast-start failover has occurred.

■ **Fast-Start Failover SCN**   Shows the SCN when a fast-start failover occurred. The fast-start failover SCN must be initialized to a value before the metric will alert.

■ **Fast-Start Failover Time**   Shows the time when a fast-start failover occurred.

Data Guard Performance

All charts on the Performance Overview page are represented by the following metrics:

■ **Apply Lag (seconds)**   Shows the approximate number of seconds the standby is behind the primary database.

■ **Estimated Failover Time (seconds)**   The approximate number of seconds required to fail over to this standby database. These account for the startup time, if necessary, plus the remaining time required to apply all the available redo on the standby. If a bounce is not required, it is only the remaining apply time.

■ **Redo Apply Rate (KB/second)**   Displays the Redo Apply Rate in KB/second on this standby database.

■ **Transport Lag (seconds)**   Shows the approximate number seconds of redo not yet available on the standby database.

Data Guard Status

If the Data Guard Status metric contains Warning, a warning alert is triggered. If the metric contains Error, a critical alert is triggered.

Configuring a Physical Standby for a RAC Database

In addition to assisting with creating a standby database from a single instance database, Enterprise Manager can help with the same option for a RAC database. Adding a standby RAC database to an existing RAC database target is a bit more complicated, but essentially, you would provision a two-node cluster including CRS, ASM, and RAC databases to another node, then create the standby database. In Grid Control 10.2.0.5 this is done in a series of steps best outlined in a workshop.

GRID CONTROL WORKSHOP

Configure a Physical Standby for RAC

Workshop Notes

In this workshop, we utilize Grid Control to assist in the extended set of steps required to create physical standby database for a RAC database.

Step 1.   From the Deployments tab, select RAC Provisioning Procedures under the Deployment Procedure Manager section. Use the second option in the next page,

Oracle Clusterware / RAC Provisioning for UNIX. Now, click the Schedule button at the top of the screen so you can initiate the Provisioning job.

■ Select the source target from the Software Library for CRS and RAC.

■ Use the RAC install to provision ASM.

■ Select the hosts to use as the target for the installation.

■ Select the correct network interfaces for both the interconnect and public and ensure the correct Virtual Host Name for the VIP is used.

■ Specify target host credentials.

■ Specify the software home locations and work areas, whether to create a starter database and its credentials, and whether to create an ASM instance and its credentials.

■ Specify the shared storage location for OCR (and mirrors), Voting Disk(s) and Datafiles. (Note: If using raw devices, you have the option to clear them as part of installation. This will ensure that installation does not fail due to leftover information from previous installs.)

■ Configure the Bonding Interface (if necessary).

■ Specify whether to install and initiate the configuration manager (receive security updates from My Oracle Support).

■ Review and submit.

Step 2. Now, you can create a single-instance physical standby database using the newly installed RAC home. Select the database to be used as the primary database from the Targets list in Grid Control.

Start by selecting Add Standby Database. From the Home page, choose the Availability tab and then the Data Guard section. A dialog screen appears with information and a link to Add Standby Database.

Step 3. Select Create a New Physical Standby Database. The rest of the screens are similar to the previous "Add Physical Standby" Workshop:

■ Determine the type of backup you want to perform.

■ Specify the location of the standby database (sid name, host, database home, storage type).

■ Specify the file location on the standby site; this should be shared storage (ASM).

■ Specify configuration parameters (database unique name, Grid Control target name, standby archive location, Use Data Guard Broker).

■ Review settings and submit.

Step 4. Convert this newly created standby database into RAC with no downtime to the primary database. First, perform prep work on the environment prior to conversion of this database to RAC.

■ Verify initialization parameter `STANDBY_FILE_MANAGEMENT=AUTO` on the primary database and the standby database to be converted.

(continued)

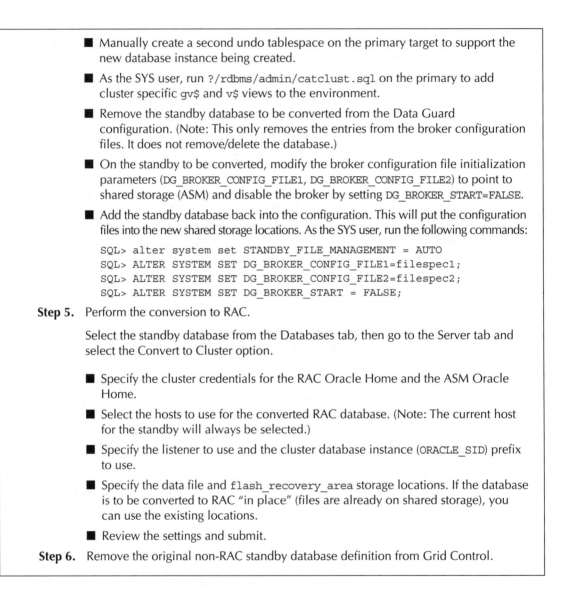

- Manually create a second undo tablespace on the primary target to support the new database instance being created.
- As the SYS user, run `?/rdbms/admin/catclust.sql` on the primary to add cluster specific gv$ and v$ views to the environment.
- Remove the standby database to be converted from the Data Guard configuration. (Note: This only removes the entries from the broker configuration files. It does not remove/delete the database.)
- On the standby to be converted, modify the broker configuration file initialization parameters (`DG_BROKER_CONFIG_FILE1`, `DG_BROKER_CONFIG_FILE2`) to point to shared storage (ASM) and disable the broker by setting `DG_BROKER_START=FALSE`.
- Add the standby database back into the configuration. This will put the configuration files into the new shared storage locations. As the SYS user, run the following commands:

```
SQL> alter system set STANDBY_FILE_MANAGEMENT = AUTO
SQL> ALTER SYSTEM SET DG_BROKER_CONFIG_FILE1=filespec1;
SQL> ALTER SYSTEM SET DG_BROKER_CONFIG_FILE2=filespec2;
SQL> ALTER SYSTEM SET DG_BROKER_START = FALSE;
```

Step 5. Perform the conversion to RAC.

Select the standby database from the Databases tab, then go to the Server tab and select the Convert to Cluster option.

- Specify the cluster credentials for the RAC Oracle Home and the ASM Oracle Home.
- Select the hosts to use for the converted RAC database. (Note: The current host for the standby will always be selected.)
- Specify the listener to use and the cluster database instance (`ORACLE_SID`) prefix to use.
- Specify the data file and `flash_recovery_area` storage locations. If the database is to be converted to RAC "in place" (files are already on shared storage), you can use the existing locations.
- Review the settings and submit.

Step 6. Remove the original non-RAC standby database definition from Grid Control.

Summary

While there is no room here to discuss in great detail the degree of help that Grid Control provides over a Data Guard environment, we have tried to summarize the features and monitoring options available so that you can dig deeper and maximize your disaster recovery capabilities. We provided a walk-through of adding a physical standby database, configuring fast-start failover (FSFO), and we ended with the steps required to add DG functionality to your RAC environment.

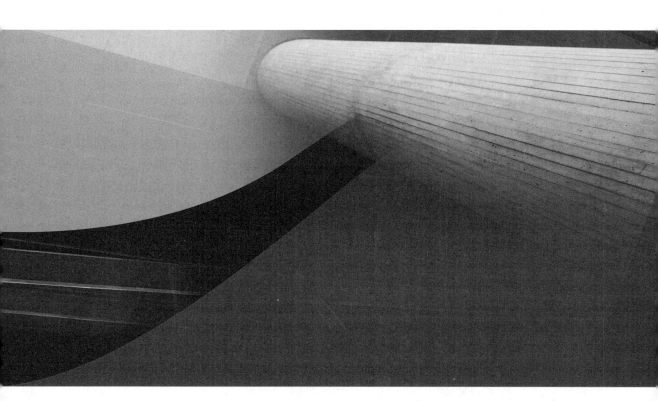

CHAPTER
17

Application Monitoring

t has long been established in the world of online operations, that having even the slightest monitoring practice for deployed applications grants certain bragging rights. However, such practices generally fall short once the extent goes beyond the basic health checks of the application server. Nowadays, when you go from simple application deployments to modeling service level agreements, it requires that monitoring production-grade environments be *proactive*, thereby detecting and responding to problems—before an end user is even aware that a problem exists. Although this sounds overly obvious, it is quite unorthodox in practice to pick up on indicators from a continual stream of data and apply a fix to an environment in anticipation of a problem. This chapter offers prescriptive guidance toward delivering better quality of service from the consumer's perspective, including the use of beacons, a tools-based monitoring feature built into Grid Control.

The Complexity of Online Operations

It wasn't long ago that avoidance of application failure was the sole incentive shared by every operations, business, and development team. Momentum has not slowed, though, since the many great minds behind Enterprise Manager speak to the evolution of Grid Control as it seeks to address a new set of challenges and trends in online operations today:

- The expectations of how a service should perform are increasing as IT investments are being squeezed.

- Interoperability, portability, and service diversity lead to configuration, deployment, and production issues that impact performance.

- Outsourcing, hosting, cloud computing, and virtualization opacity present a new set of management challenges.

Ironically enough, the user community still refuses to finger any other suspects than the application itself for their service performance and availability woes. When the chief complaint is performance related, avoid the long and arduous path of having your developers scour through code looking to optimize at every turn. Although there is a tremendous amount of literature available on developing elegant code, your time as a system administrator is better spent diagnosing the outlying factors critical to the execution of the code. In fact, a recent study by Forrester reveals that 74 percent of problems are reported by end users, rather than by the tools put in place to detect problems during development. When it comes to performance-related issues, it generally boils down to a mashup of causes, assumptions, and misconceptions that are involved when addressing the problem.

First, so many developers are pressured to meet design and functional requirements that emphasis is taken away from the art of performance tuning. The true difference between good code and a good application is when developers spend less time focusing on the slowest segments of code and shift their focus toward optimizing the most commonly executed paths instead. In software engineering, this approximation rests on the notion that by simply optimizing 10 percent of the code, you can effectively address 90 percent of the execution time required by those who make the most use of the application. This notion stems from the law of the vital few, better known as Pareto's Law, or the law of 90/10, in this context. In other words, by improving 50 percent of code that executes 0.2 percent of the time, the result will be an improvement of 0.1 percent to your overall business. On the other hand, by improving 50 percent of the code that executes 10 percent of the time, an improvement of 5 percent will take place. Now that's maximizing value.

Second, many believe that throwing more hardware at the problem improves performance, which is truly a band-aid approach to a terminal disease. More often than not, organizations simply double their existing infrastructure to solve an acute scaling need. Although versatile (the band-aid, that is), there are fundamental truths that come from adding additional hardware:

- The environment grows in complexity, making manageability an issue.
- Capital investments must be made.
- Additional time is required to act.

Naturally, environments are unavoidably complex, but before you take the opportunity to add hardware, let's take a step back and closely inspect the relationship that exists between *scaling* and *complexity*. When you add independent architectural components to your environment, such as Linux servers, your environment's complexity climbs in a linear fashion. Now, when you scale components that are dependent on each other to function—like application and database servers used to host web applications—the complexity becomes an order of magnitude higher. Complex systems are difficult to operate, extend, diagnose, and simply manage. As requirements evolve and modifications need to be made, additional time and investment will be required to alter the environment to accomplish new tasks. Herein lies the painful relativity between the relationship between scaling and complexity—sure, both scenarios scale, but by no means do both scale well. As a result, consider spending the necessary time to pinpoint the root cause behind your performance dilemmas before acting on any opportunity to deploy additional hardware into the mix.

Finally, performance enhancements can only be made after the fact. It is easier to detect performance problems once the system is built and put into place. Avoid the historical tendency of many IT shops to suboptimize. The many parts that make up an online environment form a tangle that leads administrators to optimize through decomposition as the only way to marginalize complexity. Optimization by decomposition begins by breaking complex situations into smaller pieces, followed by the measurement and optimization of each. When this process is taken too far, a false expectation surfaces that when all of the individual measurements are optimized, then the overall environment is optimized too. In the case of a performance dilemma, optimization focuses on improving just one or two aspects of performance: execution time, memory consumption, disk usage, or bandwidth. Optimizing one usually requires a trade-off— where one factor optimized comes at the cost of another. For example, increasing the size of a web cache to improve performance requires the investment of additional memory. Furthermore, premature optimization leads to designs that are unnecessarily complex, the result of overengineering a solution in anticipation of circumventing certain outcomes. In practice, you will profit the most by optimizing the whole. Specifically, tuning activities should only take place once the system is in place and there is an opportunity to see the application in use. This equalizes efficiency across the entire application life cycle by keeping performance goals in mind when designing the solution, without introducing early risks that might jeopardize the end result.

Servicing Applications

Hopefully, the previous discussion highlights the nuances that stem from our modern-day deployments as we struggle to narrow down the avenues where performance gremlins dwell. Barriers aside, the art of performance tuning remains a perpetual cycle and only serves as a notice when you go from just deploying applications to modeling them as a service. Recall, if you will, that a service in Grid Control is a model of a business function or deployed application that *services* end users. In the past, application logging was the sole trusted methodology for capturing events that took place in client-server scenarios. Today, with thin clients dominating the scene, the focus moves to capturing the frequency, response, and other related statistics based on the *user's experience* and storing the results in centralized server locations for review. These statistics are then applied against service level agreements, which define the *availability*, *performance*, and *usage* objectives expected from a service.

As we venture into the remaining part of this chapter, look for the distinct parallel that is being drawn between what has traditionally taken place (including the disappointments that result) and the approach that Grid Control is taking to address these disappointing issues with holistic precision.

Justifying Service Availability

Service performance is subject to the interpretation of the response time a user experiences. For a service to be considered online, a user must be able to access the application and perform a set of tasks in a set amount of time. In other words, service performance is tied closely to availability, such that, if performance degrades beyond a particular point, the service is thought to be unavailable. Using Grid Control, you now have a means of modeling a service's availability and quantifying performance grievances by collecting performance and response metrics from service test runs executed from beacons strategically placed within user communities. Grid Control's beaconing technology carries significant benefits, most notably, the ability to quickly add new metric collections without application code changes or additional hardware, and to do so while the application remains in use.

Working with Beacons

Beaconing is part of Grid Control's proactive application-monitoring system that sends data, ostensibly for the purpose of adding metric collection to *virtual* users as their experiences are evaluated by administrators. A beacon can be best described as a remote target that allows the Management Agent to monitor specific services. Beacons are, therefore, an integral part of modeling a service because of the following characteristics and features:

- Beacons can simultaneously monitor the availability and performance of multiple services or web applications.

- Beacons automatically record and play back web transactions of user actions at specified intervals from chosen user communities. A web transaction is a service test that allows a beacon to emulate a client to test an enabled service.

- Beacons offer basic network monitoring, including the ability to ping any network device or host and find network problems using interactive trace routing.

- Beacons are capable of testing various protocols: infrastructure (DNS, FTP, ICMP Ping, Ports), database (SQL timing, TNS ping, JDBC), middleware (SOAP, HTTP ping), and collaboration (POP, SMTP, IMAP, LDAP).

- By default, the only beacon enabled is the one that comes with the OMS install and the accompanying Management Agent. Other beacons must be added to other Agents, as you would do for any other Grid Control target.

- The closest beacon is the benchmark against which you can compare the performance of service tests run from remote beacons farther away from the service you intend to test in your enterprise.

- When adding beacons, you designate one or more of them as key beacons to determine the availability of the service. The service is considered available if at least one key beacon can execute one or more service tests.

Where to Put Beacons

The placement of beacon targets in the enterprise is crucial for monitoring the true performance of any service. You should consider deploying beacons around main concentrations of consumers on the network, together with a list of potential hotspots where bottlenecks are likely to occur. Although there is no strict rule or regulation on the number of beacons that a service may need, the number is more or less in relation to how your environment is scaled: the larger the enterprise, the larger the network, or the larger the adoption of your service, the more areas to consider when deploying your beacons. To follow the high-availability rule of two, consider using at a minimum two beacons for smaller environments—one as close to the principal components of your system and the other where the highest concentrations of consumers are expected to be. As previously hinted, this approach helps to ensure that any localized network outage will not trigger a complete outage of the entire application if another key beacon is capable of successfully accessing the same service. As the size of your deployments increases, the key will be to strategically deploy several beacons per (geographical) continent, per data center, or at an office with a larger community base, whatever makes the most sense based on the topology of your enterprise.

GRID CONTROL WORKSHOP

Creating a Beacon

Workshop Notes
Unless you have explicitly created beacons on other Management Agents, the only existing beacon will be the one that came from the initial Oracle Management Server install. This workshop will guide you through the steps for adding additional remote beacons, which are used to determine the availability of a service.

Step 1.   Access the Enterprise Manager configuration and system monitoring functions by clicking the top-right Setup link.

Step 2.   To see the listing of all Management Agents in the enterprise, click the Management Agents subtab and then select a Management Agent you want to add a beacon to, as shown in Figure 17-1.

(continued)

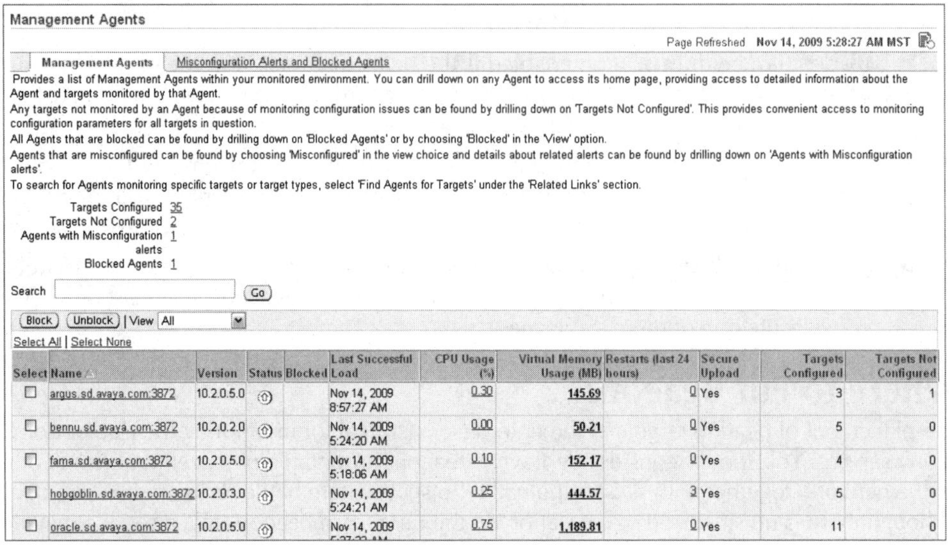

FIGURE 17-1.   *A listing of all Management Agents discovered in the enterprise*

Step 3.   Under the Monitored Targets section, select Beacon from the drop-down menu and click Go.

Step 4.   The Create Beacon page is displayed for you to enter beacon information, including any proxy settings required for the beacon to run service tests. See Figure 17-2. For the Name field, we suggest that you enter a descriptive name followed by the beacon's geographical location; such as *genisys.acme.com_vietnam* or *sylvia.acme. com_datacenter-east.*

Step 5.   If this beacon resides on a Windows platform, additional user credentials must be submitted in the section labeled "Miscellaneous Information" for web transaction playback to take place successfully.

Step 6.   Click OK to complete the Beacon Wizard.

Step 7.   You should now see the newly added beacon, which later will be designated as a key beacon when modeling a service.

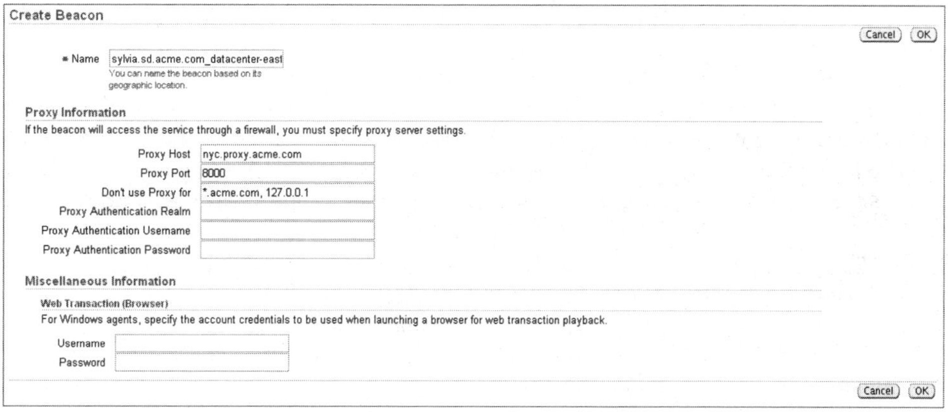

Create Beacon

Cancel   OK

* Name   sylvia.sd.acme.com_datacenter-east
You can name the beacon based on its
geographic location.

Proxy Information
If the beacon will access the service through a firewall, you must specify proxy server settings.

Proxy Host   nyc.proxy.acme.com
Proxy Port   8000
Don't use Proxy for   *.acme.com, 127.0.0.1
Proxy Authentication Realm
Proxy Authentication Username
Proxy Authentication Password

Miscellaneous Information

Web Transaction (Browser)
For Windows agents, specify the account credentials to be used when launching a browser for web transaction playback.

Username
Password

Cancel   OK

FIGURE 17-2.   *Adding beacons to a Management Server*

NOTE
*Pay attention to the shift of beacon terminology within Grid Control.
No longer does the notion of local versus remote beacons exist, even
though technology remnants are littered throughout Grid Control
(purely for backward compatibility*). Understand that, starting in
10gR2, all beacons are actually remote, and the best way to describe
the concept of local is to say that certain beacons are placed as close
as possible to the principal components of a system (including placing
the beacon on the same machine as the middle tier). This local
beacon is useful to test properties such as up/down at the functional
level while remote beacons scattered throughout the network can be
used to test the traffic, latency, and availability of the network.
cough

There are many reasons for using multiple beacons in selected geographical communities; the
following are some of the more common ones:

■   To compare service test performance against benchmarked results from the local beacon.

■   To accurately reflect the user communities represented. For example, you may need to
add beacons that run unique service tests in certain user communities, thereby broadening
the list of representative user actions.

■   To bring new hardware online, for which you need to designate new key beacons to
determine service availability.

■   To run ping tests to network devices and hosts to gauge network latency.

SSL Monitoring with Beacons

When you start modeling service tests, you can manually create transaction steps or use the Web Transaction Recorder to automatically record the process and let Grid Control construct the transaction steps taken during the session. It is important to note that the creation and playback of web-based transactions may include the use of SSL over HTTP. For the beacon to be able to log in and communicate with secured web applications, the certificate used by the application has to be available for the beacon to use. All the available certificates recognized by the beacon are stored in the b64InternetCertificate.txt file in the $ORACLE_HOME/sysman/config directory.

NOTE
On cluster machines (with CRS installed), or with state-deployed agents, make sure to save the certificate information in the state directory of the Management Agent and not in the default $ORACLE_HOME/sysman/config location.

To get the runtime state directory of the agent, issue the following command:

```
[oracle@lxclu1 ~]$ emctl getemhome
```

This will return the root directory where the agent state files exist:

```
Oracle Enterprise Manager 10g Release 5 Grid Control
10.2.0.5.0.
Copyright (c) 1996, 2009 Oracle Corporation. All
rights reserved.
EMHOME=/u01/app/oracle/product/agent10g/lxclu1
.us.oracle.com
```

GRID CONTROL WORKSHOP

Adding SSL Certificates for Beacon Playback

Workshop Notes
Add additional certificates to the b64InternetCertificate.txt file in order to create and play back SSL web-based transactions:

Step 1.   Once your web browser of choice is launched, visit the secure web site.

- As soon as the first page comes up, click the security lock icon at the bottom of the web browser application screen.

- When using a Mozilla-based browser such as Firefox: Click the security icon. When the security dialog comes up, click the View Certificate button to see the details of the certificate. From the Details tab, export the certificate to a file on your local hard drive, as shown in Figure 17-3.

- If you're using Internet Explorer, click the security icon at the bottom of the page. When the certificate dialog box comes up, navigate to the Details tab, and click the Copy To File button to export the certificate to a file on your local hard drive, as shown in Figure 17-4. Save the certificate as Base-64 encoding.

FIGURE 17-3. *Export certificate in Mozilla-based browsers*

Step 2. Open the saved certificate file, and grab the certificate data, including the BEGIN CERTIFICATE and END CERTIFICATE delimiters.

```
-----BEGIN CERTIFICATE-----
<... the b64 encoded certificate ...>
-----END CERTIFICATE-----
```

Step 3. Paste the certificate in the b64InternetCertificate.txt file.

Step 4. Restart the Agent.

```
[oracle@uyendex ~]$ emctl stop  agent
[oracle@uyendex ~]$ emctl start agent
```

(continued)

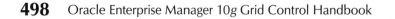

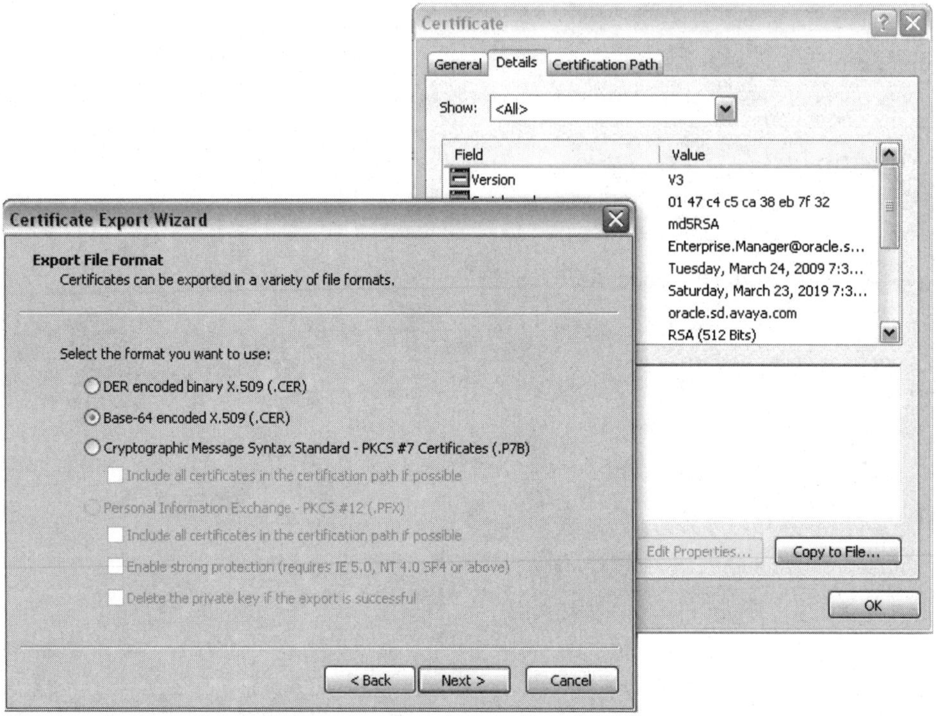

FIGURE 17-4. *Export certification in Internet Explorer*

If an SSL-based web transaction is defined, and the beacon does not have the certificate to use to initiate the SSL communication, the beacon will report the following error:

```
javax.net.ssl.SSLException: SSL handshake failed:
    X509CertChainInvalidErr -- <the HTTPS url>
```

GRID CONTROL WORKSHOP

Modeling a Service Using an Out-of-Box Web Application: Enterprise Manager Web Site

We decided that the best approach was to leverage an out-of-box web application and that was none other than the existing EM Website. At first glance, this might seem a bit redundant from the workshops outlined in Chapter 13, but rest assured we are expanding on what you have learned so far. The Create Service Wizard is the main throughway for defining a service, and it is important that we drive home a process that is representative of the majority of services you and many others will have modeled.

Step 1. *Create the system*. We are going to create the underlying system in Grid Control to host a service we will call *Enhanced EM Website System,* which will be like the default EM Website but with additional service features. Using Internet Explorer, click the Targets tab and then the Systems subtab to navigate to the Systems summary table. Leave System selected in the Add field and click Go to enter the following information into the wizard:

Component Page:

a. **Name:** For this exercise, we will provide the unique name: *Enhanced EM Website System.*

b. **Components:** To match the existing EM web site, the Grid Control Hosts, Web Cache, and Application Servers must be added. Based on the request flow, select the additional components outlined in the following illustration so that it becomes easier to narrow down the cause of service failure using a feature like Root Cause Analysis (described later).

c. **Time Zone**: We recommend that you choose the time zone closest to your Grid Control Database Repository.

Topology Page:

a. The default EM Website does not have any topology associations, but the relationships between the system components chosen earlier should take place in order to take advantage of the following benefits:

■ Indicators over each icon will quickly depict which components are down or have alerts, providing a quick avenue to drill down and review the details.

(continued)

■ Root Cause Analysis uses the topology viewer to highlight the causes of service failures, as shown in the following illustration.

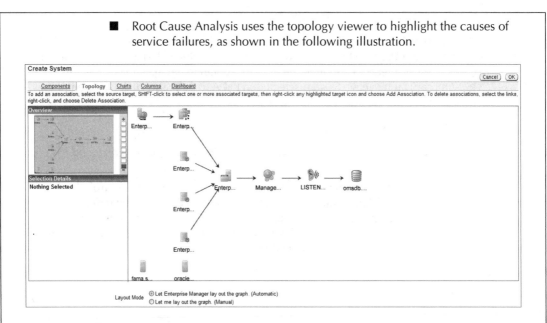

Charts Page:

a. Again, the default EM Website does not contain any charts, so it would be beneficial to depict the overall performance of the system. By default, you will get a listing of charts for the system's target types, as shown in the following illustration. Feel free to add, remove, order, or edit the charts. When editing the chart of a specific component, click Selected Targets followed by the Grid Control target name.

Create System

Components Topology Charts Columns Dashboard

Specify the charts that will be shown in the System Charts page. By default, the commonly used charts for the target types contained in this System are added.

Edit Remove | Add Reorder

Select Metric Name	Chart Description
○ Host: Total Disk I/O Per Second	Selected Targets
○ Host: CPU Utilization (%)	Selected Targets
○ Host: Memory Utilization (%)	Selected Targets
○ Database Instance: Active Sessions Waiting: Other	3 Targets with Highest Average
○ Database Instance: Active Sessions Waiting: I/O	3 Targets with Highest Average
○ Database Instance: Active Sessions Using CPU	3 Targets with Highest Average
○ Database Instance: Wait Time (%)	Selected Targets
◉ Listener: Connections Refused (per min)	3 Targets with Highest Average
○ Listener: Connections Established (per min)	3 Targets with Highest Average
○ Listener: Response Time (msec)	Selected Targets

Edit Remove | Add Reorder

Components Topology Charts Columns Dashboard

Cancel OK

Columns and Dashboard Pages:

a. The Columns Page sets the column names that appear in both the Columns and Dashboard Pages. Be sure to include the same metrics used in the Charts Page alongside the default Name, Type, Status, Alerts, and Policy Violations.

b. The System Dashboard provides the executive roll-up view of the health of managed targets in this system. Select the parameters that best fit how you would like the Dashboard to be displayed, and click OK to create the system. You will see a confirmation page, as shown in the following illustration.

Step 2. ***Create the service.*** Once the system is in place, it is time to create the service that runs on it. This wizard is quite lengthy; so ensure that you are not prone to network hiccups—because your input will only be saved after you complete the entire process! At a minimum, enter only the information the wizard requires, commit, and then circle back and customize to your heart's content. There are six service models to choose from, each model meant to closely emulate a specific class of application. Based on your choice, the wizard will guide you through the creation process specific for that model. The original EM Website is modeled after the Web Application service model and is probably the most widely used in Enterprise Manager. Click the Targets tab and then the Services subtab to navigate to the Services summary table. Select Web Application from the Add drop-down menu and click Go to enter the following information into the wizard:

(continued)

General Page:

a. **Name:** For this exercise, we will provide the unique name: Enhanced EM Website.

b. **Time Zone:** We recommend that you choose the time zone closest to your Grid Control Database Repository, but remain consistent with what you chose for your *Enhanced EM Website System.*

c. **Home page URL:** Enter the login page for your web application, for instance, **https://oms.acme.com:1159/em**.

d. **System:** Click Select System to choose an underlying system for the service, as well as the key components considered critical for the availability of this service. In this exercise, select the system we just created: *Enhanced EM Website System.* The default EM Website selected the Oracle Application Server, Web Cache, and OMS/OMR Hosts as critical components. We will follow the same selection criteria (for now).

Availability Page:

a. Decide whether you want to use service-based or system availability. It is recommended that you always select Service Test unless no such tests exist. The rough definitions of each are as follows:

- Service Test: Your service availability is based on one or more key beacons capable of executing a service test.

- System: Your service availability is based on the status of one or more key system components.

Since there are going to be suitable service tests for this web application, choose Service Test.

Service Test Page:

a. For now, we are going to outline the main test for how clients access the service, which for our web application is the application login URL. After you create the service, we will stipulate additional service tests, but for now we will mimic the default EM Website and create only one.

b.   Enter a name for this service test, an optional description, and a Collection Frequency.

c.   The transaction type will be the Basic Single URL, for which you should find the home page URL autopopulated based on what was provided on the General Page.

Beacons Page:

a.   This page enables you to add or create one or more beacons to execute the service test you just created. Click Add to select any of the beacons created in the previous workshop. Again, unless you have explicitly created beacons on other Management Agents, the only available beacon will come with the Management Agent that was part of your OMS install.

b.   Once your desired beacons have been selected, check the Key Component box to volunteer the beacons used in determining service availability. Remember, at least one of these key beacons must be able to access the service test in order to consider the service online.

c.   Next, from the Local Beacon drop-down menu, select the closest beacon that you can use to verify service availability.

d.   Confirm that the service test succeeds by clicking the Verify Service Test button. Statistical results are displayed for those metrics listed on the Services Test page.

Performance Metrics Page:

a.   This page allows you to select metrics used to measure the performance of the service. To avoid clustering all metrics under a cloud of "performance metrics," segment performance metrics as service-based and usage metrics as system-based. The only exception to this best practice is if the value from a usage metric will impact service level calculations.

Usage Metrics Page:

a.   This page helps measure user load on the underlying system by adding usage metrics relating to the performance of one or more system components. By default, the EM Website does not employ any usage metrics, but we plan to cover adding usage metrics in a later workshop.

(continued)

Review Page:

a. Review your entries as shown in the following illustration. When you're satisfied, click Finish to complete the creation of your service.

This concludes the basic creation process for our service and lays the foundation for the remaining workshops, which will further tweak the monitoring capabilities for the web application and service that it models.

Exposing Monitoring Configuration Tasks

Now that all our bases are covered, we can truly expose the application monitoring functionalities specific to Grid Control. To navigate to the Monitoring Configuration tab (which exposes the links to all the configuration steps of our workshops below), select a service from the Services summary page (*Enhanced EM Website* in our case), and click Configure. We are going to tweak this service by performing the following tasks:

- Add additional Service Tests using the Web Transaction Recorder
- Change system configurations
- Add performance and usage metrics
- Manage beacon watch lists
- Perform Root Cause Analysis (RCA) configurations

GRID CONTROL WORKSHOP

Add Additional Service Tests Using the Web Transaction Recorder

Workshop Notes

Since the Service Creation Wizard only allows you to create one service test, we will walk you through the steps to create additional service tests and leverage the Web Transaction Recorder to record and play back HTTP or HTTPS web transactions. It is much easier to reproduce the steps in a recording session, as Grid Control automatically constructs the URLs for each step. For this workshop, we are going to record a typical process that an administrator would use to evaluate the performance of the Grid Control Repository Database. Before proceeding, ensure that you have added the necessary SSL certificates for beacon playback, turned off client-side pop-up blockers, and are using Internet Explorer as your Console browser.

Step 1. Log in to the Console using the protocol (HTTP or HTTPS) you want the service test to use. This is because the recorder, which opens a spawned browser window, will inherit the credentials used; otherwise, there is no other mechanism to which you can resupply them.

Step 2. From the Monitoring Configuration page of your Enhanced EM Website service, click the **Service Tests and Beacons** link to create an additional service test.

Step 3. Click **Add** next to the Web Transaction Test Type.

Step 4. From the Create Service Test page, shown in the following illustration, you will need to manually enter the information required to identify the Service Test (for example, Name, Description, and Collection Frequency), but instead of manually specifying our transaction steps, we will reproduce the steps in a recording session.

(continued)

To demonstrate, we will record the steps needed to display the top activities for the Repository Database by clicking the Go button on this page.

Step 5. As instructed on the Record Web Transaction page, click Record to spawn the pop-up window used to record the transaction.

Step 6. In the URL address field of the new browser, access the target web site and click through the desired actions. However, since we are essentially turning EM on itself, log in using a different port; such as port 4444, to avoid losing your original session state. Pull up the Top Activity page as follows: click the Targets tab, click the Database subtab, select the name of the Grid Control Repository Database target, click the Performance page, and click the Top Activity link under the Additional Monitoring Links section. Observe the following points during the recording:

- For our *Enhanced EM Website* service test, enter the Console login URL using the HTTPS protocol, which you are currently logged in to.

- After you enter the Console URL, the address and menu bars are hidden.

- We recommend that you *never* click the browser's Back button.

- If your web transaction ever requires a login, upon completion log out (in the case of our example, do not log out or you will also exit from the original session).

- As you step through the recording, ensure that each action is being recorded by the "Page Loaded" message under the Logging section of the Web Transaction Page before proceeding.

- Do not close the window manually. The Continue button does this in the next step.

Step 7. Return to the Transaction Recording page and click Continue. This concludes the transaction and the browser window from which you performed a series of actions should now close.

Step 8. As the following illustration shows, Grid Control has constructed all the URLs used during the recording. Select all strings to verify that the beacon can play them back, and click Continue. For certain browsers, warnings about SSL certificates may be recorded as part of your session. If you successfully followed the previous workshop to add SSL certificates for beacon playback, then uncheck the first step and proceed without worry.

Web Application: Enhanced EM Website > Service Tests and Beacons > Create Service Test >
Success Strings Suggestion
Select those strings that you would like beacon to check for existence. This ensures the beacon plays back the web transaction correctly. You can change this later for each step under Success Strings. [Continue]

Select All | Select None

Select	Step	Success Strings
☐	Certificate Error: Navigation Blocked	
☑	Oracle Enterprise Manager (SYSMAN) - Hosts	
☑	Databases	
☑	omsdb.sd.avaya.com	
☑	Performance	
☑	Top Activity	

[Continue]

Home | **Targets** | Deployments | Alerts | Compliance | Jobs | Reports | Setup | Preferences | Help | Logout

Step 9. The Create Service Test page now should contain service test information. For all releases after 10.2.0.4.0, a new section appears allowing two additional selections to consider: Playback Mode and Collection Granularity.

- **Playback Mode**   Based on the heuristic of the actions performed, Grid Control automatically selects one of the following playback modes:

  - **Request Simulation**   This default selection is equivalent to Web Transaction monitoring in Grid Control Release 3. This mode is more platform-independent, but not appropriate for applications based on the use of Asynchronous JavaScript (AJAX) and XML technologies. The shortcoming of this mode is that it only measures server response time, not browser rendering time.

  - **Browser Simulation**   This mode's playback is done via a browser-based engine simulating actions from the keyboard and mouse. For AJAX applications this is the most appropriate and allows for the capturing of both server response and browser rendering time. The prerequisite for such activity includes: Internet Explorer 6.0 or greater and a 10.2.0.4.0 or greater Oracle Beacon on the Windows operating system.

    Manually make any modifications to the playback mode if needed, and click the corresponding Play button to verify that the chosen mode can successfully play back the transaction. *If you are following along with the example in this chapter, keep the default selection of Request Simulation.*

  - **Collection Granularity**   The granularity setting influences the amount of data a beacon will collect. In the example of a web transaction, each transaction consists of a series of steps with each step corresponding to a

(continued)

single or series of HTTP/S requests. The option is to record a transaction (as in this workshop), create one or more steps, or create step groups.

■ **Transaction** Collects data for the overall transaction only. This is the default granularity level.

■ **Step** Collects data for the overall transaction, the step groups, and each step in the transaction. To manually create a step, select this level, click the Steps page, and click Create.

■ **Step Group** Collects data for the overall transactions and step groups in this transaction. To manually combine a set of steps into a Step Group, select this level, click the Steps Groups tab, and click Create.

If you are following the example within this chapter, use Transaction, the default Collection Granularity as the following illustration shows.

Step 10. For Request Simulation mode only, you can confirm that the transaction runs successfully by clicking Verify Service Test here. On the results page, make note of the value for Perceived Total Time (ms). This metric outlines how long it would take a web browser to play the transaction, which simulates the user experience.

As such, this is a game-changing metric on which to set thresholds for the service test. Click Continue on the Verify Service Test page, shown in the following illustration.

Step 11. Click OK on the Create Service Test page to save the web transaction.

Step 12. Select the service test and click Enable to activate it, as shown in the following illustration. If the status of this service test does not show "UP," you will need to go through the Verify Service Test steps again.

An alternative to the Verify Service Test button is to replay the J2EE transaction. To do so, click the service test name on the Service Tests and Beacons page. Click Play to rerun performance results on the client-side or Play with Trace for results on the server side. To elaborate on this workshop and generate alerts for service tests, reference Enterprise Manager's online material to set thresholds at various granularity levels for transaction, step, or step group.

Service Tests tie in beautifully to previous discussions around performance detection of applications and systems once placed in play. With the completion of this workshop, a foundation exists to appropriately bring web applications online, baseline results that a consumer should come to expect, and the metrics to pinpoint areas of corrections should those expectations go awry. Once automatic notifications are enabled, you have come full circle and successfully modeled a true service.

GRID CONTROL WORKSHOP

Change System Configuration

Workshop Notes
Sometimes there is a need to change the service definition by altering the system or changing the definition of a component by classifying which ones become key components. Elevating components helps to accurately reflect that these components must be running for your services to be fully functional, and accurately permits Root Cause Analysis to automatically test the availability of these components.

Step 1. From the Monitoring Configuration page of our Enhanced EM System service, click the System Configuration link to begin identifying the targets critical for running our service.

Step 2. Using our example, we are going to select the following Grid Control target types as additional key components: OC4J_EM, OC4J_EMPROV, Oracle HTTP Server, Database, and Listener.

Step 3. After you have selected each of the listed components, click OK and Yes to save the system configuration, as shown in the following illustration.

Web Application: Enhanced EM Website >
System Configuration

Cancel   OK

Select the Enterprise Manager system that will host this service, then identify the targets critical for running this service.

System   **Enhanced EM Website System**   (Change System) (Remove System)
Time Zone   **(UTC-07:00) US Mountain Time**

Tip
A "system" is the infrastructure used to host one or more services. A system consists of components such as hosts, databases, and other targets.

The system components that you mark as "Key Components" may be used to determine service availability, or, in case of service failure, to perform root cause analysis.

Click **Help** for details.

Previous | 1-10 of 11 | Next 1

Component	Type	Key Component
oracle.sd.avaya.com	Host	☑
fama.sd.avaya.com	Host	☑
Management Services and Repository	OMS and Repository	☑
EnterpriseManager0.oracle.sd.avaya.com_Web Cache	Web Cache	☑
EnterpriseManager0.oracle.sd.avaya.com_HTTP Server	Oracle HTTP Server	☑
EnterpriseManager0.oracle.sd.avaya.com	Oracle Application Server	☑
omsdb.sd.avaya.com	Database Instance	☑
LISTENER_fama.sd.avaya.com	Listener	☑
EnterpriseManager0.oracle.sd.avaya.com_home	OC4J	☑
EnterpriseManager0.oracle.sd.avaya.com_OC4J_EMPROV	OC4J	☑

Previous | 1-10 of 11 | Next 1

GRID CONTROL WORKSHOP

Add Performance Metrics

Workshop Notes

Sometimes you need to add or change performance metrics used to determine service performance. This workshop will walk you through adding additional performance metrics to be run by your Grid Control beacons.

Step 1. From the Monitoring Configuration page, click the Performance Metrics link to begin adding a performance metric for our *Top Database Activity* service test.

Step 2. From the Add drop-down menu, select your preferred type of service test: Based on System or Based on Service Test. For this particular exercise, we will choose Based on Service Test. Click Go.

Step 3. From the Metric creation page, as shown in the following illustration, make the following choices:

■ **Source** Transaction or Step.

■ **Metric** Determine the metric against which you want to base service performance.

■ **Beacons** Choose to use the metric from a single beacon or across multiple beacons in an aggregated fashion.

Step 4. Click Continue to return to the Performance Metrics page. From here, you can enter comparison operators, warning, and/or critical threshold values.

Remember, these threshold values can be used to trigger notifications for out-of-bound conditions.

GRID CONTROL WORKSHOP

Add Usage Metrics

Workshop Notes

Sometimes there is a need to add or change usage metrics that determine the workload of a service. This workshop will walk you through adding additional usage metrics to be run by your Grid Control beacons.

Step 1. From the Monitoring Configuration page, click the Usage Metrics link and Add to begin adding a usage metric for our *Top Database Activity* service test.

Step 2. From the Add Usage Metric based on the System page, make the selections for the following:

- **Target Type** Choose any target type. For the purposes of this workshop, select OC4J.
- **Metric** Based on the target type, listings of available metrics are made available for selection.
- **System Components** Choose to apply this metric against a specific component or across components in an aggregated manner. If you choose to spread across multiple components, select the aggregation method and specific components you want to aggregate.

  Make the necessary selections including the System Components, as shown in the following illustration (in our case, we need to select "em;em" in the Object field, since this corresponds to selecting the specific component OC4J_EM) and click Continue.

Step 3. Returning to the Usage Metrics page, you can enter comparison operators, warning, and/or critical threshold values as with the Performance Metrics workshop.

Step 4. Click OK to save changes.

Step 5. Click the Charts subtab to see your metrics being represented in graphs.

When you return to Metric and Policy Settings for a service, the metrics listed on the Metric Threshold page combine both configured Performance Metrics and Usage Metrics—without making a distinction between the two. This emphasizes the rationale earlier by using selected service-based availability, then coming in later to add Usage Metrics. If you selected system-based availability, then this combination could never be available.

Setting Up Watch Lists

Besides the information that beacons provide for the web application that they monitor, beacons can also be used to watch parts of the network or perform ad-hoc monitoring. These queries can be defined in a beacon *watch list*. These queries are not directly related to an application or service defined within Grid Control, but they are additional metrics that can be used to corroborate the results received from the monitoring of other services and applications on the network.

GRID CONTROL WORKSHOP

Setting Up Beacon Watch Lists

Workshop Notes

This workshop will guide you through the necessary steps to create a beacon watch list for checking the network response time for a particular host or other network components. After adding attributes on the beacon watch list, at predefined intervals, the beacon will ping the target and register the time it takes to receive a response. If the average time exceeds the threshold set during creation, an alert will be triggered.

Step 1. The quickest way to access a listing of available beacons in your network is by clicking the Targets tab followed by the All Targets subtab.

Step 2. From the All Targets Summary page, get a listing of discovered components alphabetically by clicking Type, as shown in the following illustration.

(continued)

All Targets

Page Refreshed   Nov 9, 2009 9:35:05 PM MST

Targets Not Configured   1

Search All   [   ]   (Go) Advanced Search

(Remove) (Configure) | Add Database Instance   [   ] (Go)   ◁ Previous 1-25 of 42 ▼ Next 17 ▷

Select	Name	Status	Type △
○	argus.sd.avaya.com:3872		Agent
○	bennu.sd.avaya.com:3872		Agent
○	fama.sd.avaya.com:3872		Agent
○	hobgoblin.sd.avaya.com:3872		Agent
○	oracle.sd.avaya.com:3872		Agent
○	vala.sd.avaya.com:3872		Agent
○	yeti.sd.avaya.com:3872		Agent
○	bennu.sd.avaya.com_australia		Beacon
○	hobgoblin.sd.avaya.com_beacon_india		Beacon
○	oracle.sd.avaya.com_oms		Beacon
○	oracle.sd.avaya.com_oms_csa_collector		CSA Collector
○	genesis.sd.avaya.com		Database Instance
○	omsdb.sd.avaya.com		Database Instance
○	onex.sd.avaya.com		Database Instance

Step 3.   Click the name of your desired beacon to reach its home page.

Step 4.   Click the Watch Lists subtab.

Step 5.   This page is broken down into three sections: Network Watch List, URL Watch List, and Test:

- ■ **Network Watch List**   This option can be used to check specific machines on the network. Basic statistics, like the number of hops, the packet drop rate, and the response time, are measured for each connection request.

- ■ **URL Watch List**   Any specific web sites that have to be available, or need to be reachable through the network can be specified here. The beacon will check the connectivity of these URLs, and report any response times that have violated specific thresholds set.

- ■ **Test**   Use this option to perform an ad-hoc request for a host or an URL and measure the network response (Figure 17-5). There is no historical recordkeeping with this feature.

Step 6.   To add a Network Watch List Item, click Add in the top section and follow the wizard to completion.

Step 7.   To add a URL Watch List Item, click Add in the middle section and follow the wizard to completion.

Step 8.   In the last section, supply either a URL or host, followed by a selection of test type from the drop-down menu, and click Go to issue a manual test on the spot.

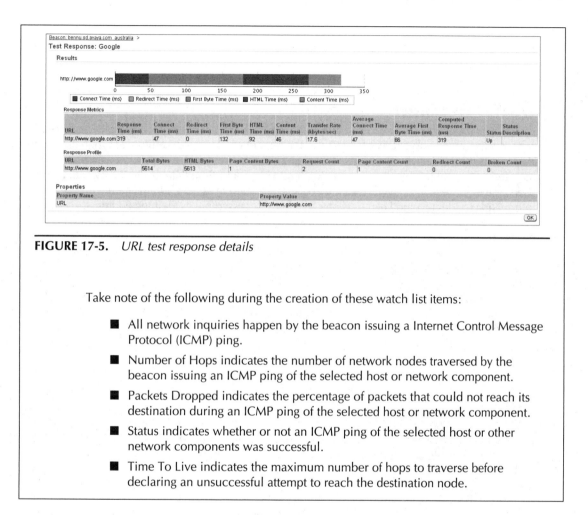

FIGURE 17-5. *URL test response details*

Take note of the following during the creation of these watch list items:

- All network inquiries happen by the beacon issuing a Internet Control Message Protocol (ICMP) ping.

- Number of Hops indicates the number of network nodes traversed by the beacon issuing an ICMP ping of the selected host or network component.

- Packets Dropped indicates the percentage of packets that could not reach its destination during an ICMP ping of the selected host or network component.

- Status indicates whether or not an ICMP ping of the selected host or other network components was successful.

- Time To Live indicates the maximum number of hops to traverse before declaring an unsuccessful attempt to reach the destination node.

The details beacons are capable of showing can be very useful for debugging network-related performance and latency issues.

Root Cause Analysis

If any of your critical components were ever to go offline, there is a high likelihood that a flurry of alerts will be coming down the pipeline demanding your attention. Narrowing down the list of alerts to the primary causes of failure may have you stumbling as if in a drunken haze. We often label these events as a fire drill, and one where gallons of water won't do the job. Fortunately for us, Grid Control offers a feature called Root Cause Analysis (RCA) that helps filters out all such alerts and user symptoms. RCA prioritizes the alerts and flags system components responsible for the failure, tying the topology page used from our previous workshop as the backdrop to graphically illuminate component interrelationships. In theory, this analysis allows you to quickly address the failures as it pertains to bringing your most significant applications back online.

To take advantage of this, you must first define the relevant metrics and thresholds that are likely to be the root cause of failure for each component, decide which analysis mode RCA should take, and expect to view the results from the home page or topology page of your service—when you're offline.

Duality Explained

For true end-to-end application monitoring to exist, managing web server data collections and subsequently managing page watch lists are the remaining pieces of the puzzle. When used with Web Cache or the Apache-based HTTP Server, Enterprise Manager taps the end-user performance monitoring capabilities by allowing you to monitor response time data generated by actual end users as they access and navigate your web site. Afterward, a system administrator can use the information to identify and keep tabs on commonly accessed pages (helping address the law of the vital few) by entering those pages into a watch list. At a glance, you can see how specific pages of your application are performing, starting with the login page, which many visitors use as a litmus test for each repeat visit to the site. There was even a time when Oracle claimed to service the fastest-loading web site, which should leave very little doubt to the technologies that made this true.

For adopters of Release 5, staying ahead of the power curve has some inherent risks, which unfortunately include the set of functionality just described. A significant number of enhancements are being made in this area, so we felt that it would be a disadvantage to cover its contents only to see it significantly change in the upcoming release. For those with older releases, refer to Oracle's online documentation for up-to-date information and examples.

Summary

In the pursuit of optimal performance, the realization that comes from a best-in-class application monitoring practice using Grid Control may bring tremendous gratification—but do not lose sight of the deeper meaning. You see, we are fervent believers that in time, the most valuable lessons that come from performance monitoring, whether at the functional level or behind a development practice, come from doing things incorrectly and then addressing the issues even in the face of opposition. If your organization were only offered the tasks and tools that led up to successful results from the word "go," it would lack the cultivation of problem-solving skills that your team needs and that helped others formulate the best practice in the first place. It is these critical behaviors that are needed to support the creation of a result-oriented culture, and Grid Control is a reflection of such a practice. While other application management solutions are tailored specifically to address a wide breadth of issues, when combined they become fragmented and only aggravate the problems rather than solving them. Unlike these vendors, Oracle's core business centers on applications, so for now and future releases, you can expect that Oracle will seek to provide their customers with a top-down application management approach that seeks to address the problems that come from deploying and managing Oracle applications.

CHAPTER
18

Troubleshooting
and Diagnostics

ou've made it to the last chapter in the book, and this one is meant as a reference to diagnose and troubleshoot issues encountered with Grid Control.

Operational issues are a fact of life: There will be always something going wrong, or not happening quite the way you want it in a large data center. The trick to successfully navigate the minefield of problems is to know where to look and what to do to get the right information.

Troubleshooting the Install

Logging and tracing are necessary tools for debugging, since there is always some corner condition or some environmental issue that causes a problem and requires more information to find out what's going on.

The trick with debugging, though, is to debug just what is needed, and not to blindly start debugging everything in the hope of finding some shred of evidence of the problem.

And it starts with the installation of the software: Knowing what is where, and where to look for the debug information is the first step. Getting specific additional information when needed in case of a problem is the next step.

Log and Trace Files

All installs done with Oracle Universal Installer (OUI) log their actions in the log directory of the OUI inventory directory.

The location of this directory depends on the operating system:

- On UNIX, the file `oraInst.loc` will contain the pointer to the OUI inventory.

  This file will be in the `/etc` directory on most UNIX platforms. On Sun Solaris, the file is located in the `/var/opt/oracle` directory.

- On Windows, the location will be stored in the registry:

  ```
  HKEY_LOCAL_MACHINE
    \Software
      \Oracle
        inst_loc    Location of the OUI inventory
  ```

A subdirectory of the inventory directory will contain all log and trace files of every install action performed while operating with this inventory.

This directory can contain the following files:

- **`OPatch<timestamp>.log`**   Log file of the `OPatch` operation done.

- **`installActions<timestamp>.log`**   Log file with an overview of all actions done while running `runInstaller`. For every timestamp, there will also be a corresponding `.err` and `.out` file.

- **`oraInstall<timestamp>.err`**   STDERR output of all commands executed by `runInstaller`. Also look for the corresponding `.out` file with the same timestamp, to get the STDOUT output.

- **oraInstall\<timestamp\>.out** STDOUT output of all commands executed by runInstaller. Also look for the corresponding .err file with the same timestamp, to get the STDERR output.

There are additional log and trace files stored in the *ORACLE_HOME* of the software being installed or changed.

The $ORACLE_HOME/cfgtoollogs will contain the following directories:

- **$ORACLE_HOME/cfgtoollogs/cfgfw** Logs for configuration tools run by install, configuration, or patch operations.

  A cumulative log for each action will also be written in this directory, which lists the individual configuration tools that were run for that particular operation.

- **$ORACLE_HOME/cfgtoollogs/opatch** Logs for all OPatch operations done in this *ORACLE_HOME*

- **$ORACLE_HOME/cfgtoollogs/oui** Logs for all install operations done in this *ORACLE_HOME*

How to Debug OUI

All install and major upgrade operations of Oracle software on UNIX are done with the runInstaller script. On Windows, the main install executable is called setup.exe. Both of these programs will be installed in the $ORACLE_HOME/oui/bin directory.

Useful Command-Line Parameters

There are a few command-line switches that can be used to get additional logging and tracing from an install session:

-debug	Report additional messages while installing.
-invPtrLoc	Location of the Oracle inventory. If the software inventory is not in the default location pointed to by the oraInst.loc file, specify this command-line switch to point to the correct inventory to use.
-logLevel	Level of logging and tracing for runInstaller. Possible levels are: severe, warning, info, config, fine, finer, finest.
-paramFile	Location of the oraparam.ini file. This file controls all the startup parameters the OUI will use. The default location of this file will always be in the install subdirectory of the CD/DVD/Staging area. Any kind of Java debugging or setting additional switches to start the Java installer will have to be specified in this file.
-printdiskusage	Log debug information for disk usage.
-printmemory	Log debug information for memory usage.
-printtime	Log debug information for time usage.

-waitforcompletion   This switch will force the `runInstaller` script to wait until the install operation (done by the Java program) has completed. Without this script, the `runInstaller` shell script will return to the shell as soon as it starts the Java part of the install. When you are using the install in a script, this can cause synchronization problems trying to determine when the install actually finished.

To get all the debug info, the following command can be used:

```
$ ./runInstaller -debug –printdiskusage –printmemory –printtime
       -waitforcompletion -logLevel finest >install.out 2>install.err
```

Java Startup Changes

The Oracle installer uses Java to run. The Java startup parameters, including some basic OUI parameters, are all specified in the `oraparam.ini` file. This file will always be located in the `<software staging directory>/install` directory.

To change the startup parameters to use for the installer, make a copy of the `oraparam.ini` file and edit the Java options.

Example:

```
[Oracle]
... other parameters ...
JRE_MEMORY_OPTIONS=" -mx96m -verbose"
... other parameters ...
```

This modified version of the parameter file can then be passed to the command-line for the installer to use.

Example:

```
$ ./runInstaller -debug -paramFile /tmp/oraparam.ini
```

Inventory Manipulation

The central inventory contains the list of all Oracle products installed on the box, and serves as the source of truth for various tools (not just the installer) for obtaining a list of available software. As soon as the installer touches or upgrades an *ORACLE_HOME*, or adds/removes software, the inventory is updated to reflect those changes.

To see the current list of all known homes in the inventory, look in the `inventory.xml` file. This file will be in a subdirectory of the inventory directory called `ContentsXML`.

Example file:

```
<INVENTORY>
  <VERSION_INFO>
    <SAVED_WITH>10.2.0.5.0</SAVED_WITH>
    <MINIMUM_VER>2.1.0.6.0</MINIMUM_VER>
  </VERSION_INFO>
  <HOME_LIST>
    <HOME NAME="oms10g" LOC="/u01/10gr5/oms10g" TYPE="O" IDX="1"/>
```

```
    <HOME NAME="agent10g" LOC="/u01/10gr5/agent10g" TYPE="O" IDX="2"/>
  </HOME_LIST>
</INVENTORY>
```

In case of a (crash) recovery, where software was restored from a backup, or the inventory has to be updated again (because an older version of the inventory got restored from backup), the required changes to the inventory will have to be updated manually.

There are a few commands available to allow this kind of inventory manipulation:

- Add an *ORACLE_HOME* to the inventory:

  ```
  ./runInstaller -silent -local –noconsole -attachHome
      ORACLE_HOME=<home directory> ORACLE_HOME_NAME=<home name>
  ```

- Remove an *ORACLE_HOME* from the inventory:

  ```
  ./runInstaller -silent -local –noconsole -detachHome
      ORACLE_HOME=<home directory> ORACLE_HOME_NAME=<home name>
  ```

How to Debug OPatch

Whenever a one-off patch or a small update to a product needs to be done, OPatch is used to apply (or roll back) the one-off patch.

OPatch Dependencies

OPatch depends on a couple of settings and requires access to certain files on the machine:

- A distribution of Perl needs to be available. All database and Application Server installs have a copy of Perl distributed with it that OPatch can use. If Perl is not installed in the *ORACLE_HOME* of the Oracle software, OPatch will need access to any Perl installation present on the system.

- *ORACLE_HOME* environment variable must be set to a valid directory. The OPatch utility is designed to patch an Oracle software home. This means that prior to invoking the tool, the *ORACLE_HOME* variable has to point to a valid location.

- OPatch needs access to the central inventory. The central inventory is the pointer specified in the /etc/oraInst.loc file (or /var/opt/oracle/oraInst.loc on some UNIX platforms). If the central inventory that requires patching is in a different location, use the -invPtrLoc switch to specify an alternate location of the oraInst.loc file.

- On RAC systems, OPatch will need access to the libraries in the $ORACLE_HOME/lib and $ORACLE_HOME/srvm/lib. These two directories will have to be present in the library search environment variables (like *LD_LIBRARY_PATH* or *SHLIB_PATH)* prior to launching OPatch.

Command-Line Usage

If OPatch is used in the context of an *ORACLE_HOME,* it will recognize and use the settings of that install. There are command-line switches available, though, to deviate from the default settings OPatch is using.

-force	In case of a patch conflict during an `apply` or `napply` operation, force the rollback of the conflicting patch automatically.
-help	To get some more details about a certain option, or to find out the exact usage of an OPatch command, use the `-help` switch:

```
$ $ORACLE_HOME/OPatch/opatch -help
```

This switch can also be used for a specific command.

Example:

```
$ORACLE_HOME/OPatch/opatch apply -help
```

-invPtrLoc	OPatch expects to find the `oraInst.loc` file in the standard location (either `/etc/oraInst.loc` or `/var/opt/oracle/oraInst.loc` depending on the OS). However, in cases where this file is present in other locations, the switch `-invPtrLoc` can be used to overrule the default location.
-jdk	Alternate location for JDK. OPatch will always first look for a JDK install in `$ORACLE_HOME/jdk`. If none is found, it will look for a JRE install also in the *ORACLE_HOME*. Both the `-jdk` and `-jre` switch cannot be used at the same time.
-jre	Alternate location for JRE. OPatch will always first look for a JDK, and if not found for a JRE install in `$ORACLE_HOME/jre`. The `-jdk` and `-jre` switches cannot be used at the same time.
-ocmrf	New switch, available in the 10.2.0.4 (or higher) version of OPatch, to specify the OCM response file to use for the patch operation.
-oh	Force a different *ORACLE_HOME* to be used for the patch operation.
-silent	Suppress any user input during the application of the patch. Starting from 10.2.0.4, this switch will also need the `-ocmrf` switch to be specified.

OPatch uses the following environment variables:

ORACLE_HOME	Home for the Oracle software to work with.
OPATCH_DEBUG	Optional debugging flag. When this flag is set to `TRUE`, OPatch will write additional information to the log and trace files.
OPATCH_PLATFORM_ID	The unique ID of the platform the Oracle installer used to install. This identifier is an internal Oracle code representing the operating system.
PERL_DL_DEBUG	Debug dynamic library loading in Perl. Set this variable to 1 to enable.

Some Useful Commands

The simplest command to verify OPatch is to request the version of the tool:

```
$ $ORACLE_HOME/OPatch/opatch version
```

If this command completes successfully, OPatch is installed correctly.

To keep track of all patches installed in an *ORACLE_HOME*, use the `lsinventory` command:

```
$ $ORACLE_HOME/OPatch/opatch lsinventory -patch
```

If the optional -details switch is added to the command-line, the details of all files modified by a patch will be displayed, too.

Logging and Tracing the Infrastructure

In this section, we'll just give an overview of all the possible logging and tracing facilities that the infrastructure has. The next section will then use these logging and tracing facilities to debug real-life issues, and give guidelines on what (and more importantly where) to enable the logging and tracing.

Logging and Tracing the Agent

We will start with the last tier in the infrastructure: The Agent. Although there is only one main process to trace (The 'emagent' executable), there are more areas to be traced in more detail independently. For more details on how to diagnose Agent problems, refer to the section "Diagnosing Agent Problems."

Agent Process

All logging and tracing for the Agent is done through settings in the emd.properties file. The tracing follows the basic rule of inheritance: tracelevel.main is the main module, and the first module in the tree. Whatever level of debugging is specified at this level will be used by all modules used by the Agent, unless otherwise specified in the emd.properties files. Submodules can also be specified. The submodules can then overrule the main trace level, and trace in a different way.

All trace information will be written in the emagent.trc file. No debug information will be written to the emagent.log file.
Example:

```
tracelevel.main=WARN
tracelevel.ssl=INFO
tracelevel.ssl.io=DEBUG
```

In this example, the whole Agent is tracing in WARN mode. Except for the SSL module, which is in INFO mode. The ssl.io submodule is overruling the parent again, and puts the tracing in DEBUG mode.

Each of these modules can have a "level" of monitoring. These levels follow the log4j definitions:

ERROR	Error messages only
WARN	Warning and error messages only
INFO	All informational, warning, and error messages
DEBUG	All debug, info, warning, and error messages

After every change to these tracelevels parameters, the Agent will have to be either reloaded or restarted. A reload is the recommended mechanism, compared to a full stop and restart. If the intent is just to change the trace levels, informing the Agent just to reload the properties will be faster and more efficient compared to re-initializing all the Agent operations.

```
$ emctl reload agent
```

Every module in the Agent can be traced individually, removing the need to put the entire Agent process in debug mode to triage an issue. The following modules are available at the Agent side for debugging in the `emd.properties` file:

`tracelevel.Authentication`	OS Authentication Module (Jobs).
`tracelevel.blackouts`	Blackout Management.
`tracelevel.browser`	Metric browser.
`tracelevel.collector`	Collection Manager.
`tracelevel.command`	Internal Command Executor. Executes OS commands and Perl scripts, and handles all commands to be executed for jobs.
`tracelevel.credproviders`	Credential handling.
`tracelevel.Dispatcher`	OMS server request dispatcher.
`tracelevel.emSDK`	Main OMS server API calls.
`tracelevel.engine`	Metric evaluation engine.
`tracelevel.fetchlets`	Fetchlets. Specific modules to execute metrics for targets.
`tracelevel.http`	HTTP Listener and client. Performs all basic HTTP operations, and handles all unsecure communication between the OMS and the Agent.
`tracelevel.javavm`	Java Virtual Machine monitoring.
`tracelevel.javaproc`	Java Procedures/Java Interface.
`tracelevel.metadata`	XML Metadata Parser.
`tracelevel.NLS`	NLS handling and debugging.
`tracelevel.pingManager`	Ping Manager/Heartbeat Manager.
`tracelevel.recvlets`	Metric recvlet. Specific modules to listen for incoming traffic from targets, to be uploaded as metrics. Examples are the SNMP recvlet listening for incoming SNMP traps, and the database AQ recvlet listening for database-generated alerts.
`tracelevel.reload`	Information reload manager (EMCTL reload agent).
`tracelevel.resman`	OS Resource Manager. Handles all resources like file descriptors, sockets, and virtual memory.
`tracelevel.ResMonitor`	Resource Monitor.
`tracelevel.scheduler`	Threadpool scheduler. Makes sure all threads operating on a schedule (like metric evaluation and XML uploads) are happening on time.
`tracelevel.ssl`	SSL interface. Handles all the secure communication between the Agent and the OMS.
`tracelevel.TargetManager`	Target metadata manager. Handles all XML files related to target managed and metric collection handling.

`tracelevel.targets`	Target manipulation handler. Handles all operations performed on a target.
`tracelevel.ThreadPool`	Thread Pool Manager. Manages all threads used for evaluating metrics, executing jobs, and performing the Agent housekeeping tasks.
`tracelevel.upload`	XML file upload manager.
`tracelevel.utils`	Utilities and common Agent routines.
`tracelevel.vpxoci`	OCI8 interface. Used by the SQL fetchlet and AQ recvlet for database monitoring.

Fetchlet Tracing

All external fetchlets can be traced using the properties in the `emagentlogging.properties` file (as opposed to the parameters listed in the preceding table, in the `emd.properties` file). There is only one module with one trace level that can be specified in this file.

This logging level will be used for all Java-based fetchlets:

`ExtJavaWrapper`	Generic enhanced Java Interface
`JavaWrapper`	Generic simple Java Interface
`SNMP`	SNMP request handling
`DMS`	iAS performance instrumentation
`URLXML`	URL operations and XML parsing

The trace levels that can be used are the same as the Agent ones:

`ERROR`	Error messages only
`WARN`	Error and warning messages only
`INFO`	Informational, warning, and error messages
`DEBUG`	All messages, including the debug messages

Example:

```
log4j.rootCategory=INFO,emagentlogAppender,emagenttrcAppender
```

All log and trace information will be written to the files `emagentfetchlet.log` and `emagentfetchlet.trc` in the `<EMHOME>/sysman/log` directory.

There are two fetchlets the Agent itself is executing, and they will not be affected by any of the logging and tracing parameters specified in the `emagentlogging.properties` file. They are part of the main Agent process, and the tracing of these two fetchlets is controlled by the `emd.properties` settings:

■ **SQL fetchlet** SQL command executions in Oracle databases. Tracing is done through the `vpxoci` Agent module.

■ **OS commands** Execution of OS scripts. Tracing is done through the `command` Agent module.

Perl Script Tracing

A substantial number of metrics are being collected via Perl scripts. These scripts can be debugged separately, in separate log and trace files.

The settings for the Perl debugging are specified in the `emd.properties` file:

`EMAGENT_PERL_TRACE_FILESIZE`	Maximum size in MB for the metric Perl trace file. Default value is 5 (MB).
`EMAGENT_PERL_TRACE_DIR`	Directory where the metric Perl trace file is stored. Default location is `<EMHOME>/sysman/log`.
`EMAGENT_PERL_TRACE_LEVEL`	Tracing level used by the metric Perl scripts. Default value is `WARN`.

The possible trace levels are the same as with the other tracing facilities: `ERROR`, `WARN`, `INFO`, and `DEBUG`.

Although an alternate directory to put the Perl trace file in can be specified in the `emd.properties` file, the name of the trace file cannot be changed: All trace information will be written in the `emagent_perl.trc` file.

EMCTL Tracing

EMCTL is the main script to start the Agent and the OMS. In the rare case that the script itself needs to be debugged, a special environment variable named *EMCTL_DEBUG* can be used. If this variable is set to any value (the value itself is irrelevant, as long as the environment variable exists, and contains something), additional messages will be printed on `STDOUT` about the operations EMCTL is doing.
Example:

```
$ EMCTL_DEBUG=TRUE
$ export EMCTL_DEBUG
```

Tracing the Secure Operations

Secure operations can also be performed on both the Agent and the OMS. And for both these tiers, the same method can be used to get more information. The `secure` and `unsecure` commands of EMCTL can be traced separately, using the *EM_SECURE_VERBOSE* environment variable. As with the *EMCTL_DEBUG* variable, any value can be used to enable the debugging. As long as the variable exists and contains something, the tracing will be enabled.
Example:

```
$ EM_SECURE_VERBOSE=TRUE
$ export EM_SECURE_VERBOSE
```

All log information will be written in the `secure.log` file, in the `<EMHOME>/sysman/log` directory.

SNMP Subagent

The SNMP subagent is an Agent module that will only be started in very specific environments. The purpose of this extra process is to respond to all SNMP requests issued to the targets the Agent is monitoring. The subagent does not manage SNMP traps, only incoming SNMP requests.

If the SNMP subagent is used, three more files are created:

`emsubagent.log`	Log file for the SNMP subagent
`emsubagent.nohup`	File with SNMP subagent `STDOUT` and `STDERR` messages
`emsubagent.trc`	Trace file for the SNMP subagent

All logging and tracing parameters for the subagent are controlled by the `snmp_rw.ora` file. To enable the logging, modify the following files in the `$ORACLE_HOME/network/admin` or the value of the *TNS_ADMIN* environment variable if specified:

■ First create a `sqlnet.ora` file (an empty one if none is present).

■ Make sure the subagent can read and write to the file `snmp_ro.ora`.

■ Create a file `snmp_rw.ora` file with the following line:

```
snmp.trace_level=15
```

The trace level follows the Oracle Net standards, with values ranging between 0 (no tracing) and 15 (highest level of tracing).

Logging and Tracing the Management Server

The OMS is working on top of an Application Server, which has its own set of log and trace files, and its own debugging facilities.

For more details on how to diagnose OMS problems, refer to the section, "Diagnosing OMS Problems."

All the logging and tracing parameters for the Application Server components that are part of the OMS install can be specified in the AS Control Console:

■ Make sure AS Control is started. If needed, start AS Control:

```
$ emctl status iasconsole
$ emctl start  iasconsole
```

■ Use a web browser to connect to AS Control, and navigate to the component to set the tracing parameters:

```
https://<host>:1157/
```

■ Log in to the iAS console using the ias_admin account (or any other administrator account defined).

■ For each of the iAS components, go to the Administration tab. One of the administration links for the components will be the Logging setup and configuration.

The iAS Log Files

All files created by OPMN (the process starting the Application Server), and all the messages written to `STDOUT` by all modules started by OPMN, are stored in the `$ORACLE_HOME/opmn/logs` directory. This includes:

■ **Application Server log files** Includes the files `ipm.log`, `ons.log`, `opmn.log`, and `service.log` These files are created by OPMN itself, and are used while performing operations on the entire application stack (like stopping and starting the Application Server).

- **Application Server modules** Each module OPMN starts will also create a log file: `HTTP_Server~1`, `OC4J~home~default_island~1`, `WebCache~WebCache~1`, and `WebCache~WebCacheAdmin~1`.

- **Grid Control–specific log files** The two OC4J applications that Grid Control deploys will also have their own log files in the OPMN directory:

  `OC4J~OC4J_EM~default_island~1` (OMS server) and `OC4J~OC4J_EMPROV~default_island~1` (Agent provisioning)

To increase the logging levels for the `ipm.log` and `ons.log` file:

- Edit the file `$ORACLE_HOME/opmn/conf/opmn.xml`.

- Change the level tag for IPM or ONS to 9.
  Example for the ONS logging:

  ```
  <log-file path="$ORACLE_HOME/opmn/logs/ons.log" level="9"
            rotation-size="1500000"/>
  ```

- Save the configuration:

  ```
  $ dcmctl updateconfig -ct opmn
  ```

- Stop and restart the OPMN services:

  ```
  $ opmnctl stopall
  $ opmnctl startall
  ```

The HTTP Server Log Files

The Apache log and trace files are written in the `$ORACLE_HOME/Apache/Apache/logs` directory.

Logging to these files can be controlled from the Apache configuration scripts. Special macros can be added to the configuration to modify or change the default logging, and prevent certain URL requests from being populated in the log files.
Example:

To prevent all image requests from being logged in the `access_log` file, add this in the Apache `httpd.conf` file:

```
SetEnvIF Request_URI .*/em/images.* no-log
CustomLog "|<ORACLE_HOME>/Apache/Apache/bin/rotatelogs
          <ORACLE_HOME>/Apache/Apache/logs/access_log 86400"
          common env=!no-log
```

The Webcache Log Files

The Webcache server log and trace files are written in the directory `$ORACLE_HOME/webcache/logs`.

`access_log`	List of all requests made to Webcache.
`event_log`	List of all the internal events encountered by Webcache.
`io_log`	Log file for the IO logger. This is a Webcache feature used for diagnostics and debugging that has to be enabled separately. See the *Application Server Administration* guide for more information on this feature.

A special subdirectory will also be present on the OMS that has the archived `access_log` files: Every day, the current file is archived to `$ORACLE_HOME/webcache/logs/archive`.

Neither the Application Server nor Grid Control needs these backup files. They are only used when uploading end user-monitoring information from the Grid Control website.

The OC4J Log Files

The OC4J applications (home, OC4J_EM, and OC4J_EMPROV) also write log and trace files when running. For the each of the OC4J applications, the files will be stored in the following directories:

Home	`$ORACLE_HOME/j2ee/home/log/home_default_island_1`
OC4J_EM	`$ORACLE_HOME/j2ee/OC4J_EM/log/OC4J_EM_default_island_1`
OC4J_EMPROV	`$ORACLE_HOME/j2ee/OC4J_EMPROV/log/OC4J_EM_default_island_1`

Each OC4J application will have its own set of log files, and its own definition of how to log and trace the application:

`Default-web-access.log`	Text log file with all the access requests made to the OC4J application.
`em-application.log`	Text log file used by the OC4J_EM application only. This file contains all error messages logged by the deployed OMS application.
`global-application.log`	Text log file containing all messages about the start and stop of the deployed application.
`jms.log`	Text log file containing all messages from the JMS service.
`rmi.log`	Text log file containing all messages from the RMI service.
`server.log`	Text log file containing all messages from the ONS service.

The Main OMS Server Log and Trace Files

The log and trace information written by the OMS server operations are written in the directory `$ORACLE_HOME/sysman/log`:

`emca_repos_create`	Log file with all messages from the repository creation made during the install
`emca_repos_drop`	Log file with all messages from the repository drop made by RepManager
`emctl.log`	Log file with a list of all EMCTL invocations
`emoms.log`	Log file with only the WARN and ERROR messages in English only
`emoms.trc`	Trace file with all trace messages, in local language
`emrepmgr.log`	Log file with all the messages from a repository upgrade

To control the level of logging done for the OMS, the logging parameters in the `emomslogging.properties` files can be changed.

The default settings used after the install affect the whole of the OMS application:

```
# Edit the line below to change the trace level. Valid values are
# DEBUG, INFO, WARN, and ERROR
#
log4j.rootCategory=WARN, emlogAppender, emtrcAppender
```

The possible values for the logging are the standard ones for the Java logging:

ERROR	Error messages only
WARN	Error and warning messages only
INFO	Informational, warning and error messages
DEBUG	All messages, including the debug messages

For debugging specific issues with the OMS, just the part to be debugged can be added to the `emomslogging.properties` file.
Example:

```
log4j.category.eml.XMLLoader=INFO
log4j.category.em.blackouts=DEBUG
```

The following high-level categories can be used to specify this more fine-grained logging:

em.blackouts	Internal blackout operations
em.console	Internal Console/UI-based operations
em.db	Internal database maintenance and monitoring operations
em.ecm	Internal Configuration Management operations
em.failover	OMS failover system
em.jobs	Job engine
em.notification	Notification handler
em.sec	Security Engine
ems.SDK	Grid Control SDK routines
eml.XMLLoader	XML loader engine
eml.adm	All Console-based administration pages
eml.jobs	All Console-based job pages
eml.mntr	All Console-based monitoring pages

After each change of the properties file, the OMS will have to be restarted, to pick up the new tracing settings.

Starting from 10.2.0.4, the OMS is capable of generating a Java thread dump on each abnormal termination of the OMS application. To enable the generation of these stack dumps, set the following property in the `emoms.properties` file:

```
em.oms.dumpModules=omsThread,repos
```

Provisioning Log and Trace Files

Provisioning logs will be in a subdirectory, `$ORACLE_HOME/sysman/log/pafLogs`.
For every execution of a Deployment Procedure, a file will be created in the form:

```
<Procedure Name>_<Instance Guid>.log:
```

- The procedure name is the name of the Deployment Procedure used
- The instance GUID is the internal ID of the DP used

The logs will only contain Deployment Procedure–specific information. To get more information about the EM jobs the Deployment Procedures are using and executing, enable job debugging on the OMS in the `emomslogging.properties` files:

```
log4j.category.em.jobs=DEBUG
```

The AS Control Agent

AS Control is the main Application Server administration tool. Its primary function is to provide a framework to perform basic administration functions to the Application Server stack. Under the covers, besides the main AS Control program (which is just an OC4J application), there is also an Agent that works hand in hand with AS Control. It behaves in the same way as a standard Grid Control Agent, with the exception that it will not upload any data to a repository for historical tracking: All the data the Agent gathers and calculates is for real-time purposes online. All logging and tracing operations are the same, and the same log and trace files are created. The AS Control agent writes all files to the `$ORACLE_HOME/sysman/log` directory.

Logging and Tracing the Repository

There are numerous ways to trace and debug the database, all of which can be used with Grid Control as well: Events can be set in the database to trace specific database actions, `oradebug` can be used in SQL*Plus to trace a specific session or get sessions specific information, and so on.

NOTE
Since the OMS is using connection pools for the connections for both the processing of data from the Agents, or doing the user interaction from the browsers, doing a SQL trace on a particular session is not always going to have the desired effect: There is no guarantee that the traced session will always be used for the operation that needs to be traced on the OMS.

Tracing PL/SQL Routines

The PL/SQL code the OMS is executing can be traced and debugged starting from 10*g*R2. This is a very little-known feature, but it can be quite useful when debugging some SQL exception, or trying to narrow down a problem with one of the internal OMS server subsystems.

To view the current PL/SQL tracing levels and see which modules have tracing enabled, issue this SQL command:

```
SELECT context_type_id id, context_type name, trace_level lvl,
       TO_CHAR(last_update_date,'DD-MON-YYYY HH24:MI:SS') last_update
FROM   emdw_trace_config
ORDER BY context_type_id;
```

The output will always contain the same nine modules. The tracing levels for each module can be changed to trace a specific part of the PL/SQL code:

```
ID NAME                      LVL LAST_UPDATE
-- ---------------------     --- --------------------
 1 DEFAULT                     0 02-JAN-2009 07:52:17
 2 TRACER                      0 02-JAN-2009 07:52:17
 3 LOADER                      0 02-JAN-2009 07:52:17
 4 NOTIFICATION                0 02-JAN-2009 07:52:17
 5 REPOCOLLECTION              0 02-JAN-2009 07:52:17
 6 EM.JOBS                     0 02-JAN-2009 07:52:17
 7 EM.BLACKOUT                 0 02-JAN-2009 07:52:17
 8 SVCTESTAVAIL                0 02-JAN-2009 07:52:17
 9 COMPLIANCE_EVALUATION       0 02-JAN-2009 07:52:17
```

The trace levels can have the following values:

0	No tracing
1	Error messages only
2	Warning (includes error messages)
3	Information (includes error and warnings messages too)
4	Debug (all messages)

PL/SQL tracing can be enabled for any of these named modules using the following routine:

```
SQL> exec emdw_log.set_trace_level('<name>',<level>);
```

Example:

```
SQL> exec emdw_log.set_trace_level('LOADER',4);
```

BEST PRACTICE
Don't leave modules in trace mode for prolonged periods of time. Enable the tracing to get more information about a specific issue, and deactive the tracing again, by calling the `set_trace_level` *routine again with a value of 0 (zero).*

The actual stored trace information can be retrieved from the repository by querying the EMDW_TRACE_DATA table:

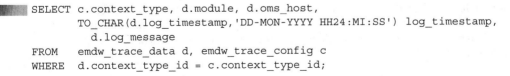

```
SELECT c.context_type, d.module, d.oms_host,
       TO_CHAR(d.log_timestamp,'DD-MON-YYYY HH24:MI:SS') log_timestamp,
          d.log_message
FROM   emdw_trace_data d, emdw_trace_config c
WHERE  d.context_type_id = c.context_type_id;
```

Purging the PL/SQL Tracing

The information is this table is not truncated. All trace data in this table will have to be deleted manually after debugging (and resolving) an issue.

Example: SQL code to remove all messages older than a month:

```
DELETE
FROM   emdw_trace_data
WHERE  log_timestamp < ADD_MONTHS(SYSDATE,-1);
```

Diagnosing Agent Problems

Going through log and trace files is one thing. Debugging issues and triaging the problems you encounter is another. While triaging, the log and trace files are just a source of information and typically are not sufficient by themselves to come to a resolution of the problem. Some additional tips and tricks are needed to help dig deeper, and get to the core of the problem.

Agent Hang/Restart

The Agent watchdog checks the state and condition of the main Agent process regularly. If it finds that either the Agent is not responding, or an operation is taking too long to complete with the Agent signaling a restart, it will dump the process statistics of the Agent process, and force a shutdown and restart of the Agent.

Example: Watchdog intervention entry in the `emagent.nohup` file:

```
Tue May  6 17:32:43 2008::Checking status of EMAgent : 19818
Tue May  6 17:32:43 2008::Abnormality reported for EMAgent : 19818
...
Tue May  6 17:32:55 2008::EMAgent either hung or in abnormal state
Tue May  6 17:32:55 2008::EMAgent will be restarted/thrashed
```

For a hang detected by the watchdog, a message like this will be present in the `emagent.trc` file:

```
ERROR Dispatcher: The remote api of type 10624 has timed out.
   We will bounce the agent
```

A unique number in the trace files identifies each of these remote API calls. The following table contains the most common potentially lengthy operations the OMS server can send to the Agent:

10624	Update target configuration
10634	Remove target from Agent
10635	Update target configuration
10648	Get blackout details (single blackout)
10649	Get blackout details (multiple blackouts)
10650	Remove blackout from Agent
10651	Create new blackout

10658	Reset target state on Agent
10661	Recompute the target properties on Agent
10662	Set new master Agent for cluster target

Whenever the watchdog intervenes, it will write out the process statistics of the Agent process in the `<EMHOME>/sysman/emd` directory. The following files will be generated:

`core.hung.<pid>_<time>`	If GCORE executable is available
`core.hung.<pid>.lsof.1`	If LSOF executable is available

To get more information about what the Agent is executing, and where the time is spent, enable the following tracing in the `emd.properties` file:

```
tracelevel.Dispatcher=DEBUG
tracelevel.resman=DEBUG
tracelevel.TargetManager=DEBUG
```

TIP
If the Agent restarts repeatedly, the log and trace information of the Agent can also be segregated to have a unique set of files for each execution of the Agent. Change the following parameter in the `emd.properties` *file:*

LogFileWithPID=TRUE

The Agent watchdog can also cause a recycle of the Agent if it detects an abnormal increase in either memory or CPU usage. If the watchdog does intervene, a message will be written to the nohup file, with the details of the intervention:

```
Recycling process. VMSize is 371.9765625 MB increased by 7.296875 MB in past 1
```

In cases when there are many targets being monitored, the default values might not be sufficient, leading the watchdog to assume that the Agent is consuming "too many" resources. The following environment variables can be used to change the default behavior:

EMAGENT_MAXMEM_INCREASE	Maximum amount of virtual memory in MB that the Agent can increase since the last check. In the Agent is monitoring a lot of targets, after starting up the Agent, the memory usage can increase with more than the default 1MB.
EMAGENT_RECYCLE_MAXMEMORY	Maximum amount of virtual memory in MB that the Agent can consume on a machine. The default value for this is quite sufficient for normal monitoring. However, if there are a lot of targets discovered, the default value might need to be increased.

Target Discovery Debugging

Firstly, we need to set the stage properly for the discovery: The Agent discovery scripts are making a best effort to find and discover targets on a box. With endless possibilities for setting up and configuring targets on a machine, the discovery scripts will try to figure out all the different ways and different configurations. But there will be cases where the discovery will not find every target on the box. This is exactly the reason why there is always a way to add a target either via the Console or via EMCLI commands.

Common Discovery Problems

The most common problem is a hostname mismatch between the host that was used during the install of the Agent, and the hostname that is used for the configuration of the Agent targets. If the hostname used for the discovery does not match the one used in the configuration files, all involved targets will not be discovered. This is a frequent problem in failover scenarios, and machines that have a virtual hostname, or have multiple NIC cards defined.

When installing the Agent on a machine with a virtual hostname, always use the *ORACLE_HOSTNAME* variable to specify the virtual hostname:

```
$ ORACLE_HOSTNAME=virtual.acme.com
$ export ORACLE_HOSTNAME
$ ./runInstaller -debug ORACLE_HOSTNAME=virtual.acme.com
```

For machines with RAC and CRS installed, the discovery scripts will try to get the configuration details from both CRS and RAC.

The first step is to get the list of all databases known in CRS. If the CRS command fails to report the data, the discovery will not be able to discover all cluster targets correctly.

```
$ <CRS_HOME>/bin/cemutlo -n
```

The *CRS_HOME* environment variable should be set prior to installing the Agent, to point to the correct CRS installation.

For each *ORACLE_HOME* with a RAC database running, the Agent has to be capable of running the `svrctl` command to get the details of the RAC database. For each RAC database, the discovery script will execute this command:

```
$ <DB_HOME>/bin/svrctl config database -d <RAC Database>
```

Additional Logging and Tracing

The discovery scripts will use the same debugging logic as the Perl scripts. All the parameters to control the Perl debugging are located in the `emd.properties` file of the Agent:

```
EMAGENT_PERL_TRACE_LEVEL=DEBUG
EMAGENT_PERL_TRACE_DIR=<EMHOME>/sysman/log
```

After you have made these changes, the discovery scripts can be rerun manually. The Perl scripts from the `$ORACLE_HOME/sysman/admin/discover` directory can be run manually to get the output of that specific discovery script.
Example:

```
$ /bin/sh
$ . $ORACLE_HOME/bin/emctl
```

```
$ cd $ORACLE_HOME/sysman/admin/discover
$ $ORACLE_HOME/perl/bin/perl oracledb.pl $ORACLE_HOME `hostname` $CRS_HOME
```

The following discovery scripts are available:

`csa_collector.pl`	Discovery of the Client Side Analyzer for this machine.
`host.pl`	Discovery for host and cluster targets.
`ocs_mailstore_discovery.pl`	Discovery for Collaboration Suite and all related targets.
`oracle_apache.pl`	Discovery of standalone HTTP Servers.
`oracle_beehive.pl`	Discovery of Oracle Beehive Application and all related targets.
`oracledb.pl`	Discovery for database targets.
`oracle_ias.pl`	Discovery of Application Servers and all related AS targets.
`oracle_webcache.pl`	Discovery of standalone Webcache servers.
`sap_discovery.pl`	SAP discovery. This script cannot be run using the mentioned set of commands.
`siebelDiscovery.pl`	Siebel Enterprise discovery. This script cannot be run using the mentioned set of commands.

Target Monitoring Debugging

Discovering the target is only the beginning. As soon as a new target is registered, the Agent has to start monitoring the target. The first thing an Agent calculates and computes for each target is a set of properties needed to monitor the target. These targets, referred to as *dynamic properties*, define how the target will be monitored. These properties contain settings like the version of the target, the platform the target is running on, and so on. Since the values of these properties can change over time (like the version of a target after an upgrade), the Agent recalculates these values after each Agent restart, and after each downtime of the target.

Debugging the Dynamic Properties

If there is a problem determining the properties of a target, the target will be marked as `broken` internally, and no monitoring will happen for this target. In the console, the availability status of the target will be set to `Unknown`. To get the list of all broken targets (excluding targets in blackout), issue this SQL query:

```
SELECT t.host_name, t.target_name, t.target_type, t.broken_str
FROM   mgmt_targets t, mgmt_current_availability a
WHERE  t.broken_reason  > 0
  AND  t.target_guid    = a.target_guid
  AND  a.current_status != 5
  AND  BITAND(t.broken_reason,1167) != 0
ORDER BY t.host_name, t.target_type, t.target_name
```

There are two possible reasons for problems with the properties:

■ There is an error calculating the properties, usually due to a configuration problem with the target itself (like a bad password, or the wrong *ORACLE_HOME*). The only way to fix these issues is by updating the monitoring settings of the targets via the Console.

■ A timeout while trying to calculate the properties. Out of the box, there is a limit of 30 seconds set at the Agent to calculate all the properties for a single target. On a heavily loaded machine, with large targets, this time might not always be enough to get the properties calculated in time. This timeout, specified in seconds, can be increased at the Agent side in the `emd.properties` file. It can be specified for all targets, or for a specific target type. The overall timeout is controlled by this property:

```
dynamicPropsComputeTimeout=30
```

Increasing the overall property sets the timeout for all types of targets the Agent is monitoring. There are also timeouts possible for each target type individually. Example for the database:

```
dynamicPropsComputeTimeout_oracle_database=120
```

This value will overrule the default one, and set the timeout for all databases the Agent is monitoring to 120 seconds.

There is a third parameter in the `emd.properties` file that influences the calculation of the target properties. For host targets, a special executable in the `$ORACLE_HOME/bin` called nmupm is used to get some OS-specific values for the Agent. The default timeout for this executable is set to 15 seconds by default. It can be increased in the `emd.properties` file by setting the *NMUPM_TIMEOUT* variable. Example:

```
NMUPM_TIMEOUT=30
```

In case of a timeout or a transient error with the calculation of the target properties, EMCTL can be used to force the agent to recompute all the properties for the targets:

```
$ emctl reload agent dynamicproperties [<Target_name>:<Target_Type>]
```

Additional Logging and Tracing

To get more information about the target management, and the way the Agent determines the target properties, specify the following debugging parameters in the `emd.properties` file:

```
tracelevel.targets=DEBUG
tracelevel.TargetManager=DEBUG
```

Agent Metric Debugging

In order for the Agent to evaluate metrics on a target, there are a couple of prerequisites:

■ *The target must be discovered properly.* A complete definition of the target must be present in the `targets.xml` file.

■ *The target must be configured correctly.* All configuration parameters have to be correct, and the Agent must be able to contact the target.

■ *The target must be up and running.* If the target is not available, no metrics will be executed. If any of these conditions is not met, the Agent will not be executing metrics for this target, and no data will be generated or uploaded to the OMS. So the first step in debugging a metric problem should always be to verify that the target is indeed up and running, and running properly for the Agent to monitor it.

Verifying Metric Schedules and Executions

Once the target has been validated, and it's available for monitoring, check to see if the Agent does indeed have metrics scheduled for this target. A special EMCTL command is available to dump out all the metrics the Agent is scheduling:

```
$ emctl status agent scheduler
Oracle Enterprise Manager 10g Release 4 Grid Control 10.2.0.4.0.
Copyright (c) 1996, 2007 Oracle Corporation.  All rights reserved.
-----------------------------------------------------------
Scheduler status at 2008-05-09 16:11:13
Running entries::
Ready entries::
Scheduled entries::
2008-05-09 16:11:31 : Ping Manager
2008-05-09 16:12:05 : Upload Files Recount
2008-05-09 16:14:07 : host:mybox.acme.com:Load
2008-05-09 16:14:14 : host:mybox.acme.com:Network+ProgramResourceUtilization
2008-05-09 16:23:50 : oracle_emd:mybox.acme.com:3872:ProcessInfo
2008-05-09 16:23:55 : host:mybox.acme.com:Filesystems+DiskActivity+
                      PagingActivity+CPUUsage+proc_zombie
2008-05-09 16:24:25 : Upload Manager
2008-05-09 16:24:26 : host:mybox.acme.com:FileMonitoring
2008-05-09 16:25:00 : oracle_emd:mybox.acme.com:3872:EMDUploadStats
2008-05-10 11:13:57 : host:mybox.acme.com:Inventory
2008-05-10 11:14:17 : host:mybox.acme.com:oracle_security
2008-05-10 11:14:27 : host:mybox.acme.com:host_storage
2008-05-10 11:25:41 : host:mybox.acme.com:Swap_Area_Status
2008-05-15 11:14:07 : oracle_emd:mybox.acme.com:3872:EMDIdentity+EMDUserLimits
-----------------------------------------------------------
```

To see what metrics the Agent has already executed, and what the current values and the current violations are for these metrics, two special EMCTL commands are available. The first is just a dump of the metrics the Agent has already executed for a given target. The target is specified in the form `<target_name>,<target_type>`:

```
$ emctl status agent mcache mybox.acme.com,host
Oracle Enterprise Manager 10g Release 4 Grid Control 10.2.0.4.0.
Copyright (c) 1996, 2007 Oracle Corporation.  All rights reserved.
-----------------------------------------------------------
Metric cache contains value for following metrics at 2009-01-10 12:06:17
CPUUsage
DiskActivity
FileMonitoring
```

```
Load
Network
PagingActivity
-------------------------------------------------------------------
Agent is Running and Ready
```

The second command is to give a dump of all the metrics and the outstanding alerts generated for those metric data-points, for a given target. The target to debug in this command is also specified in the form <target_name>,<target_type>:

```
$ emctl status agent mcache mybox.acme.com:3872,oracle_emd
Oracle Enterprise Manager 10g Release 4 Grid Control 10.2.0.4.0.
Copyright (c) 1996, 2007 Oracle Corporation.  All rights reserved.
-------------------------------------------------------------------
Target Name : mybox.acme.com:3872
Target Type : oracle_emd
Current severity state
--------------------------
```

Metric	Column name	Key	State	Timestamp
ProcessInfo	HostInfovszGrowth	n/a	CLEAR	2009-01-10 11:18:07
ProcessInfo	HostInfocpu	n/a	CLEAR	2009-01-10 11:18:07
ProcessInfo	HostInforegf	n/a	CLEAR	2009-01-10 11:18:07
ProcessInfo	HostInfosza	n/a	CLEAR	2009-01-10 11:18:07
ProcessInfo	HostInfoszp	n/a	CLEAR	2009-01-10 11:18:07

```
-------------------------------------------------------------------
Agent is Running and Ready
```

Metric Execution Debugging

Metrics are executed on a regular basis by the Agent to get the up-to-date data from the target. Each metric has a schedule to be used. However, if the metric itself takes longer than the interval used to schedule the metric again, collection delays will start to occur.

There are two types of delays possible:

- The time it takes to execute the metrics is just a little longer than the scheduled interval. For those cases, the Agent will log a warning message in the log and trace files. Metric timeout example from the emagent.trc file:

    ```
    SchedEntry{<type>:<name>:<metric>} exceed next scheduletime, delay=15
    ```

    (Delay is specified in seconds.)

BEST PRACTICE
Any metric taking longer than its scheduled interval will continuously consume a lot of resources on the box. For all these metrics, the schedule should be revised to collect that metric on a less frequent basis.

■ If a metric takes three times longer than its specified interval, the Agent will assume that the metric is hung, and will abort the metric collection. The hung thread will be killed and restarted. These conditions should be avoided at all costs, since they cause a restart of the Agent scheduling, and in case of a systemic problem with the monitored target, will most likely just stumble on the same timeout again. Metric timeout example from the emagent.trc file:

```
ERROR engine:[<type>,<name>,<metric>] : nmeegd_GetMetricData failed :
    Metric execution timed out in <n> seconds
```

BEST PRACTICE
The out-of-box default collection frequencies for the metrics are based on an average load on the machine and the monitored target, and will be more than adequate for most targets. If a metric is timing out, it indicates a case of severe load on either the box or the monitored target (or both) that will need to get investigated. If this load is considered normal and will most likely continue as-is, the collection interval of the affected metrics will need to be altered.

Metric Errors

Each time the Agent runs a metric, it executes some kind of statement or command on behalf of a target. But these commands can fail and report errors. If the execution of the metric is not successful, the Agent will write an error message in the agent trace file in the following form:

```
ERROR engine:[<target type>,<target_name>,<metric name>]:<error message>
```

In case of a configuration error, or an environmental issue on the machine, as soon as the underlying problem is resolved, the next scheduled execution of the metric will clear the error. If the cause is known and cannot be fixed, the metric can be disabled from the Console to prevent the Agent from continuously reporting failures for this metric.

Additional Logging and Tracing

To get additional information about what metrics the Agent is scheduling, and how these metrics are being executed, additional logging and tracing can be enabled.

The following modules can be traced:

```
tracelevel.collector=DEBUG
tracelevel.engine=DEBUG
tracelevel.scheduler=DEBUG
```

For SQL metrics, standard database tricks like SQL tracing or database events can be used to get more details about the SQL statements the Agent is executing.

In case of a Perl metric—a metric that uses a Perl script to get the data—special debugging can be activated to get more details about the execution of the Perl script. In the emd.properties file, the following parameters are available:

`EMAGENT_PERL_TRACE_LEVEL`	Tracing level used by the metric Perl scripts. The values to be used for the level are the `log4j` levels: ERROR, WARN, INFO, and DEBUG. Default value is WARN.
`EMAGENT_PERL_TRACE_FILESIZE`	Maximum size in MB for the metric Perl trace file. Default value is 5 (MB).
`EMAGENT_PERL_TRACE_DIR`	Directory to store the metric Perl trace file. Default location is `$ORACLE_HOME/sysman/log` or `$EMSTATE/sysman/log` if the agent is using a runtime state directory.

Metric Browser

The Agent has a build-in metric debugger, to run some basic tests. This debugger is called the *metric browser*, and can be used to verify some of the values the Agent is collecting for metrics. This is a useful feature, which not only can confirm or deny the fact that the Agent is executing the metric, but can also validate the data that the metric is collecting. To enable the metric browser, enable or uncomment this flag in the `emd.properties` file:

 `EnableMetricBrowser=TRUE`

After the Agent has been reloaded (or restarted), the metric browser will be accessible on the main Agent port. Use this URL to access the information:

 `http[s]://<agent_host>:<port>/emd/browser/main`

> **NOTE**
> *The metric browser will only show those metrics that are reporting basic values to the OMS server. Complex metrics, like configuration metrics that can report complex data structures, or aggregate metrics that depend on other metrics to get the values, will not be available through the metric browser.*

> **BEST PRACTICE**
> *The metric browser can be used to debug a specific issue, but should never be kept operational in a production environment. When the browser is enabled, the Agent starts an extra thread, which listens for the incoming browse requests. This means extra work the Agent may be doing, which serves no real purpose.*

Forcing an Execution of a Metric

There are several ways to force a metric to be re-executed (see Chapter 9 for all the details). One of the ways is to rerun the collection on the Agent using EMCTL. This can be useful to get the extra logging and tracing that has been enabled to debug a particular issue.

■ The metric browser can be used to force any normal data metric to be executed on the Agent. Just click on the metric of interest for the specified target, and the Agent will re-evaluate the metric then and there. Conditions and threshold are not re-evaluated for metrics run through the metric browser. Even though no alerts will be generated by using the metric browser, if the metric does write out state while executing, that state will be affected when an execution of that metric is forced through the metric browser. The logfile-based metrics (like alertlog and listener log analyzers) are good examples of metrics that can have their state changed because of this. To prevent these side effects from impacting the normal monitoring that Enterprise Manager is doing, the general recommendation is *not* to use the metric browser, unless instructed to do so by Oracle Support, to debug a specific metric or metric.

■ EMCTL can be used to rerun a collection of metrics:

```
$ emctl control agent runcollection
        <target_name>:<target_type> <collectionName>
```

The collection names to use are the ones listed in the output of the `scheduler` command:

```
$ emctl status agent scheduler
```

Agent Upload Debugging

As soon as there are target configuration changes, new threshold violations, or new metric data to upload, the Agent will upload the pending XML files. Files will be uploaded using the following rules:

■ Any change in the monitoring configuration of the target will be uploaded immediately. This includes adding or removing targets, changing properties like passwords, and so on, or any major change in the target (like an upgrade of an Oracle database). These settings are all target metadata, stored in A files.

■ Any change in the monitoring of the targets will be uploaded immediately. This includes any change in the metrics that need to be collected, like collection intervals, or the thresholds that need to be evaluated. These settings are all metric metadata, stored also in A files.

■ Any state change or any threshold violation found while collecting a metric will also be uploaded immediately, but after the metadata. These state changes and alerts are stored in B files.

■ All metric data collected for the configured targets will be uploaded only after all A and B files are uploaded. Metric data is stored in C, D, and E files. Every 15 minutes, if no A or B file was generated in the meantime, the Agent will upload all metric data. This default of 15 minutes can be overruled by the `UploadInterval` parameter in the `emd.properties` file:

```
# How long, in minutes, collector will wait until next load.
UploadInterval=15
```

Debugging Communication Problems

The main function the Agent does when uploading the XML file is to establish a connection to the OMS. In most cases, if there is a problem with uploading data, the problem is exactly this: The Agent was not able to create a new HTTP or HTTPS connection to the OMS.

Common Problems

■ Agent cannot reach the OMS. This is the typical network routing issue. Standard TCP tools like nslookup, ping, tracert, and wget can help here. If an invalid hostname is used for the OMS, the following error message will be written in the emagent.trc file:

```
ERROR http: snmehl_connect: Failed to get address for <machine>:
    Authoritive Answer Host not found (error = 1)
```

■ Agent is not allowed to make a connection to the OMS. Example message from the emagent.trc file:

```
WARN  http: snmehl_connect: connect failed to (<machine>:<port>):
    Connection refused (error = 111)
```

There are a couple of potential reasons for this error:

■ The Agent is using the wrong port to talk to the OMS. The Agent uses the REPOSITORY_URL property from the emd.properties as the destination for the HTTP and HTTPS requests. If the port specified in that URL is not the correct one, this error will be reported.

■ The Apache server on the OMS machine is rejecting the communication. In cases where the Apache server is configured to do IP filtering, the incoming connection will never reach the OC4J application, and will be rejected immediately.

■ A firewall between the Agent and the OMS is rejecting the connection. Firewalls need to have rules set up to allow traffic on certain ports. If the port the Agent is using to talk to the OMS is not allowed by the firewall, the communication will be rejected.

■ For secure agents (using SSL), the Agent key that is stored on the disc has to match the key the OMS has stored for this Agent. If they don't match, KEY_MISMATCH and internal SSL errors will be reported by the OMS when the Agent tries to establish a new connection. Workarounds:

■ Stop and start the Agent, to make sure there is no read failure of the Agent key.

■ If the error persists, resecure the Agent:

```
$ emctl secure agent
```

■ Check the secure.log in <EMHOME>/sysman/log for errors.

If the Agent has not been able to talk to the OMS at all since it started, any attempt to try to upload the XML files will return this message:

```
$ emctl upload
Oracle Enterprise Manager 10g Release 4 Grid Control 10.2.0.4.0.
Copyright (c) 1996, 2007 Oracle Corporation.  All rights reserved.
--------------------------------------------------------------
EMD upload error: uploadXMLFiles skipped :: OMS version not checked yet...
```

This means there is a systemic problem with the Agent not being able to make a connection to the OMS. Check the Agent log and trace files for more information about the exact reason of the failure.

Debugging A-file Upload Errors

Since A files contain all the metadata Grid Control needs to properly identify the target in the Console, this information is crucial and always needs to be uploaded first. Any failure to upload an A-file causes blocking: No more uploads will happen until all the A-files are uploaded to the repository. A failure at this level is typically a configuration issue, where the Agent and the OMS have not been configured properly, or the information the Agent has about the targets and metrics does not match, and cannot be synchronized with the information in the repository.

Common Problems

- If the EMD_URL of the Agent has changed, the OMS will not be able to correctly identify the source of this XML file, and will reject any metadata upload from this Agent. Check the agntstmp.txt file and the EMD_URL, and compare it with the EMD_URL definition in the repository for this agent.

- In case of manual changes, or changes made to the targets.xml file outside of the standard APIs, the target information might not be synced with what the repository already knows about this Agent. The error messages associated with the upload will then pinpoint the exact problem area to look at.

Debugging B-file Upload Errors

Like the A-files, the info from the B-files is crucial for Grid Control. Availability state changes or new threshold violations or errors need to be reported ASAP to alert the administrators in a timely fashion.

Common Problems

- The same basic problems that A-files have can also cause B-files to not get loaded. So first check those conditions.

- If the state of the target known to the Agent does not match the state in the repository, B-files can be rejected. This is a situation that can happen with blackout corruptions, or when a target has been forced without the Agent being able to pick up this new state. For false-target states, this command can be used to force a re-evaluation:

  ```
  $ emctl reload agent dynamicproperties <Target_name>:<Target_Type>
  ```

  This will force the re-evaluation of the state of the target, and reschedule the metrics for this target.

- In case of state corruptions (like a missing blackouts.xml file), issue this command:

  ```
  $ emctl clearstate agent
  ```

  This will force the Agent to disregard all state for this target, and start re-evaluating all metrics from scratch.

  When issuing a clearstate command, *always* make sure the Agent is up and running:

  ```
  $ emctl status agent
  ```

Debugging C-, D- and E-file Upload Errors

Unlike the A- and B-files, there is no blocking validation done for this type of data with C-, D-, and E-files. As long as the Agent can communicate with the OMS, and the OMS can identify the Agent, the data will be uploaded.

Common Problems

- The Agent is not able to establish an HTTP[S] connection to the OMS. To debug these kinds of issues, trace the network configuration, to make sure the Agent is able to create a new connection with the OMS.

Agent Job Debugging

The Agent does not keep any kind of state or schedule information about jobs locally. It just listens for requests coming from the OMS servers to execute job tasks.

To get more information about the incoming request the Agent is receiving from the OMS server, enable the dispatch tracing in the `emd.properties` file:

```
tracelevel.Dispatcher=DEBUG
```

After the Agent has reloaded, the incoming requests from the OMS servers will be logged in XML format in the `emagent.nohup` file.

As soon as the Agent receives a valid job request, it will run the `nmo` executable to validate and verify the username and password specified to run this command. To enable the authentication tracing in the `emagent.trc` file, change the following in the `emd.properties` file:

```
tracelevel.Authentication=DEBUG
```

On Windows, an extra switch is present, to give more details about the user authentication process. The parameter is available starting from 10gR2, and is especially useful when debugging issues with domain users and Domain Controllers (PDC and BDC machines).

```
nmotracing=TRUE
```

GRID CONTROL WORKSHOP

Setting Up the Agent to Run Jobs and Commands

On UNIX platforms, if `root.sh` has not been run after the Agent got installed, the `nmo` executable will not have the `setuid` bit set. In that case, `nmo` will not be able to validate the credentials, and the following error message will be sent back to the OMS server:

```
ERROR: NMO not setuid-root (Unix-only)
```

On Windows, the user executing the job commands must have the `Log on as batch job` system privilege set.

If the Agent was not started as the system user, the following system privileges will have to be granted to the user who started the Agent in order to give that user the ability to submit commands as another user:

```
Act as part of the operating system
Adjust memory quotas for a process
Log on as batch job
Replace a process level token
```

The privilege `Adjust memory quotas for a process` will be named `Increase memory quotas` on Windows 2000.

The extra debugging information will be written in the `nmo.trc` file, in the directory `<EMHOME>/sysman/log`.

Once the command is ready to be executed, the `command` Agent module takes over, and executes the specified command. To enable the additional tracing in `emagent.trc` for this module, change this parameter in the `emd.properties` file:

```
tracelevel.command=DEBUG
```

To get a list of all jobs the Agent is currently running, use this EMCTL command:

```
$ emctl status agent jobs
```

This will return a list of all job process IDs the Agent is executing. Use standard OS commands to get more details about the state and conditions of these processes.

Time Zone Debugging

The time zone (TZ) the Agent is using and reporting back to the repository is essential for the data upload. All timestamps the Agent is sending over are stored together with the time zone of the Agent, in order to be able to retrieve and compare the data with targets in other time zones. If the time zone is specified incorrectly on the Agent, the data will not line up any more, and the repository might even make wrong decisions for aggregate metrics (like availability of the container targets, or beacon performance and availability data).

Determining the Time Zone

During the install of the Agent, the time zone of the operating system is used to determine the time zone the Agent will use for its operations.

NOTE
The environment variable TZ can be used on UNIX systems to overrule the operating-system–specific value. When the install is done, the value of the TZ variable (if specified in the environment) has to match the value of the agentTZRegion variable in the emd.properties *file.*

Once the install is completed, the value will be stored in the `emd.properties` file, and can be verified in one of two ways:

- Using EMCTL:
  ```
  $ emctl config agent getTZ
  agentTZRegion=US/Pacific
  ```
- Directly in the `emd.properties` file:
  ```
  $ grep TZ emd.properties
  agentTZRgion=US/Pacific
  ```

The value used by the Agent needs to match the value in the repository.

```
SELECT  agent_name, timezone_region
FROM    mgmt_targets
WHERE   target_type = 'oracle_emd'
  AND   target_name = '<agent_name>'
```

Validating the Time Zone

Before a new time zone is forced on the Agent, always first validate the time zone, to make sure the Agent accepts this new value, and can actually use this for its operations. Any new value used has to be a valid one, specified in the `supportedtzs.lst` file from the `$ORACLE_HOME/sysman/admin` directory.

To validate the time zone at the Agent:

```
$ EMDROOT=$ORACLE_HOME
$ EMSTATE=$ORACLE_HOME
$ export EMDROOT EMSTATE
$ emdctl validateTZ agent <TZ region from emd.properties>
```

Changing the Time Zone

If the machine the Agent is running on is moved, or placed in a different time zone, the Agent configuration will have to be updated to reflect this change. The recommended way of updating the time zone for the agent is by using the `resetTZ` command:

```
$ emctl resetTZ agent
```

After a new time zone has been specified on the Agent, use this PL/SQL routine in the repository to update the target data and metadata in the repository:

```
SQL> exec mgmt_target.set_agent_tzrgn
        ('<agent name>:<agent port>','<new timezone value>')
```

This step is required to update the repository pointers, and make the loaders of the OMS aware that the Agent has switched time zones: The timestamps the Agent will generate after the change might be from the past, and, therefore, the loaders have to be made aware of this time change, to prevent them from rejecting the information from the past that the Agent is sending.

Dumping the Agent State

A new feature was added in 10.2.0.5 to generate diagnostics information from a running Agent. These dumps are low-level diagnostic dumps that should only be run at the request of Oracle Support or Oracle Development to diagnose issues. The dump information will be written to a special file with the `.diagtrc` extension. If no parameter is specified to overrule the dump location, the `<EMHOME>/sysman/dump` directory will be used to store the diagnostic files.

Available Dump Components

This diagnostics feature can be used to dump several components:

`activities`	Details for the activity manager. This thread keeps track of the execution statistics of a task the Agent is executing. It keeps track of the CPU and memory utilization, as well as the elapsed time of the task.
`blackouts`	Details of all blackouts known to the Agent.
`clusterproviders`	Details for the cluster manager.

collections	Details for the collection manager. This thread makes sure all metric collections are getting scheduled, and the data is correctly evaluated and thresholded if needed.
Health	Details for the health manager. This thread in the Agent keeps track of all running threads, and makes sure none of them are either timing out, or are running rampant.
httpclient	HTTP and HTTPS communication details.
Jobs	Details for the job manager.
metricengine	Details on what the metric engine is executing.
Ping	Details for the ping manager. This thread is responsible for the heartbeating the Agent does to the OMS.
recvlets	List of all known modules to read metric data from other targets.
Refcnt	Internal list of all allocated regions of memory the Agent is using.
Reload	Details for the reload manager.
resources	Details for the resource manager. The resource manager keeps track of the open network connections, the files in use, memory allocated, and so on.
scheduler	Details for the Agent task scheduler. The scheduler is responsible for making sure all the tasks the Agent needs to run are run at the appropriate time.
Targets	List of all targets known to the Agent.
threadpool	Details for the Agent thread manager.
Upload	List of all files the upload manager is working on.

The dump commands can be executed in this way:

 `$ emctl dumpstate agent <component>`

> **NOTE**
> *If no component is specified for the `dumpstate` command, all the components will be dumped.*

Configuration Parameters

A few new parameters were added in the `emd.properties` file to influence the dumping of information:

DUMPDIR	An alternate directory the Agent will use for the diagnostics files. If this parameter is not specified, the default location `<EMHOME>/sysman/dump` will be used.
MaxDumps	The number of diagnostic files the Agent will keep in the dump directory. If more files are present in the directory, the oldest one will be removed.

MaxSizeDumps   Maximum size in MB for all the files in the dump directory. If the total size of all the files in the dump directory exceeds the limit, the oldest file will be removed. The default limit is set to 500MB.

Diagnosing OMS Problems

The Management Servers are the heart and soul of the EM infrastructure: All the information going in and out of Enterprise Manager passes through the Management Server. This then already assumes that there will be two distinct types of debugging:

- The debugging of the Management Server and the execution of the code the OMS runs (JAVA debugging).
- Debugging of the data and the data processing the OMS does.

Java Debugging

Debugging the JAVA part of the Management Server is focused more on the execution of the code and the interaction with the Java Virtual Machine (JVM). The processing of the data from the Agents and the repository is less important for these triaging operations.

OC4J Debugging

The startup commands used for the two OC4J containers are defined in the `opmn.xml` file. Separate options can be specified for the startup and shutdown commands of each of the OC4J applications deployed on the Application Server.

```
<category id="start-parameters">
  <data id="java-options" value="-server
      -Djava.security.policy=<ORACLE_HOME>/j2ee/OC4J_EM/config/java2.policy
      -Djava.awt.headless=true -Xmx512M -XX:MaxPermSize=256m
      -DORACLE_HOME=<ORACLE_HOME> -Dajp.keepalive=true "/>
  <data id="oc4j-options" value="-properties"/>
</category>
<category id="stop-parameters">
  <data id="java-options"value="
    -Djava.security.policy=<ORACLE_HOME>/j2ee/OC4J_EM/config/java2.policy
    -Djava.awt.headless=true"/>
</category>
```

For large Grid Control deployments, with a large number of Administrators working on a large number of targets, the memory parameters for the OC4J_EM application can be increased. Increase the Java parameters for the startup command:

```
<process-type id="OC4J_EM" module-id="OC4J">
    ...
    <category id="start-parameters">
      <data id="java-options" value="-server
          -Djava.security.policy=<ORACLE_HOME>/j2ee/OC4J_EM/config/java2.policy
          -Djava.awt.headless=true -Xmx1024M -XX:MaxPermSize=256m
          -DORACLE_HOME=<ORACLE_HOME> -Dajp.keepalive=true "/>
```

```
        <data id="oc4j-options" value="-properties"/>
    </category>
    ...
</process-type>
```

On a heavily loaded size, the maximum heap size (the –Xmx parameter) can be easily increased to 1GB (1024MB). However, it can never grow beyond approximately 1.7GB: This is a limitation of the 32-bit Java distribution. The buffer for the permanent generation heap (the -XX:MaxPermSize parameter) should never be increased. The value of 256MB is sufficient for the OMS, regardless of the use or load put on the Management Server or the rest of the infrastructure.

It is possible to add debug parameters to those startup commands (like the -verbose Java flag). Any kind of debugging done, though, will add the log and trace messages from the Java process to the OPMN log file. Since you know that this file should not become bigger than 2GB in size, any debugging flags added to the Java command-line should only be used for a short period of time, to avoid overflow of the log file.

Java Stack Dump on UNIX

A Java stack trace can be forced on UNIX by sending a SIGQUIT signal to the main OMS server process.

- Use the opmnctl command to get the main process ID of the OMS server:

  ```
  $ $ORACLE_HOME/opmn/bin/opmnctl status -l
  ```

  Send a SIGQUIT signal to that process:

  ```
  $ kill -3 <oms pid>
  ```

- When using Grid Control 10.2.0.4 or higher, there is an EMCTL command available that will force a Java thread dump of the OMS:

  ```
  $ emctl dump omsthread
  ```

  The Java stack dump will be written to the OC4J_EM application log file OC4J~OC4J_EM~default_island~1 in the $ORACLE_HOME/opmn/logs directory.
  The start of the Java dump will be at the end of the OC4J_EM log file. The Java dump will look something like this:

  ```
  Oracle Application Server Containers for J2EE 10g (10.1.2.0.2) initialized
  Full thread dump Java HotSpot(TM) Server VM (1.4.2_14-b05 mixed mode):
  ...
  <information for all threads in the OMS>
  ...
  "VM Thread" prio=1 tid=0x080ba448 nid=0x663d runnable

  "VM Periodic Task Thread" prio=1 tid=0x080c3940 nid=0x664f waiting on con-
  dition
  "Suspend Checker Thread" prio=1 tid=0x080be9e8 nid=0x664a runnable
  ```

Java Stack Dump on Windows

On Windows, there is no equivalent of a kill command by default. To still be able to get a Java dump, check out this note from *My Oracle Support*:

Note 437464.1: How to capture a Java Stack Dump on the Windows Platform

The `thdump` utility mentioned in that note can be used to get a Java thread dump of a running Java program. It works the same way as on UNIX platforms: The dump will be sent to `STDOUT`, which will be written to the OPMN log files.

OMS Target Debugging

All monitoring and administration in Grid Control is done in the context of a target. This makes it essential that a target can be discovered correctly in Grid Control, and that it can be reached properly.

Discovery of Targets

Discovery of new targets can happen in several ways:

- During the install of the Agent, the default targets will be discovered and added to Grid Control.

- In the Console, an Administrator can add targets to an Agent. For the standard target types (like databases and Application Servers), the Console will ask the Agent to auto-discover the targets again on the machine, and show a list of any potential new ones. There is always an option to manually add a new target.

- EMCLI can also be used to add a target. In this case, however, it is the responsibility of the Administrator to specify all the relevant parameters, and provide all the information the Agent needs to monitor the target.

There are a couple of rules an Enterprise Administrator should pay attention to, in order to successfully discover new targets:

- Target names in Grid Control are case-sensitive. `ORCL.WORLD` and `orcl.world` will be considered two different targets, although they might be pointing to the same database on the same machine. It's, therefore, essential to have a well-defined naming convention for the discovered targets. Any convention is fine, as long as it's followed consistently throughout the deployment.

- Duplicate targets cannot be added. If a target with the same name already exists, any attempt to discover this new target again using the Console will result in an error, and the operation will not complete. However, if the Agent uploads new metadata containing a new target that is already present in the repository, it will be added to the duplicate target list.

    `https://<host>:<port>/em/console/health/healthDupTarget`

    A duplicate target can be resolved in two ways:

    - The original Agent has the correct target. The target marked as a duplicate must be removed from the Agent. Go to the Agent home page of the Monitoring Agent (the Agent with the duplicate target), and remove the target.

    - The duplicate target is the correct one. Go to the Agent home page of the Conflicting Agent (the Agent that had this target already discovered), and remove the target.

- A target can only be re-added again after the delete operation completes. If a target is deleted from Grid Control, that same target cannot be rediscovered again until the delete operation has completed. To verify the delete operation, go to the Deleted Targets page:

    `https://<host>:<port>/em/console/health/healthDeletedTargets`

Unless the column `Time delete completed` contains a value, the delete operation is still busy and has not completed yet.

Communication Between OMS and the Agent

The quickest way to verify if the OMS can communicate with the Agent is to go to the Agent home page. If that home page is showing the real-time data for the Agent, the OMS was able to initiate a connection with the Agent and obtain the latest metric data. In case of a communication failure, the home page will not show any real-time data, and a communication error will be displayed on the page, as shown in Figure 18-1.

To determine the reason for the failure, a couple of simple tests can be performed:

■ See if the Agent is up and running:

```
$ emctl status agent
```

If the Agent is not running, start the Agent, and make it upload any pending data, to make sure the Agent can communicate with the OMS:

```
$ emctl start  agent
$ emctl upload agent
```

■ If the Agent is running just fine, and the OMS still has a problem establishing a connection with the Agent, either the network route from the OMS to Agent is not okay, or some network device, like a firewall, is blocking or preventing the traffic to go through. Tools like `traceroute`, `wget`, and `ping` can be used to debug the network route.

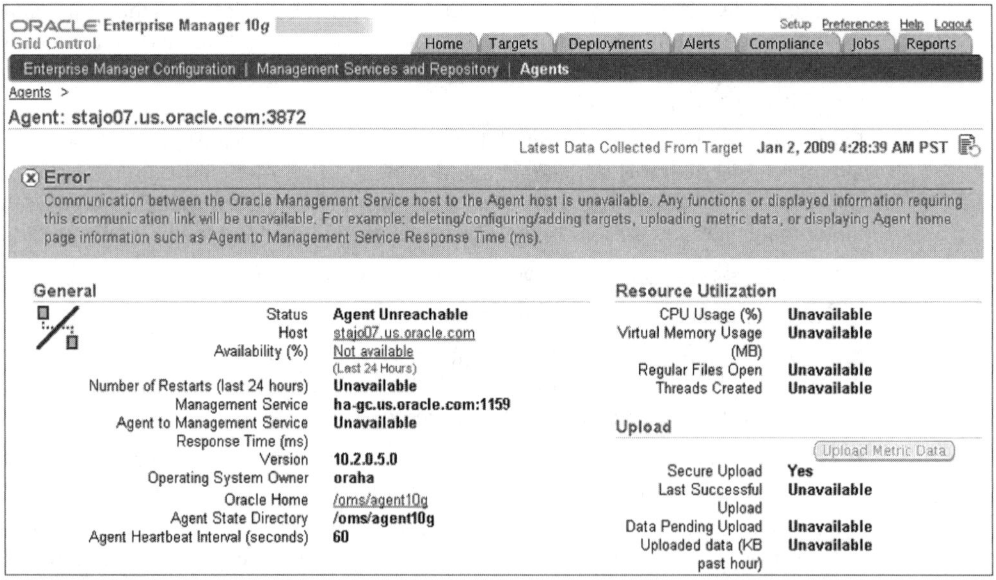

FIGURE 18-1. *Agent communication failure*

Examples:

```
$ traceroute <agent machine>
$ ping <agent machine>
$ wget --no-check-certificate https://<agent name>/emd/main
```

Secure Communication Between the Agent and OMS

In a secure environment, where both the Agent and the OMS are operating in secure mode (SSL-based communication), the OMS will check the SSL key the Agent sends, and will compare it with the value it has. If those values do not match, the OMS will reject the communication from the Agent, and log this message in the emoms.trc file:

```
OMSHandshake failed.(AGENT URL=<Agent URL>)(ERROR = KEY_MISMATCH)
```

Things to check if these errors pop up:

- Run this query in the repository as SYSMAN:

```
SELECT  emd_url,
        DECODE(a.agent_key,NULL,'Missing','Available') key_status
FROM    mgmt_targets t, mgmt_agent_sec_info a
WHERE   t.target_name = '<<agent hostname>>:<<agent port>>'
  AND   t.target_type = 'oracle_emd'
  AND   t.target_guid = a.target_guid (+)
```

If the query returns no rows, the Agent is not discovered in Grid Control. This means that there is a rogue unknown element trying to upload data into the repository. Either stop this Agent on the machine, or rediscover the Agent again in Grid Control. To rediscover the Agent back in Grid Control:

```
$ emctl stop agent
$ emctl secure agent
$ emctl start agent
```

If the query returns the row for the Agent, check to see if the protocol used in the emd_url (the Agent URL) is set to https. If it still says http, then the repository is expecting an unsecure Agent, and therefore cannot accept the secure communication from this Agent. This can happen in cases of a restore of the Agent software, where the state of the Agent software is not the same as the state of the OMS.

If the key_status column returns missing, the secure key for that Agent is not present in the repository. If an administrator manually removed the Agent directly from the repository, without cleaning up the Agent, any subsequent restart of the Agent will cause this problem.

For both these cases, simply resecure the Agent to get the correct SSL information in the repository:

```
$ emctl secure agent
```

- Starting from 10.2.0.5, there is a new command available on the Agent to verify the SSL key from the Agent side:

```
$ emctl verifykey
```

This command will use the wallet the Agent has and try to establish a connection to the OMS. It will verify the connection, and if there is a problem, it will give the details on what part of the communication is not working.

Even if this command is used, the repository side still needs to be verified, to make sure the key is still present.

XML Loader Debugging

The loading of data uploaded by the Agent is a crucial part of Grid Control. Any repeating error or performance bottleneck will have a huge impact on the infrastructure.

Loader Log and Trace Messages

Every Grid Control administrator should perform daily checks to make sure all files are loaded properly.

- **System Errors**   Part of the self-monitoring is the system error log, where all warnings and errors are recorded.

  ```
  https://<host>:<port>/em/console/health/healthSystemError
  ```

  Look for messages from the `Loader` component. If necessary, further filtering can be done per Agent.

- **The OMS Log and Trace Files**   All loader errors are reported in the `emoms.log` and `emoms.trc` files of the Management Server. For all XML handling, the following loader references can appear in the log and trace files:

  - **[XMLLoader<*number*> 1234567890.xml]**   The filename referenced in the message is the name of the file locally, as it is known by the OMS. It has no reference with the name of the file the Agent has sent over. The module name (XMLLoader<*number*>) points to the thread that was processing the file: The number specified in the tag is the loader thread number of the Management server.

  - **[MetadataLoad http://<<agent>>/emd/main/:A0123456789.xml]**   The metadata loader handles all target and metric definitions. All metadata files will always start with an "A" (to indicate the A-channel or metadata channel the Agent is using to upload the file). The filename is again a locally generated one, and has no relevance or significance to the filename sent by the Agent.

  - **[SeverityLoad http://<<agent>>/emd/main/]**   A state change from the Agent cannot be processed in the repository. The accompanying message in the trace file will point to the exact cause of the error. An additional message will also be inserted in the system error log.

XML Loader Debugging

There is no need to put the entire OMS in debug mode just to verify something for the XML loaders. Specific tracing modules can be enabled to debug just those modules working on loading files in the repository. To enable the specific debugging in the `emoms.log` and `emoms.trc` files, add these entries to the `emomslogging.properties` file:

```
log4j.category.emdrep.LoadCoordinator=DEBUG
log4j.category.emdrep.TargetDirectLoader=DEBUG
```

```
log4j.category.emdrep.XMLLoaderContext=DEBUG
log4j.category.eml.XMLLoader=DEBUG
```

After making the change to the properties file, restart the OMS server.

```
$ emctl stop  oms
$ emctl start oms
```

If a consistent error is thrown by a PL/SQL routine when loading an XML file, the PL/SQL debugging can be enabled for the loaders, to get more information:

```
SQL> exec emdw_log.set_trace_level('LOADER',4);
```

After the debugging session has completed, turn off all tracing, and restart the OMS again, to revert to the normal operations without all the changes enabled.

XML Loader Backlog

As already discussed in the previous chapters of this book, an XML backlog is typically a performance bottleneck somewhere, preventing the optimal throughput of the files.

To start debugging backlog issues:

- Always start by looking in the OMS log and trace files to see if there is a repeating error happening.

- Then check the system error log in the console, to see if any repeating loader errors are reported there.

- Check the loader connections in the database:

  ```
  SELECT machine, COUNT(*) cnt
  FROM   gv$session
  WHERE  username = 'SYSMAN'
    AND  action LIKE 'XML%'
  GROUP BY machine
  ORDER BY machine
  ```

- And finally, look at the performance statistics, to see if you can spot a bottleneck using the metrics the OMS is collecting.

The ORA-14400 Error

The following error can appear while loading metric data in the repository:

```
ERROR eml.XMLLoader run.1180 - Exception caught while loading:
   ORA-14400: inserted partition key does not map to any partition
```

The cause for this error is pretty simple: The loader cannot upload data in the repository, because the partitions needed to store the data in do not exist. There are only two possible explanations for this problem:

- The Agent is running in the future. The DBMS_JOBS will already create partitions for five days in the future. However, if the Agent is reporting a timestamp for metric data that is more than five days ahead of the time the repository is using, the data cannot be stored in the repository, and the ORA-14400 error will be thrown. To stop this error from happening again, the OS clock on the Agent machine will need to be synchronized again, to put it in the proper time.

■ The necessary partitions are not created. Partitions are always created five days in advance. A DBMS_JOB will run each day, and truncate the old partitions, and create new ones. The status of this job can be verified in the Console: Look for the Maintenance (Analysis) job in the Repository Operations tab of the Management Services and Repository page:

```
https://<oms URL>:<oms port>/em/console/health/healthRepOp
```

To check this directly in the database, use this SQL:

```
SELECT job, failures, broken, next_date
FROM   USER_JOBS
WHERE  what = 'emd_maintenance.analyze_emd_schema(''SYSMAN'');'
```

To check the number of partitions, and the timestamp of the last partition for each of the partitioned metric tables, you can use this query:

```
SELECT table_name, COUNT(*) cnt, MAX(partition_name) last_partition
FROM   user_tab_partitions
WHERE  table_name IN
       ('MGMT_METRICS_RAW','MGMT_METRICS_1HOUR','MGMT_METRICS_1DAY')
GROUP BY table_name
ORDER BY table_name
```

If there are no current partitions available in the system to load the data, a set of PL/SQL routines can be used to create the partitions. This can be used to get the system operational again, and give the Enterprise Administrator time to locate the exact problem with the DBMS_JOBS.

```
SQL> exec emd_maintenance.add_partitions('MGMT_METRICS_RAW'  ,5,FALSE);
SQL> exec emd_maintenance.add_partitions('MGMT_METRICS_1HOUR',5,TRUE);
SQL> exec emd_maintenance.add_partitions('MGMT_METRICS_1DAY' ,5,TRUE);
```

EM Job Debugging

All the job messages are also stored in the usual places: They're either in the system error log in the console, or in the emoms log and trace files.

Job Log and Trace Messages

There are two places where log and trace messages can be found for the Job system:

■ All failures for the PL/SQL jobs operations are also logged in the system error log:

```
https://<host>:<port>/em/console/health/healthSystemError
```

Use the Jobs component to filter the messages to get just the ones from the Grid Control job handling.

■ If the job tracing is enabled, look for these types of messages in the emoms.log and emoms.trc file:

■ **[Job Dispatcher Thread]**   All work the dispatcher does to pick up the steps to be dispatched and executed.

■ **[Job Worker 1234:Thread-789]**   These are messages from a Job Worker thread handling a specific step of a job. The thread number (789) is a Java-generated thread number for the thread on the OMS. That number can also be found in a thread dump of the OMS. The step the Job Worker is working on is the number associated with the

Job Worker (1234), a unique number to identify that piece of work for the job that is being executed. A dump of this job step can be obtained via EMDIAG for this:

```
$ repvfy dump step -id 1234
```

- **[Job Receiver 1234 5678:AJPRequestHandler-ApplicationServerThread-90]**   The first number (1234) is again the unique ID for the work that the Job Worker is doing. The same EMDIAG command can be used to dump the details of that job step. The second number is a sequence number used by the communication from the Agent to the OMS to keep track of the sequence of the updates. This is particularly important when saving job output in the repository, which has to be saved in the right order. That number is an internal number only, and has no significance for the working of the job, or the way the job is getting executed.

Debugging the Job System

If there is not enough information available from both the error log and the messages in the OMS log and trace files, additional job-specific debugging can be enabled in the emomslogging.properties file. Add these two lines in the file, and restart the OMS:

```
log4j.category.em.jobs=DEBUG
log4j.category.oracle.sysman.eml.jobs=DEBUG
```

All log and trace messages related to the job system will be written to the emoms.log and emoms.trc file.

NOTE
Since any OMS can pick up steps of a job, putting just one of the OMS servers in debug mode to trace a job issue is rarely sufficient. If there are multiple Management Servers active, all the OMS servers will need to have the job debugging enabled to trace the job workflow.

As with the XML loaders, it is possible to do PL/SQL tracing for the job system. To enable the tracing for that, issue the following command in the repository:

```
SQL> exec emdw_log.set_trace_level('EM.JOBS',4);
```

Repository Validation

The repository database is the heart and soul of Grid Control. Without the database to store and retrieve the information, there is no application to work with. Besides the usual ways of debugging the database, like checking the alertlog, and viewing the ADDM and AWR reports, a couple of Grid Control–specific checks can be performed too.

Checking the DBMS_JOBS

Grid Control relies on a set of database jobs (DBMS_JOBS) that perform some key housekeeping tasks. If any of them are not working, various areas of Grid Control will be impacted. The status of these jobs is shown in the Console on the Repository Operations tab of the Management Services and Repository page: Any of the jobs that are marked as "down" have a problem and are not getting run on their designated schedule.

```
https://<host>:<port>/em/console/health/healthRepOp
```

The status of the database jobs can also be queried directly in the database from the standard DBA views available:

```
SELECT job, DECODE(this_date,NULL,'No','Yes') running,
       broken, failures, what
FROM   user_jobs
```

There are several possible ways messages could get reported for these database tasks:

- **In the alertlog of the database**   The database will report any errors or messages encountered during the scheduling and execution of the jobs in the alertlog.

- **In the system error log**   For all application-level messages, or any anomalies encountered during the execution of the tasks, messages will be written to the system error log. These messages can be found in the Console on the Errors tab of the Management Services and Repository pages. Each job will have its own module name that can be used to filter out the messages for that job only. The list of these module names, and the DBMS_JOB they are associated with, can be found in the repository:

  ```
  SELECT display_name, dbms_jobname
  FROM   mgmt_performance_names
  WHERE  is_dbmsjob = 'Y'
  ```

  There is no routine or call to resubmit one or a few of the necessary Grid Control database jobs. There are only two routines: one to remove all the jobs, and another one to resubmit them.

- To remove the DBMS_JOBs from the repository:

  ```
  exec emd_maintenance.remove_em_dbms_jobs;
  COMMIT;
  ```

- To resubmit the DBMS_JOBs in the repository:

  ```
  exec emd_maintenance.submit_em_dbms_jobs;
  COMMIT;
  ```

Checking the AQs

A lot of functionality in the repository database uses Advanced Queues (AQ). The following queues are created in the repository:

MGMT_ADMINMSG_BUS	Queue for all repository administration messages to be executed.
MGMT_LOADER_Q	Queue used when the Shared File System loader mechanism is used on the Management Servers. This queue will contain the list of all metric files to upload in the repository.
MGMT_HOST_PING_Q	New in 10.2.0.5. Queue for all Host ping requests.

MGMT_NOTIFY_INPUT_Q	New in 10.2.0.5. All alerts passed to the notification system to verify if the alert requires a notification.
MGMT_NOTIFY_Q	Queue with all the alerts that need require a notification to be delivered.
MGMT_PAF_REQUEST_Q	All the request messages sent by the Provisioning framework.
MGMT_PAF_RESPONSE_Q	All the response messages sent by the Provisioning framework.
MGMT_TASK_Q	Queue for all internal repository operations (like repository metrics).

All these queues need to be enabled for both enqueue and dequeue. To verify the state of all the AQs in the repository, use this SQL query:

```
SELECT name, queue_type, enqueue_enabled, dequeue_enabled
FROM   user_queues
WHERE  queue_type = 'NORMAL_QUEUE'
```

All the AQs should have both the enqueue and dequeue enabled. If one of the queues is not enabled properly, use the DBMS_AQADM package to start the queue properly in the database:

```
$ exec dbms_aqadm.start_queue('<queue name>',TRUE,TRUE);
```

Using EMDIAG

EMDIAG is a name used for the collection of scripts and tools used to debug all the tiers of Enterprise Manager. The module people will recognize (and most likely will be using already) is repository verification part: repvfy. Specific Agent (agtvfy) and OMS (omsvfy) debugging are on the drawing board.

What Is EMDIAG?

EMDIAG as a tool grew out of a set of SQL scripts and SQL commands that both Oracle Support and Oracle Development would ask people to run to debug issues involving the OMS and the repository. All those debugging scripts have been combined in one tool, with a wrapper around it to provide a single point of entry for all the debugging. Over time, extra debugging steps were added to it, and the ability to dump certain data structures and certain objects from the repository was added.

EMDIAG Versions

The diagnostic toolkit is released on its own schedule, and is refreshed regularly. The version of the kit is always in this format: `<year>.<month><day>`.

Example: 2009.0201
Means: The kit released on February 1, 2009.

To check on the current version of EMDIAG, and get details on how to download and install the kit, with all the information about how to use it, read the following note on *My Oracle Support*:

```
Note 421053.1: EMDiagkit Download and Master Index
```

Using the Command-Line Options

There are two types of options that can be specified on the command-line: generic ones, which apply to all commands and function executed by `repvfy`, and command-specific ones. The typical command-line to run EMDIAG looks something like this:

```
$ repvfy [options] <command> [options]
```

The common generic options are as follows:

`-h`	Help pages. Also available: `h0`, `h1`, `h2`, ... `h9`. These screens provide a quick reference of all the options and capabilities of EMDIAG.
`-i`	Read the password from `STDIN`. Use this parameter when using an external command to provide the password for the repository connection.
`-pwd`	Password to be used for the repository owner.
`-t`	Trace level to use for debugging. The tracing levels map to those of Oracle Net, going from 0 (no tracing) all the way to 16 (maximum tracing).
`-tns`	TNS descriptor to connect to the repository database. There are three ways available to connect to a database via EMDIAG:

- A TNS alias, defined in the `tnsnames.ora` file, or a full TNS descriptor to use. If EMDIAG is run from an OMS *ORACLE_HOME*, the connect descriptor for the database will be read from the `emoms.properties` file.

- If no TNS alias is defined or present and the repository database can be reached using an SID, the connection can be specified in the form `host:port:sid`.

- If no TNS parameter is specified on the command-line, and an *ORACLE_SID* environment variable is set, EMDIAG will try to make a connection to the local machine using the value of the *ORACLE_SID* variable. This way of connecting will only work if EMDIAG is run using the *ORACLE_HOME* of the repository database.

`-usr`	Owner of the repository schema in the database. This value will default to SYSMAN if nothing is specified.
`-v`	Verbose logging. More information will be printed on `STDOUT` if this option is used.

Common options to specify directories and file locations:

`/d`	Location of the main EMDIAG directory, used to extract the EMDIAG software. The environment variable *$EMDIAG_HOME* can also be used to specify this value.
`/log`	Location of the EMDIAG log directory, where all the log and trace files will be written to. The environment variable *$EMDIAG_LOG* can also be used to specify this value.
`/o`	Location of the Oracle software to use. This overrules the value of the *ORACLE_HOME* environment variable, and should only be used when you are told to do so by Oracle Support or Oracle Development.
`/sid`	Value for the *ORACLE_SID* environment variable. This switch is only useful when running EMDIAG on the repository database machine, using the *ORACLE_HOME* of the database.

Specifying Passwords

Security is always a concern when rolling out an application in an enterprise. To meet the security requirements, EMDIAG has several options available to pass in the password for the repository connection:

- *Pass it on the command-line.* The easiest option, but the least secure one. Various OS tools can inspect the typed-in commands, making this a very unsecure solution. Example:

  ```
  $ repvfy -pwd my_password <command>
  ```

- *Store it in the repvfy.cfg file.* This is a special file in the `<EMDIAG_HOME>/cfg` directory that EMDIAG looks at when it is launched, and it contains the common properties. Information like the repository connect string, the default user, and the password can be stored in this file. This is a more secure option, since the security on the password can be set to allow only the owner of the EMDIAG to read the filename. Still, some (super-user) accounts can read all files, making this a potential security problem.
  Example to change in the `repvfy.cfg` file:

  ```
  ora_pwd=<my_password>
  ```

- *Stream it via the command-line.* This can be useful when the password can be retrieved via a third-party tool, making it therefore not visible on the command-line, or anywhere in the environment.
  Example:

  ```
  $ get_the_password -user SYSMAN | repvfy -i <command>
  ```

- *Don't specify anything.* If no password is specified anywhere, or no input is streamed to the tool, it will ask for the password.
  Example:

  ```
  $ repvfy <command>
  Please enter the SYSMAN password:
  ```

Installing EMDIAG

EMDIAG can be installed on any box and in any location. The best locations to put it are naturally on any of the infrastructure machines: either the OMS servers or the repository database servers. At a minimum, EMDIAG needs SQL*Plus and Perl to be present in the *ORACLE_HOME* it is run from. If EMDIAG is installed in an `$ORACLE_HOME`, in the `emdiag` directory, no special environment variables will need to be set to make the kit find the necessary executables and specific Oracle software files. If EMDIAG is installed standalone, the environment variable *EMDIAG_HOME* will need to be specified, to point to the location of the kit.

BEST PRACTICE
Install EMDIAG in the ORACLE_HOME of the OMS servers. If you have multiple OMS servers, install it on each server. The extra work to install it on the different servers and keep it all on the same version, will pay off if you have to use EMDIAG when debugging issues on specific OMS server.

Installing and Upgrading EMDIAG

The installation of EMDIAG happens in two phases:

1. Install the software. EMDIAG is distributed as a ZIP file. To install the kit, simply extract the contents of the ZIP file in an empty directory (the directory `$ORACLE_HOME/emdiag` on the OMS is the recommended location). There are some OS-specific steps that need to be followed to complete the installation. All of this is specified in the `README.TXT` file in the root directory of the EMDIAG software.

   On UNIX:

   ■ Make the `repvfy` and `emdiag` shell scripts from the `<EMDIAG_HOME>/bin` directory executable.

   On Windows:

   ■ Update the `repvfy.bat` file from the `<EMDIAG_HOME>/bin` directory, and specify the correct *ORACLE_HOME* of the OMS software or the database software to be used.

   ■ Create a `commonenv.bat` file, in the `$ORACLE_HOME/bin` directory EMDIAG is pointing to, that contains the version and the location of Perl in that *ORACLE_HOME*. Example:

   ```
   set EMPERLVER=5.6.1
   set EMPERLOHBIN=perl\5.6.1\bin\MSWin32-x86
   ```

2. Install the necessary PL/SQL packages in the repository. The typical four commands are there to do the maintenance operations:

   ```
   $ repvfy install
   $ repvfy upgrade
   $ repvfy deinstall
   $ repvfy version
   ```

   The difference between `install` and `upgrade` is just to retain all settings, and keep the details of all the logged actions. When the `install` option is used, all EMDIAG objects are dropped first (if they exist in the repository), and then re-created. With an upgrade only the PL/SQL and the test signatures are reuploaded.

BEST PRACTICE
Before any major update of Grid Control, deinstall EMDIAG. After the upgrade has completed, reinstall EMDIAG. This way, any changes in the code and the checks of EMDIAG will be adjusted automatically with the reinstall.

The EMDIAG Directory Structure

After the contents of the EMDIAG zip file have been extracted, the following directories will be created:

10gR1 This directory will contain all the Grid Control 10*g*R1–specific scripts and test signatures.

10gR2 This is the directory with all the 10*g*R2–specific scripts and test signatures.

bin This directory will contain the script files `repvfy` (for UNIX) and `repvfy.bat` (for Windows).

cfg   The only file in this directory by default is the `repvfy.cfg.template` file. To use a startup configuration file, rename this file to `repvfy.cfg`, and update the settings in this file. Each time EMDIAG is used, it will read the `repvfy.cfg` file first, and use all the settings and parameters specified in this file.

doc   Release notes and specific information about EMDIAG.

log   Every operation and command that EMDIAG executes will write a log file in this directory.

tmp   This is a placeholder directory. If EMDIAG cannot find any workable directory to create temporary files, it will use this directory to store temporary files (and remove them when the command finishes). When EMDIAG is not running, this directory should always be empty.

Verifying EMDIAG

The easiest way to verify if EMDIAG is working properly is by simply requesting the versions of EMDIAG and Grid Control infrastructure:

```
$ repvfy version
Category                      Info
---------------------------   ----------
Linux                         2.6.9-78.0.0.0.1.ELsmp
PERL                            5.6.1
repvfy                        2009.0201
SQL*Plus Version              10.2.0.4.0
Database Version              10.2.0.4.0
EMDIAG Version                2009.0129
Number of object tests             214
Number of repository tests         420
Repository Type               CENTRAL
Repository Version            10.2.0.5.0
Total enabled object tests         212
Total enabled repository tests     414
---------------------------   ----------
```

This will not only verify the setup of EMDIAG, but also retrieve the necessary information from the repository.

Using Verify Commands

The most common command used will be the `verify` command, to check all the known signatures and see which ones are showing a violation in the repository. The verification process is run as a series of SQL statements in the repository. The statements are defined as *test signatures*: If the signature does not find anything, a count of zero will be returned for that test, and no problem is found. If the signature does pick up an issue, a nonzero count is returned, and the test will show up in the output, together with the number of violations for that test.

Test Signatures

All the test signatures EMDIAG has defined are catalogued using two attributes:

- A level, signifying the criticality of the problem. The level can be specified on the command line by adding the `-level` parameter. If no level is specified, level 2 is assumed. Example:

```
$ repvfy -level 7
```

The level feature is a way to restrict the number of tests and be able to focus more on the problem. When the critical issues are all fixed and dealt with, a higher level can then be used. The following levels are available for use:

0	Critical issues, blocking functionality	Tests 1 to 99
1	Critical issues, severely limiting functionality	Tests 100 to 199
2	Issues, potentially impacting functionality	Tests 200 to 299
3	Warnings, requiring attention	Tests 300 to 399
4	Informational messages	Tests 400 to 499
5	Currently not used	
6	Best practice violations	Tests 600 to 699
7	Purge and cleanup issues	Tests 700 to 799
8	Failure reports	Tests 800 to 899
9	Reserved for internal use and testing	

- The module (functional area of Grid Control) this test belongs to. This can be specified either as an additional command-line parameter when specifying, or as the `module` option. Example:

```
$ repvfy -module targets
```

or:

```
$ repvfy verify targets
```

A *verification* can either be run on the complete repository (the virtual module `all`), or against a specific feature (a single module). The following verification modules are available:

ALL	A virtual module: Run verifications on all modules. If no module is specified on the command-line, this module is assumed.
AGENTS	All Agents of the infrastructure
ASLM	Application Server–level monitoring
AVAILABILITY	Availability subsystem
BLACKOUTS	Blackout subsystem
CA	Corrective Actions
CREDENTIALS	Credentials
ECM	Configuration Management

JOB	Job subsystem
LOADER	XML Loader
METRICS	Metrics and metric metadata
NOTIFICATIONS	Notification subsystem
PLUGIN	Plug-in and extensions
POLICIES	Policies and violations
PROVISIONING	Patching and Provisioning subsystem
RCA	Root Cause Analysis Engine
REPORTS	Reporting framework
REPOSITORY	Repository and repository database
ROLES	Roles and privileges
SYSTEM	EM infrastructure
TARGETS	Targets
TEMPLATES	Templates
USERS	User subsystem

Running a Verification

The default out-of-box way of running verification can be specified on the command-line, like this:

```
$ repvfy verify all -level 2
```

BEST PRACTICE
Always run EMDIAG against a specific module when debugging a specific issue. Only in case of a generic problem (like a performance problem), or when performing a health-check of the system, is a `verify all` *command the option to use. When debugging a job system issue, for instance, there is no point in getting distracted by an issue EMDIAG picks up about the ECM configuration. Always start with a verification of the module. More information can always be obtained later on, to do a health-check of the system.*

Just knowing the numbers of violations is almost never enough information to know what the actual issues are. In order to get more information about the specific violation, the `-details` switch can be added on the command-line:

```
$ repvfy verify all -level 2 -details
```

When this switch is used, after completing the normal verification run, a detailed report of all tests will be run in SQL*Plus, and the SQL script with the statements to verify these tests, as well as the log file with the output of these statements, will be stored in the log directory.

BEST PRACTICE
Get the details of the violating tests when diagnosing a specific
test. With the details, more specific details will be available to help
diagnose the problem.
Example:

```
$ repvfy verify ecm -test 100 -details
```

Fixing Issues

For some of the tests, there is a fix available, capable of cleaning up the reported violations. The fix routines always follow a strict protocol:

- No data is removed or destroyed automatically.

- These fixes are very strict and intended to correct the very specific problem identified in the test. They will double-check the conditions, and only clean up those problems that exactly match the pattern.

To get details on how to fix issues with EMDIAG, contact Oracle Support or Oracle Development. There is no guarantee that all violations reported by the test will actually be fixed by the cleanup routine: Some violations will require more debugging to find the underlying cause of the problem.

An audit trail is left behind of every action and every fix that EMDIAG has run. To get a list of all actions and fixes run, use this command:

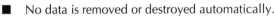

```
$ repvfy audit
```

Dumping Reports

A very useful option in EMDIAG is the ability to dump data structures and repository objects via the dump command. These reports can then be used to check this object, and the related information. There are two types of reports that can be generated:

- **System reports**   These provide information about the infrastructure, or generic information about the repository. The available system reports are:

addm	ADDM report of the repository, if applicable. This report can only be used if the repository is created in a 10gR1 (or higher) database.
ash	ASH report of the repository, if applicable. This report can only be used if the repository is created in a 10gR2 (or higher) database.
awr	AWR report of the repository, if applicable. This report can only be used if the repository is created in a 10gR1 (or higher) database.
health	Overall health-check of the repository.
loader	Overview of the XML loaders.
mtm	Overview of the Monitor the Monitor settings (Grid Control health-checks).

performance	Performance report on the repository, and the tasks the repository is performing.
space	Overview of the size and fragmentation of the repository objects.
system	Overview of the infrastructure.
trace	Dump PL/SQL trace information.

Example:

```
$ repvfy dump system
```

■ **Object reports** To get details about a target, a job, a template, and so on, these kinds of reports can be used. They will dump the main object and all related information in one report. Possible objects to dump are:

agents	Agents
availability	Availability of a target
blackout	Blackout definition and metadata
Ca	Corrective Actions (10*g*R2 onward)
cluster	Cluster definition and metadata (10*g*R2 onward)
credential	Credential Set Info (10*g*R2 onward)
execution	Job execution details
Job	Job definition and metadata
metric	Metric definition and metadata
output	Job execution output
plugin	Plug-in definition and metadata (10*g*R2 onward)
Rac	RAC database definition and metadata
report	Report definition and metadata (10*g*R2 onward)
Role	User role definition and metadata
severity	Alert/severity information
snapshot	ECM data snapshot definition
step	Job Step
target	Target definition and metadata
template	Template definition and metadata (10*g*R2 onwards)
user	User definition

All EMDIAG object reports will require more switches to be provided on the command-line, to identify the exact object that needs to be dumped. For a target, this will be the name and type of the target. For a job, it will be the job name and owner. This information can be specified on the command-line when requesting a dump:

```
$ repvfy dump target -name <name> -type <type>

$ repvfy dump job -name <name> -owner <owner>
```

More information on all the available command-line options, and which parameters to specify for each of the object reports, is available in the README.TXT file (but since we all read and study this file as soon as we install a piece of software, this should already be common knowledge).

Reporting on EMDIAG Findings

Creating reports either for management executives, or simply to check on the overall status of things is always a big thing. It's no different with EMDIAG. When the kit gets installed, a couple of views are created on top of the repository tables EMDIAG adds to the repository. These views were created specifically with the Reporting Framework in mind. Based on the EMDIAG views, a simple, yet very useful report can be created.

1. **Create the report.**

    First provide the title and a descriptor of the report.

    Title: EMDIAG Repository Diagnostics

    Description: EMDIAG Repository Diagnostics

    Since this is a diagnostics report, doing some basic health-checks, we'll create a new category and subcategory for this report:

    Category: EM Diagnostics

    Subcategory: EMDIAG

    EMDIAG does not need specific information from any of the targets discovered in the repository.

    To simplify matters with running the report, always specify the target for this report. Set it to the OMS and Repository target. Another tip to save some page real estate: Uncheck the This Report Has a Time Period checkbox at the bottom of the General tab while defining the report. When this option is left checked (the default), you will always get two extra lines at the top of the generated report specifying the time boundaries for the report. Since the EMDIAG report does not have time boundaries, there is no point in displaying those timestamps.

2. **Create the elements.**

    The report contains just two tables with EMDIAG information from the repository. To specify the details about each of these two report elements, click the Set Parameters icon.

3. **First element: Version overview of EMDIAG**

    Header: EMDIAG version overview

    Type: Table From SQL

    Rows to display: 5

    SQL statement to use:

```
SELECT category, info
FROM   sysman.mgmt$diag_info
```

4. **Second element: Log of all tests run by EMDIAG in the last 30 days**

   Header: Overview of tests run by EMDIAG

   Type: Table From SQL

   Rows to display: 100

   SQL statement to use:

   ```
   SELECT module, label,
          TO_CHAR(vfy_tstamp,'DD-MON-YYYY HH24:MI:SS') last_verified, vfy_cnt,
          TO_CHAR(fix_tstamp,'DD-MON-YYYY HH24:MI:SS') last_fix, fix_cnt
   FROM   sysman.mgmt$diag_results
   WHERE  vfy_tstamp > ADD_MONTHS(SYSTIMESTAMP,-1)
   ORDER BY module, label
   ```

5. **Finish the report.**

   This report will be run on demand, and no schedule or special access restrictions are needed. The only thing left to do at this point is to preview the report, to make sure all the definitions are entered correctly, and click the OK button to save the report in the library. When this new report is saved, the new category and subcategory will now be part of the reporting tree, and the new report will be available for administrators to use.

Summary

As stated in the opening of this chapter, the key to success while triaging and debugging issues is to get to the right information (preferably in a timely fashion). Finding the right information means you need to have the knowledge of all the key players involved and know the break-down of how the data flows through the system. And that is the purpose of this chapter: To give a reference of all the options and possibilities available to an administrator to get additional information, if needed. Sometimes, additional logging and tracing is all it takes: Getting that extra piece of data from a more detailed log and trace file can already make a huge difference. In other cases, some scripts or additional tools will be needed to get the information, or mine the existing information to filter out the necessary piece of data.

PART
IV

Appendixes

APPENDIX

A

Configuration Files

Agent

The directory `<EMHOME>` is the state directory the Agent will use to store the runtime information in. This directory can be retrieved in two ways:

- Either by issuing this command:

  ```
  $ emctl getemhome
  ```

- Or by getting this property from the `emd.properties` file:

  ```
  agentStateDir=<runtime state directory>
  ```

`agntstmp.txt`	Directory: `<EMHOME>/sysman/emd` Text file with the `EMD_URL` and the date and time of the last heartbeat the Agent has sent over to the OMS server. This file is created and updated by the Agent at runtime, and will be regenerated if this file is removed.
`blackouts.xml`	Directory: `<EMHOME>/sysman/emd` XML file containing the list of all blackouts known by the Agent. This file cannot be modified by users. It is maintained by the Agent, and cannot be regenerated or re-created.
`clusters.reg`	10*g*R2 onward. Directory: `$ORACLE_HOME/lib` Text file with the definition of all routines and functions used in monitoring and administration of cluster targets. This is a fixed file, which cannot be changed or updated.
`discover.lst`	Directory: `$ORACLE_HOME/sysman/admin/discover` Text file with the list of all services that will be discovered during install time. This file cannot be changed or modified.
`emagentlogging.properties`	Directory: `<EMHOME>/sysman/config` Text file with the logging and tracing parameters for the Java fetchlet.
`emd.properties`	Directory: `<EMHOME>/sysman/config` Text file with all the configuration settings for the Agent. This file can be modified by users.
`emd.properties.template`	Directory: `<EMHOME>/sysman/config` Text file with all the configuration settings for the Agent, used during the install and cloning of the Agent. Properties will be instantiated at install time. This file can be modified by users.

`fetchlet.reg`	Directory: `$ORACLE_HOME/lib` Text file with the definition of all fetchlets an Agent can use to collect metrics. This is a fixed file, which cannot be changed or updated.
`nsupportedtzs.lst`	Directory: `$ORACLE_HOME/sysman/admin` Text file with the list of all supported time zones. This is a fixed file, which cannot be changed or updated.
`OUIinventories.add`	Directory: `<EMHOME>/sysman/config` Text file containing the location of all OUI software inventories, and their real locations on the disc. This file can be updated by users.
`portlist.ini`	Directory: `$ORACLE_HOME/install` Contains the port numbers assigned during the installation. This file is not updated if port numbers are changed after the installation.
`protocol.ini`	Directory: `<EMHOME>/sysman/emd` Text file with the protocol settings the Agent will use to communicate with the OMS server. This file is created and updated by the Agent at runtime, and will be generated if this file is removed.
`recvlets.reg`	10gR2 onward. Directory: `$ORACLE_HOME/lib` Text file with the definition of all routines and functions used by the metrics listening for data points to be sent to the Agent. (Examples are the AQ for database monitoring and the SNMP trap functions.) This is a fixed file, which cannot be changed or updated.
`setupinfo.txt`	Directory: `$ORACLE_HOME/sysman` Text file with a summary of the Agent installation. This file is instantiated at install time, and does not get updated if subsequent changes are made to the Agent configuration.
`supportedtzs.lst`	Directory: `$ORACLE_HOME/sysman/admin` Text file with the list of all supported time zones. This is a fixed file, which cannot be changed or updated.
`targets.xml`	Directory: `<EMHOME>/sysman/emd` XML file with the list of all discovered targets. This file cannot be modified by users. It is maintained by the Agent, and cannot be regenerated or re-created.
`tzmappings.lst`	Directory: `$ORACLE_HOME/sysman/admin` Text file with the complete list of all mappings between the user-friendly time zone names, and the matching internal time zone name to be used for this name. This is a fixed file, which cannot be changed or updated.

OMS: Management Server

In the context of the Oracle Enterprise Manager environment, an Oracle Management Server (OMS) functions as the middle-tier between Management Agents and the Management Console, where administrators can view and control the enterprise. The OMS has special links with a repository database, used for storing details related to Enterprise Manager. The following is listing of configuration files that can be used to tailor the OMS to an environment.

`emoms.` `properties`	Directory: $ORACLE_HOME/sysman/config Text file with the list of all OMS server configuration parameters. This file can be modified by users. It will be rewritten by the OMS on startup.
`emomsintg.xml`	Directory: $ORACLE_HOME/sysman/config XML file containing the list of additional plugins and extentions installed. This file should never be changed by an end-user. Only install actions should update this file.
`emomslogging` `.properties`	Directory: $ORACLE_HOME/sysman/config Text file containing the Java logging and tracing settings to be used. This file can be modified by users.
`httpd.conf`	Directory: $ORACLE_HOME/Apache/Apache/conf Text file with the standard settings for the Oracle HTTP Server. This file can be updated by users.
`httpd_em.conf`	Directory: $ORACLE_HOME/sysman/config Text file with the Grid Control–specific information for the Oracle HTTP Server. This file can be updated by users.
`opmn.xml`	Directory: $ORACLE_HOME/opmn/conf XML file with the definition of all the Application Server components OPMN will need to manage. This file can be updated by users. After a change to this file, the `dcmctl updateConfig` command will need to be run to make these changes permanent in the AS configuration.
`portlist.ini`	Directory: $ORACLE_HOME/install Contains the port numbers assigned during the installation. This file is not updated if port numbers are changed after the installation.
`setupinfo.txt`	Directory: $ORACLE_HOME/sysman Text file with a summary of the OMS server installation. This file is instantiated at install time, and does not get updated if subsequent changes are made to the OMS server configuration.
`ssl.conf`	Directory: $ORACLE_HOME/sysman/config Text file with the SSL settings and configuration for the Oracle HTTP Server. This file can be updated by users.
`targets.xml`	Directory: $ORACLE_HOME/sysman/emd XML file with the list of all targets used by the AS Console. This file cannot be modified by users. It is maintained by the AS Console Agent, and cannot be regenerated or re-created.

APPENDIX
B

Configuration Parameters

Agent: Properties in the emd.properties File

This is a list of all the properties in the `emd.properties` file that an administrator should be aware of.

The directory `<EMHOME>` is the state directory the Agent will use to store the runtime information in. This directory can be retrieved in two ways:

- Either by issuing this command:

  `$ emctl getemhome`

- Or by getting this property from the `emd.properties` file:

  `agentStateDir=<runtime state directory>`

NOTE
Not all of these values can be modified or changed.

`agentJavaDefines`	Additional parameters to be specified to the Java command line when the agent uses the Java Native Interface (JNI) to call a Java metric. This value is generated during the install and should never be changed or modified.
`AgentListenOnAllNICs`	Boolean value specifying whether the agent should allow all local NIC/IP addresses to be used for incoming requests. When this value is set to `FALSE`, only the hostname specified in the `EMD_URL` will be used to listen for incoming requests. Default value is `TRUE`.
`agentSeed`	Sequence to use for generating the encryption key. This value is generated during the install and should never be changed or modified.
`agentStateDir`	Runtime directory for the Agent to store all configuration, log, and state files. This directory has to be the same as the directory returned by the following command: `$ emctl getemhome` This value is generated during the install and should never be changed or modified.
`agentTZRegion`	Time zone where the agent is working. The value for this parameter should be present in the `supportedtzs.lst` file. The value for this is determined from the OS during install.

agentVersion	This string is used by the Agent to determine which algorithm to use for encrypted data. The string value will be same as in the release version. This value is generated during the install and should never be changed or modified.
altAdminPath	Alternate location for the machine-specific information. Used in clustering environments.
backupUploadedFiles	Boolean flag, indicating whether uploaded XML files are backed up to an alternate location before being erased. If this flag is enabled, the XML files will be copied to the directory <EMHOME>/sysman/emd/upload/succbkup Default value is FALSE.
cannotScheduleThreadTimeout	Timeout in minutes to prevent metric thread starvation. Default is 20 (minutes).
chronosRoot	Directory specifying the location of the Chronos files. This value is generated during the install and should never be changed or modified.
CLASSPATH	Java-required parameter specifying the set of JAR files and directories of dependent modules. This value is generated during the install and should never be changed or modified.
data_buffer_delay	Number of seconds to delay before sending data to the OMS after a severity has triggered. This is used to allow batching of data in case several severities are generated at the same time. Default is 30 (seconds).
DbHangTimeout	Time in seconds the Agent will wait for establishing a connection to a monitored database. If after the timeout has expired, the connection was not established, the Agent will mark the database as down. Default value is 200 seconds.
disableDuplicateCollection ItemDetection	Boolean flag. Disables duplicating metric check for every collection on the Agent. Do not use when beacons, targets, and UDMs are used on the Agent. Default value is FALSE.
dontProxyFor	Domain specification for hosts that do not require the proxy server. By default this value is disabled.
dynamicPropsCompute Timeout	Timeout in seconds for the computation of dynamic properties for a target. Default value is 30 seconds.

`disableECIDGeneration`	Boolean flag. Controls the generation of ECID for every collection. The ECIDs are only used for Application Server management or web transaction management. This means that this parameter can be enabled on all Agents not doing any Application Server or web transaction work. Do not use when beacons or targets are used on the Agent. Default value is FALSE.
`disableCollectionState`	Boolean flag. Controls the update of the state directory containing the last known state. Do not use this parameter unless instructed to do so by Oracle Support or Oracle Development. Default value is FALSE.
`DUMPDIR`	New in 10.2.0.5. Alternate directory location for the diagnostics files. This variable is not set by default, and does not have a default value.
`EMAGENT_PERL_TRACE_LEVEL`	Tracing level used by the metric Perl scripts. Default value is WARN.
`EMAGENT_PERL_TRACE_FILESIZE`	Maximum size in MB for the metric Perl trace file. Default value is 5 (MB).
`EMAGENT_PERL_TRACE_DIR`	Directory to store the metric Perl trace file. Default location is $ORACLE_HOME/sysman/log
`Emd_email_address`	Address to use for out-of-bounds critical Agent messages. There is no default value for this parameter.
`emd_email_gateway`	Gateway to use for out-of-bound critical agent messages. There is no default value for this parameter.
`EMD_ENV`	OS command to use to get and set environment variables. This value is OS specified, and will be instantiated during the install.
`emd_from_email_address`	Return email address to use for out-of-bound critical agent messages.
`EMD_URL`	The unique URL definition the Agent will use to identify itself. Default port used for the URL is 3872 (10gR2) or 1830 (10gR1).
`emdFailureScript`	The script to run if disk space usage exceeds parameters or if certain other error conditions occur. No default value specified for this parameter.

`emdRoot`	Directory location specifying the root of the Agent software. By default, the value of this parameter will be the same as the `ORACLE_HOME` environment variable. This value is generated during the install and should never get changed or modified.
`emdRootCertLoc`	File with the SSL certificates to use.
`emdWalletDest`	Directory with the SSL security files.
`emdWalletSrcUrl`	URL definition.
`enableMemoryTracing`	Boolean value. Enabled additional memory tracing used with the command `emctl status agent memory`.

`enableMetricBrowser`	Boolean value. Determines whether the metrics results are accessible via an URL.
	When this value is activated, you can view the metric data via this URL:
	`https://<machine>:<port>/emd/browser/main`
	If the agent is unsecure, the URL will be:
	`http://<machine>:<port>/emd/browser/main`
	Default value is `FALSE`.

`hostConfigClasspath`	Java classpath for host config collection. This value is generated during the install and should never be changed or modified.
`httpTimeoutBody`	Timeout value in seconds for reading HTTP body. Default is 60 seconds.
`httpTimeoutPrimaryHeader`	Timeout value in seconds for reading HTTP primary header. Default is 30 seconds.
`httpTimeoutSecondaryHeaders`	Timeout value in seconds for reading HTTP secondary headers. Default is 30 seconds.
`JAVA_HOME`	Directory location specifying the root of the JDK software. The default value is `$ORACLE_HOME/jdk`. This value is generated during the install and never be changed or modified.
`JAVA_OPTIONS`	Additional `JAVA_OPTIONS` to use when calling Java program/classes.
`KeepAliveIdleThreads`	Boolean value. Specifies whether the threads in the Agent need to exit after their work is done. The default value is `FALSE` to have a low memory footprint for the Agent. Users can configure it to `TRUE` if thread creation is expensive. Default value is `FALSE`.

`LogFileMaxRolls`	Number of backup copies of the agent log files. Default value is 5.
`LogFileMaxSize`	Size (in KB) of a log file. Default value is 256.
`LogFileWithPID`	Boolean value. When this value is set to TRUE, the process ID of the Agent process is appended to the log and trace files of the Agent, to make these files unique across different runs. Default value set to FALSE.
`MaxDumps`	Maximum number of diagnostic trace files the state manager will keep in the dump directory. If more files are in the directory, the oldest ones will be purged. Default value is 10.
`MaxInComingConnections`	Limit the maximum number of incoming HTTP connections. If this number is reached, no more incoming HTTP requests can be accepted, except the shutdown request from emctl. Default value is 25.
`MaxItemsPerThread`	Maximum number of metrics that will be executed by a thread at a particular interval. By default the Agent will put all metrics for a particular target, executed at the same interval, together in the same run. By default, this parameter is disabled, keeping all metrics scheduled with the same schedule grouped together.
`MaxOCIConnection`	Maximum number of OCI connections to ASM or database instances created by the Agent for the SQL fetchlet. If this limit is reached, no connection can be created for monitoring databases. Default is 100.
`MaxOCIConnectionPerTarget`	The Max OCI sessions that an Agent will create for a target (Include Active+Idle). Default value is 7.
`MaxOCIIdleConnection PerTarget`	Maximum number of idle connections that the Agent will keep per target. Default is 2.
`MaxSizeDumps`	New in 10.2.0.5. The maximum size of diagnostic dump in MB. Default value is 500MB.

MaxSpawnedProcesses	The maximum number of processes that can be created. This includes job processes and processes created for collection threads. If we reach this limit, new processes will not be created; collection will be delayed until the outstanding threads are below this number again. The default value for the parameter will be calculated at startup time as follows: maximum number of file descriptors / 4.
MaxThreads	Maximum number of threads the Agent will used. Minimum value of 4 required. By default this value is disabled.
NormalThreadPoolMax	Internal parameter. Only specify this value when debugging and diagnosing problems. Maximum number of threads the Agent will allow. Has to be at least 8.
NormalThreadStackSize	Size of the stack size (in bytes) for the Agent threads in bytes. By default disabled.
nmotracing	Windows NT only. Boolean flag, to specify additional authentication tracing. Useful for debugging domain vs. local user account authentication problems. Default value is FALSE.
OCIMaxIdleTime	Maximum amount of idle time in minutes. If the maximum is reached, the Agent will disconnect the idle connection. Default is 10 minutes.
ouiLoc	Location of the OUI Java libraries. This value is generated during the install and should never be changed or modified.
perlBin	Directory location specifying the location of the Perl package. Default value is $ORACLE_HOME/perl/bin. This value is generated during the install and should never get changed or modified.
PingHangMaxAttempts	Number of attempts by the Health Monitor when a ping request to the OMS times out, before finally shutting down the EMD process. Default is 3 times.
PingMaxTime	Timeout for ping operation. Health Monitor will abort the EMD process if PingManager does not finish a ping request within this time. Unit is minutes, the default value is 15 minutes.

`proxyHost`	Host machine acting as a proxy server. Used by the fetchlets when monitoring targets. By default disabled.
`proxyPort`	Port to be used on the proxy server. Used by the fetchlets when monitoring targets. By default disabled.
`REPOSITORY_PROXYHOST`	Proxy machine to use when communicating with the OMS. There is no default value for this parameter.
`REPOSITORY_PROXYPORT`	Port on the proxy machine to use when communicating with the OMS. There is no default value for this parameter.
`REPOSITORY_PROXYPWD`	Password for the authentication. There is no default value for this parameter.
`REPOSITORY_PROXYREALM`	String assigned by proxy server to indicate the protected space that needs authentication. There is no default value for this parameter.
`REPOSITORY_PROXYUSER`	User name for the authentication. There is no default value for this parameter.
`REPOSITORY_URL`	URL definition. Used by the Agent to contact the OMS to upload data. Default port used is 4889 for HTTP (unsecure) and 1159 for HTTPS (secure).
`scriptsDir`	Directory location specifying the location of the metric scripts. Default value is `ORACLE_HOME/sysman/admin/scripts`.
`severity_buffer_delay`	Number of seconds to delay before sending severities to the OMS. This is used to allow batching of severities in case several severities are generated at the same time. Default is 3 (seconds).
`SnmpRecvletListenNIC`	This property is used by the SNMP `recvlet` module of the agent to listen for SNMP traps on UDP/IP. If this property is not defined, then the emd port will be used to listen for traps. Default port for SNMP traps is 162.
`SSLSessionCache`	Boolean value specifying whether or not to cache the SSL connections to the OMS. Possible values are `TRUE` and `FALSE`. Default is `TRUE`.

`ThreadPoolModel`	This parameter indicates the thread model to use. If this parameter is not specified, the Agent will determine the optimal thread model itself based on the number of targets it is monitoring. Possible values: SMALL, MEDIUM, LARGE. By default this value is disabled.
`TrcFileMaxRolls`	Number of backup copies of the agent trace files. Default value is 5.
`TrcFileMaxSize`	Size (in KB) of a trace file. Default value is 256.
`UploadFileSize`	Maximum size (in KB) for the metric XML file to be uploaded to the OMS. The value specified is only a guide for the Agent, to close the file and start a new one as soon as the size has been reached. The actual size of the XML file can be a little bigger. Default value is 2048 (2MB).
`UploadFailBackoffPct`	Percentage that will be added to the upload interval time, to calculate the next upload time in case of an upload failure. Default is 20 (percent).
`UploadInterval`	Number of minutes to wait before the Agent uploads the XML files to the OMS. Default value is 30 (minutes).
`UploadMaxBytesXML`	Maximum size (in MB) the upload manager will support in the upload directory before temporarily being disabled. Default value is 50 (MB).
`UploadMaxDiskUsedPct`	The maximum amount (in percentages) of disk space that can be used on the EMD file-system before the following is disabled: Collection of data (upload manager) Logging and tracing The default value is 98.
`UploadMaxDiskUsedPctFloor`	The percentage of disk space that can be used on the EMD file-system before the following is re-enabled after being previously disabled: Collection of data (upload manager) Logging and tracing The default is 95.
`UploadMaxNumberXML`	The maximum number of files the upload manager will support in the upload directory before temporarily being disabled: Default value is 5000.

`UploadMaxTime`	Timeout in minutes used by the Health Monitor to time out an upload request. If the file is not uploaded within this interval, the Health Monitor will time out the upload. Default value is 15 (minutes).
`UploadTimeout`	Maximum amount of time, in seconds, upload will wait for response from repository before timing out. (0 means infinite) Default value is 1800 (seconds) = 30 minutes.

OMS: Properties in the emoms.properties File

`CommitInterval`	Number of metric data rows inserted into the repository before the Loader commits. Default is 500.
`DontProxyFor`	List of comma-separated values of domains not to proxy for. Not used by default. This parameter should not be used. All proxy settings should be specified in the Console UI.
`em.failover.heartBeatInterval`	Number of seconds that dictates how often the OMS server should heartbeat. Default value is 30 (seconds).
`em.jobs.disable`	Internal. Boolean flag. Can be used to disable the job system. Possible values are TRUE and FALSE. Default value is FALSE.
`em.jobs.longPoolSize`	Long-term thread pool for repository side operations. These are synchronous operations. Default is 12.
`em.jobs.shortPoolSize`	Short-term thread pool for "short" agent operations. These are asynchronous remote operations for Agents. Default is 25.
`em.jobs.systemPoolSize`	Internal thread pool for internal operations. System jobs. Default is 8.
`em.loader.disable`	Internal. Boolean flag. Can be used to disable the loader system. Possible values are TRUE and FALSE. Default value is FALSE.

`em.loader.enableMetadataCache`	Boolean property, which controls whether the loader should use a metadata cache. If enabled, the loader skips over rowsets for which it detects that the metadata is already present. Default is FALSE.
`em.loader.errorDirPurgePeriod`	Time in seconds to wait in between purge cycles. Default is one day (86,400 seconds).
`em.loader.loaderCoordinator`	Type of XML loader mechanism used by the loaders. If no value is specified, the value of nonSharedFilesystem is assumed.
`em.loader.maxAgeErrorFiles`	Maximum age in seconds an error file can reside in the errors subdirectory of the receive directory before purging will occur. Default is 30 days (2,592,000 seconds).
`em.loader.maxDirectLoadFileSz`	Maximum size in bytes the OMS will allow for metadata uploads. Default value is 5,242,880 (5MB).
`em.loader.maxMetadataThreads`	Maximum number of metadata loader threads the OMS will spawn. Default is 10.
`em.loader.maxNumErrorFiles`	Maximum number of files allowed in the errors subdirectory of the receive directory before purging will occur. Default value is 10,000.
`em.loader.threadPoolSize`	Number of threads used for loading data files into the repository. Possible values are in the range of 1 to 10. Default value is 1.
`em.notification.cmds_per_minute`	The maximum number of OS commands that can be sent in a minute. Default is 30.
`em.notification.emails_per_ connection`	The maximum number of emails that can be sent in a single connection to an email server. Default value is 20.
`em.notification.emails_per_minute`	The maximum number of emails that can be sent in a minute. Default value is 250.
`em.notification.max_delivery_ threads`	The maximum size of the thread pool for handling notification delivery. Default value is 24.
`em.notification.min_delivery_ threads`	The minimum size of the thread pool for handling notification delivery. Default value is 6.

`em.notification.os_cmd_timeout`	Amount of time in seconds after which an OS command started by the notification system will be killed if it has not exited. Default value is 30 seconds.
`em.notification.plsql_per_minute`	The maximum number of PL/SQL procedures that can be executed in a minute. Default value is 250.
`em.notification.queue_timeout`	The timeout (in seconds) for which the `NotificationMgr` thread blocks waiting for a notification to be queued. Default value is 30 (seconds).
`em.notification.short_format`	The format of the short email. It can be set to `subject`, `body`, or `both`. When set to `subject`, the entire message is sent in the subject, for example: `EM:<severity>:<tgt>:<msg>:<time>` When set to `body`, the entire message is sent in the body, for example: `EM:<severity>:<tgt>:<msg>:<time>` When set to `both`, the message is split, that is, the subject contains `EM:<severity>:<tgt>` and the body contains `<msg>:<time>`. Default value is `subject`.
`em.notification.short_format_length`	The maximum size of a short format email. This limit is imposed by the SMS protocol. Default value is 155.
`em.notification.traps_per_minute`	The maximum number of SNMP traps that can be sent in a minute by the notification system. Default is 250.
`em.notifications.disable`	Internal. Boolean flag. Can be used to disable the notification system. Possible values are `TRUE` and `FALSE`. Default value is `FALSE`.
`em_email_address`	Email address to use to send OOB messages. Not specified by default.
`em_email_gateway`	Email gateway server to use for the OOB messages. Not specified by default.
`em_from_email_address`	Email address to use when as source email address in OOB messages. Not specified by default.
`em_oob_crash`	Boolean flag. Send OOB messages on crash/restart. Default is `FALSE`.

`em_oob_shutdown`	Boolean flag. Send OOB messages on shutdown. Default is FALSE.
`em.oms.dumpModules`	Modules to dump each time the OMS server encounters an abnormal termination.
`em_oob_startup`	Boolean flag. Send OOB messages on startup. Default is FALSE.
`em.oms.dumpModules.defaultTimeout`	Maximum time in seconds any dump of an OMS module can take. If it takes longer, it will get aborted. Default is 240 seconds.
`em.oms.dumpModules.omsThread.timeout`	Maximum time in seconds the thread dump of the OMS can take. If it takes longer, the operation will be aborted. This value will overrule the default dump timeout. Default is 120 seconds.
`em.oms.dumpModules.repos.timeout`	Maximum time in seconds the repository threads dump can take. If it takes longer, the operation will be aborted. This value will overrule the default dump timeout. Default is 180 seconds.
`em.omsbackup_dir`	New parameter in 10.2.0.5. The default directory to use when exporting the OMS configuration. If nothing is specified for this parameter, the default location $ORACLE_HOME/sysman/admin/backup is assumed.
`emctl.watchdog.hang_timeout`	Timeout in seconds for EMCTL. If the OMS does not respond within this timeout period on a command, the watchdog will assume the OMS is hung and will abort. Default value is 120.
`emctl.watchdog.startup_timeout`	The timeout before the watchdog gives up waiting on a response from the Console when it has just been started. Value must be given in multiples of 120 seconds and must be greater than 360 seconds (6 minutes). The default value is 360 seconds.
`emdrep.ping.heartbeatRecordInterval`	Number of seconds used by the heartbeat recorder to batch the incoming heartbeats before writing them to the database. Default is 10 seconds.
`emdrep.ping.pingAgentTimeout`	This property defines the timeout in seconds to be used while reverse-pinging the Agent. Default value is 40 (seconds).

`emdrep.ping.pingCommand`	Command use to reverse-ping a host. The command should wait no more than 30 seconds before timing out. Use the literal `<hostname>` to specify the hostname in the `ping` command. EM will replace `<hostname>` with the real hostname at runtime. Note that you must specify `<hostname>` literally in the command. This command is OS specific.
`emdrep.ping.pingDirectory`	Location to find the `ping` OS command.
`emdrep.ping.pingHostTimeout`	This property defines the timeout in seconds to be used while reverse-pinging the host. Default value is 40 (seconds).
`LargeRepository`	Boolean value. When this value is set to TRUE, the Grid Control home page will not show any of the policy or configuration overviews, to speed up the display of the home page. Default value is FALSE.
`NoHeartbeatRecorder`	Internal. Boolean flag. Can be used to disable the ping system. Possible values are TRUE and FALSE. Default value is FALSE.
`oracle.net.CONNECT_TIMEOUT`	Timeout interval in milliseconds used by JDBC connections. Default is 15.000 (15 seconds).
`oracle.net.crypto_checksum_client`	This property defines the client's (in this case OMS's) checksum encryption requirement. Possible values are: REJECTED ACCEPTED REQUESTED If the server supports secure connection, then OMS uses secure connections; otherwise, it uses unsecure connections. REQUIRED The default value is REQUESTED. This value is only used when ANO is enabled. (Secure Oracle*Net)
`oracle.net.crypto_checksum_types_ client`	Crypto-checksum algorithm to use for client-initiated connections. Possible values are: md5 (RSA Data Security's MD5 algorithm) sha1 (Secure Hash algorithm) The default value is md5. This value is only used when ANO is enabled. (Secure Oracle*Net)

`oracle.net.encryption_client`	This property defines the client's (in this case OMS's) encryption requirement. Possible values are:
	`REJECTED`
	`ACCEPTED`
	`REQUESTED` If the server supports secure connection, then OMS uses secure connections; otherwise, it uses unsecure connections.
	`REQUIRED`
	The default value is `REQUESTED`.
	This value is only used when ANO is enabled. (Secure Oracle*Net)

`oracle.net.encryption_types_client`	Client-initiated encryption method to use. Possible values are: `3des112` (triple DES with a two-key [112-bit] option) `3des168` (triple DES with a three-key [168-bit] option) `des` (standard 56-bit key size) `des40` (40-bit key size) `rc4_40` (40-bit key size) `rc4_56` (56-bit key size) `rc4_128` (128-bit key size) `rc4_256` (256-bit key size) By default, all algorithms are enabled. This value is only used when ANO is enabled. (Secure Oracle*Net)
`oracle.sysman.db.adm.conn` `.statementCacheSize`	Number of DB admin SQL statements to keep in the OMS cache. If this value is not specified, zero (0) is assumed.
`oracle.sysman.db.isqlplusUrl`	URL for iSQL*Plus.
`oracle.sysman.db.isqlplusWebDBAUrl`	URL for the DBA part of iSQL*Plus.
`oracle.sysman.db.perf.conn` `.statementCacheSize`	Number of SQL statements to keep in the OMS cache. If this value is not specified, zero (0) is assumed.
`oracle.sysman.db.rac` `.DefaultInstNum`	Specify the total number of cluster nodes the performance pages will show for a RAC database. Default value is 4. Only valid for 10.2.0.3 and above.
`oracle.sysman.emkeyfile`	Location of the secure EMKEY file. There is no default value for this. The location of the `emkey` file has to be set by an `emctl config` command.

`oracle.sysman.eml.app.noLicensing`	Boolean value. Flag to determine whether to show the licensing page or not on login. Possible values are TRUE or FALSE. Default is TRUE.
`oracle.sysman.eml.ecm.clone .tryFtpCopy`	Boolean flag. Set to TRUE to allow home cloning jobs to first try using FTP for pulling the home archive from source host to destination host. This defaults to FALSE.
`oracle.sysman.eml.maxInactiveTime`	Time in minutes before an idle session is logged out. Default value is 5 minutes.
`oracle.sysman.eml.mntr .emdRepConnectDescriptor`	TNS connect descriptor to use when connecting to the repository database. This value overrules the SID value.
`oracle.sysman.eml.mntr.emdRepPort`	The port on which the listener of the repository is listening.
`oracle.sysman.eml.mntr.emdRepPwd`	The password of the repository owner, to be used when connecting to the repository. This value can be an encrypted value, based on the value of the emdRepPwdEncrypted flag.
`oracle.sysman.eml.mntr .emdRepPwdEncrypted`	Boolean flag. This property defines whether the password of the repository user is encrypted or not. Possible values are TRUE and FALSE. The default values is FALSE.
`oracle.sysman.eml.mntr .emdRepServer`	Machine on which the repository database is running.
`oracle.sysman.eml.mntr.emdRepSID`	SID of the repository database.
`oracle.sysman.eml.mntr.emdRepUser`	Username to use to connect to the repository.
`oracle.sysman.emRep.dbConn .enableEncryption`	Boolean flag. This property defines whether encryption between OMS and repository is enabled. Possible values are TRUE and FALSE. The default values is FALSE.
`oracle.sysman.emRep.dbConn .maxConnForDataLoad`	Number of database connections used for loader uploads to the repository. This includes Agent metadata, Agent state changes, and severities and Job notifications. Default is 25.

`oracle.sysman.emRep.dbConn` `.maxConnForJobWorkers`	Maximum number of allocated DB connections to handle job execution. If the site is intended to run several jobs of different magnitudes (long-running vs. short-running), then tune this parameter for effective DB connection utilization. Default value is 10.
`oracle.sysman.emRep.dbConn` `.maxConnForNotifications`	Maximum number of allocated DB connections to handle alert notifications. This should be set to accommodate the number of notification queues being handled by the OMS. If more than one OMS is sharing the same repository, then the number of queues can vary. Default value is 12.
`oracle.sysman.emRep.dbConn` `.maxConnForReceiver`	Maximum number of allocated DB connections to handle incoming XML files from the Receiver. Default value is 25.
`oracle.sysman.emRep.dbConn` `.numConnForUILoad`	Maximum number of allocated DB connections to handle agent uploads. No further DB connections will be established beyond the prescribed number. The agents will retry to upload during a quieter time. Default value is 10.
`oracle.sysman.emRep.dbConn` `.statementCacheSize`	Number of SQL statements that will be cached in the OMS. Default value is 30.
`oracle.sysman.emSDK.emd` `.httpConnectionTimeout`	Timeout set for creating an HTTP connection and reading the response. Used by internal jobs used by Grid Control. Default value is 180 seconds.
`oracle.sysman.emSDK.emd` `.rt.useMonitoringCred`	Controls the sharing of credential information for real-time metric collection. Default is TRUE.
`oracle.sysman.emSDK.eml.maxRows`	The maximum number of rows that to allow a single query in the Console return. Default value is 2,000 (rows).
`oracle.sysman.emSDK.sec` `.DirectoryAuthenticationType`	SSO setup parameter. Possible values are: EnterpriseUser None: No SSO setup SSO Default value is None.

`oracle.sysman.emSDK.svlt` `.ConsoleMode`	Force the Console to run in certain mode. Possible values are: `enterprise`: Grid Control `standalone`: Grid Control without a repository `dbStandalone`: Database Control `singleNode`: AS Control
`oracle.sysman.emSDK.svlt` `.ConsoleServerHost`	Host on which the server is running. This value *always* needs to be specified, and cannot be changed by a user.
`oracle.sysman.emSDK.svlt` `.ConsoleServerHTTPSPort`	Port to use for SSL communications. Value will be -1 if no SSL is used. This value *always* needs to be specified, and cannot be changed by a user.
`oracle.sysman.emSDK.svlt` `.ConsoleServerName`	Name of the OMS, as it will identify itself. This name has to be unique across all OMS servers in the infrastructure. This value should *never* be changed manually!
`oracle.sysman.emSDK.svlt` `.ConsoleServerPort`	Port to use for the regular HTTP communication. This value *always* needs to be specified, and cannot be changed by a user.
`oracle.sysman.emSDK.svlt` `.disableClassLoading`	Boolean flag. This property allows you to disable the preloading of UI classes during servlet context initialization. Possible values are `TRUE` and `FALSE`. The default value is `FALSE`.
`oracle.sysman.emSDK.svlt` `.PublicServletEnabled`	Boolean parameter. When this value is set to `TRUE`, public reports will be accessible on the OMS. Possible values are `TRUE` and `FALSE`. The default value is `FALSE`.
`oracle.sysman.signon.username`	Default username to use for all pages. By default this value is not set, forcing a logged-in user for all pages.
`patchCacheTempLocation`	Temporary location the OMS will use when downloading patches from My Oracle Support.
`proxyHost`	Machine to use to proxy HTTP requests. Not used by default. This value should not be specified in the properties file. Proxy setting should be specified in the Console UI.

`proxyPort`	Port to use to proxy HTTP requests. Not used by default. This value should not be specified in the properties file. Proxy setting should be specified in the Console UI.
`proxyPropsEncrypted`	Boolean flag indicating whether `proxyUser` and `proxyPwd` are encrypted values. This needs to be set to `FALSE` initially. Once the username and password have been obfuscated, this parameter will be set to `TRUE` automatically.
`proxyPwd`	Password for proxy server authorization. This value should not be specified in the properties file. Proxy setting should be specified in the Console UI.
`proxyRealm`	Proxy server realm. This value should not be specified in the properties file. Proxy setting should be specified in the Console UI.
`proxyUser`	User name for proxy server authorization. This value should not be specified in the properties file. Proxy setting should be specified in the Console UI.
`ReceiveDir`	Directory to place the XML files retrieved from the agents. Default location is `$ORACLE_HOME/sysman/recv`.

APPENDIX
C

Log Files

his appendix gives an overview of the various log and trace files of the Grid Control environment.

Agent

The directory `<EMHOME>` is the state directory the Agent will use to store the runtime information in. This directory can be retrieved in two ways:

- Either by issuing this command:

  ```
  $ emctl getemhome
  ```

- Or by getting this property from the `emd.properties` file:

  ```
  agentStateDir=<runtime state directory>
  ```

Agent Log and Trace Files

The agent log and trace files are stored in the `<EMHOME>/sysman/log` directory.

`agabend.log`	10gR3 (10.2.0.3) onward. Contains all the Agent startup errors. Errors will be added for each failed startup to this file. The Agent watchdog mines this file, to report on an abnormal end of the Agent.
`apmeum.log`	Log and trace information from the end-user monitoring (EUM - Chronos) scripts.
`e2eme.log`	Log file for the end-to-end (E2E) tracing of OC4J.
`e2eme.trc`	Trace file for the end-to-end tracing of OC4J.
`emagent.log`	Log file used by the Agent process. Contains all informational messages in local language.
`emagent_memdump_<time>.trc`	Optional trace file, generated by an `emctl status agent memory` command. Contains the overview of the memory usage of the Agent at that point in time.
`emagent.nohup`	Log file for the Agent watchdog. This will contain all actions the watchdog has performed.
`emagent_perl.trc`	Trace file for the Perl scripts. This includes the Perl metrics and the discovery.
`emagent.trc`	Trace file used by the Agent process. Contains all the trace messages in English only.

`emagentfetchlet.log`	Log file used by the external fetchlets.
`emagentfetchlet.trc`	Trace file used by the external fetchlets.
`emdctl.log`	Agent control utility log file.
`emdctl.trc`	Agent control utility trace file.
`emsubagent.log`	SNMP sub-Agent log file.
`emsubagent.nohup`	SNMP sub-Agent log file with the STDOUT and STDERR messages.
`emsubagent.trc`	SNMP sub-Agent trace file.
`nmei.log`	Log file for the ilint XML file validation.
`nmei.trc`	Log file for the ilint XML file validation.
`nmo.trc`	This trace file will be used on Windows platforms only. It contains the additional tracing for the authentification (both local and via a domain server). The level of debugging written to this file is controlled by the 'nmotracing' parameter from the emd.properties file.
`secure.log`	Log file with all secure operations done from the Agent.

Oracle Net Log Files

By default, the Oracle Net log files are stored in the `$ORACLE_HOME/network/log` directory.

`sqlnet.log`	Log file with a list of all failed SQL*Net logins into the monitored databases, performed by the Perl scripts.

OMS: Management Server

The following section lists the log and trace files for the middle tier.

Oracle HTTP Server Log Files

The Oracle HTTP Server log files are stored in the `$ORACLE_HOME/Apache/Apache/logs` directory.

`access_log`	Log file with all completed HTTP requests made to OHS.
`error_log`	Log file with all failed HTTP requests made to OHS.
`ssl_engine_log`	List of all SSL errors reported by the Oracle HTTP server.
`ssl_request_log`	List of all failed SSL requests to the Oracle HTTP server.

AS Control Agent Log Files

The AS Control Agent log files are stored in the `$ORACLE_HOME/sysman/log` directory.

`em.nohup`	The output of the process that starts AS Control.
`em-application.log`	Main log file with all AS Control messages.
`em-web-access.log`	Log file with all requests users have submitted to AS Control.
`emagent.log`	Log file with English-only messages of the AS Agent.
`emagent.trc`	Trace file with all AS Agent messages.
`emagentfetchlet.log`	Log file for the execution of metrics of the external fetchlets of the AS Agent.
`emagentfetchlet.trc`	Trace file for the execution of metrics of the external fetchlets of the AS Agent.
`emctl.log`	Log file with a list of all EMCTL commands issued for either the OMS server and the AS Agent.
`emdctl.log`	Log file for AS Control Agent control utility.
`emdctl.trc`	Trace file for AS Control Agent control utility.
`emias.log`	Log file for the AS Control application.
`rmi.log`	OC4J interprocess communication log.
`secure.log`	Log file with all secure operations done from the Agent.
`server.log`	Server log file for the AS Control and the interaction with the standalone OC4J container.

OC4J Applications

The log files for OC4J applications are stored in the following directory

`$ORACLE_HOME/j2ee/<OC4J app>/log/<OC4J app dir>`

`default-web-access.log`	Access log with all HTTP requests made to this application.
`em-application.log`	OC4J_EM only. Log for the OMS server application.
`global-application.log`	Main OC4J application log files.
`jms.log`	Java messaging information.
`rmi.log`	Remote command log for this application.
`server.log`	Server log file for the application and the interaction with the application server.

If ODL is enabled for any of these log files, a file called `log.xml` will be used in a separate directory for that module.

OMS Server (OC4J_EM) Log and Trace Files

The log and trace files for OMS Server (OC4J_EM) are stored in the `$ORACLE_HOME/sysman/log` directory.

`emoms.log`	Log file with only the English ERROR and WARN messages.
`emoms.trc`	Trace file with all messages logged by the OMS server.
`repmgmr_create.log`	Log file created during the installation of Grid Control, containing details about the repository creation.
`repmgmr_drop.log`	Log file created during the running of the installer or EMCA (Enterprise Manager Configuration Assistant), containing details about the repository deletion.
`emrepmgr.log.<version>`	Log file for the repository upgrade of Grid Control.
`emrepmgr.log.<version>.errors`	Log file with just the ORA errors filtered from the upgrade log file.
`secure.log`	Log file with all the secure operations performance on the OMS.

Agent Push Installs (OC4J_EMPROV) Log and Trace Files

All log and trace files for the prerequisite checks the Agent Push install performs will be written in the following directory:

`$ORACLE_HOME/sysman/prov/agentpush/<timestamp>/prereqs`

`prereq<timestamp>.log`	Application log messages for the prerequisite check.
`prereq<timestamp>.out`	Standard output of the prerequisite checks (`STDOUT`).
`prereq<timestamp>.err`	Error output of the prerequisite checks (`STDERR`).

The log files for the install operation itself will be written in the following directory:

`$ORACLE_HOME/sysman/prov/agentpush/logs`

`EMAgentPush<timestamp>.log`	Log file of the install operation initiated by the OC4J_EMPROV application.
`remoteInterfaces<timestamp>.log`	Log messages of the remote interfaces layer.

All the messages and output from the commands executed on the target machine are written to the following directory:

`$ORACLE_HOME/sysman/prov/agentpush/<timestamp>/logs/<hostname>`

`agentStatus.log`	Status of Agent after the install operation completes.
`clusterUpgrade.log` `clusterUpgrade.err`	Log and error messages of the cluster upgrade operation.
`config.log` `config.err`	Log and error messages of the configuration of an install on a shared cluster.
`install.log` `install.err`	Log and error messages of the install operation.

`installActions<timestamp>.log`
`oraInstall<timestamp>.err`
`oraInstall<timestamp>.out`
	Oracle Universal Installer logs from the install session.

`nfsinstall.log` `nfsinstall.err`	Log and error messages of the Shared Agent install.
`postinstallscript.log` `postinstallscript.err`	Log and error messages of the specified postinstall scripts executed after the install operation.
`preinstallscript.log` `preinstallscript.err`	Log and error messages of the specified preinstall scripts executed before the install operation.
`rootsh.log` `rootsh.err`	Log and error messages from running `root.sh`.
`sharedClusterUpgradeConfig.log` `sharedClusterUpgradeConfig.err`	Log and error messages of the configuration of an upgrade on a shared cluster.
`upgrade.log`	Log messages of the upgrade operation.
`upgrade.err`	Log error messages of the upgrade operation.

DCM Log Files

All DCM operations will log files in the `$ORACLE_HOME/dcm/logs` directory. For Grid Control, DCM is only used during the install and upgrade, when infrastructure changes are made to the Application Server stack.

`log.xml`	File with all the messages reported during the install (or upgrade) of Grid Control.

OPMN Log Files

The OPMN log files are stored in the $ORACLE_HOME/opmn/logs directory.

HTTP_Server~1	Log file for HTTP Server.
ipm.log	Inter Process Management (AS housekeeping).
OC4J~home ~default_island~1	Log file for the default "home" OC4J application.
OC4J~OC4J_EM ~default_island~1	Log file for the OC4J_EM application (OMS server).
OC4J~OC4J_EMPROV ~default_island~1	Log file for the OC4J_EMPROV application (Agent provisioning).
ons.log	Notification server log file.
opmn.log	Log file for OPMN itself.
service.log	Microsoft Windows platforms only. Log file with the OPMN service messages.
WebCache~WebCache~1	Log file for the Webcache server.
WebCache~WebCacheAdmin~1	Log file for the Webcache administration server.

Webcache Server Log Files

The standard log files are written to the $ORACLE_HOME/webcache/logs directory. If End-User Monitoring is used, this directory will also have an archive subdirectory, with all the archived access_log files the End-User Monitoring has processed.

Access_log	Log file with all completed Webcache server requests.
event_log	Log file with all failed Webcache server requests.
io_log	IO logger file. This is a transient file, which contains only temporary data.

Install, Configure, and Patch

The following section lists all the log and trace files for the middle tier.

Installer

Every time the installer is used to add, upgrade, or delete software in the *ORACLE_HOME*, the details for that install session will be written in the $ORACLE_HOME/cfgtoollogs/opatch directory:

configActions<timestamp>.err	File with all error output (STDERR) of configuration tools run by the Installer.
configActions<timestamp>.out	File with all normal output (STDOUT) of configuration tools run by the Installer.
installActions<timestamp>.log	Details of the install session.
oraInstall<timestamp>.err	File with all error output (STDERR) of the installer.
oraInstall<timestamp>.out	File with all the normal output (STDOUT) of the installer.

Configuration Tools

Every time the installer calls a configuration tool or an external command, the details for that command will be written in the $ORACLE_HOME/cfgtoollogs/cfgfw directory:

CfmLogger_<timestamp>.log	File for the install or configuration action that is run on the *ORACLE_HOME*. This will contain the list of all the commands and configuration tools run for this action.
<command>_cmd_<timestamp>_ERR.log	All the error output (STDERR) of an external command called by the installer.
<command>_cmd_<timestamp>_OUT.log	All the regular output (STDOUT) of an external command called by the installer.
<component>_<timestamp>.log	Log file, created when using the Oracle Installer, with all actions done for a specific installable component.

OPatch

All patch applications run in a particular *ORACLE_HOME* will write a log file in the $ORACLE_HOME/cfgtoollogs/opatch directory:

Opatch<timestamp>.log	Log file with the opatch operation details.

APPENDIX
D

Environment Variables

Environment Variables Used by EMCTL on the Agent

CLUSTER_NAME	Name of the cluster. Only to be used on machines with Cluster Ready Services (CRS) software installed and running.
CONSOLE_CFG	Type of installation. Possible values are: agent Grid Control Agent central Application Server Agent This variable is an internal value. It is set by the EMCTL script, and should *not* be set in the environment prior to using EMCTL.
CRS_HOME	Location of the CRS cluster software. This variable should be set prior to installing the Agent, to have the install instantiate the location of the CRS software correctly in the EMCTL script.
EM_ADMIN_PORT	TCP port the agent should work on.
EM_CHECK_INTERVAL	Polling frequency in seconds of the watchdog. Can be specified as <num><unit>, with the time unit being: S Seconds M Minutes H Hours Default value is 30 seconds (30s).
EM_DESCRIPTORS	Number of file descriptors needed. Default value is 1024.
EMAGENT_MAX_CORES	Maximum number of core files the Watchdog will keep. If there are more core files present, the oldest ones will be removed by the Watchdog. Default value is 3.
EM_MAX_RETRIES	Maximum number of times the Watchdog will restart the Agent. Default value is 3.
EM_RETRY_WINDOW	Time interval in seconds between restart attempts.
EM_SECURE_VERBOSE	Flag to enable additional tracing during securing of the Agent. By default this value is not set.
EM_STANDALONE	Internal variable defined during the installation of the Enterprise Manager software. This variable should never be changed or updated.
EM_THREAD_STACK_SIZE	Size in KB for Agent threads. Default is 3072KB.
EMAGENT_LANG_DEBUG	Flag to enable NLS debugging. By default, this variable is not specified.

EMAGENT_MAX_CORES	Maximum number of core files allowed in the emd directory. If there are more core files present, they will be removed. Default is 9.
EMAGENT_MAXMEM_INCREASE	Maximum size in MB allowed for the Agent to increase in between memory checks. Default is 20 MB.
EMAGENT_MEMCHECK_HOURS	Number of hours between checks for virtual memory size. Default is 1 hour.
EMAGENT_RECYCLE_DAYS	Number of days before Watchdog shuts down and restarts Agent.
EMAGENT_RECYCLE_MAXMEMORY	Maximum virtual memory size in MB an Agent can reach before it will be recycled. Default value is 200MB on most platforms, 350MB on LINUX.
EMCTL_DEBUG	Flag to enable tracing for EMCTL. By default this value is not set.
EMDROOT	Internal value. Set by the EMCTL script, and should *not* be set in the environment prior to using EMCTL.
EMHOSTNAME	Hostname to be used for state file location (DBConsole only).
EMPERLOHBIN	Location of the bundled Perl software. Set in the commonenv file in $ORACLE_HOME/bin during the install. This value should not be changed or set outside EMCTL.
EMPERLVER	Version of the Perl software. Set in the commonenv file in $ORACLE_HOME/bin during the install. This value should not be changed or set outside EMCTL.
EMPRODVER	Version of the EM software. Set in the commonenv file in $ORACLE_HOME/bin during the install. This value should not be changed or set outside EMCTL.
EMSTATE	Starting point for the EM state files. This value should match the agentStateDir parameter from the emd.properties file.
LOCAL_EMDROOT	Internal value. Set by the EMCTL script, and should *not* be set in the environment prior to using EMCTL.
NLS_LANG	Standard Oracle environment variable to specify the National Language Support (NLS) settings of the machine to be used by the Oracle software.

NMUPM_TIMEOUT	Timeout for the NMUPM program, used to gather OS-specific metric data.
ORACLE_HOSTNAME	Hostname the Agent is to use to identify the machine it is running on. This name should match the name of the Agent and Host target used in the `targets.xml` file.
ORATAB	UNIX systems only. Location of the `oratab` file, to be used during the discovery of targets on the machine.
REMOTE_EMDROOT	Internal value. Set by the EMCTL script, and should *not* be set in the environment prior to using EMCTL.
TNS_ADMIN	Standard Oracle environment variable to identify the location of the Oracle Net files, used to resolve any TNS alias used in the monitoring configuration.
TZ	UNIX only. Value of this variable will control the time zone the system is using. This value has to match the *agentTZRegion* variable in `emd.properties`.

Environment Variables Used by EMCTL on the Oracle Management Server (OMS)

CONSOLE_CFG	Type of installation. Possible values are: `agent` Grid Control Agent `central` Application Server Agent Internal value. Set by the EMCTL script, and should *not* be set in the environment prior to using EMCTL.
EM_DESCRIPTORS	Number of file descriptors needed. Default value is 1024.
EM_OC4J_HOME	Location of the Application Server files.
EM_OC4J_OPTS	Additional Java flags for OMS to be used on startup.
EM_STANDALONE	Internal variable defined during the installation of the Enterprise Manager software. This variable should never be changed or updated.
EMCLI_OPTS	Additional Java flags for EMCLI to be used. This variable can be used and changed to specify additional Java variables to debug or change the default behavior of the JVM (Java Virtual Machine) used by the OMS.
EMCTL_DEBUG	Flag to enable tracing for EMCTL. Any value assigned to this variable will enable the tracing. By default this value is not set.
EMDROOT	Internal value. Set by the EMCTL script, and should *not* be set in the environment prior to using EMCTL.

EMPERLOHBIN	Location of the bundled Perl software. Set in the `commonenv` file in `$ORACLE_HOME/bin` during the install. This value should not be changed or set outside EMCTL.
EMPERLVER	Version of the Perl software. Set in the `commonenv` file in `$ORACLE_HOME/bin` during the install. This value should not be changed or set outside EMCTL.
EMPRODVER	Version of the EM software. Set in the `commonenv` file in `$ORACLE_HOME/bin` during the install. This value should not be changed or set outside EMCTL.
LOCAL_EMDROOT	Internal value. Set by the EMCTL script, and should *not* be set in the environment prior to using EMCTL.
NLS_LANG	Standard Oracle environment variable to specify the NLS settings of the machine to be used by the Oracle software.
REMOTE_EMDROOT	Internal value. Set by the EMCTL script, and should *not* be set in the environment prior to using EMCTL.
TNS_ADMIN	Standard Oracle environment variable to identify the location of the Oracle Net files, used to resolve any Transparent Network Substrate (TNS) alias used in the monitoring configuration.

APPENDIX
E

Standard Repository Views

he repository views are designed to get information from the Grid Control repository in the context of a given target, user, job, blackout, and so on. Unless you want to give the database a real workout and stress-test the IO subsystem, dumping the content of all violations or all notifications is not a wise idea. Not all views created in the Grid Control repository are covered in this section. Only a couple of common ones that can be easily used in reports are listed in this section. Use your favorite tool (like SQL*Developer or SQL*Plus) to experiment with these views, in a test environment. Always be careful when running complex SQL commands directly in a production environment: Check them out on a test system first (with SQL tracing enabled if necessary), to see how they are behaving!

MGMT$APPLIED_PATCHES

List of all one-off patches applied on ORACLE_HOMEs
Example: List all patches applied on the OMS running on oms1.acme.com:

```
SELECT home_location, patch, installation_time
FROM   mgmt$applied_patches
WHERE  home_name = 'oms10g'
  AND  host      = 'oms1.acme.com'
```

MGMT$APPLIED_PATCHSETS

List of all patchsets applied on ORACLE_HOMEs
Example: List all patchsets applied on the Management Servers:

```
SELECT host, home_location, version, TIMESTAMP
FROM   mgmt$applied_patchsets
WHERE  name      = 'Enterprise Manager Patchset'
  AND  home_name = 'oms10g'
```

MGMT$APPL_PATCH_AND_PATCHSET

List of all outstanding critical patch advisories for the targets
Example: Rollup for each patch to apply, per product, per OS:

```
SELECT platform, product, patch_id, COUNT(home_location) no_homes,
       COUNT(DISTINCT host_name) no_hosts
FROM   mgmt$appl_patch_and_patchset
GROUP BY platform, product, patch_id
```

MGMT$AUDIT_LOG

Log of all operations audited by Grid Control
Example: List all failed operations of the last 24 hours:

```
SELECT user, operation, "OPERATION MESSAGE"
FROM   mgmt$audit_log
WHERE  "OPERATION STATUS"    != 'SUCCESS'
  AND  "NORMALIZED TIMESTAMP" > SYSDATE-1
```

MGMT$AVAIL_ALERT_HISTORY

List all availability outages
Example: List the reasons for host outages that lasted longer than a day:

```
SELECT target_name, target_type, collection_timestamp, message
FROM   mgmt$avail_alert_history
WHERE  violation_level IN (20,25,125,325)
  AND  alert_duration > 1
  AND  target_type    = 'host'
```

MGMT$AVAILABILITY_CURRENT

Overview of the current state of all targets
Example: List of all targets currently blacked out:

```
SELECT target_name, target_type, start_timestamp
FROM   mgmt$availability_current
WHERE  availability_status = 'Blackout'
```

MGMT$AVAILABILITY_HISTORY

History of all availability state changes for all targets in the repository
Example: List of availability state changes for the repository in the last 30 days:

```
SELECT start_timestamp, end_timestamp, availability_status
FROM   mgmt$availability_history
WHERE  target_type   = 'oracle_emrep'
  AND  end_timestamp > SYSDATE-30
ORDER BY start_timestamp
```

MGMT$BLACKOUTS

Definition of all blackouts known in the system
Example: List of all future blackouts:

```
SELECT blackout_name, reason, created_by, schedule_type, scheduled_time
FROM   mgmt$blackouts
WHERE  status = 'Scheduled'
```

MGMT$BLACKOUT_HISTORY

Overview of all finished blackouts per target
Example: Number of targets blacked-out in the last 30 days:

```
SELECT target_type, COUNT(*) cnt
FROM   mgmt$blackout_history
WHERE  start_time > SYSDATE-30
GROUP BY target_type
```

MGMT$CONNECTOR

Overview of all connectors installed in Grid Control. This view has changed in newer versions: Starting in 10gR5, the status column is now a number field with the values of 0 (used to be Disabled) and 1 (used to be Enabled).

Example to get the list of connectors in 10*g*R4:

```
SELECT  connector_name
FROM    mgmt$connector
WHERE   status = 'Enabled'
```

Example to get the list of connectors in 10*g*R5:

```
SELECT  connector_name
FROM    mgmt$connector
WHERE   status = 1
```

MGMT$CONNECTOR_TYPE

Details of all connectors installed in the repository
Example: List all operational connectors:

```
SELECT  connector_type_name, version
FROM    mgmt$connector_type
```

MGMT$DB_CONTROLFILES

Control file information for databases in the enterprise
Example: List all databases with only one control file:

```
SELECT  host_name, target_name
FROM    mgmt$db_controlfiles
GROUP BY host_name, target_name HAVING COUNT(*) = 1
```

MGMT$DB_DATAFILES

Data file information for databases in the enterprise
Example: All databases with data files approaching the maximum size (+90 percent):

```
SELECT  host_name, target_name, tablespace_name,
        file_size, max_file_size
FROM    mgmt$db_datafiles
WHERE   file_size > max_file_size*0.90
```

MGMT$DB_INIT_PARAMS

All `init.ora` parameters for databases in the enterprise
Example: List all databases with hidden (underscore) parameters specified:

```
SELECT  host_name, target_name, name, value
FROM    mgmt$db_init_params
WHERE   SUBSTR(name,1,1) = '_'
```

MGMT$DB_OPTIONS

Installed database options for databases in the enterprise
Example: List all databases with label security installed:

```
SELECT  host_name, target_name
FROM    mgmt$db_options
```

```
WHERE  name     = 'LABEL_SECURITY'
  AND  selected = 'TRUE'
```

MGMT$DB_SGA

   SGA details for all databases in the enterprise
Example: List all databases with an SGA larger than 4GB:

```
SELECT host_name, target_name, sgasize
FROM   mgmt$db_sga
WHERE  sganame = 'Total SGA (MB)'
  AND  sgasize > 4096
```

MGMT$DB_TABLESPACES

   Tablespace details for all databases in the enterprise
Example: List all dictionary-managed user tablespaces:

```
SELECT host_name, target_name, tablespace_name
FROM   mgmt$db_tablespaces
WHERE  status            = 'ONLINE'
  AND  contents          = 'PERMANENT'
  AND  extent_management = 'DICTIONARY'
  AND  tablespace_name NOT IN ('SYSTEM','SYSAUX')
```

MGMT$ECM_VISIBLE_SNAPSHOTS

   All configuration snapshots for all targets
Example: All current snapshots for the emrep database:

```
SELECT snapshot_type, start_timestamp
FROM   mgmt$ecm_visible_snapshots
WHERE  target_name = 'emrep'
  AND  target_type = 'oracle_database'
  AND  is_current  = 'Y'
```

MGMT$HW_NIC

   Network interface details for every host
Example: List of all hosts with standard ethernet cards that don't have a subnet mask set to 255.255.248.0:

```
SELECT host_name, inet_address, mac_address, host_aliases
FROM   mgmt$hw_nic
WHERE  mask != '255.255.248.0'
  AND  name LIKE 'eth%'
```

MGMT$JOBS

   Definition of all the jobs defined in the system
Example: List of all running repeating jobs:

```
SELECT job_name, job_owner, job_type, start_time,schedule_type
FROM   mgmt$jobs
```

```
WHERE   NVL(end_time,SYSDATE+1) > SYSDATE
  AND   is_library      = 0
  AND   schedule_type != 'One Time'
```

MGMT$JOB_ANNOTATIONS

Overview of all the notifications sent out for job state changes
Example: Number of notifications send for failed jobs per job owner:

```
SELECT job_owner, COUNT(*) cnt
FROM   mgmt$job_annotations
WHERE  job_status = 'FAILED'
  AND  occurrence_timestamp > SYSDATE-30
GROUP BY job_owner
```

MGMT$JOB_TARGETS

List of all targets used in the defined jobs
Example: List all jobs that have the repository itself as a target:

```
SELECT job_name, job_owner, job_type
FROM   mgmt$job_targets
WHERE  target_type = 'oracle_emrep'
```

MGMT$METRIC_CURRENT

Last known data-points for all metrics on all targets
Example: All hosts with more than 90 percent CPU utilization:

```
SELECT target_name, collection_timestamp, value
FROM   mgmt$metric_current
WHERE  target_type   = 'host'
  AND  metric_name   = 'Load'
  AND  metric_column = 'cpuUtil'
  AND  value         > 90
```

MGMT$METRIC_DAILY

Daily rollup data of all metrics for all targets
Example: Min/max number of sessions for all OMS applications in the last 30 days.

```
SELECT target_name, MIN(MINIMUM) min_val, MAX(maximum) max_val
FROM   mgmt$metric_daily
WHERE  target_type   = 'oc4j'
  AND  target_name LIKE '%OC4J_EM'
  AND  metric_name   = 'oc4j_instance_rollup'
  AND  metric_column = 'session.active'
  AND  rollup_timestamp > SYSDATE-30
GROUP BY target_name
```

MGMT$METRIC_DETAILS

Metric data points uploaded by the Agent
Example: Loader throughput of the OMS last day:

```
SELECT key_value,
       ROUND(MIN(value),2) min_val, ROUND(MAX(value),2) max_val
FROM   mgmt$metric_details
WHERE  target_type    = 'oracle_emrep'
  AND  metric_name    = 'Management_Loader_Status'
  AND  metric_column = 'load_processing'
  AND  collection_timestamp BETWEEN SYSDATE-2 AND SYSDATE-1
GROUP BY key_value
```

MGMT$METRIC_ERROR_CURRENT

All outstanding metric errors
Example: List all metric errors for metrics on Agents:

```
SELECT target_name, metric_name, collection_timestamp, error_message
FROM   mgmt$metric_error_current
WHERE  target_type = 'oracle_emd'
```

MGMT$METRIC_ERROR_HISTORY

Overview of all resolved metric errors
Example: Number of UDM metric errors on host targets in the last 30 days:

```
SELECT target_name, COUNT(*) cnt
FROM   mgmt$metric_error_history
WHERE  target_type = 'host'
  AND  metric_name = 'UDM'
  AND  error_message IS NOT NULL
  AND  collection_timestamp > SYSDATE-30
GROUP BY target_name
```

MGMT$METRIC_HOURLY

Hourly rollup data of all metrics for all targets
Example: Min/max number from the last full day for the performance of GC:

```
SELECT MIN(MINIMUM) min_val, MAX(maximum) max_val
FROM   mgmt$metric_hourly
WHERE  rollup_timestamp BETWEEN TRUNC(SYSDATE-1) AND TRUNC(SYSDATE)
  AND  target_name   = 'Grid Control'
  AND  target_type   = 'website'
  AND  metric_name   = 'Performance'
  AND  metric_column = 'PerformanceValue'
  AND  key_value     = 'Perceived Time per Page (ms)'
```

MGMT$OC4J_CONFIGFILES

Details of all deployed OC4J applications per AS Control install
Example: List all OC4J configuration files modified in the last three days:

```
SELECT host_name, oc4j_name, filepath, filesize
FROM   mgmt$oc4j_configfiles
WHERE  modificationtime > SYSDATE-3
```

MGMT$OC4J_DEPLOYEDAPPS

Details of all deployed OC4J applications per AS Control install
Example: List all Application Stacks with more than three OC4J applications deployed:

```
SELECT host_name, oc4j_name, COUNT(*) cnt
FROM   mgmt$oc4j_deployedapps
WHERE  is_current = 'Y'
GROUP BY host_name, oc4j_name HAVING COUNT(*) > 3
```

MGMT$OC4J_PORTRANGES

Details of the entire range of ports the OC4J features use
Example: List all OC4J setups that are not using the default `ajp` port ranges:

```
SELECT host_name, oc4j_name, range
FROM   mgmt$oc4j_portranges
WHERE  id        = 'ajp'
  AND  range     != '12501-12600'
  AND  is_current = 'Y'
```

MGMT$OS_PATCHES

Patch information for all hosts
Example: Number of patches applied per type of OS:

```
SELECT os_extended, MIN(cnt) min_cnt, MAX(cnt) max_cnt
FROM   (
         SELECT os_extended, COUNT(*) cnt
         FROM   mgmt$os_patches
         GROUP BY host, os_extended
       )
GROUP BY os_extended
```

MGMT$OS_PROPERTIES

OS-specific properties for all host machines
Example: All Linux hosts that have the `kernel.shmmax` set lower than 4GB:

```
SELECT host, value
FROM   mgmt$os_properties
WHERE  name  = 'kernel.shmmax'
  AND  value < 4294967295
```

MGMT$POLICIES

All policies defined in the repository
Example: List all critical security polices for host targets:

```
SELECT policy_name, description
FROM   mgmt$policies
WHERE  category          = 'Security'
  AND  target_type       = 'host'
  AND  condition_operator = 'Critical'
```

MGMT$SOFTWARE_COMPONENTS

Version details of Oracle components installed
Example: List JDK versions for all 10.2.0.4 Agents:

```
SELECT base_version, host_name, home_location, version
FROM   mgmt$software_components
WHERE  name             = 'oracle.jdk'
  AND  home_name        = 'agent10g'
  AND  installer_version = '10.2.0.4.0'
```

MGMT$SOFTWARE_HOMES

Details of Oracle software installed on all the host targets
Example: Directory per host of all OMS installations known in the repository:

```
SELECT host_name, home_location
FROM   mgmt$software_homes
WHERE  home_name = 'oms10g'
  AND  home_type = 'ORACLE_HOME'
```

MGMT$SOFTWARE_ONEOFF_PATCHES

Details of Oracle software installed on all the host targets
Example: List of all ORACLE_HOMEs with patch 6109764 installed:

```
SELECT host_name, home_name, home_location, install_timestamp
FROM   mgmt$software_oneoff_patches
WHERE  patch_id = '6109764'
```

MGMT$SOFTWARE_OTHERS

Details of non-Oracle software installed on all the host targets
Example: List the version of emacs installed on all the host machines:

```
SELECT host_name, software_version
FROM   mgmt$software_others
WHERE  software_name = 'emacs'
```

MGMT$SOFTWARE_PATCHSETS

Details of patchsets applied on Oracle software
Example: List of all patchsets installed on Management Servers:

```
SELECT host_name, home_location, version, install_timestamp
FROM   mgmt$software_patchsets
WHERE  home_name = 'oms10g'
```

MGMT$TARGETS

All targets defined in Grid Control
Example: Number of hosts, grouped by operating system

```
SELECT type_qualifier1, COUNT(*) cnt
FROM   mgmt$target
WHERE  target_type = 'host'
GROUP BY type_qualifier1
```

MGMT$TARGET_COMPOSITE

All members of every group target defined in Grid Control
Example: List of targets used in the "Grid Control" web site definition:

```
SELECT member_target_name, member_target_type
FROM   mgmt$target_composite
WHERE  composite_name = 'Grid Control'
  AND  composite_type = 'website'
```

MGMT$TARGET_MEMBERS

All members of all container targets defined in Grid Control
Example: Number of targets grouped per type for the GC Infrastructure group:

```
SELECT member_target_type, COUNT(*) cnt
FROM   mgmt$target_members
WHERE  aggregate_target_name = 'GC Infrastructure'
  AND  aggregate_target_type = 'composite'
GROUP BY member_target_type
```

MGMT$TARGET_METRIC_COLLECTIONS

All metric collection settings for all targets in the repository
Example: List all targets with the Response metric disabled:

```
SELECT target_name, target_type, collection_frequency
FROM   mgmt$target_metric_collections
WHERE  is_enabled  = 0
  AND  metric_name = 'Response'
```

MGMT\$TARGET_METRIC_SETTINGS

All metric threshold settings for all targets in the repository
Example: List all database or RAC targets that have the tablespace thresholds set to less than 85 for warning and 95 for critical:

```
SELECT target_name, target_type, warning_threshold, critical_threshold
FROM   mgmt$target_metric_settings
WHERE  target_type IN ('oracle_database','rac_database')
  AND  metric_name   = 'problemTbsp'
  AND  metric_column = 'pctUsed'
  AND  NVL(TRIM(warning_threshold),0)  < 85
  AND  NVL(TRIM(critical_threshold),0) < 95
```

MGMT\$TARGET_PROPERTIES

Monitoring properties for every target
Example: Number of Agents grouped per version:

```
SELECT property_value, COUNT(*) cnt
FROM   mgmt$target_properties
WHERE  property_name = 'Version'
  AND  target_type = 'oracle_emd'
GROUP BY property_value
```

MGMT\$TARGET_POLICIES

All policies defined per target
Example: Number of distinct security policies enabled on databases:

```
SELECT COUNT(DISTINCT policy_name) cnt
FROM   mgmt$target_policies
WHERE  is_enabled  = 1
  AND  target_type = 'oracle_database'
  AND  category    = 'Security'
```

MGMT\$TARGET_POLICY_SETTINGS

Policy rule defines per target
Example: List all databases for which the password lifetime is not defined as 60 days:

```
SELECT target_name, policy_threshold
FROM   mgmt$target_policy_settings
WHERE  category     = 'Security'
  AND  policy_name = 'Password_Life_Time'
  AND  policy_threshold != 60
```

MGMT$TARGET_TYPE

All metrics collected for each target

Example: List all metrics for the Agent on the machine `oms.acme.com`:

```
SELECT metric_label, column_label
FROM   mgmt$target_type
WHERE  target_type = 'oracle_emd'
  AND  target_name = 'oms.acme.com:3872'
  AND  TRIM(metric_column) IS NOT NULL
```

MGMT$TARGET_TYPE_PROPERTIES

All internal monitoring properties for all targets

Example: List all clustered targets in the repository:

```
SELECT target_name, target_type
FROM   mgmt$target_type_properties
WHERE  property_name  = 'is_cluster'
  AND  property_value = 1
```

MGMT$TEMPLATES

All templates defined in Grid Control

Example: List all public templates:

```
SELECT target_type, template_name, owner, created_date
FROM   mgmt$templates
WHERE  is_public = 1
```

APPENDIX
F

Command-Line Tool
Options

he following pages have a small reference of the most commonly used command-line tools, and the available options for those commands.

EMCTL: Agent-Side Commands

```
$ emctl clearstate [agent]
```

Clear all state for all the targets. This means that the first evaluation of each metric after issuing this command will send over the state of that metric again. This command should be only be run when the Agent is up and running. Only use this command when instructed to do so by Oracle Support or Oracle Development.

```
$ emctl clearsudoprops
```

Remove the properties for PDP commands executed by the Agent. This is for Agent internal use only, and should not be run on its own.

```
$ emctl config agent getlocalhost
```

Return the hostname the Agent is currently using. This can be either the primary hostname of the box, or the value of *ORACLE_HOSTNAME* if specified in the environment.

```
$ emctl config agent credentials <Target_name>[:<Target_Type>]
```

Change the monitoring username and password for the specified target. Only targets that have credentials specified can be used with this command.

```
$ emctl config agent getTZ
```

Return the time zone the Agent is currently using.

```
$ emctl config agent listtargets
```

Return the list of all targets the Agent is currently monitoring (all targets in the `targets.xml` file).

```
$ emctl config agent runcollection <tgt name>:<tgt type> <collection>
```

Run the specific collection at that time for the specified target, regardless of what the actual schedule for this metric really is. This will execute the metric collection, and evaluate the thresholds if there are any defined for the collection.

```
$ emctl config agent updateTZ
```

The command `emctl resetTZ agent` should be used instead when changing the time zone of an Agent.

```
$ emctl deploy agent [-s <install-pwd>]
        <deploy-dir> <deploy-host>:<port> <src-host>
```

Internal command used by the `nfsagentinstall` script to stage another Agent using the shared Agent installation.

```
$ emctl dumpstate agent <component>
```

New in 10.2.0.5. Dump the current state of the Agent. If no component is specified, all the components are dumped. The dump file will be located in the `<EMHOME>/sysman/dump` directory. The available components are: `activities`, `blackouts`, `clusterproviders`, `collections`, `health`, `httpclient`, `jobs`, `ping`, `metricengine`, `recvlets`, `refcnt`, `reload`, `resources`, `scheduler`, `targets`, `threadpool`, and `upload`.

```
$ emctl gensudoprops
```

Generate the properties for PDP commands executed by the Agent. This is for Agent internal use only, and should not be run on its own.

```
$ emctl getemhome
```

Return the directory with the runtime state information. For a normal standalone Agent, this directory will be the same as the `$ORACLE_HOME`. On a cluster machine, this directory will be `$ORACLE_HOME/<hostname>`. For a state-deployed Agent (NFS agent), this will be the directory specified during the deploy with the `nfsagentinstall` command.

```
$ emctl getversion [agent]
```

Return the current version of the Agent.

```
$ emctl ilint <...options...>
```

XML validation of the Agent files. This is for Agent internal use only.

```
$ emctl reload [agent]
```

Force rereading the `targets.xml` file and all the custom collection files. Use this command after each change to the logging and tracing parameters of the Agent.

```
$ emctl reload agent dynamicproperties [<Target_name>:<Target_Type>]
```

Reload the target definition, and recompute the dynamic properties of either all targets (if no target specified), or the specific target specified on the command-line.

```
$ emctl resetTZ agent
```

Update the time zone the Agent will use. This command can be run only if the Agent is down. If the time zone offset has changed, a PL/SQL routine will need to be run on the repository to sync-up the last known timestamps sent by this Agent, to reflect the time zone change.

```
$ emctl secure add_trust_cert -trust_certs_loc <loc>
```

New in 10.2.0.5. Use this command to add third-party certificates to the Agent. For more information, see the chapter on "Advanced Configuration" in the *Installation and Configuration Guide*.

```
$ emctl secure agent [-emdWalletSrcUrl <url>]
```

Request an SSL wallet from the OMS, to secure the communication between the Agent and the OMS. If the Agent is not yet secured, the Agent will switch from HTTP to HTTPS and use the downloaded SSL wallet from the OMS. If the Agent is already secured, it will request a new wallet from the OMS, and use that for the communication. If this command is issued while the Agent is running, the Agent will be stopped first. After the SSL wallet has been downloaded, the Agent will then get restarted.

```
$ emctl start agent
```

Start the Agent.

```
$ emctl start blackout <name> [-nodeLevel]
        [<target_name>[:<type_type>]].... [-d <Duration>]
```

Create a new blackout with the given name on the specified target(s). The duration option should always be specified last on the command line. The value of the duration option is in the form <days> <hour>:<min>. Zero values for days and hours can be omitted when specifying the duration.

```
$ emctl start subagent
```

Start the SNMP sub-Agent.

```
$ emctl status agent
```

Show the current status of the Agent.

```
$ emctl status agent jobs
```

Show the list of job processes the Agent is currently running.

```
$ emctl status agent -secure [-omsurl <url>]
```

Validate the secure communication between the Agent and the OMS.

```
$ emctl status agent mcache <target_name>,<target_type>
```

Show the list of all metrics the Agent has in memory for the given target.

```
$ emctl status agent memory
```

Overview of the memory the Agent is currently using. The information will be dumped in a file called emagent_memDump_<timestamp>.trc in the <EMHOME>/sysman/log directory. If the enableMemoryTracing parameter is enabled in the emd.properties file, additional memory will be dumped in the memory trace file.

```
$ emctl status agent oci
```

New in 10.2.0.5. List all connections made to the database for monitoring.

```
$ emctl status agent scheduler
```

List of the scheduled tasks the Agent is currently maintaining. This will contain all the scheduled metrics to be executed, as well as some internal housekeeping tasks like the XML upload.

```
$ emctl status agent target <target_name>,<target_type>
```

Show the current values and current violations for all metrics the Agent has in memory for the given target.

```
$ emctl status blackout [<Target_name>[:<Target_Type>]]
```

Either show current status of all blackouts if no target is specified, or report only on those blackouts affected by the target specified on the command-line.

```
$ emctl status subagent
```

Show the current status of the SNMP sub-Agent.

```
$ emctl stop agent
```

Stop the Agent.

```
$ emctl stop blackout <Blackoutname>
```

Stop the Agent-side blackout specified on the command-line. The blackout name has to be a valid active blackout from the blackouts.xml file. Blackouts submitted via the Console UI cannot be used with this command.

```
$ emctl stop subagent
```

Stop the SNMP sub-Agent.

```
$ emctl unsecure agent
```

Fall back to HTTP when communicating with the OMS. If the Agent is secured, the configuration will be changed to switch to HTTP.

```
$ emctl upload [agent]
```

Force upload of all pending XML files.

```
$ emctl verifykey
```

New in 10.2.0.5. Command to verify the SSL key to communicate with the OMS.

EMCTL: OMS Server-Side Commands

```
$ emctl abortresync repos {-full|-agentlist="agent names"}
      -name "resync name"
```

New in 10.2.0.5. Stop any running repository resynchronization operations.

```
$ emctl config emkey -emkeyfile <path> [-force] [-sysman_pwd <pwd>]
```

Specify the location of the EMKEY file to use on the filesystem. If there is already an EMKEY file stored, the -force option will need to be added to force the new location of the file.

```
$ emctl config emkey -copy_to_repos [-sysman_pwd <pwd>]
```

Upload the EMKEY back into the repository. This requires a valid EMKEY to be present on the filesystem, pointed to by the `oracle.sysman.emkeyfile` parameter.

```
$ emctl config emkey -repos [-emkeyfile <path>] [-force]
                            [-sysman_pwd <pwd>]
```

Store the EMKEY on the file system of the OMS. This command should be run on all the OMS servers. As soon as this is done, the key should be removed from the repository using the `emctl config emkey -remove_from_repos` command.

```
$ emctl config emkey -remove_from_repos
```

Store the EMKEY from the repository in an external file on the disc. The location of the EMKEY file will be specified by the setting in the `emoms.properties` file. The default location for this file is $ORACLE_HOME/sysman/config/emkey.ora.

```
$ emctl config emrep [-sysman_pwd <pwd>] [-agent <new agent>]
                     [-conn_desc [<tns>]]
```

New command introduced in 10.2.0.5. Update the monitoring properties for the OMS and Repository target.

```
$ emctl config oms -change_repos_pwd [-change_in_db]
       [-old_pwd <pwd>] [-new_pwd <pwd>]
       [-use_sys_pwd [-sys_pwd <pwd>]]
```

New in 10.2.0.5. Command to change the password of the SYSMAN user.

```
$ emctl config oms -change_view_user_pwd [-sysman_pwd <pwd>]
                   [-user_pwd <pwd>] [-autogenerate]
```

New in 10.2.0.5. Command to change the password of the MGMT_VIEW user, used by the Reporting framework. After this command has run, the OMS will have to be restarted to make the OMS pick up the new password, and re-create the MGMT_VIEW database connections.

```
$ emctl config oms loader -shared <yes|no> -dir <loader dir>
```

Configure the loader mechanism used by the OMS server. If a shared loading mechanism is used, the load directory must be a shared directory, visible on all OMS servers as the same location.

```
$ emctl config oms sso -host <host> -port <port> -sid <SID>
          -pass <pwd> -das <URL> -u <user>
```

Set up the OMS to use Single-Sign-On for authentication of Grid Control users.

```
$ emctl create service [-user <name>] [-pwd <pwd>] -name <servicename>
```

Windows NT only. Creates the specified Grid Control service.

```
$ emctl delete service [-user <name>] [-pwd <pwd>] -name <servicename>
```

Windows NT only. Deletes the specified Grid Control service.

```
$ emctl dump [-log] omsthread
```

Force a Java dump in the OPMN log file for the OC4J_EM application.

```
$ emctl exportconfig oms [-dir <dir>] [-keep_host] [-sysman_pwd <pwd>]
```

New in 10.2.0.5. Exports all OMS configuration, and creates an encrypted file with all the configuration settings in the specified directory. The filename will be in the form `opf_<date>_<time>.bka`.

```
$ emctl getmessagedetails oms -id=<id>
```

New in 10.2.0.5. Display information about the specified Grid Control error message.

```
$ emctl getversion [oms]
```

Return the current version of the OMS server.

```
$ emctl importconfig oms -file <bka file> [-key_only] [-noresecure]
        [-sysman_pwd <pwd>] [-reg_pwd <pwd>]
```

New in 10.2.0.5. Exports all OMS configuration, and creates an encrypted file with all the configuration settings in the specified directory. The filename will be in the form `opf_<date>_<time>.bka`.

```
$ emctl resync repos {-full|-agentlist="agent names"} [-name "name"]
```

New in 10.2.0.5. Initiate a repository synchronization from either all Agents, or just the Agents specified on the command line.

```
$ emctl secure lock
```

Allow only HTTPS traffic from the Agents reporting to this Grid Control environment. All Agents still trying to contact the OMS via an unsecure way (using HTTP without SSL), will get rejected.

```
$ emctl secure oms -sysman_pwd <pw> -reg_pwd <pwd>
        [-host <hostname>] [-reset] [-secure_port <port>] [-lock]
        [-slb_port <port>] [-root_dc <dc>] [-root_country <country>]
        [-root_state <state>] [-root_loc <loc>] [-root_org <org>]
        [-root_unit <unit>] [-root_email <email>]
```

Secure the OMS, and generate an SSL wallet using the specified information.

```
$ emctl secure setpwd [authpasswd] [newpasswd]
```

Set the password for AS Control. This password is needed to log in and perform the administration functions of the Application server.

```
$ emctl secure unlock [-console]
```

Allow both HTTP and HTTPS traffic from the Agents reporting to this Grid Control environment. If the -console switch is used (new in 10.2.0.5), only the Oracle HTTP Server configuration is changed to allow HTTP access via browsers for Administrators to use Grid Control.

```
$ emctl start oms
```

Start the OMS server. If OPMN or the HTTP Server is not started, it will get started first before starting the OC4J_EM application. The OC4J_EMPROV application is not started with this command.

```
$ emctl status emkey [-sysman_pwd <pwd>]
```

Report the status of the secure EMKEY.

```
$ emctl status oms
```

Report the status of the OMS server. This command does check for the AS application stack.

```
$ emctl statusresync repos -name "resync name"
```

New in 10.2.0.5. Report the status of the running resynchronization operation.

```
$ emctl stop oms
```

Stop the OMS server. Only the OC4J_EM applications will be stopped with this command.

EMCTL: AS Control Commands

```
$ emctl secure em
$ emctl secure iasconsole
```

Switch to secure HTTPS access for AS Control.

```
$ emctl set password <old> <new>
```

Change administrator login password of AS Control.

```
$ emctl start em
$ emctl start iasconsole
```

Start the AS Console Agent.

```
$ emctl status em
$ emctl status iasconsole
```

Report the status of AS Control.

```
$ emctl stop em
$ emctl stop iasconsole
```

Stop the AS Console Agent.

```
$ emctl unsecure em
$ emctl unsecure iasconsole
```

Switch back to HTTP traffic for AS Control.

APPENDIX
G

Acronyms

f you read any kind of technical document these days, you'll notice that it is literally filled with abbreviations and acronyms. Although many of them will sound familiar, and might even be used daily in "casual computer conversation," it's still amazing just how many of these things *do* creep into technical documentation. And for some, they have become so commonplace that we don't even realize that they are in fact an acronym. To clarify this point, and to give a reference of all these abbreviations used in this book, this list has been compiled.

3DES	Triple DES (Data Encryption Standard—168-bit)
AD4J	Advanced Diagnostics For Java
ADDM	Automatic Database Diagnostic Monitor
AIX	Advanced IBM UNIX (Advanced Interactive eXecutive)
AKA	Also Known As
ANO	Advanced Networking Option
API	Application Programmable Interface
AQ	Advanced Queuing
AS	Application Server
ASAP	As Soon As Possible
ASH	Active Session History
ASM	Automatic Storage Management
ASO	Advanced Security Option
AWR	Automatic Workload Repository
BDC	Backup Domain Controller
BLOB	Binary Large Object
CA	Certificate Authority
CA	Corrective Action
CBO	Cost-Based Optimizer
CD	Compact Disc
CEO	Chief Executive Officer
CIO	Chief Information Officer
CLI	Command-Line Interface
CPIO	Copy In/Out archives
CPU	Central Processing Unit
CPU	Critical Patch Update
CRS	Cluster Ready Services

CSR	Certificate Signing Repository
CSV	Comma-Separated Values
DAS	Distributed Application Services
DB	Database
DBA	Database Administrator
DBCA	Database Configuration Assistant
DBI	Database Interface
DBMS	Database Management System
DCM	Distributed Configuration Management
DES	Data Encryption Standard
DG	Data Guard
DMS	Dynamic Monitoring System
DMZ	Demilitarized Zone
DNAT	Destination Network Address Translation
DNS	Domain Name Server
DP	Deployment Procedure
DR	Disaster Recovery
DST	Daylight Savings Time
DTD	Document Type Definition
DVD	Digital Versatile Disc
E2E	End-To-End (Monitoring)
ECID	Execution Context ID
ECM	Enterprise Configuration Management
EE	Enterprise Edition
EM	Enterprise Manager
EOF	End Of File
ER	Entity Relationship
ESA	Enterprise Security Advisor
EUM	End User Monitoring
EUS	Enterprise User Security
FQDN	Fully Qualified Domain Name
FRA	Flash Recovery Area
FTP	File Transfer Protocol
GC	Grid Control

GIF	Graphical Image File
GMT	Greenwich Mean Time
GUID	Global Universal ID
HA	High Availability
HTML	Hypertext Markup Language
HTTP	Hypertext Transport Protocol
HW	Hardware
IDM	Identity Management
IMAP	Internet Mail Access Protocol
IO	Input/Output
IP	Internet Protocol
IPM	Inter Process Management
IPW	Initial Password
IT	Information Technology
ITIL	Information Technology Infrastructure Library
JAR	Java Archive
JDBC	Java Database Connectivity
JDK	Java Development Kit
JMS	Java Message Service
JNI	Java Native Interface
JRE	Java Runtime Engine
LAN	Local Area Network
LDAP	Lightweight Directory Access Protocol
LOB	Large Object
LOB	Line Of Business
MAA	Maximum Availability Architecture
MAN	Metropolitan Area Network
MIB	Management Information Base
MTM	Monitor The Monitor
NAS	Network Attached Storage
NAT	Network Address Translation
NFS	Network File System
NIC	Network Information Center

NIC	Network Interface Card
NLS	National Language Support
NTP	Network Time Protocol
NTPD	NTP Daemon
OC4J	Oracle Container For Java
OCFS	Oracle Cluster File System
OCI	Oracle Call Interface
OCM	Oracle Configuration Manager
OCS	Oracle Collaboration Suite
ODBC	Open Database Connectivity
ODL	Oracle Diagnostic Logging
OHS	Oracle HTTP Server
OID	Object ID
OLTP	On-Line Transaction Processing
OMA	Oracle Management Agent
OMR	Oracle Management Repository
OMS	Oracle Management Server
ONS	Oracle Notification Service
OOB	Out Of Band
OPMN	Oracle Process Management and Notification
OPN	Oracle Partner Network
OS	Operating System
OTN	Oracle Technology Network
OUI	Oracle Universal Installer
OWM	Oracle Wallet Manager
PAF	Provisioning Application Framework
PAM	Pluggable Authentication Modules
PAR	Provisioning Archive
PAT	Port Address Translation
PDC	Primary Domain Controller
PDP	Privilege Delegation Provider
PERL	Practical Extraction and Report Language
PID	Process Identifier
PING	Packet Internet Grouper

PITR	Point-in-Time Recovery
PKI	Public Key Infrastructure
PL/SQL	Procedural Language/Structured Query Language
PM	Process Management
POP	Post Office Protocol
RAC	Real Application Cluster
RAT	Real Application Testing
RBS	Rollback Segment
RCA	Root Cause Analysis
RCP	Remote Copy
RFC	Request For Comment
RMAN	Recovery Manager
RMI	Remote Method Invocation
RPM	RPM Packet Manager (yes, it is a recursive acronym)
RSA	Rivest-Shamir-Adleman (encryption technology)
SA	System Administrator
SAN	Storage Area Network
SCM	Software Configuration Manager
SCN	System Change Number
SCP	Secure Copy
SDK	Software Development Kit
SE	Standard Edition
SGA	System Global Area
SID	Service Identifier
SLA	Service Level Agreement
SLB	Server Load Balancer
SLM	Service Level Management
SMP	System Management Products
SMS	Short Message Service/Short Message System
SMTP	Simple Mail Transfer Protocol
SNAT	Secure Network Address Translation
SNMP	Simple Network Management Protocol
SO	Shared Object
SOA	Service Oriented Architecture

SOAP	Service Oriented Architecture Protocol
SOX	Sarbanes-Oxley
SQL	Structured Query Language
SR	Service Request
SSE	Systems and Solutions Engineering
SSH	Secure Shell
SSL	Secure Socket Layer
SSO	Single Sign-On
SUN	Stanford University Network
SW	Software
TAF	Transparent Application Failover
TAR	Tape Archive
TAR	Technical Assistance Request
TCP	Transport Control Protocol
TCP/IP	Transport Control Protocol/Internet Protocol
TLA	Three-Letter Abbreviation
TNS	Transparent Network Substrate
TTL	Time To Live
TZ	Time Zone
UDM	User Defined Metric
UDP	User Datagram Protocol
UI	User Interface
UIX	User Interface XML
UNIX	Uniplexed Information and Computing System
URI	Uniform Resource Identifier
URL	Uniform Resource Locator
UTC	Coordinated Universal Time (yes, the acronym is not "CUT"!)
VPD	Virtual Private Database
VPN	Virtual Private Network
WAN	Wide Area Network
WWW	World Wide Web
XML	Extended Markup Language
YP	Yellow Pages

Glossary

Administrator   A user of Grid Control. Someone who should typically be responsible for the administration and management of a group of targets.

Agent   The third tier in the Enterprise Manager architecture. An Agent is responsible for the monitoring of its assigned target, and responds to the requests users send over to manage and maintain these targets.

Alert   An alert is a violation of a threshold for a given metric. The alert can be either in "warning" or "critical" state, depending on the severity of the threshold violation.

Beacon   A virtual user, defined on an Agent, that is responsible for periodically checking the availability of applications and services in the enterprise.

Blackout   A maintenance window to be applied on one or more targets. A blackout can be a one-time thing, or a recurring blackout (for example, every Friday from 9 P.M. to midnight).

Blackout Window   Period of time for which monitoring of a target should be suspended. This usually indicates a time window for the administrator to perform some work on the target.

Certificate   An encrypted definition of a secure password or passphrase to allow access to an HTTP server to log in to an application.

Cluster   A group of physical machines, capable of running applications and software at the physical level, while advertising the service at the logical (group) level to the outside world. Each cluster will also have a target called a "cluster," which has two or more physical machines as member targets.

Collection   See *Metric Collection.*

Compliance Score   The level of compliance of a target based on the number of outstanding policy violations that target has.

Components   The individual targets that are used in systems and services.

Composite Target   See *Container Target.*

Container Target   A container target is a special type of target. It is defined in the repository, not managed by an Agent, and is a logical definition used to group several other targets together. Examples of container targets are groups, systems, and services.

Corrective Action (CA)   A Grid Control job submitted in response to a threshold violation. The CA is submitted from the OMS to the Agent in response to an alert.

Credentials   A username and password to use for authorization. Credentials can be specified for a machine (a physical box), for a target (to do monitoring or perform administrative tasks), for a job (so it can run in the context of a particular target), or for an *ORACLE_HOME* (so the software can be patched).

Critical Alert   A violation of the critical threshold for a given metric.

Dashboard   In essence, dashboards are nothing more than a special kind of rollup report defined in Grid Control. Any report a user makes in Grid Control can be defined with the Dashboard layout.

Demilitarized Zone (DMZ)   In computer security, a demilitarized zone, or DMZ, is a physical or logical subnet that contains and exposes an organization's external services to a larger untrusted network, usually the Internet.

Deployment Procedure (DP)   A set of actions to take in order to roll out a new target, or upgrade/patch an existing target in Grid Control. The actions can be logical in nature (like running internal prerequisite checks), or physical (like copying a zip file over to the Agent to patch with, or executing an `opatch` command to patch an *ORACLE_HOME*).

Gold Image   To expedite the provisioning of new environments, gold images, or provisioning templates, are often used to reduce the time of deployment into the environment. The idea behind a gold image is to have a pristine system configuration that can be customized as needed for deployment to the target environment, usually in a matter of minutes.

Group   A container target. A set of targets put together in one logical "container."

Heartbeat   Timestamp that a component registers to let the infrastructure know it is still alive. Both the Agents and the Management Servers will send over and record heartbeats.

Home Page   Starting point in the Console for all the information available for a given target. Each target type will have its own specific home page. All targets of the same type will, therefore, have a similar *home page* with the same information displayed.

Job   The definition of a set of commands to run: Every job will have a schedule and a set of commands to be run on one or more targets using the specified schedule. A job will have one or more job runs.

Job Execution   The grouping of a set of job steps to be run in the specified order against the specified targets. A job execution will have one or more steps.

Job Run   A set of executions scheduled for the same time. For daily jobs, you would have the Monday run, the Tuesday run, and so on. A job run will have one or more job executions.

Job Schedule   The definition of when the job has to run. This can be immediate, one-time only (somewhere in the future), or on a repetitive basis (daily, weekly, monthly, and so on).

Job Step   The smallest unit of work a job can do. A single command/operation that a job can do against a target.

Key Components   Critical components needed to guarantee the uptime of a system or service: Any outage of a key component has an effect on the rest of the system or service.

Lifecycle Management   Lifecycle management loosely encompasses all the required facets that make up a business service. This means collaborating and integrating components for the purpose of managing things like:

- Service and artifact versioning
- Lifecycle information (for example, development, test, production, deprecated)
- Lifecycle status and state of the service (availability) compliance or governance

Loader   The module on the Management Server, responsible for loading the XML files the Agent has sent over.

Management Server (OMS)   The middle tier of the Grid Control infrastructure. The OMS is the central information broker, accepting requests from the Agents and the Administrators, and storing and retrieving the information in the repository.

Metric   Every data point collected for a managed target is called a metric. Metrics are collected on a regular basis, defined by the frequency of the metric definition.

Metric Collection   A set of metrics, grouped together to report on a specific set of data points for a given target.

Monitor The Monitor (MTM)   The subsystem of the Management Server responsible for keeping an eye on the Grid Control infrastructure itself.

Notification   A message sent out from Grid Control to notify an administrator of a certain alert or message that happened. Notifications can be triggered by alerts (threshold violations), or from actions happening in the console (like job status notifications).

Notification Method   A way to deliver a notification. This can be done via email, an OS command, an SNMP trap, or with a PL/SQL procedure.

Plug-in   An extension that can contain both monitoring and administration capabilities to be added to the Agent to monitor a new target type.

Policy   Also referred to sometimes as a Policy Rule. A business rule, to be evaluated based on metric data-points. There are three types of policies: Configuration, Security, and Storage.

Policy Violation   A violation of a business rule: an alert for a policy rule.

Preferred Credentials   A username and password to use by default when accessing a particular target in the Console.

Purge   The DBMS_JOB running in the repository database, responsible for the cleanup of old data.

Repository Metric   A data point, or set of data points, evaluated in the repository database itself, without any intervention from the Agent.

Response Action   An OS command executed by the Agent in response to a threshold violation. Response actions are executed directly by the Agent without any intervention of the OMS.

Rollup   The DBMS_JOB running in the repository database, responsible for the aggregating of the metric data to an hourly and a daily level.

Server Load Balancer (SLB)   Virtualization layer for the OMS. It can be either a dedicated hardware device or a software solution running on a machine. An SLB is the single point of contact for the Agents, and will forward the Agent requests to one of the available Management Servers.

Super-User   Special type of Grid Control administrator, with the privileges to access and manage everything defined in the Grid Control repository, including other administrators.

Target   A managed entity in Grid Control, visible in the Console.

Target Type   A classification for targets. Every target of the same type will have the same monitoring and administration capabilities in the Console.

Template   Metric and policy settings can be grouped together into a template. Templates can be applied on targets via the console, to replicate the settings specified in the template on the target.

Threshold   A metric can have thresholds defined to alert in case the data returned by the metric violates the specified values. Thresholds can be numerical or contain string values. A metric can have two thresholds defined: one for a warning alert, and one for a critical alert.

Transaction   Also sometimes referred to as a web transaction (although a beacon can perform transactions that are not web-based too!). A set of instructions that the virtual user (the beacon) has to execute to mimic real end-user activity in an application.

Service   The definition of an application in Grid Control. Services are business applications or business services present in the enterprise that require monitoring, such as email servers, HR databases, and web sites.

System   A System is a group of Grid Control targets representing the physical components of an application.

User-Defined Metric (UDM)   An extension, specified by an administrator, to the monitoring that Agents already do for the targets they are responsible for.

Wallet   A container for SSL certificates, present on both the Agent and the OMS. It is used to initiate communication between the Agent and the OMS.

Warning Alert   A violation of the warning threshold for a given metric.

Web Application   A special kind of service, accessible in the enterprise via an HTTP Server.

Index